To Larry!
My favorite tropical
herpetologist!

Como Siempre

James R. Dixon

TEXAS SNAKES

IDENTIFICATION, DISTRIBUTION, AND NATURAL HISTORY

John E. Werler and James R. Dixon

Line drawings by Regina Levoy

University of Texas Press ⌄⌄ *Austin*

This book has been published

with the assistance of a grant from

the Zoo Friends of Houston, Inc.

Fourth printing, 2004

Requests for permission to reproduce material
from this work should be sent to Permissions,
University of Texas Press, Box 7819, Austin, TX
78713-7819.

∞ The paper used in this book meets the minimum
requirements of ANSI/NISO Z39.48-1992 (R1997)
(Permanence of Paper).

LIBRARY OF CONGRESS CATALOGING-IN-
PUBLICATION DATA
Werler, John E.
    Texas snakes : identification, distribution,
and natural history / John E. Werler and James R.
Dixon ; line drawings by Regina Levoy. — 1st ed.
    p.   cm.
Includes bibliographical references and index.
ISBN 0-292-79130-5 (hardcover : alk. paper)
1. Snakes—Texas.   I. Dixon, James Ray.
II. Title.
QL666.06 W42 2000
597.96·09764—dc21
                              99-6329

We dedicate this book to our wives,

Ingrid Werler and Mary Dixon,

and to our children,

who participated in nearly all

of our field activities throughout our careers.

∼

It is a paradox that so many human beings agonize over the well-being of an individual animal, yet ignore the millions daily brutalized by the destruction of their habitats. We are inspired by the wildness, equating it with freedom and beauty, and each day we destroy more wildness. We are touched with sadness at the plight of vanishing species but much more readily brought to tears by the difficulties of E.T., Dumbo, or Simba. We are as concerned with Star Wars' Wookie as with Australia's wallabies, with Ninja Turtles as with vanishing turtles. We populate our concept of the world with caricatures that differ not only from culture to culture but also from time to time. We depend upon short-term perceptions in a long-term world.

And so, among the most serious threats to the well-being of wild creatures today is that they will be ignored; condemned by growing, shifting masses of humanity to the same closets of irrelevance as corset stays and trilobites.

—William G. Conway *Wildlife Conservation* 98 (1995), no. 2

CONTENTS

ILLUSTRATIONS

PREFACE

The notion to write a book about Texas snakes first surfaced in the mind of the senior author, John E. Werler, during the late 1940s when he was serving as reptile curator for the San Antonio Zoo and Aquarium. Although the idea of such a volume seemed plausible at the time, a review of the literature revealed a remarkable absence of details concerning the life histories of the state's serpent fauna, and so, discouraged by a lack of natural history studies from which to draw, he put the project aside. It surfaced again several years after he joined the staff of the Houston Zoological Gardens in 1954 as the zoo's general curator. The idea became more focused in the 1970s, and the actual work began in 1980. The early efforts consisted of assembling photographs, reviewing the scientific literature, and enlisting the aid of friends and colleagues who kept snakes in captivity. Along the way, the task of gathering information about the natural history and distribution of Texas' large and diverse snake fauna became so arduous that in 1984 the junior author, James R. Dixon, was asked to join the effort, and he agreed. Since then, we have tried to assemble the latest information about the distribution, natural history, and taxonomy of our subjects. The senior author wrote virtually all of the species and subspecies accounts and the sections dealing with conservation, snake classification, myths and misinformation, and the snakebite hazard, whereas the junior author produced some of the text, as well as the checklist, the sections on amphibian and reptile organizations in Texas, history of Texas herpetology, organization of the book, biotic provinces of Texas, and taxonomic issues. He also produced the key to the species of Texas snakes and all of the distribution maps. Since computer mapping programs were not available when the junior author entered the project, the detailed state maps were produced without the benefit of computers. They contain well over 10,000 Texas localities, representing 46,655 specimens of 72 snake species.

Although this book was written for a broad readership, it is directed primarily at the novice, the amateur naturalist, and the person who maintains live snakes as a hobby. It is expected, however, that the species distribution maps and the bits of new natural history information it contains will be of interest to both the serious student and the professional herpetologist.

While we feel that a useful purpose of the book is to help the reader identify the various species and subspecies of Texas snakes, we have made a special effort to showcase their natural history—what they do, how they do it, when they do it, and why. We believe such information, although either inadequately known or lacking altogether for the vast majority of Texas snakes, will move the reader to see these creatures in a new light. This is the first step toward building an awareness of the need to conserve them, for with knowledge comes understanding. Two other goals of the book are to inspire others to join in the fascinating hobby of snake study and responsible snake keeping, and to encourage the serious amateur to submit significant and previously unreported natural history notes and range extensions for publication in appropriate journals or regional herpetological society newsletters. Even anecdotal observations may provide useful supplements to more formal, organized field studies. By reviewing the species and subspecies accounts in this book, the reader will readily detect the lapses of life history and distributional information that need further investigation.

ACKNOWLEDGMENTS

To the many persons who assisted us in the preparation of this book, we owe a profound debt of gratitude. Some, whose names are listed below, offered details of unreported personal observations. Others, whose published works on the taxonomy and natural history of serpents, particularly those in Texas, provided the major sources of information for this volume, are listed in the reference section at the back of the book together with the titles of their contributions. They are no less collaborators on this book than are those who offered us unpublished material.

To our wives, Ingrid Werler and Mary Dixon, who gave so generously of their time and understanding so that we could devote our own time to this project, there is no way to express adequately the measure of our gratitude. They also filed reprints, assisted with clerical work in general, and shared with us both the joys and tribulations of many field trips. Sincere thanks also to John Henry Werler, not only for his constant encouragement and companionship in the field but also for introducing his father to the world of computers, and to LeeAnn Werler for her comments on certain species accounts.

David Johnson was particularly helpful in providing specimens and literature during virtually the entire time the book was in progress. He also served as our unofficial contact person with private reptile collectors throughout the state, whose cooperation he enlisted for the loan of live specimens to illustrate the book. To him we owe a special debt of gratitude.

Clay Touchstone and Kerry Touchstone, keen naturalists and longtime friends of the senior author, also provided numerous live snakes for use as photographic models and over the years eagerly and unfailingly offered other assistance whenever it was needed.

Marinelle Stone not only typed the early drafts for many of the species and subspecies accounts but also made numerous editorial suggestions to improve their clarity. Her contribution to this project has been significant.

We especially thank Dr. Sherman A. Minton, Jr., for reviewing the venomous snakes accounts and for suggesting ways to improve them.

Since illustrations represent an important ingredient in a book of this kind, it was our good fortune early in the project to enlist the services of Regina Levoy to prepare the line drawings. We believe her talent speaks for itself. One other drawing, depicting colonial crayfish burrows, appeared in "Notes on the burrows, behavior, and color of the crayfish *Fallicambarus (F.) devastator* (Decapoda: Cambridae)," by Horton H. Hobbs and Mike Whiteman, in the *Southwestern Naturalist*, volume 36, no. 1, March 1991, pp. 127–135, and is reproduced here with permission of the authors.

As would be expected, obtaining live photographic models of all the species and subspecies of snakes in a state as large and ecologically diverse as this one proved difficult—a task accomplished only with the help of the following herpetologists, both professional and amateur: Johnny Binder, Patrick Burchfield, William Dege, the late Thomas Dieckow, James Dunlap, John Flury, Michael Forstner, Richard Funk, Ed Guidry, David Gyre, Gordon Henley, Charles Hoessle, David Johnson, Tim Jones, Tommy Jones, Jack Joy, Frank Judd, Stephen E. Labuda, Jr., Gerald Lentz, Rusty Martin, Greg Mengden, Hugh Quinn, Gus Rentfro, Buzz Ross, James Schwartz, Kelvin Scott, Norman Scott, Jr., Clay Touchstone, Kerry Touchstone, Bern Tryon, John Tveten, Robert G. Webb, Larry White, Richard Worthington, and Jim Yantis.

Most of the photographs in the book were made at the Houston Zoo by staff members Michael Bowerman, Andrew Odum (now curator of reptiles at the Toledo Zoo), and John E. Werler and are used here courtesy of the Houston Zoological Gardens and its director, Donald G. Olson. We are especially indebted to R. L. Stanley Photography for the photos of two male western diamondbacked rattlesnakes engaged in springtime combat, which were taken in southwestern Atascosa County by R. L. Stanley. To complete the list of illustrations, the following persons offered their own slides for use in the book: Dave Barker, Jonathan Campbell, Suzanne Collins, Paul Freed, Emmett Haddon, Toby J. Hibbitts, William W. Lamar, Andrew Odum, Wayne Van Devender, and Jim Yantis.

We are also grateful to the following individuals who offered their personal observations about the natural history of Texas snakes: Colette Adams, Ted Beimler, Patrick Burchfield, Roger Conant, Richard Etheridge, Michael Forstner, Gordon Henley, Tim Jones, Tommy Jones, John V. Rossi, Clay Touchstone, Kerry Touchstone, Larry White, Richard Worthington, and Jim Yantis.

Completing the maps illustrating the localities of all known museum records for Texas snakes would have been impossible without the help of the many museum curators and their staffs, who gave freely of their time and effort to provide the various Texas snake records for the second author. We thank them, one and all: Pere Alberch, Walter Auffenberg, Robert L. Bezy, Bryce C. Brown, Stephen D. Busack, Jonathan A. Campbell, David Canatella, Charles C. Carpenter, Alan H. Chaney, Charles J. Cole, Walter W. Dalquest, B. G. Davis, William G. Degenhardt, William E. Duellman, Harold A. Dundee, Robert R. Fleet, M. Jack Fouquette, Neil B. Ford, Thomas H. Fritts, Daniel A. Gallagher, Jimmy Green, Harry W. Greene, Stephen Hammack, Laurence M. Hardy, W. Ronald Heyer, Robert F. Inger, Sarah Kerr, Flavius C. Killebrew, Arnold G. Kluge, John M. Legler, David Lentz, Alan E. Leviton, Carl S. Lieb, Ernest A. Liner, Carol Malcom, Edmond V. Malnate, the late Robert F. Martin, Hymen Marx, Terry Maxwell, the late C. Jack McCoy, Roy W. McDiarmid, Ronald A. Nussbaum, William J. Pyburn, Fred Rainwater, Jose Rosado, Norman J. Scott, James F. Scudday, Wayne Seifert, C. B. Smith, Hobart M. Smith, the late Philip W. Smith, Steve Smith, Fred Stangl, Thomas Uzzell, Jens V. Vindum, William J. Voss, David B. Wake, Robert G. Webb, Kenneth L. Williams, John W. Wright, George R. Zug, and Richard G. Zweifel.

Many colleagues and graduate students offered encouragement, provided records and reports of sightings, and furnished unpublished local names of hard-to-find localities. A number of graduate students went out of their way to visit sites where we suspected certain species occurred and either confirmed or denied their presence. For these and other courtesies we gratefully acknowledge the following persons: F. Andett, Ralph W. Axtell, David G. Barker, the late Richard J. Bauldauf, George Baumgardner, Patrick M. Burchfield, Roger Conant, Kurt Cornelison, Rob H. Dean, Curtis T. Eckerman, Carl H. Ernst, Edward Farmer, George W. Ferguson, Tony Gallucci, Brian D. Greene, Michael Haiduk, Chris Harrison, Fred S. Hendricks, Terry Hibbitts, Toby Hibbitts, Kelly J. Irwin, John B. Iverson, Jerry D. Johnson, Frank W. Judd, John P. Karges, Brian Keeley, Kenneth King, David Kizirian, Travis LaDuc, William W. Lamar, Harry Longstrom, John Malone, William L. McClure, Hugh McCrystal, Jenna McKnight, Edwin J. Michaud, Edward O. Moll, James

Mueller, Roy Murray, Keith Nietman, William F. Parker, Ray Pawley, Karl Peterson, the late Floyd E. Potter, Andrew H. Price, Hugh R. Quinn, Gus Rentfro, Francis L. Rose, Michael E. Seidel, Jack W. Sites, Jerry R. Smith, Douglas Stine, Steve Stone, Robert A. Thomas, Okla W. Thornton, Thomas Vance, R. Kathryn Vaughan, Thomas G. Vermersch, Jack Ward, and Martin J. Whiting.

TEXAS SNAKES

INTRODUCTION

CONSERVATION

The loss of a single snake, or a dozen snakes, or even a hundred in one year will probably not seriously impact the balance of a particular ecosystem, at least not in the long term. Most natural changes occur slowly, over prolonged periods, like the rhythm of the seasons or the process of aging, so that their effects are usually not immediately apparent. But it is clear that over time the cumulative consequences of snake bashing, coupled with habitat destruction and environmental pollution, have taken a heavy toll of most native serpents, as probably has the insidious and sometimes equally devastating damage inflicted by the imported fire ant. Although habitat degradation and pollution are the chief causes of decline in local serpent populations statewide, it is not our intention to address these issues at length, since the resolution of such threats resides largely in the political arena and is therefore beyond the scope of this book. This is not to suggest, however, that interested persons should avoid becoming involved with local or national conservation groups to influence government policy makers in wildlife conservation matters. Indeed, doing so is often the best way to achieve significant and lasting results.

But to anyone with a clutching fear of snakes (which includes most of us), any idea of conserving these creatures will seem ludicrous or, at the very least, a misplaced prior-

ity. What is the compelling reason for this antiserpent bias? If we can accept that the great majority of snakes are incapable of causing us serious harm and that by reason of their feeding habits most of them are beneficial to our interests, by what logic do we feel obliged to destroy them on sight? The obvious answer is that a great majority of us lack even a basic understanding of these essentially timid and benign animals.

Our information about them often comes from those whose bias, like our own, is based primarily on the same myths and misconceptions that have confounded the subject since ancient times. Although erroneous, such implausible tales pique our interest, and their telling makes for lively after-dinner conversation. Unfortunately, however, by masking the truth they make more difficult the task of getting to the facts. The challenge then is to present the facts about these generally innocuous animals in such a way that even the snake haters among us will see these reptiles for what they really are—not vengeful creatures lurking in the brush to ambush the next human victim but another life form no more villainous than any of the others. Indeed, the life of a snake is basically not much different from that of other animal species. Like them it must find food, reproduce, protect itself from its enemies, and maintain a comfortable body temperature in the face of the changing seasons. How serpents fulfill these life functions can be as interesting as the bizarre snake stories we often hear and accept as fact. Only when we can cast aside such misinformation and replace it with an objective view of our subjects are we likely to entertain the idea of conserving snakes. That, it seems to us, is where the conservation ethic begins.

MYTHS AND OTHER MISINFORMATION

Most of the fictitious snake stories and misconceptions that follow have been part of our culture since at least colonial times, having been chronicled as fact in newspapers, magazines, books, and even in state publications. Others not listed here (but mentioned in the main text under the appropriate species or subspecies accounts) include those of the hoop snake (under western mud snake), spreading adder (under eastern hog-nosed snake), milk snake (under Central Plains milk snake), and whipsnake (under eastern coachwhip). Finally, the erroneous belief that one can determine the age of a rattlesnake by the number of segments in its rattle is discussed under the account for the western diamond-backed rattlesnake.

Snakes are slimy. Unlike fish, whose slimy bodies help to reduce resistance as they move through the water, snakes have skin that is quite dry. Since they have no internal resource with which to control their body temperature, snakes often feel cold to the touch, a condition that may be misconstrued as sliminess.

The snake's forked tongue is a venomous stinger. Nothing could be farther from the truth, since the soft, fleshy tongue—a delicate organ associated with the snake's senses of taste and smell—is no more dangerous than our own. It is found in all snake species, even those that are nonvenomous.

Snakes have hidden legs. A male snake that is thrown into a fire may evert its hemipenes in agony. During its frantic attempts to escape the flames, these exposed, paired copulatory organs will probably be perceived as legs.

Snakes do not die until sundown. A wounded snake, even a seriously injured one, may hold on to life for hours or even days before succumbing to its wounds, though it will quickly die if decapitated, cut in two, or crushed under a large rock.

Snakes always travel in pairs. During the breeding season, which generally occurs in the spring, male and female snakes of the same species can be found together during the short time it takes them to consummate the mating act. After that, they usually go their separate ways. According to this myth, a snake whose mate is killed as the two are traveling together will avenge the act by attacking the perpetrator. Although none of that is true, it has been confirmed that a male racer, particularly of the northeastern subspecies, *Coluber c. constrictor*, when interrupted during courtship or mating, sometimes vigorously attacks a human interloper. Such an assault should be of little concern, however, for a snake of this kind is incapable of inflicting serious injury.

Snakes chase people without provocation. It is true that some native snakes defend themselves aggressively when they are provoked and unable to flee, but none is known to pursue a human being. When, as occasionally happens, an intruder comes between a snake and its refuge, the snake may dash right by the startled onlooker to reach its nearby shelter. In these circumstances, it would be difficult to convince anyone that the snake was not making a direct attack.

Snakes routinely crawl into sleeping bags. Although snakes have been known to enter sleeping bags to escape the chill of evening, such events are extremely uncommon. To avoid this possibility it is suggested that the sleeping bag be placed on a cot or used inside a tightly zippered tent.

Snakes will not cross a horsehair rope. The belief, once common in the Southwest, that a rattlesnake will not crawl over a horsehair rope placed around a campsite can be dangerously misleading. As the story goes, the stiff protruding hairs of the rope stick the snake's belly as it attempts to cross, causing the reptile enough discomfort or pain to make it turn back. Yet most rattlesnakes are desert dwellers that live among spiny plants, including cactus, over which they sometimes crawl without hesitation. A snake that is not deterred by cactus spines will hardly be discouraged by the presence of a horsehair rope.

A snake's detached fang can kill. This legend, dating back to at least the early 1700s, describes the death of a man who was struck through one of his boots by a rattlesnake. The same boot was later worn by the victim's son, who was pricked by a fang still embedded in the leather and suffered the same fate that befell his father. After his death, a second son eventually put on the fatal boot, only to succumb to the poisonous fang as well. While it is true that when quickly dried and properly stored, the venom of a rattlesnake can maintain its potency for many years, the small amount of venom, if any, that would reside in the detached fang under the circumstances described above would hardly be enough to cause death in even one person, let alone three. Moreover, in an actual rattlesnake bite, the venom is forced under pressure through the hollow fang and into the victim. In the case of a detached fang, any small amount of venom that may still reside in the fang would simply remain there, unable to be expelled, since there is no mechanism to force it out through the orifice near the fang's pointed tip. On the other hand, there is a real danger in handling the recently severed head of a venomous snake, since it can still see, flick its tongue, and inflict a poisonous bite for up to an hour after having been separated from its body.

Mother snakes swallow their young to protect them. One of the oldest of all snake myths, this one has been traced back to the early Egyptians (about 2500 BC), though it is among the most incredible stories of snake behavior repeated in the United States today. It details how a mother snake, confronted by danger, emits a warning hiss or whistle to alert her young, whereupon she opens her mouth and allows the infants to enter and hide in her throat. If such an event is as common as the many eyewitness accounts would have us believe, why has it not been observed by even one herpetologist, professional or amateur? After all, many hundreds of snakes are born in captivity every year, yet not one of the female parents of these broods has ever been seen to swallow her young. Nor has this behavior been observed in the wild by trained field zoologists, either in this country or elsewhere. One likely explanation for this popular myth is that when a female snake carrying nearly full-term young is killed, the infant snakes, still alive, may be expelled through her cloaca or escape from

her ruptured body. To some, this confirms the notion that just before her death, the mother snake senses the potential danger, prompting her to swallow the young as a way to protect them.

For further information about this topic, we suggest the following books and pamphlets: L. M. Klauber, *Rattlesnakes: Their Habits, Life Histories, and Influence on Mankind* (1956); C. H. Curran and C. F. Kauffeld, *Snakes and Their Ways* (1937); K. P. Schmidt, *The Truth about Snake Stories* (1929); J. A. Oliver, *Snakes in Fact and Fiction* (1958); J. K. Strecker, *Reptiles of the South and Southwest in Folklore* (1926b); and E. Wigginton, *The Foxfire Book* (1972), especially the chapter on snake lore.

THE SNAKEBITE HAZARD

To a large extent, our fear of snakes is based on the knowledge that a few of them are venomous and capable of causing us serious bodily injury and sometimes even death. This fear, while logical enough when based on the facts of the matter, is usually so exaggerated that it can become unreasonable or, in the extreme, even grotesque, leaving little or no opportunity for rational dialogue. Some people have such an overwhelming fear of snakes that getting them to talk about the animals that cause them so much mental anguish may be impossible without professional help. Psychologists explain that ophidiophobia is among the more difficult fears to overcome. Such practitioners estimate that more than 50 percent of our population experience some anxiety in the presence of snakes, and another 20 percent are terrified by them. Extreme examples of the latter include those who become terror-stricken when they so much as see the picture of a snake in a magazine, a book, or on television, and others who avoid outdoor activities altogether for fear of encountering a snake, even a harmless one. Sadly, most of these people retain their morbid fear for life. But there are hopeful signs that the 50-plus percent— those with only a moderate fear of serpents —are slowly but surely being reduced in number as both public and private institutions and organizations concerned with natural history education reach ever more people with their hands-on programs. Probably at the forefront in molding such attitudinal changes are the country's zoological parks (and aquariums), which, through live exhibits and informal teaching programs, annually expose their nearly 120 million visitors to wildlife conservation messages. Science museums, nature centers, and wildlife organizations are fulfilling a similar role. As a direct result of such efforts, one encouraging sign of the change taking place in our attitude about snakes is the phenomenal growth of the pet-snake hobby; having gained prominence only about 20 years ago, it continues to expand at an accelerated pace, with devotees nationwide numbering in the many thousands.

Despite such progress, a great deal of apprehension and misunderstanding still exist among Texans about their native serpents. In the minds of most persons, snakes are still the enemy. They are seen as mysterious and menacing, to be killed wherever and whenever they are encountered. The truth is that snakes—even the dangerous ones—are fundamentally shy and retiring, more than willing to avoid a confrontation with mankind by fleeing when given the chance. Only as a last resort will they bite in self-defense. The notable exceptions are assignable not to our native serpents but to a few exotic species such as the giant king cobra of southeastern Asia, the deadly black mamba of Africa, and the fearsome taipan of Australia—all highly dangerous venomous snakes whose occasional lack of tolerance for man's intrusion into their territory can result in an aggressive confrontation.

Our native venomous serpents do not display such overtly offensive behavior; they nevertheless pose a potential risk for those engaged in outdoor activities. This is, after all, a large state with a diverse snake fauna, consisting of 72 species (by our count), 11 of which are considered dangerous to man. Ranking the states by raw figures, Parrish (1964) estimated that Texas suffered more venomous snakebites in a single year than any other state nationwide, although when the number of such accidents was calculated per 100,000 residents, Texas ranked third, with an incidence rate of 14.70 percent, trailing behind North Carolina at 18.79 percent and Arkansas at 17.19 percent. Moreover, based on actual and projected snakebite in-

cidents for 1958 and 1959, he estimated that approximately 1,408 snakebite victims were treated in Texas in each of those years, consisting of 784 inpatients and 624 outpatients. An average of only 2.4 fatalities occurred annually—a mortality rate of just one-fourth of one percent of those bitten. Even more encouraging are the mortality figures for the last 18 years (1978 through 1995), which according to the Texas Department of Health, Bureau of Vital Statistics, averaged only one death a year. These figures hardly classify venomous snakebite as a high-mortality occurrence, at least in the United States. Outdoor hazards more likely to cause human death in Texas are the stings and bites of insects and arachnids, lightning strikes, hunting accidents involving firearms, and drownings.

Among our dangerous snake species, two in particular are responsible for the greatest number of bites inflicted on humans. They are the copperhead and the western diamondbacked rattlesnake, both abundant and wide-ranging in the state. Although copperheads accounted for 22 percent of the bites reported by Parrish, they caused no fatalities, whereas the western diamondback, which was blamed for nearly all of the bites included in the rattlesnake category (47 percent of the bite total), was responsible for some human deaths. The cottonmouth ranked next in order of frequency but inflicted only 7 percent of the bites.

Reducing the risk of snakebite is largely a matter of learning to recognize the dangerous species in your part of the state, becoming familiar with their habits, and observing some commonsense safety practices, a few of which are listed below.

1. The first rule should be, never handle a venomous snake unless you are qualified by training or experience to do so. This admonition, while it may seem self-evident, deserves emphasis, for an ever-increasing number of snakebites are being inflicted on inexperienced amateur herpetologists and reckless adventurers. Other bites are the result of mistaken identification. In one such incident, a Houston radio announcer encountered a coral snake on a city jogging trail. Believing the snake to be a harmless species, he picked it up and was promptly bitten on the hand,

whereupon, momentarily startled by the reptile's reaction, he quickly dropped it to the ground. Still not convinced that the snake was dangerous, he handled it a second time and was bitten again. Also to be carefully avoided is a dead venomous snake, for such a creature often can bite reflexively for periods lasting up to an hour after death, as can its decapitated head, a reaction Klauber (1956) elicited many times from experimentally beheaded rattlesnakes. One of the most sobering examples of such an accident is the case reported by Kitchens and his colleagues (1987) in which a Florida man died after having been bitten by the severed head of a large canebrake rattlesnake.

2. Since nearly all snakebites occur on the arms and legs of human victims, avoid placing your hands in places where you cannot see, and wear protective footwear on the lower half of your legs when venturing into areas known to harbor venomous snakes. Be particularly alert when climbing rocky ledges or when walking near old logs and decaying tree stumps, places often favored by certain venomous species. It also makes sense when crossing a log to first step onto it in order to see what is behind it, then to step down on the other side when it appears safe to do so. Never reach into mammal burrows, especially in arid habitats where aboveground shelters are scarce, for such tunnels are frequently occupied by rattlesnakes. Since one of the leading causes of snakebite is the practice of lifting or turning surface objects with the bare hands, a sensible rule to follow is to move these items (rocks, boards, logs, brush, construction debris, etc.) with a long-handled tool such as a hoe, shovel, axe, or broomstick.

3. To discourage snakes from maintaining permanent residence close to a home or vacation cottage, it is advisable to keep the premises free of debris. Rock piles, trash piles, stacked lumber, and various forms of junk not only provide the serpents with shelter but also often harbor the rats and mice that constitute the principal food of most venomous species. Removing such debris helps to eliminate the snake's cover and that of its rodent prey.

4. If you must kill a venomous snake that is a threat to human safety, do so out of range of the snake's strike, which ordinarily is less than its own body length. To attack the reptile with a short-handled weapon such as a knife, hatchet, or hammer is simply to invite an accident. Although this word of caution may seem too obvious to bear mentioning, it is clear from our review of Texas snakebite cases that accidents from this cause happen with some frequency.

For most people, snakebite is a terrifying experience that finds the victim both emotionally and intellectually unprepared to deal with such an emergency. Usually fear and extreme apprehension result from such an accident, when what is most needed at this time is a sense of calm. Despite the rarity of human death from envenomation in the United States, convincing a fearful snakebite victim that he or she has an excellent chance to recover from such a mishap is difficult. Nevertheless, every attempt should be made to convey this information to the victim, since to do so may relieve his or her anxiety and thereby expedite the victim's recovery.

Reaching medical aid as quickly as possible should be the first objective, but with a minimum amount of physical exertion on the part of the victim, who, if alone and on foot, should not run. If the bite is on an extremity, immobilize the bitten limb or at least avoid moving it, since muscular activity hastens the spread of venom through the lymphatic channels. Moreover, when the bite is on a hand or arm, take off any rings and tight bracelets before swelling makes their removal difficult.

Other, more aggressive first-aid measures —including incision and suction, with or without a constricting band or tourniquet; application of cold to the bite site; compression wrapping of the extremity; or stun gun electroshock—may or may not be used, depending on the knowledge and decision of the victim. However, such procedures, some of which are potentially harmful, have not been embraced with equal enthusiasm among the best-informed medical specialists, although the same experts agree that the several preliminary steps mentioned earlier (reassurance, prompt transport to medical aid without undue exertion, immobilization of the bitten limb, and removal of rings and tight bracelets) are beneficial. One expert, Dr. D. L. Hardy (1992), reviewed several commonly recommended first-aid methods for North American pit viper bites and presented his evaluation of their effectiveness. Anyone with a serious interest in snakebite first aid is encouraged to read this article.

TEXAS HERPETOLOGY

Early native Americans were well acquainted with their local snake fauna, but their interest in them appears to have been more a matter of veneration than of specific knowledge about their behavior. The Spanish explorers who encountered reptiles in Texas during the period from about 1650 to 1700 were especially impressed with the large and dangerous noise-making snake they called the cascabel (meaning tinkle bell or jingle bell). Since the classification scheme of Linnaeus was not published until 1758, there was no formal designation of snake names. To the Spaniards, however, "vibora," or viper, was the name for any snake believed venomous, and "culebra" was any nonvenomous species. These terms are still widely used by Spanish-speaking native Texans. Perhaps the first European to have written scientific articles about Texas amphibians and reptiles was Jean L. Berlandier, a French botanist who, as he traveled across the state between 1828 and 1834, recorded his encounters with snakes in his field journal.

Prior to 1900, the collection of Texas amphibians and reptiles for scientific study was accomplished primarily by professional employees of the United States government, particularly those whose duties involved land exploration and survey work in the then largely unfamiliar territories of the Southwest, including Texas. Two such pioneers, John Russell Bartlett and William Emory, who conducted a railroad survey for the U.S. Army from 1850 to 1854, amassed a rather significant study collection of amphibians and reptiles from across the state (between Indianola in Calhoun County and El Paso), which was the source for most Texas-related herpetological publications issued between 1852 and 1854. During the next 15 years, because of the difficulties of conducting faunal surveys, little fieldwork was accomplished; hostile native forces, the distractions of the Civil War, and the stresses that followed the war were all contributing factors.

Dr. Benno Matthes, a German physician who had traveled to Texas on several occasions before settling here in 1865, was described by Geiser (1941) as one of the state's earliest resident herpetologists. The results of his studies, mostly published in German scientific journals, included a monograph of North American salamanders and the osteology and natural history of certain Texas snakes, especially those from Central Texas, where he lived.

By the late 1870s, following that period of inactivity, the acquisition of specimens for study collections was again being actively pursued. Most of the material acquired during this period was forwarded to some of the leading herpetologists in the northeastern states, resulting in the publication of approximately 40 scientific papers between 1876 and 1899. In 1895, John K. Strecker, who was to become the father of Texas herpetology, began his field surveys in the state, eventually producing 60 articles dealing with the state's herpetofauna, among which was his 1915 checklist of Texas reptiles and amphibians, the first such comprehensive summary to be published. His work continued until 1935. Despite the creation of the Texas Herpetological Society in 1937, little fieldwork or other herpetological research was conducted in Texas between 1935 and 1946, partly as a result of the Second World War and the restrictions it had placed on automobile travel. After the war there was a renewed interest in the subject. A number of Texas universities appointed appropriate professors of zoology to inaugurate doctoral programs with an emphasis on herpetology. Among them were W. Frank Blair at the University of Texas and Hobart M. Smith and William B. Davis at Texas A&M University. Since then, generations of doctoral students in herpetology have walked the halls of Texas universities. Some have pursued their professional careers in the state or have left and returned to do so later. Among those still involved in the science of herpetology, either in Texas or elsewhere, are Ralph W. Axtell, Royce E. Ballinger, James P. Bogart, Lauren E. Brown, Jeffrey D. Camper, William G. Degenhardt, Benjamin E. Dial, James R. Dixon, Robert R. Fleet, Alvin G. Flury, M. Jack Fouquette, Daniel S. Gallagher, William Garstka, Brian D. Greene,

Sheldon H. Guttman, Louise Hayes, Fred S. Hendricks, David L. Jameson, Jerry D. Johnson, Frank Judd, J. Patrick Kennedy, Christopher P. Kofron, Chris T. McAllister, Wayne McAllister, John S. Mecham, William W. Milstead, Craig E. Nelson, David Pettus, Kenneth R. Porter, William F. Pyburn, Carlos Rivero-Blanco, Richard D. Sage, Joseph J. Schall, James F. Scudday, Kyle W. Selcer, Jack W. Sites, Robert A. Thomas, R. Kathryn Vaughan, Aron O. Wasserman, and probably others.

Largely because of the work of many zoologists, our knowledge of Texas amphibians and reptiles has expanded at an accelerated pace over the past four decades. Each new book on the subject, particularly if it contains species distribution maps, invariably leads to additional short notes on distribution or natural history by those who can add to this body of knowledge with contributions of their own. During the 45 years prior to Strecker's *Reptiles and Amphibians of Texas*, issued in 1915, only 85 articles had been published about the state's amphibians and reptiles. Yet, from 1915 until the appearance in 1950 of *An Annotated Checklist of the Reptiles and Amphibians of Texas*, by Bryce Brown, 453 articles concerning these animals appeared in print. From 1950 to 1994, 2,116 additional works were published, many of them no doubt inspired by several recent books: Raun and Gehlbach's *Amphibians and Reptiles in Texas* (1972), Tennant's *Snakes of Texas* (1984), Dixon's *Amphibians and Reptiles of Texas* (1987), Vermersch and Kuntz's *Snakes of South-central Texas* (1987), and Garrett and Barker's *A Field Guide to Reptiles and Amphibians of Texas* (1987).

Much of the recent increase in the publication of locality reports and brief natural history notes can be attributed to the relative ease with which such information can be published in national and state journals, as well as in regional herpetological society newsletters. As examples of this incessant growth, Raun and Gehlbach's 1972 book referenced 1,108 articles about Texas amphibians and reptiles published through 1967. Dixon's 1987 volume contained an additional 990 articles, and by the middle of 1996 there was a total of 2,769 separate articles spanning 146 years of herpetological investigation in Texas. References to individual species of Texas snakes, published between 1828 and 1996, number 4,736 citations, representing an average of 66.7 references per species.

The five snakes most frequently mentioned in these reports, in descending order of frequency, are the western diamond-backed rattlesnake, coachwhip, Texas rat snake, copperhead, and plain-bellied water snake, followed by the bull snake, ribbon snake, racer, common king snake, and checkered garter snake. Discounting any recent name changes, those mentioned least often include the Trans-Pecos black-headed snake, red-bellied snake, worm snake, plains garter snake, and Mexican black-headed snake. Venomous snake species represent only 15.5 percent of the Texas snake fauna but are mentioned in 21.6 percent of the literature, whereas aquatic and semiaquatic snakes comprise 21.1 percent of the Texas serpent fauna and are mentioned in 20.6 percent of the Texas snake literature. Coachwhips, racers, rat snakes, king snakes, and bull snakes together amount to 18.3 percent of the snake fauna and are mentioned in 23.3 percent of the literature. The seven snakes found most commonly in yards represent 9.8 percent of the state's snake fauna but are noted in 13.4 percent of the articles, whereas the ten rarest and most secretive serpents—those with a limited Texas distribution—represent 13.4 percent of the serpent fauna but are included in only 3.5 percent of the literature.

Those wishing to pursue their interest in reptiles may join one of several state, regional, or local herpetological societies scattered throughout the state. Catering to mixed groups of amateur, student, and professional members, such nonprofit organizations promote the study and conservation of amphibians and reptiles through regular meetings and newsletters. One of them, the Texas Herpetological Society, established in 1937, sponsors an annual spring field trip within the state at a different site each year, as well as an annual fall meeting of speakers, most of them specialists in their field. For anyone with a serious interest in herpetology, participation in these meetings is indispensable.

The principal Texas herpetological organizations are the Texas Herpetological Society, the East Texas Herpetological Society, the El

Paso Herpetological Society, the North Texas Herpetological Society, the South-central Texas Herpetological Society, and the South Texas Herpetological Society. Since most, if not all, of these groups frequently change officers by due process of periodic elections, changes of address are not unusual. To obtain current names and addresses, contact the nearest museum, zoo, nature center, or university biology department.

In addition, the serious student and the professional may wish to belong to one or more of the following North American herpetological organizations, each of which provides regular issues of its scientific journal as a benefit of membership: American Society of Ichthyologists and Herpetologists, publishers of *Copeia*; Herpetologists League, publishers of *Herpetologica*; Society for the Study of Amphibians and Reptiles, publishers of *Journal of Herpetology* and *Herpetological Review*.

Texas universities offering both graduate and undergraduate courses in herpetology include the University of Texas colleges at Arlington, Austin, El Paso, and Tyler; Texas A&M University colleges at College Station and Kingsville (formerly Texas A&I); Baylor University; Texas Tech University; Southwest Texas State University; Sul Ross State University; Angelo State University; and Midwestern State University. Lower-division (two-year) colleges with herpetologists on staff include El Paso Community College, Hill Junior College, Temple Junior College, and Navarro Junior College.

BIOTIC PROVINCES OF TEXAS

By our count, 72 snake species inhabit Texas, more than reside within the borders of any other state in the Union. This is not surprising, since Texas is so large, is located far enough south to enjoy a relatively warm year-round climate, and contains a wide diversity of environments ranging from moist East Texas pine-oak forest, which receives an annual 40 to 55 inches (102–140 cm) of rainfall, to the arid Trans-Pecos region in the west, some parts of which normally get as little as 8 inches (20 cm) of precipitation a year. Elevation, which also affects the distribution of Texas snakes, varies from sea level to as high as 8,749 feet (2,667 m) at Guadalupe Peak,

though much of the state is relatively flat or consists of rolling prairies. To help define the distribution of small vertebrate animals (including snakes) within this mosaic of diverse climatic, physiographic, and vegetational conditions, biologists have divided the state into several rather distinct natural regions called biotic provinces.

One of the first to define such regions in Texas was L. R. Dice (1943), who described a biotic province as "a considerable and continuous geographic area . . . characterized by the occurrence of one or more ecologic associations that differ, at least in proportional area covered, from the associations of adjacent provinces. In general, biotic provinces are characterized by peculiarities of vegetation type, ecological climax, flora, fauna, climate, physiography, and soil." In his review he recognized seven provinces. Not long thereafter, W. F. Blair (1949), using terrestrial vertebrate animals (including snakes) as indicator species, refined Dice's arrangement but did not change the number of provinces. He did, however, change the name of one of Dice's provinces, in part, from the Comanchian to the Kansan.

Much of the following information is based on Blair's study. We have also referred to Richard Phelan's book, *Texas Wild*. For an interesting and easy-to-read introduction to Texas' wilderness areas, their effect on mankind, and humanity's impact on them, we recommend this publication.

Blair recognized seven biotic provinces in Texas, only six of which were large enough to have been adequately defined by their faunal elements. The seventh, the Navahonian, was later invalidated by Mecham (1979), who demonstrated that the overwhelming majority of reptile and amphibian species in this region inhabiting elevations below 6,000 feet (1,829 m) actually belong in the Chihuahuan biotic province, mixed with some Texan and Balconian forms. Of the small number of reptiles and amphibians identified as belonging in the Navahonian biotic province, only a few occur in the Guadalupes above 6,000 feet (1,829 m). Since at best this province represents a transitional zone in the state, we support Mecham's suggestion that it not be recognized as a legitimate Texas biotic province.

Blair listed the following numbers of snake

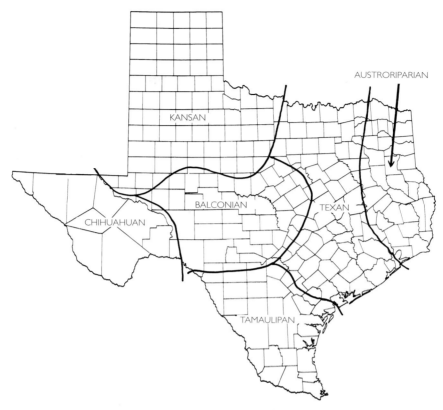

Map 1. *The state of Texas, with major plant and vertebrate divisions that correspond to the biotic provinces of Texas.*

species in each of the six biotic provinces de-scribed in this section (the numbers known from these regions today appear in parenthe-ses): Chihuahuan, 38 (40); Balconian, 36 (40); Tamaulipan, 36 (38); Kansan, 31 (35); Texan, 39 (41); and Austroriparian, 29 (33).

However distinct these provinces, none is inhabited exclusively by a unique set of ani-mals, for many species occur in two or more such regions. Unlike the narrow lines used to separate these regions on a physiographic map, the real boundaries are ordinarily wide and inexact, the product of intermingling ecological conditions between adjacent prov-inces. Thus, some snakes that are confined largely to one region often cross over into an-other without having to forsake suitable habitat. Certain other species, such as garter, ribbon, and water snakes, which ordinarily thrive in the wetter provinces, sometimes manage to make their way into an adjacent

drier region by following the edges of rivers or streams that flow from one into the other. One biotic province in particular, the Kansan, serves as a broad distributional crossroads for eastern and western species, whose ranges fall chiefly in other provinces. Despite the inexact nature of these somewhat artificially defined natural regions, they serve as useful tools to help us more easily visualize the overall, sometimes complex distributions of Texas snakes.

THE CHIHUAHUAN PROVINCE Beginning west of the Pecos River and including all of the Big Bend region of Texas, this is physiographi-cally the most diverse of all Texas biotic provinces. It is essentially an arid region of dry, rocky mountains, separated by hot desert plains and basins, whose soils range from ig-neous and basaltic to sedimentary. Its moun-tain ranges—more than 30 in all—reach a maximum elevation of 8,749 feet (2,667 m) on Guadalupe Peak in the Guadalupe Mountains, 8,381 feet (2,554 m) on Mount Livermore in the Davis Mountains, 7,730 feet (2,356 m) on Chinati Peak in the Chinati Mountains, and rise to just over 6,000 feet (1,829 m) in a few of the remaining mountain groups. Some of the highest elevations, whose north-facing slopes receive about twice as much rainfall as the surrounding lowlands, support cool, montane forests of juniper, Ponderosa pine, and oak, although such tree growth, more sparse than at the top, extends down the slopes of some mountains to approximately 4,500 feet (1,371 m). On the mountain foothills, at and below 3,500 feet (1,064 m), grow mostly desert plants including dense stands of sotol, yucca, lechuguilla, agave, and various cacti, as well as creosote bush, leatherstem, and blackbrush. There are also grasslands in the Trans-Pecos, which occur most conspicuously at elevations between 3,500 and 5,200 feet. According to Powell (1988), the best stands of grass, consisting mainly of blue grama, can be found in the Davis Mountains around the towns of Valentine, Marfa, Alpine, and Fort Davis, where soils are rather deep and fertile.

THE BALCONIAN PROVINCE Situated in the south-central part of the state, this is a limestone plateau with elevations ranging between 1,500 feet (457 m) and 3,000 feet (914 m). Its most clearly defined boundary is the Balcones Escarpment, a wide, ragged band of exposed limestone that forms the canyons and breaks along the southern and eastern edge of the Edwards Plateau from Del Rio to Austin. Elements of these limestone extrusions also appear sporadically from Austin to Dallas, with a rather large outcrop within the city of Dallas itself, which lies outside the Balconian province. Throughout the province, the southeastern part of which is often called the Hill Country, the soil is primarily of limestone origin, with some igneous extrusions and sediments. Since it rests on solid rock, the soil is usually only a few inches deep, except where it has accumulated in cracks, depressions, and low-lying areas. Despite its sparse rainfall and resulting aridity, the region has an abundance of underground water, which surfaces as springs and rivers, with tall sycamore and cypress trees typically lining the banks of the latter. Where surface water is absent, the vegetation consists chiefly of short-tree forest—oak, cedar, ash, hickory, cedar elm, hackberry, and mesquite, with an understory of arid-resistant grasses, catclaw, agarita, Texas persimmon, and cactus.

THE TAMAULIPAN PROVINCE An essentially dry, rocky, low-lying region characterized by flat or only slightly rolling terrain, this province covers nearly all of South Texas from the Balcones Escarpment to the southernmost tip of the state. Its northeast boundary lies along an indistinct transition zone where the aridland brush intermingles with the sacahuista grass of the adjoining coastal marshes. Its eastern border is the Gulf of Mexico; its western, the Rio Grande. The region's soils are mostly sedimentary, with some Cretaceous limestone outcroppings along the upper Rio Grande Valley, but in Kenedy, Brooks, and parts of some neighboring counties the substrate is predominantly sand, some of it reaching a depth of 60 feet (18.3 m). Rainfall in the Tamaulipan province is scarce, annually averaging about 25 inches (63.5 cm) in counties remote from the Gulf, though the hurricanes and violent storms that occasionally sweep across South Texas can cause severe flooding in low-lying areas, adversely affecting the local fauna. In response to the region's semiarid climate, the native vegetation consists largely of drought-resistant species armed with needle-sharp spines or thorns, hence the term "thornbrush." The predominant species include catclaw acacia, mesquite, huisache, Texas ebony, white brush, prickly pear, tasajillo, cenizo, wild olive, retama, and granjeno, with grasses growing in the open spaces. The Chihuahuan province also contains a wide variety of spiny plant species, but those in the Tamaulipan province frequently grow close together to form large, tangled masses of impenetrable brush that may stand as much as 20 feet (6.1 m) tall. Such thornbrush reaches its greatest luxuriance on the floodplain of the lower Rio Grande Valley, where, in addition to the typical plant species seen elsewhere in the province, large elms occur in places. The sabal palm, a typically Mexican species, reaches the northernmost end of its range along the Rio Grande in the vicinity of Brownsville.

THE KANSAN PROVINCE The largest and one of the most varied of all such regions in

Texas, this province extends across the entire Panhandle, then continues eastward through the Rolling Plains of north-central Texas to the western edge of the Cross Timbers, its southern boundary more or less following the course of the Colorado River. To a large extent it is a region of transition in which woodland species from the east intermingle with western grassland forms. Responsible for this faunal mixing are the region's rather diverse environmental components of physiography, vegetation, and climate, which have prompted ecologists to divide the province further into three subregions called biotic districts. From west to east, they are as follows:

Short-grass Plains District. Better known as the High Plains or the Llano Estacado, this western portion of the Texas Panhandle, the driest of the three, is situated at elevations between 3,000 feet (912 m) and 4,000 feet (1,219 m) above sea level. It was formed by the action of rainwater and melting snow that over time systematically washed away sand, gravel, shale, and clay from the slopes of New Mexico's adjacent Rocky Mountains and left the displaced material on the flatter Texas plains. Over these deposits lies several feet of rich soil, blown there by southwest winds, once covered with native grass but now supporting mostly a variety of agricultural crops. Along the eastern edge of this district is the Caprock Escarpment, a natural, uneven boundary between it and the mixed-grass plains district immediately to the east. The leading edge ascends from 200 to 800 feet or more above the base. Its scalloped outline, made jagged by the forces of erosion, is also dissected by the region's major streams, which have cut canyons back into the Caprock. The most notable is Palo Duro Canyon, carved out of the Caprock by a tributary of the Red River. In it grow juniper, mesquite, and cottonwood trees.

Mixed-grass Plains District. Bounded on the west by the Caprock Escarpment and on the east by the mesquite plains district, this division of the Kansan province is characterized by rolling hills. In many places it is covered with grama grass, beardgrass, and buffalograss, though the floodplains of streams that drain southeast through the district support stands of oak, elm, hackberry, and maple. Those moist woodlands create habitable avenues for the westward dispersal of moisture-dependent reptiles and amphibians from the east.

Mesquite Plains District. This, the easternmost district in the Kansan province, borders the Texan province on the east and the Balconian on the south. Its most common plant association is mesquite and a few shrubs, which grow in clusters and alternate with open areas of grass, mostly grama and three-awn. In many instances, the same stream systems that occur in the mixed-grass plains district also pass through this one, creating continuous corridors of streamside woodland that facilitate the dispersal of moisture-loving reptiles and amphibians into the drier parts of the Kansan province from the east.

THE TEXAN PROVINCE In Texas, this variable region, trending from north to south, extends all the way from the Red River to the Gulf Coast. It is bounded on the west by the Kansan, Balconian, and Tamaulipan provinces and on the east by the moist pine-oak forests of the Austroriparian province. It includes both the East and West Cross Timbers, whose essentially sandy soils support the growth of post oak–blackjack oak–hickory savannahs interspersed among tallgrass prairies. The Grand Prairie, which lies between the two, has thinner, rockier soil, exposed limestone hills, and cedar brakes but also contains significant areas of tallgrass prairie, as do both the Blackland and Coastal prairies. The Texan province additionally includes some of the state's better interior wetlands, with numerous freshwater marshes and peat bogs scattered along a line stretching from Leon County to Gonzales County, where some typically eastern species of reptiles and amphibians occur. A number of moisture-dependent reptiles and amphibians have entered the drier parts of the province from the east by moving along the major river systems, whose wet woodlands of oak, hackberry, elm, and pecan trees provide the necessary moisture and leaf-litter shelter that are necessary to the survival of such species. Their overland entry into or through the province would otherwise be unlikely.

THE AUSTRORIPARIAN PROVINCE Because of its sandy soils and high annual rainfall—conditions that promote tree growth—this province contains the largest, most luxuriant woodlands in the state, the pine and pine-hardwood forests of East Texas. Its western boundary in Texas runs approximately along a line drawn from the western end of Red River County in the north to Harris County in the south; its eastern boundary in the state is the Louisiana border. The southernmost part of the province is coastal prairie. To describe the region simply as a pine and pine-hardwood forest is to understate the spectacular diversity of this most complex mosaic of plant life. While the northern upland part of the province contains fewer kinds of trees per acre (mostly longleaf pine together with some oaks and sweet gum) than the southern, the region to the south, particularly in the Big Thicket, is believed to contain more separate ecosystems than any other area of similar size in North America. Altogether, the bountiful flora of this province comprises hundreds of plant species, some derived from eastern and northern forests and a few whose origins are represented in the barren deserts to the west. Oaks, hickories, and sweet gums, with some ash, sycamore, alder, river birch, black willow, maple, water hickory, and swamp tupelo, grow in the bottomlands; bald cypress and swamp tupelo, together with some water hickory and water elm, constitute the region's cypress sloughs; dwarf palmettos growing among hardwood trees in wet flatlands characterize the palmetto swamps; American beech and southern magnolia, along with a few white oak and loblolly pine, grow on the drier slopes and ridges, as do some prickly pear cactus and yucca; and there are even more plant associations that form additional biotic subdivisions.

Neither the Chihuahuan nor the Balconian biotic province contains a characteristic group of snakes within its borders, but together they share the following 12 species: Baird's rat snake, Trans-Pecos rat snake, Trans-Pecos blind snake, Central Texas whipsnake, gray-banded king snake, Big Bend patch-nosed snake, Trans-Pecos black-headed snake, Texas lyre snake, northern black-tailed rattlesnake, Mojave rattlesnake, banded and mottled rock rattlesnake, and western and eastern black-necked garter snake. The Tamaulipan biotic province, where part of the serpent fauna is of tropical origin, includes a number of snakes that in Texas are found only in this region: indigo snake, speckled racer, black-striped snake, Mexican hook-nosed snake, northern cat-eyed snake, Schott's whipsnake, and Mexican black-headed snake. Although the Kansan biotic province contains a large complement of snakes (35 species), only the western plains garter snake is confined to this province in Texas. The Texan biotic province contains an even greater number of serpent species (41), of which only the midland water snake is restricted to it in Texas. The Austroriparian biotic province contains only three characteristic serpents—Louisiana pine, Florida red-bellied, and Gulf crayfish snakes. When combined with those of the Texan province, the following six serpents can be added—western mud snake, canebrake rattlesnake, western pygmy rattlesnake, Mississippi green water snake, broad-banded water snake, and western earth snake.

We would be remiss if we did not discuss aquatic habitats in Texas, for no less than 24 Texas snake species and subspecies (22 percent) are aquatic or semiaquatic. Texas contains nine major river basins: the Rio Grande, Nueces, San Antonio–Guadalupe, Colorado, Brazos, Trinity, Neches-Sabine, Canadian, and Red River systems. The Canadian and Red rivers drain most of North Texas; the Trinity and Neches-Sabine basins drain East Texas; the Brazos basin drains central and northwestern Texas; the San Antonio, Guadalupe, and Nueces basins drain southern Texas; and the Colorado and Rio Grande basins drain parts of central and western Texas.

Only two native aquatic serpents, the Brazos and Concho water snakes, are narrowly restricted to limited sections of particular river systems, whereas each of the others is distributed between and among two or more river systems. All of the garter snakes are semiaquatic, and although several of them are found in very dry habitats, they seldom stray far from moisture. The checkered garter snake, which seems able to tolerate arid conditions for relatively long periods, is the single exception. On the other hand, the Gulf salt marsh snake, which is restricted to the Gulf coastal marshes, is the only native serpent wholly adapted to a saltwater existence, although even the cottonmouth demonstrates a degree of tolerance for brackish and saltwater Gulf Coast marshes. Most of the aquatic snakes are habitat generalists, in that they occur in aquatic conditions but these conditions can occur from eastern to southern Texas and from the Sabine system to the Pecos River and Rio Grande.

SNAKE CLASSIFICATION AND IDENTIFICATION

Taxonomy is the science of classifying and naming animals and plants—the foundation for the development of biological knowledge. The history of classifying animals is perhaps nearly as old as man himself. Even natives of various primitive tribes were good naturalists, with specific names for local trees, flowers, mammals, birds, fishes, and other species. Their health—sometimes even their lives—depended on their ability to distinguish between harmless and venomous (or toxic) plants and animals. To survive in nature, they frequently learned the subtle differences between such things as edible mushrooms and deadly toadstools, milk snakes and coral snakes, and a host of other "good-bad" species that they encountered in the wild.

Perhaps the first modern taxonomist was Aristotle (384–322 BC), who brought together the knowledge of his time and formulated it into the beginnings of a science of classification. He categorized animals by larger groupings and even classified them according to their actions, habits, and where they lived. But the real father of taxonomy is considered to be Carolus Linnaeus, a Swedish naturalist who in the mid-1700s consistently used the binomial system of nomenclature in his pioneer work; that is, he assigned both a generic and specific name to each animal. In those days, taxonomy was a relatively simple science that required only a careful examination of the organism's body parts and a comparison of such features with those of other closely related animals. Since then, however, the science of taxonomy has changed dramatically. Today, instead of relying only on morphological characters to compare species, the taxonomist uses a variety of other, more sophisticated, tools to accomplish the task. Among them are biochemistry, histology, cytology, genetics, and, in the case of venomous snakes, analysis of their venoms by electrophoresis and chromatography.

Beginning at the highest level of animal classification, snakes are grouped with the vertebrates, since they have a backbone consisting of individual segments, or vertebrae. Together with the crocodilians, turtles, lizards, and tuataras (all of which are cold-blooded and share the characteristic of dry, scaly skin), they are included in the class Reptilia. Defining their taxonomic status even more narrowly, snakes are sorted with lizards in the order Squamata, then placed in their own suborder, Serpentes. This suborder is generally considered to be divisible into 13, 14, or 15 living families (depending on which authority one follows), 4 of which occur in Texas. In the main body of this book, the species and subspecies accounts are grouped by family, and each of the four groups is preceded by a brief definition of the relevant family.

DEFINING THE SNAKE Snakes are essentially highly specialized lizards without limbs, movable eyelids, and external ear openings (though some lizards also lack limbs, movable eyelids, and external ear openings). Furthermore, they have neither a sternum nor a urinary bladder, and most species possess only a single functional lung, which is extremely elongated to conform to the snake's long, slender body shape. In snakes, the two lower jaw bones are separated at the front and united there by a flexible ligament, whereas in lizards they are solidly fused at that point. In addition, the quadrate bones of snakes are typically long and loosely connected to the skull, permitting flexibility of movement, but those of lizards are firmly attached to the skull. While lizards have only a few pairs of ribs, those of snakes are numerous and in some species can number more than 300 pairs.

MAKING AN IDENTIFICATION Before attempting to identify a snake, it is necessary to become familiar with some simple terms used to define various external features of this animal group. Among the most obvious and useful are those of coloration and markings. A glance at the photographs in this book will quickly show that Texas snakes come in a bewildering array of patterns and colors, ranging from unicolored on top (green and earth snakes) to complex dorsal patterns combining both blotches and spots (long-nosed snake and rock rattlesnake).

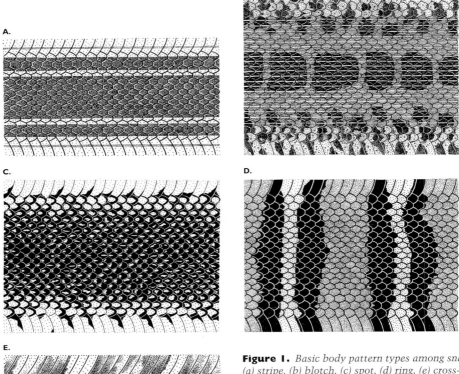

Figure 1. *Basic body pattern types among snakes: (a) stripe, (b) blotch, (c) spot, (d) ring, (e) cross-band.*

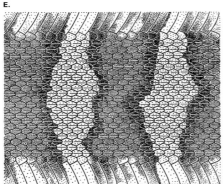

Some of the basic pattern types can be defined as follows:

Unicolor. A single, solid dorsal color, but with a generally paler hue on the belly.

Stripe. A narrow, lengthwise line of color, which, if wide, may be called a band.

Blotch. A large oval, rectangular, squarish, or diamond-shaped marking, usually arranged with numerous others in a single, lengthwise row along the back. One or more secondary longitudinal rows of blotches often occur on either side of the body below the main series of blotches, although these are sometimes small enough to be considered spots.

Spot. A marking not as large as a blotch, but one that can be smaller than a single dorsal scale or occupy an area the size of six or eight dorsal scales.

Ring. A band of color that completely encircles the body.

Crossband. Similar to a ring, in that it crosses the back and sides of the snake's body, but it fails to cross the belly.

Besides color and pattern, other characteristics that may help to make a positive identification include the size and shape of the snake's head, as well as its markings, if any; unusual features of the snout, such as an upturned or enlarged rostral scale; the presence or absence of a facial pit on either side of the head, in addition to a nostril opening; and whether the eyes have round or elliptical pupils. Another clue is the shape of the snake's body, whether slender, of moderate girth, or heavy-bodied.

Although scale characteristics (expressed by kind, number, shape, and arrangement) may prove more reliable for distinguishing certain species and subspecies than either color or markings, such features are not easily recognized by those unfamiliar with them. Furthermore, they are not readily observed, especially in smaller snakes. Yet some scale characteristics, when considered together with other morphological features, often are important aids for identifying snakes, and they are therefore included in the description of each species and subspecies. Among the more important of these are the number of scale rows, called dorsals, that wrap diagonally around the top and sides of the snake's body (usually counted near the middle of the trunk) and the condition of the anal plate (the scale covering the anal opening), which is either single (undivided) or double (divided). An even more fundamental character used to help sort out species is whether a snake has lengthwise-keeled or smooth body scales, though in some snakes the keels are not pronounced and may occur only on the upper few rows of the body.

The simplest and most practical way to begin the task of making an identification is to review the color photographs in the book, keeping in mind the various features that are most important for such purposes. When a match has been found, verify the snake's identification by turning to the text account for that species or subspecies. Compare its key characters with those mentioned in the Description section, and eliminate from consideration any look-alikes by reading the Comparable Snakes section in the same account. The line drawings throughout the book that compare patterns and other features of certain species or subspecies to one another should serve to confirm your choice. If, after completing this procedure, you are still unable to identify the specimen, the next step

is to use the taxonomic key, beginning on page 25, which is designed to help trace the snake to the species level. From there, the text descriptions and line drawings should lead you to the correct subspecies. In most instances, the final part of the task will be simplified if you know precisely where the snake was found, since each subspecies — except for intergrade populations between adjoining subspecies — occupies a separate geographic territory.

ABERRANT SNAKES Unfortunately, it is not possible for a novice to identify by such means every snake encountered in the wild, for in nature we can expect each organism to show varying degrees of color and pattern deviation. Moderately atypical specimens, which nevertheless fall within the normal range of variation for their kind, are mentioned in the appropriate species and subspecies text descriptions and should, therefore, present no real obstacle in one's efforts to identify them. Others may be more troublesome. At times, for example, different but usually closely related species may breed with one another and produce offspring, called hybrids, which share certain characteristics of both parents. But since such progeny are themselves generally incapable of producing young, they rarely become established as viable local colonies. Because they do not exactly match the descriptions or illustrations depicted in most field guides, they are normally difficult to identify, even by the experts. Fortunately, such species crosses are rare, and the possibility of encountering one in the wild is extremely remote.

Equally uncommon in nature are snakes with extreme color or pattern abnormalities. Even professional herpetologists, who probably find more snakes in several seasons of fieldwork than most persons see in a lifetime, rarely encounter them in the wild. Among these curiosities, the most frequently reported are partial or complete albinos. Although we usually think of an albino animal as one totally lacking in melanin, Bechtel (1995) defines albinism as either the absence or deficiency of melanin, a condition occurring in approximately one of every 10,000 to 40,000 individuals of a given species.

Over the last 40 years we have seen a number of such aberrant, wild-caught snakes in Texas. Among the harmless species were an albino prairie king snake, a snow-white (leucistic) Texas rat snake with dark eyes, and a white Texas rat snake with an irregular band of pale, gray-brown scales reaching down the middle of its back. Of the venomous species, four were Texas coral snakes: two from Channelview in Harris County, one from Lufkin in Angelina County, and another from Wilson County, 30 miles (48 km) southeast of San Antonio, each of which exhibited the normal complement of red and yellow colors but lacked all traces of black pigment. Then there are golden yellow (xanthic) variants with vague patterns, like the western diamond-backed rattlesnake collected near Austin.

At the other end of the spectrum are all-black individuals whose normal body patterns have been virtually obliterated by black pigmentation. Two such unusual coral snakes are known from Texas, one of which was found at Lackland Air Force Base near San Antonio. The second, reported by Gloyd (1938), was a melanistic specimen encountered near Victoria by a woman familiar with the local serpent fauna. After concluding from the snake's all-black color that it did not fit the description of any local venomous species known to her, she picked it up, whereupon the reptile bit her on a finger. Although the bite proved serious, the victim recovered.

Just as bewildering as all-black coral snakes are the occasional patternless examples of ordinarily well-marked species, like the completely pale gray mottled rock rattler found near Juno in Val Verde County, the lengthwise-striped western diamond-backed rattlesnakes sometimes reported from Central and West Texas, and the piebald western diamond-backed rattlesnake from Bosque County.

Considering the great odds against finding an aberrantly colored or patterned snake in the wild, it may seem trivial to devote so much space to a discussion of such abnormal specimens. Nonetheless, we feel that the reader should at least be aware of their existence, so that an unexpected encounter with one of these odd serpents, should it be venomous, does not become a medical emergency. Since the striking coloration of an all-white or golden yellow snake is unlike that of any normally colored Texas snake species, it will more than likely be recognized for what it is—an aberrant specimen—and should therefore not be handled unless and until it is determined to be a harmless kind. There is, however, no easy solution for identifying some of the other bizarre color and pattern mutations. By observing many snakes over a period of time, an experienced herpetologist, amateur as well as professional, eventually learns to recognize most native species—even the strange out-of-character individuals—from their general, overall appearance and behavior. Any person seriously interested in the subject can in time achieve the same objective.

If all attempts to classify a particular unfamiliar specimen prove futile, we suggest you take the puzzling reptile to a local zoo, nature center, museum of natural science, or university zoology department, where the staff can assist you in making a determination. Under no circumstances, however, should you risk a venomous snakebite by picking up such an animal by hand, for at this point you will not know if your mystery specimen is harmless or dangerous.

NAMING THE SNAKE Once the snake has been identified, it will be assigned a name, which will probably be a vernacular name (otherwise known as the common name). Because such designations often vary greatly from one part of the continent to another, Collins (1990) has attempted to standardize the common names of all North American snakes. We have, with some exceptions, followed his recommendations. Even more meaningful than a serpent's vernacular name is its scientific name, for not only is such a Latinized designation accepted and understood by scientists and naturalists worldwide, but it also reveals the reptile's relationships with other closely related snakes.

The novice usually finds scientific names intimidating, but they need not be. Early in life, without ever knowing it, we were already using the scientific names of certain familiar zoo animals: alligator, as in *Alligator mississippiensis*; boa constrictor, as in *Boa constrictor*; giraffe, as in *Giraffa camelopardalis*; and hippopotamus, as in *Hippopotamus amphibius.*

Composed of at least two separate words

(genus and species) and sometimes three (genus, species, and subspecies), the scientific name may also include the name of the person (the author) who first formally described the snake, in which case his or her name will appear at the end. When the author's name is enclosed in parentheses, it means the snake has been assigned to a different genus from the one in that author's original description. In more formal listings, the year in which the animal was first described will follow the author's name.

The generic name, which always begins with a capital letter, is the first element in a snake's scientific name. It is followed by the species name, which always begins with a lowercase letter. Both are printed in italics, and together they identify a specific kind of organism—the species. Considered the basic unit of classification, a species can be defined as a distinct group of similar organisms capable of interbreeding among themselves but reproductively isolated from other species. An example of a species with no described subspecies is *Crotalus atrox*, the western diamond-backed rattlesnake. In some instances, a species is further divided into two or more geographically different local populations, called subspecies (or races), in which case the scientific name will be composed of three parts, the last part also beginning with a lowercase letter and italicized. For example, the rock rattlesnake consists of several subspecies, two of which, the mottled rock rattlesnake (*Crotalus lepidus lepidus*) and the banded rock rattlesnake (*Crotalus lepidus klauberi*), occur in Texas, each occupying a different segment of the species' range. Subspecies can therefore be defined as geographically distinct populations of a species that are still recognizable at the species level but differ in certain characteristics from other races within the same species. Unlike species hybrids, however, they freely interbreed and produce fertile offspring. The area where two subspecies meet and intermingle reproductively, known as a zone of intergradation, can be as narrow as a few miles or as broad as a couple of hundred miles. Because there are inadequate specimen samples from many such areas, the zones are not always well defined. Within these zones, individual animals can look like either of the two involved subspecies, or they can share certain characteristics of both races.

TAXONOMIC ISSUES

At the beginning of this project, we had to make some decisions about the scientific names of several species of Texas snakes whose taxonomic status is in dispute. Most involve the classification of subspecies within a single species, whose individual geographic ranges apparently do not converge and whose evolutionary pathways seem to be in isolation from those of their closest relatives.

Since evolution is a continuing biological process, the science of classifying snakes is often complex and open to differing taxonomic interpretations. As a result of its dynamic nature, there is frequent disagreement among taxonomists about whether a particular population of snakes represents a subspecies or is, in fact, more correctly classified as a species. For example, when two subspecies (races) of the same species are sufficiently isolated from one another by an impassable geographic barrier (a large body of water, mountains, etc.), preventing any genetic exchange between them, they will probably evolve independently and may over time become separate and distinct species. One issue then is whether there is sufficient evidence to support the contention that the two populations are already completely isolated from one another geographically and therefore reproductively separated. Which raises the question, are they indeed genetically isolated, or have we, as the result of a collecting bias, overlooked areas of contact between them? If they are completely isolated from one another, at what point in time can we conclude that they have, in fact, evolved into separate species? We should also remember that evolutionarily speaking, such decisions are being made in a tiny slice of time. Who can say whether in the next 500 years, 1,000 years, or longer, the two subspecies will remain separate races, eventually merge again into a single population, or continue on their present evolutionary course to become individual species? Some herpetologists argue that when two adjacent but geographically separated populations of a single species (presently regarded as subspecies) are iso-

(a) Prairie king snake. Lampropeltis calligaster calligaster. *Albino adult from Brazoria County.*
(b) Texas rat snake. Elaphe obsoleta lindheimeri. *Leucistic adult from Brazos County.*
(c) Texas rat snake. Elaphe obsoleta lindheimeri. *Adult with color-pattern anomaly from Fort Bend County. Photo by R. A. Odum.*
(d) Texas coral snake. Micrurus fulvius tener. *Albinistic adult from Angelina County.*

A.

B.

C.   D.

E.   F.

(e) Western diamond-backed rattlesnake. Crotalus atrox. *Xanthic adult
from Travis County. (f) Mottled rock
rattlesnake.* Crotalus lepidus lepidus.
*Patternless adult from Val Verde
County. (g) Western diamond-
backed rattlesnake.* Crotalus atrox.
*Patternless adult. Photo by P. Freed.
(h) Western diamond-backed rattlesnake.* Crotalus atrox. *Piebald adult
from Bosque County. Photo by
J. E. Werler.*

G.

H.

lated from one another, they are well on their way to becoming species and should therefore automatically be given species status. We have taken a more conservative approach. It is our belief that before all such subspecies are summarily elevated to species rank, they must be evaluated case by case, using all of the data available. Only then can we adequately decide the outcome of such taxonomic controversies.

Based on that position, we have adopted the proposed change of status for three snakes from subspecies to species rank: Louisiana pine snake from *Pituophis melanoleucus ruthveni* to *P. ruthveni*, *Tantilla rubra cucul-lata* to *T. cucullata*, and *Carphophis amoenus vermis* to *C. vermis*. We are retaining the subspecies designation for the northern scarlet snake (*Cemophora coccinea copei*) and Texas scarlet snake (*C. c. lineri*); eastern yellow-bellied racer (*Coluber constrictor flaviventris*); Texas indigo snake (*Drymarchon corais erebennus*); corn snake (*Elaphe guttata guttata*), Great Plains rat snake (*E. g. emoryi*), and Southwestern rat snake (*E. g. meahllmorum*); Texas coral snake (*Micrurus fulvius tener*); Brazos water snake (*Nerodia harteri harteri*) and Concho water snake (*N. h. paucimaculata*).

CHECKLIST OF TEXAS SNAKES

FAMILY LEPTOTYPHLOPIDAE

Plains blind snake
  Leptotyphlops dulcis dulcis (Baird and
  Girard) 1853
New Mexico blind snake
  Leptotyphlops dulcis dissectus (Cope)
  1896

Trans-Pecos blind snake
  Leptotyphlops humilis segregus Klauber
  1939

FAMILY COLUBRIDAE

Kansas glossy snake
  Arizona elegans elegans Kennicott 1859
Texas glossy snake
  Arizona elegans arenicola Dixon 1960
Painted Desert glossy snake
  Arizona elegans philipi Klauber 1946
Trans-Pecos rat snake
  Bogertophis subocularis subocularis
  (Brown) 1901
Western worm snake
  Carphophis vermis (Kennicott) 1859
Northern scarlet snake
  Cemophora coccinea copei Jan 1863
Texas scarlet snake
  Cemophora coccinea lineri Williams,
  Brown, and Wilson 1966
Buttermilk racer
  Coluber constrictor anthicus Cope 1862
Tan racer
  Coluber constrictor etheridgei Wilson
  1970

Eastern yellow-bellied racer
  Coluber constrictor flaviventris Say 1823
Mexican racer
  Coluber constrictor oaxaca Jan 1863
Southern black racer
  Coluber constrictor priapus Dunn and
  Wood 1939
Black-striped snake
  Coniophanes imperialis imperialis
  (Kennicott) 1859
Prairie ring-necked snake
  Diadophis punctatus arnyi Kennicott
  1858
Regal ring-necked snake
  Diadophis punctatus regalis Baird and
  Girard 1853
Mississippi ring-necked snake
  Diadophis punctatus stictogenys Cope
  1860
Texas indigo snake
  Drymarchon corais erebennus (Cope) 1860

Speckled racer
Drymobius margaritiferus margaritiferus
(Schlegel) 1837
Baird's rat snake
Elaphe bairdi (Yarrow) 1880
Corn snake
Elaphe guttata guttata (Linnaeus) 1766
Great Plains rat snake
Elaphe guttata emoryi Baird and Girard
1853
Southwestern rat snake
Elaphe guttata meahllmorum Smith,
Chizar, Staley, and Tepedelen 1994
Texas rat snake
Elaphe obsoleta lindheimeri (Baird and
Girard) 1853
Western mud snake
Farancia abacura reinwardti (Schlegel)
1837
Mexican hook-nosed snake
Ficimia streckeri Taylor 1931
Western hook-nosed snake
Gyalopion canum Cope 1860
Plains hog-nosed snake
Heterodon nasicus nasicus Baird and
Girard 1852
Dusty hog-nosed snake
Heterodon nasicus gloydi Edgren 1952
Mexican hog-nosed snake
Heterodon nasicus kennerlyi Kennicott
1860
Eastern hog-nosed snake
Heterodon platirhinos Latreille 1802
Texas night snake
Hypsiglena torquata jani Duges 1866
Gray-banded king snake
Lampropeltis alterna (Brown) 1902
Prairie king snake
Lampropeltis calligaster calligaster
(Harlan) 1827
Speckled king snake
Lampropeltis getula holbrooki Stejneger
1902
Desert king snake
Lampropeltis getula splendida (Baird and
Girard) 1853
Louisiana milk snake
Lampropeltis triangulum amaura Cope
1860
Mexican milk snake
Lampropeltis triangulum annulata
Kennicott 1860

New Mexico milk snake
Lampropeltis triangulum celaenops
Stejneger 1903
Central Plains milk snake
Lampropeltis triangulum gentilis (Baird
and Girard) 1853
Northern cat-eyed snake
Leptodeira septentrionalis septentrionalis
(Kennicott) 1859
Western smooth green snake
Liochlorophis vernalis blanchardi
Grobman 1941
Eastern coachwhip
Masticophis flagellum flagellum (Shaw)
1802
Western coachwhip
Masticophis flagellum testaceus Say
1823
Schott's whipsnake
Masticophis schotti schotti Baird and
Girard 1853
Ruthven's whipsnake
Masticophis schotti ruthveni Ortenburger
1923
Central Texas whipsnake
Masticophis taeniatus girardi Stejneger
and Barbour 1917
Gulf salt marsh snake
Nerodia clarki clarki (Baird and Girard)
1853
Mississippi green water snake
Nerodia cyclopion (Dumeril, Bibron, and
Dumeril) 1854
Yellow-bellied water snake
Nerodia erythrogaster flavigaster
(Conant) 1949
Blotched water snake
Nerodia erythrogaster transversa
(Hallowell) 1852
Broad-banded water snake
Nerodia fasciata confluens (Blanchard)
1923
Florida water snake
Nerodia fasciata pictiventris (Cope) 1895
Brazos water snake
Nerodia harteri harteri (Trapido) 1941
Concho water snake
Nerodia harteri paucimaculata (Tinkle
and Conant) 1961
Diamond-backed water snake
Nerodia rhombifer rhombifer (Hallowell)
1852

Midland water snake
Nerodia sipedon pleuralis (Cope) 1892
Rough green snake
Opheodrys aestivus (Linnaeus) 1766
Sonoran gopher snake
Pituophis catenifer affinis Hallowell 1852
Bull snake
Pituophis catenifer sayi (Schlegel) 1837
Louisiana pine snake
Pituophis ruthveni Stull 1929
Graham's crayfish snake
Regina grahami Baird and Girard 1853
Gulf crayfish snake
Regina rigida sinicola (Huheey) 1959
Texas long-nosed snake
Rhinocheilus lecontei tessellatus Garman
1883
Big Bend patch-nosed snake
Salvadora deserticola Schmidt 1940
Mountain patch-nosed snake
Salvadora grahamiae grahamiae Baird
and Girard 1853
Texas patch-nosed snake
Salvadora grahamiae lineata Schmidt
1940
Great Plains ground snake
Sonora semiannulata semiannulata Baird
and Girard 1853
Taylor's ground snake
Sonora semiannulata taylori (Boulenger)
1894
Marsh brown snake
Storeria dekayi limnetes Anderson 1961
Texas brown snake
Storeria dekayi texana Trapido 1944
Florida red-bellied snake
Storeria occipitomaculata obscura
Trapido 1944
Mexican black-headed snake
Tantilla atriceps (Gunther) 1895
Trans-Pecos black-headed snake
Tantilla cucullata Minton 1956
Flat-headed snake
Tantilla gracilis Baird and Girard 1853

Southwestern black-headed snake
Tantilla hobartsmithi Taylor 1937
Plains black-headed snake
Tantilla nigriceps Kennicott 1860
Western black-necked garter snake
Thamnophis cyrtopsis cyrtopsis
(Kennicott) 1860
Eastern black-necked garter snake
Thamnophis cyrtopsis ocellatus (Cope)
1880
Checkered garter snake
Thamnophis marcianus marcianus (Baird
and Girard) 1853
Western ribbon snake
Thamnophis proximus proximus (Say)
1823
Arid land ribbon snake
Thamnophis proximus diabolicus
Rossman 1963
Gulf coast ribbon snake
Thamnophis proximus orarius Rossman
1963
Red-striped ribbon snake
Thamnophis proximus rubrilineatus
Rossman 1963
Western plains garter snake
Thamnophis radix haydeni (Kennicott)
1860
Eastern garter snake
Thamnophis sirtalis sirtalis (Linnaeus)
1758
Texas garter snake
Thamnophis sirtalis annectens Brown
1950
Red-sided garter snake
Thamnophis sirtalis parietalis (Say) 1823
Texas lyre snake
Trimorphodon lambda vilkinsoni Cope
1886
Lined snake
Tropidoclonion lineatum (Hallowell) 1856
Rough earth snake
Virginia striatula (Linnaeus) 1766
Western earth snake
Virginia valeriae elegans Kennicott 1859

FAMILY ELAPIDAE

Texas coral snake
Micrurus fulvius tener (Baird and Girard)
1853

FAMILY VIPERIDAE

Southern copperhead
  Agkistrodon contortrix contortrix
  (Linnaeus) 1766
Broad-banded copperhead
  Agkistrodon contortrix laticinctus Gloyd
  and Conant 1934
Trans-Pecos copperhead
  Agkistrodon contortrix pictigaster Gloyd
  and Conant 1943
Western cottonmouth
  Agkistrodon piscivorus leucostoma
  (Troost) 1836
Western diamond-backed rattlesnake
  Crotalus atrox Baird and Girard 1853
Canebrake rattlesnake
  Crotalus horridus atricaudatus Latreille
  1802
Mottled rock rattlesnake
  Crotalus lepidus lepidus (Kennicott) 1861

Banded rock rattlesnake
  Crotalus lepidus klauberi Gloyd 1936
Northern black-tailed rattlesnake
  Crotalus molossus molossus Baird and
  Girard 1853
Mojave rattlesnake
  Crotalus scutulatus scutulatus
  (Kennicott) 1861
Prairie rattlesnake
  Crotalus viridis viridis (Rafinesque) 1818
Desert massasauga
  Sistrurus catenatus edwardsi (Baird and
  Girard) 1853
Western massasauga
  Sistrurus catenatus tergeminus (Say) 1823
Western pygmy rattlesnake
  Sistrurus miliarius streckeri Gloyd 1935

KEY TO THE SPECIES OF TEXAS SNAKES

This key is written for persons not familiar with identification keys. It is essentially a numbered list of opposing pairs of characteristics, or couplets. To determine the species of a particular specimen, choose the characteristic from the first couplet that most closely fits the snake. At the end of the characteristic is a number that refers to the next couplet relevant to your snake. Proceed to that couplet, choose the closest characteristic, and continue in that fashion until your choice of characteristic ends in the name of a species.

To aid in your choices, the names for the various scales on the snake's head and body are presented in Figure 2, and other helpful figures are scattered throughout the key.

The key identifies only species found in Texas, and it does not distinguish between subspecies. Species common names, however, are followed in parentheses by the names of subspecies described in this book, to help the reader find the appropriate accounts for subspecies identification.

1. Belly scales about same size as dorsal scales (Fig. 3a)...2
   Belly scales much larger than dorsal scales (Fig. 3b) 3
2. Supraoculars absent (Fig. 4a); a very small, pinkish snake, with blackish eye spots beneath the scales; body scales all the same size; length about 6 inches, maximum length around 11 inches

....Western blind snake (Trans-Pecos), *Leptotyphlops humilis*

Supraoculars present (Fig. 4b); color and scales similar to above; length about 9 inches, maximum length around 13 inches
....Texas blind snake (plains, New Mexico), *Leptotyphlops dulcis*
3. A facial pit between eye and nostril (Fig. 5a) 4
   No facial pit between eye and nostril (Fig. 5b) 13
4. No rattle or button on end of tail........5
   Rattle or button on end of tail.............6
5. Loreal scale present (Fig. 6a), maximum of 23 dorsal scale rows; copper color, dorsal saddles dark to moderate brown, narrow along the middle of the back and frequently not meeting dorsally; dorsal scales weakly keeled, elliptical pupil, and tip of tail frequently yellow, belly pinkish brown; length ranges between 24 and 36 inches, maximum length about 42 inches ....Copperhead (southern, broad-banded, Trans-Pecos), *Agkistrodon contortrix*

No loreal scale (Fig. 6b), maximum of 25 dorsal scale rows; young occasionally copper colored, but belly dark brown to black; black cheek stripe in young and adults, but frequently faded in adults; black dorsal transverse bands are quickly lost as individual grows; general adult color dark brown to black; frequently swims with most of body visible above water; averages about 36 inches in length, maximum length about 62 inches .... Cottonmouth (western), *Agkistrodon piscivorus*

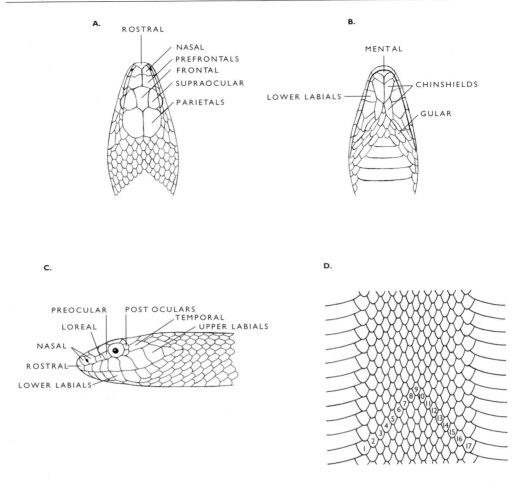

Figure 2. *Basic head and body scale arrangement of a typical snake: (a) dorsal head scales, (b) ventral head scales, (c) lateral head scales, (d) method of counting dorsal body scale rows.*

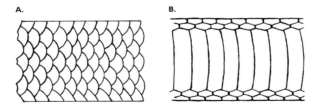

Figure 3. *Reduced (a) and normal (b) size of belly scales.*

6. Head scales generally very small (Fig. 7a) 7

    Head scales consist of nine large plates (Fig. 7b) 12

7. Upper preocular divided vertically, anterior division being somewhat higher than posterior part and curved over the snout in front of the supraocular (Fig. 8a); body pattern of widely separated transverse dark bands, occasionally intermixed with dark spots; length about 20 inches, maximum length about 32 inches ....Rock rattlesnake (mottled, banded), *Crotalus lepidus*

    Upper preocular not divided vertically

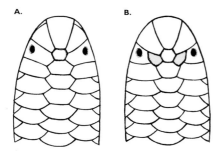

Figure 4. *Supraoculars absent (a) or present (b).*

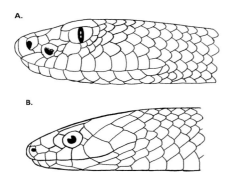

Figure 5. *Facial pit present (a) or absent (b).*

(Fig. 8b), or if divided the anterior division not noticeably higher than the posterior part and not curved over the snout in front of the supraocular..8

8. Anterior body pattern of dark blotches that grade into bands on rear part of body and tail; length around 40 inches, maximum length about 57 inches

.... Western rattlesnake (prairie), *Crotalus viridis*

Not patterned as above 9

9. Dorsal pattern of diamond-shaped blotches, tail with black and white bands 10

Dorsal pattern of transverse dark bands or diamonds; tail black 11

10. Dark and pale tail bands of about equal width; white cheek stripe extends to mouthline; scales between supraoculars small; length about 48 inches, maximum length about 84 inches

.... Western diamond-backed rattlesnake, *Crotalus atrox*

Dark tail bands about half the width of pale bands; white cheek stripe passes behind

the mouthline; scales between supraoculars larger than those on rear of head; length around 30 inches, maximum length 51 inches ....Mojave rattlesnake, *Crotalus scutulatus*

11. Anterior dorsal pattern with chevron-shaped bands, tail black; length about 48 inches, maximum length around 74 inches ....Timber rattlesnake (canebrake), *Crotalus horridus*

Anterior body pattern with an interconnected chain of dark blotches or diamonds, tail black; length around 38 inches, maximum length about 49 inches

..................................Black-tailed rattlesnake (northern), *Crotalus molossus*

12. Upper preocular in contact with post-nasal; a series of dark brown to brown body blotches outlined in pale brown, with a lateral alternating series of pale brown spots with ventrolateral darker spots alternating with the pale brown spots; rattles relatively

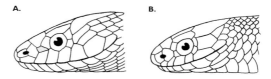

Figure 6. *Loreal scale present (a) or absent (b).*

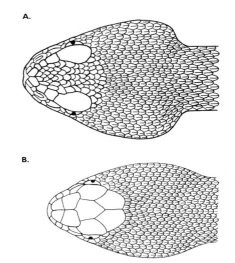

Figure 7. *Small (a) or large (b) scales on crown of rattlesnakes.*

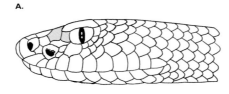
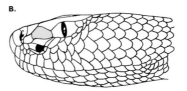

Figure 8. *Upper preocular vertically divided (a) or not (b).*

large for a small rattlesnake with a length of 23 inches, maximum length about 34 inches ....Massasauga (desert, western), *Sistrurus catenatus*

Upper preocular not contacting post-nasal; usually a pale reddish brown dorsal longitudinal stripe, interrupted by a series of short transverse blackish markings; one or two rows of lateral or ventrolateral blackish spots in addition to the dorsal bands; ground color gray to grayish pink; rattles very small; length around 18 inches, maximum length about 25 inches
.... Pygmy rattlesnake (western), *Sistrurus miliarius*

13. Rings completely encircle the body, red rings alternate with yellow rings that are separated by black rings; snout and anterior head black, followed by a yellow ring, then a black ring; an erect fang at the anterior end of upper jaw; length about 25 inches, maximum length around 47 inches
...........................Eastern coral snake (Texas), *Micrurus fulvius*

Body not as above, ringlike crossbands never completely encircle the body; no permanently erect fang at anterior end of upper jaw 14

14. Prefrontals more than two (Fig. 9a)...15
Prefrontals two (Fig. 9b); color patterns highly variable; small or large snakes........16

15. A large snake with more than 41 large dark body blotches on a yellowish ground color that contrast more strongly with the ground color at each end of the snake; the dor-

sal blotches may or may not fuse on the neck; belly marked laterally with large blackish marks on a yellow ground color; tendency to hiss (expel air) loudly; size around 48 inches, maximum length about 100 inches
.... Gopher snake (Sonoran, bull), *Pituophis catenifer*

A large snake with 42 or fewer body blotches; neck blotches normally brown, somewhat obscure, and frequently fusing on the anterior body; blotches just in front of the vent and on the tail brownish red, distinct, and well separated; belly mottled with pale yellow and dark brown spots; length about 51 inches, maximum length around 70 inches......................Louisiana pine snake, *Pituophis ruthveni*

16. Scales beneath tail normally in a single row (Fig. 10a); nose appears long; black transverse dorsal bands separated by red ground color; red scales often obscured with black flecks; belly pale yellow to cream; length about 26 inches, maximum length around 41 inches .... Long-nosed snake (Texas), *Rhinocheilus lecontei*

Scales beneath tail normally in two rows (Fig. 10b); color pattern variable........17

17. Loreal scale absent (Fig. 6b)..............18
Loreal scale present (Fig. 6a).............26

18. Number of middorsal scale rows normally two more than in front of vent; upturned pointed nose 19

Number of middorsal scale rows the same as those in front of vent; nose neither upturned nor pointed...................................20

19. Prefrontal scales in contact, separating rostral from frontal scale; color pattern of narrow transverse brown bands on a grayish ground color; head also banded; adults usually less than 12 inches in length but may reach 15 inches
.... Western hook-nosed snake, *Gyalopion canum*

Prefrontal scales not in contact, ros-

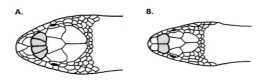

Figure 9. *Prefrontals more than two (a) or only two (b). (After Conant and Collins 1991.)*

A.

B.

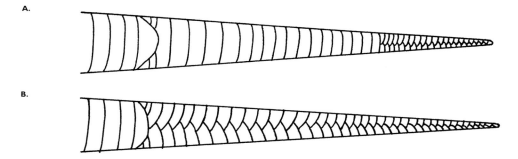

Figure 10. *Scales beneath tail in a single row (a) or a double row (b).*

A.

B.

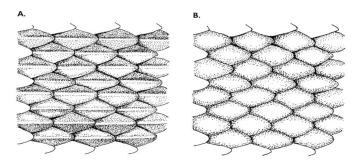

Figure 11. *Body scales keeled (a) or smooth (b).*

tral contacts frontal; body with small and usually obscure transverse brownish bands or blotches; ground color grayish brown to pale brown; head seldom has bands; adults usually less than 12 inches but may reach 19 inches

.... Mexican hook-nosed snake, *Ficimia streckeri*

20. Body scales with keels (Fig. 11a).......21
    Body scales smooth (Fig. 11b)............22

21. Body scales in 15 rows; belly yellowish, dorsal color tan or reddish tan, faint yellowish transverse band behind head, head usually dark reddish brown to dark brown; usually a white spot on the edge of the upper lip below and behind the eye; adults usually 10 inches but may reach 16 inches

.... Red-bellied snake (Florida), *Storeria occipitomaculata*

Body scales in 17 rows; belly grayish; dorsal body with tan or pale tan middorsal longitudinal stripe from rear of head to tail, with a series of small black or dark brown dots along each side of stripe; rear of head

with a pair of dark spots; adults usually about 12 inches in length but occasionally 19 inches ....Brown snake (marsh, Texas), *Storeria dekayi*

22. Head brown, tan, or slightly darker than body color, upper lip scales six per side; belly bright pink to almost red; length around 7 inches, maximum length about 9 inches

.... Flat-headed snake, *Tantilla gracilis*

Head with black cap, contrasting with body color; upper lip scales normally seven per side 23

23. Black head cap with a straight or slightly convex posterior margin, extending only about three scales beyond posterior edge of parietals, usually followed by pale border...24

Black head cap with a V-shaped posterior margin, extending four to eight scales beyond posterior edge of parietals; the black cap may or may not be interrupted by a white neck band 25

24. Normally one postocular, rear of black

head cap straight; mental usually separated from chin shields; length less than 12 inches ....Mexican black-headed snake, *Tantilla atriceps*
Normally two postoculars, rear of black head cap straight; mental usually in contact with chin shields; length less than 12 inches ....Southwestern black-headed snake, *Tantilla hobartsmithi*

25. Black cap not extending below end of mouthline, posterior margin V-shaped; body pale brown or tan, midventral area of belly pinkish red; length about 10 inches, maximum length around 15 inches
....................Plains black-headed snake, *Tantilla nigriceps*
Black cap extending below end of mouthline and 4 to 8 scales behind parietals, dorsal and ventral surfaces of head completely black, no white cheek patch; or black cap rarely extends beyond posterior tips of parietals, followed by narrow white band, which in turn is followed by a broad black band; snout usually white, a white cheek patch below and behind eye; chin shields white; white band across neck usually one to two scale rows in longitudinal width, occasionally with a longitudinal black line from parietal to black band, or a black dot, or an interrupted line from parietal to black band; length about 12 inches, maximum length around 25 inches
..................Trans-Pecos black-headed snake, *Tantilla cucullata*

26. Two loreals, pupil of eye elliptical; body with about 20 dark brown to brown transverse bands on a gray ground color; the broad dorsal blotches narrow laterally; belly white or cream to dirty yellow; usually three obscure dark spots on back of head; length about 24 inches, maximum length around 41 inches ....Lyre snake (Texas), *Trimorphodon lambda*
One loreal, pupil variable, color pattern variable, size variable....................27

27. Preocular absent, loreal enters orbit (Fig. 12a) 28
Preocular present, loreal not entering orbit (Fig. 12b) 31

28. Dorsal scale rows smooth, in 19 rows; dorsal body glossy black, belly red and black; body stout; tail short with horny tip; neck not distinguishable from rest of body; usually

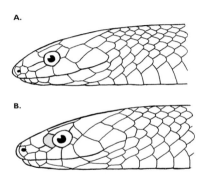

Figure 12. *Preocular scale absent (a) or present (b).*

found around swamps, often burrows in mud; length about 45 inches, maximum length around 81 inches....................Mud snake (western), *Farancia abacura*
Dorsal scale rows keeled or smooth, in fewer than 19 rows....................29

29. Dorsal scale rows 13; dorsum black to purplish black, belly pinkish, belly color extends up the sides to the third scale row; 10–12 inches in length, occasionally reaching 15 inches
....................Western worm snake, *Carphophis vermis*
Dorsal scale rows 17; dorsal surface gray, brown, or reddish brown; pointed head; length less than 15 inches 30

30. Postocular single, five upper lip scales; pointed snout; scales strongly keeled; a very plain, small brown snake with pale brown to gray belly; length about 8–9 inches, maximum length about 12 inches
....................Rough earth snake, *Virginia striatula*
Postoculars two, six upper lip scales; scales smooth or weakly keeled; gray, brown, to reddish snake; length 8–9 inches, maximum length around 15 inches
....................Smooth earth snake (western), *Virginia valeriae*

31. Anal plate entire (single scale, Fig. 13a) 32
Anal plate divided (two scales, Fig. 13b) 44

32. Dorsal scales keeled....................33
Dorsal scales smooth....................38

33. Belly pattern consisting of two parallel rows of black half-moon spots; three pale longitudinal lines of yellow, orange, white,

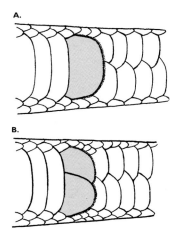

Figure 13. *Anal plate single (a) or double (b).*

or gray; length 10–12 inches, occasionally reaching 21 inches..................... Lined snake,
Tropidoclonion lineatum
Belly without two rows of black half-moon spots 34
34. Pale lateral stripe on anterior body involving fourth scale row (Fig. 14a).............35
Pale lateral stripe on anterior body absent or not touching fourth scale row (Fig. 14b) 36
35. Upper lips, lower lips, and belly with some dark markings, a double row of black spots between pale stripes; lateral pale line

on scale rows 3 and 4; outer edge of belly with obscure blackish spots on each side; length around 20–24 inches, maximum length about 41 inches
..........................Plains garter snake (western),
Thamnophis radix
Upper lips, lower lips, and belly without dark markings; three pale stripes, the median one highly variable in Texas populations, from pale yellow or grayish white to orange red; two pale spots on the parietal scales; a thin, long-tailed garter snake about 25 inches long, but may reach 48 inches
.....................Western ribbon snake (western,
arid land, Gulf coast, red-striped),
Thamnophis proximus
36. Lateral pale stripe on third scale row only near head; checkerboard pattern of squarish black and white spots, black spots frequently invade lateral pale lines; yellowish crescent mark behind the corner of the mouth followed by a large black spot; scales in 21 rows, anal plate single; about 21 inches in length, maximum length around 41 inches
..................................Checkered garter snake,
Thamnophis marcianus
Lateral pale stripe on second and third scale rows on neck 37
37. Upper lip scales eight to a side; a white to pale yellow mark on the side of the head preceded by a pair of large black neck blotches that may or may not unite across

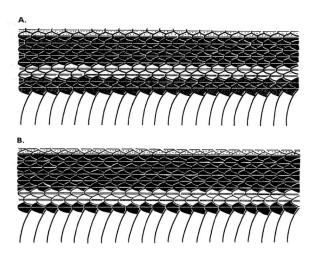

Figure 14. *Lateral pale stripe on third and fourth scale rows (a) or on second and third scale rows (b) in garter snakes.*

the back of the neck; head usually gray or bluish gray, contrasting with the black neck blotches; an orange longitudinal stripe from rear of head to tail, but may turn yellowish posteriorly; one or two rows of lateral black blotches between the middorsal and the ventrolateral pale stripes; scale rows usually 19 at midbody, anal plate single; length about 24 inches, maximum length around 41 inches ....Black-necked garter snake (western, eastern), *Thamnophis cyrtopsis*

Upper lip scales seven to a side; no pale crescent or paired black blotches behind head; lateral longitudinal pale stripes confined to scale rows 2 and 3; basic colors highly variable, the three longitudinal pale stripes varying from yellow (usual color) to gray, yellowish orange, greenish, or bluish, or occasionally absent; usually two rows of black spots between pale stripes; may have red on scales or skin; belly with a lateral series of small black marks; length about 24 inches, maximum length about 48 inches ....Common garter snake (eastern, Texas, red-sided), *Thamnophis sirtalis*

38. Dorsal scale rows 17; a large bluish black snake with some indication of black marks below the eye; young with anterior to middle of body brownish yellow to brown, with some indication of an obscure pattern of darker marks; length around 4–5 feet, maximum length about 100 inches ....Western indigo snake (Texas), *Drymarchon corais*

Dorsal scale rows 19 or more; always some pattern of blotches, spots, or bands present 39

39. Dorsal scales in 19 rows; snout pointed and red; transverse bands of red bordered with black, and yellow bands between the black-edged red bands; belly immaculate white to cream; length about 18 inches, reaching a maximum length of about 32 inches ....Scarlet snake (northern, Texas), *Cemophora coccinea*

Dorsal scale rows 21 or more 40

40. Dorsal scale rows 29 or more; pale brown to tan, moderately large transverse body blotches, with alternating smaller brown body blotches on sides of body; belly white to cream; snout pointed, head with two preoculars; length about 30 inches, with maximum length about 54 inches ....Eastern glossy snake (Kansas, Texas, painted desert), *Arizona elegans*

Dorsal scale rows 27 or less; dorsal body pattern, if consisting of a series of blotches or spots, accompanied by a blotched belly pattern; preoculars single 41

41. Dorsal pattern of narrow blackish gray to gray transverse bands, alternate bands being mixed or split with red color, or a pattern of alternating black-bordered red or orange saddles and white-bordered gray saddles; belly blotched with black or sometimes almost entirely black; length about 25 inches, maximum length about 57 inches ....Gray-banded king snake, *Lampropeltis alterna*

Dorsal pattern not as described above 42

42. Dorsal pattern of small yellow or yellowish white dots on each scale, or obscure black transverse blotches with yellow or pale yellow borders, occasionally forming a chain-like pattern, or a series of transverse black blotches separated by white or yellow bands or spotted scale rows; belly mostly black but may be blotched with yellow and black; scales smooth, anal plate single; length about 40 inches, maximum length about 72 inches ....Common king snake (speckled, desert), *Lampropeltis getula*

Dorsal pattern of dark brown to brown transverse blotches with alternating small spots on the sides of the body, or pattern of red, black, and yellow to white transverse bands that extend onto the belly and may occasionally reach across the belly................43

43. Dorsal pattern of brown to dark brown transverse body blotches; belly with squarish brown blotches alternating with pale tan to cream ground color; length about 36 inches, maximum length around 56 inches ....Prairie king snake, *Lampropeltis calligaster*

Dorsal pattern consisting of various widths of red, black, and yellow (occasionally white) transverse bands that may form rings around the body; belly is typically colored like the dorsum, but bands usually do not meet across the belly; red bands are always bordered by black bands, which alternate with yellow or white bands; length around 24 inches, maximum length about 42 inches....................Milk snake (Louisiana, Mexican, New Mexico, Central Plains), *Lampropeltis triangulum*

44. Dorsal scales keeled...........................45
    Dorsal scales smooth..........................60
45. Dorsal color a uniform green to bright green in life, no other pattern; belly whitish to pale yellow to white or pale green cast; long and slender body and tail; length about 26 inches, maximum length around 45 inches .... Rough green snake, *Opheodrys aestivus*

Dorsal surface with some pattern; old individuals may appear unicolored, pattern may be lined, blotched, or spotted.............46
46. Nose scale (rostral) turned up............47
    Nose scale (rostral) normal, not turned up...48
47. Prefrontal scales separated by small scales; nose scale turned up sharply and keeled; underside of tail not paler than belly; belly and undertail usually black, marked with yellow areas; dorsum with five rows of brown blotches, a larger middle row and two smaller rows per side; length about 22 inches, maximum about 39 inches ....Western hog-nosed snake (plains, dusty, Mexican), *Heterodon nasicus*

Prefrontal scales contact one another,

underside of tail paler than belly; belly often mottled with gray or greenish on yellow-gray or rose; dorsum normally with transverse brown to black blotches in a single or double row, background color sometimes reddish; occasionally the dorsum appears uniform black or gray; length about 25 inches, maximum length about 45 inches .... Eastern hog-nosed snake, *Heterodon platirhinos*

48. Dorsal scales in 19 rows 49
    Dorsal scales in 21 or more rows 50
49. Dorsum with distinct yellow longitudinal lines on lowermost three scale rows (Fig. 15a); a distinct black line on outer edge of belly adjacent to lowermost body scale row; occasionally a faint series of dark spots down the center of the belly; scales keeled; belly usually yellow, buff, or grayish yellow; length around 24 inches, maximum length about 45 inches ....Graham's crayfish snake, *Regina grahami*

Dorsum unicolored, occasionally glossy brown, dark brown, or almost black; scales keeled; two rows of distinct black spots down the belly, almost meeting at midline, but with a pale space between each pair of dark spots (Fig. 15b); length about 18 inches, maximum length about 31 inches .... Glossy crayfish snake (Gulf), *Regina rigida*

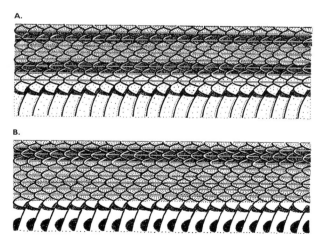

Figure 15. *Graham's crayfish snake (a), with dark lateral line and no bold belly spots, and the Gulf crayfish snake (b), with bold belly spots but no dark lateral stripe.*

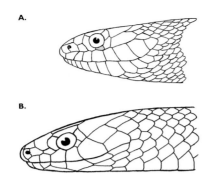

Figure 16. *Subocular scales present (a) or absent (b).*

50. Subocular scales present (row of scales separating upper lip scales from eye, Fig. 16a) 51

Subocular scales absent (Fig. 16b) 52

51. Dorsal pattern rarely blotched, usually consisting of a series of longitudinal H-shaped blotches; a pair of black neck stripes that extend posteriorly to form the outer segments of the H pattern; desert form, nonaquatic; occasionally a blond form with pale yellowish brown blotches in the Lajitas area of West Texas; length about 40 inches, maximum length around 66 inches
....Trans-Pecos rat snake, *Bogertophis subocularis*

Dorsal pattern usually greenish or brownish with dark brown or blackish markings intermixed; belly with distinctive mottling of dark and light, but color variable; strongly keeled scales; aquatic form; length about 36 inches, maximum length around 50 inches
........................Mississippi green water snake, *Nerodia cyclopion*

52. Large aquatic form with strongly keeled scales; dorsal pattern of chainlike dark brown to black markings; each dark loop of the chain extends down the sides to the belly, forming a somewhat loose diamond mark; general ground color olive green or dark green to brownish; belly strongly marked with black spots on the outer edge and scattered smaller black spots down the center; length about 40 inches, maximum length around 63 inches
........................Diamond-backed water snake, *Nerodia rhombifer*

Small to large aquatic snake with strongly keeled scales; pattern of transverse blotches, bands, or spots 53

53. A double row of somewhat small, reddish brown to pale brown spots on each side of dorsum, on a pale brown to pinkish brown ground color; a row of obscure to distinct dark spots along each side of the belly (known only from middle Brazos, Concho, and Colorado river drainages); length about 22 inches, maximum length about 39 inches
......................................Harter's water snake (Brazos, Concho), *Nerodia harteri*

Dorsum never with four rows of small spots; belly pale or dark, never with small obscure dark spots along the sides on a pinkish or tannish background 54

54. Belly pale yellow, yellow, or with a slight orange tinge, occasionally with dark markings laterally; dorsum with dark brown to blackish blotches that may fade in larger snakes, usually some indication of pattern remaining even in old snakes; colors often variable in different parts of the state; length around 40 inches, maximum about 59 inches
.... Plain-bellied water snake (yellow-bellied, blotched), *Nerodia erythrogaster*

Belly never pale colored; dorsum blotched, banded, or striped 55

55. Ventrals number 160 or fewer 56
Ventrals number 190 or more...........58

56. Dorsum with two yellowish stripes and two brown stripes on each side of the body; belly reddish brown or blackish brown with a longitudinal central row of whitish dots; in addition, there may be a pair of whitish dots along the outer row of belly scales; length about 28 inches, maximum length about 36 inches ....Salt marsh snake (Gulf), *Nerodia clarki*

Dorsum with 30 or fewer reddish brown to blackish brown transverse bands...........57

57. Dark stripe from eye to angle of mouth; anterior part of body with 17 or fewer broad brown to rich reddish brown bands separated by spaces usually some blend of yellow; belly yellow with squarish red to rust-red spots, occasionally scattered and not uniform in size; scales strongly keeled; length about 30 inches, maximum length around 45 inches
....................................Southern water snake (broad-banded, Florida), *Nerodia fasciata*

Dark stripe absent from eye to angle of mouth; anterior of body has a few brown bands, remainder of body shows a series of alternating brown to gray blotches, dorsal bands and blotches usually fewer than 30; series of dark markings on belly, often paired; length about 40 inches, maximum length around 59 inches
..................Northern water snake (Midland), *Nerodia sipedon*

58. Dark stripe behind eye normally crosses the end of the mouthline and frequently extends onto neck; number of brown to grayish brown body blotches variable, 28 to 56; belly with extensive dark squarish blotches, fewer blotches in South Texas and more numerous in North Texas; tail with or without a pair of ventral stripes, but stripes more common in East Texas; length about 40 inches, maximum around 72 inches
.....................Corn snake (corn, Great Plains, southwestern), *Elaphe guttata*

Dark stripe behind eye, when present, stops near the end of the mouthline, never crossing or extending onto neck 59

59. Young gray with brownish blotches, as they mature the blotches become dark brown to black and frequently disappear; head usually black in adults; length about 45 inches, maximum size around 86 inches
...............................Eastern rat snake (Texas), *Elaphe obsoleta*

Young grayish to greenish brown, with more than 47 narrow brown crossbands; adults with four dark stripes, the two lateral stripes frequently obscure and the two upper ones more distinct but occasionally absent; length about 54 inches, maximum around 62 inches ....Baird's rat snake, *Elaphe bairdi*

60. Same number of dorsal scale rows throughout the body (occasionally 14 or 13 at vent in South Texas) 61

Two fewer dorsal scale rows in front of the vent than at midbody 62

61. Dorsal color tan, brown, reddish brown, with or without small and narrow black transverse bands, or orange or reddish orange longitudinal stripe down the back; length about 10 inches, maximum size around 15 inches
.........................Ground snake (Great Plains, Taylor's), *Sonora semiannulata*

Dorsal color uniform green, scales smooth; long, slender body and tail; belly white to pale yellow; length around 15 inches, maximum length about 26 inches
.......................Smooth green snake (western), *Liochlorophis vernalis*

62. Dorsal scale rows 19 or more 63
Dorsal scale rows fewer than 19 65

63. Dorsal pattern of broad, dark brown to black longitudinal stripes that alternate with tan or pale brown stripes; a white or yellowish line from snout, over eye, to rear of head; belly orange or reddish, without other markings; about 15 inches in length, maximum length around 20 inches
....Black-striped snake, *Coniophanes imperialis*

Dorsal pattern with blotches or bands, no stripes 64

64. Dorsal pattern of large, dark brown to black, roundish blotches or saddles, extending down sides almost to belly, blotches contrast with ground color; pupil elliptical; neck narrow, head broad; belly white or cream to pale yellow; about 22 inches in length, maximum length around 38 inches
.... Northern cat-eyed snake, *Leptodeira septentrionalis*

Dorsal pattern of small, brown to dark brown, irregularly shaped blotches that may be in one, three, or more rows; neck and middorsal blotches may be large and fused, while remainder may be paired and much smaller; black stripe from snout, through eye, to side of neck; neck pattern usually of three longitudinal black marks; lateral dark neck marks may fuse with lateral head stripe; belly cream to white; pupil of eye elliptical; about 15 inches in length, maximum length around 20 inches.......................Night snake (Texas), *Hypsiglena torquata*

65. Nose scale (rostral) much enlarged, shieldlike and with free edges (Fig. 17)......66
Nose scale not enlarged, not with free edges 67

66. Upper lip scales eight per side; posterior chin shields usually in contact or separated by a single scale (Fig. 18a); dorsum with broad dark brown to blackish longitudinal stripes strongly contrasting with yellowish tan ground color; paler middorsal stripe may be similar in color to or brighter than the sides of the body; occasionally with a dark

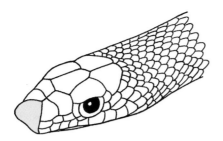

Figure 17. *Large rostral scale of patch-nosed snake.*

longitudinal line on the third row of scales; belly pale yellow to cream; length about 30 inches, maximum length around 47 inches ....Mountain patch-nosed snake (mountain, Texas), *Salvadora grahamiae*

Upper lip scales nine per side; posterior chin shields separated by two or three scales (Fig. 18b); two broad blackish lines on the back; a thin dark line usually on scale row 4, but posteriorly on scale row 3; lower edges of the broad blackish stripes often interrupted with ground color, having a zigzag appearance; belly peach to rose; length around 27 inches, maximum length about 40 inches .... Big Bend patch-nosed snake, *Salvadora deserticola*

67. Preocular single; body and tail long and slender; throat yellowish, ventral surface fading to whitish posteriorly; dorsum with a single yellow dot in the center of a black scale, the base of each scale blue; a black stripe from eye to neck; some blackish marks may be present on the ventral surface of body, most frequently under the tail; length

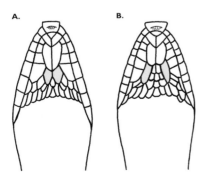

Figure 18. *Posterior chin shields touching or separated by a single row of scales (a) or separated by two or more rows (b). (After Conant and Collins 1991.)*

about 35 inches, maximum length around 50 inches................................Speckled racer, *Drymobius margaritiferus*

Preoculars two.....................................68

68. Anterior temporal scale single; lower preocular almost equal in size to upper preocular, not wedged between adjacent upper lip scales; a small snake with a bright orange or orange-yellow neck band in most populations, neck ring may be interrupted by dorsal ground color; dorsal color gray, blue, bluish green, tan, or brown; belly bright orange to yellow, with a series of black spots scattered or densely spaced on the belly, spots may be in a single or paired row; length about 12 inches, maximum length around 19 inches ....Ring-necked snake (prairie, regal, Mississippi), *Diadophis punctatus*

Anterior temporal scales in two or three rows; lower preocular smaller than upper preocular and wedged between adjacent upper lip scales...69

69. Dorsal scale rows just in front of the vent 15; dorsal color highly variable, black, blue, tan, green, bluish green, with or without brown or reddish brown transverse blotches or bands (especially in young); belly pale yellow, cream, bright yellow, or lemon yellow; normally unicolored dorsally as adults, but some populations may have individual white scales scattered over the dorsal surface; length highly variable by population, usually about 38 inches, maximum length around 73 inches....................................Eastern racer (buttermilk, tan, eastern yellow-bellied, Mexican, southern black), *Coluber constrictor*

Dorsal scale rows 11, 12, or 13 just in front of the vent 70

70. Dorsal scale rows at midbody 17; dorsal color pattern highly variable throughout the range of the species, bright red, brown, tan, or black anteriorly to brown, tan, or pale yellow posteriorly; some populations may be completely black; rear of body appears braided to the human eye, resembling a leather whip; belly usually one color, cream, pinkish, or reddish; young have anterior brownish transverse bands or blotches, resembling young racers; length around 48 inches, maximum length about 102 inches ....Coachwhip (eastern, western), *Masticophis flagellum*

Dorsal scale rows at midbody 15 71

71. Uniformly black scales predominate on dorsal surface; head black with some scales outlined in white; narrow white transverse band or paired white nape spots across neck, and normally five (0–10) white bands over the body; eight longitudinal black lines (four per side) on scale rows 1, 2, 3, and 4 within white areas; anterior two-thirds of belly black, including throat; posteriorly, the ventral black pigment shifts to coral red near the vent and on the ventral surface of the tail; length about 48 inches, maximum length around 72 inches
.... Striped whipsnake (Central Texas), *Masticophis taeniatus*

Uniformly bluish gray to greenish gray scales on dorsal surface, each scale with a pair of white, cream, or yellow marks on its anterolateral surface; usually two white stripes on scale rows 3 and 4 on each side of the body (usually absent in Rio Grande Valley, where it occasionally has a pale stripe at the edge of the belly); throat and neck whitish, sides of neck reddish orange; belly with some speckled bluish marks throughout but turning salmon pink toward the tail; length about 48 inches, maximum length around 66 inches
.... Schott's whipsnake (Schott's, Ruthven's), *Masticophis schotti*

ORGANIZATION OF SPECIES
AND SUBSPECIES ACCOUNTS

In organizing the species and subspecies accounts in the main text, we have used the standard arrangement found in most general books about snakes. Families are listed first, according to their phylogenetic position, followed by their respective genera, in alphabetical order, then the species, also listed alphabetically. When a Texas species is represented by more than one subspecies, such races are arranged alphabetically as well, unless the nominate race is included (the one in which both species and subspecies names are the same), in which case it comes first regardless of alphabetical order.

Each snake account begins with the serpent's common name, followed immediately by its scientific name. Thereafter, each account is organized into six main headings: "Description," "Comparable snakes," "Size," "Habitat," "Behavior," "Feeding," and "Reproduction." In the case of venomous snakes, these are followed by an additional heading, "Venom and bite." Occasionally a special heading is added for a topic that does not properly fit in any of the other categories, particularly when the discussion is lengthy.

Unless a more recent record length is noted, the maximum measurement mentioned herein for each species and subspecies generally is that listed in Conant and Collins (1991). We have not accepted every new maximum length report, however, particularly if it is unsupported by a voucher specimen.

The amount of natural history information presented for individual species and subspecies is largely a reflection of the documented knowledge available for that snake. An account is long when the published information about it is plentiful and brief when such data are sketchy. Whenever possible, we have based our information about a given species or subspecies on studies conducted in Texas, but when such knowledge was scanty or lacking altogether, we turned to observations made in other parts of the serpent's geographic range. The behavior of a few of Texas' uncommon serpents (such as the western smooth green snake, Florida red-bellied snake, eastern garter snake, red-sided garter snake, and western plains garter snake, which are found only peripherally in the state) has been well documented with a substantial amount of information, such bodies of knowledge having been derived from studies conducted outside Texas where they are widespread and plentiful. What has been observed about their behavior in other parts of their range may or may not differ from that within their marginal Texas domain. A notable exception might be the length of the snake's active season, which typically is longer at the southern end of the snake's geographic range than at more northern latitudes. Likewise,

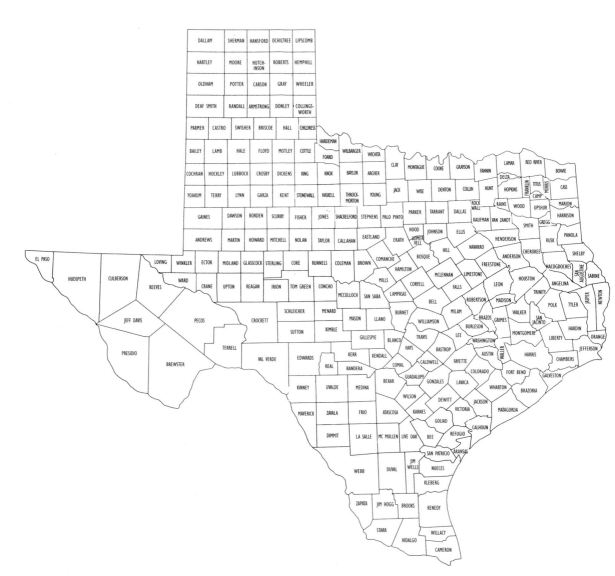

Map 2. *The 254 counties of Texas.*

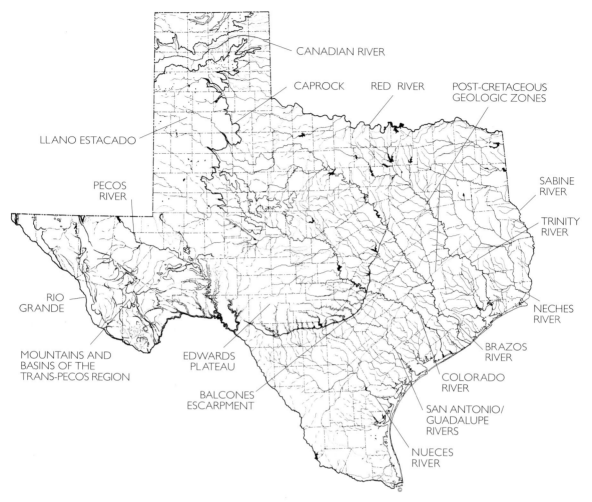

Map 3. *The base distribution map of Texas, with major streams, mountains, lakes, fault zones, and ancient ocean beaches that left large and deep sand deposits across Texas.*

timing of a snake's reproductive cycle may also vary somewhat according to latitude.

THE MAPS Two kinds of maps accompany the species and subspecies accounts. One defines the general distribution of a particular snake species, together with all of its races, if any, in the United States, Mexico, and Central America as far south as Honduras. Although some species range beyond these latitudes, illustrating such extralimital distributions is not feasible in the space available. The other map shows the species' Texas distribution. Unlike the previously published state maps prepared by Raun and Gehlbach (1972) and by Dixon (1987), whose locality data were based on literature records as well as museum specimens, the maps in this book are based solely on actual preserved specimens held in museum, university, and other scientific collections throughout the United States. Since some locality records reported in certain earlier publications were not supported by voucher specimens, we have decided not to include them in the maps, for we cannot verify identification of the snakes on which they were based. For the same reason, we have ignored most records of collected specimens that have subsequently been lost or destroyed, just as we have rejected locality records based on apparently erroneous collecting data, such as those for pet snakes liberated into alien wild habitats. A classic example of released reptilian pets that have found their way into museums from habitats far outside their natural range are Texas tortoises encountered in Houston, Dallas, El Paso, Austin, Fort Worth, and Galveston, though this species occurs naturally only in South Texas. Of concern as well are museum specimens with apparently erroneous collecting information. One such snake, a speckled racer in the Texas A&I University collection, is reported from Kingsville, Texas, although to our knowledge this species does not range north of the Sabal Palm Grove in Cameron County. Other illegitimate records involve hitchhiker snakes, those that have been relocated to a place outside their natural range by accident. Included in this category are earth snakes that arrived in El Paso after having been transported from South and East Texas in the soil of potted plants, and a copperhead

relocated from Junction to Lubbock in a load of fenceposts.

Raun and Gehlbach and Dixon used county boundaries as units of distribution (one dot per county per species), which not only failed to account for the unequal sizes of such political land areas but also neglected to identify certain major physiographic features that effectively limit the range of some snakes, even within a single county. For example, Rockwall County, which encompasses only about 129 square miles (334 km²), is relatively unvaried in physiographic features and vegetation types, whereas Brewster County, with a land area of approximately 6,193 square miles (16,040 km²), is about 48 times larger than Rockwall County and embraces a variety of physiographic features. Thus, to define the distribution of Texas snakes more clearly, in this book each dot represents a single location from which a specimen(s) was collected.

A glance at the state maps demonstrates that few Texas snakes are shown to be evenly distributed throughout their respective ranges. Such spotty patterns can sometimes be real, reflecting a species' absence from certain local areas of unsuitable habitat, for few serpents are adaptable enough to occupy all of the varied environments within their territories. Inhospitable areas within a snake's range can be smaller than a square mile or involve several hundred square miles. Nevertheless, many of the distributional gaps evident on the maps are not the result of such natural barriers but are traceable to a collecting bias on the part of zoologists and others who capture voucher specimens for university and museum collections. Such voids are particularly evident in West Texas, and to a lesser degree in South Texas, where vast tracts of privately owned land are fenced and therefore not readily accessible to collectors. In these areas, where off-road collecting is prohibited, snakes were found chiefly along the main roads and highways. As a result, when plotted on the maps, the collecting localities of some snake species precisely follow these nearly straight stretches of asphalt, their arrangement curiously resembling long strings of beads.

The base map of Texas and the smaller associated map of North America, drawn and produced by Ralph W. Axtell, are used here with his permission. The Texas map delineates political boundaries (counties); details rivers, major streams, and lakes; and indicates the approximate locations of certain geological features such as faults and ancient beach lines that affect or limit the distribution of some snake species.

SPECIES ACCOUNTS

Family Leptotyphlopidae
BLIND SNAKES

This family of small, slender, wormlike snakes contains two genera, one of which is confined to West Africa. The other, *Leptotyphlops,* embracing more than 80 species, has a worldwide distribution that takes in Africa, southern Asia, Arabia, Pakistan, and the Americas, including the southwestern part of the United States. Two species are found in Texas, one of which contains two subspecies. Features that distinguish this nonvenomous family of snakes are the rather solidly constructed skull, an adaptation for burrowing; the presence of teeth only in the lower jaw; the degenerate eyes, which can be seen only as small black dots beneath the translucent ocular scales; the absence of broad abdominal scales; and the presence of a rudimentary pelvic girdle. Also notable are the small blunt head (which is no wider than the snake's body), the reduced size of most of the plates on the crown, and the extremely short spine-tipped tail that is present in most species.

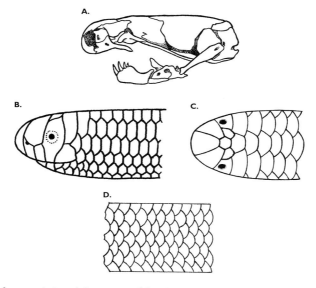

Figure 19. *Family characteristics of the Leptotyphlopidae: (a) solid skull with teeth only in the lower jaw, (b) degenerate eyes nearly hidden beneath large ocular scales, (c) small blunt head no wider than neck or body, (d) belly scales same size as dorsal scales.*

PLAINS BLIND SNAKE
Leptotyphlops dulcis dulcis
PLATE I

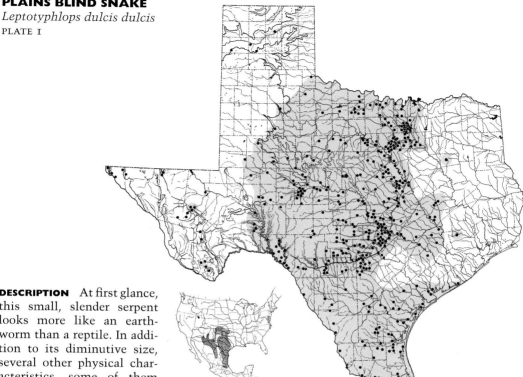

DESCRIPTION At first glance, this small, slender serpent looks more like an earthworm than a reptile. In addition to its diminutive size, several other physical characteristics, some of them unique among Texas snakes, help to emphasize this similarity. The serpent's coloration, like that of a nightcrawler, is earthy and virtually patternless, and the luster of its small, shiny scales resembles the glistening surface of a wet annelid. In addition, its body is cylindrical, being the same diameter throughout, beginning with a blunt head and ending in a very short, stubby tail. Unlike the slender neck of most other serpents, that of the blind snake is just as thick as the reptile's head and trunk, making its appearance even more wormlike. Finally, the snake's tiny, vestigial eyes, barely visible as black dots beneath semitransparent scales, are noticeable only upon close examination. The upper trunk is light brown, reddish brown, or dull pink, while the lower sides and belly are pale gray to pinkish; the entire body of some specimens displays a silvery sheen or delicate iridescence. In this subspecies, three small scales occur on top of the head between the eye plates, and only one upper lip scale is present between the lower part of the eye plate and the lower nasal scale. Moreover, the body scales, which in blind snakes are perfectly smooth and all of equal size (including those on the belly), normally are arranged in 14 rows around the trunk.

COMPARABLE SNAKES The Trans-Pecos blind snake has only a single small scale on top of the head between the eye plates (see illustration in Trans-Pecos blind snake account). The New Mexico blind snake differs from the closely related plains subspecies in that two upper lip scales instead of one are present between the lower portion of the eye plate and the lower lip scale. Besides the blind snakes, no other Texas serpent has degenerate, scale-covered eyes and belly scales that are no larger than the dorsals. Unfortunately, such details of scale arrangement in so small a snake are visible only under magnification.

SIZE Among the smallest of all Texas snakes, the adults of this subspecies are no thicker than a shoelace and usually range in length from 5 to 8 inches (12.7–20.3 cm). The largest known specimen measured 10¾ inches (27.3 cm) long.

HABITAT Strictly a snake of arid to semiarid regions, it typically occurs in sandy or loamy soils, usually near moisture, for there it can easily dig its way below the surface, where it is safe from numerous predators that search for it above ground. Where those requirements are satisfied, it is found in a variety of habitats, including rocky and sandy desert, rock-strewn hillsides and mountain slopes, thornbrush, live oak and juniper woodlands, and open grassy plains. Milstead and his colleagues (1950) collected two specimens on the Blackstone Ranch in northern Terrell County. One came from the cedar savannah plant community; the other was found in the stomach of a roadrunner killed in the cedar-ocotillo plant association. From the southwestern corner of the Panhandle in Dawson County, Fouquette and Lindsay (1955) collected two specimens along a mesquite-lined creek bank.

BEHAVIOR A serpent more harmless than this can hardly be imagined. Its mouth gape is much too small to engage even a human finger, and in the unlikely event that it should succeed in doing so, there would be no cause for alarm, since the snake's teeth are much too small to penetrate the skin. Besides, it has only a few teeth, all in the lower jaw. Poorly adapted to defending itself, this innocuous little reptile uses means more devious than biting to repel its adversaries. When first handled, its most common tactic is to expel from the cloaca a mixture of feces and foul-smelling musk, which is then spread liberally over the captor's hand by the snake's frantic writhing. At the same time, the serpent may partially raise the tips of its dorsal scales, giving its body a peculiar silvery look. This particular behavior allows the gooey secretions to reach the soft skin between the reptile's scales, apparently as a defense against the bites and stings of the ants on whose pupae and larvae it feeds, but it plays no useful role in dispelling other, larger an-

tagonists. This is not its only reaction in the face of danger. In a study of the blind snake's defensive responses, Gehlbach (1970) found that after being roughly handled, the snake sometimes reacted by crawling away energetically in serpentine fashion, but with a strangely semirigid motion. Some handheld specimens then went completely limp and hung from the fingers like a piece of soft cord, apparently as a way to feign death. Another way a captured blind snake discourages its enemies is by using its tail spine. Rigid but completely harmless, this barely visible little thornlike projection is pressed firmly against the captor's skin. Although painless, the thrust of the prodding spine may briefly demoralize the startled handler, who will, if unfamiliar with this tactical bluff, automatically release the snake. The reaction is not much different from the response to an insect crawling on the back of the neck. The unidentified intruder may be harmless or it may be capable of a painful sting or bite, and so we involuntarily swat it away.

Although the blind snake's existence centers around its subterranean life, this reptile is not perfectly adapted for digging. It lacks the more specialized modifications of certain other burrowing serpents, such as the enlarged nose scale of patch-nosed snakes or the flared and sharply upturned snout of hog-nosed snakes, each in its own way an effective digging tool. Yet the blind snake is not entirely without special tunneling adaptations. Perhaps most obvious is the contour of its jaws, in which the upper mandible substantially overlaps the lower one, allowing the snake to push headfirst through loose substrate without getting soil in its mouth. Another is the serpent's solidly constructed skull, a useful modification for a burrowing creature that thrusts its head forcefully into the ground as it works its way through the earth. Most other serpents, endowed with a less rigid skull, are not so well suited for digging. In addition, the blind snake is covered with relatively hard, sleek scales that help reduce friction as the creature pushes its way underground. While not considered a functional burrowing adaptation, a sure sign of the reptile's subterranean life are its degenerate, scale-covered eyes, the same sort of habitat-derived modification found in several other

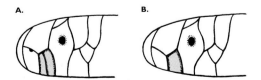

Figure 20. *Differences in lateral head scales between the subspecies of the Texas blind snake,* Leptotyphlops dulcis: *(a) New Mexico blind snake,* L. d. dissectus, *(b) plains blind snake,* L. d. dulcis.

lower vertebrate animals that dwell in the eternal darkness of Central Texas' underground aquifers. (Among them are five different salamanders and two species of catfishes, all equipped with degenerate, sightless eyes or none at all.)

Although it is an accomplished burrower, the blind snake does not always create its own tunnels, for such a small serpent can easily slip underground through any number of small openings at the surface. Earthworm tunnels and the burrow systems of ants and other insects offer easy access to subterranean refuges, as do the spaces created by the decaying roots of trees and shrubs. Where there are old buildings, this serpent may follow foundation cracks into the soil. Above ground, blind snakes are discovered most often after a shower, hidden under flat rocks scattered across dry, sandy hillsides; several specimens frequently congregate beneath the same rock. In such a treeless environment one zoologist found 13 of these little serpents clustered under a single sandstone slab that measured just over 12 inches square. It might be added that blind snakes often gather under one particular rock while ignoring other equally suitable shelters nearby, though it is still unclear what specific attribute makes one rock a better refuge than its neighbors.

How the serpents manage to find their way to a common shelter is no mystery; they simply follow one another's scent trails. This trailing ability, which is especially well developed in blind snakes, is considered important for bringing together males and females during the breeding season, and it may also aid in conserving the snakes' body moisture by facilitating their clustering behavior in times of drought.

By no means does the blind snake restrict itself to rock shelter. It also hides under logs, compost piles, leaf mold, and trash; in fact, it can be expected to crawl under any kind of surface debris that rests on damp soil. Some have been discovered by collectors in rotting tree stumps and rock crevices, others in flower beds and on lawns. From Vermersch and Kuntz (1986) we learn that in the San Antonio area these reptiles frequently find their way into homes and other man-made structures, particularly in the rainy season.

Surprisingly, some Bexar County specimens were found in buildings several stories above street level, a remarkable feat for such a small, subterranean serpent.

There is ample evidence to show that these ordinarily terrestrial and subterranean serpents sometimes climb tree trunks bearing active ant columns. Gehlbach and Baldridge (1987) were the first to report the presence of blind snakes in the nests of screech owls. Because most of the blind snakes found in the owl nests showed only superficial injuries, it is believed they were intentionally carried there by the adult birds, not to serve as food for the nestling owls (in which case they would probably have first been killed) but specifically to help control the soft-bodied insect larvae that infest the plant and animal debris of the nest floor. By eating and thus reducing the larval insect population that plagues the baby screech owls, the snakes may contribute to the growth and general health of the birds. In turn, the snakes, no longer considered owl prey, enjoy a safe haven and a steady source of insect food, at least for a while. When the owls have left the nest the supply of insects diminishes significantly, and the snakes probably crawl back to the ground to resume their normal subterranean activities.

Seldom observed above ground by day, this burrowing species sometimes comes to the surface in the early evening, especially after the ground has been dampened by summer showers. Active thereafter for only a relatively brief time, it is rarely seen out in the open later than nine or ten o'clock at night. During early summer, when a lack of rain and a scorching sun have parched the uppermost layer of soil, the moisture-dependent blind snake, unwilling to risk dehydration at the surface, moves down into the damper earth. The snake's annual active season generally begins in March and ends in November.

On top of the ground, the blind snake's crawling movements are much like those of most other snakes, but less graceful, for instead of having the wide side-to-side abdominal plates of typical serpents, its belly scales are small, about the same size as the scales circling the rest of its body, and so they provide less traction. Another encumbrance to surface movement is the snake's perfectly rounded bottom, which compared with the more flattened bellies of most serpents allows less body surface to contact the ground. This reduces the snake's ability to move forward, particularly on smooth surfaces, resulting in occasional side-slipping.

One of the strangest things about this unusual reptile is the way it uses its tail spine to help move itself along the ground. Inching its tail ahead a short distance, the snake presses the terminal spine lightly but firmly into the soil, where it provides an anchor point that the creature can push against. Whether or not the blind snake uses the same tactic to aid its travels in underground burrows is unknown.

FEEDING Adult termites, plus the eggs and larvae of both ants and termites, are the favorite prey of the blind snake. Abundant, soft-bodied, and helpless, they represent an ideal source of food for a snake so small and with such a limited mouth gape. Just how this sightless little reptile manages to find such prey remained a mystery until the observations of Watkins (1964) and the subsequent laboratory experiments of Watkins and his colleagues (1967) and Gehlbach and his coworkers (1971) provided the answer. Their research revealed that instead of wandering aimlessly on the surface until it encounters ants by accident, the snake need only locate the residual scent trail of the worker ants, which it is then able to follow to their underground nests. Such a trail is laid down by the insects as they travel over the ground. For the ants it is a means of chemical communication—a kind of trail marker—by which they coordinate their circuitous travels. Surprisingly, the same pheromonal substance that attracts the blind snake (particulary the important ingredient known as skatole) was found to have just the opposite effect on certain snake-eating and insect-eating serpents. Ophiophagous species such as the coachwhip, racer, and copperhead were repelled by it, as were the little insectivorous flat-headed and ground snakes.

Once a blind snake encounters a vacated army ant trail, it hesitates momentarily. Then, with its head held close to the ground for a minute or less, as if to test the substrate more intimately, the reptile significantly increases its rate of tongue flicking, apparently to verify the lingering scent. As it moves along the trail, the snake's tongue stays in motion, picking up minute chemical particles, which it then transmits to the Jacobson's organ in the roof of the serpent's mouth. There they are processed and identified. Occasionally the snake arches its head, neck, and forebody so its snout contacts the ground, bringing the nostrils close to the soil, a behavior that serves to orient the reptile through its more direct sense of smell. Steadily flicking its tongue to maintain direction, the serpent continues on its course. When the snake reaches the underground ant nest, its reward is a veritable bonanza, for such a nest contains thousands of eggs, larvae, or pupae—more food than the tiny reptile can possibly eat at one time. Incidentally, the blind snake's ability to track army ants better than other ants or termites suggests that army ants probably constitute this snake's chief prey.

Even more surprising than its ability to track an abandoned ant trail is the blind snake's willingness to enter the raiding columns of army ants in its quest for food. Such nocturnal columns, often stretching out more than 150 feet (45.7 m) from home base, contain thousands of scurrying ants. Their mission is to plunder the nests of other ants. However, the blind snake ordinarily shows little interest in the endless ribbon of ants or in the captured brood that the returning members of the raiding detail are bringing back to their own nest site. Its goal apparently is to follow the column until it reaches the army ant nest. There it evidently feasts on the storehouse of army ant brood and the captured brood of other ants.

How, one may ask, does this seemingly defenseless little serpent manage to invade a raiding column of ants without being attacked and killed by the alert participants? When it has reached the insects' nest, how is it able to exploit such a tempting food supply before it is overwhelmed by the teeming horde of pugnacious defenders? For reasons still unknown, a blind snake traveling on its own initiative among a raiding colony of army ants is not likely to be attacked, although one manually placed in such a column is promptly set upon by the quick-tempered insects. When attacked by them, for whatever reason, the snake is at serious risk unless it can quickly protect itself. The serpent responds to such an assault with the same kind of defensive behavior it uses when it is handled, twisting and turning energetically, discharging feces and a clear viscous liquid from its anal opening, then liberally smearing both substances over its body by its animated writhing. At the same time, the snake raises the ends of its body scales, allowing the gooey mixture to infiltrate to the sensitive underlying skin, which is more vulnerable to attack than the serpent's coating of scaly armor. During this particular maneuver, the snake's normally brown or grayish coloration gives way to a dull silvery hue, and soon the mucuslike material (which contains a remarkably effective ant repellent) covers the creature's entire body. The blind snake is now prepared to travel unchallenged along the army ant raiding column for periods lasting from 3 to 30 minutes. Just how this slimy overlay works to ward off the troublesome insects is still a mystery. We do know, however, that it is the clear liquid originating in the serpent's cloacal sac that repels the ants and not, as one might expect, the foul-smelling fecal discharge.

Once the snake is safely on the trail, how does it know which way to go? Traveling in one direction will eventually lead it to the army ant nest; going in the other will take it farther away from its objective. The raiding army ants are moving in both directions along the column; some are headed for the nests of other ants, while an equal number may be returning to their own nest with captured brood. To explain how the blind snake orients itself in the right direction to reach the coveted cache of ant food, Watkins and his coworkers suggested that this image-blind predator may somehow follow the scent of captured brood, which are always transported in only one direction along the raiding column, from the plundered nursery to the army ant nest.

Ant larvae and pupae, incapable of defending themselves, are vulnerable targets for the marauding blind snake, and they are soft-bodied enough to be easily swallowed. Yet adult ants seem rarely to be eaten. Clad in chitinous body armor and in some cases armed with fearsome biting jaws, they are probably too difficult to overcome and to swallow. Adult termites, on the other hand, represent one of the snake's choice foods, for while they have a hard head and sharp jaws, the abdomen is soft and vulnerable. In its assault on such prey, according to Reid and Lott (1963), the blind snake approaches the victim from behind, seizes the termite by the abdomen, engulfing it nearly to the head, and then, with vigorous twisting movements, forcefully rubs the insect's protruding crown against the ground, wrenching it from its body. To finish it off, the serpent will ingest the prey or puncture the termite's soft body and suck out its fluid contents before discarding the victim's spent carcass.

REPRODUCTION Despite the prevalence of blind snakes throughout the Southwest, few details of their breeding behavior are known, for besides spending most of their lives below ground, they are too small to attract attention even when they do appear at the surface. Mating, which occurs sometime in late March, April, or May, results in the laying of individual clutches of 2 to 7 thin-shelled eggs, each egg about ⅝ inch (1.6 cm) long, in June or July. When they hatch during late August or early September, the baby snakes, which are then no thicker than a pencil lead, measure from 2½ to 3 inches (6.3–7.2 cm) long.

NEW MEXICO BLIND SNAKE
Leptotyphlops dulcis dissectus
PLATE 2

DESCRIPTION The New Mexico and plains blind snakes are subspecies of a single species, differing from one another only in minor details of scale arrangement. In fact, they are so small and look so much alike that they can be identified only by examining the side of the head under magnification. In the New Mexico blind snake, two upper lip scales separate the eye plate from the lower nasal scale, whereas in *L. d. dulcis*, only one does so. At first glance, the snake appears to be uniformly dark brown, but a closer look often

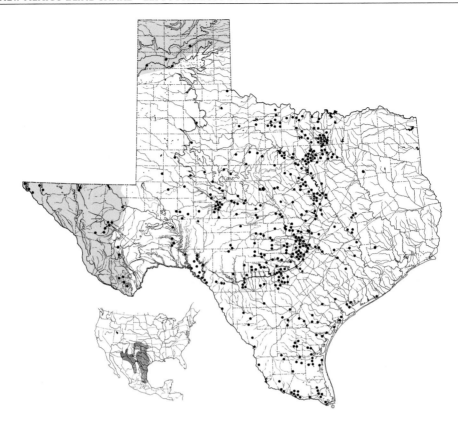

reveals a two-toned creature, one that carries a dark brown band (4 to 6 scale rows wide) down the middle of its back, flanked on either side by a cream or pinkish hue, which continues downward onto the belly. Some individuals even acquire an overall silvery sheen. See plains blind snake description.

COMPARABLE SNAKES   The Trans-Pecos blind snake has only one scale between the plates covering the eyes; the New Mexico and plains blind snakes possess three. Except for other *Leptotyphlops*, no Texas serpent has degenerate eyes and belly plates as small as its upper body scales.

SIZE   Although this subspecies reaches a maximum length of about 10 inches (25.4 cm), most adult New Mexico blind snakes are between 5 and 8 inches (12.7–20.3 cm) long. They are the tiniest of all Texas serpents, more apt to be viewed by the layman as earthworms than reptiles.

HABITAT   Usually confined to more arid terrain than that inhabited by the plains blind snake, this serpent nevertheless prefers to establish residence in loose soil where its burrowing tendencies can best be accommodated. Such places, often occurring near permanent or transient sources of water, include arroyos, streams, and canyon bottoms. In the absence of lingering moisture, the snake can frequently be found on sandy soil beneath boulders and large stones, which, shaded from the relentless sun, often retains a certain degree of dampness, however small, not to mention an equable temperature that tends to attract the snake.

BEHAVIOR   Small, secretive, and leading a largely subterranean life, this inconspicuous creature has so far managed to conceal from prying zoologists most details of its natural history. What little we know about it has been learned primarily from individuals held in captivity. Indeed, our meager knowledge concerning the behavior of other kinds of native blind snakes has been gleaned in much the same way and for the same reasons.

Secretive though it may be, the blind snake is occasionally observed above ground during the early evening hours, especially after the ground has been soaked by a heavy summer rain and when the air temperature is between 78 and 82 degrees F. At such times it is most likely to be discovered under some large, flat rock, its slender body partially buried in the damp soil. Then it may reveal its gregarious tendencies, for often several specimens will cluster under a single large rock, as witnessed on one occasion by Rundquist and his co-workers (1978), who discovered 11 individuals of this subspecies beneath one limestone slab in Clark County, Kansas. Others have been found in rock crevices and tree stumps, under logs and cactus litter, among the root systems of trees and bushes, and in ant burrows.

For more information about this snake's behavior, see the account for the plains blind snake. Since the two are closely related, they probably differ little in their life histories.

FEEDING This serpent's chief prey consists of termites and the larvae and pupae of ants, although other small, soft-bodied insects are probably eaten as well. See the plains blind snake account.

REPRODUCTION Surprisingly little information is available about the breeding habits of blind snakes in general and about this subspecies in particular. Mating in the species occurs in late March, April, or May, after which the females deposit individual clutches of 2 to 7 eggs in June or July. The elongated, thin-shelled eggs, each about $5/8$ inch (1.6 cm) long, hatch in late August or early September, producing young barely as

thick as a pencil lead and measuring only $2\frac{1}{2}$ to 3 inches (6.3–7.6 cm) in length.

It was not until 1964 that communal nesting by female New Mexico blind snakes was first reported. While engaged in digging a new stone quarry in Meade County, Kansas, Hibbard (1964) encountered several female blind snakes as he broke pieces from a large slab of fossil-bearing rock at the base of a shallow gully. Covered with 14 inches (35.6 cm) of silty clay, 4 to 7 inches (10.2–17.8 cm) of sandstone, and a layer of silt and topsoil 2 feet (61 cm) deep, the communal nest site was situated at the base of the stony formation and contained a number of narrow fractures in which the snakes had convened to lay their eggs. Two of the female snakes, each confined to a different crack, were loosely coiled about their clutches, one of which consisted of 5 eggs, the other of 6. As the surface rocks were being dismantled, three groups of unattended eggs were found in nearby joint cracks, but it could not then be determined if they too had been originally sheltered by guardian females. Altogether, 42 apparently viable eggs were found at the site. A number of these were discovered on the quarry floor, probably after having been dislodged from the stone matrix during its excavation. In addition, spent eggshells from previous hatchings were found in the slim stone crevices just below the latest clutches, tangible evidence that this was a perennial communal nest site for blind snakes of the area.

TRANS-PECOS BLIND SNAKE
Leptotyphlops humilis segregus
PLATE 3

DESCRIPTION Often mistaken for an earthworm, this small, slender reptile can easily be recognized as a snake both by the scales that cover its body, and by the two small dark spots on either side of its head, which are vestigial eyes embedded beneath large, partially transparent scales. Even the snake's dark-hued, cylindrical body has the look of a worm, for it changes little in girth from the blunt snout to the end of the tail. The neck, which in most snakes is narrower than the head and body, is not distinctive in this species. The serpent's other novel features include the short spine at the end of its tail and the small belly scales, which are the same size as the body scales.

The three kinds of blind snakes found in Texas look so much alike superficially that to tell them apart requires an examination of their head scales, a task that in so small a snake is accomplished only under magnification. In the Trans-Pecos blind snake, there is but one scale on top of the head between the plates covering the eyes. The 14 rows of smooth, tightly fitting scales that encircle its body give the blind snake a highly polished

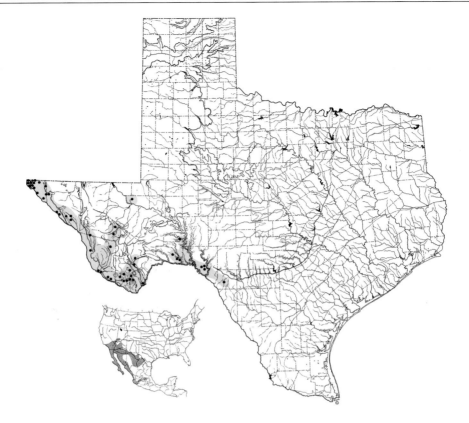

look. The upper 5 or 7 dorsal scale rows are usually brown or purplish, often with a silvery tint, while those along the sides and on the belly are subdued pale purple or pinkish.

COMPARABLE SNAKES The plains and New Mexico blind snakes, although similar in coloration to the Trans-Pecos blind snake, generally display a more uniform body pigmentation. In addition, they have three small scales on top of the head between the eye plates instead of one. Blind snakes can be distinguished from all other Texas serpents by their vestigial, scale-covered eyes and by the size of their abdominal plates, which are no larger than the dorsal scales.

SIZE The greatest length reported for this subspecies is 13⅛ inches (36.2 cm), making it the largest of all blind snakes inhabiting Texas. Adults of average size measure between 7 and 10 inches (17.8–25.4 cm) long.

HABITAT Although essentially an aridland serpent of deserts, dry brushland, and regions of desert-grassland transition, the Trans-Pecos blind snake is partial to localities with either permanent or residual moisture, such as those containing springs, streams, arroyos, or canyon bottoms, for it readily succumbs to excessive dehydration. To survive the intolerably hot daytime temperatures of the desert floor, it burrows down into the soil, which in choice habitats is mostly gravelly or sandy and, therefore, easily penetrated. In fact, specimens are regularly plowed up in fields or discovered during routine excavat-

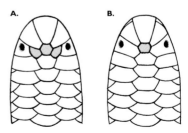

Figure 21. *Differences in head scales between blind snake species: (a) Texas blind snake, three scales between eyes, (b) western (Trans-Pecos) blind snake, one scale between eyes.*

ing activities. More specific habitat descriptions for Texas specimens include those of Jameson and Flury (1949), who found a Trans-Pecos blind snake in a plant community of catclaw acacia and grama grass, and of Milstead and his coworkers (1950), whose Terrell County specimen was collected in a cedar-ocotillo plant association. In describing the habitat of western forms of this species, Klauber (1940a) states that the ideal terrain is generally a bit more arid than that occupied by *L. dulcis* and its subspecies and that, at least in San Diego County, California, stony substrate is favored over sandy terrain. The snakes' preferred territories include rocky canyons and mountain slopes where the vegetation typically consists of mesquite, mountain ash, cottonwood, or ocotillo, although they generally avoid sandy flats, dry lake basins, and alluvial fans.

BEHAVIOR Small, sightless, and completely inoffensive toward man, the blind snake must be considered among the most harmless of all Texas serpents. In the first place, its tiny teeth, found only in the creature's lower jaw, are not large enough to penetrate human skin, and even if they were, the snake's limited mouth gape prevents them from being engaged defensively. Despite its apparent vulnerability to attack, this helpless little reptile has an ingenious way to repel its adversaries. Instead of instantly biting when first picked up, its typical response is to writhe vigorously while simultaneously smearing its captor and itself with a foul-smelling goo that is discharged from its cloacal opening. The feel and smell of this disgusting slime often is enough to gain the snake its release. In another defensive tactic, which does not necessarily coincide with the one just described, the serpent presses its tiny tail spine firmly against the handler's skin. While not forceful enough to achieve penetration, the pressure of the hard little spike against a hand or finger is startling to the uninitiated, often resulting in the snake's quick liberation.

Below ground, where it lives most of its life, the blind snake is reasonably safe from the many predators that search for it on the surface. It can, of course, be scooped out of the soil by any number of different digging mammals such as coyotes, skunks, and badgers, although in such a subterranean refuge the serpent's chances of becoming a victim are greatly reduced. Above ground, where a wide variety of mammals, birds, reptiles, large amphibians, and arachnids all consider it a tasty meal, its attrition rate from predation is believed to be relatively high. This probably accounts for the snake's incessant restlessness when fully exposed at the surface, for in such circumstances, unless preoccupied with some important task such as following an ant trail or searching for a mate, it makes every effort to burrow.

Although this and other blind snakes are reasonably well adapted for digging, they lack the more sophisticated burrowing modifications of certain other desert-dwelling serpents, whose specialized nose scales make them more efficient excavators. Among the blind snake's burrowing attributes are smooth scales that help reduce friction as the reptile moves through the soil, an underslung lower jaw designed to prevent soil from entering the serpent's mouth as it moves forward, and a rigidly constructed skull that serves to absorb the jab of a prodding head. Where the soil is loose enough for burrowing, the snake simply pushes its way through the substrate. In more unyielding soil, it is apt to slip below the surface through existing tunnels, such as those created by insects or small animals, just as it sometimes makes its way along the channels that follow decaying plant and tree roots into the ground.

In rocky deserts where large boulders dominate the arid landscape, the blind snake can be found in their cracks and in the narrow spaces between boulders, both above and below the ground. There too, especially in the presence of damp soil, *L. humilis* hides under displaced rock flakes lying flat on the ground or beneath those resting at an angle against the parent boulders, the thin, slightly curved slivers of stone having been peeled from the massive granite rocks by the sustained effects of alternating torrid days and near-freezing nights. It can also be found under rock flakes previously detached from the boulders' surface but still resting in place. Blind snakes are most likely to be discovered hiding under rocks near or in contact with the ground, or in the cleft between flake and boulder, where soil and debris have accumulated. Indeed, stones, which occur in practically every one of the snake's varied habitats, represent the most important surface shelters for this species. In fact, Klauber was convinced that in one way or another, rocks and boulders are essential to the blind snake's environment.

In many parts of the arid Southwest, according to Fowlie (1965), especially around Tucson and Phoenix, *L. humilis* and its several subspecies are commonly attracted to gardens and farmland that are irrigated year-round, although they carefully avoid regions of moderate to heavy annual rainfall, for they do not tolerate continually soggy ground. Thus it may seem odd that they are most often discovered at the surface following heavy summer rains, yet that is generally when they leave their underground retreats. At such times they do not randomly crawl about in the daylight but instead find refuge under stones lying on top of the ground, where they remain until after sundown. Their early evening forays are not extensive, however, lasting only a couple of hours before the snakes retreat again to the safety of their rock shelters. Most such activity takes place in May and June, usually when the temperature ranges between 78 and 82 degrees F, although the more western subspecies of *L. humilis* have been found moving about even when the temperature has dropped to a low of 64 degrees F, and also when it reached a high of 88 degrees F.

FEEDING While the food of this species, like that of other native blind snakes, consists chiefly of termites, plus the pupae and larvae of ants, the Trans-Pecos blind snake also eats other small invertebrates and their larvae, including spiders, millipedes, and centipedes. In Arizona, where both this species and the plains blind snake occur together in the same habitat, Punzo (1974) found that their diets were not exactly alike. Although both species fed largely on ants and termites, the menu of *L. humilis* contained a greater percentage of surface-inhabiting arthropods than did the plains blind snake, whose diet included more subterranean-dwelling prey. Since both snakes appear to be opportunistic in their feeding habits, and based on the difference in their diets, he concluded that while *L. humilis* shares the same microhabitat with the plains blind snake, it spends more time foraging above ground than its cohabiting cousin. For a description of blind snake feeding behavior, see the Feeding section under the plains blind snake.

REPRODUCTION Mating in this species takes place during spring or early summer, after which the females lay individual clutches of 2 to 6 eggs sometime in July or August, each elongated egg measuring about $\frac{3}{5}$ inch (1.5 cm) long and $\frac{1}{5}$ inch (0.5 cm) in diameter. Hatchlings are 3 to $3\frac{1}{2}$ inches (7.6–8.9 cm) long.

Family Colubridae
COLUBRIDS

Of all snake families, this is by far the largest and most varied, containing more than 280 genera and about 1,600 species. It is also the most perplexing, for it includes snakes that do not exactly fit in this family but are included here as a matter of convenience. Indeed, few internal or external characteristics can be used consistently to define all members of the family or those of its subfamilies. Colubrids, which inhabit all of the continents except the polar regions, display their greatest diversity in North America, Eurasia, and tropical Asia but are found only marginally in Australia, whose serpent fauna is dominated by elapid species.

In this large, diverse family, species range from diminutive snakes less than 12 inches (30.5 cm) long to those exceeding 11 feet (3.35 m) in length. All colubrids have large ventral scales; some have smooth dorsal scales, and others are covered with strongly keeled dorsal scales; most possess a conventionally rounded snout, while a small number have an oddly modified rostral scale, like those of bull, hog-nosed, and patch-nosed snakes; the vast majority have round eye pupils, but in a few the pupil is vertically elliptical; and though most of them possess upper jaw teeth of nearly equal length, some have enlarged (grooved or ungrooved) teeth at the rear part of the upper jaw, including species with modified salivary glands that produce toxic saliva. In Texas, however, such rear-fanged snakes present no danger to mankind.

The family Colubridae is divided into four subfamilies, one of which, the Lycodontinae, is not represented in Texas. The largest subfamily, the Colubrinae, contains the following Texas genera: *Arizona* (glossy snakes), *Bogertophis* (Trans-Pecos rat snake), *Cemophora* (scarlet snakes), *Coluber* (racers), *Drymarchon* (indigo snake), *Drymobius* (speckled racer), *Elaphe* (rat snakes), *Ficimia* (Mexican hook-nosed snake), *Gyalopion* (western hook-nosed snake), *Lampropeltis* (king and milk snakes), *Liochlorophis* (smooth green snake), *Masticophis* (whipsnakes), *Opheodrys* (rough green snake), *Pituophis* (bull and pine snakes), *Rhinocheilus* (long-nosed snake), *Salvadora* (patch-nosed snakes), and *Sonora* (ground snakes). The subfamily Natricinae includes the Texas genera *Nerodia* (water snakes), *Regina* (crayfish snakes), *Storeria* (brown and red-bellied snakes), *Thamnophis* (garter and ribbon snakes), *Tropidoclonion* (lined snakes), and *Virginia* (rough and smooth earth snakes). In the subfamily Xenodontinae, we find the Texas genera *Farancia* (mud snake), *Carphophis* (worm snake), *Coniophanes* (black-striped snake), *Diadophis* (ring-necked snakes), *Heterodon* (hog-nosed snakes), *Hypsiglena* (night snake), *Leptodeira* (cat-eyed snake), *Tantilla* (black-headed and flat-headed snakes), and *Trimorphodon* (lyre snake).

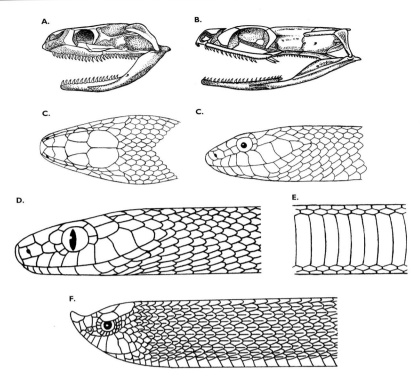

Figure 22. *Family characteristics of Colubridae: (a) Small solid teeth in both upper and lower jaws or (b) last two teeth of upper jaw enlarged and sometimes grooved. The majority of colubrids have (c) an unmodified head shape and round eye pupils; some possess (d) elliptical eye pupils. All colubrids possess (e) large ventral scales. A few, like the hog-nosed snakes, have (f) modified rostral scales for digging.*

KANSAS GLOSSY SNAKE

Arizona elegans elegans
PLATE 4

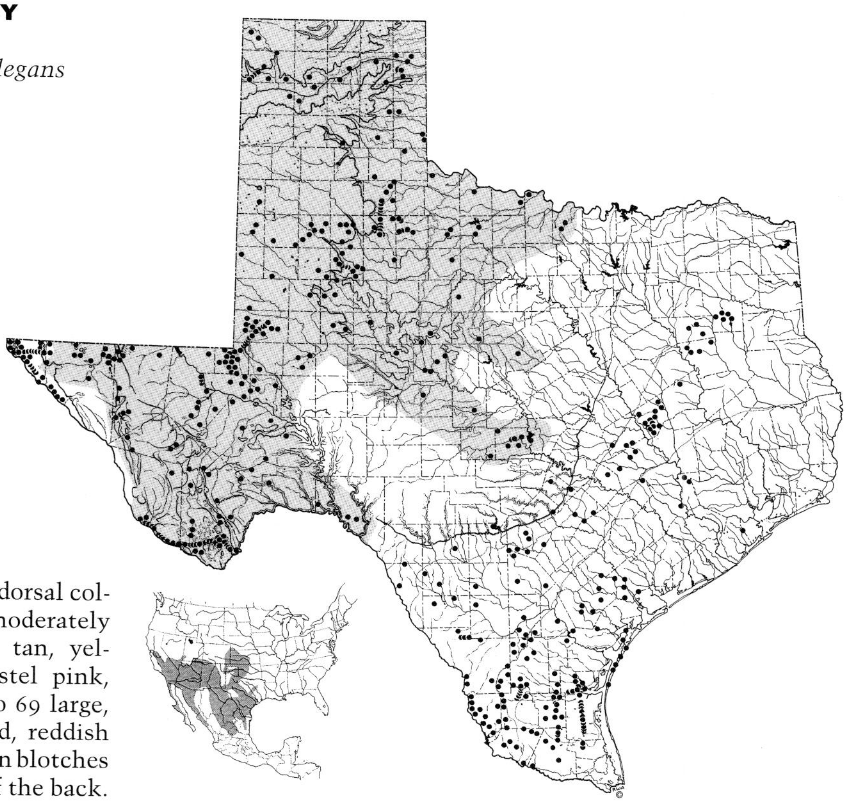

DESCRIPTION The dorsal coloration of this moderately slender serpent is tan, yellowish tan, or pastel pink, with a row of 39 to 69 large, distinct, dark-edged, reddish brown to dark brown blotches down the middle of the back. Each blotch is wider than long and narrowly separated from its neighbors. The intervening spaces of pale ground color, which are most vivid along the midline of the back, become darker on the sides, especially in older specimens. Flanking the primary markings on either side of the body is an alternating row of smaller circular spots, shadowy in outline, below which is yet another lengthwise series of even smaller, irregular ones, which are often indistinct. The white or yellowish white abdomen is unmarked. Although neither the serpent's pattern nor coloration is particularly bold, its scaly covering is as shiny as though it were painted with clear acrylic, giving it a distinctive glossy appearance.

The snake's relatively small head, which is not much wider than the neck, begins with a somewhat pointed snout, and the pupil of the eye, unlike that of most nonvenomous serpents, is slightly elliptical. A dark brown bar crosses the crown just forward of the eyes, while on either side of the face a dark stripe extends from the eye to the end of the mouthline. The dorsal scales, all smooth, are in 29 or 31 midbody rows, and the anal plate is single.

The Kansas glossy snake, the Texas glossy snake, and the Painted Desert glossy snake are all subspecies of a single species and differ from one another only in minor details of scalation and color pattern. In the Kansas glossy snake, the primary row of body blotches (not counting those on the tail) usually numbers more than 50 (50 or fewer in *A. e. arenicola*), and the dorsal scales are usually in 29 to 35 midbody rows (only 29 in the Texas glossy). The Painted Desert race, on the other hand, is a paler subspecies whose primary body blotches ordinarily number more than 62 and whose midbody dorsal scales are in no more than 27 rows.

COMPARABLE SNAKES Except for the Texas night snake (which can be identified by its 21 midbody dorsal scale rows), all similar Texas serpents have either keeled body scales *and* a divided anal plate, or the body blotches are squarish *and* the belly is marked with some form of dark pigmentation. Furthermore, the bull snake and Sonoran gopher snake have 4 prefrontal scales (2 in glossy snakes) and an enlarged nose scale, while the crown of the Great Plains rat snake is distinctly marked with a large, dark, forward-directed, spearpoint-shaped marking, and the underside of its tail is light-and-dark striped.

SIZE A snake of moderate size, it attains a usual adult length of 20 to 39 inches (66–99.1 cm), though a record-size specimen measured 55¾ inches (141.6 cm) long.

HABITAT The Kansas glossy snake is encountered in a variety of arid and semiarid regions in the western part of Texas, where the substrate consists of sandy or loamy soils, for this snake, like all species of the genus *Arizona*, is an inveterate burrower. Preferred habitats include sagebrush slopes, sand dunes, pastures, and grass-covered slopes of the Canadian Breaks region in the Panhandle, as well as creosote bush flats of Trans-Pecos Texas. In Big Bend National Park, according to Easterla (1989), it is found from the Rio Grande floodplain to the foothills (Panther Junction and lower Green Gulch). Much farther north, in the Panhandle county of Hutchinson, Fouquette and Lindsay (1955) found it primarily in the deep sand formation above a creekbed floodplain where sage and scattered clusters of cottonwood trees were the principal vegetation on the area's sand dunes and sand flats. But at the bottom of the Panhandle, in Dawson County, they encountered the glossy snake only in the mesquite-grassland area above the rimrock. According to recent records, it has also been found in the east-central portion of the Edwards Plateau, where sandy soils border some of the region's major stream systems.

BEHAVIOR A generally mild-mannered reptile, the glossy snake normally does not bite in self-defense, even when handled for the first time. On the ground, it is less likely than many other native serpents to flee swiftly from danger, nor does it then instantly gather its body into a protective posture of tight, S-shaped coils from which to strike. Instead, it may simply lie motionless in its original traveling position, hoping to be overlooked, or in a behavior described by A. J. Kirn (in Klauber 1946) draw itself together slightly so that its whole body takes on a continuous succession of short lateral bends or kinks, though the usefulness of this curious behavior is still unclear. In response to

fear or anger, an aroused glossy snake may do no more than vibrate its tail, and one that is picked up may thrash its body about as a way to gain its freedom. Despite these frantic actions, this is a benign creature.

There is some disagreement among zoologists about when the glossy snake comes out of hiding to wander about on the surface. Most naturalists describe it as chiefly nocturnal but sometimes also active during the twilight hours of dawn and dusk. Yet south of San Antonio, near the town of Somerset, in an area of gently rolling sandy soils dominated by cultivated fields and scattered stands of oak and hickory, Kirn invariably encountered it during the day. By most accounts, however, the reptile's daytimes are spent under surface objects (primarily rocks) or in the vacant burrows of small mammals. At other times, especially when such shelters are not handy, the snake simply tunnels a few inches down into the sandy soil until it is out of sight, for it is an accomplished digger.

Its chief burrowing adaptation is the unusual modification of its jaws (a feature found in most serpents that tunnel below the surface), in which the leading edge of the lower jaw is recessed firmly under the front of the upper jaw, so that when the snake pushes headfirst through the substrate, sand is not inadvertently forced between the lips and into the mouth. Sand-burrowing serves not only as a way to avoid surface predators but also as a means to escape the calamitous effects of excessive solar radiation. On two separate occasions, Fouquette and Lindsay watched a glossy snake tunnel in the sand at the base of a sage bush, disappearing below the surface in just a short time, with not as much as a ripple in the sand to pinpoint its location. The shade of the bush, they suggested, may have added an extra measure of thermal protection against the daytime heat. That the glossy snake does not dig deeply into the soil (at least during its active season of May to September in the Panhandle and from April to October in the Big Bend region) is indicated by the frequency with which farmers unearth specimens while tilling their fields.

In winter, to avoid the peril of prolonged cold weather, the snake undoubtedly seeks a deeper refuge. Then it probably crawls into abandoned animal burrows that extend two or more feet below the surface, where the temperature stays above the freezing mark. Yet this is a relatively cold-tolerant species, which sometimes prowls at night when the air temperature is below 65 degrees F. More remarkable, however, are the results of laboratory experiments by Cowles and Bogert (1944), whose research demonstrated that the glossy snake can endure short-term exposure to temperatures near 107 degrees F.

FEEDING The diet consists chiefly of small rodents and lizards, most of which no doubt are attacked in their underground tunnels. Collins and Collins (1991) speculate that this species may also consume small snakes and owls (probably burrowing owls, the only tunnel-dwelling species). In specimens from Andrews and Winkler counties, McKinney and Ballinger (1966) found side-blotched and earless lizards, an unidentified lizard, small mammals, beetles, and orthopteran insects. We suspect that the insects were not directly consumed by the snakes but were the prey of lizards that were later devoured by the serpents, for no other study mentions invertebrates as the natural food of this species.

Large prey, whose struggles make them difficult to control, are effectively subdued by being constricted within the snake's strong body coils.

REPRODUCTION Nothing is recorded about the subspecies' reproductive biology in Texas, nor is there much information about this aspect of the snake's natural history from elsewhere in its range. Mating in the species ordinarily occurs sometime in May or June, after which the female deposits a clutch of 3 to 23 (usually 8 or 9) eggs during June or July.

Captive glossy snakes (subspecies not reported) maintained by Rossi and Rossi (1995) in Florida invariably mated in May and laid their eggs in mid-June. In August, 57 days on average after deposition, the eggs produced hatchlings measuring 9½ to 11 inches (24.1–27.9 cm) long. While Kansas glossy snakes bred in captivity by Ball (1990) also mated only in May, they consistently laid their eggs in mid-July, a month later than those reported by Rossi and Rossi. The eggs hatched in September or October, following an unusually lengthy incubation of 90 days.

TEXAS GLOSSY SNAKE
Arizona elegans arenicola
PLATES 5, 6

DESCRIPTION The overall hue of this shiny-looking serpent is yellowish tan to tannish red, with a row of 41 to 58 prominent, dark-edged, reddish brown blotches down the middle of the back, which contrast sharply with the paler ground color. On either side of the primary markings is an alternating row of small, dark, circular spots, below which is still another row of even smaller, irregular ones. The white abdomen is unmarked.

The snake's relatively small head, which is not much wider than the neck, begins with a moderately pointed snout, and the pupil of the eye, in contrast to that of most nonvenomous serpents, is slightly elliptical. A dark brown bar crosses the crown just forward of the eyes, while a dark stripe reaches from the eye to the end of the mouthline. The dorsal scales, all smooth, are in 29 to 35 midbody rows, and the anal plate is single.

Apparently *A. e. arenicola* from South

Texas are paler than those from the San Antonio region, while individuals from the northeastern end of the range are the darkest of all.

COMPARABLE SNAKES *See Kansas glossy snake account.*

SIZE Most adult Texas glossy snakes are from 27 inches to 3 feet (68.6–91.4 cm) long, although the largest known specimen measured nearly 55½ inches (141 cm) in length.

HABITAT This snake is usually found wherever there is deep, sandy soil, its rather wide range of habitats including open scrubland, prairies, farmlands, beachfronts, sand dunes, and open woodland. While chiefly an inhabitant of the semiarid South Texas thornbrush environment, it also follows the Carrizo Sands geological formation from Central Texas to the northeastern part of the state, where a few specimens have been found in Henderson and Smith counties. The dominant vegetation of this formation, where soils

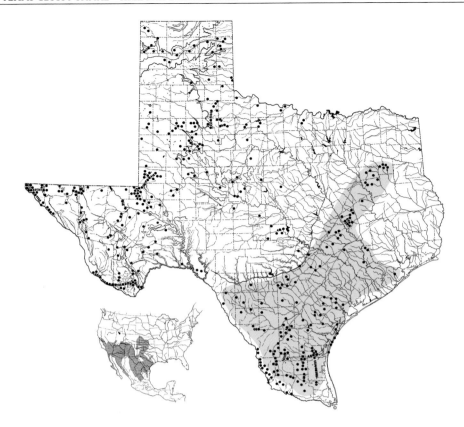

consist of fine to loosely coarse sand from one to several feet deep, is oak-hickory. There are also isolated records for the Texas glossy snake from Waller and Brazoria counties.

BEHAVIOR *See Kansas glossy snake account.* Once a common serpent in South Texas, the Texas glossy snake has declined noticeably over the years. At least until the 1960s, it was among the most frequently encountered snakes along Interstate Highway 35 between San Antonio and Laredo, especially on the stretch of road south of Cotulla, where it was not uncommon to see more than a dozen specimens on the pavement in one night, many of them the victims of vehicular traffic. Today it is seen crossing this highway only occasionally.

We found two specimens at different times loosely coiled under dead, recumbent prickly pear leaf pads. This is a relatively cold-tolerant serpent whose annual active season in Texas, according to museum collection records, lasts from February through September.

FEEDING What sketchy information there is about the dietary preferences of the Texas glossy snake suggests that small mammals, particularly rodents and moles, represent the serpent's chief prey, with a variety of terrestrial lizards constituting the rest. Although there is no documentation to support such speculation, it would come as no surprise to learn that like other glossy snake subspecies, it also consumes small snakes. To constrain large, struggling animals, the snake constricts its prey within the strong coils of its muscular body.

REPRODUCTION Few details about this snake's reproductive biology have been reported. For the species as a whole, there are records of spring mating, followed by egg-laying in June or July. Altogether, clutch size varied from 3 to 23 (usually 8 or 9), with hatching occurring sometime during August, September, or, uncommonly, in October. The 8½ to 11 inch (21.6–27.9 cm) long babies, paler in coloration than their parents, otherwise resemble the adults.

PAINTED DESERT GLOSSY SNAKE

Arizona elegans philipi

PLATE 7

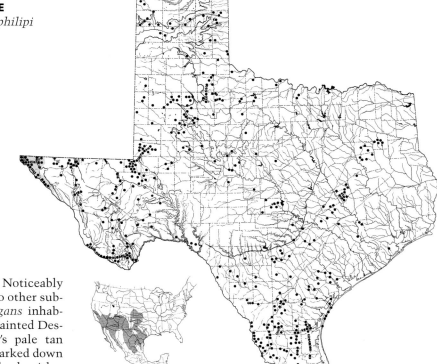

DESCRIPTION Noticeably paler than the two other subspecies of *A. elegans* inhabiting Texas, the Painted Desert glossy snake's pale tan ground color is marked down the center of the back with a row of 53 to 80 (usually 62 or more) fawn to nearly brick-red blotches, whose outer margins are only slightly darker than the centers. Flanking them on either side is another longitudinal row of smaller dark spots, somewhat circular in shape, while below these is an additional one or two rows of even smaller dark spots of irregular size and shape. There is a tendency for some of the primary markings to split along the spine so as to form a pair of separated and sometimes offset half-blotches. The belly is white and unmarked.

The snake's rather small head, which begins with a somewhat pointed snout, is little wider than the neck, while the pupils of the eyes are slightly elliptical, a rare condition among local nonvenomous snakes. The dark bar that in other native glossy snakes typically crosses the crown just forward of the eyes is normally faded or absent in this subspecies, as is the dark stripe that runs backward from each eye to the end of the mouthline. The snake's smooth and unusually glossy scales normally occur in 27 rows at midbody, and the anal plate is single.

COMPARABLE SNAKES *See Kansas glossy snake account.*

SIZE The adults of this, the smallest native glossy snake subspecies, are usually 15 to 37 inches (38.1–94 cm) long, although the largest known specimen measured 39 inches (99.1 cm) in length.

HABITAT Inhabiting the extreme western end of the state, where it occurs in El Paso County and along the adjacent borderland of Hudspeth County, the Painted Desert glossy snake is found primarily in the sand dunes east and southeast of the city of El Paso and along the creosote- and mesquite-covered benches above the dune areas. Although primarily a snake of moderate to low altitudes, outside Texas it has been encountered at elevations exceeding 6,000 feet (1,829 m).

BEHAVIOR In Texas, the Painted Desert glossy snake begins its annual active season in late April or early May and returns to its winter refuge sometime in September or early October. This generally agrees with the seasonal activity cycle reported for the snake in

New Mexico by Aldridge (1979), where 243 specimens were collected in the months of April (11), May (114), June (47), July (22), August (35), and September (14). See Kansas glossy snake account.

FEEDING Small mammals and lizards are its favorite prey, although small snakes are sometimes eaten as well. The larger animals are usually subdued by constriction, while smaller prey is normally swallowed soon after it is seized. See Kansas glossy snake account.

Evidence that glossy snakes sometimes devour horned lizards is indicated in a photograph taken in El Paso County near Fort Bliss in 1925 and later reproduced by Wright and Wright (1957), which shows a glossy snake in the act of swallowing a large horned lizard, belly-side up. Apparently unable either to swallow or to regurgitate its spiny victim, both the predator and its prey died at the site of their desperate encounter.

REPRODUCTION Nothing is known about the reproduction of this subspecies in Texas, although elsewhere the females lay their single clutches of 6 to 12 eggs during the first half of July. When they hatch sometime in late August or September, the babies are 8 to 10 inches (20.3–25.4 cm) long.

TRANS-PECOS RAT SNAKE
Bogertophis subocularis subocularis
PLATES 8–12

DESCRIPTION One of Texas' most strikingly patterned serpents, this relatively slender snake is easily recognized in its typical form by the conspicuous dark brown or black H-shaped dorsal blotches, which stand out boldly against a contrasting background color of tan, yellow, or pale orange. In a departure from the norm, specimens from the Franklin Mountains near El Paso may display a steel-gray ground color instead. Whatever the snake's overall dorsal hue, the central core of each H marking is paler than its lateral horizontal arms and is flecked with both pale and dark scales, while in the midportions of the arms themselves some scales are edged in white. On the neck and forebody, the outer arms of the blotches are connected, forming two bold, continuous, though sometimes irregular, parallel dark lines that extend down either side of the spine and between which only remnants of the blotches remain. The arms of the other dorsal H markings may be similarly connected, though the intervening horizontal links that unite them are generally obscure. A row of small, indistinct dark spots occurs beneath the larger dorsal series, with every other spot located directly below a primary blotch and each alternate lying between two adjacent blotches.

Not all Trans-Pecos rat snakes fit this description, for specimens from the lower Trans-Pecos River drainage system are quite unlike typical examples. Instead of displaying the characteristic H blotches, the pattern of this blond variety consists of pale, often indistinct, dark-edged oval or vaguely diamond-shaped blotches set against an even paler background hue of yellowish tan.

It is in certain specialized features of the head that the Trans-Pecos rat snake best displays its uniqueness. One is the arrangement of scales around the eye. Whereas in all other native rat snakes, and in most other serpent species for that matter, the lower border of the eye directly meets the upper lip scales, that of *B. subocularis* is separated from them by an intervening row of small scales. Of special note also are the serpent's large, somewhat bulging eyes, a useful adaptation for a creature whose aboveground activities are limited mostly to the hours after sundown.

The pale-colored head, rather wide and flat on top, bears no markings. Its upper surfaces are nearly the same pale hue as the background body color, but the chin, throat, and neck are white. The belly, however, is olive buff, usually with some discreet dark mottling, which may consolidate on the underside of the tail to form a pattern of dusky stripes. At midbody, the dorsal scales are arranged in 31 to 35 rows. Like other native rat snakes, this species has faint keels only on the upper body scales, the others being smooth. The anal plate is divided.

COMPARABLE SNAKES The pattern of an adult Baird's rat snake consists of four dark, lengthwise stripes, whereas the young of this species are marked along the back with a series of narrow, dark crossbars. The blond variety of *B. subocularis* can be distinguished from other blotched snakes within its range by its pale, rounded dorsal blotches (none of which is linked with either of the adjoining spots) and its unmarked, light-colored head.

SIZE Adults are usually between 3 and

Figure 23. *Head of Trans-Pecos rat snake showing the row of small subocular scales separating the orbit from the upper lip scales.*

4½ feet (91.4–137.2 cm) long, although the maximum length recorded for this subspecies is 5½ feet (167.4 cm).

HABITAT Dry, rocky terrain between 1,500 and 5,000 feet (457–1,520 m) elevation is the preferred habitat of this aridland dweller. In Texas it occurs chiefly within the confines of the Chihuahuan Desert in a variety of environments, ranging from low basins and valleys where mesquite is the dominant vegetation; through the intermediate regions of chiefly creosote bush in association with tarbush, prickly pear cactus, and ocotillo; to the higher desert slopes where the widely scattered vegetation consists of sotol, lechuguilla, ocotillo, agave, and yucca; and still higher to the more moist oak and juniper woodlands of the mountains. In such environments, where aboveground shelter is often severely limited, the snake finds refuge in the labyrinth of honeycombed or fractured rock formations that lie beneath the desert floor, though it seems not to favor any particular type of rock formation. In the Chisos Mountains it occurs among the region's igneous rocks, while along the stretch of the Rio Grande that delineates the southern border of the Big Bend, it occupies pure limestone formations. In New Mexico it is even found in the Tularosa Valley lava beds. Although in such habitats it may occasionally be found in streambeds, the presence of permanent water is not a necessary ingredient for the snake's well-being; most specimens have been taken on arid, rocky slopes devoid of surface water.

BEHAVIOR Few large Texas snakes are as docile as this one. Rarely biting in self-defense, even when first captured, the Trans-Pecos rat snake generally shows little resentment to being handled, other than sometimes to struggle halfheartedly in attempting to free itself. Its noncombative response in the face of danger represents a startling contrast to the volatile and sometimes vicious defensive reaction of the Texas rat snake under similar circumstances. Even when caught in the powerful beam of automobile headlights, this serpent generally remains motionless, whereas most other snakes are inclined to escape quickly to the side of the road. Illuminated at night in this way, the snake's eyes appear to emit a very noticeable shine, similar to the reflected ocular light that is so well-known in cats and to a lesser extent in some reptiles such as alligators. Kauffeld (1957), however, did not believe this was "eyeshine" in the true sense. He concluded that since a snake's eyes lack the tapetum lucidum, a layer of mirrorlike cells behind the retina, the reflected light is merely the result of the protruding character of the rat snake's eyes, which simply causes focused light to be deflected from their unusually rounded outer surfaces. Like most cold-blooded desert dwellers, this species is primarily nocturnal, its period of aboveground activity narrowly restricted to the hours between sunset and midnight, although the majority of specimens taken by collectors apparently have been discovered wandering above ground between 10 and 11 PM. Calm, warm nights without a full moon seem the best time to look for it. In Kauffeld's view, a bright moonlit night generally is an unfavorable time to search for Trans-Pecos rat snakes; perhaps sensing that they are then more easily detected by their natural enemies, the snakes prefer to remain in their subterranean shelters. When it is out searching for prey, this relatively fast-moving serpent travels over considerable distances. One specimen was found a quarter-mile from the nearest conceivable shelter. Unlike certain other desert serpents that are drawn to the surface by summer rains, this species is not so affected.

Though apparently well adapted to a desert environment, which has permitted it to survive in a hostile setting in which few other rat snakes have dared to venture, this aridland serpent is nevertheless plagued by a peculiar parasite that attaches itself only to individuals of this species. The host-specific tick *Aponomma elaphensis*, first discovered and named in 1958 and later studied by De-genhardt and Degenhardt (1965), belongs to a genus of hard tick not previously reported in North America. In fact, its closest relative is found in Australia, half a world away. This shelter-seeking parasite finds the snake an ideal host, for not only does the reptile support the tick's critical need for darkness and humidity by passing the hot, dry daytime hours underground, but it also nearly always emerges from its refuge at night, when the fierce desert temperatures have moderated. For the tick, such conditions of darkness and moisture become even more important for the successful development of its eggs. Annoying as it may be to its host, this unique little parasite is probably never life-threatening. Instances of tail-tip loss in Trans-Pecos rat snakes are not uncommon, because large numbers of engorged ticks will concentrate on that part of the serpent's caudal appendage where they are less likely to be rubbed off than when they are attached to the snake's body. Deprived of blood, the affected tail-end eventually mortifies and drops off.

FEEDING Adults of this species consume mostly small mammals, some birds, and even fewer lizards, whereas very young Trans-Pecos rat snakes devour primarily lizards. From a detailed study of the snake's food habits in the northeastern Mexican state of Chihuahua, Reynolds and Scott (1982) found that this species and the cohabiting black-tailed rattlesnake both confine themselves largely to the region's rockiest habitats where the number of rodent prey species is somewhat limited. Their survey revealed that the following animals were eaten by 12 wild-caught rat snakes (percentage of occurrence in parentheses): cactus mouse (25), rock pocket mouse (16.7), Merriam's kangaroo rat (16.7), white-throated wood rat (16.7), birds (16.7), and the plains pocket mouse (8.3). Outside this study, other species mentioned as having been eaten by the Trans-Pecos rat snake include deer mice, bats, roadrunners, and cliff swallows.

This serpent not only kills its prey by constriction but also, like the bull snake, simultaneously can wrap two or three adult rodents in its powerful coils. When several prey animals are encountered together in a confined area such as a nest, they are seized in rapid succession, the first one enveloped in a forebody coil while still gripped in the snake's mouth. Almost immediately and without being set free, it is shifted backward toward the rear of the serpent's body as a second victim is grabbed and enfolded in a forebody loop. The same process is repeated again for a third rodent. Baby rodents, however, are simply swallowed alive without being constricted.

REPRODUCTION Reaching sexual maturity at two to three years of age, this serpent mates annually between mid-June and early July, the female producing a clutch of 2 to 11 eggs (average about 5) sometime between mid-July and mid-August. Measuring between 2 and 2¾ inches (5.1–7 cm) long (the longer eggs are generally smaller in diameter than the shorter ones), they hatch 73 to 105 days later, yielding baby snakes that are 11 to 14⅞ inches (27.9–57.8) in length. Near-replicas of the adults, the hatchlings differ chiefly in their paler yellowish or pinkish ground color.

WESTERN WORM SNAKE
Carphophis vermis
PLATE 13

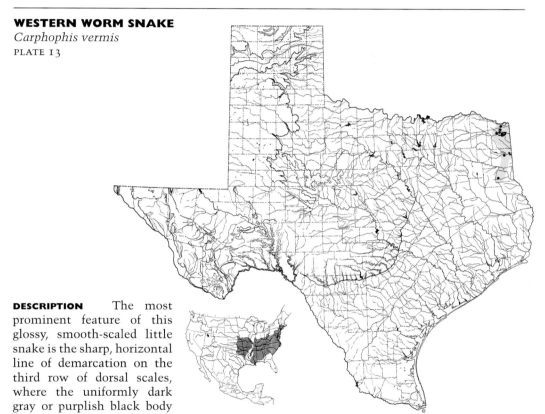

DESCRIPTION The most prominent feature of this glossy, smooth-scaled little snake is the sharp, horizontal line of demarcation on the third row of dorsal scales, where the uniformly dark gray or purplish black body hue meets the contrasting salmon-pink belly color. Just days before the snake sheds its skin and until the epidermis is discarded, the dark dorsal tone fades to ashen gray, masking its true color. The serpent's bluntly pointed head is no wider than its neck, its eyes are small, and its short tail ends in a sharp little spine. There are but 13 midbody rows of dorsal scales, and the anal plate is divided.

COMPARABLE SNAKES When first hatched, the mud snake is nearly the same length as an adult worm snake, but with a much thicker body. Although both species are shiny and blackish on the back and sides, the red color of the mud snake's belly extends up along the lower sides of the body as vertical bars instead of terminating in a sharp, horizontal line of demarcation. The ring-necked snake, whose slate gray to blackish dorsum is similar to that of a worm snake, has a narrow, pale-colored ring on the neck and black spotting on its yellowish belly. The Florida red-bellied snake may have a pale orange abdomen, but its color does not extend upward to the third row of body scales. Moreover, it has 15 rows of *keeled* dorsal scales at midbody and a conspicuous pale spot covering all of the fifth upper lip scale.

SIZE   Although the known record length for this snake is 14¾ inches (37.5 cm), most adults are between 7½ and 11 inches (19–27.9 cm) long.

HABITAT   In northeastern Kansas, according to D. R. Clark (1970), the snake's distribution is closely tied to stream valleys adjacent to forested or grassy hillsides where elevations generally rise above 100 feet (30.5 m). Such areas, while damp, contain well-drained, organically rich soils littered with rocks or logs, under which the snake can take cover, and are shaded either by trees or dense ground cover, leafy umbrellas that help to conserve soil moisture. Black, clay-loam soils containing from 10 to 30 percent water, by weight, are preferred, whereas neighboring patches of more cohesive, light-brown clay substrate are avoided. Some open habitats near Lawrence, Kansas, characterized by sparse ground cover as the result of moderate cattle grazing, actually attracted greater numbers of worm snakes than did other, more natural, nearby habitats.

BEHAVIOR   An altogether harmless reptile, the worm snake neither strikes nor bites when handled. Like many other snake species, it does employ a defensive strategy that may repel small predators, although the same tactic probably has limited success against larger adversaries. Combining musk from its scent glands with waste from its cloacal opening, it smears the smelly material over its captor as it struggles to free itself. Meanwhile, it may firmly press its sharp tail tip into one part of a person's hand while its head is busily probing in another. To the captor, such persistent poking can be alarming, for when the snake's terminal tail spur is unexpectedly forced against the skin, the sensation is like the jab of a dull needle. This strange feeling, while not painful, may nevertheless be startling enough to cause the handler to pull back suddenly and drop the snake to the ground. Since the serpent's tail-tip maneuver ordinarily is not directed at the part of the hand grasping the snake, the tail thrusts are perhaps intended to find an escape route or to

assist the snake's forward motion. Almost nothing is recorded about the western worm snake's natural history in Texas, for the serpent is rare in the state, having been reported so far in only two northeastern counties, Bowie and Red River. Consequently, most of the data presented below are from field studies conducted by D. R. Clark in northeastern Kansas, where the snake occurs so commonly that it is often found there at the rate of 150 to 300 individuals per acre. The study, from which we have drawn freely, remains the primary source of information about the snake's natural behavior.

The worm snake's small narrow head, smooth glossy scales, and short pointed tail all suggest a fossorial existence, yet this reptile has no outstanding physical or behavioral attributes that would allow it to bore easily into packed soil, although it can readily penetrate loose substrate. When approached, a worm snake usually tries to escape by quickly crawling under a rock or some other form of surface debris. In the absence of such cover, it places its snout against the loose soil, if there is any, seeking some small opening into which it can poke its snout. By rotating its head from side to side, up and down, in a rolling motion, or in a combination of such movements, it makes a hole large enough for its body to enter, then soon disappears below the surface.

Above ground it can be found wandering about either by day or at night, so long as the air temperature is between 58 and 78 degrees F and the ground is warm and damp. This small serpent normally travels over surprisingly short distances. One marked specimen was recaptured nearly two and a half years later just 12 feet from the same spot where it was initially liberated. There are also records of unusually long treks. One, involving an adult female worm snake that wandered 410 feet in only 19 days, represents a record travel distance for this species. In northeastern Kansas the male occupies a home range estimated to be approximately one-sixth of an acre maximum, minuscule compared to the large home territories inhabited by the males of other species living in the same region: copperhead, 24.4 acres; racer, 26.3; rat snake, 29; and garter snake, 35. (Females occupy smaller home ranges.)

The snake's annual activity cycle is influenced largely by temperature and precipitation. Thus, when rising spring temperatures and increased rainfall accelerate the decomposition of leaf litter deposited the previous fall, earthworms rise to the surface and are soon followed by the worm snakes that feed on them. Later in the year (notably in August), as temperatures rise and the surface mulch dries, the earthworms move deeper into the ground, and the worm snakes follow them. This is illustrated by Clark's comment that 94 percent of all *C. vermis* he discovered during the year in an Osage County, Kansas, field survey were encountered in March, April, and May. Before the end of October, the serpent's wanderings are over and it prepares for winter. In most cases the worm snake hibernates in minute burrows whose entryways are located under rocks, although it also seeks winter refuge in ant mounds, rock crevices, rotting logs, and tree stumps, or even under loose tree bark. Johnson (1987) mentioned hibernacula in which the snakes crawled into deep accumulations of leaf litter that filled the basins of dark, steep-sided ravines, and he noted that other worm snakes found winter shelter in a cave.

FEEDING Though it sometimes consumes other small invertebrate prey, earthworms constitute the primary diet of this leaf-litter inhabitant of the forest floor. The ring-necked snake, another small serpent living in the same damp woodlands, hides under the same logs, rocks, and pieces of loose bark with its smaller neighbor and even competes with it for the same annelid prey.

REPRODUCTION Two mating periods occur in this species, one in April and May and another in September and October. The fall copulation results in the storage of viable sperm in the female's body until the following spring, when the eggs are fertilized and embryonic development begins. Sometime between mid-June and early July the female lays 1 to 8 (normally 2 or 3) oval eggs, 1 to 1½ inches (2.5–3.8 cm) long, beneath rocks or in tiny underground burrows. They incubate over the next seven weeks, hatching during the period of mid-August to early September. The baby snakes, which measure 3½ to 4 inches (8.9–10.2 cm) long, look much like the adults but show more contrast between the dark dorsal hue and the reddish pink undercolor.

NORTHERN SCARLET SNAKE
Cemophora coccinea copei
PLATE 14

DESCRIPTION The dorsal markings of this moderately small, white or tan snake consist of wide, black-encircled crimson to red-orange saddles that extend down either side of the body to the first or second scale row. Alternating with and located just below them is a series of dark, irregularly shaped spots. The snake's small head is scarcely wider than its neck, and its sharply pointed red or orange snout juts forward prominently beyond the end of the lower jaw. The forward edge of the black rim that encloses the first scarlet body blotch usually reaches the parietal scales and contacts or nearly meets (shy one scale width or less) the transverse black band on the forecrown. This condition is relatively inflexible, despite a wide range of minor variations in the serpent's head markings. Even more constant is the scarlet snake's white or yellow unmarked belly. The

smooth dorsal scales are usually arranged in 19 rows, and the anal plate is single.

Not every scarlet snake precisely fits this description, for the species undergoes a remarkable color transformation from the time it first emerges from the egg until it is aged. First of all, the hatchling's red colors are more muted than those of the adult, and there is more white in its coloration. Extending downward on either side of the body to the second or third scale row above the abdomen, the young snake's soft-pink saddles, black-edged front and back, are separated from one another by immaculate white spaces. An intermittent row of black flecks borders the lower edges of the saddles, including a black spot at each white interspace just above the belly line. At this age the scarlet snake appears distinctly blotched.

After it reaches a foot (30.5 cm) in length,

it experiences a gradual pale yellowing of the white dorsal spaces between the saddles, which hue gradually expands laterally. At the same time, the pinkish saddles become more red and, together with their lateral black margins, gradually extend farther down along the sides of the body nearly to the abdomen. Later the black margins converge under the saddles to encircle them completely, whereas the black flecks between the blotches gradually diminish. By the time it is fully adult, the northern scarlet snake, even when seen from the side, looks like it is completely encircled by rings of deep red, bright yellow (paler near the belly), and black. But this is only an illusion, for none of the colors extends across the reptile's pure white belly. Still different looking is the very old scarlet snake, whose colors have gradually darkened over time—eventually becoming somber red-brown instead of scarlet on the saddles and tan or pale gray instead of yellow in the interspaces—and its number of dark-centered, pale-colored scales has increased. The dorsal

scales, all smooth, are arranged in 19 rows at midbody, and the anal scale is single.

COMPARABLE SNAKES The coral snake's ringed dorsal pattern continues across its abdomen, the red and yellow markings are side by side, its snout is all black, it has only 15 rows of dorsal scales at midbody (19 in the scarlet snake), and its anal plate is divided. Another species likely to be confused with *Cemophora coccinea copei* is the Louisiana milk snake, whose black, yellow (or whitish), and red body bands reach well onto its belly and whose midbody dorsal scales are arranged in 21 rows.

SIZE Adults generally range in length from 14 to 20 inches (35.6–50.8 cm). The largest known example of this subspecies measured 32½ inches (82.5 cm) long.

HABITAT Like most other burrowing serpents, the scarlet snake prefers areas of well-drained, sandy or loamy soil, usually in pine, hardwood, or pine-oak forest, where it can easily dig into the relatively loose substrate. Despite the traditional notion that the species restricts itself to a woodland environment, there is sufficient evidence to show that it frequently inhabits open places as well, provided the soils there are penetrable. In the most comprehensive study yet made of the scarlet snake's behavior and occurrence in the wild, Nelson and Gibbons (1972) reported that of 49 specimens collected in pitfall drift fence traps during a survey near the U.S. Department of Energy's Savannah River Plant below Aiken, South Carolina, 28 were taken in woodland and 21 in open areas (abandoned fields, grassy tracts, and roadsides). It is also evident from this and other studies that the scarlet snake often is found in the vicinity of marshes, swamps, or ponds, though we can find no report that this species enters the water. At more northern latitudes it sometimes inhabits rocky, wooded hillsides and even rugged, nearly treeless, slopes.

BEHAVIOR This docile species rarely bites when provoked, its first line of defense being to burrow into the sand or to crawl under leaf litter. It may respond to further harassment by hiding its head beneath one of its body coils, then lifting its tail, apparently to focus the predator's attention on this caudal appendage and away from its more vulnerable head. Sometimes during such a head-hiding posture, the snake's tail, instead of being elevated, is simply moved about. This action, it seems, like the first, would also serve to protect the snake's head at the expense of its less vital tail.

Until the appearance of the Nelson and Gibbons study of the northern scarlet snake in South Carolina, very little was known about the natural history of this species. Their report gives us the first glimpse into the snake's basic ecology. Despite that information, many details of the serpent's behavior remain a mystery, for this secretive little snake is seldom encountered above ground over most of its geographic range, except only occasionally at night.

By day it usually remains below the earth's surface, concealed in a self-made tunnel or hidden in an underground passageway created by another animal. An efficient burrower equipped with a compact skull and a recessed lower jaw to facilitate digging, the scarlet snake easily penetrates loose soil. First it

presses its pointed snout firmly into the substrate, moving its head from side to side to create an initial opening, then pushes the soil upward with its forebody as it penetrates deeper.

Reports of finding it deep in the ground, both in summer and winter, are prevalent. In North Carolina, according to Palmer and Tregembo (1970), a specimen was excavated from a sandy winter den that was four feet below the surface, and another was removed in the spring at a similar depth, but from red clay soil. More novel circumstances that have led to the discovery of this species in its underground shelters include road construction, the removal of soil to accommodate building foundations, and grave digging. Yet it is not unusual for farmers plowing their fields to uncover scarlet snakes from shallower depths. In Alabama, one was even found in an abandoned fire ant mound. When not hiding below the surface, it may spend brief periods beneath rocks, logs, and boards; in rotting logs and tree stumps; or under the loose bark of dead trees, where it can find aboveground security from predators and perhaps also capitalize on small prey animals that use the same shelters.

Aside from those gathered in pitfall drift fence traps near Aiken, South Carolina, most of the northern scarlet snakes captured over the years by field collectors in all parts of its range were encountered at night on blacktop roads. Even those removed from the traps each day probably entered the pitfalls after

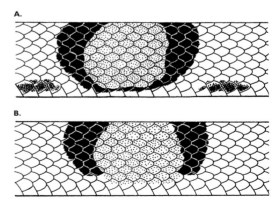

Figure 24. *Lateral body markings of (a) northern scarlet snake and (b) Texas scarlet snake.*

sundown and before dawn. Though some say the species is likely to come out of hiding during summer showers, most of the Aiken specimens (29 of 49) were encountered in the open when there had been no rainfall over the previous 24 hours.

At South Carolina's Savannah River study site, this serpent first ventured above ground as early in the year as May 2, was active during the next five months, and was not seen again after September 6, until the following spring. This three-year study revealed that unlike many other snake species, which are seen in greatest numbers in the spring, the peak of scarlet snake activity at this location came in June. According to the survey, 17 specimens were trapped in May, 44 in June, 28 in July, 22 in August, and only 2 in September. Wright and Wright (1957) mention one that was found above ground in South Carolina by J. D. Dickson as early as April 1 and a Mississippi specimen taken as late in the year as December 10. It seems likely, therefore, that scarlet snakes living in the relatively mild climate of southeastern Texas are apt to maintain a similar seasonal activity cycle of early emergence and late retirement, at least during mild winters.

According to Nelson and Gibbons, this subspecies ordinarily travels moderate distances when on the move. They found that several marked individuals wandered roughly 50 feet (15.2 m) per day and that one specimen covered 1,968 feet (600.2 m) in 25 days, or a calculated distance of 75½ feet (23 m) each day. Unlike certain other snake species in the area (particularly ring-necked and red-bellied snakes), whose seasonal activities are evidently closely correlated with certain climatic changes such as increased dryness and noteworthy variations in temperature, this serpent's wanderings apparently were not directly influenced by such factors.

At the approach of winter, most scarlet snakes retreated several feet into the ground to avoid freezing temperatures, though some hibernated in decaying logs and tree stumps.

FEEDING Since few field reports detail the snake's diet and feeding behavior, most such information comes from observations of captive specimens. Reptile eggs, which appear to constitute a major portion of the serpent's menu, are either swallowed whole, if they are small enough, or seized at one end and pulled into the snake's mouth until the two enlarged, bladelike teeth at the rear of each upper jaw can pierce the shell. Firmly pressing a loop of its body against the egg to prevent it from moving, the snake vigorously chews on the shell, forcing the fluid contents into its mouth, while often further immobilizing the egg by wedging it between a body coil and some nearby solid object.

In southern New Jersey, Burger et al. (1992) encountered a northern scarlet snake in the nest burrow of a northern pine snake, where it was eating the contents of a pine snake egg. Surprisingly, the scarlet snake may even eat its own eggs. As observed by Ditmars (1936), a captive female *Cemophora* in his care consumed her entire clutch of eight eggs about a month after she had laid them in her cage. Another important prey item in the scarlet snake's diet is lizards (especially skinks), which are first killed by constriction, like the small snakes and diminutive mammals it also eats. Small amphibians and insects appear on the menu as well, but it is likely that such prey are consumed only rarely.

REPRODUCTION Like so much else about this species, information concerning its reproduction is based on a few anecdotal reports, some of which are derived from instances of egg-laying by captive specimens. Neither the precise time nor the details of copulation are known, but mating presumably takes place in early spring. The eggs, numbering 3 to 9 per clutch and measuring 1¼ to 1⅜ inches (3.2–3.5 cm) long, are ordinarily laid sometime during June or July in moist soil, under damp humus, or in moist rotting logs; one clutch was discovered beneath a layer of pine straw and humus on a red-clay embankment. In late summer or early fall, approximately 70 to 80 days after deposition, the eggs hatch, producing babies 5 to 6 inches (12.7–15.2 cm) long. It must be added that based on reports of nesting dates spanning a considerable time—from June 23 to August 24—there is the possibility that a single snake may lay more than one clutch of eggs in a season.

TEXAS SCARLET SNAKE
Cemophora coccinea lineri
PLATE 15

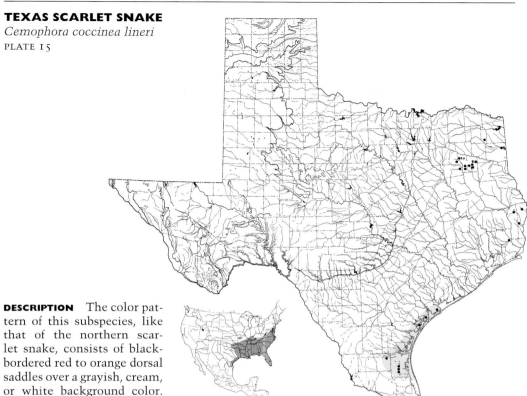

DESCRIPTION The color pattern of this subspecies, like that of the northern scarlet snake, consists of black-bordered red to orange dorsal saddles over a grayish, cream, or white background color. There is no black border across the lower edge of the red blotches as there is in *C. c. copei,* and the saddles extend down either side only to the fourth or fifth scale row above the belly (to the first or second row in the northern scarlet snake). Moreover, the leading black edge of the Texas scarlet snake's first red body blotch does not reach as far forward on the head as the parietal scales, although it nearly always does in the northern subspecies. Other features common to all *Cemophora* are the serpent's pointed red snout, the distinctly recessed lower jaw, the transverse black marking on the crown, and the unmarked white belly. The smooth dorsal scales are in 19 rows at midbody, and the anal plate is single.

During its lifetime this subspecies experiences the same gradual color transformation described in the northern scarlet snake account.

COMPARABLE SNAKES *See northern scarlet snake account.* The Texas long-nosed snake's yellow dorsal coloration is confined mostly to narrow lines of demarcation between its much wider black and red crossbands and to dots of similar color in the black markings. Its dorsal scales are arranged in 23 midbody rows; among all of our harmless serpents, only the longnose has most of the scales on the underside of the tail in a single row.

SIZE The known maximum length for this subspecies is 26 inches (66 cm).

HABITAT Although the snake's South Texas coastal habitat is clearly different from the pine-hardwood forest environment of its close relative to the northeast, it is nevertheless restricted largely to areas of loose, sandy soils. Of several specimens collected within the city limits of Rockport, two were found near live oaks scattered across the coastal sand dunes, while two others were dug from the sandy substrate of watermelon patches. Stephen E. Labuda Jr. (pers. com:) discovered one on the Aransas Wildlife Refuge as it crawled over the sand in a cluster of red bay trees and scattered American beauty berry plants. This subspecies may even occupy dry, sandy flatland where the dominant vegetation is mesquite, black huisache, and prickly pear cactus.

BEHAVIOR Only a few Texas scarlet snakes have been encountered in the wild or been maintained in captivity, so little is known regarding its natural history. The small amount of behavioral information we have comes from studies of the other subspecies, discussed in the northern scarlet snake account.

Rarely seen in the open, the scarlet snake is occasionally unearthed by farmers tilling their soil or by construction crews excavating land for development. It does come to the surface to forage, but almost always at night. Specimens are sometimes found beneath objects on the ground, like the scarlet snakes Auffenberg (1948) discovered under scrap piles at the Corpus Christi Naval Air Station many years ago. In fact, the five specimens he collected there were the first examples of this species ever reported from Texas, which led him to believe incorrectly that they were Florida scarlet snakes accidentally introduced to the Lone Star state by

military aircraft hauling large crates of cargo from Pensacola.

FEEDING This serpent's feeding habits are probably no different from those of the two other subspecies of scarlet snake, consisting primarily of small lizards and the eggs of reptiles. See the northern scarlet snake account.

A Texas scarlet snake kept at the Houston Zoo for several months initially consumed nearly a quarter of the contents of a domestic hen's egg from a shallow dish placed in its cage, but over the next eight days it swallowed whole nine eggs of a Texas spiny lizard. That the same snake refused all other offerings of various small lizards and snakes during its long confinement demonstrates its preference for eggs. The scarlet snake does not limit its diet to such food, however, for the species is also known to eat snakes, lizards, amphibians, small rodents, and insects.

REPRODUCTION Nothing is recorded about the reproduction of this subspecies, although the details of its breeding habits probably are similar to those described in the northern scarlet snake account.

BUTTERMILK RACER
Coluber constrictor anthicus
PLATE 16

DESCRIPTION No other adult Texas racer is as curiously marked as this one, its steel-blue, blue-green, slate, or dark olive dorsal color randomly speckled with a hodgepodge of white, gray, tan, or pale yellow scales, most of which are of a single, solid hue and arranged both individually and in clusters of diverse sizes. So variably complex is this pattern that no two specimens exhibit exactly the same markings. Some display just a few pale-colored scales, while others are densely speckled over nearly their entire bodies; in all cases the rear part of the racer's trunk, as well as the tail, is some shade of pale brown. The white or pale gray belly is usually marked with a small number of pale yellow spots, and the racer's snout, throat, and lips are white. The dorsal scales, all smooth, are in 17 rows at midbody, and the anal plate is divided. Like the young of most other racer subspecies, the juvenile buttermilk's grayish ground color is conspicuously marked with a row of reddish

brown saddles down the middle of the back, which are flanked on either side by two or three longitudinal rows of smaller dark spots. During a brief interval in the racer's early life (at a length of approximately 20 inches, when the juvenile loses its baby pattern of bold, dark blotches but before it develops its light dorsal spotting) it is essentially unicolored.

COMPARABLE SNAKES Because its body is heavily flecked with dark spots, the speckled king snake is the serpent most likely to be mistaken for an adult buttermilk racer, although its spots are small (not covering an entire scale), its yellow abdomen boldly checked with black, and its anal plate undivided. The juvenile buttermilk racer can be distinguished from other small, blotched serpents by the following combination of features: it has smooth dorsal scales, no more than 17 dorsal scale rows at midbody, and a divided anal plate.

Bounded on all sides by several other closely

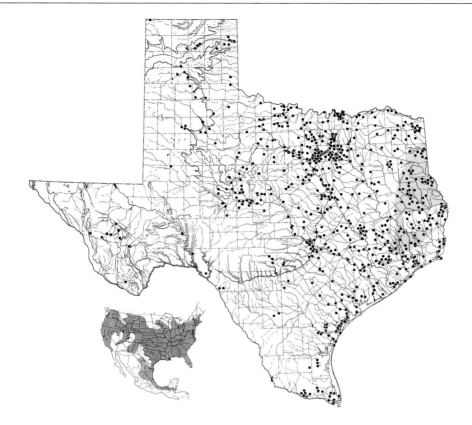

related subspecies whose geographic ranges overlap its own, the buttermilk racer in such places often exhibits features of coloration intermediate between it and its nearest neighbor, making a precise subspecies identification difficult. The most practical course in such cases is to identify the mystery specimen according to geography, assigning it by its collecting locality to the closest ranging subspecies. When it shares equally the color and pattern characteristics of two adjacent races, the only realistic option is to call the specimen what it is—an intergrade between the two.

SIZE This subspecies approaches in maximum size the yellow-bellied racer, whose greatest known length of 71 inches (180.3 cm) is only 1 inch longer than that of its speckled cousin. Most adult buttermilk racers, however, are between 30 and 60 inches (76.2–152.4 cm) long.

HABITAT Restricted to the longleaf pine and mixed pine-hardwood forests of East Texas and adjacent Louisiana, the buttermilk racer is most likely to be encountered in places that have been cleared by man but not so sanitized as to be without some form of brushy ground cover. Little-used agricultural and urban areas adjacent to woodlands are especially favored. Such forest-edge clearings include pastureland, abandoned farm fields, old oil-field sites, powerline rights-of-way, sawmill sites (especially those no longer in use), and certain open spaces devoted to outdoor recreation, where the buttermilk racer can at times be unexpectedly plentiful. During a single week in mid-May, for example, nine of these elusive reptiles were captured along the brushy perimeter of a golf course in northeastern Harris County by an amateur snake collector employed there as a groundskeeper. All but two were spotted out in the open, where they apparently were sunning themselves. Thirty-nine of 40 specimens collected by R. F. Clark (1949) in the Hill parishes of Louisiana were found in woodlands near brier patches or other brushy ground cover.

BEHAVIOR Like all racers, the buttermilk is nervous and quick to flee when approached, but it has been our experience that this subspecies is not as combative as the others when picked up. Unless severely provoked or roughly handled, it shows considerable restraint, biting in self-defense only as a last resort. With only a mouthful of small, needle-sharp teeth with which to defend itself, a racer is no match against a large aggressor. To escape danger, it streaks away into the brush with a sudden burst of speed that usually leaves its foe momentarily bewildered, for this is one of Texas' fastest snakes. A few seconds later it is out of sight. Surprisingly little detailed information is reported about the natural history of the buttermilk racer, whose large size, abundance, and terrestrial habits should make it an easy subject for investigation. It almost certainly shares many of the behaviors of other *C. constrictor* subspecies. For more information about racers in general, see the account for the eastern yellow-bellied racer.

FEEDING In the only known survey of the buttermilk racer's food habits, conducted by Clark in northern Louisiana, the following prey items were found in the stomachs of sample specimens: mice in 25, rats in 5, lizards in 8, frogs in 7, and birds in 3. Curiously, none contained insects, a dominant food item in the diets of most other racers.

REPRODUCTION Clark states that in the Hill parishes of Louisiana, the female of this subspecies lays her eggs in soft, moist soil (like that found next to old rotting logs), in individual clutches of 6 to 18 eggs. The only other clues to the reproductive biology of this subspecies, based on captive-laid and -hatched egg clutches, were reported by Werler (1970). They include three clutches (two from Harris County and one from Liberty County) deposited at the Houston Zoo on May 25, May 26, and May 29, respectively. They represent earlier laying dates than were reported by Fitch (1963b) for all other subspecies of *C. constrictor*, both in Texas and elsewhere. For a yellow-bellied racer from Texas, his earliest record was June 1; for a Mexican racer from South Texas, June 5. Two of the buttermilk racers mentioned by Werler laid 18 eggs each; the third deposited 27. A little more than an inch long at the time of deposition, the successfully incubated eggs hatched 46 days later, producing babies $9\frac{1}{3}$ to 11 inches (22.9–27.9 cm) long.

TAN RACER
Coluber constrictor etheridgei
PLATE 17

DESCRIPTION This long, slender racer has a pale tan to brown body, usually randomly speckled with a few small, pallid spots or, less often, none at all. Its chin, throat, and belly are even paler. The snake's dorsal scales are smooth and arranged in 17 rows at midbody. The anal plate is divided. A very young specimen shows little resemblance to the adult. Like the hatchlings of most other racer subspecies, its pale gray ground color is conspicuously marked with a row of reddish brown saddles down the middle of the back, on either side of which are two or three lengthwise rows of smaller dark spots. All of these markings become gradually more indistinct on the rear of the body, finally fading altogether long before they reach the end of the tail.

COMPARABLE SNAKES Although the speckled king snake is heavily spotted, its overall coloration is dark brown to black instead of light brown. Moreover, virtually every one of its dorsal scales contains a small central light spot, whereas the spots of the tan racer, when present, are randomly distributed over the back and sides; each typically occupies an entire scale. Another similar snake, the adult eastern coachwhip, is generally much darker than a tan racer and unspotted; it also has fewer midbody rows of dorsal scales (13 rather than 17) and a subtle crosshatched pattern on its tail. The juvenile racer can be distinguished from other small, spotted snake species by a combination of characters: it has smooth scales, a divided anal plate, and no more than 17 rows of dorsal scales at midbody.

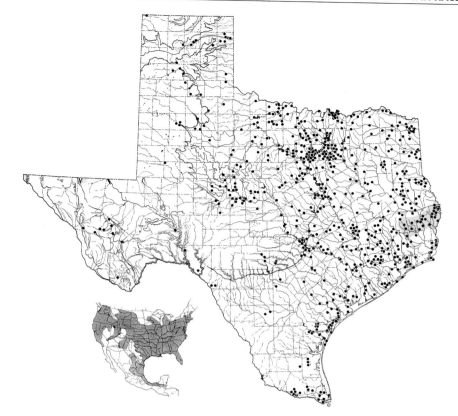

SIZE Most adults of this uncommon subspecies are 3 to 4½ feet (91.4–137.2 cm) long, although large examples may reach a length of nearly 6 feet (182.9 cm).

HABITAT While most other racer subspecies occurring in Texas inhabit primarily open spaces, this one dwells chiefly among the longleaf pine flatwoods that dominate the eastern part of the state along its south-central border with Louisiana. Land clearing is inexorably reducing its prime habitat. Richard Etheridge (in Fitch 1963b) suggested that as ever more prime forest is converted to brushy space by logging, the buttermilk racer, a resident of open habitat, invades the cleared land at the expense of the forest-dwelling tan racer.

BEHAVIOR Judging from the dearth of specimens in museum collections, this seems not to be an abundant serpent. The reptile's small geographic range, its concealing coloration (which makes it difficult to detect), or both may account for its apparent scarcity. Lying in shaded woods among grasses and shrubs,

the tan racer is difficult to recognize, its slender brownish form blending intimately with the layer of dead pine needles that carpets the sandy forest floor. The relatively low light level of such a shadowy habitat would also make the racer more difficult to spot than if it were in an open, weedy field.

Like its relatives, the tan racer is quick to escape when threatened, its slim body coursing easily over the ground until it is safely out of sight. Except for its characteristically nervous *Coluber* disposition, we have found it to be a relatively mild-mannered racer, whose reaction to being picked up is more controlled than that of other Texas racer subspecies, with the possible exception of the buttermilk racer. Those we handled, both in the field and in captivity, neither struck nor bit. Likewise, Larry N. White (pers. com.), who captured the pair of tan racers mentioned in the Reproduction section of this account, commented that even when interrupted during mating and subsequently handled, neither snake attempted to use its teeth defensively. For more information about the species in general, see the eastern yellow-bellied racer account.

FEEDING Although the composition of this snake's diet has not been identified, racers in general consume a wide variety of both invertebrate and vertebrate prey that includes insects, spiders, lizards, turtles, snakes, birds, and mammals. A tan racer collected by Larry White in northeastern Hardin County on April 22 had the following invertebrates in its stomach: common crickets; short-horned, banded-winged, and slant-faced grasshoppers; spider fragments; and a large quantity of other unidentifiable orthopteran remains, but no vertebrate prey.

REPRODUCTION Virtually no documented information is available about the snake's reproductive biology, but Larry White (pers. com.) observed a copulating pair in north-

eastern Hardin County on April 22, 1984, at about 10:30 AM, at which time the Fahrenheit temperature was in the low seventies. The mating location was described as somewhat open woodland with a ground cover of grass 12 inches (30.5 cm) high and scattered brush. Forty days after copulation, on June 1, the female laid 17 eggs, ranging in length from 1 to 1¼ inches (2.5–3.2 cm), which were artificially incubated at the Houston Zoo. Only 4 hatched—on July 14, 15, and 16—producing babies that were 7½ to 8⅛ inches (19–20.6 cm) in length. The only other record of egg laying for this snake is that of a captive female tan racer from a locality east of Woodville; on May 28 she deposited 20 eggs at the Houston Zoo, each measuring more than 1 inch (2.5 cm) long, none of which hatched.

EASTERN YELLOW-BELLIED RACER
Coluber constrictor flaviventris
PLATE 18

DESCRIPTION The unpatterned olive-brown to grayish green dorsal hue of adult Texas specimens contrasts with the cream to yellow belly color, which is especially bright under the snake's chin, across its upper lip scales, and on the sides of its neck. The snake's dorsal scales are smooth and arranged in 17 rows at midbody, there are usually 7 upper lip scales on either side of the head, and the anal plate is divided.

The juvenile racer (at least for the first two or three years of its life) looks strikingly different from the adult. Its back is boldly marked with a longitudinal row of dark, light-edged blotches and two or more rows of alternating small dark spots along the sides, all of which become indistinct and finally fade altogether before reaching the end of the tail. On the abdomen are scattered dark speckles.

COMPARABLE SNAKES An adult coachwhip snake with no appreciable change of color from head to tail (some are banded or bicolored) can be distinguished from a grown adult yellow-bellied racer by its fewer rows of dorsal scales (13 rather than 17), and by the distinct pale and dark crosshatched pattern

on its tail. The rough green snake is an emerald color in life (dark blue after death) and has keeled scales. The similarly hued (though sometimes olive colored) smooth green snake has no more than 15 rows of dorsal scales at midbody. Among several small serpent species whose dorsal markings resemble the blotched pattern of the juvenile racer, none has the following combination of characters: smooth scales, a divided anal plate, and no more than 17 dorsal scale rows at midbody.

SIZE This subspecies usually attains an adult length between 23 and 50 inches (63.5–127 cm), although the largest known specimen measured 70 inches (177.8 cm) long.

HABITAT Occupying much of Texas from the Panhandle and the Red River south to the northern edge of the coastal plain and the upper Gulf Coast (but excluding southwestern Texas, most of South Texas, and the pine and pine-hardwood forests of East Texas), this adaptable racer utilizes a wide variety of habitats. In a comprehensive, long-term study of its natural history conducted primarily in northeastern Kansas, Fitch (1963b) described in detail the snake's choice habi-

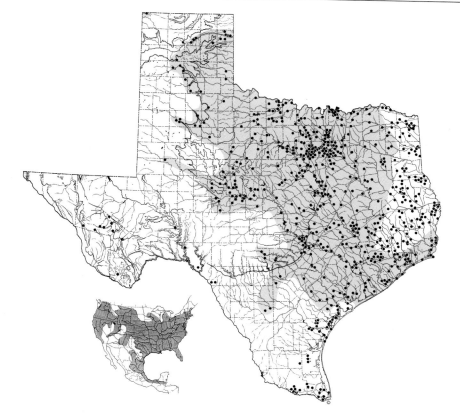

tats, which are scarcely different from those in Texas. We have therefore included some of the Kansas information here and have also drawn freely from his extensive observations to complete all other sections in this account.

Generally avoiding heavily shaded forest in favor of open, brushy areas, this racer shows a definite preference for tallgrass prairie, pastureland overgrown with high weedy vegetation, brush-covered ravines, brushy woodland edge, streamside thickets, weed-covered fields, and sparse woodland. In southeastern Texas it also favors abandoned farmland and the edges of both active grain fields and old oil-field sites, while along the coast it frequently occupies marshland levees. When choosing a grassland habitation, the snake usually avoids areas that have been closely cropped by man, for where there is inadequate ground cover, the snake tends to move elsewhere.

At more northern latitudes it sometimes changes habitat according to season, migrating each fall from lowland meadows to hill-top rock outcroppings in or near dense woods, where it overwinters in rock crevices below ground.

BEHAVIOR The eastern yellow-bellied racer, along with its close relatives the coachwhips and whipsnakes, is among the fastest of Texas serpents. A full-gaited specimen traveling across uneven terrain where it can gain a firm grip with its belly scales appears to be moving even faster than it really is. Gliding over the ground at top speed, however, it crawls at only about 4 or 5 miles (5.5–8 km) per hour, a good speed for a serpent but not nearly as fast as the average man can run. Such a seemingly high velocity results in part from the racer's ability to slip through dense brush without slowing and from the elongated shape of its body—all large, slender serpents in motion convey a sense of rapid forward movement.

To increase its survival opportunities, the racer employs several different defensive strategies, each one used in a particular circumstance. The snake's first line of defense, given adequate warning of an impending threat, is to dart for the nearest shelter (usually a patch of shrubbery, a rock, a log, or the dark interior of a convenient animal burrow), where it remains until the danger is past. It may even try to evade its foe by climbing into bushes or the lower limbs of trees. If compelled by circumstances, it will take to water without hesitation, swimming with its head held several inches above the surface. If suddenly confronted at close range by a large foe, the startled reptile generally uses one of two survival strategies to avoid a direct confrontation. In the first, which is infrequently executed, the racer stands pat instead of retreating, pulls its body into a tangle of slowly writhing coils, and with its head tucked beneath them discharges a musky, cream-colored slime from its cloaca, which it then liberally smears over itself by its animated movements. In one case, reported by Lynch (1978), a snake of this subspecies that was picked up after displaying such behavior twice feigned death by turning over onto its back and remaining there for about 30 seconds. These tactics, used as a second line of defense when the snake has been cornered, captured, or injured, apparently are meant to confuse and thereby discourage a predator.

If unfettered by such constraints, however, the same snake makes a determined effort to flee. When startled by the sudden appearance of a human in relatively unobstructed terrain, it instantly streaks away at full speed, flailing its tail from side to side as it disappears into the underbrush, its trail marked only by a zigzag line of wavy grass. While the commotion immediately attracts the interloper's attention to the site of the original disturbance, the snake, without any further turmoil, quickly glides unnoticed from the scene. In a move that typifies the racer's innate curiosity, it may execute a wide half-circle a few minutes later and slowly return to the area where it was first flushed, coming in from the direction opposite its original escape route. At this point it is apt to climb into a tree or bush and drape itself along an outermost branch where, apparently feeling secure among the sheltering leaves, it can be closely approached before it will flee.

When a racer encounters a creature or condition about which it is apprehensive but that appears not to be immediately threatening, the snake takes a different approach. This is especially true if the suspect object stands between the snake and its refuge. With its slightly arched forebody held high off the ground in a rigid stance and its neck flattened horizontally, the alarmed serpent cautiously moves away from the object, extending its forked tongue frequently and waving it slowly up and down as it tries to assess the danger. At best only a threat display, the racer will abandon this pretentious bluff and flee at the first sign of overt movement.

An eastern yellow-bellied racer that has been cornered is not so timid; in fact, it can actually be quite fierce in its self-defense. If unable to escape, it puts up a determined fight, lashing out vigorously time and again from a slightly elevated S-shaped forebody stance, its tail whirring and its anal opening occasionally exuding feces and musk. If it hits its mark, the snake has a peculiar way of yanking its head back from a bite that causes its teeth to be raked across the skin, inflicting on its victim a series of long, parallel scratches that in some cases will bleed excessively. As a result of this insidious biting style, there is always the possibility that some of the snake's small, needle-sharp teeth will be torn from their sockets and remain firmly embedded in the skin. Like minute cactus spines, they may not be noticed until they fester and become painful a day or two later.

If facing an agitated racer on the ground is an unpleasant experience, picking one up can be unnerving. So determined is this snake to escape one's grasp that if it is lifted off the ground by the rear portion of its tail, it is likely to twirl its body with such vigor that the seized tail end twists free from the rest, gaining the reptile its freedom at the expense of part of its lost caudal member. When picked up near midbody, the captured racer spews body wastes and musk from its cloaca as it thrashes violently from side to side, striking out furiously in an attempt to gain its freedom. When it seizes a hand, it is not always satisfied to disengage its jaws quickly; instead it sometimes keeps a firm grip on its captor, releasing its hold only after it has fully embedded its small teeth by chewing in place for several seconds. Such injuries, while they may be somewhat painful, are not serious.

A strictly day-active serpent whose preferred ambient air temperature lies between 78 and 80 degrees F, the yellow-bellied racer usually remains active when most other snakes avoid the midday heat by retiring to some shady spot; its wanderings may continue even after the thermometer reaches a high of 90 degrees F. Indeed, when the others are out of sight, the racer may still be encountered crawling in the open or perhaps even stretched out on a shrub, tree limb, rock, or log, basking in full sunlight. In one example of the snake's exceptional heat tolerance, Fitch tells of a large female yellow-bellied racer that was released from a live trap and came to rest in a cluster of sunflower stalks 50 feet away with half her body directly exposed to the sunlight where the air temperature registered more than 93 degrees F. Although she steadfastly maintained this position for several minutes, the racer indicated no discomfort, nor did she immediately move from the spot.

To avoid excessively hot or cold temperatures temporarily during its active annual season (which at more northern latitudes lasts from early April to late August or mid-November, and in South Texas from mid-March to mid-November), the racer crawls under any of a variety of surface objects. Depending on the available habitat, they can include large rocks, rock piles, logs, boards, and sheet-metal siding. It also seeks shelter in animal burrows, decaying tree stumps, old building foundations, and rock crevices. We have found, too, that in many parts of Texas the racer is especially attracted to abandoned farmhouses and their associated barns, whose tumbledown structures provide the snake with a generous array of sheltering objects. In the opinion of many naturalists, such a refuge (a rock, log, board, or like article) located within the racer's home range may serve as a specific homing nook to which the snake returns each night for as long as it occupies a particular territory and to which it flees for protection when it is foraging nearby.

As reported by Fitch, the reptile's territory, or home range, contains about 25 acres (11.4 ha). It is within this relatively limited space that some racers spend virtually their entire lives, while others, perhaps in response to a food shortage or a significant change in environmental conditions, sometimes permanently shift their territories. At least in the more northern parts of its range, a racer may leave this area only temporarily as it seeks a mate or engages in seasonal migrations to and from a more distant winter denning site.

For most yellow-bellied racers in Fitch's northeastern Kansas study area, such migrations were routinely conducted each spring and fall between the snakes' summer grassland homes and their more elevated rocky hibernacula, covering an average distance of approximately ¼ mile (402 m). In regions like those in South Texas and along the Gulf Coast, where rock formations are generally absent, the serpents spend their winters underground primarily in animal burrows and above ground in rotting logs and tree stumps. Faced with generally mild winters and plenty of shelters from which to choose, such racers nearly always hibernate singly. At more northern latitudes, where winters are longer and more severe and where suitable denning sites are sometimes scarce, the serpents may be compelled to den communally; a single, deep rock-crevice chamber sometimes contains as many as several dozen snakes. In some instances this number may be even greater, for according to Collins and Collins (1991), in Kansas more than 100 racers have been known to occupy the same den. There is also ample evidence to show that in such northerly winter refuges, other snakes, including ring-necked, garter, rat, and bull snakes, as well as copperheads and rattlesnakes, often share the same underground shelters with the hibernating yellow-bellied racers.

FEEDING In a lengthy study of the eastern yellow-bellied racer's food habits, conducted in Kansas over a span of 14 years, Fitch identified in the snake's diet a wide assortment of prey that included virtually everything from insects to small mammals, but not fishes. Except for insects, all of the listed items seem like usual fare for a snake of this size. Although the copperhead (a serpent of moderate length that only sporadically dines on a variety of arthropods) will eagerly gorge on cicada imagoes as they periodically emerge in vast numbers from their underground chambers, the racer (including its various subspecies) is probably the only large native snake that regularly consumes substantial numbers of insects. While such prey represented the racer's most frequently consumed food (about 76 percent of the total), mammals (at 66 percent) exceeded them as prey when the two categories were compared by weight. These figures, of course, are only approximations of the reptile's menu, since the kinds of animals eaten by this far-ranging snake will vary from place to place, depending on their local abundance and seasonal availability. Ranking high on the list of insect prey were grasshoppers, katydids, and crickets, with caterpillars, moths (and their larvae), and cicadas constituting less important menu items. Among mammals, voles and white-footed mice were most frequently devoured, the former encountered during the day in the racer's grassy habitat and the primarily nocturnal mice plucked from their underground nests as they slept by day. Other mammals often consumed by the snake include a variety of rodent species (especially harvest mice), shrews, and baby cottontail rabbits—all of them small and relatively defenseless. Prey much larger than this are usually avoided as being too bulky to be easily swallowed and, perhaps just as important, too dangerous to confront. Although an adult racer is not foolish enough to attack large rats or squirrels, whose sharp, chisellike incisor teeth make them dangerous adversaries, it willingly raids their nests to devour the helpless young. Similarly, ground-nesting birds that fall prey to the snake are generally the nestlings, fledglings, or eggs.

More common in the racer's diet than birds, however, are several kinds of ground-dwelling lizards, including certain species of scaly and earless lizards, in addition to race runners and skinks. Other reptiles are also important menu items, particularly small serpents such as ring-necked, green, and garter snakes, as well as young rat snakes and bull snakes. In the digestive tract of an Arkansas yellow-bellied racer, Plummer (1990b) found a keeled green snake egg, in addition to an adult keeled green snake and a large number of grasshoppers. Even juvenile copperheads and rattlesnakes are known to have been eaten by this indiscriminate carnivore. Of all the serpents consumed by the eastern yellow-bellied racer in Fitch's study, the majority were smaller examples of its own kind. Perhaps the most unusual prey items reported

were hatchling turtles, both land (tortoises) and water (painted turtles) species, whose hard shells and cumbersome shapes must make them acceptable meals for only the largest racers. Frogs, where they are abundant, particularly those of the genera *Hyla* and *Rana*, often constitute an important food source for this snake.

With its head held as much as a foot off the ground, a racer glides through the underbrush at a lively pace, its large eyes scanning the immediate surroundings for some sign of movement. By frequently changing direction, the snake tries to flush from hiding any concealed prey. Stealth and keen eyesight are especially important to its foraging success. So is speed. The instant the snake spots movement, it responds. Indeed, one of the most impressive things about a racer is its sudden acceleration, which, although not fast when measured in miles per hour, is quick enough to close the gap between itself and its fleeing prey.

Frogs are particularly elusive targets whose nimble, erratic movements, together with their sudden stops and starts, make them difficult to follow. One that suddenly becomes motionless during a chase, especially if it comes to rest in concealing vegetation, is likely to escape its pursuer, at least momentarily, for the snake relies primarily on the prey's movement to keep it in sight. To the racer, a stationary frog is virtually invisible. Only by diligently searching the area where the amphibian was last seen can the serpent expect to find its lost quarry and renew the pursuit by setting it in motion again.

Small animals that have no effective means to retaliate are simply seized in the snake's jaws and promptly swallowed alive. Larger prey whose vigorous struggles are difficult to control may be pinned to the ground by a segment of the serpent's muscular body. Despite the species' misleading scientific name, *constrictor*, this serpent does not suffocate its victim with constricting coils, as do king, rat, and bull snakes. To subdue certain larger animals, such as adult rodents and snakes, it may chew viciously as it holds its victim's head in its jaws.

REPRODUCTION Like most Texas snakes, racers mate not long after they emerge from hibernation in April or May, at which time two or more males, attracted to the same female by her scent, may all court her simultaneously. As described by Fitch, courtship in this subspecies is a lively affair. It begins with the male maintaining close physical contact with his mate by extending his body alongside hers (sometimes by draping himself along the length of her trunk) as brief spasmodic rippling movements periodically pass through his body, gradually increasing in their intensity and duration. Each cycle of such writhing movements ends with the male excitedly jerking his head forward and backward. During this phase of courtship, the female remains relatively passive, though she occasionally streaks ahead of her suitor, stopping just as abruptly as she began, 4 or 5 feet (1.2–1.5 m) away. Such actions, instead of discouraging the male, tend to arouse him. The male responds by darting right along with her, staying so close by her side that the two snakes appear to be moving as one. At approximately 10-minute intervals he initiates his own ritualistic withdrawals, briefly circling his mate with quick, spirited movements. As much as an hour later, when she finally accepts the male's advances, the female raises her tail so that the snakes' cloacal openings are in alignment for mating, allowing copulation to occur. After mating has been achieved and the female begins to crawl away, the male is unceremoniously dragged along with her, his engorged, spine-covered hemipenis still firmly held in place within her cloaca.

Probably no other North American serpent is as likely as a male racer to respond aggressively when disturbed by humans during its courtship or copulation, although nearly all accounts of such hostile behavior by this species are attributable to the northern black racer, a large, pugnacious subspecies inhabiting the northeastern part of the United States (Fitch 1963b, Ernst and Barbour 1989). Fitch does tell of a captive eastern yellow-bellied racer that turned aggressively to face a human intruder who approached as it was mating with a female cagemate in a large outdoor enclosure, but the snake failed to follow with an outright attack. Is it possible that under such circumstances the males of this subspecies, like those of *C. c. constrictor*, sometimes react with even greater hostility, ad-

vancing on or striking repeatedly at an interloper? This is, after all, a relatively large racer whose courage and willingness to defend itself in stressful situations are well known.

When the eggs are ready to be laid, the female must find a suitable nest site that is both warm and moist. As with virtually all snake eggs, their successful incubation is not the result of maternal care but of the right ambient conditions. In regions where the soil is heavy with moisture, as it is in swamps, marshes, and certain other low-lying areas, the ground is usually too wet for the proper long-term development of the eggs, and so the female living in such an environment selects a somewhat drier place in which to deposit her clutch. In a Louisiana swamp, for example, Tinkle (1959) found two clutches of racer eggs under man-made objects lying on the ground, one beneath old newspaper and the other under a small, thin board. In more arid regions, however, such as those in Central and West Texas, where dry surface conditions are even less favorable for egg development, the yellow-bellied racer probably lays her clutch underground in the burrows of small mammals, where moderate temperatures and adequate levels of moisture offer a more satisfactory microenvironment for their long-term growth than do surface sites. In eastern Kansas such burrows are also the most common places for local racers to lay their eggs. Consisting of abandoned tunnels that were probably originally excavated by moles and voles in or near fields and pastures, they are usually 4 to 8 inches below the surface. Elsewhere in its geographic range the racer is reported to have laid its eggs in piles of sawdust, in the soft soil next to a rotting log, in decaying stumps, and under flat rocks lying on hillsides.

In none of those instances was more than a single clutch laid at any one location. Near Boulder, Colorado, however, Swain and Smith (1978) reported the discovery of an apparent communal nest in which 89 viable eggs and 29 spent eggshells were found under a pile of large rocks, suggesting that in areas where adequate nest sites are scarce, two or more racers may be obliged by circumstances to lay their eggs together in precisely the same place. Although 5 to 26 eggs, each measuring 1¼ to 1½ inches (3.2–3.8 cm) long, may be deposited at a time by a female eastern yellow-bellied racer, 12 is considered the usual clutch size. Laid sometime in June or July, the yellowish, oval eggs, with saltlike granules scattered over their leathery shells, hatch in late August or early September, producing young that measure on average about 10¾ inches (27.3 cm) in length.

MEXICAN RACER
Coluber constrictor oaxaca
PLATES 19, 20

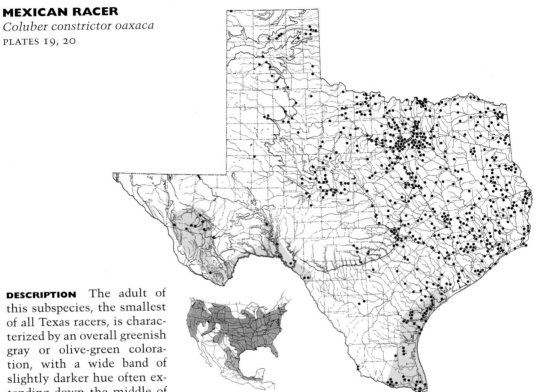

DESCRIPTION The adult of this subspecies, the smallest of all Texas racers, is characterized by an overall greenish gray or olive-green coloration, with a wide band of slightly darker hue often extending down the middle of the snake's back. The skin between the dorsal scales, and sometimes even the leading edges of the scales themselves, exhibit a dark blue, almost black color that is most evident when the skin is stretched after the snake has taken a large meal. Normally the throat is whitish or pale yellow, though in some specimens this area is pastel pink; the rest of the abdomen is yellow to yellowish green. The dorsal scales are smooth and arranged in 17 rows at midbody, there are usually 8 upper lip scales on either side of the head, and the anal plate is divided. Bearing no resemblance to their plain-colored parents, very young examples of this subspecies are conspicuously marked with narrow dark crossbars on the forebody, which become gradually less distinct toward the rear of the trunk and disappear altogether before they reach the tail. Below them on either side of the tan body are two or more irregular rows of small dark spots, giving the juvenile snakes a distinctly speckled look.

The infant Mexican racer differs from juveniles of other Texas subspecies of *C. constrictor* in the shape of its dorsal blotches, which are jagged in outline and pointed at their lateral edges; those of other native racers are oval with rounded ends.

COMPARABLE SNAKES A plain-colored adult western coachwhip snake (some are banded) differs from a Mexican racer by its fewer rows of middorsal scales (13 rather than 17) and by the distinct light and dark crosshatched pattern of its tail. The rough green snake has keeled dorsal scales and is vivid green in life (dark blue after death). Among several other small serpent species whose dorsal markings somewhat resemble those of a very young Mexican racer, none has the following combination of characters: smooth scales, a divided anal plate, and no more than 17 dorsal scale rows at midbody.

SIZE This, the smallest of all Texas racers, reaches an adult length between 20 and 40 inches (50.8–101.6 cm).

HABITAT Primarily a Mexican serpent whose geographic range reaches northward into the dry South Texas thornbrush and extends northeast along the Gulf Coast to Corpus Christi, C. c. oaxaca generally avoids the more arid sections of the Rio Grande Valley and those that are heavily wooded. Its choice habitats include areas of sparse or scattered brush and open woodland, with a secondary preference for terrain supporting either heavy brush or bare grassland. A couple of hundred miles to the northwest, the snake occurs again in widely scattered populations throughout the Trans-Pecos region of Texas, its highly intermittent distribution there probably representing isolated remnants of a once much wider ranging population that occupied the area in the wetter climate of an earlier geological age. Most of these western locality records, in fact, are associated with some form of natural surface water.

BEHAVIOR Auffenberg (1949) was the first to describe in any detail the snake's habitat and behavior, basing his information on specimens he encountered within a 50-mile (80.6 km) radius of the U.S. Naval Air Station near Corpus Christi, Texas. During a span of 18 months, he observed 291 Mexican racers, documenting their life styles and habitat preferences. Today, more than 50 years later and despite the snake's relative abundance in parts of South Texas, little new information about its natural history has been reported. This account, therefore, is based largely on Auffenberg's study.

Like most subspecies of C. constrictor, this one is nervous and quick-tempered, streaking out of sight at the first sign of danger. Yet in the Brownsville area, where Mulaik and Mulaik (1942) found it to be largely arboreal, the snake often remained still when approached, its dark green coloration apparently providing an effective camouflage as it rested along the tops of bushes. One that is picked up will flail about and bite viciously, clamping its jaws onto its captor's hand, at least briefly, as it embeds its teeth by chewing repeatedly. Meanwhile, the harried snake may expel musk and feces from its cloacal opening in a further attempt to discourage its foe.

This is strictly a day-active serpent. Except in October, when the racer was slightly more visible than during its more idle months of September, March, and April, most specimens were observed in May, June, and July, their daily periods of prowling activity typically separated into morning (7 AM to noon) and afternoon (3 PM to 7 PM) cycles, usually at temperatures between 70 and 85 degrees F. As would be expected of such a cold-blooded animal, it limited its springtime movements to the warmer midafternoon hours and confined its midsummer prowling activities to mornings and late afternoons. In the Brownsville area, Mulaik and Mulaik observed this snake chiefly in the tops of bushes. Auffenberg, on the other hand, while admitting he may have overlooked specimens that were camouflaged in such elevated niches, nevertheless considered this an essentially terrestrial snake, whose forays into bushes and trees are infrequent. In support of this conviction, he points to the large number of earless lizards, a strictly terrestrial species, found in the snakes' stomachs. Most of the Mexican racers he encountered around Corpus Christi were discovered crossing sandy roads, lying under shrubs or trees, resting along the edge of tall grass, or coiled in or next to cactus clumps. He also noted the racer's ability when traveling over loose, sandy soil to use the same lateral looping style of locomotion employed by the sidewinder rattlesnake in the shifting sands of its southwestern desert habitat.

FEEDING In a study of 206 wild-caught Mexican racers from the Corpus Christi area (considering the feeding habits of adult and juvenile individuals together), this snake had eaten chiefly grasshoppers (42.5 percent), crickets (13.5), miscellaneous insects (0.6), earless lizards (40.1), scaly lizards (2.1), frogs (10.0), and rodents (2.2). When the sampled snakes were separated by age, the diet of very young specimens proved to differ significantly from that of the adults. Snakes up to

18 inches long had consumed mostly insects, some frogs, but very few lizards, whereas the full-grown racers ate primarily lizards, some insects, even fewer frogs, and only a small number of rodents. Curiously, no snakes were found in the stomachs of the racers examined, although such reptilian prey is at least occasionally consumed by the other racer subspecies. See eastern yellow-bellied racer account.

REPRODUCTION During June or early July, female Mexican racers migrate from more open terrain to areas of heavier vegetation, a move apparently associated with the egg-laying season. Like other racer subspecies living in relatively dry environments, they probably deposit their clutches underground, particularly in the abandoned subterranean burrows of small mammals, where both the ambient moisture and temperature are more favorable for egg development than they are above ground. Auffenberg mentioned a clutch of 10 eggs laid on June 5 by a female from the Corpus Christi area, 9 of which hatched 73 days later. The largest hatchling was 14½ inches (36.8 cm) long.

SOUTHERN BLACK RACER
Coluber constrictor priapus
PLATES 21, 22

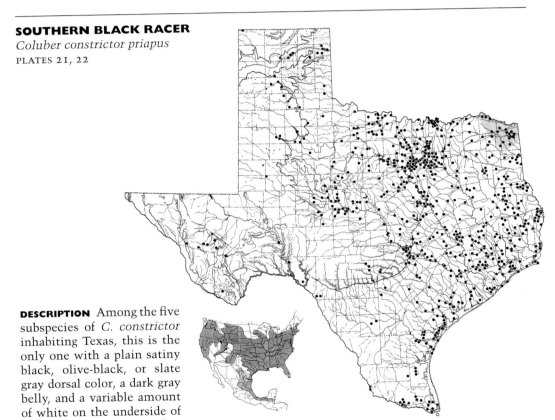

DESCRIPTION Among the five subspecies of *C. constrictor* inhabiting Texas, this is the only one with a plain satiny black, olive-black, or slate gray dorsal color, a dark gray belly, and a variable amount of white on the underside of its head and throat. The dorsal scales are smooth and arranged in 17 rows at midbody, and the anal plate is divided. The hatchling of this subspecies looks nothing like the unpatterned adult. Its dorsal row of reddish brown saddles, which stand out conspicuously against a light gray background color, is flanked on either side by two or more rows of smaller dark spots. Toward the rear of the body the markings become gradually less distinct and more closely aggregated, until they finally disappear altogether before reaching the end of the tail. The abdomen is pale gray and marked along its outer edges with small dark spots.

COMPARABLE SNAKES An adult eastern coachwhip, while sometimes nearly all black, will usually have some reddish brown color on the rear part of its body, especially on the tail. Furthermore, its dorsal scales, when counted at a point just ahead of the tail, are in 13 rows (15 in the racer). The Texas rat snake, whose typically blotched pattern may occasionally be obscured by an unusual amount of dark pigmentation, can be distinguished most readily by the shape of its body, which in cross-section resembles a loaf of bread instead of a cylinder, and by the keeled scales across the back of its trunk. No other small, blotched snake species in northeastern Texas shares the juvenile racer's combination of features: smooth scales, a divided anal plate, and no more than 17 rows of dorsal scales at midbody.

SIZE Adults range from 20 to nearly 65 inches (50.8–165.1 cm) in length. The largest known specimen of this subspecies was collected in Indiana.

HABITAT In Texas the southern black racer is known only from the northeastern corner of the state, where it resides in a rather wide assortment of habitats, including tree-studded pastureland, pine and pine-hardwood forest clearings, grassy hillside rock outcroppings dotted with oak trees, and, according to Jim Yantis (pers. com.), brush-covered terraces along the Red River. In other parts of its geographic range it has commonly been observed in rocky highlands, along brushy stream and lake edges, in the vicinity of limestone bluffs near swamps, and around disturbed areas close to water.

BEHAVIOR All racer subspecies are nervous, quick-tempered reptiles that will defend themselves fiercely when caught unawares and unable to flee from danger. A provoked individual strikes repeatedly, its head and forebody slightly raised off the ground, its tail frequently whirring or swishing nervously back and forth as an explicit warning of its intentions. The snake's striking distance, incidentally, is excellent, often approximating more than half its own length. Some racers are more temperamental than others. According to Jim Yantis, then a Texas Parks and Wildlife Department biologist assigned to Mount Pleasant, southern black racers inhabiting northeastern Texas are notably more pugnacious and more easily aroused than the eastern yellow-bellied subspecies he encountered in the central part of the state.

Despite its more aggressive behavior, even *C. c. priapus* prefers to avoid a confrontation with man. Given the opportunity, it will immediately streak away to a place of refuge— a log, rock crevice, stone pile, tangle of brush, or mammal burrow. Even so, Yantis never saw one in a bush or tree, as is often reported for this snake in other parts of its range, but always on the ground, where it remained motionless until almost stepped on, when, at the last moment, it streaked away into the underbrush. In winter it is said to hibernate in the crevices of rock outcroppings, mammal burrows, rotting logs, or the cavities of decaying tree stumps, either singly or with other snake species. See also the eastern yellow-bellied racer account.

FEEDING Although nothing is known of the southern black racer's food habits in Texas, Minton (1972) obtained dietary information from 38 Indiana specimens (including both *C. c. priapus* and *C. c. flaviventris*). Of that sample, 14 snakes contained insects (grasshoppers, crickets, cicadas, caterpillars, and beetle larvae), 12 had eaten mammals (field mice, unidentified mice, and a chipmunk), 4 held nestling birds or bird eggs, 8 had taken serpents (garter, keeled green, and some unidentified snakes), 3 had consumed tree and leopard frogs, 3 contained skinks, and 2 had devoured baby turtles. Mount (1975) says that in Alabama this snake is also known to have eaten lizards and toads, and Cook (1954) remarked that in Mississippi it takes eggs and small chickens from farmyards.

The racer hunts both by stealth and speed. Moving easily through brush or grass, its head held several inches above the ground for better viewing, the snake seeks to flush its quarry from hiding, for it seems not to notice motionless prey. The moment it detects movement, the racer dashes forward in a sudden burst of acceleration, relying on its speed and agility to overtake its prey. Once captured, the victim may be dealt with in either of two ways. A small, innocuous animal such as a frog is promptly swallowed with no further preliminaries, whereas an adult rodent, whose sharp incisor teeth present a potential risk to the snake, is usually pressed firmly against the ground or a solid object by a segment of the predator's body while still held fast in the snake's jaws. Meanwhile, to subdue a combative victim more quickly, the racer may viciously chew on its head.

REPRODUCTION No observations of reproductive behavior have been reported for the southern black racer in Texas, but in other parts of its range the snake typically mates during the latter part of April or early May. Then sometime between early June and early July, the female deposits her clutch of 7 to 22 (usually 10 to 18) eggs in a warm, damp spot, such as in loose soil, a mammal burrow, a decaying log or tree stump, a pile of sawdust or decomposing vegetation, or beneath a rock or other large surface object. There is evidence that a single female will sometimes use the same nest site year after year and that two or more females may deposit their eggs communally in the same nest cavity. The eggs are 1¼ to 1½ inches (3.2–3.8 cm) long, with granular shells. With known incubation periods of 41 to 64 days, they hatch between early June and early July, producing baby racers 9 to 13 inches (22.9–33 cm) long.

BLACK-STRIPED SNAKE
Coniophanes imperialis imperialis
PLATE 23

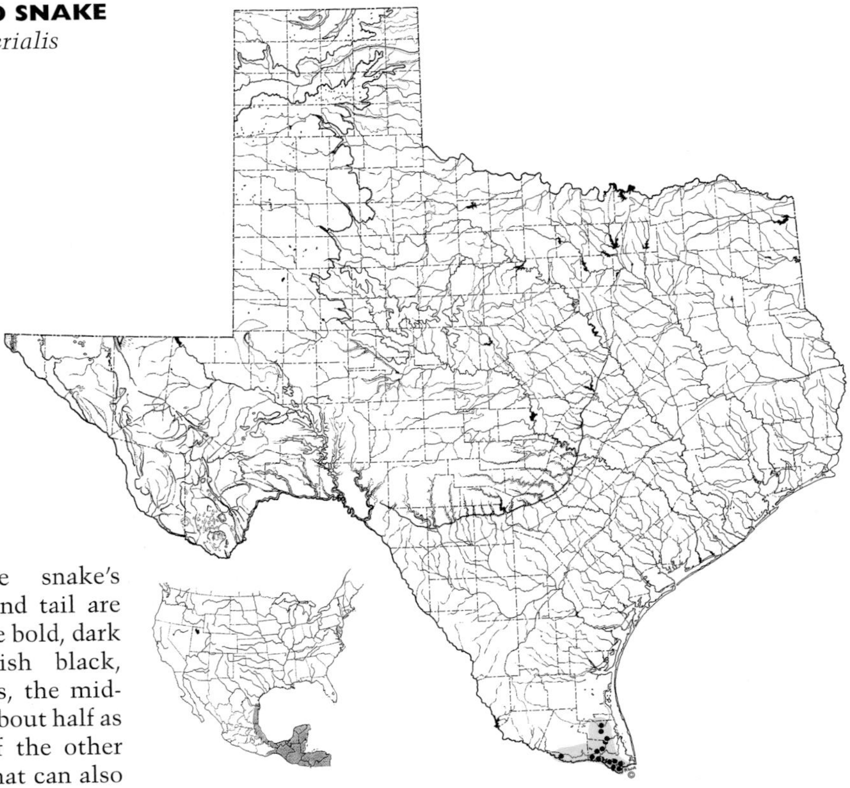

DESCRIPTION The snake's tan upper body and tail are marked with three bold, dark brown or purplish black, lengthwise stripes, the mid-dorsal one being about half as wide as either of the other two—a pattern that can also be described as a series of alternating dark and pale brown longitudinal stripes. The serpent's belly, unlike the rest of its mostly brown body, is pinkish, orange, or scarlet. A pale, narrow line on either side of the face extends backward from the snout, crosses the top of the eye, and ends at the back of the head. Also distinctive are the white, black-dotted upper lip scales. The dorsal scales are smooth and in 19 rows at midbody; the anal plate is divided.

COMPARABLE SNAKES The Texas patch-nosed snake's longitudinal pattern consists of four dark lengthwise stripes, not three; its median stripe is light-colored instead of dark; its belly is white or cream-colored, never pink, orange, or red; its dorsal scales are keeled; and its anal plate is single. Ribbon and garter snakes have a pale spinal stripe, white or pale green bellies, keeled scales, and a single anal plate.

SIZE The adults of this moderately small snake are usually 12 to 18 inches (30.5–45.7 cm) long, although a specimen of record size measured 20 inches (50.8 cm) in length.

HABITAT In the lower Rio Grande Valley live several typically Mexican reptiles, including this one, whose predominantly Latin American ranges continue northward to the southern tip of Texas. Fifty years ago, before intensive agricultural and urban development consumed so much of the Valley's indigenous scrub forest and tropical woodland, the black-striped snake was more widely dispersed throughout the region encompassing Cameron, Hidalgo, and Willacy counties, the only part of the state where it has so far been found. As a result of such widespread disturbance, its habitat has no doubt been considerably reduced. Yet even today, according to Burchfield (pers. com.), it is still relatively common in many Brownsville back yards, being found there in patches of moist humus or leaf litter.

BEHAVIOR Most specimens are nervous creatures that twist vigorously when first restrained or picked up. B. C. Brown (1939) observed that although young individuals were sometimes inclined to bite in self-defense under such circumstances, the adults used their teeth only when forced to do so. Equipped with small, grooved teeth at the back of the upper jaw and a venom of low toxicity, the snake, although able to subdue small vertebrate prey, is no real threat to man, its bite producing no serious or lasting medical consequences in a human victim.

To learn something about the venom's effect on man, Brown allowed one of these snakes to bite him on the skin between the second and third fingers of his left hand. He described the initial pain as sharp, like that of a bee sting, and he experienced some itching at the site of the bite. Within an hour the pain had reached the elbow, and the hand, which was now reddish, particularly at the fang punctures, eventually became numb, swollen, and nearly useless. Five hours after the bite, the pain had subsided somewhat on the forearm but persisted in the still swollen and discolored hand. Twenty-four hours after the experiment began, the hand remained numb and swollen, although no longer painful. Two days later, only a small amount of swelling and some muscle lameness remained.

Another of the snake's defensive strategies is to wave its elevated, pink-bottomed tail slowly back and forth in the face of danger, an apparent diversionary tactic intended to focus a predator's attention on the snake's animated tail and away from its more vulnerable head, and perhaps also to startle and thus frighten away its enemy. Rossi and Rossi (1995), basing their theory on the apparent ease with which this snake loses its seized tail, suggested that the elevated tail-waving behavior invites a predator to attack the caudal member, so that when part of it is unwittingly torn from the rest, the assailant's attention is distracted long enough for the snake to escape unnoticed from the scene. Although lizards of many species regularly lose their tails to attacking predators and grow new ones, we doubt that this is the intended function of the tail display in the black-striped snake. Frequent tail loss in this serpent can probably be attributed to the condition called tail rot.

Active primarily at dusk and dawn but occasionally also at night, the black-striped snake usually hides during the day beneath debris resting on damp soil. Most specimens have been found under accumulations of moist, decomposing vegetation, particularly those in drying streambeds, where bottom layers typically hold more moisture than those at the top. Others have been discovered beneath fallen palm fronds and logs and even beneath the loose bark of dead trees. The serpent carefully selects places that are neither too wet nor too dry. For example, when the base of its plant litter refuge becomes saturated, the snake moves upward into the drier levels of the heap, returning again to the bottom of the pile as the topmost layers desiccate. In response to surface drying conditions, it may burrow into loose, sandy soil or hide in deep earthen cracks created by the dehydrating effects of prolonged hot weather.

FEEDING Although this snake occasionally eats small lizards, snakes, and mice, its chief prey consists of small frogs and toads. Specific food items reported to have been consumed by it in the wild include the Gulf Coast toad, Blanchard's cricket frog (Ted Beimler pers. com.), narrow-mouthed toad, Rio Grande chirping frog, white-lipped frog, and four-lined skink. The snake subdues such animals with the aid of its short, primitive, rear-positioned fangs and a venom that although relatively weak when injected into larger animals, is capable of incapacitating the much smaller prey. As reported by Brown, this was convincingly demonstrated in the case of a black-striped snake that seized a large toad by one leg. After escaping its captor, the amphibian, seemingly uninjured,

died a few minutes later, apparently from the effects of the serpent's venom.

REPRODUCTION The only information about the breeding habits of this snake in Texas are two reports of captive females: one that laid 4 eggs in early June, the other 5 eggs on May 3 and 4. Eggs of the first group measured about 1 inch (2.5 cm) in length; those of the second clutch were nearly ¾ inch (1.9 cm) long. Alvarez del Toro (1960) reported that in the Mexican state of Chiapas, where this species lays as many as 10 eggs per clutch, incubation lasts approximately 40 days, resulting in hatchlings that measure about 6½ inches (16.5 cm) in length.

PRAIRIE RING-NECKED SNAKE
Diadophis punctatus arnyi
PLATES 24, 25

DESCRIPTION The only dorsal marking on this gray, dark olive, or nearly black snake is a prominent yellow or orange-yellow neck ring, which is usually separated from the body hue by a narrow black border; the ring's front edge meets the solid black or dark brown dorsal head color. In some specimens this nuchal collar is interrupted along the top of the neck. The snake's pale-colored lips, chin, and throat are speckled with black dots, and the bright yellow belly, grading to pale orange toward the tail, is randomly covered with numerous small black spots. The undertail, by contrast,

is scarlet red. The smooth body scales are usually arranged in 17 rows on the forward part of the body (sometimes 15), and the anal plate is divided.

COMPARABLE SPECIES The rough earth snake often is born with a pale-colored band across the back of its head, and the juvenile brown snake enters the world with a pale-hued nuchal ring; both species lose such markings long before they reach maturity. Both can be distinguished from the ring-necked snake by their keeled body scales, whitish unmarked abdomens, and brown dorsal color. The Florida red-bellied snake, whose yellowish to reddish orange abdomen sometimes resembles that of a ring-necked snake, differs from *Diadophis* in typically having three small nuchal blotches, keeled body scales, and a virtually immaculate belly. Finally, the three imitator species have a suedelike dorsal surface unlike the glossy appearance of the ring-necked snake.

SIZE Adults of this subspecies usually are 10 to 14 inches (25.4–35.5 cm) long; the largest specimen on record measured 16½ inches (41.9 cm) in length.

HABITAT Much of the information for this account comes from the field studies of Fitch (1975), who has contributed more to our understanding of this snake's natural history than anyone else.

The prairie ring-necked snake lives in a variety of habitats, most of which meet the following requirements: moist, but not wet or soggy soil; an adequate surface layer of plant litter, or flat rocks, boards, logs, or other debris under which it can hide; and a canopy of vegetation that while providing some shade allows considerable sunlight to reach the ground. Within those limits it is found most abundantly in old sparsely wooded and brushy hillside pastures, in bottomland pasture dotted with small trees and shrubs, along hilltop limestone outcroppings littered with loose rocks and supporting a modest growth of underbrush, in prairie gullies containing rock outcroppings and brush patches, near streams and ponds, and in old fields carpeted with ground cover. Curiously, in areas impacted by moderate to heavy cattle grazing, Fitch found that prairie ring-necked snakes occurred in higher densities than in similar ungrazed habitat. It so happens that in such places cattle feed on and trample the underbrush, eventually creating open spaces where the sun can filter through to the ground, resulting in more basking opportunities for the snakes.

BEHAVIOR This gentle serpent rarely, if ever, bites defensively. When provoked, it raises its tail off the ground and curls it into a tight spiral, exposing the bright red underside, a behavior most likely intended to startle an attacker or to direct the assailant's attention to the snake's tail and away from its vitally important head (which it sometimes hides under one of its body coils). Startled by this sudden and unexpected gaudy display, particularly when it is performed by such a somber-looking serpent, the predator may react by momentarily delaying its attack, giving the serpent a few more seconds to crawl beneath some nearby shelter and out of harm's way. Greene (1973) proposed another, though not mutually exclusive, interpretation of the tail-display function. In it he suggested that certain predators, instead of being intimidated by the ringneck's brightly colored tail (which begins at the anus), might indeed be attracted to it, their curiosity drawing them close enough to receive the full impact of the snake's odious cloacal discharge. Further experiences of the same kind would no doubt eventually condition a predator to avoid any snake whose bright red undertail is tightly curled and held aloft. Still others believe the display is intended to draw the predator's attack, if there is to be one, away from the serpent's head and focus it instead on the snake's more expendable tail. Whichever interpretation is correct—and they may all be—there is every reason to believe that tail-curling in the ring-necked snake is an antipredator strategy. Not every ring-necked snake engages in such caudal display. Only those subspecies with a red undertail do so; those with yellow beneath the tail do not.

Another deception sometimes employed by this snake is to play dead by turning over on its back and remaining motionless. If either of these strategies fails and the snake is then seized, it discharges the foul-smelling contents of its cloaca, smearing the loathsome material over itself and its captor as it twists convulsively to escape. Often it is this liberal coating of slime that prompts the assailant to release its victim.

As it is in Texas, the prairie ring-necked snake is considered uncommon to rare over most of its geographic range, but in some places such an erratic distribution may be more a reflection of its secretive habits than a case of meager numbers. Fitch found the snake to be so abundant in a particular northeastern Kansas study site that he concluded it must outnumber all other serpent species in the area combined. The site, a nearly flat hilltop field of 9⅓ acres (4.2 ha) adjacent to some steep, rocky slopes, produced 279 ring-necked snakes in just half an hour of collecting—a phenomenal number of serpents to occupy so limited a plot of ground. In this instance the snakes were hiding in variously sized groups beneath two dozen or so pieces of corrugated sheet metal scattered across the field. As another example of the snake's abundance in some parts of the High Plains, Dundee and Miller (1968) collected 300 specimens in Douglas County, Kansas, in one hour. Even more amazing is a report of 238 ring-necked snakes taken from an area just 10 feet (3 m) wide and 400 feet (121.7 m) long by the same herpetologists in no more than 50 minutes. More sociable than most other serpents, *Diadophis* habitually aggregates in groups under pieces of surface shelter, usually in the spring and fall. Such behavior has resulted in the discovery of as many as 44 snakes under a single stone. It is probable that these gatherings develop when the snakes follow each other's scent trails to a common shelter.

Seldom seen in the open, this shy, terrestrial snake spends most of its time under rocks, logs, strips of bark, or leaf litter, although objects discarded by man, such as boards, sheet metal, plastic, and tarpaper often represent the snake's preferred shelter. Because sheet-metal strips absorb solar radiation more quickly than do most other materials, in time of cold it holds a special attraction for the ring-necked snakes. When both air and ground temperatures are uncomfortably low, the snake lies under the sun-warmed metal with its body in a flat, horizontal spiral, the length of its back pressed gently against the sheet-metal undersurface to absorb its heat. In this way a snake can easily raise its body temperature while safely hidden from predators. In fact, one individual thus elevated its body temperature 13.6 degrees F above that of the ambient air temperature. On the other hand, as the air temperature turns overly hot or cold, the metal strips become uncomfortable, causing the snakes to avoid them. Although essentially a night-active reptile, the ring-necked snake occasionally basks in direct sunlight when the temperature is cool. Fitch mentions a bask-ing individual of this subspecies whose body temperature at the time registered 85.5 degrees F, 25.2 degrees higher than the ambient air temperature.

More sensitive to drying conditions than most native snake species, the ring-necked snake generally retreats to underground shelters during the hot summer months of July and August when the land becomes relatively dry from rising temperatures and reduced rainfall. This it does by following existing subterranean pathways or by pushing through loose soil, for unlike the burrowing blind snake, it is not an accomplished digger. In many parts of its range it enters the underground tunnel systems of moles (primarily in woodland), voles (chiefly in grassland), pocket gophers, and other small burrowing mammals. Perhaps even better shelters for this purpose are the numerous emergence tubes of cicada nymphs, whose modest burrows are snug enough to exclude larger predators yet of sufficient diameter for this small snake to turn in and deep enough to provide the resident with optimum conditions of temperature and humidity. The ring-necked snake also avoids desiccation by living close to ponds and streams or by hiding in the moisture-laden nooks of eroded banks, decaying vegetation, or exposed tree roots.

In Kansas the snake's usual home range has a diameter of about 230 feet (70 m), and the diameter of a particularly large one is twice that long. The snake wanders even greater distances when it shifts its home range or undertakes seasonal migrations to and from hibernating and egg-laying sites. Fitch discovered that despite such journeys, the snake was often found a year or more later at the same spot where it was originally collected. He also learned that adult females traveled nearly twice as far as their male counterparts, presumably because some of them covered greater distances to reach special nesting sites, and perhaps, being larger, they have the energy to cover more territory.

In Kansas (approximately the middle of the snake's geographic range) the prairie ring-necked snake's active season begins during the third or fourth week of March, though in southeastern Texas it may leave hibernation several weeks sooner.

By early May the snakes become increasingly secretive. In response to progressively warmer and drier weather, they retreat to underground shelters, which provide more moderate temperatures and a higher humidity. By midsummer they are seldom seen at the surface. With the arrival of heavy fall rains and cooler temperatures in September, the snakes emerge from their subterranean retreats to revisit in numbers particular sites unoccupied since spring.

Their annual active season finally ends in late September and October, when most of them begin a leisurely exodus to their hilltop hibernacula, whose deep crevices provide ideal conditions for overwintering. Here they may spend the cold weather in the company of other serpents, including racers and rat snakes. Not all ring-necked snakes migrate from their summer homes to distant hibernacula; some find winter shelter close by, individually or in small groups, wherever they can obtain adequate shelter from below-freezing temperatures. In Kansas such underground sites, which generally are 1 to $2\frac{1}{2}$ feet (30.5–76.2 cm) beneath the surface, include mammal burrows, old wells, rock crevices, and probably even the numerous tunnels of cicada nymphs; aboveground shelters may be found in stone walls, gravel banks, old wells, decaying logs and tree stumps, sawdust mounds, and leaf piles.

FEEDING This species eats a wide variety of small animals, including earthworms, slugs, grubs, insects and their larvae, salamanders and their eggs, frogs, lizards, and snakes. For most ring-necked snakes, earthworms are standard fare. In northeastern Kansas, for example, Fitch reported that it fed on earthworms almost exclusively, but in Virginia, Uhler and his associates (1939) found the diet to consist mostly of salamanders (80 percent by volume), ants (15 percent), and assorted other insects and arthropods (5 percent). In another departure from the norm, ring-necked snakes sampled at Big Black Mountain in eastern Kentucky also contained primarily salamander prey, as did a certain northern Michigan population of this species. Those living in the more arid regions of Texas, where earthworms and salamanders may be less abundant, subsist largely on lizards and small snakes.

Gehlbach (1974) observed that ring-necked snakes, after seizing smaller serpents, maintained a tenacious grip on their struggling victims, chewing on their prey until they became immobile, some 40 to 375 minutes later. Based on those and similar reports, it is probable that the prey animals that died or were paralyzed during such episodes were poisoned by the ring-necked snake's toxic saliva, which was introduced into the victim's tissues by the repeated penetration of the snake's slightly enlarged rear teeth. Although longer, thicker, and with a more backward slant than the snake's other upper-jaw teeth, these diminutive fanglike spikes are neither hollow nor grooved. As a result, they are incapable of injecting the salivary toxins into the victim's flesh with any precision; they merely create puncture wounds that allow the debilitating substance to seep, almost by chance, into the victim's tissues. Dangerous only to its small prey, such toxins present no medical risk to humans.

REPRODUCTION By the second or third spring of their lives, the females of this egg-laying species are sexually mature, their first mating usually occurring in March or April, soon after they have come out of hibernation. Observations of captive ring-necked snakes revealed that the male is often sexually stimulated immediately after the female has shed her skin, presumably by the chemical scent created during the sloughing process. Accordingly, breeders of captive reptiles, who for some time have been aware of this particular reproductive cue, carefully schedule the introduction of opposite sexes to coincide with spring skin shedding in the female. It is likely that the same or a similar pheromone derived from the serpent's skin is responsible for drawing together groups of ring-necked snakes containing both sexes, usually in the spring and fall. It is during such springtime aggregations that mating usually occurs. For reasons not well understood, except perhaps as a way for several gravid snakes to benefit from the use of a single choice site, two or more (up to several dozen) females may lay their eggs in the same nook during the same nesting season; in one instance, a single nest held 55 eggs. Such communal nest sites, which above all else must contain adequate moisture to insure successful egg development, have been located under flat stones, in crevices of hill-top outcroppings, in the cracks of old stone structures, in decaying logs and tree stumps, in the walls of mammal burrows, and perhaps also in the tunnels of cicada nymphs. The female may likewise deposit her eggs in leaf litter and sawdust mounds or under pieces of fallen tree bark. The usual complement of eggs laid by one female is 3 or 4, but a single clutch may contain from 1 to 10. Elongated, slightly curved at either end, and somewhat sausage-shaped, the eggs are comparatively thin walled, so that the enclosed yolks can frequently be identified through the somewhat translucent shells. Moreover, their em-

bryos are in a more advanced state of development when first laid than those of most other egg-laying species. When initially deposited at a nest site, sometime between late June and mid-July, the eggs are $^{15}/_{16}$ to $1^{1}/_{8}$ inches (2.4–2.9 cm) long. They slowly gain size during the 46 to 60 days of incubation, their continuous growth promoted by indirect solar heat or by heat generated from the decaying vegetation in which they lie. The eggs hatch sometime between late August and early September, and the young ring-necked snakes, which then measure $4^{15}/_{16}$ to $5^{3}/_{8}$ inches (12.6–13.7 cm) long, look much like the adults.

REGAL RING-NECKED SNAKE
Diadophis punctatus regalis
PLATE 26

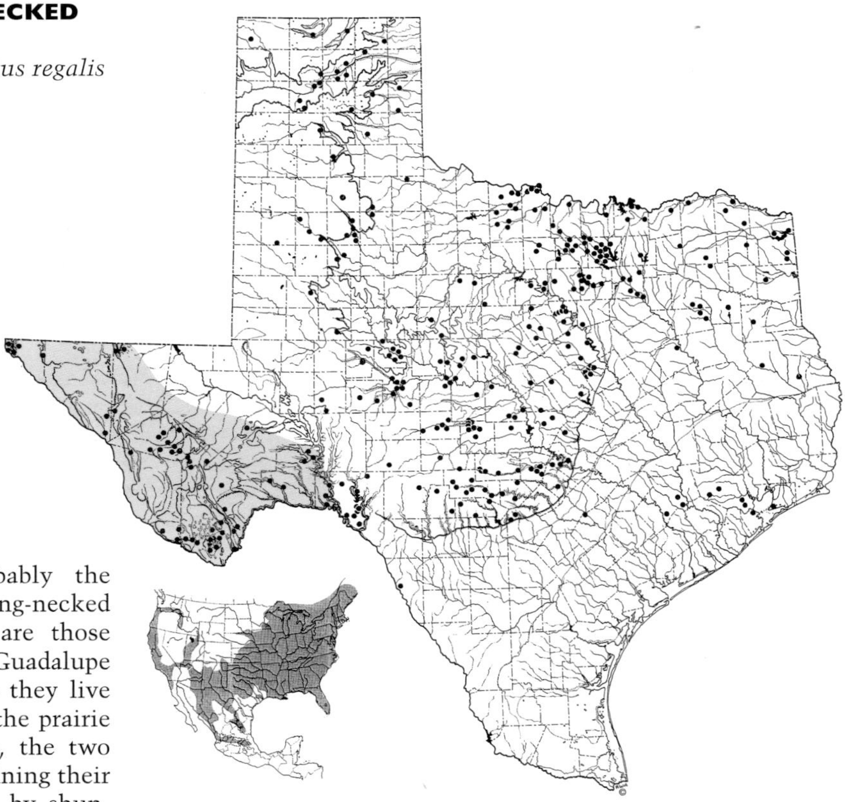

DESCRIPTION Probably the only pure regal ring-necked snakes in Texas are those found in the Guadalupe Mountains, where they live side by side with the prairie ring-necked snake, the two subspecies maintaining their separate identities by shunning one another as mates. The remaining Trans-Pecos populations are considered by Gehlbach (1974) to be intergrades between it and the prairie ring-necked snake, although they more closely resemble *D. p. regalis*. In its unadulterated form, the regal ring-necked snake has an unmarked greenish gray, gray-

ish olive, or slate gray upper body color but lacks the pale-hued nuchal ring that is the hallmark of other native ring-necked subspecies. Yet across the vast area of intergradation between the two involved subspecies, the neck ring may be complete in some specimens, broken along the middle of the back in others, or absent altogether. The belly color, which reaches up along either side of the trunk onto the first row of dorsal scales, is yellow on the forebody but changes gradually to orange-yellow along midbody, then to bright scarlet red near and on the tail. The vividly hued abdomen is randomly decorated with prominent black spots.

The top of the head is usually a bit darker than the upper body, and the lower lips, chin, and throat are sparsely covered with small dark spots. The dorsal scales, all smooth, are arranged in 17 midbody rows, and the anal plate is divided.

COMPARABLE SNAKES The Trans-Pecos black-headed snake possesses a brownish instead of grayish dorsal color, and its whitish abdomen has no bold, dark spotting. Although species of black-headed snakes living within the geographic range of the regal ring-necked snake ordinarily display a pinkish belly, this surface area is not spotted, nor is the underside of the tail bright red. The solid color phase of the Great Plains ground snake, which has no prominent black spots on its abdomen, also lacks a bright red undertail, and its dorsal scales occur in only 14 or 15 midbody rows. In the collared variety, the nuchal marking is an abbreviated *dark* bar.

SIZE This, the largest subspecies of ring-necked snake in Texas, reaches a record length of 19½ inches (49.5 cm) in the state but attains an even greater size (33⅝ inches, 85.4 cm) elsewhere within its range. The usual adult length is between 15 and 18 inches (38.1–45.7 cm).

HABITAT Although better adapted to a dry environment than its eastern relatives, the regal ring-necked snake nevertheless prefers moist habitats, steadfastly avoiding the extreme aridity of shrub desert. Suitable habitat, which is discontinuous throughout the snake's geographic range, occurs primarily within the sparse mountain or scarp woodland between about 3,900 and 7,200 feet elevation. In a study of the snake's evolutionary history, which involved a survey of its ecological distribution, Gehlbach encountered intergrade specimens in the following Trans-Pecos habitats: evergreen woodland (21 specimens), deciduous woodland or forest (15), succulent desert (3), and desert grassland (1). But in the Guadalupe Mountains, where the

two subspecies have essentially retained their respective identities, he found that they mostly inhabited separate and distinctly different sites. The smaller prairie ring-necked snake occupied the damper regions of deciduous woodland, while the larger regal ring-necked snake preferred the drier oak-juniper habitat or occasionally even the more arid succulent desert environment.

BEHAVIOR See prairie ring-necked snake account. Active annually from late March to mid-October, this chiefly nocturnal creature normally spends its daytime hours concealed beneath a rock or some form of plant debris. It occasionally also comes out of hiding early in the morning, and during cool, wet days may be encountered in the open even later.

FEEDING This subspecies, like Texas populations of the prairie ring-necked snake, consumes virtually nothing but small snakes and lizards, which it apparently subdues with its toxic saliva, aided by the enlarged but ungrooved teeth at the back of its upper jaw. Among specific prey items taken by it in captivity are rough earth, ground, flat-headed, and southwestern black-headed snakes, as well as skinks and spiny lizards.

From Gehlbach's observations we learn that this snake ordinarily makes no attempt to swallow its prey immediately; instead, the victim is either held firmly in the serpent's jaws at the point where it was initially grasped, or chewed on at the same place for periods lasting anywhere from 40 minutes to as long as several hours. During this time it apparently is sufficiently paralyzed by the serpent's salivary toxins to be easily swallowed. The venom of a ring-necked snake is not considered dangerous to man, but Shaw and Campbell (1974) noted that a person bitten by one of these snakes experienced a localized burning sensation after the bite.

REPRODUCTION Although the female is known to lay 2 to 5 eggs sometime in June or July, surprisingly little other information is recorded about the reproductive biology of this subspecies. It is also evident that the larger snakes deposit bigger clutches of eggs: small females lay 1 to 3, those between 14 and 16 inches long deposit 3 or 4, and females 17 or more inches long lay 5 or 6. Vitt (1975) described a clutch of 3 large eggs laid by a captive Arizona regal ring-necked snake on

July 25, each of which was about 1¾ inches (4.4 cm) long. When they hatched 52 days later, the baby snakes measured between 6⅘ and 7½ inches (17.3–19 cm) in length. Almost immediately after leaving their eggshells they raised and curled their red undertails in the same kind of stereotyped defensive be-

havior practiced by the adults. A female of this subspecies collected by Minton (1959) in the Big Bend region of Texas deposited 5 eggs on June 14, none of which hatched. Slightly bowed like a sausage, they were about 1⅕ inches (3 cm) long.

MISSISSIPPI RING-NECKED SNAKE

Diadophis punctatus stictogenys

PLATE 27

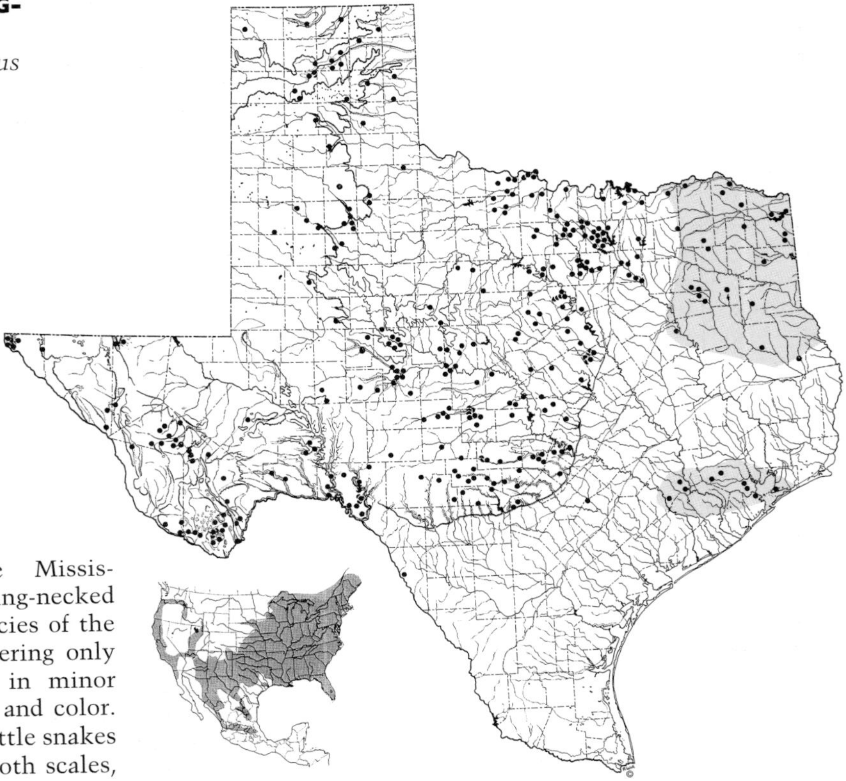

DESCRIPTION The Mississippi and prairie ring-necked snakes are subspecies of the same species, differing only in scalation and in minor details of pattern and color. Both are slender little snakes covered with smooth scales, whose glossy quality gives them an overall satiny look. Although both have a light-colored neck ring, the nuchal collar of the Mississippi ring-necked snake is narrower than that of the prairie subspecies. In certain individuals of both races, the collar is incomplete at the top of the neck. In addition, *D. p. stictogenys* has a bright yellow instead of scarlet undertail, and the small, black abdominal spots are not randomly scattered, as in the prairie subspecies, but tend to form an irregular line of pairs down the belly midline. As far back as the yellow neck ring, the top of the head is a bit darker than the bluish slate upper body hue, while the lower lips and underside of the chin are unevenly

speckled with small black spots. The body scales are usually arranged in 15 rows on the forebody, and the anal plate is divided.

COMPARABLE SNAKES *See prairie ring-necked snake account.*

SIZE A bit smaller than the prairie ring-necked snake, this subspecies reaches a maximum length of about 14 inches (35.6 cm).

HABITAT Essentially a snake of pine forest and pine-oak woodland, this secretive reptile also occurs in adjacent unwooded habitats such as weedy fields and ravine bottoms, provided such places offer both sufficient moisture to prevent the snake's dehydration during times of dry weather and adequate surface debris under which it can hide. It is most often associated with sparse timberland abundantly littered with hollow logs, rotting tree stumps, and other forest-floor debris, all of which it uses as places of shelter. Though it is generally absent from the coastal prairie, Guidry (1953), after nearly half a lifetime of diligent collecting efforts over a large portion of southeastern Texas, discovered only a single specimen of this subspecies in sparse woodland near Port Arthur.

BEHAVIOR This mild-mannered little reptile rarely bites in self-defense, but even when it does, its diminutive teeth are scarcely large enough to make a noticeable impact on most predators, especially if the antagonist is much bigger than the snake itself. Instead, like so many other serpent species, both large and small, harmless and venomous, it responds to being captured by expelling from its cloacal opening a foul-smelling combination of musk and feces, while simultaneously twisting and turning its body. In just a few seconds the loathsome material covers the captor's hand, often resulting in the snake's quick release.

Tail-spiraling, a defensive behavior probably intended to startle and perhaps confuse a predator, ordinarily is not practiced by the Mississippi ring-necked snake, whose underside, including the tail, normally is some shade of yellow.

Rarely observed in the open by day, this nocturnal little serpent discreetly hides in or under some moist shelter that most commonly includes decaying logs, rotting tree stumps, or the space beneath the loose bark of fallen trees. In an unidentified southern state, Ditmars (1936) was able to collect more than 50 examples of this species in just half a day by systematically peeling the loose bark from such tree trunks, most of which were found to be teeming with ants. On another occasion he found a specimen inside a large, active anthill. The Mississippi ring-necked snake has also been found under flat stones, moss, piles of leaf litter, boards, railroad ties, and other human-generated debris.

To avoid the dehydrating effects of midsummer heat during July and August, the Mississippi ring-necked snake, like the prairie subspecies, probably enters the burrows of other animals or stays close to permanent

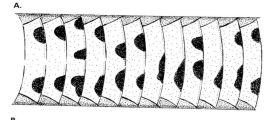

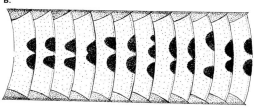

Figure 25. *Spotted belly patterns of (a) prairie ring-necked snake and (b) Mississippi ring-necked snake.*

bodies of water, for it is unable to excavate its own underground tunnels. Despite the serpent's inability to dig, the ring-necked snake's subterranean lifestyle is reflected in its flattened head, small eyes, and uniformly slender body.

Over much of its range, the Mississippi ring-necked snake ordinarily emerges from hibernation between late March and early April, although in southeastern Texas, at least during mild winters, it may periodically come to the surface at any time. Though chiefly active after dark, on cold nights it may reverse its normal activity cycle by basking in direct sunlight, even when daytime air and ground temperatures are disagreeably cool. More often, however, it warms itself at such times by coiling under some object on the ground that has first been warmed by the sun, favoring large, flat stones lying on open slopes. Not only are the stones directly exposed to solar radiation, but they also naturally absorb such heat more quickly than do logs, bark, and leaf litter.

By late October the snakes have returned to their winter shelters to spend the next several months in hibernation, sometimes singly, though more often in groups and not infrequently with other snake species. Some choose to escape the rigors of winter by traveling several hundred feet from their summer territories to a favorite rocky hilltop outcropping where sunken crevices reach far into the ground, offering the serpents a safe haven from below-freezing temperatures. Others hibernate in small mammal and insect burrows, and some enter decaying logs, tree stumps, and piles of vegetative debris.

FEEDING The diet of this woodland carnivore is a varied one, but most Mississippi ring-necked snakes show a definite preference for earthworms, whereas others consume primarily salamanders. Other animals devoured by this species include slugs, grubs, insects and their larvae, salamander eggs, frogs, lizards, and other snakes. See prairie ring-necked snake account.

REPRODUCTION The female ordinarily produces her first clutch of eggs in her third year of life, at which time she is about 12½ inches long. Although mating usually takes place soon after the snakes have left their winter dens in late March or early April, fall copulations have also been reported. Such matings generally occur after male and female are drawn together by a chemical scent trail left on the substrate as they move over the ground. See prairie ring-necked snake account.

Sometime between late June and the end of July, the female lays a clutch of eggs, each egg measuring ¹⁵/₁₆ to 1⅛ inches (2.4–2.9 cm) long. The nest site, which must contain adequate moisture for the proper development of the eggs, may be located in the crevices of hilltop outcroppings, in the cracks of deteriorating stone structures, under flat stones, in rotting logs and tree stumps, in the walls of mammal burrows, in piles of leaf litter, in sawdust mounds, or under fallen tree bark. When a particular nook in a given area provides ideal conditions for egg development, it is often shared by several females during the same nesting season.

A single female lays 1 to 10 eggs per clutch, but the usual number is 3 or 4. Most often elongated and slightly bowed like a sausage, the thin-shelled eggs contain rather large embryos when first laid. Since they are initially in such an advanced stage of development, they hatch in less than half the time required for egg incubation in most other snake species. Following a 46- to 60-day incubation, they hatch during late August and early September, producing babies that are about 4⅜ inches (11.1 cm) long.

TEXAS INDIGO SNAKE

Drymarchon corais erebennus
PLATES 28, 29

DESCRIPTION Most adult Texas indigos, which at first glance look like large, shiny, all-black serpents, prove on close examination to be blue-black only on the rear half of the body and the tail; on the forward half of the trunk, that color is mottled or discreetly banded with gray-brown. Some specimens from the Brownsville area, according to Patrick M. Burchfield (pers. com.), are glossy indigo blue with a reddish blush, resembling somewhat the eastern subspecies of the indigo snake. The chin, throat, and sometimes even the belly as far back as midbody, although generally brown to orange-brown, occasionally display a distinct reddish hue, whereas the rear half of the abdomen is gray, shading to blue-black near the tail. The uniformly dark brown or black color of the crown fades to a paler tone along the sides of the face, where most of the upper lip scales are edged in black. The most prominent of these dark streaks are the two or three that radiate downward from the eye. The large, smooth dorsal scales are in 17 rows at midbody (14 near the tail), and the anal plate is single. A newly hatched Texas indigo snake, however, is dark gray-brown to black, with widely separated, small, white, dashlike spots feebly arranged along the sides of the body as thin, diagonal lines. Evident even at this age are the bold black bars directly below each eye. The young snake's face, as well as its chin and throat, which are whitish or buff-colored, will turn reddish or reddish orange as the snake reaches maturity but will thereafter become dark and nearly colorless.

COMPARABLE SNAKES An especially dark specimen of the Texas rat snake may have its

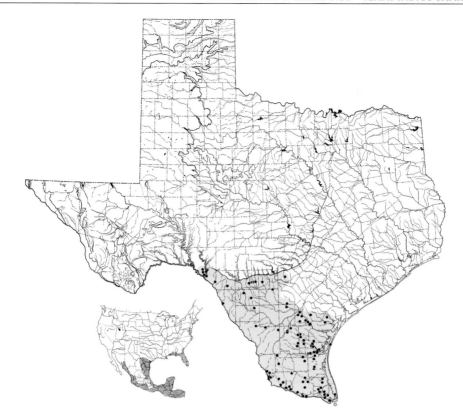

dorsal markings so obscured as to result in a virtually all-black serpent. Unlike the indigo, it will have at least some keeled body scales, a divided anal plate, and no bold vertical dark bars lining its upper lip scales.

SIZE One of Texas' largest serpents, both in length and weight, this snake rivals several other native species as the state's biggest ophidian. Its usual adult length is between 5 and 6½ feet (152.4–198.1 cm); Conant and Collins (1991) give the maximum length for this subspecies as 8 feet 4¼ inches (254.6 cm). An even larger specimen, reported to have measured 9 feet 5 inches (287 cm), was mentioned by Vermersch and Kuntz (1986), although the authors gave no specific reference for such a record. In either case, among our nonvenomous species, only the bull snake grows as long. The western diamond-backed rattler, at an approximate maximum length of 7 feet 4 inches (223.5 cm), is not as long as a Texas indigo, but with a maximum weight of about 16 pounds, it can be more than three to four times as heavy.

HABITAT Primarily a resident of Mexico, the snake we call the Texas indigo occurs only peripherally in the United States, where its distribution is limited to the thornbrush country of South Texas. This semiarid environment, best characterized as a vast mesquite grassland savannah, will support indigo snake populations only where there is adequate moisture, such as in areas near streams, ponds, resacas, and windmill seeps, for the long-term well-being of this drought-sensitive reptile is intimately associated with water.

Much of the thornbrush that constitutes suitable wildlife habitat on the Gulf Coast Plain has disappeared, especially in the lower Rio Grande Valley, and as the Valley's remaining brushland succumbs to the unrelenting encroachment of agriculture and urban development, ever more wildlife is displaced. The first to be affected are large species such as this. Despite the ongoing alteration of so much South Texas wilderness, significant parcels of favorable habitat remain, though some of them represent only small isolated pockets. Among the largest of such sanctuaries is the Santa Ana National Wildlife Refuge, a nearly 2,000-acre expanse of brush, trees, and ponds lying along the Rio Grande south of McAllen, where wildlife of all kinds, including the indigo snake, is permanently protected. Below it, near the southernmost end of the state, is the National Audubon Society's Sabal Palm Grove Sanctuary, a unique 172-acre (68.8 ha) tract of remnant subtropical forest whose principal hallmark is the indigenous sabal palm. Within its borders this native palm, together with the indigo and a handful of other distinctly Mexican animal and plant species, enjoys protection from indiscriminate exploitation.

From this coastal thornbrush habitat, the snake has traced the major bands of riverine woodland northwestward, extending its range as far inland as Val Verde, Kinney, Uvalde, and Medina counties. Though it occurred along the southern border of Bexar County as recently as the early 1950s, it apparently is no longer found there.

BEHAVIOR It is surprising that a serpent so large, with a real potential to inflict a nasty bite, should normally behave with such restraint when handled, yet seldom does the indigo snake bite in self-defense. At worst, the impatient serpent is likely to smear its captor with a liberal quantity of feces and musk as it struggles to escape. One that is provoked and unable to flee is more likely to show its resentment by flattening the neck vertically (not horizontally like a threatening hog-nosed snake); it may also bow the neck slightly. This may be followed by loud hissing and tail-shaking, all part of a spectacular display intended to frighten away its foe. The bluff is especially effective if the tail, as it is set in motion, strikes a hard object or moves rapidly against a layer of dead leaves, creating a whirring sound like that made by an aroused rattlesnake.

Especially susceptible to dehydration, the indigo snake must have access to a certain degree of moisture if it is to survive in its relatively dry South Texas environment. Above ground it generally stays close to natural or artificial bodies of water. Ponds, streams, resacas, cattle tanks, drainage ditches, and even windmill seeps offer suitable sources of day-

time humidity, but at night, when the snake is at rest and an easy target for a myriad of nocturnal predators, it retires to an underground refuge that provides a safe haven from its enemies as well as a certain amount of dampness. Unlike the digging-adapted bull and pine snakes, which can excavate their own subterranean tunnel systems, the indigo is unable to dig and so must find such shelter in the burrows of small mammals, whose tunnels are abundantly scattered throughout South Texas. In the absence of such animal burrows, it may crawl into other available underground spaces. Near Laredo we watched a large specimen disappear deep down between the nearly horizontal slabs of soft, sedimentary rock forming the layered shelves of a river terrace and observed another as it slipped into an opening at the base of a tall, uprooted tree whose displaced roots created several large holes where they had been pulled out of the soil. Otherwise, sizable natural objects such as boulders and logs—items that might furnish good aboveground cover—are generally scarce or absent in the snake's scrubby environment; even if present, they would at best offer only temporary shelter, as do the omnipresent clumps of prickly pear cactus that form an integral part of this landscape. Eight large specimens of this subspecies (perhaps the greatest number of Texas indigo snakes observed together in one place on the same day), were encountered by Robert Dooley and David Klemmer (pers. com.) in the mesquite grasslands near Riviera in Kleberg County. Following several days of heavy rains that extensively flooded the low-lying areas, they discovered the snakes basking quietly atop the plant-litter mounds of packrat nests tucked into the bases of prickly pear clumps scattered along slightly elevated ridges.

During its daytime wanderings, *D. c. erebennus* is essentially a ground-dwelling serpent that can move surprisingly fast for such a large snake, often traveling a considerable distance from its burrow in its quest for food, then returning again before the end of the day, usually to the same underground lair. Despite its large size, it is occasionally found in bushes and on tree branches near the ground. In Mexico, according to Ruthven (in Wright and Wright 1957), one was seen 4 or

5 feet (1.2–1.5 m) off the ground, basking on top of bushes along a riverbank.

As the winters in the lower Rio Grande Valley often are mild, the Texas indigo snake frequently remains active there on at least some days during every month of the year, although especially cold weather promptly sends it down into the same deep animal burrows it used as temporary shelters throughout the warmer months. During periods of severe midsummer drought as well, when much of the surface water has evaporated from intense solar radiation, this moisture-dependent reptile retires to damp underground shelters to prevent unnecessary loss of body moisture through its skin.

FEEDING Not too particular about its choice of prey, the Texas indigo eats a wide variety of vertebrate animals ranging from frogs, toads, lizards, baby turtles, and snakes to birds and small mammals. Young ones have also been reported to eat fish. Further evidence of its aquatic foraging tendency is apparent in a statement by Ruthven, who reported in 1912 that the stomach of a specimen found foraging along the margin of a pond in southern Mexico contained two small snapping turtles in addition to three mice and two Mexican burrowing toads (Wright and Wright 1957). One of us (Dixon) found four hatchling Texas tortoises in the stomachs of two indigo snakes from the vicinity of Lake Falcon.

Considered a useful ally by many South Texas farmers and ranchers familiar with its bold attacks on rattlesnakes, *D. c. erebennus* is often spared the relentless persecution suffered by other native ophidian species, harmless as well as venomous. Not only do they allow it to roam their lands unrestrained and unharmed, for it is still commonly portrayed as the avowed enemy of venomous snakes, but in the past they have actually imported specimens from distant sites, releasing them locally to help increase their numbers. Although the indigo is a fearless predator quite capable of subduing rattlesnakes and other venomous serpents, even those larger than itself, there is no truth to the notion that it preys solely on such pit vipers. Odds are that it attacks them infrequently. Nevertheless, its prodigious rodent-eating habits alone provide a useful service to the farmer, which from a pragmatic point of view is reason

enough to conserve it. Another is that under state law the indigo snake is designated a protected species.

When it does target a rattlesnake, the indigo moves quickly alongside its victim until it reaches the rattler's head, which is then seized in a sudden sideward snap of its powerful jaws. With its head held firmly shut in this vicelike grip and its fangs still folded in the at-rest position, the venomous creature is unable to retaliate. After some minutes of repeated vicious chewing, the indigo snake finally wears down its struggling quarry, which, though alive and still active, is then swallowed head first. Not every feeding attack is so carefully executed, though. Sometimes the victim is seized near midbody, leaving its head free to inflict venomous bites on its assailant. The indigo snake seems not to be seriously affected by the rattler's assault, though it may be injected repeatedly with the pit viper's lethal toxins; if it is not totally immune to such venom, it clearly shows a high degree of resistance to it.

Bird eggs, not previously mentioned as part of the snake's menu, may in fact constitute a significant percentage of the serpent's diet. In a study of wild turkey predator control on the King Ranch, Beasom (1974) stated that poisoned chicken eggs placed along the area's roads in 1971 and 1972, and subsequently consumed by the serpents, killed 11 indigo snakes. Because it is likely that after eating the toxic eggs some of the snakes may have crawled into animal burrows and died there without being found or tallied, the actual death toll may have been even greater than reported. The evidence that the indigo snakes in this experiment readily consumed egg baits, coupled with the abundance of ground-nesting birds in the serpent's mesquite-brushland habitat, strongly suggests that bird eggs are routinely eaten by this large, terrestrial serpent.

The snake's usual method of subduing prey is simply to seize the animal in its mouth and begin to swallow, using its strong, flexible jaws and rows of needlelike teeth to pull the victim quickly into its throat. Larger prey, particularly if it struggles vigorously, is pressed firmly against the ground under a segment of the snake's muscular body as it is held in the snake's mouth. Never is it wrapped in the serpent's coils and killed by constriction.

REPRODUCTION Only meager bits of information about this snake's reproductive biology have been reported. Wright and Wright (1957) mention seeing captive Texas indigo snakes in a Brownsville animal dealer's compound, some of which had recently laid eggs that they reported were at least 4 inches (10.2 cm) long. Considering the known size of such eggs, which are generally about $2\frac{1}{2}$ inches (6.3 cm) long, their estimate was no doubt an exaggeration.

According to Gordon Henley, director of the Ellen Trout Zoo in Lufkin, a pair of Texas indigo snakes in that institution's collection bred on four separate occasions. The first mating, which was not documented in detail, produced 10 eggs on March 3, 1984, but none hatched. The second pairing, on September 8, 1984, yielded no eggs. Another, on January 8, 1985, resulted in the deposition of 12 eggs on April 3, 1985. The most recently observed copulations, on January 9 and 10, 1986, produced at least 7 eggs, probably in early April, 1986, although precise details of this mating and the subsequent egg-laying event were not recorded. The eggs in this clutch hatched on June 22 and 24, 1986, but the young were not measured. Average length and width of the eggs laid in 1984 was $2^{25}/_{64}$ by $1^{3}/_{8}$ inches (6.1 × 3.5 cm), while those deposited in 1985 measured $2^{5}/_{8}$ by $1^{1}/_{2}$ inches (6.7 × 3.8 cm). From Colette Adams, curator of herpetology at Brownsville's Gladys Porter Zoo (pers. com.), we learn that copulation in captive *D. c. erebennus* held at that zoo has occurred over a span of several months, beginning as early as November and as late as January. The female of a pair of indigo snakes introduced to each other in November and caged together for the next few months laid a clutch of eggs on March 19, 1991. The same regimen, repeated again in another year, produced a clutch of 7 eggs on April 13. However, Adams believes that in the wild, breeding among these serpents is probably stimulated by the year's first spell of prolonged warm weather, usually in February but sometimes as early as January. This was verified by Ted Beimler (pers. com.), who observed mating specimens in the Brownsville area on January 1, sometime during the 1950s. He also saw another pair mating in the wild during the month of April.

A gravid female Texas indigo captured in the Brownsville area by Ted Beimler laid 6 eggs on April 20, 1990. Measuring $2\frac{1}{2}$ inches (6.3–6.4 cm) long and $1\frac{1}{4}$ to $1\frac{1}{2}$ inches (3.2–3.9 cm) wide, the eggs were uniformly covered with extracalcified dots. They hatched on June 24 after incubating for 65 days at temperatures ranging from 84 to 88 degrees F. A female Texas indigo snake maintained as a captive by Rossi and Rossi (1995) mated in January. On April 11 she deposited 7 eggs, one of which was infertile. The fertile eggs, which averaged about $2\frac{1}{2}$ inches long (6.4 cm) and a little more than 1 inch (2.6 cm) wide, began to hatch on June 27, after incubating for 76 days at temperatures ranging between 78 and 84 degrees F.

SPECKLED RACER

Drymobius margaritiferus margaritiferus
PLATE 30

DESCRIPTION Each dorsal spot of this moderately slender, dark green snake contains a horizontal, yellow to faded orange, dartlike spot near its center; blue edging at its base; and a black border along its exposed outer edges. Toward the belly these pale spots are more greenish than yellow and slightly larger than they are on the upper body; those on the neck and tail usually are pale turquoise green.

In a newly shed specimen, the overall effect is that of a daintily jeweled piece of oriental ceramic finished in lacquer. A wide, dark, horizontal band extends backward from the eye, and the scales of both the upper lips and crown are delicately edged in black. Except for the scales under the tail, which are black-edged on their rear margins, the abdomen is usually all white or yellowish. The

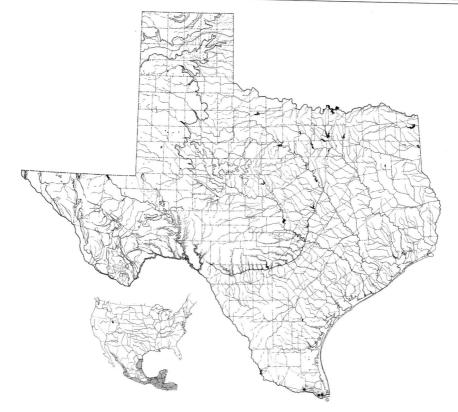

dorsal scales are only weakly keeled and are aligned in 17 rows at midbody; the anal plate is divided.

COMPARABLE SNAKES The only other serpent in the area with a dark ground color and numerous small, light-colored dorsal spots is the desert king snake, which can be distinguished by the dark chainlike pattern on its back, the 23 or 25 midbody rows of smooth dorsal scales, and the single anal plate.

SIZE Thirty to 40 inches (76.2–101.6 cm) is the usual adult length for this subspecies, but a specimen of maximum size measured 50 inches (127 cm) long.

HABITAT This is essentially a Latin American serpent whose distribution brings it northward to the very tip of South Texas, the only place in the United States where it occurs. North of the border it is found primarily in the few areas of remnant subtropical forest that remain intact in Cameron County. The most notable remnant is the National Audubon Society's Sabal Palm Grove Sanctu-

ary (6 miles southeast of Brownsville), which probably harbors more speckled racers than any other area in South Texas. Even in such prime habitat the snake remains uncommon to rare. Nevertheless, Pat Burchfield (pers. com.) noted that it is not unusual to see specimens along drainage ditches and low, swampy places in the Southmost area of Brownsville. According to Mrs. L. Irby Davis, naturalist and longtime resident of Harlingen (in Wright and Wright 1957), this snake apparently never was plentiful in the lower Rio Grande Valley. She reported it from only two Valley locations: among the grove of sabal palms below Southmost and in hackberry woodland along the river near La Feria.

By contrast, the speckled racer is abundant over much of its Latin American range. In Mexico and Central America, living in a variety of moist to wet habitats ranging from sea level to about 4,750 feet (1,453 m) elevation, it favors areas of relatively dense vegetation where leaf litter and other plant debris provide adequate ground cover. It also occurs in open savannahs, especially around marshland pools, and it can even be found in the vegetative debris of village back yards, provided there is some nearby moisture to sustain its amphibian prey. According to Stuart (1935), it was so plentiful in central Petén, Guatemala during the 1930s that in a single day the natives of the area collected as many as a dozen specimens for a visiting naturalist.

BEHAVIOR   This is an alert, agile serpent, which, like racers of the genus *Coluber*, reacts to nearby movement by promptly flicking its head to face the action. If the motion appears threatening, the speckled racer darts into the nearest patch of grass or brush without hesitation, preferring to flee rather than fight. When first picked up, however, a wild-caught specimen is usually quick to seize the restraining hand in its jaws, hanging on and chewing briefly but viciously. As the snake disengages its jaws, it yanks the head sharply to one side, inflicting a series of freely bleeding but superficial slashing cuts on its captor as the long, needle-sharp teeth rake across the skin.

Although the speckled racer is locally abundant in tropical Mexico and Central America, we know little about its natural history. This species is a fast, active reptile that seems frequently to be on the prowl, often entering aquatic environments in its search for food. Its fondness for water is mentioned by several zoologists, one of whom found a specimen fully submerged in a pool of water where it apparently was searching for frogs. In the Mexican state of Michoacán, a closely related subspecies, *D. m. fistulosus*,

consistently avoided capture by darting into the water of an old channel cluttered with water hyacinths. So closely is this snake associated with water that Peters (1954) considered it to be semiaquatic.

FEEDING   The chief prey of this moisture-loving serpent consists almost entirely of amphibians. Among 36 speckled racers from Guatemala and Mexico with food in their stomachs, Seib (1984) found that 86 percent contained anurans (mostly frogs of the genus *Eleutherodactylus*), 8 percent had lizards, 4 percent held reptile eggs, and 2 percent contained small mammals.

REPRODUCTION   The female of this species often lays her eggs in the spring, although in Costa Rica, Solorzano and Cerdas (1987) found one clutch as early in the year as February 19 (which hatched April 18) and another on March 29 (which hatched June 1–3). A speckled racer from an unknown locality in Mexico deposited 7 eggs on April 22, 2 of which hatched on June 9 and 11. Another Mexican female of this subspecies laid 2 eggs on July 29 (Werler 1951). Infants have also been observed in March, July, and September, suggesting that at least in the southern part of the snake's range, the breeding season may not follow the usual cyclical pattern. Recently, a gravid female was found dead in the Audubon Nature Preserve at Brownsville. She was found in July 1997 with 4 shelled eggs. Each egg was 2 inches (5.1 cm) long and ⅝ inch (1.6 cm) wide. The nonadherent eggs, from 2 to 8 in a clutch, usually measure about 1½ inches (3.8 cm) long when laid and incubate for 8 or 9 weeks before producing hatchlings 6 to 10⅞ inches (15.2–27.6 cm) long.

BAIRD'S RAT SNAKE
Elaphe bairdi
PLATES 31–33

DESCRIPTION   The adult is a lengthwise-striped, grayish brown snake with an infusion of golden yellow on the forebody and burnt orange toward the rear; the rich highlighting is created by a pale-hued crescent at the base of each dorsal scale. The essential pattern elements are four dark, shadowy stripes running the length of the body and tail. The up-

permost pair of stripes is the more prominent; between them sometimes lies a row of indistinct dark crossbars, remnants of the serpent's blotched juvenile pattern. Present also may be a series of smaller but equally vague lateral spots. Aged specimens, however, can be virtually patternless. The head, which is often a subtle bluish gray on the

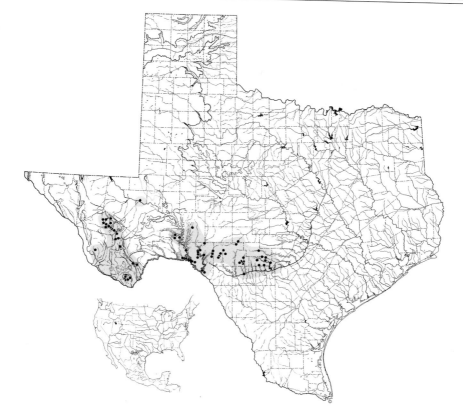

crown, fades to a russet or yellowish hue along the sides but in some specimens is overall pale gray. The snake's underside, often exhibiting small, ill-defined dark blotches, is usually pale yellow on the chin and neck, becoming orange-tan on the rear part of the abdomen. Arranged in 27 midbody rows, the dorsal scales are only slightly keeled. The anal plate is divided. The juvenile, paler in color than the adult, lacks lengthwise stripes and is strongly blotched; its 48 or more dark brown to black body crossbars (sometimes dumbbell-shaped) stand out clearly against the snake's ground color of pale gray. Similar, though progressively smaller, markings occur on the tail. Alternating with the crossbars is a row of much smaller dark spots low on either side of the body. The head markings consist of a dark transverse band between and just forward of the eyes and a dark line on each side of the face that begins at the orbit and slants back to the mouthline. Also evident may be a pair of longitudinal dark bars, one on either side of the neck directly

behind the head. According to Olson (1977), the juvenile pattern of bold, dark crossbars persists until the snake reaches a length between 27 and 31 inches, and the adult pattern of lengthwise stripes becomes evident in serpents over 38 or 39 inches long. He considered specimens in between (those displaying both stripes and crossbars at the same time) to be young adults. Then there are the occasional very large Baird's rat snakes, whose dark stripes have disappeared altogether, resulting in uniformly gray or yellowish orange individuals.

COMPARABLE SNAKES The typical adult Texas rat snake can be distinguished from a mature Baird's rat snake by the median row of large, dark blotches along its back, though some specimens display dark lengthwise body striping as well, and others appear nearly all black, their blotched patterns barely visible through the overall dark pigmentation. Even so, the crown of a Texas rat snake is almost invariably all black or dark gray, whereas that of a Baird's is much paler, particularly along the edges. Although the juveniles of both species are strongly blotched, there are some conspicuous differences between them. The Texas rat snake has only 27 to 37 dorsal body markings (48 or more in Baird's), they are longer than wide (much wider than long in Baird's), and their color is generally a rich brown (gray in Baird's). The dark H-shaped blotches of the Trans-Pecos rat snake, particularly those on the forebody, often merge to give the appearance of lengthwise striping, but in this species the midbody dorsal scales are in 31 to 35 rows, and in a condition unique among our native rat snakes, a row of small scales separates the eye from the upper lip scales. Patch-nosed snakes, also lengthwise striped, have 17 rows of midbody scales, all smooth, and a head not distinctly wider than the neck (clearly so in Baird's). Moreover, the uppermost dark stripes on the body of a patch-nosed snake begin at the snake's eye, while those of E. bairdi originate on the neck.

SIZE Most adults are between 28 and 42 inches (71.1–106.7 cm) long. A maximum-size specimen of 63½ inches, collected by John Malone in Bandera County, is in the Texas Cooperative Wildlife Collection at Texas A&M University.

HABITAT One of Texas' uncommon serpents, Baird's rat snake has a limited distribution across the west-central part of the state, beginning near the south-central edge of the Edwards Plateau and extending westward through the Stockton Plateau and the Big Bend region to the Davis Mountains. In a recent study, Lawson and Lieb (1990) described the snake's ecology in some detail. Most of the following habitat information is derived from their report.

At the easternmost end of its range, this serpent is confined primarily to the wooded limestone ridges and precipitous canyon walls of the Nueces River, the headwater zones of the Llano and Guadalupe rivers, the high ground separating the Guadalupe and Medina river valleys, and the ridges running along the Medina valley as far east as Medina Lake. Here, where Baird's rat snake is encircled on three sides by populations of the Texas rat snake, the two species occasionally meet and hybridize. For unknown reasons, E. bairdi apparently is absent from similar choice habitat in the eastern and northern parts of the Edwards Plateau. In contrast to the limestone-dominated eastern part of its range, the westernmost portion of the snake's environment in Texas is characterized by the igneous rock formations of the Davis Mountains, especially along the region's wooded canyons and forested uplands. No matter where it occurs, whether at 1,000 or 10,000 feet (305–3,050 m) elevation, this species favors rough, rocky habitats, particularly those containing caves, deep fissures, and steep canyon walls, although it is more catholic in its choice of plant associations, occupying a variety of vegetation types ranging from Chihuahuan desert scrub to Sierra Madrean pine forest (in south-central Tamaulipas, Mexico).

BEHAVIOR A Baird's rat snake is difficult to spot in its West Texas habitat. Wright and Wright (1957) described an encounter with a specimen at Green Gulch in the Chisos Mountains that perfectly illustrates the effectiveness of the serpent's camouflage. At the time of the encounter, the reptile was crawling leisurely through a low oak shrub along a small wash. In this setting it precisely resembled a dead branch, gray and twisted, among the reddish orange rocks. Furthermore, the dark salmon tinge of many Baird's rat snakes—an impression created by the pale orange crescent at the base of each body scale—would also serve to camouflage the creature in regions covered with iron-red rubble, as it did in this case. Apparently aware that they are not easily detected in their matching background environment, most E. bairdi move rather leisurely over the ground and are not inclined to flee at the first sign of danger. Nor are they apt to strike or bite, even when picked up. In fact, not one of the dozens we have encountered over the years ever used its teeth defensively. Chiefly a day-active species (except during the unbearably hot midsummer weather, when it becomes largely nocturnal), this snake, like so many other serpents of the arid Southwest, is drawn to the surface by heavy summer rains. At such times it is most likely to be found on the ground, though at other times it readily climbs into bushes and the lower limbs of trees. Lawson and Lieb mentioned that it also hides in the eaves of ranch outbuildings and between the structural timbers of such shelters. Collecting records show that its annual active season begins in late April and ends in October.

FEEDING   Like all native rat snakes, this species is a constrictor. Its broad-based diet consists of lizards, birds and their eggs, and a variety of small mammals, including bats and small rodents.

REPRODUCTION   Combat between adult male snakes, especially prevalent during the spring mating season, is documented for a number of native species, including this one. In it, the opponents engage in a suite of stereotypic actions as each tries to assert dominance over the other. At no time is this behavior life-threatening to the snakes, nor does it ever result in their serious bodily injury. It is simply a kind of physical competition, intense and animated, by which the contenders settle the question of dominance. In most cases it is the larger male who prevails.

Brecke, Murphy, and Seifert (1976) were the first to describe combat behavior between male Baird's rat snakes. Their observations were based on an encounter between two captive specimens that lasted about 20 minutes. When the snakes were first placed together, the slightly smaller serpent approached the larger one, rapidly flicking his tongue to investigate. He then aligned his body over the length of the other in a series of broad, lateral, S-shaped loops, at the same time crawling forward as he tried to bring his head beyond that of his opponent. This apparently gave him a strategic advantage for the next phase of the encounter. Without ever stopping, he raised his forebody 6 or 8 inches above ground level at a 30-degree angle, the goal being to gain ascendency so as to force the opponent's head to the ground. In response, the larger male elevated his own forebody to a plane nearly parallel to that of the opponent. Meanwhile, both snakes continued to move forward. Frequently the larger serpent, seeming to ignore the aggressive approaches of the more dominant smaller male, tried unsuccessfully to escape, only to have his head eventually forced to the ground by the pressure of the assailant's lateral body loops—but only briefly, before the subdued snake jerked free. Finally, after 15 minutes of such sparring, the submissive male no longer responded to the aggressor's overtures. At this point the dominant reptile assumed his normal horizontal stance, crawled directly to the other male, briefly touched him with the tongue, then seized him at midbody, maintaining a firm grip for several seconds. It was not until the victim snapped a loop of his body forcefully sideways toward the aggressor that the smaller male let go. This episode was repeated twice more before the snakes were separated.

Courtship and mating, which ordinarily take place during May and mid-June, may also occur earlier in the year, as reported by Brecke and his coworkers. A pair of *E. bairdi* in their collection copulated on March 25, resulting in the deposition of 5 eggs on May 6 and 7, which hatched 83 days later. Even more interesting was the mating of the same pair of snakes again on May 13, a month and a half after their first successful pairing, producing another clutch of eggs—the second in one season. Laid on June 21, they hatched between July 28 and July 31. This is the first evidence of multiple clutching in this species. The granular-surfaced eggs, 4 to 10 per clutch, measure $1\frac{7}{8}$ to $2\frac{1}{4}$ inches (4.8–5.7 cm) long and produce young between 11 and 15 inches (27.9–38.1 cm) in length.

CORN SNAKE
Elaphe guttata guttata
PLATES 34–36

DESCRIPTION   In a recent study of *E. guttata* and its subspecies in Texas, Vaughan, Dixon, and Thomas (1996) confirmed the presence of the corn snake in the state, although here it is not the usual vivid red or bright orange reptile commonly found in the eastern part of the serpent's range. Such brightly hued corn snakes apparently occur no farther west than the Louisiana parishes of Iberia, Pointe Coupee, and West Baton Rouge. Texas specimens, as well as those in western Louisiana, while they do not display the gaudy colors, nevertheless fit the description of *E. g. guttata* in other important characteristics.

Texas corn snakes are tan, grayish tan, or orangish tan, with a dorsal row of large brown to reddish brown dark-edged blotches down the middle of the back, below which is another row of smaller alternating blotches, followed by a third series of even smaller spots at the belly line. Their combined dorsal body and tail blotches are fewer (44–59, average 51) than those of either the Great Plains (57–81, average 67) or southwestern (39–67, average 55) rat snakes. Moreover, their combined belly (ventral) and undertail (subcaudal) scales average only 282, which is 13 fewer than the southwestern rat snake but the same as the Great Plains rat snake. *E. guttata*'s numerous squarish, black belly markings, each of which involves at least three ventral scales in a row, are set against a whitish background, giving the abdomen a conspicuously checkered appearance, and the stripes under the tail are bold and black. A characteristic pattern element of all *E. gut-*

tata subspecies is the conspicuous dark, dorsal, spearpoint-shaped marking that begins on the neck as two nearly parallel dark stripes and ends in a point on the crown between the eyes. In the middle of this dark outline is an area of light background color. Just ahead of it, a dark transverse bar connects the eyes, then slants backward along each side of the head past the end of the mouthline, where it sometimes joins the first body blotch. Another short, dark bar may cross the top of the snout. The body scales, of which only the upper several rows are keeled, occur in 27 (rarely 29) middorsal rows, and the anal plate is divided.

COMPARABLE SNAKES No other East Texas serpent within the corn snake's range has a distinct, dark, forward-directed spearpoint marking on the crown and two distinct, lengthwise dark stripes under the tail. The prairie king snake has perfectly smooth scales and a single anal plate. On the adult Texas rat snake, the dorsal blotches often are poorly defined, the top of its head is uniformly dusky, and the underside of its tail lacks two bold, dark lengthwise stripes. The juvenile Texas rat snake also lacks the dark undertail stripes, and the dark stripe behind its eye fails to reach backward past the end of the mouthline.

SIZE Throughout its range, the usual adult length of this snake is 30 to 48 inches (76.2–121.9 cm); the largest specimen on record measured 72 inches (182.9 cm) long. Five corn snakes collected in Texas from Brazos, Grimes, Milam, and San Augustine counties were 41 to 55 inches (104.1–139.7 cm) in length and averaged 47.2 inches (119.9 cm) long.

HABITAT The corn snake reaches the westernmost limit of its extensive geographic range in the east-central and southeastern parts of Texas, where it has been found primarily in pine-oak habitat from the eastern edge of the post oak savannah, north to the town of Big Sandy, east to the Louisiana border, and south to Hardin County. It has not been found west or south of Brazos and Grimes counties or more than 20 airline miles (32.2 km) west of the natural pine-oak woodlands of East Texas. For the most part, collecting records in the state are widely scattered, with most specimens of this subspecies having been obtained in Brazos County. Outside Texas it is encountered in a wide variety of habitats that include sparse woodland, forest edge, rocky hillsides, dry fields, and open grassy areas but is seldom found in wet bottomlands. Despite its secretive lifestyle, the corn snake is attracted to agricultural and urban areas, especially those in which dilapidated old buildings provide shelter for the snakes themselves and for the small rodents on which they feed.

BEHAVIOR Armed only with relatively small teeth, the corn snake, like most serpents its size, is no match against a large adversary. In the face of danger, it ordinarily does not seek to escape by dashing for the nearest shelter (a strategy used effectively by such species as the coachwhip, racer, and ribbon snake, among others). Instead, when suddenly confronted by man, especially in the open, it is likely to pull its entire body together slightly into a series of short, lateral, wavelike kinks and remain that way without taking any further action. An aroused corn snake is not so passive. When closely approached, it gathers its forebody into several tight, elevated S-loops, pulls its head back to somewhere near the top of the coils, then often leans backward so that a portion of its boldly checkered belly is visible to its foe. In this position, its body tense and waiting, the snake holds its ground, sometimes vibrating its tail as a further signal of its intentions. At the first threatening move, the snake delivers a quick strike that is often punctuated with a brief, sharp hiss, but seldom do the reptile's jaws engage the intended victim, for the attack is intended primarily to discourage the snake's adversary, not to injure it. When first picked up, some corn snakes bite with determination and expel feces on their captor; others are more docile, never showing hostility, even when initially captured. Virtually all corn snakes become tractable soon after their first few days in captivity, which (in addition to their usual stunning roseate

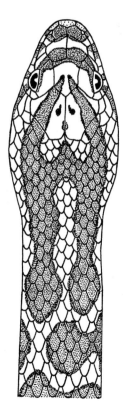

Figure 26. *Long, spearpoint marking on head typical of the corn snake and its subspecies.*

coloration and ease of maintenance in captivity) is why they are typically the snake of choice among reptile hobbyists around the world.

Since next to nothing is known about this snake's natural history in Texas, the following information is based on the subspecies' behavior as reported in other parts of its range.

The corn snake is active from April to October or early November, but in the South, particularly in southern Florida, it may be encountered year round. Chiefly nocturnal, it is likely to be seen crossing country roads during the hours of sunset and early evening, a dangerous habit that frequently causes it to become the victim of vehicular traffic. By day the corn snake usually remains out of sight in natural shelters that include hollow logs, rotting stumps, stump holes, channels left by the decay of dead tree roots, piles of leaf litter, and the tunnels of burrowing animals; in the spring, young specimens have been collected from under the loose bark of standing trees, stumps, and logs. Around old abandoned houses and farm buildings, it hides under boards, sheet metal, and trash piles and in or beneath the structures themselves.

Even though this species, like other rat snakes, possesses a body shape uniquely adapted for climbing (see Texas rat snake account), it is seldom found in trees or bushes and almost never in the attics of barns, a favorite hideout for the highly arboreal Texas rat snake. Palmer and Braswell (1995) mention a corn snake that was coiled nearly 8 feet above the ground in a large oak and another that was found nearly 12 feet (3.7 m) off the ground in the hollow of a dead tree. Even trees of large diameter present no serious impediment to the snake's arboreal tendencies. According to Oliver (1955), one corn snake made its way up the trunk of a tall, smooth-barked coconut tree, another scaled a sweet gum 3 feet in diameter, and a third, without ever making a slip, expertly traveled head first down the trunk of an elm tree 3½ feet (1.1 m) in diameter.

With the arrival of cold weather, the corn snake retires to a sheltered refuge to avoid the lethal effects of subfreezing temperatures. Such a hibernaculum can take the form of a hollow tree, a decaying log or tree stump, the channels left by the decay of dead tree roots, a rock crevice or stone wall, the spaces beneath building foundations, or the tunnels of burrowing animals.

FEEDING Like most of its rat-snake kin, this powerful constrictor feeds primarily on small mammals, which, after being seized with a quick snap of its jaws, are suffocated in the serpent's muscular body coils. Farmers with a knowledge of its feeding habits welcome this efficient rodent killer because it devours so many rats and mice harmful to crops. The down side is that the corn snake sometimes also captures birds and their eggs. Other prey items consumed by it include shrews, moles, voles, bats, lizards, small snakes, and frogs.

REPRODUCTION Mating in this subspecies, which usually occurs sometime in April or May, may be preceded by a stereotypic combat behavior between two rival males, each seeking to court and mate with the same receptive female. During such lively altercations, the serpents follow a predictable scenario, as each snake tries to gain a postural advantage that will permit him to pin his adversary's body to the ground. In most cases it is the larger male that prevails. The subdued contestant, having suffered no physical harm during the encounter, quickly departs the area, leaving the victor to search out his new mate.

Sometime from May to July, the female lays 3 to 31 eggs per clutch, which hatch during late July to late September. Although the coloration of infant Texas corn snakes is unknown, elsewhere the hatchlings are patterned like the adults but with a more reddish overall hue. They are 11 to 15 inches (27.9–38.1 cm) long.

Natural nest sites have been discovered in riverbanks, abandoned mammal burrows, rotting stumps and logs, and sawdust piles, but never has more than one clutch of eggs been found at a single location. Palmer and Braswell were the first to report communal egg-laying in this subspecies. They described two such sites, both discovered in North Carolina in sawdust piles. One consisted of a large mound surrounded by marshland, which on July 8, 1961, was found to contain six groups of corn-snake eggs, each clutch containing 8 to 11 eggs. On July 3, 1965, the same sawdust pile held four clutches of 8 to 12 eggs each and spent eggshells from past years. In a similar mound of sawdust—this one located in dense pine woods—Palmer and his colleagues found four clutches on July 9, 1961, each containing 6 to 14 eggs. The clutches were always found in damp sand 6 to 15 inches (15.2–38.1 cm) below the mound's surface and on the south and southeast sides of the sawdust piles, where presumably they would receive the longest daily exposure to the sun's warming rays. Although no clutch was closer than 8 inches (20.3 cm) to any other in the same mound, in at least one instance the distance between them was as much as 25 feet (7.7 m).

GREAT PLAINS RAT SNAKE
Elaphe guttata emoryi
PLATES 37, 38

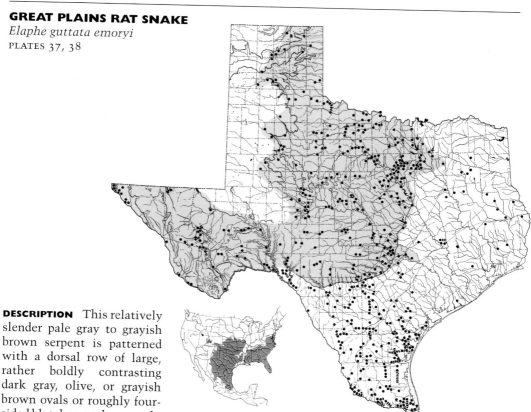

DESCRIPTION This relatively slender pale gray to grayish brown serpent is patterned with a dorsal row of large, rather boldly contrasting dark gray, olive, or grayish brown ovals or roughly four-sided blotches, each narrowly outlined in dark brown or black. Two more lengthwise rows of smaller dark blotches occur on either side of the body. In old specimens, however, the usual bold pattern of dark blotches may be largely replaced by four shadowy lengthwise stripes. The underside of the serpent's tail features a pair of dark stripes that extend its full length, sometimes discontinuously.

The snake's most easily observed hallmark, present in all *E. guttata* subspecies, is the dark spearpoint-shaped marking on top of its head, which, despite its general usefulness as a species characteristic, may be indistinct in very old specimens. *See corn snake description and illustration.*

COMPARABLE SNAKES Among our native serpent species, only the Great Plains rat and corn snakes have both a bold, dark, forward-pointing spearpoint marked on the head *and* a distinctly dark-striped undertail. The prairie king snake, which is easily confused with *E. g. emoryi,* has perfectly smooth body scales and a single anal plate, as do the glossy snakes, whose undersides are unmarked. The strongly keeled dorsal scales of the bull snake are arranged in 28 to 37 midbody rows, and the anal plate is single. In the adult Texas rat snake, the dark dorsal blotches do not stand out boldly against the background color, the top of the head is dusky and virtually patternless, there is no downward-slanting dark stripe behind the eye, and the underside of the tail lacks dark striping. Although the juvenile Texas rat snake—with its pale background color, contrasting dark brown blotched pattern, and bold head markings—closely resembles the Great Plains rat snake, it lacks both the dark, forward-pointing spear-point design on the head and the striped un-dertail of *E. g. emoryi*. Furthermore, the dark stripe behind each eye does not extend past the end of the mouthline. The adult Baird's rat snake displays four dark stripes along the full length of its body and has an unpatterned head; the juvenile is marked with numerous narrow, dark crossbars, and the scattered dark markings on its crown do not take the shape of a spearpoint. The blond color phase of the Trans-Pecos rat snake carries no distinct markings on either its head or neck.

SIZE   A snake of moderate size, the adult usually attains a length between 24 and 48 inches (61–121.9 cm), although a speci-men of record length measured 72 inches (182.9 cm).

HABITAT   Generally absent from the western Panhandle and regions east of the limestone extrusions that sporadically surface between Waco and Dallas, this adaptable serpent ranges widely across Central and North Texas, being associated with every major vegetational community in this part of the state. Its distribution stretches from the Ed-wards Plateau, north through the southern Great Plains of Texas and Oklahoma, and in-cludes the Rolling Plains, Cross Timbers, and grassland prairie, although it generally avoids the Staked Plain. Its preferred microhabitats include rocky bluffs and slopes, partially wooded hillsides, and even caves. In other-wise arid environments, it frequently occurs near springs, streams, and rivers; across the grassy plains, it is often found along dry gul-lies. Though less disposed than the more pre-cocious Texas rat snake to occupy sites near human habitations, this species sometimes inhabits rural areas where the scattered re-mains of abandoned farm buildings and simi-lar unoccupied structures harbor an abun-dance of rodent prey.

BEHAVIOR   Although by no means vicious, this serpent occasionally strikes out when provoked, but rarely with the same frenzied vigor displayed by its short-tempered rela-tive, the Texas rat snake. In fact, handled for the first time, most wild-caught specimens refuse to bite in self-defense. Instead of using its teeth in such circumstances, it is more likely to surprise its foe by expelling a pun-gent, unpleasant-smelling liquid from a pair of musk glands in the base of its tail and even feces from its cloacal opening. Separately these substances may be offensive to the senses of touch and smell; together they can be almost sickening, which is precisely the point. Liberally covered with the smelly goo, the attacker is apt to release its struggling victim. If simply disturbed but not picked up, the snake may gather its forebody to-gether into an S-shaped loop and prepare to deliver a defensive strike, simultaneously vi-brating its tail. When the tail strikes against a hard object, the sound can easily be mis-taken for the strident buzz of a rattlesnake's caudal appendage.

In Central Texas, the Great Plains rat snake leaves its hibernaculum sometime in late February or early March, though during un-usually mild winters it can often be found at the surface even earlier, periodically basking in the warm midday sun. In the more tem-perate climate of the Panhandle, 400 miles to the north, where winters are cold and pro-tracted, it normally makes its initial spring-time appearance more than a month later. Except for such brief day-active periods in early spring and again in late fall, it is al-most exclusively nocturnal, avoiding diurnal predators by hiding under rocks, logs, boards, and other surface objects or by crawling into animal burrows. With the first chill of fall (as early as September in the northern part of its range and as late as November in the south-western portion), it retires to a deep rock fis-sure, quarry, cave, or mammal burrow where it can safely pass the winter, sometimes in small groups and frequently in association with other serpents, including ring-necked snakes, yellow-bellied racers, and copper-heads. One such communal den, located in a rocky ravine near Winfield, Kansas, held a dozen Great Plains rat snakes, numerous yel-low-bellied racers, and a few prairie ring-necked snakes (Burt and Hoyle 1935).

FEEDING   Rodents and other small mammals apparently make up the bulk of the snake's diet, but ground-nesting birds and their eggs are also important menu items. Lizards are consumed only occasionally. In what is perhaps a typical representation of the kinds of prey items usually devoured by this species, R. F. Clark (1949) examined the stomach contents of specimens from northern Louisiana and found rats in six individuals, rabbits in three, and birds in six. Although the relatively large number of birds in this sample is consistent with the high percentage of avian prey items reported for the species by others, it is difficult, even in the face of such numbers, to accept Davenport's (1943) suggestion that this serpent is more injurious to birdlife than the Texas rat snake, a skilled tree climber whose keen appetite for feathered prey is well documented. Be that as it may, the Great Plains rat snake is indeed an effective predator of ground-nesting birds, which raises the question, how did a specimen of this ordinarily terrestrial serpent, collected in the northeastern corner of the Panhandle by Fouquette and Lindsay (1955), manage to capture two northern orioles, a tree-dwelling species that builds a hanging nest some distance above the ground at the farthest end of a tree limb? Excluding the unlikely possibility that the snake had climbed high enough to reach an oriole nest, it is of course imaginable that the reptile somehow chanced upon two baby birds after they had accidentally fallen to the ground. On the other hand, since the orioles' age is not mentioned in the report, perhaps these were adults, ambushed as they engaged in some infrequent terrestrial pursuit.

Bats, especially those living in large nursery colonies in certain Central Texas caves, are also captured and eaten by the Great Plains rat snake, as they are by several other serpent species of the region. At such locations, Herreid (1961) found their most important ophidian predator to be the western coachwhip, not *E. g. emoryi*. Yet in the gypsum caverns of Kansas, Twente (1955) identified the Great Plains rat snake as the serpent most responsible for such predation, noting that several specimens were found to be living within the cave interiors, where they apparently satisfied their appetites by dining on the resident free-tailed bats.

REPRODUCTION Details about this snake's reproductive biology are still not well known. The female, which can reach sexual maturity as early in life as 18 months of age, mates soon after leaving hibernation, with copulation occurring in southwestern Texas as early in the season as March but at more northern latitudes not until May. Sometime in June or July she will deposit her clutch of eggs, which can number anywhere from 3 to 27, in some relatively damp location where they will incubate for approximately the next 53 to 70 days. In the beginning, each egg is about $1\frac{5}{8}$ inches (4.1 cm) long, but like all snake eggs it will significantly increase in size over time. When it first passes from the female's cloaca, it is covered with a wet, sticky substance that causes it, as it dries, to adhere with any other eggs it may initially touch, eventually resulting in the formation of a single, large, rigid mass as one egg after the other is added to the cluster. The survival value of such a mass is obvious; a single egg can easily be swallowed whole by other snakes, but when firmly bound together the entire clutch is much too large to be ingested. At hatching, usually in late August or September, the baby snakes are between 10 and $15\frac{1}{2}$ inches (25.4–39.4 cm) long.

SOUTHWESTERN RAT SNAKE
Elaphe guttata meahllmorum
PLATE 39

DESCRIPTION This somewhat slender snake has a pale gray ground color and a lengthwise row of large, contrasting grayish brown to pale brown oval or nearly four-sided dorsal blotches, each margined with a darker color. The combined number of dorsal body and tail markings of this subspecies (39–67, average 55) has an average intermediate between the corn snake's (44–59, average 51) and the Great Plains rat snake's (57–81, average 67). In about half the specimens, a light gray transverse bar crosses through the middle of each dorsal blotch. Usually two more rows of smaller spots lie on either side of the body below the large primary series.

On the forebody the abdomen is white or cream colored, with normally few if any dark markings except for dark spots along the outer edges of the belly plates, beginning after about the first 50 ventral scales. The degree of ventral spotting, however, can vary from none to moderate. The underside of the tail is irregularly marked with small dark spots, which are seldom arranged in two well-defined lengthwise stripes. Furthermore, of the three subspecies of *E. guttata*, the southwestern rat snake shows the highest average number of belly (ventral) plus undertail (subcaudal) scales, more than 290 in 86 percent of the specimens as opposed to about 282 in both corn and Great Plains rat snakes.

In common with other members of the *E. guttata* group, the southwestern rat snake has a dark, forward-directed, spearpoint marking on the crown. See corn snake description and illustration. In old snakes, this

marking may be indistinct. Just ahead of it, a dark transverse bar connects the eyes and continues diagonally along each side of the head before terminating at or beyond the end of the mouthline, where it may merge with the first body blotch. Another short, dark bar may cross the top of the snout. The body scales, of which only the upper several rows are weakly keeled (the others being smooth), occur in 27 (rarely 29) middorsal rows, and the anal plate is divided.

COMPARABLE SNAKES In no other Texas snake species do we see the distinct, dark, forward-directed, spearpoint head marking that characterizes the three subspecies of *E. guttata*. The prairie king snake has perfectly smooth body scales and a single anal plate. Glossy snakes, which display the same scale characters, have an immaculate belly and undertail surface. Bull snakes possess strongly keeled dorsal scales, arranged in 28 to 37 midbody rows, and a single anal plate. On the adult Texas rat snake, the dark dorsal blotches usually are not as well defined as those of the southwestern rat snake, the top of its head is uniformly dark, there is no distinct dark stripe behind the eye, and the undertail lacks dark spots. On the other hand, the boldly blotched juvenile Texas rat snake does not appear greatly different from the southwestern rat snake, but it lacks a spearpoint marking on the crown and the dark stripe behind its eye fails to reach beyond the end of the mouthline.

SIZE Adults of this moderately sized subspecies generally range from 24 to 48 inches (61–121.9 cm) long. The maximum known length for the species is 72 inches (182.9 cm).

HABITAT An inhabitant of the South Texas brush country, it occurs as far north as the Balcones Escarpment (along a line extending from Del Rio to San Antonio to Austin), west into the eastern portion of the Chihuahuan Desert, and east to a line between Austin and Corpus Christi. In south-central Texas, according to Vermersch and Kuntz (1986), it is found in juniper, oak, and hackberry woodlands, as well as in the more open adjacent grasslands that support stands of mesquite and scattered yucca. They also note that it is attracted to suburban gardens, drawn there by the moisture derived from the constant watering of cultivated plants.

BEHAVIOR Like almost all native serpents, the southwestern rat snake tries to avoid man. When provoked, however, it is apt to assume a defensive S-shaped forebody stance with its head pulled back and its tail vibrating rapidly, from which position, if further annoyed, it may deliver a menacing strike. When directed at a human, such a blow is more bluff than substance, for the snake's relatively small teeth are unable to inflict serious wounds on so large an adversary. Even so, it has been our experience that most wild-caught specimens of this subspecies do not bite when first handled, choosing instead simply to void a foul-smelling musk and feces from the cloacal opening at the base of the tail.

In South Texas, where it usually spends the winters in animal burrows, this rat snake ordinarily leaves its hibernaculum sometime in late February and early March, though during unusually mild winters it can periodically be found at the surface even earlier, briefly basking in the warm midday sun. It continues its daytime prowling activities into the succeeding cool days of early spring. With the arrival of oppressively hot summer temperatures, it becomes nocturnal, remaining night-active until the return of cool autumn weather, when it again comes to the surface during the day.

Chiefly a ground-dwelling reptile, it can often be found hiding beneath a variety of surface objects, including large stones and stacks of dead plant debris, as well as rock piles, boards, and other discarded construction material. It is also an efficient climber, a trait shared with other native rat snake species; the convergence of its flat abdomen and nearly straight sides forms right angles that improve the serpent's clinging ability and prevent the body from slipping as it ascends a vertical surface such as a tree trunk. In spite of the southwestern rat snake's capacity to climb, however, we believe it seldom moves into the uppermost branches of trees. The few we have encountered on elevated perches were discovered in bushes only a foot or two above the ground, and one was coiled on top of a pack rat nest in a prickly pear cactus clump.

FEEDING What little published information is available about the dietary preferences of this subspecies suggests that small mammals, especially rodents, represent its chief prey, with birds and their eggs, lizards, and occasionally other snakes constituting the rest. This corresponds closely with the food habits of the serpent's close relatives, the Great Plains rat and corn snakes. Like them, it uses its muscular body to constrict prey that is too large to be otherwise easily subdued.

REPRODUCTION With the recognition by Smith and his colleagues (1994) of the southwestern rat snake as a subspecies distinct from the Great Plains rat snake, the natural history information previously reported for the latter race does not necessarily apply to *E. g. meahllmorum*, since most of those behavioral observations and field studies were conducted in regions other than South Texas. Essentially, all of the published records concerning the reproductive biology of this species, of which there are many, apply to the Great Plains rat snake and corn snake. Only one, reported by Werler (1951), described egglaying and hatching by the southwestern rat snake, the details of which were not different from those of the two other subspecies. It involved a large female from the Brownsville area, which laid 15 smooth-shelled, adhesive eggs on June 14 and 15. Ranging from 1½ to 2 inches (3.8–5.1 cm) long, 7 of them hatched over a period of several days (August 7–12), producing young that measured 17⅓ to 18½ inches (44–47 cm) long.

TEXAS RAT SNAKE
Elaphe obsoleta lindheimeri
PLATES 40–44

DESCRIPTION Except for the occasional adult specimen whose dorsal markings are obscured by the snake's overall black coloration, the typical pattern of this subspecies consists of a median row of large, dark brown to purplish blotches displayed against a background color of yellowish to grayish brown or, on occasion, even reddish. Below and alternating with them is another row of smaller dark blotches. Owing to considerable variation in body color among individual specimens, the dorsal and lateral markings either stand out boldly against the background hue or appear almost to blend with it. In some older Texas rat snakes the chief pattern element consists of lengthwise dark stripes, with or without indistinct dorsal blotches.

Despite such diversity, there is, according to Lawson and Lieb (1990), a tendency for the overall base coloration of this subspecies to be dark gray in the forested eastern portions of its range and yellowish in the oak savannah, riparian, and juniper woodland regions to the west. Whatever the serpent's basic hue, all adult Texas rat snakes have one thing in common: the skin between the body scales and many of the scale edges themselves bear reddish pigmentation. In some individuals, orange-, yellow-, or white-tipped scales appear as well. The head, which is uniformly dark gray on top, is white on the lip scales, across the lower jaw, and on the throat. Squarish dark blotches tinted with gray usually mark the pale-colored belly, and the underside of the tail is normally solid gray. At midbody, 27 rows of dorsal scales encircle the snake; only those near the spine bear weak keels, the others being smooth. The anal plate is divided.

A very young rat snake scarcely resembles the adult. Its large, dark brown dorsal saddles stand out boldly against the snake's light gray background color, as do its smaller lateral blotches. On the pale-colored crown, which is only a shade darker than the light gray body, a dark bar crosses the forehead just in front of the eyes. A similar bar extends obliquely backward from each eye, almost reaching the end of the mouthline, while a pair of dark streaks runs back from the rear of the crown to join the first neck blotch. A few small dark spots of diverse shapes and sizes also mark the top of the head.

COMPARABLE SNAKES Nearly all adult Baird's rat snakes have lengthwise dorsal striping, although a few mature Texas rat snakes are also faintly striped. Juvenile *E. bairdi*, with their numerous narrow dorsal crossbars (44–61 bars, 2–3 scale rows in length, measured front to back), can easily be distinguished from young Texas rat snakes, which have only 27 to 37 middorsal body blotches that are 4–6 scales long. In both juvenile and adult Great Plains rat snakes, a dark, forward-pointing, spearpoint marking decorates the top of the head, the postocular stripe extends backward onto the neck, and two bold dark stripes occur on the underside of the tail. Bull and pine snakes have a pale-hued crown, 28 or more strongly keeled dorsal scale rows at midbody, and a single anal plate. In glossy snakes, the belly is white and unmarked, the body scales are smooth, and the anal plate is single. The body scales of the prairie king snake are all smooth, and its anal plate is also single.

SIZE This is one of Texas' longest serpents. Most adults are between 42 and 72 inches (106.7–182.9 cm) in length; a record individual measured 86 inches (218.4 cm) long.

HABITAT Throughout eastern Texas, this serpent is found most commonly in brushy or wooded areas, particularly those containing large trees, for it shows a strong tendency to climb. In such an arboreal niche, it finds not only refuge from ground-dwelling predators but also a convenient source of birds and their eggs, both favored prey items. It utilizes a wide variety of other East Texas habitats,

such as rocky hillsides, grasslands, cultivated fields, marshland, and even wooded suburban lots and inner-city parkland. From there it ranges westward through the prairies and Cross Timbers; to the south it penetrates the predominately grassy and brushy parts of south-central Texas by keeping mostly to the area's countless oak savannahs and mottes and to the woodlands that border the region's numerous watercourses. In the northern part of the Edwards Plateau, according to Lawson and Lieb, it occurs chiefly in the floodplain and along the riverine woodlands of the Colorado River drainage system (including the Llano, San Saba, and Concho rivers), as well as in the valley floodplains of the Guadalupe, Medina, and Sabinal rivers.

BEHAVIOR The Texas rat snake is bold and deliberate. When suddenly confronted, its tendency is not to flee (as is the rule among the more lively racers, coachwhips, and whipsnakes) but to hold its ground. Pulling its forebody together into a tight S-shaped configuration at an oblique angle above the ground, the snake locks its gaze on the intruder. At this point the head is cocked back and the mouth may be held open in readiness to strike. At the same time, the reptile often vibrates its tail nervously, sounding a clearly audible staccato if the caudal appendage strikes a nearby hard object or dead leaves, producing a noise that in some cases sounds frighteningly like a rattlesnake's buzzing. If an intruder approaches too close, the rat snake unleashes its forebody coils in a sudden forward strike, sometimes accompanied by a brief, sharp hiss. This is more a threatening gesture than a genuine attempt to inflict injury, for despite the reptile's savage lunge, its head often falls short of the target. Even a successful strike inflicts no serious injury. Engaged only briefly, the serpent's numerous needlelike teeth are quickly withdrawn as the snake pulls its head back to its original defensive position. The result is a cluster (or two, if both upper and lower jaws are engaged) of shallow punctures that will heal in a day or two.

When deliberately handled, however, an angry Texas rat snake will not only bite but also often maintain its hold as it chews on its assailant, inflicting more and perhaps deeper puncture wounds than during a strike; still, they are not of a serious nature. It also responds to being captured by ejecting fecal matter from its cloacal opening and a musky spray from a pair of glands at the base of its tail. These foul-smelling substances, when spread over a captor's hands by the snake's writhing body, are sometimes deemed so offensive by the handler that they gain the serpent its immediate release.

Despite the snake's large size, abundance, and wide distribution in Texas and Louisiana, no comprehensive, long-term study has been made detailing any aspect of its natural history; even the pattern of its daily or seasonal movements is not well understood. Most of the information we have about it comes from scattered anecdotal reports.

The Texas rat snake ordinarily remains active from April through October, although in the southern part of its range it can be found abroad in any month, even during the brief interludes of unseasonally warm weather that sometimes occur during mild winters. Strecker (1926a), for example, collected active specimens in Central Texas up to the last week in November and as early in the year as the second week in February. In south-central Texas, Vermersch and Kuntz (1986) occasionally found young ones in midwinter, coiled at the surface beneath a variety of man-made objects and natural vegetative debris. In northern Louisiana, R. F. Clark (1949) collected at least one specimen in each week of the year; those he observed in winter were generally basking on sunny wooded hillsides during spells of warm weather.

To survive freezing temperatures, the rat snake must find a suitable frost-free refuge. Appropriate hibernation sites include the interiors of rotting logs and tree stumps, the elevated cavities of tree trunks, discarded mammal burrows (especially those under large fallen trees), rock crevices, caves, and even old wells, where it may spend the winter underwater. It is not unusual for the snake to hibernate in barns. It may also share its winter quarters with other reptiles and amphibians, such as copperheads, brown snakes, leopard frogs, and toads.

Except during unbearably hot summer months, when it often ventures out at night, the Texas rat snake can generally be found wandering about by day. Specimens observed by Davenport (1943) in the San Antonio area were described as most active between 3 PM and 10 PM. Although we have no specific information about this subspecies' home range or movements, studies by Fitch (1963a) and Fitch and Shirer (1971) made in Kansas of the closely related black rat snake, *E. o. obsoleta*, show that its travels averaged approximately 146½ feet (44.6 m) per day and that it generally maintained a home range of 25 to 30 acres (10–12 ha), which it occupied continuously for many years, possibly even for life.

Like the cohabiting rough green snake, this skillful climber spends much of its time in bushes and trees. Its muscular trunk and the sharp perpendicular angle created by the juncture of each body flank with the belly greatly increase the snake's ability to scale trees, cliffs, and walls. It is mostly this body shape that enhances the reptile's climbing agility. Visualized in cross-section, the serpent's trunk is shaped like a loaf of bread; in other snakes it is more circular. Thus, as the serpent inches upward along a tree trunk (even one that is absolutely vertical), the angular, slightly outward-projecting belly scales press firmly against irregularities in the bark, like cleats, providing sufficient traction to hold the snake's body securely against the trunk—a structural peculiarity found in all North American species of rat snakes.

To the rat snake, trees are a matter of considerable importance; in them it finds a haven from natural ground-dwelling enemies as well as a source of prey, such as birds and squirrels, whose nests it plunders for their young. When the trees have died and fallen to the ground, their rotten, hollow interiors are used by the snake for egg-laying, temporary shelter, and occasionally as a place in which to hibernate. According to Lawson and Lieb, large trees, particularly oaks and mulberrys (which are intimately associated with the snake's more arid western habitats), appear to be essential to the serpent's existence. Choice trees are those with natural, elevated trunk cavities. From such a hole, sometimes as much as 50 feet above the ground, the forebody of a rat snake can occasionally be seen idly extended, the rest of its body concealed

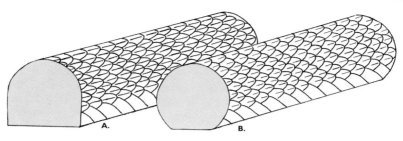

Figure 27. *Cross section of body of (a) rat snake and (b) most other snakes.*

within the trunk hollow. More often, however, one of these serpents can be observed resting with its long body draped loosely across a leafy branch or coiled ball-like on a limb.

Not every forest provides adequate natural shelter for the cavity-dependent wildlife living within its borders. A case in point, according to McComb and Noble (1981), are the vast tracts of once unspoiled bottomland hardwood forests in Louisiana (and East Texas) that have been converted to soybean farms or monoculture woodlands and in whose artificial environments scarcely any natural shelter remains. Most of their old or dying trees, logs, and rotting stumps are constantly being removed, eliminating much of the cover vital to the survival of many small vertebrate animals.

Despite all of that, the rat snake frequently benefits from man's interference. The same biologists, studying the use of nest boxes by species other than the birds and squirrels for which they were erected, found that Texas rat snakes sheltered in such structures more than twice as often as they did in natural tree cavities. This prompted them to suggest that in commercially managed woodlands inhabited by cavity-dependent wildlife, the judicious use of nest boxes can partly compensate for the loss of natural shelters.

The snake is often attracted to human habitations, sometimes with fatal results. Poultry ranchers, who view it as one of their greatest enemies, kill it on sight. Considering the great risk to itself in such surroundings, it seems strange that a snake as big as this would choose to live so close to man, for its large size makes it highly conspicuous. Why is it so drawn to farms and homes, both

occupied and abandoned? One reason seems to be its lusty appetite for the poultry and rodent prey that usually occur there in abundance; the other is the ready supply of elevated shelters, such as rafters and upper-story wood flooring, where the serpent can find a convenient refuge and a comfortable place to digest its periodic meal.

Despite its propensity to climb, the Texas rat snake is also a good swimmer that willingly enters the water. It does so to escape its enemies or, when cruising slowly along a lakeshore or riverbank, to search for prey animals along the water's edge. Although it may seldom swim below the surface, this species is evidently well equipped to remain underwater for more than an hour at a time, owing primarily to the large and numerous air pockets in its single functional lung.

FEEDING There is no denying that this serpent's vernacular designation "chicken snake" is based on the species' particular fondness for birds (including domestic poultry) and their eggs, but considering its useful role as a capable destroyer of rodents harmful to our interests, a good argument can be made to defend it from senseless persecution. Just as birds of prey once were regarded as marauders of the henhouse, rat snakes are often considered the scourge of the farmer. Since we have finally come to the realization that most hawks destroy as many or more rodents than birds, we should also appreciate that the chief prey of rat snakes is mammals, most of which are clearly detrimental to agriculture. This was verified by R. F. Clark (1949) in a study of the reptile's food habits in northern Louisiana. His survey of 100 wild-caught specimens showed that mice were contained in 35 of the stomachs, rats in 20, rabbits in

18, and squirrels in 10. Birds were discovered in only 17.

There can be no doubt, however, that where avian prey is locally more abundant or more accessible than mammalian food, birds will often constitute the bulk of the serpent's diet. This is especially true during the avian nesting season, when baby birds, not yet fledged, are confined to the nest and unable to escape such predators. Young domestic fowl are especially vulnerable. In unguarded coops filled with chicks, the rat snake quickly indulges its ravenous appetite, gorging on as many birds as it can hold, and coils sluggishly in some nearby nook for the next several days until its bloated trunk returns to near-normal size. It is often under such circumstances that the serpent is discovered and instantly destroyed. That barn-nesting wild birds are also at risk was mentioned by Strecker (1926a), who described how three cliff swallows, sleeping under the eaves of a barn in their gourd-shaped mud nests, were attacked and devoured by a marauding rat snake.

No doubt many more wild birds are captured in their tree nests than are domestic poultry in chicken yards. According to Rudolph, Kyle, and Conner (1990), the red-cockaded woodpecker, which nearly always nests in living pine trees, has managed to reduce its losses from rat-snake predation by carefully selecting trees with specific characteristics, then modifying the area around the nest cavity entrance hole to prevent easy access by ophidian predators. Living pines are the tree of choice because they produce significant resin flows, an important ingredient for creating snake-free roost and nest sites. After excavating the entrance hole, which is sloped upward to prevent the resin from flowing into the woodpecker's chamber, the bird punches several small auxiliary holes into the tree trunk not far from the entryway. These secondary holes, called resin wells, are routinely worked by the woodpeckers so that a generous flow of resin constantly exudes from them, effectively coating the trunk with the sticky substance, particularly the area extending several feet below the cavity entrance. By extensively scaling loose bark from around the opening, the birds create a smoother trunk surface and insure a more

even coverage of the flowing resin. The surface area around and below the roost or nest cavity entrance is eventually surrounded by a continuous smooth, sticky outer coating that is difficult for a snake to cross. This was confirmed in a series of field experiments conducted by Rudolph and his coworkers, who found that only 3 of 18 trial attempts by Texas rat snakes to climb over such resin barriers proved successful.

Even birds as large as a full-grown domestic hen can be subdued by this powerful constrictor, although smaller birds are the snake's prey of choice, for they are more easily swallowed. Occasionally larger birds do fall victim to this voracious predator. G. G. Williams (1951), for instance, tells of an encounter between a large Texas rat snake and a red-shouldered hawk at the San Jacinto Battleground near Houston, in which the snake completely immobilized its adversary with two loops of its body, one of which was wrapped tightly around the bird's neck. After it was rescued, the hawk at first hung limply in Williams' hand, but following a brief struggle it flew away. Despite the snake's dominant role in this instance, it seems likely that in a more typical life-and-death struggle between the two, the hawk (a relatively large bird with a sharp beak and strong talons) would have a decided physical and strategic advantage over the reptile, which is high on the hawk's list of prey. This encounter, therefore, raises the question, was the snake initially the predator or the prey? Did it coil about the hawk to defend itself from the bird's attack, or was it the aggressor? There can be no doubt, judging from the outcome of this particular encounter, that the rat snake has within its well-muscled body the power to subdue relatively large and potentially dangerous prey.

As many Texas farmers know from experience, bird eggs are an especially vulnerable target for this expert climber. The snake probably finds them by their odor or perhaps by the smell of the female, which over time permeates the nest. Each egg is swallowed whole, its shell broken by the serpent's muscular contractions before it reaches the stomach, after which the spent shell is either consumed or regurgitated. In this way, a large rat snake can easily ingest half a dozen hen's eggs in one meal.

Even more remarkable is the snake's ability to detect avian nest sites that are completely surrounded by water (if, indeed, it does not locate them simply by a process of random trial-and-error searching). In one case, reported by Ridlehuber and Silvy (1981), a Texas rat snake managed to reach an artificial wood-duck nest erected atop a pole 2 feet (61 cm) high in a large pond 16½ feet (5 m) from shore. When it was killed and examined, the reptile had in its digestive tract not only 10 of 22 wood duck eggs known to have been in the box but also a Mexican free-tailed bat that apparently was using the nest as a day-time roost. Similar examples are not uncommon. In South Texas, for instance, Bolen, McDaniel, and Cottam (1964) frequently found this snake in waterbound trees containing black-bellied tree duck nest cavities. In one case they discovered two snakes in a single nest from which 16 eggs had disappeared; although they found the remains of 5 eggs in one specimen, they failed to mention the fate of the others.

A peculiar habit of this and other large rat snakes is that of swallowing egg-sized foreign objects associated with poultry nests. The variety of such items is surprising; according to Davenport, it includes darning eggs, door knobs, and large smooth stones. The item ingested most frequently, however, has been the artificial hen's egg, typically made of glass, sometimes of wood, that the farmer routinely placed in a chicken's nest to encourage egg-laying. Under ordinary circumstances, such an undigestible article was simply regurgitated, with no harm or discomfort to the involved reptile, but there have been some notable exceptions. One, reported by Strecker (1927), concerned a Texas rat snake whose skeletal remains were discovered hanging from both sides of a barbed-wire fence. After swallowing a glass egg, it apparently tried to crawl between two closely spaced strands of the wire but was prevented from doing so by the bulging meal. Unable to free itself, the unfortunate reptile died there from starvation. When its remains were found, the artificial egg was still in its original position within the dead snake's body, held in place by a strip of dried skin. In another well-documented account, H. M. Smith (1953) recorded the case of a large Texas rat snake, caught near College Station, that had swallowed a wooden nest egg at least four months earlier and had been unable to regurgitate it. Why it could not rid itself of the stubborn barrier was uncertain. Despite the obstruction, the serpent subsequently ingested a number of meals as a captive, digesting some but regurgitating others.

Juvenile rat snakes too small to swallow the mammals and birds consumed by their parents feed instead on small amphibians (mostly tree frogs) and diminutive lizards, as well as lizard eggs. An additional diet item in nature could well be newborn mice, which even the smallest captive rat snakes eagerly devour.

REPRODUCTION Mating in this subspecies, which ordinarily takes place in April and May, produces single clutches of 5 to 20 eggs in June or July. The white, nongranular eggs, each measuring 1⅝ to 2¾ inches (4.1–7 cm) long, are laid in a variety of nooks that include hollow logs and stumps, mounds of decaying vegetation, old sawdust heaps, and manure piles. They have also been found in loose soil and under large rocks. At hatching, sometime in August or September, the infant snakes are 10 to 16 inches (25.4–40.6 cm) long.

Recently, Brothers (1994) found 14 spent eggshells of this species in a rotten cavity of a beech tree near Elizabeth City, North Carolina. Nearly 20 feet (6.1 m) above the ground in what may originally have been a squirrel nest, the chamber was half full of rotting wood. In another example of tree nesting, described by D. R. Clark and Pendleton (1995), a group of 52 Texas rat snake eggs was found 4 feet (1.2 m) above the ground in the rotting interior of a chinaberry tree in Caldwell, Burleson County, Texas. This report is significant not only because it verifies the tree-nesting behavior of the Texas rat snake but also because it represents the first documented example of communal nesting by this subspecies. Based on their sizes and incubation dates, the eggs were believed to belong to four different clutches.

WESTERN MUD SNAKE
Farancia abacura reinwardti
PLATES 45, 46

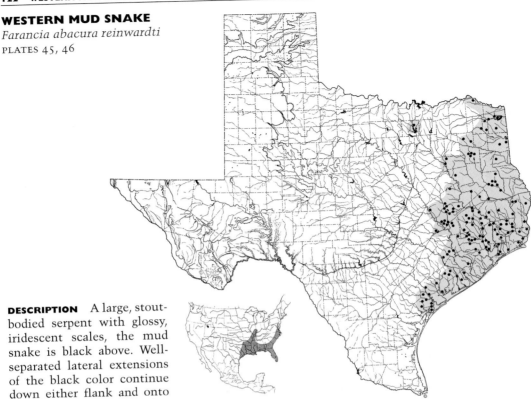

DESCRIPTION A large, stout-bodied serpent with glossy, iridescent scales, the mud snake is black above. Well-separated lateral extensions of the black color continue down either flank and onto the snake's abdomen; between them are red interspaces that reach upward as extensions of the snake's red or pink belly. In some specimens the black bars cross the abdomen in regular sequence, and in others they break up to form a red and black checkered pattern. Among the mud snake's other distinctive features are a somewhat flattened head that is no wider than its neck, tiny eyes, and a sharp spine on the end of its short, stout tail. The head is mostly black on top, whereas the center of each light-colored upper and lower lip scale contains a distinct central dark spot. Similar dark markings occur on the yellow or orange chin and throat. The smooth dorsal scales are arranged in 19 rows at midbody, and the anal plate is nearly always divided.

COMPARABLE SNAKES Within the mud snake's range, the only other serpent having a similar color pattern is the western worm snake, but it has a nearly straight line of demarcation between its contrasting dorsal and ventral coloration, and its dorsal scales are in 13 midbody rows. Although the undertail color of ring-necked snakes is red or orange-red, the belly is never pink or scarlet, the neck is nearly always circled by a partial or complete light-colored ring, and there is a double row of small dark spots along the length of the abdomen.

SIZE The usual adult length for this subspecies is 3 to 4 feet (91.4–121.9 cm); how-

Figure 28. *Dorsal view of mud snake head, with small eyes and head no wider than neck.*

ever, Guidry (1953) reported a record specimen from southeastern Texas that measured 6 feet 2 inches (188 cm) long.

HABITAT This semiaquatic snake is most likely to be found in or near still or slow-moving bodies of water with muddy bottoms and an abundance of aquatic and shoreline vegetation, usually in the vicinity of open woodland. Its favorite haunts are wooded swamplands littered with rotting logs, but it also frequents mud- or sand-bottomed lakes, ponds, marshes, sloughs, ditches, and sluggish streams, particularly those surrounded by muddy lowlands. It is also known to inhabit brackish marshes and tidal streams.

BEHAVIOR Few large serpents are as inoffensive as this one; in fact, a mud snake never attempts to bite when handled, despite the potential of its powerful jaws to inflict a painful injury. If lifted off the ground, the reptile is likely to become completely limp or to twist feebly in an attempt to escape one's grasp. Despite its docile nature, this creature has long been one of the most feared inhabitants of southern swamps. Its evil reputation derives from two persistent myths, one of which is based entirely on circumstantial evidence. It stems from the snake's unorthodox defensive behavior, in which a seized specimen wraps the rear part of its body around the captor's hand or arm, then presses its stiff, pointed, and presumably venomous tail spine firmly against the assailant's skin. The unexpected pressure of the hard spine against bare, tender skin is usually enough to unnerve even the boldest handler, whereupon the snake is ordinarily released, its bluff having succeeded. Far from being a venomous stinger, the mud snake's rigid tail tip is merely a probing tool used by the serpent primarily to help control the movements of its struggling prey. The second and more fearsome of the two myths attributes to the mud snake the astonishing ability to form a hoop of its body by placing its tail in its mouth, then rolling swiftly downhill in pursuit of its fleeing victim. When the reptile finally overtakes its quarry, it makes a remarkable postural adjustment. Without ever slowing its forward momentum, it abruptly straightens its trunk so that it assumes the shape of a javelin with its venomous tail spine pointing

forward. In an instant the hurtling snake drives home its deadly tail stinger, and in a matter of seconds the unfortunate victim is dead. Clearly both stories are without substance, and they persist today merely as interesting examples of early American folklore. The truth is that the mud snake can neither roll like a hoop nor inject venom with its tail or any other part of its body.

What is no myth is the snake's remarkable flash display, a real-life behavior meant to startle an adversary into temporary inaction or retreat. It is not unusual for a mud snake under attack to hide its head beneath one of its body loops, and at the same time raise its tail in a spiral coil with the colorful underside turned upward—an unexpected and unsettling turn of events. To suddenly see the reptile's brilliant crimson and black ventral coloration, where just a moment before there was only a somber-hued serpent, leaves the observer startled and perhaps even bewildered. Sometimes further prodding of an already annoyed mud snake causes it to turn over onto its back and flatten the rear part of its body so as to expose its red and black underside fully, enhancing the effectiveness of the display. Such behavior is more apt to be practiced by very young snakes than by adults.

Seldom found far from water, except when it moves about on the surface after rains, this semiaquatic species is also partial to muddy ditches. Otherwise, it is likely to be discovered beneath soggy, decaying logs scattered throughout moist bottomlands or under logs partly submerged in water. It is also known to take refuge in plant debris lying in shallow water and in mats of wet vegetation on shore. When not engaged in aboveground activity, it is believed to spend most of its time buried in the mud, for in such soft substrate it is an accomplished burrower.

The snake's annual active season in Texas normally extends from March into October, although in the absence of harsh winter weather it may be found under logs as early in the year as late February or as late as November. During this period, the mud snake is chiefly night-active; its infrequent aboveground forays are often associated with nocturnal rains, when it is likely to be encountered on roads running through or adjacent to wet areas. With the advent of cool fall weather, it seeks shelter in loose soil, pine stumps, rotting logs, or animal burrows.

FEEDING The snake's favorite prey consists of aquatic eellike salamanders called amphiumas, whose slippery bodies, once seized, are difficult to control and to maneuver for swallowing. It is for such occasions that the mud snake may bring its tail spine into play. Evidence suggests that by probing the salamander's soft, sensitive skin with its hard, sharp tail tip, the snake forces its struggling prey to make postural adjustments that facilitate ingestion. Enlarged teeth in the back of each upper jaw apparently also help the reptile hold its slippery quarry. Besides amphiumas, this species eats sirens and other kinds of salamanders, frogs, fish, and tadpoles. Neill (1951) stated that mud snakes living in or near brackish water may feed entirely on fish, including saltwater kinds. He cited as examples two Georgia specimens, one of which was seen dragging a flatfish (probably a flounder) across the road and another with a large mulletlike fish in its mouth.

Judging from eyewitness accounts of feeding episodes, encounters between mud snakes and their sizable amphiuma prey are usually violent confrontations that test the fitness of both participants. George P. Meade (1934), one of Louisiana's pioneer naturalists, described an occasion in which a captive 5½-foot (167.6 cm) long snake with a 2-inch (5.1 cm) body diameter attacked a 25-inch (63.5 cm) long amphiuma of similar girth. Placed in a water dish within the serpent's cage, the amphibian was detected immediately and promptly seized near its hind legs. The ensuing struggle was so violent that it thrust both animals out of the container and onto the ground, where the conflict continued with unabated intensity. Although the amphiuma bit the snake time and again, both on its head and body, the tenacious reptile never released its firm grip, despite efforts by several onlookers to prod and move the combatants for better photo opportunities. Not until the victim was finally subdued and well on the way to being swallowed, more than an hour and a quarter after the struggle began, did the defiant salamander end its biting attempts. What most im-

pressed Meade was the startling contrast between the mud snake's ordinarily timid and lethargic nature and the savage, unrelenting behavior it demonstrated during this and several other feeding engagements with amphiumas. Further evidence of the reptile's vicious feeding response was noted by Rossman (in Dundee and Rossman 1989), who watched a captive mud snake constrict a siren in the water, then inflict deep gashes along the length of the salamander's back with constant, vigorous chewing motions.

REPRODUCTION Little is known about the snake's mating behavior beyond the occurrence of copulation in spring and summer. During July or August, the female lays 6 to 104 eggs per clutch in some moist location, usually within or beneath rotting logs or in dirt mounds, piles of decaying vegetation, or animal burrows. Each egg measures about 1½ inches (3.8 cm) long.

A more unusual nest site was recently described by Hall and Meier (1993), who discovered four clutches of western mud snake eggs in alligator nest mounds at Lacassine National Wildlife Refuge in southwestern Louisiana. Each of two mounds examined by the zoologists contained two separate clutches of snake eggs. Constructed of maiden cane along the edge of a large, shallow marsh, each mound was about 5½ feet (167.6 cm) in diameter at the base and approximately 10 to 20 inches (25.4–50.8 cm) high at the center. One was an active nest that held 33 alligator eggs, prompting Hall and Meier to suggest that such a mound, actively guarded against predators by the resident female crocodilian, might afford the snake eggs a degree of protection not otherwise available. That may be true, but it is also conceivable that upon hatching, the infant snakes would become an easy source of prey for the adult alligator, for serpents are an important part of its diet.

It also seems likely that the egg-laying female mud snake would be at risk from alligator predation, since she usually remains with her eggs during their incubation (mud snakes are one of the few serpent species worldwide to do so). She normally remains inconspicuous within the mound during the 60 to 80 days it takes the eggs to hatch, leaving the nest site only briefly to eat, defecate, or shed her skin. Just what benefit the developing eggs may derive from her presence is not clear. Some believe she coils about her eggs to protect them from predators, yet among the handful of zoologists who have observed such nest sites in the wild or in captivity, none has reported any active behavior on the part of the female to defend her nest, either by striking, biting, or displaying her colorful red and black undertail as a warning. For example, one of the specimens Hall and Meier found tightly coiled around a clutch of eggs merely hid her head from view when the nest was uncovered, then escaped through

the bottom of the nest material as the eggs were being examined. There is also no evidence to suggest that the female raises her body temperature above that of the immediate surroundings to increase the temperature of the incubating eggs, the way some brooding pythons do by inducing periodic body contractions. The reason for this nesting behavior, therefore, is still not apparent. When the eggs finally hatch, usually sometime between mid-August and October, the infant snakes are 7 to 9 inches (17.8–22.9 cm) long.

MEXICAN HOOK-NOSED SNAKE
Ficimia streckeri
PLATE 47

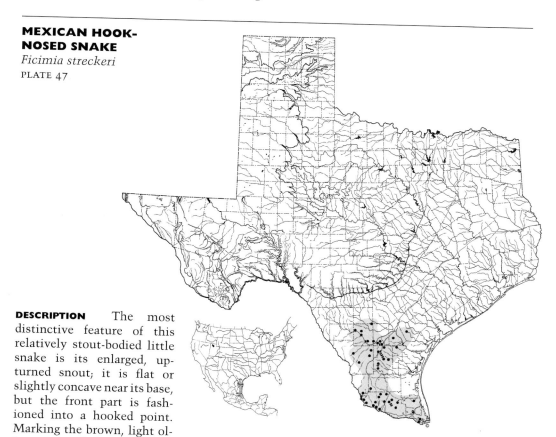

DESCRIPTION The most distinctive feature of this relatively stout-bodied little snake is its enlarged, upturned snout; it is flat or slightly concave near its base, but the front part is fashioned into a hooked point. Marking the brown, light olive, or grayish dorsal color is a row of narrow, dark brown crossbars, each of which reaches down along the sides of the body to about the second row of scales above the belly, where the dorsal color fades to a paler hue. In some specimens these markings are reduced to large spots, and in others they are obscured by a darkening of the snake's ground color. In addition, most specimens display one or more

lengthwise rows of small, irregular dark spots low on each side of the body along the edge of the pale lateral hue. Some of the spots are aligned directly under the ends of the crossbars; others occur between them.

The snake's head and neck are the same width. The crown, usually unpatterned, is generally a bit darker than the dorsal body coloration, and on the upper lip scales beneath and behind each eye there is often an indistinct dark brown spot. Like the belly, the lower lip scales and throat are immaculate white or pale yellow. In the absence of internasal scales, the rostral plate makes direct contact with the frontal scale. There are 17 rows of smooth dorsal scales at midbody, and the anal plate is divided.

COMPARABLE SNAKES The strongly keeled dorsal scales of hog-nosed snakes occur in 23 or 25 midbody rows, and the upturned rostral plate bears a lengthwise keel down its center.

SIZE Although most adult hook-nosed snakes are between 7 and 11 inches (17.8–27.9 cm) long, the greatest length reported for this species is 19 inches (48.3 cm).

HABITAT Chiefly an inhabitant of the South Texas thornbrush woodland, this burrowing serpent also occurs in the floodplain of the lower Rio Grande Valley. Low in elevation, covered mostly with tight gravelly soil, and generally dominated by endless thickets of mesquite and prickly pear cactus, the region contains relatively few natural bodies of standing water, though man-made tanks, ponds, and resacas are common. It is near such sources of moisture that the Mexican hook-nosed snake is most likely to be encountered. During the spring and summer of 1935, Mulaik and Mulaik (1943) found this ordinarily secretive species in greatest numbers in the vicinity of Edinburg, stranded in concrete irrigation canals from which the snakes apparently had been unable to escape. Axtell (1969) states that this species prefers tight alluvial and even stony soils, avoiding the sizable areas of dune sands and sandy loam that occur in Kenedy, Brooks, east Jim Hogg, and north Willacy and Hidalgo counties. Similar kinds of sandy barriers in La Salle and Dimmit counties, he believes, may effectively limit the snake's spread any farther northwest.

BEHAVIOR Except to burrow quickly into the gravelly soil when threatened, this peaceful, slow-moving reptile has no real defense against a large enemy. It does not bite humans, nor does it challenge an adversary in any combative way. Unlike hog-nosed snakes, which attempt to frighten their foe through bluff and intimidation (hissing, spreading the forebody into a wide hood, and often striking aimlessly), the hook-nosed

snake responds to harassment in its own strange way. It twitches and writhes its body about in an alarming display as it alternately extends and retracts the lining of its cloacal opening, producing a popping sound that can be heard several feet away.

Mexican hook-nosed snakes spend most of their lives underground, except when numbers of these little snakes come to the surface after drenching spring or summer rains, or when they are lured above ground by the watering of lower Rio Grande Valley lawns and gardens. Those discovered above ground are usually encountered at night.

The hook-nosed snake's rigid, upturned, pointed snout, together with its thickset, well-muscled body, clearly equip this species for a burrowing existence. Rooting its way into the gravelly soil with strong, abbreviated side-to-side and rocking head motions, it quickly disappears below the surface, where it is usually safe from predators. For such a small snake, these head thrusts are remarkably strong, enabling it to squeeze through exceptionally small spaces. More than once has a Mexican hook-nosed snake escaped from a collector's bag by thrusting its head forcefully through the overhand knot tied at the open end.

FEEDING This snake preys chiefly on spiders and is also known to eat centipedes. Beyond that, little is recorded about its natural diet or how it catches and subdues its quarry. One captive specimen is said to have consumed cave crickets.

REPRODUCTION Since the only reference to this species' breeding habits is that it lays eggs, the following information may fill in some of the missing details about its reproductive biology. A female collected in Harlingen by Maurice J. Fox III (pers. com.) deposited 5 eggs sometime during March or April. According to Fox, they were probably laid in March, although a photograph he took of the clutch is stamped with the date "April, 1954." The eggs could have been laid in either month, of course, depending on how soon after deposition the photo was taken. Although no measurements were made of the eggs, judging from a tape measure shown in the photograph, each appears to have been about 3/4 inch (1.9 cm) long.

WESTERN HOOK-NOSED SNAKE

Gyalopion canum
PLATE 48

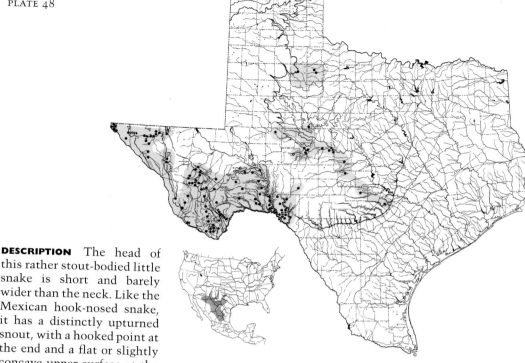

DESCRIPTION The head of this rather stout-bodied little snake is short and barely wider than the neck. Like the Mexican hook-nosed snake, it has a distinctly upturned snout, with a hooked point at the end and a flat or slightly concave upper surface at the base. The snake's overall color, which can vary from pale yellow to pinkish brown, is usually pale brown to gray-brown and marked with 25 or more jagged, distinctly black-edged darker dorsal crossbands. These markings become progressively narrower as they approach the belly and may even break up into small spots low on the sides of the body. Sometimes also present on or near the belly line is an irregular series of small dark spots or clusters of spots which alternate with the crossbands. The unmarked abdomen is white or cream.

The most prominent markings are on top of the head, where a dark brown bar crosses the snout between the eyes, followed by another dark bar, sometimes interrupted medially, that crosses the crown behind the first one. Following the last marking is a large, lengthwise nape blotch colored like the body crossbands; on either side of the head, a large dark brown spot occupies the upper lip scales just below the eye. There are two internasals, and the rostral plate makes contact with the pre-frontal scales. The dorsal scales are smooth and in 17 midbody rows. The anal plate is divided.

COMPARABLE SNAKES Hog-nosed snakes have strongly keeled dorsal scales in 23 or 25 midbody rows; they are patterned with large, dark body blotches; and their oversized, upturned rostral plates have a lengthwise keel down the center.

SIZE Although the record length for this species stands at 15⅙ inches (38.5 cm), adults are generally between 7 and 11 inches (17.8–27.9 cm) long.

HABITAT Essentially an inhabitant of the Chihuahuan Desert, the western hook-nosed

Figure 29. *Moderately upturned snout of western hook-nosed snake. (After Stebbins 1985.)*

snake ranges northward from Mexico into Trans-Pecos Texas and the central and western parts of the Edwards Plateau, with a few isolated records from as far north as the southern Panhandle counties of Dickens, King, and Scurry. A single Wise County record from the western Cross Timbers is questionable and requires further confirmation. In Texas it has typically been found in plant associations of mesquite, mesquite-creosote, creosote-agave, persimmon–shin oak, oak-juniper, and the pinyon-juniper woodland of Big Bend National Park. In the prairie grasslands of the southern Panhandle, where this species reaches the northernmost limit of its distribution in the state, Ferguson (1965) described the topography as normally flat to rolling, with some gypsum and limestone outcroppings. In addition to various grasses, the vegetation consisted of mesquite, often interspersed with lotebush, and juniper.

BEHAVIOR Small and inoffensive, the snake's first line of defense against a predator is to remain still, for it is neither fast enough to outdistance its enemy nor large enough to engage its foe in combat. If touched or otherwise provoked, its strategy is to confront the enemy with an unexpected and bizarre behavior, one that may tend to startle and distract the interloper just long enough for the serpent to make an escape. The charade begins with convulsive writhing and flopping, so vigorous that the snake appears to be in torment. As the snake continues its violent twisting, it rapidly extends and retracts the lining of its cloacal opening, each cycle creating a popping or bubbling noise that, coming from such a small creature, might very well have a sobering effect on its foe.

Rarely seen wandering above ground in daylight, the western hook-nosed snake is a burrowing species that spends nearly all of its time below ground, under rocks, in the crevices of boulders, or beneath the remains of dead cacti and succulents. It emerges at night, usually after the ground has been dampened by rain. So secretive is the western hook-nosed snake that from the time it was first described as a new species, in 1860, until 1960, a hundred years later, only 24 specimens had been mentioned in published reports, despite intensive collecting efforts in parts of its range. Then it was considered one of North America's rarest snakes. With the

advent of new collecting techniques, particularly night cruising along desert roads by automobile, the western hook-nosed snake was turning up with ever greater frequency. Today it is no longer regarded as rare, though the chances of finding a specimen on any given field trip can be compared to the likelihood that a nonprofessional golfer will hit a hole in one. The time to look for it is from April to September, its annual active season.

The snake's muscular, smooth-scaled body and its modified, upturned snout are adaptations for burrowing, tools it uses effectively to dig through loose rocky or gravelly soil. It employs the same kind of forceful head thrusts when picked up. Jabbing its nose between a captor's fingers in an apparent effort to lever its way out of sight, it rocks its head firmly from side to side, creating an unnerving sensation that can easily be misconstrued as biting. This can often gain the snake its prompt release.

FEEDING Living in underground burrows and in shallow depressions beneath stones and other surface objects is an array of small invertebrates on which the western hook-nosed snake feeds. Among them are spiders, believed to be the snake's chief prey, as well as scorpions and centipedes. To reach its quarry in such hidden places, the little hook-nosed snake depends on its digging capabilities, using its modified snout and well-muscled body to thrust its way underground and through debris.

In one instance, which may represent an anomaly, a captive western hook-nosed snake ate a dead ring-necked snake but was itself found dead three days later. Its death was suspected to have been caused by its having consumed a meal too large for its size or perhaps by the effects of the prey's toxic saliva, which is known to inhibit the actions of the small vertebrates on which it feeds.

REPRODUCTION Like so much else about the natural behavior of the western hook-nosed snake, we know almost nothing concerning its reproductive biology. The only report lists a single egg, about 1⅛ inches (2.9 cm) long, laid on July 1, 1970, by a captive female from Big Bend National Park. Since the egg failed to hatch, we are left to speculate about the period of egg incubation and the size of the hatchlings.

PLAINS HOG-NOSED SNAKE

Heterodon nasicus nasicus
PLATES 49, 50

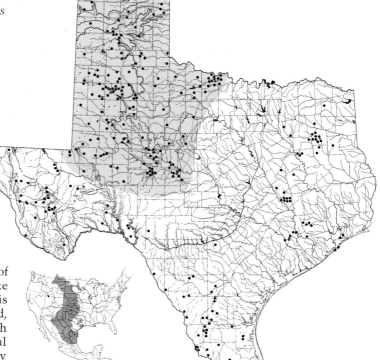

DESCRIPTION Three races of the western hog-nosed snake are recognized, and this is one. All are medium-sized, heavy-bodied serpents with 23 rows of keeled dorsal scales at midbody, a sharply upturned snout bearing a lengthwise keel on top, and large areas of coal-black pigment on the belly and underside of the tail that are irregularly margined with white, yellow, or pale orange. The snake's overall dorsal ground color, which varies in individual specimens from pale brown to brownish gray or reddish brown, is patterned with a row of sharply contrasting dark blotches ranging from grayish brown or olive to deep cinnamon or chocolate brown. The blotches are sometimes edged in black, especially along the front and back. Counted from the neck to a point above the anal scale, they number more than 35 in males and more than 40 in females. One to three rows of smaller dark spots occur below the primary series, each spot alternating with the one just above it.

The snake's pale-colored head is conspicuously marked with a white-edged, transverse, dark brown bar on the crown between the eyes; a wide, dark brown cheek mask that reaches obliquely downward from each eye to the end of the mouthline; and a large, V-shaped mark of the same color, whose apex lies on top of the head between the eyes and whose arms slant downward and backward to either side of the neck. In this subspecies, as in the dusty hog-nosed snake, the small scales on top of the head just behind the large nose scale number 9 or more. The anal plate is divided.

COMPARABLE SNAKES The larger eastern hog-nosed snake resembles the western species in its heavy build and general head configuration but differs in its less sharply upturned snout and uniformly pale-colored tail undersurface. (See Dusty hog-nosed snake account and illustration.) The western hook-nosed snake, which looks like a miniature hognose, possesses a shallow depression on top of the head behind the snout instead of a lengthwise keel, and its body scales are smooth and in 17 rows at midbody. The massasauga also resembles the western hog-nosed snake, but it lacks the upturned snout, has a pale-colored undertail, and a rattle.

SIZE The usual adult length for this subspecies is 16 inches to 2 feet (40.6–61 cm). A record specimen from Hale County measured 35½ inches (90.2 cm) long.

HABITAT The snake's preferred habitat in Texas is the shortgrass or mixed-grass prairie of the arid High Plains, where the ground cover is sparse and gravelly or sandy soils provide good surface drainage and a loose substrate into which the snake can easily burrow. In such an environment it is encountered chiefly in the vicinity of sandy hills, sand dunes, sandy prairies, and river floodplains. Like the eastern hog-nosed snake, it is most abundant in areas of sandy wilderness that have been disturbed by man, though it carefully avoids zones of intensive cultivation. In Hutchinson County, Fouquette and Lindsay (1955) frequently found it on the High Plains escarpment where the principal vegetation of the deep-sand habitat consisted of sage, sumac, and some grass cover; in the natural drainage systems buffalograss, goat weed, and scattered stands of mesquite replaced the sage.

Because the snake occurs in a number of isolated populations outside its known continuous range, the boundaries of its geographic distribution have not been clearly defined. To the east its range apparently is limited by the increasing plant density of the tallgrass prairie and deciduous woodland or by the more compact soil associated with such habitats. Either or both circumstances, it is believed, may in some way inhibit the snake from meeting its basic biological needs.

BEHAVIOR When first threatened, the plains hog-nosed snake, like the eastern hog-nosed snake, will often become immobile if it is on the move. If it decides to crawl away, it usually continues the escape effort for a longer time than the eastern hog-nosed snake before initiating the next phase of its defensive behavior, which is simply to hide its head beneath a coil of its body while curling the tail into a tight spiral and hissing loudly. It is less likely than its eastern cousins to spread its head, neck, and forebody. If the neck is spread at all, it is not done with the flair typical of the eastern species.

A thoroughly provoked specimen may lunge at its foe, usually with the mouth closed but sometimes with the jaws agape, though not with the intention of biting. If the bluff fails to deter its antagonist, and particularly if it is then touched, the snake may suddenly twist and turn, contorting its body

as though dying. The movements gradually increase until the snake finally turns belly up, its body now limp as if dead. Several other elements of this charade make the display even more convincing: the tongue hanging lifelessly from the snake's open mouth, the discharge of feces from the reptile's cloaca, and sometimes even the presence of blood in its mouth. The snake maintains this apparent moribund posture for several minutes or until it believes the danger is gone, at which time it slowly rights itself and nonchalantly crawls away.

One obvious flaw mars this otherwise convincing performance. If, as the reptile rests motionless on its back, it is turned right side up, it instantly flips over again. In fact, the snake will repeat this bottom-up response as often as it is rotated onto its abdomen. Since dead snakes do not make such body-posture adjustments, the hog-nosed snake's ruse is clearly revealed. Although in the usual sequence of events the neck-spreading threat display precedes death feigning, the western hog-nosed snake sometimes plays dead immediately following its initial escape effort, completely omitting the neck-spreading behavior. In captivity, most hog-nosed snakes, eastern and western alike, soon discontinue both such responses.

Like its eastern cousin, this snake is active mostly in the morning and again late in the afternoon, finding shelter at night and during cool weather by burrowing into the sandy soil or by hiding in an animal burrow; seldom does it take cover under surface objects such as logs, boards, or stones.

Although all hog-nosed snakes are accomplished burrowers, this species is better adapted for digging than its eastern relatives. Its enlarged nose scale has more of a flare along the sides, creating a thin, bladelike cutting edge that more easily penetrates the soil than does the rostral of the eastern species, and its longer, more upcurved snout forms a better scooping surface for loosening and moving sand. Other anatomical features suggesting a greater specialization for burrowing include a relatively heavier body and a shorter head and tail. For digging, the hog-nosed snake prefers fine sand to loam or coarse sand, but where such fine-textured substrate has become too dry for easy penetration, the snake may burrow into the loose substrate at the base of an anthill to reach the moist soil underneath.

Since the habits of the western hog-nosed snake presumably do not vary greatly among its three subspecies, see also the behavior section for the dusty hog-nosed snake.

FEEDING Although 35 to 50 percent of its diet consists of amphibians (mostly toads and frogs), this snake also consumes reptiles and their eggs, some mammals, and a few birds. One of the more unusual foods of the plains hog-nosed snake in a particular Nebraska locale, according to Iverson (1990), were the eggs of the yellow mud turtle, which the snakes pillaged during the turtle's nesting season. In central Kansas, Platt (1969) found that small snakes of this species ate a greater percentage of prairie lizards and their eggs than did larger specimens, but they consumed no young birds or other small serpent species, items sometimes eaten by the adults.

Like the eastern hog-nosed snake, this species locates prey through its well-developed sense of smell, often tracking the odor of an amphibian or lizard to its refuge beneath sand or loose soil. Once prey is located, the snake soon digs its victim from its underground shelter, a task for which it is remarkably well adapted. In one instance, a western hog-nosed snake was observed as it burrowed through loose soil, its body thrust into a depression containing several tiger salamanders, one of which it held resolutely in its mouth as it was pulled tail-first from the hole. Reptile eggs, also detected by their scent, are located soon after being deposited in the ground and while the odor of the female is still fresh enough to serve as a location marker.

Although the hog-nosed snake does not subdue or kill its prey by constriction, it may control a larger struggling victim by pressing it firmly against the ground with a single loop of its body as it holds the animal tightly in its jaws. The serpent's enlarged rear teeth serve as skewers that not only assist in holding the prey but also aid in its manipulation for swallowing. An additional adaptation—one without which it would be unable to consume toads—is the snake's enlarged adrenal glands, which render harmless the anuran's toxic digitaloid skin-gland secretions. Snakes without such physiological protection suffer severe systemic damage or death after eating large toads.

REPRODUCTION Since hog-nosed snakes hibernate singly, the males probably travel considerable distances after spring emergence to find females that have spent the winter, like themselves, in scattered, solitary locations. Some matings occur in the fall, however, with viable sperm retained in the female's oviducts until the next spring. There is also evidence to suggest that in some parts of the snake's range, the female breeds only in alternate years.

Sometime between early June and mid-July, the female lays a clutch of 4 to 23 (average 9 or 10) elliptical eggs with white, paper-thin shells, each about 1½ inches (3.8 cm) long, usually burying them a few inches deep in sandy or loamy soil. They hatch 52 to 64 days later, the young measuring 6 to 7¾ inches (15.2–19.7 cm) long. By the time they are 21 months old, some of the males have already reached sexual maturity, although the females usually do not attain breeding age until they are more than two years old.

DUSTY HOG-NOSED SNAKE
Heterodon nasicus gloydi
PLATE 51

DESCRIPTION In body form and scalation this subspecies of the western hog-nosed snake is identical to the closely related plains hog-nosed snake, differing from it in having fewer dorsal body blotches. It possesses fewer than 32 dark blotches down the middle of the

back in males (not counting those on the tail) and fewer than 37 in females. In common with the plains and Mexican subspecies, it displays a sharply upturned snout bearing a longitudinal keel on its upper surface, prominent black blotching on the underside of the

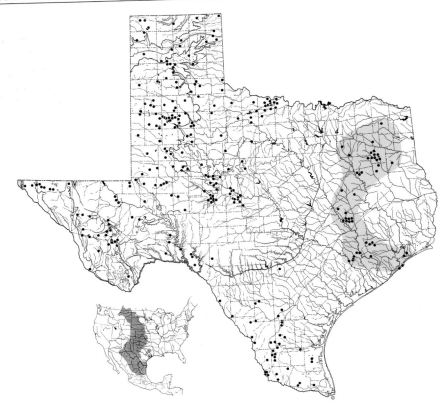

body and tail, keeled dorsal scales in 23 rows at midbody, and a divided anal plate.

COMPARABLE SNAKES The eastern hog-nosed snake is similar to the dusty hognose in body shape and general head configuration, but it has a less upturned snout and lacks bold, dark markings on the underside of its tail. The slightly upturned snout of the little western hook-nosed snake, though resembling the prominently raised rostral of a hognose, bears no longitudinal keel on its upper surface, nor is the underside of its tail pigmented with well-defined black blotches. Moreover, the hook-nosed snake has only 17 rows of midbody dorsal scales, none of which is keeled. The venomous massasauga, also relatively stout-bodied, has a narrow neck, pits between the eyes and nostrils, elliptical eye pupils, and rattles on the end of its tail.

SIZE Mature adults generally measure 15 to 25 inches (38.1–63.5 cm) long; maximum-size specimens reach a length of nearly 3 feet (91.4 cm).

HABITAT Like all subspecies of the western hognose, this one occupies relatively dry, sandy grassland, although where streams, irrigation ditches, and other bodies of water are present, it will often be encountered near their banks. Broadly distributed in Texas, often in isolated local populations, it is nevertheless rare or absent in the Blackland and Fayette prairies, the Cross Timbers, the Edwards Plateau, and the oak-hickory-pine forests of extreme eastern Texas. In cordgrass prairies and marshlands near the Gulf, where it is also scarce, the dusty hognose is recorded along the coast as far north as Chambers County.

BEHAVIOR Because the habits of the western hog-nosed snake presumably do not vary greatly, if at all, among its three subspecies, only the natural history of the dusty hog-nosed snake is discussed at any length. Field studies of this race, made by Kroll (1973) in south-central Texas and by Platt (1969) of intergrade populations between the plains and dusty subspecies in south-central Kansas, provide much detailed information about the dusty hog-nosed snake's life history and form the basis for the following synopsis.

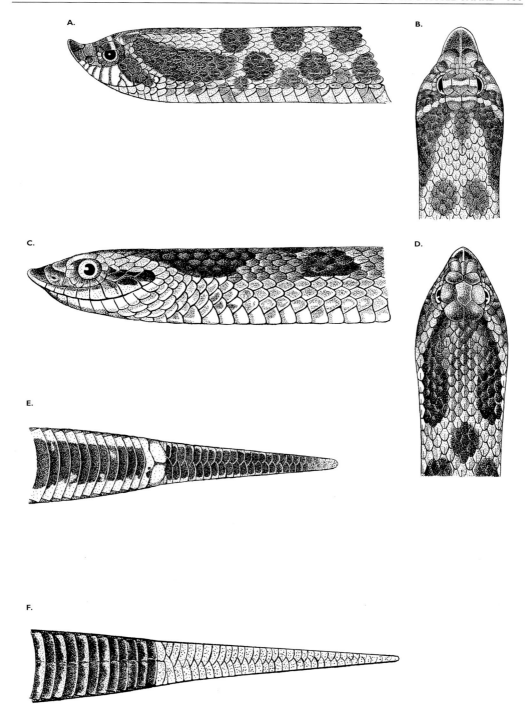

Figure 30. *Lateral and dorsal head views of native hog-nosed snakes: (a and b) the more pronounced nose scale of the western species compared to that of (c and d) the eastern species. Undertail views of (e) the black-marked western species and (f) the almost patternless eastern species.*

Though it may at first do its best to escape an antagonist, this chunky, slow-moving reptile lacks the speed and agility of the larger, more slender serpents to glide quickly out of harm's way. If its getaway is blocked, the hog-nosed snake may use another strategy to avoid immediate danger. It tries to startle and even frighten away a naive trespasser by expanding its body with air, while spreading and greatly flattening its head, neck, and part of its forebody. Following those preliminaries, it often hisses loudly and may even deliver mock strikes in a further attempt to demoralize the opponent. Such strikes are usually made with the mouth tightly closed, however, for its teeth are not used defensively. The entire performance, it turns out, is simply a bluff.

Should this frightful display fail to deter the interloper, or if the snake is then touched, it often responds with yet another elaborate masquerade; this time the idea is to play dead, convincingly enough to discourage any further interest by the curious observer. Anyone who has ever seen a hog-nosed snake in the act of simulating a dying serpent will agree that it is remarkably realistic. See also the behavior section for the plains hog-nosed snake.

What makes the dramatic demonstration even more convincing is the way some dusty hog-nosed snakes by accident bite themselves during the aimless, erratic writhing that is part of their death-feigning display. In some instances, such self-inflicted wounds, imposed by the serpent's enlarged rear teeth, have left permanent scars; one specimen bit itself critically enough to cause its own death. This curious phenomenon has been observed only in a certain Brazos County, Texas, population of the western hog-nosed snake; it has not been reported for the eastern hog-nosed snake. It may thus represent a previously unnoticed behavior of this species, or it may simply be an aberrant behavior of the local population.

Despite the elaborate sham, the western hog-nosed snake is inoffensive. Under certain unusual circumstances it has inflicted bites on humans. One such incident occurred when Kroll handled a recently captured dusty hog-nosed snake, though in this case, the snake apparently had no intention of inflicting an offensive bite on its captor. In Kroll's

view, it had simply engaged one of its rear, fanglike teeth unwittingly as it performed its vigorous death-feigning ritual. The immediate result was a sharp pain at the site of the bite (middle finger, left hand), like a needle prick. Five minutes later the pain became more severe; Kroll described it as akin to that produced by a wasp sting or ant bite. One hour after the bite, his whole finger was slightly swollen and tender to the touch, and he felt a dull ache in his left elbow near the radial nerve. Although the swelling was gone before the end of the day, the bitten area was still tender two days later; otherwise the victim suffered no serious or lasting consequences. Morris (1985), another zoologist, experienced similar local reactions after having been bitten by a western hog-nosed snake, as did Bragg (1960), whose thumb the snake tried to swallow as the reptile was being examined. Since the victim had handled frogs not long before the bizarre event took place, the confused snake evidently was merely executing a feeding reaction in response to the scent of prey.

The pain and swelling described above, however minor, are not just the result of puncture wounds inflicted by the snake's enlarged rear teeth. They come from the snake's toxic saliva. There is now sufficient evidence, based on such cases, to show that under some circumstances, snakes of the genus *Heterodon* (at least the western species) can cause mild envenomation in humans. The snake's weak toxins, produced in modified salivary glands, are used to immobilize small vertebrate animals, though in man they cause only the unpleasant but relatively trivial symptoms mentioned earlier.

For the most part, the length of the snake's annual active season depends on where the serpent lives. In Kansas, for example, Platt found that the dusty hognose's aboveground movements began as early in the year as April 24 (average date, May 9), after the ground temperature had reached 60 degrees F for several consecutive days. The last capture date was October 31 (average date, October 18). At warmer latitudes the same snake leaves hibernation earlier in the year and returns to its winter den later, resulting in a longer active annual season. This is confirmed by Kroll, whose earliest capture date for a dusty hognose in south-central Texas was March 25, a month before the first emergence of Kansas specimens. He saw the last one above ground on October 23.

Studying specimens in an outdoor enclosure, he found that from March through May, and again in September and October, the snake's aboveground activity occurred between 9 AM and as late as 6 PM; in summer (June through August) it avoided uncomfortably high midday temperatures (above 95 degrees F) by prowling on the surface between 5:10 AM and 10:15 AM and again between 6:30 PM and 11:50 PM. In Kansas, Platt (who also used an outdoor enclosure to observe captive hog-nosed snakes) never saw one out after dark. According to Kroll, once out of hibernation, free-roaming hog-nosed snakes remained in their grassland habitat through spring, engaging in movements that averaged approximately 530 feet per journey. Curiously, during these excursions the snakes returned to their original release sites about once a month.

In addition to its typical prairie haunts, in south-central Texas the dusty hog-nosed snake also occupied adjacent deciduous forest. In such places the snakes spent the summer in the wooded areas and the spring and fall in the grasslands. The reason for this dichotomy, Kroll concluded, was that during the hot summer, when temperatures often exceeded 100 degrees F, the cooler woodland environment provided more prey in the form of ground-dwelling scaly lizards, and drinking water, usually available in the grasslands only as dew, was obtainable in the woodlands from more permanent water sources. Then in late August, with the approach of fall and an attendant increase in rainfall, the hog-nosed snake returned to the grasslands, where it remained until entering hibernation sometime in November.

The dusty hog-nosed snake, like all other races of the species, is seldom seen above ground after dark. Generally active during the day or at dusk, it passes the night in underground burrows it has dug itself or that have been excavated by other animals. Naturalists have discovered that it scoops out not just one but several different kinds of tunnel. For instance, to avoid severe temperature extremes and to evade predators, it digs shallow burrows, usually an inch or two deep, that serve as temporary underground shelters. Seldom does it hide beneath rocks, logs, or other surface debris. Deeper tunnels, generally 4 to 6 inches below the surface and terminating in a small chamber, are also excavated. Such tunnels, used either intermittently over a span of weeks or months or even continuously for weeks at a time, represent more permanent sanctuaries. Even deeper burrows are dug in the sand as protection against winter's freezing temperatures.

All hog-nosed snakes are good burrowers, but *H. nasicus* is a better excavator than its larger cousin, the eastern hog-nosed snake. Equipped with a more flared and sharply upturned snout and a superior skull morphology that increases the snake's mechanical advantage for digging, the western hog-nosed snake can bury itself rather quickly in loose sandy soil. It can disappear into a shallow burrow within two minutes, although to complete a deep tunnel may take an adult from five minutes to as long as half an hour. The snake's other burrowing adaptations include a short, barrel-shaped body that fits more easily into an abbreviated tunnel and strongly keeled body scales that when pressed against a burrow wall serve as cleats to provide a firm grip against the thrusting spadelike snout.

Describing the burrowing activity of the western hog-nosed snake, Platt says that as the process begins, the snake holds the long axis of its head approximately perpendicular to the ground. The sharp, bladelike edges of its snout then push forward and sideward, cutting into the loose sand, shoving it to either side and eventually away from the excavation site. As the hole becomes larger, the snake pushes some of the sand to the rear of the tunnel, where it is pressed firmly against the burrow wall, presumably to pack and thus strengthen it. To brace itself against its own strenuous pushing, the snake shoves loops of its body tightly against the completed portion of the tunnel wall and presses other body loops against the ground.

FEEDING *H. nasicus* consumes a wider selection of vertebrate prey than its larger eastern relative. As recently summarized by Ernst and Barbour (1989), a specific list of prey animals eaten by this species in the wild includes toads (genus *Bufo*), spadefoot toads, leopard frogs and their tadpoles, tiger salamanders, whiptail and race runner lizards, skinks and their eggs, scaly lizards, side-blotched lizards, collared lizards, garter snakes, snake eggs, mud turtles, turtle eggs, meadowlarks, grasshopper sparrows, eggs of ring-necked pheasants and quail, deer mice, white-footed mice, pocket mice, meadow mice, and voles.

Although both eastern and western hog-nosed snakes commonly devour toads, such amphibians are the principal choice of only the eastern species. It is significant in this regard that all hog-nosed snakes are specifically adapted to consume toads, whose skin glands (particulary those of the adults) produce toxic secretions that when ingested prove deadly to most serpents. This adaptation is explained in the eastern hog-nosed snake account.

Like other races of the western hog-nosed snake, the dusty subspecies dines nearly as much on reptiles and their eggs as on amphibians, with birds and small mammals making up the rest of the menu.

To test the soil surface for the odor of recent prey movement, a hog-nosed snake relies primarily on its prey-detection resources—the tongue and its affiliated Jacobson's organ. If, as the snake glides over the sandy landscape, it picks up the scent of a favorite food animal, the rate of its tongue flicking increases, and the serpent diligently follows the scent trail to its destination, usually a toad or lizard hidden in a rodent tunnel or buried just under the sand. It can detect such a trail at least two hours after it has been made. Once the victim is located, the snake's spadelike snout digs into the loose soil until the prey is uncovered, whereupon it is seized in the snake's powerful jaws.

Hog-nosed snakes locate prey by sight as well as by odor, attacking such animals whenever they can be caught unawares. One would think that these ordinarily slow-moving serpents are no match for a bounding frog or fast-gaited lizard. That is true for the eastern species of *Heterodon*, but it is not necessarily so for the western, whose keen eyesight and quick response to feeding stimuli make it better suited for detecting and overtaking fast-moving prey. It can also track lizards farther than its eastern counterpart, giving it a competitive advantage in areas lacking in amphibian prey. Indeed, Kroll found that

H. nasicus, whose diet includes a significant number of active lizard species, quickly spotted such lizards as they came within sight and immediately reacted to their movements by dashing with open mouth to intercept them. However prey is located, once captured it must usually be subdued before it can be swallowed. For the snake, this can be a problem. The struggles of some large frogs and toads frequently are so vigorous that an obstinate victim may escape from the snake's grip. Other animals, such as large lizards or small mammals, are capable of retaliating with their strong jaws and sharp teeth, often inflicting serious bodily injury on their captors, but hog-nosed snakes are equipped to cope with most such contingencies.

It has already been mentioned that the western hog-nosed snake can deliver a venomous bite. To do so, the snake is provided with both a mildly toxic saliva and an enlarged rear tooth, solid and ungrooved, on either side of its upper jaw. Buried in fleshy sheaths, these fanglike teeth rest nearly parallel to the long axis of the snake's head, their pointed ends directed backward. When readied for use, special articulations of the upper jaw bones rotate them downward to a 45-degree angle so their sharp points can penetrate the body or limb of the victim. Since the fangs are not tubular, there is no forceful injection of venom through them directly and deeply into the tissues, as happens in pit-viper bites. Rather, the snake's toxic secretions are forced from the enlarged upper salivary glands, through a fleshy duct, and into the fang sheath, where they diffuse, almost by chance, into the fang-inflicted perforations. These teeth also help to hold the victim securely as it struggles to escape.

The snake gives no quarter. It hangs on tenaciously, embedding its fangs repeatedly as it works to subdue its quarry with the stupefying effects of its salivary toxins. These toxins, it should be noted, ordinarily fail to kill a toad or lizard, nor do they quickly suppress the struggling prey. Although experiments on the toxicity of *H. nasicus* venom suggest that adult lizards of the kind normally devoured by this snake can be completely immobilized within an hour, prey is usually weakened enough by the venom to be swallowed sooner.

When the victim is sufficiently benumbed, the same rear teeth that first held the prey and aided the introduction of venom into its tissues now help to manipulate the quarry into position for swallowing. Together with the smaller conventional teeth that line the upper and lower jaw bones, they not only maneuver the prey into the snake's mouth, usually headfirst, but they also pull it into the snake's gullet, engaging first the teeth on one side of the jaw, then on the other. Ingestion is completed in five minutes or less for a toad or leopard frog of average size and about 20 minutes for a moderate-sized lizard.

It has long been speculated that these fang-like teeth also function as skewers to pierce and thus collapse the bodies of captured toads, whose lungs, greatly inflated during feeding encounters, make them difficult to swallow.

Kroll conducted some simple experiments to learn if hog-nosed snakes can, in fact, puncture the lungs of toads in the way it has so often been described. After provoking the amphibians to greatly inflate their lungs (a typical reaction when they are seized), he punctured them with a sharp needle, first along their backsides, then on their bellies, in each case measuring the depth of penetration necessary to deflate them. Comparing the fang lengths of western hog-nosed snakes with the needle lengths required to reach the toad's lungs, he concluded that this snake is incapable of deflating toads by dorsal penetration but that a large hog-nosed snake might successfully achieve such penetration if its fangs entered the prey through the abdomen.

In view of these observations, added to the fact that a hog-nosed snake almost invariably seizes and swallows its prey backside up, it must be concluded that the snake does not deflate toads in this way. But it can do so in another way. Using the considerable power of its muscular jaws, the snake can apply enough pressure on a captured toad to collapse its lungs. In one instance, which may represent an extreme case, a toad being swallowed sideways by one of these snakes was held so tightly in the serpent's jaws that one of the toad's lungs was forced out of its own mouth.

REPRODUCTION Male western hog-nosed snakes reach sexual maturity at about 21 months of age, females when they are more than two years old and just over 13½ inches (34.3 cm) long. Most females of this species, particulary those living at more northern latitudes, probably mate only once every two years, usually in the spring but occasionally also in autumn. Most of those observed by Platt in Harvey County, Kansas, mated sometime between May 13 and May 29 and laid their eggs from July 2 to July 23, although in other parts of the snake's range egg-laying may occur as early in the year as June 3 (South Texas) and as late as August 4 (Iowa). Deposited in sandy or loamy soil, the 1½-inch (3.8 cm) long oval eggs, covered with white, parchmentlike shells, vary from 4 to 23 per clutch, though the average is 9 or 10. They hatch 50 to 64 days later (in August or September), revealing miniature replicas of the adults 6 or 7 inches (15.2–17.8 cm) long. As in many snake species, in relation to body length, the head of the baby snake is larger than that of its parents.

MEXICAN HOG-NOSED SNAKE

Heterodon nasicus kennerlyi
PLATE 52

DESCRIPTION The Mexican hog-nosed snake is a heavy-bodied serpent of medium length, with a wide neck and a sharply turned-up snout bearing a longitudinal keel on its upper surface. Except for the 6 or fewer small scales on top of the head directly behind the upturned rostral (9 or more in other *H. nasicus*), there is little to distinguish it from its close kin. In common with the dusty hog-nosed snake, the Mexican subspecies possesses fewer than 32 dorsal blotches in males and fewer than 37 in females, counting from just behind the head to a point above the anal plate. These sometimes indistinct,

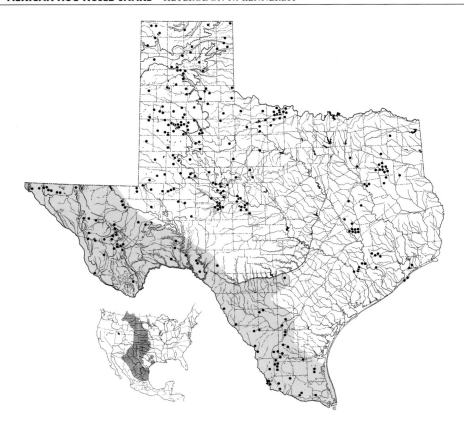

cinnamon-brown to dark brown markings, rounded or narrowly elongate, rest on a tan to yellowish background color.

Two alternating rows of smaller dark spots occur along each side of the body, the upper row usually more pronounced. As with all western hog-nosed snakes, the serpent's most distinctive color feature is the squarish black blotching on its bottom, especially under the tail, where the dark pigmentation is particularly bold. Like the other subspecies, its pale-hued head displays a dark, white-edged bar between the eyes; a large, dark V-shaped mark on the crown, with the apex between the eyes and the arms slanting backward onto either side of the neck; and a broad, dark mask that extends obliquely downward on either side of the head from the eye to the cheek. The dorsal scales are keeled and arranged in 23 rows at midbody. The anal plate is divided.

COMPARABLE SNAKES The eastern hog-nosed snake is the species most likely to be confused with *H. n. kennerlyi*, but it has a less sharply turned-up nose than its smaller counterpart, and the undersurface of its tail is uniformly pale, not boldly splotched with black. In both western and Mexican hook-nosed snakes, the snout, which is turned up only slightly, lacks a longitudinal keel on its upper surface. In addition, neither of these serpents displays conspicuous dark pigmentation under its tail, and each has but 17 rows of scales at midbody, none of which is keeled. The venomous massasauga, which bears some resemblance to the Mexican hog-nosed snake in build and coloration, is easily distinguished from its distantly related look-alike by its slender neck, heat-sensing pits between the eyes and nostrils, elliptical eye pupils, and the rattle at the end of its tail. In addition, it has neither an upturned snout nor a solid swath of black pigmentation down the center of its undertail.

SIZE The average adult length of this subspecies is between 15 and 25 inches (38.1–63.5 cm).

HABITAT Although most abundant in the mesquite grassland and thorn scrub environment of the lower Rio Grande Valley, this snake also occupies the sandy and gravelly prairies of Trans-Pecos Texas. In such habitats it can be found most frequently in the vicinity of floodplains, streams, and arroyos, where the loose, well-drained soil provides a substrate suitable for burrowing.

In Cochise County, Arizona, according to Fowlie (1965), the Mexican hog-nosed snake appears for a brief time along the edges of temporary bodies of water created when summer rains drench the parched ground; it may also appear under similar circumstances in the more arid parts of its West Texas range. It exists as well in desert scrub, dry mountain canyon basins, and open woodland associated with watercourses, not to mention areas disturbed by man. Even farmland in extremely arid country may offer the serpent an attractive habitat. This is indicated by Tanner (1985), who stated that a local farmer in western Chihuahua, Mexico, collected five of these snakes from a single cultivated field.

BEHAVIOR   See dusty hog-nosed snake account. Although natural history information about the Mexican hog-nosed snake is scarce, the serpent's behavior probably differs little from that of other *H. nasicus* subspecies.

When annoyed, members of the western hog-nosed snake subspecies are less likely than the eastern species to engage in neck-spreading. At such times, they may do no more than hide the head under their body coils, twist the tail into a compact spiral, and hiss noisily. If neither strategy succeeds, and the enemy approaches or actually nudges the snake, it is likely to feign death. See the plains hog-nosed snake account.

FEEDING   This snake dines mostly on toads, frogs, and lizards, which it usually locates through its well-developed sense of smell. It digs them out of the loose, sandy soil where

such animals are prone to hide. Other animals in its diet include frog tadpoles, salamanders, snakes, snake eggs, baby turtles, birds and their eggs, and small mammals. It is not unusual for it to eat the eggs of other reptiles, but Hammack (1991) is the first to report the ingestion by a hog-nosed snake of her own eggs. He described how a captive female of this subspecies twice devoured some of her recently laid eggs. See also the dusty hog-nosed snake account.

To test the snake's ability to detect the odor of its prey, Platt took sand from a toad cage and placed it in one holding a female western hog-nosed snake. Even as the sand was being poured, the snake detected the toad aroma and promptly increased her rate of tongue flicking as she sought to locate its source. Crawling eagerly about the cage, she explored the area around and under the newly introduced sand pile, seeking the quarry she knew from the familiar scent should be there. This crude experiment illustrates just how important the snake's sense of odor detection is for locating prey.

REPRODUCTION   Females of this species deposit 4 to 23 eggs per clutch several inches below the surface of the ground in loamy or sandy soil. The white, thin-shelled eggs measure about 1½ inches (3.8 cm) long. At hatching, 50 to 64 days later, the infants measure 6 to 7½ inches (15.2–19.1 cm) in length. Although little specific information about reproduction in this subspecies has been recorded, details of its breeding habits are probably like those for the other races. One actual report of egg-laying for *H. n. kennerlyi* is that of a female from Starr County, Texas, which laid 7 eggs on June 3 (Werler 1951), the earliest recorded date for oviposition in the species.

EASTERN HOG-NOSED SNAKE
Heterodon platirhinos
PLATES 53–62

DESCRIPTION   Since this moderately large species comes in a range of colors, it is most easily recognized by its head and body shape. Like other hog-nosed snakes, it has a stocky build, a broad head scarcely wider than its neck, an enlarged and pointed upturned

snout with a longitudinal keel on its upper surface, and keeled body scales.

The snake's overall color is commonly yellowish brown, but individual specimens can be various shades of yellow, orange, red, brown, olive, gray, or black. All-red speci-

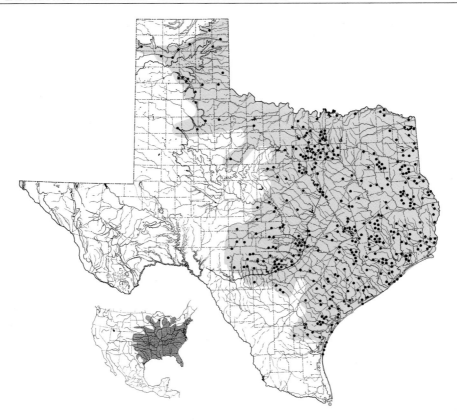

mens, for example, are sometimes found southeast of San Antonio and in southeastern Texas, and solid brown examples occur only rarely throughout the snake's range. Except for plain-colored specimens, the usual dorsal pattern consists of rather large, dark brown or black blotches or saddles typically separated from one another by interspaces of a lighter hue. On the tail's upper surface these markings become alternating light and dark half-rings; the tail's underside is nearly always lighter in color than the belly. A transverse dark bar crosses the snake's head between the eyes before slanting downward on either side of the face to the back of the mouthline. Farther back on the head a second dark bar, irregularly shaped and often segmented, parallels the first, sloping away to either side of the neck, where it ends in a large oval blotch. In the absence of such a bar, the conspicuous black or dark brown nuchal blotches stand alone. Either 23 or 25 rows of dorsal scales occur at midbody, and the anal plate is divided.

COMPARABLE SNAKES All subspecies of the western hog-nosed snake are predominantly black on the belly and underside of the tail, and they have a more sharply upturned snout. The snout of hook-nosed snakes is also slightly turned up, but instead of being dorsally keeled, it has a shallow depression behind it. The body scales of a hook-nosed snake are smooth, and the underside of its tail lacks bold, black pigmentation. Copperheads and juvenile cottonmouths, two other serpents likely to be confused with the eastern hog-nosed snake, possess clearly defined crossbands on the body and also have facial pits and elliptical eye pupils. The western pygmy rattlesnake, whose close resemblance to an eastern hog-nosed snake has been the reason for at least two human snake-bite accidents in Harris County alone, has a distinctly narrow neck, facial pits, 21 middorsal scale rows, an undivided anal plate, and a tiny rattle on the end of its tail. Furthermore, its snout is neither turned up nor pointed.

SIZE The usual adult length is between 20 and 33 inches (50.8–83.2 cm), but the largest known specimen measured 45½ inches (115.6 cm) long.

HABITAT This snake is most abundant in regions of well-drained, loose, or sandy soil for easy burrowing, where plant cover is sufficiently sparse to allow sunlight to bathe the ground and where adequate moisture guarantees a ready supply of amphibian prey. Consequently, it favors relatively open deciduous forest, sparsely wooded pine forest, and woodland edge, usually near streams, ponds, and lakes. Although it generally avoids dense, wet forest, staying more to the drier ridges and hillsides, around Beaumont and Port Arthur, according to Guidry (1953), it also inhabits moist bottomland. By following the major stream systems westward in Texas, it has managed to invade the arid grassland prairies of the state's High Plains, for it is along these ribbons of moisture that the largest concentrations of the snake's amphibian prey occur. As would be expected, the snake is not abundant in such areas of limited marginal habitat. Nor is it common on the Edwards Plateau, where scattered populations of this species occur only in locally suitable places within this essentially dry region. The species reaches the southern limit of its distribution in the mesquite-acacia savannah of the South Texas Coastal Plain, where increasing aridity confronts the snake with an unfavorable habitat. Similar environmental conditions restrict its westward movement as well.

BEHAVIOR Our understanding of this snake's natural history has been significantly improved by the excellent field studies of Platt (1969) and Kroll (1973), which have been freely used in the preparation of this account.

This shy, harmless serpent rarely attempts to bite, relying instead on an unusual three-phase defensive response to discourage its enemies. Since its crawling speed is inhibited by a cumbersome, thickset body, the snake is easily detected in its open habitat, making it vulnerable to a host of predators, including man. When suddenly confronted, it may first try to avoid detection by lying motionless, depending on its concealing markings to render it inconspicuous. If closely approached, it tries frantically to escape. If

further provoked at this stage, the snake may enter phase 2 of its predictable agenda. Assuming a threat posture that is thoroughly convincing to the uninitiated, it flattens its head and forebody, including the neck, which it spreads to nearly three times its usual width by elevating its long nuchal ribs. The spectacular display is fearsome. Even the skin between the now separated scale rows reveals startling new colors that further enhance the effectiveness of the threatening behavior. The entire body expands and contracts as the snake inhales and exhales deeply, producing a loud hiss with each breath. The head is often raised above the rest of the body, with the mouth either closed or wide open, or perhaps even tucked under one of the snake's body coils, while the short tail is often held in a tight spiral over the snake's head.

If this intimidating behavior fails to drive away its adversary, the snake adds another tactic to its masquerade, lunging repeatedly and with apparent fury at the object of its annoyance but, it should be noted, almost invariably with a closed mouth. The entire astonishing performance is strictly a bluff, meant to frighten away a predator or at least to discourage or postpone its attack. So ingrained is this practice in the snake's defensive repertoire that according to Minton (1972) even hatchlings not completely out of their eggshells engage in such behavior.

When these seemingly aggressive efforts fail, the hognose proceeds to the third stage of its antipredator routine, but usually only after it has been touched. Suddenly it twists and turns convulsively, often with the mouth held wide open, followed by the discharge of fecal material from its cloaca and a foul-scented fluid from musk glands at the base of its tail. If the snake has recently eaten, it will regurgitate its meal. In some cases, the mucous membrane around the snake's teeth bleeds, adding even more credibility to the pretended seizure. As the writhing slowly ends, the snake turns belly up and twitches a few times before becoming completely limp, its tongue drooping from the side of its partially open mouth, its breathing imperceptible. Now it lies perfectly still, as if dead.

Remaining in this simulated moribund position for as long as there is any nearby movement, the snake tries to outwait its foe, a game that in one case lasted 45 minutes. If picked up at this critical time, the hognose stoically maintains its lifeless demeanor, allowing itself to be jostled or even draped over a fence or tree limb, without ever moving a muscle, its entire body as limber as a piece of cotton rope. Should the snake be turned right side up, however, it immediately turns over again to assume the appropriate belly-up position. It will do so as often as it is righted, for it knows instinctively that to portray itself convincingly as a dead snake it must be seen on its back. Finally, when there is no further movement nearby and all seems secure, the reptile breathes normally again, the tongue is withdrawn, the mouth closed, the head cautiously righted and raised an inch or two, the tongue set in motion to test the surroundings, and the body turned right side up. The bluff ends as the snake leisurely crawls away.

The absence of movement is not the only stimulus to end the serpent's display. As Burghardt and Greene (1988) learned experimentally, a hog-nosed snake is more inclined to prolong its death-feigning behavior if a nearby human antagonist focuses its gaze directly on the snake than when it looks away. By looking away, the interloper conveys a lack of interest in its prospective victim, giving the snake enough confidence to terminate the bluff and attempt an escape.

Although most snake species hide under logs, boards, rocks, and other available objects lying on the ground, this snake seldom does so; instead, it spends most of the night and part of the day in subterranean burrows, becoming active in the morning and perhaps again late in the afternoon. It is a more zealous wanderer than the western hog-nosed snake. Typical movements noted between successive captures at two different south-central Kansas study sites averaged 682 and 951 feet (208, 290 m), respectively. During the breeding season, even greater distances were covered by the males in their search for females, some traveling approximately ½ mile (805 m) to consummate a mating.

An accomplished burrower, the eastern hog-nosed snake digs into sandy or loose soil, both to find concealed prey and to create underground excavations for shelter, egg-laying, and hibernation. Its wedge-shaped snout performs much like a double-shared ridging plow

that pushes its way through the sand, forcing the loosened material to either side. In addition to a projecting, shovellike nose, the serpent's other burrowing modifications include a short, thick body and tail that fit more easily into a shorter tunnel, and keeled scales that act like an athlete's cleats to anchor the body when the snake is digging, permitting a firmer headthrust into the substrate than would otherwise be possible.

Basically, two kinds of tunnels are excavated. One is a shallow temporary tunnel, dug an inch or two below the surface, which the snake occupies only once and which may cave in after it leaves. The more permanent burrows are deeper. To these the snake returns frequently over a period of weeks or months. One such refuge, examined by Platt, dropped downward sharply for the first 2 inches (5 cm) before continuing its descent diagonally another 4½ inches (11.4 cm), finally terminating in a small chamber that held the snake. An even deeper tunnel, discovered by other naturalists in a sandy orchard, was found to be 8 inches (20.3 cm) below ground level and 3 feet (91.4 cm) long. Where the soil is rocky, tightly packed, or otherwise unsuitable for digging, the eastern hog-nosed snake finds shelter in the burrows of other animals.

Despite its preference for dry environments, this species occasionally takes to water and may even be encountered considerable distances from shore, as reported by Barney Oldfield (in Oldfield and Moriarty 1994), who observed a large hog-nosed snake as it swam in the St. Croix River between Wisconsin and Minnesota.

That it also enters saltwater was documented by Rodgers (1985), who often saw specimens on the beach of Assateague Island, a long, narrow barrier island off the coasts of Maryland and Virginia. During the hot summer and fall months, they were seen to enter the surf. Swimming in the breakers, usually parallel to shore, the snakes remained in the water for as long as five minutes before returning to the beach on an incoming wave.

More cold tolerant than most North American snakes, the eastern hog-nosed snake leaves its hibernaculum earlier in the year than the majority of other serpent species, and it is among the last to seek shelter as winter approaches. In Harvey County,

Kansas, it hibernates for approximately six months of each year, normally entering its winter den between October 12 and 25 (average date, October 20) and emerging again sometime between April 17 and May 23 (average date, May 2). In midwinter, if the soil temperature rises as the result of a warm spell, the hognose may come to the surface to bask briefly in the midday sun, only to return to its lair again before dusk. Many such incidents have been documented, notably at more northern latitudes. One involved the sighting of several specimens above ground on December 2 in Union County, Pennsylvania; another concerned a single hognose observed in the open on January 24 in Clermont County, Ohio; and a third involved a specimen found in West Virginia in February resting on a blanket of snow.

In southeastern Texas, where this species often makes its initial appearance in late February or early March, the snake's winter dormancy lasts no longer than four or five months. During the region's especially mild winters, the eastern hog-nosed snake may be encountered at any time of year, provided the air temperature is above 75 degrees F and the sun is shining.

As a rule, this serpent does not hibernate in communal dens with other snake species, nor does it usually share a den with others of its own kind. Rather, to avoid severe winter weather, it digs 2 to 3 feet (61–91.4 cm) down into loose soil or sand, enters the burrows of other animals, or, less often, secretes itself in decaying logs or tree stumps. Those living at warmer latitudes may even take refuge beneath rocks, plant debris, or human-generated trash.

FEEDING A study of prey items consumed by this species in nature shows that it eats chiefly toads, as well as frogs and salamanders. Those amphibians together total more than 90 percent of the snake's diet in most places. Where they are plentiful, frogs, not toads, may constitute its chief quarry. In addition to anuran prey, the snake occasionally consumes lizards and their eggs, small mammals, birds, and on rare occasions even baby turtles.

Insects, spiders, and other arthropods have also been found in hog-nosed snake stomachs, though it is generally believed that most such invertebrates do not represent the serpent's actual prey but were first eaten by frogs and toads before the amphibians themselves were consumed by the snakes. That insects are indeed sometimes eaten by this species is confirmed by Conant (1951), who watched several young captive hognose snakes consume live crickets. Then again, juvenile specimens in Platt's collection rejected such insects but did not hesitate to eat small amphibians.

Above ground the eastern hog-nosed snake finds prey mostly through chance encounters, for it is primarily day-active, its prey chiefly nocturnal. Because its eyesight is not as keen as that of the western hog-nosed snake, it is less likely than its western cousin to detect active prey; nor is it as quick, making problematic the snake's successful capture of a rapidly moving target. In experimental encounters, frogs and toads easily outpaced the plodding snake on open ground, and most lizards had no trouble getting out of the snake's way. Such prey are usually captured by the snake when it digs them out of loose sand, finds them in the burrows of other animals, or takes them by surprise in places where they have limited options to escape. Kroll, for example, reports that when toads were placed in an arena with eastern hog-nosed snakes, some of the serpents had difficulty recognizing the active prey by sight alone, even after the amphibians stopped just an inch or two from the snakes. Instead of seizing the toad at such an opportune moment, the hognose chose to follow the anuran's odor trail, which often took the snake on a roundabout course that eventually led right back to the resting toad, where the snake could easily have captured it in the first place. He thus concluded that for finding prey, odor detection, not sight, is the eastern hognose's principal asset.

What the thick-bodied serpent lacks in speed and acute vision, it makes up for in other toad-eating adaptations, including a stout body, a large head, and a wide and highly flexible mouth—all of which allow it to swallow large toads with relative ease.

When actively searching for prey in the open, the snake tries to seize any nearby moving creature that is not too large to be swallowed, crawling toward the action with its

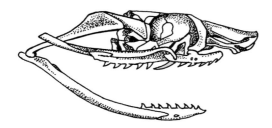

Figure 31. *Skull of eastern hog-nosed snake showing enlarged teeth on rear of maxillary bone.*

mouth wide open but never actually striking. More often, it digs toads, frogs, salamanders, and sometimes lizards from their underground daytime shelters, to which it is guided by an acutely developed sense of smell and by tiny skin sensors on its head. Once exposed, the prey is quickly captured and maneuvered to the rear of the snake's mouth, where a pair of lancelike teeth attached toward the back of the upper jawbones impales the struggling victim. These large, backward-pointing teeth effectively prevent the quarry from escaping, and they help to manipulate the prey as it is being swallowed.

Despite these useful adaptations, the snake would be unable to eat such amphibians without its remarkably enlarged adrenal glands. This special feature endows the snake with a physiological resistance to the powerful digitaloid poisons produced by the toad's skin glands, poisons so toxic that few vertebrates can consume large toads without suffering severe systemic damage or death. Since most other Texas snakes possess only small adrenal glands, they do not enjoy the same protection against toad secretions, nor do they normally eat these anurans. Species with intermediate-sized adrenals (garter snakes, ribbon snakes, water snakes, and the venomous massasauga) eat toads only occasionally. Moreover, they consume just the smaller amphibians, whose poorly developed parotoid and other skin glands produce significantly less of the dangerous secretions than do those of the larger toads. Thus, we see here an unmistakable correlation between the size of a snake's adrenal glands and its toad-eating habits.

REPRODUCTION　Both male and female hog-nosed snakes become sexually mature when they are about 21 months old. According to Plummer and Mills (1996), the male locates a receptive female by following her scent trail, which may attract two or more suitors at the same time. In southeastern Texas they breed as early in the year as late March, though in most other parts of the snake's geographic range, mating takes place between mid-April and the end of May. Copulation can also occur in the fall; the sperm maintain their viability until spring of the next year. As early as May 27 (in Texas) or as late as August 28 (in Indiana), the female scoops out a nest 4 to 6 inches (10.2–15.2 cm) deep in sand or loose soil, often along the edge of a cultivated field, where she lays a clutch of 4 to 61 eggs (average 22). At other times she may deposit them under a large rock or in a rotting log or tree stump. About 1½ inches (3.8 cm) long when first laid, the peculiarly thin-shelled, oval eggs hatch in May or June, 51 to 65 days later. More boldly patterned than the adults, the hatchlings are 6½ to 9½ inches (16.5–24.2 cm) long.

TEXAS NIGHT SNAKE

Hypsiglena torquata jani
PLATES 63–65

DESCRIPTION　In some ways the night snake resembles the venomous pit vipers. Like them, its head is rather flat on top and notably wider than its neck, and its relatively large eyes, bulging slightly from their sockets, are equipped with vertically elliptical pupils like those of a cat (when viewed in daylight).

The most distinctive markings of this relatively small, slender serpent consist of three (sometimes only two) conspicuous, large dark blotches that extend from the back of the

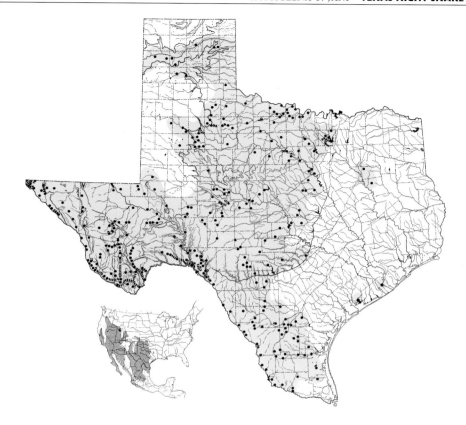

snake's head onto its neck. Running parallel to one another, these elongated spots are sometimes irregularly shaped and occasionally joined at their common borders, in which case the snake appears to have but a single large nuchal collar. Another significant pattern element on the snake's head is the lateral dark brown or nearly black bar that runs backward and slightly downward from each eye, standing out in sharp contrast against the adjacent whitish upper lip scales. The tip of the chin and sometimes even the leading edge of the throat are dark.

The body, normally gray, gray-brown, or tan in hue, carries a row of dark brown blotches down the middle of the back; a second row of alternating smaller spots lies below the first. Another series of even smaller dark spots occurs low on the sides near the belly, which is white or dull yellow and unmarked. Compared to night snakes from the central and eastern parts of the state, those from southwestern Texas have an overall faded look,

and the dorsal blotches of at least some of them are split down the midline, with one half of each divided blotch generally out of alignment with the other. Every Texas night snake possesses a divided anal plate and smooth body scales that are arranged in 21 rows at midbody.

COMPARABLE SNAKES A young glossy snake, though colored and blotched somewhat like a night snake, has a head scarcely wider than its neck. Moreover, the pupils of its eyes are round, the number of its midbody scale rows falls between 29 and 35, and the anal plate is single. Racers, which are also blotched when very young, have round pupils and 17 rows of dorsal scales at midbody. Both western and Mexican hook-nosed snakes can be distinguished from the night snake by their distinctly upturned snouts, circular pupils, and 17 rows of midbody scales. In young Baird's and Great Plains rat snakes, a distinct dark bar crosses the top of the head between the eyes, the pupils are round, and the upper rows of body scales are faintly keeled. Observed at close range, a night snake might be mistaken for a baby rattler, for it shares some of the same characteristics with that pit viper: a wide head, elliptical pupils, and a blotched body pattern. Even the dark horizontal band behind its eye is duplicated in some rattlesnake species. But every newborn Texas rattler comes into the world with a button on the end of its tail, whereas the night snake has a long, pointed tail.

SIZE Adults of this moderately small snake usually measure between 10 and 14 inches (25.4–35.6 cm) in length, although a 24-inch (61.5 cm) specimen from Brewster County is on record (Yancey 1997).

HABITAT Except for several isolated, out-of-range records for Anderson, Brazoria, Calhoun, Henderson, and Smith counties, where the surroundings are not typical for the species, this wide-ranging serpent occupies a variety of arid to semiarid environments across the western two-thirds of the state, ranging from sea level to an elevation of about 5,000 feet. Most commonly associated with rocky, dissected terrain covered with sandy or gravelly soil, it also occasionally occurs in the pine-hardwood forests of northeastern Texas. Typical natural regions in the state where it is found include the grassy, sometimes broken plains of the Panhandle and north-central Texas; the scrubby oak-juniper savannahs and hills of the Edwards Plateau; the nearly flat thornbrush country of South Texas; and the highly variable topography of the Trans-Pecos, where rugged hillsides and fractured mountain slopes, sparsely covered with desert plants, contain areas generously littered with loose flat rocks and talus slopes—favorite habitats for this retiring reptile.

BEHAVIOR Although the night snake's moderately wide head and elliptical pupils convey the look of a venomous serpent, the snake's defensive behavior in the face of danger is nothing compared to the animated reaction of a threatened pit viper. Yet the night snake can be a convincing bluffer. When first confronted, it generally tries to escape beneath the nearest surface object or, by frantically probing the ground with its head, searches for an opening into which it can disappear.

One that is sufficiently annoyed may spasmodically jerk its head and forebody about as if preparing to strike, though it rarely ever follows through by lunging. When clearly provoked, it sometimes flattens its head and trunk, lifts its forebody off the ground in an abbreviated spiral, and may actually strike at its tormentor. For emphasis, it may even add a menacing hiss to this charade. Such a foreboding display is merely a desperate attempt to frighten away its enemy, for the night snake is otherwise defenseless against an adversary much larger than itself. Even when picked up, it rarely ever bites. In a more submissive response, a provoked specimen may pull its body into a tight ball and tuck its head somewhere in the middle, maintaining this position even when handled.

In South Texas the night snake ordinarily leaves its hibernaculum in late March or early April, although during unusually mild winters it can be found at the surface even earlier, coiled under whatever surface litter is available. By the end of October, at the end of its annual active season, it returns to its winter refuge.

Essentially a nocturnal creature, the night snake avoids diurnal predators by spending the daylight hours hidden under any of a variety of surface objects, mostly flat rocks but also fallen tree limbs, dead cactus plants, or man-made debris. Because they are less yielding, rock crevices and the deep spaces under the horizontal shelves of limestone that cap many of the region's rock-strewn hillsides make even better shelters. Night snakes that are occasionally observed moving about in daylight are usually encountered on overcast or rainy days, but following a warm rain they are most likely to be found under rocks. Like many other aridland serpents, their nocturnal hunting forays frequently take them across desert roads and busy highways, where they sometimes fall victim to vehicular traffic and snake collectors.

Diller and Wallace (1986), who studied the natural history of this species in southwestern Idaho, discovered that although specimens were regularly found beneath rocks as early in the year as late April, especially during cool days, they were curiously absent from such shelter during the summer. Of 23 snakes located under rocks during the study, 16 were found in pairs (7 pairs of males, 1 pair of females), an aggregating behavior not previously reported for this species. By erecting specially designed drift fences in areas known to be inhabited by the serpents, the zoologists determined that the snake's first significant aboveground movements took place in mid-May. Strangely, and for reasons not yet understood, all but one of the serpents encountered during these travels were males. One explanation for this gender bias might well be that like most other snakes, the males of the species actively search for mates in spring after they emerge from hibernation, but the snake's peak period of activity during the study occurred in early June, when for the first time, females were caught in drift fences (strategically placed wire-mesh or metal panels that herd nearby wandering snakes into a container buried in the ground at either end of the fence). When rocks were absent from the landscape, the night snakes crawled into ground squirrel and kangaroo rat burrows.

FEEDING Lizards and small snakes apparently constitute the bulk of the snake's diet, although lizard eggs, frogs, insects, and worms are consumed as well. The last two items, because of their small size, are probably taken mostly by the younger snakes. Specific prey items known to have been eaten in nature by the Texas night snake include whiptail and desert side-blotched lizards, Texas banded geckos, and both ground and blind snakes.

Like certain other desert lizards, the Texas banded gecko is remarkably adapted to survive an attack by a predator such as the night snake, for it has a strongly banded tail that not only attracts an assailant by being elevated and waved conspicuously from side to side but also readily separates from the lizard's body when seized, allowing the gecko to escape with its life while the predator busily consumes the squirming detached member. Otherwise, this delicate little lizard is poorly equipped to defend itself against such an enemy. One of only a handful of native lizards known to be active after dark when the night snake is also out searching for prey, it presents an easy target for nocturnal predators, for its relatively short legs are not designed for speed, nor is it in any way

adapted to defend itself. Therefore, by being able to sacrifice its tail, the gecko enjoys a vital survival advantage, one that can be employed repeatedly over the span of its lifetime, for a tail that has been lost to a predator during a feeding episode is replaced by a new one in as little as seven or eight weeks.

Day-active lizards are also devoured. Based on the remains of such prey, together with the accidentally swallowed sand and plant matter found in the serpents' digestive tract and their scats, Diller and Wallace concluded that night snakes probably find these dormant reptiles after dark by probing in rock crevices or by burrowing through loose soil. To support this view, they point out that diurnal side-blotched lizards represented the chief prey of the night snakes in southwestern Idaho.

Despite its characterization as a harmless species—one incapable of seriously injuring man—the night snake is equipped with a pair of moderately enlarged teeth (one at the back of each upper jawbone) and a radically modified saliva that is toxic to the small creatures on which it feeds. Gripping a struggling lizard in its mouth, the snake manipulates the prey until the rear fanglike teeth can be successfully engaged. Embedded repeatedly by an intermittent chewing action of the serpent's jaws, these teeth produce a succession of tiny puncture wounds that admit the gradual introduction of the snake's paralyzing salivary toxins into the victim's tissues, toxins that eventually incapacitate the quarry and make it easier for the snake to handle. In one instance, reported by Goodman (1953), a young night snake was observed to seize a small sagebrush lizard and to chew forcefully at the base of its tail, effectively paralyzing its hind quarters in just a few seconds and the victim's entire body not long thereafter. Two hours later the lizard was dead. Its gasping for air, coupled with a bluish-green discoloration of its right hind leg, suggest that the snake's venom contains both a dominant nerve-attacking element (which it appears was mainly responsible for the lizard's death) as well as a secondary hemorrhagic component that damaged the victim's small blood vessels.

So gluttonous is this little snake that even when first captured and dropped into a collecting bag with other reptiles on which it normally feeds, it sometimes attacks and devours them. Under such circumstances, we have witnessed three separate attacks by night snakes on banded geckos and two on ground snakes.

REPRODUCTION One pair of Texas night snakes is known to have mated in May, although several other egg-laying dates reported for this subspecies range from as early in the year as April 25 to as late as July 15. This presents something of a contradiction, however, since the earliest date of egg deposition precedes the only known mating time by several weeks. From these facts, it may be concluded that the Texas night snake either

mates as early as March or that the April 25 laying date represents the case of a fall mating, followed by the retention of viable sperm in the female's oviducts until the next spring, when they became activated and fertilized her ovulating eggs. Another possibility is the deposition of more than one clutch of eggs per female each year. Relatively large compared to the size of the female, the eggs are about 1¼ inches (2.8 cm) long when first laid, with 4 to 6 per clutch. They hatched 54 to 59 days later (on June 18 and September 12, respectively), according to information from two clutches, and produce young that measure approximately 6⅛ to 7⅗ inches (15.6–19.3 cm) long.

GRAY-BANDED KING SNAKE
Lampropeltis alterna
PLATES 66–75

DESCRIPTION Notable for its extreme color and pattern variation, this medium-sized, often brightly hued snake comes in two basic and somewhat geographically distinct color phases. One of them, often called the *blairi* phase, occurs at the eastern end of the species' range in Terrell and Val Verde counties. Ordinarily the more colorful of the two, it is typically marked with fewer than 16 wide, reddish or orange saddles enclosed by narrow black bands, which are separated from one another by broad, dark gray saddles

thinly edged in white. Individual snakes can vary greatly. In some specimens, dark pigmentation so completely overwhelms the pattern that it obscures all of the orange and gray colors, leaving only the narrow white edges of the gray bands clearly visible. Between these two extremes, a number of other pattern variations occur as well. The second basic color type, known as the *alterna* phase, is found primarily west of Terrell County. In its typical form, which generally consists of 16 moderately narrow, white-bordered, black bands on a slate-gray background, it is the only color variety found at higher elevations in the Chisos, Davis, and Guadalupe mountains. In such snakes, the spaces between the primary dark markings are occasionally occupied by narrower, sometimes broken, secondary black bands. In some, the primary bands may be unusually wide and split across the back by varying amounts of red.

In summarizing the morphology of the gray-banded king snake, Miller (1979) reported that the greatest degree of color and pattern variation in this species was in a series of specimens collected in southern Brewster County along a 1¼-mile stretch of Texas Highway 118 that runs north to south through the Christmas Mountains. In this highly diverse group of snakes, he found specimens fitting the descriptions of both basic color phases, others with an overall brown-orange appearance, and some with deep-red saddles but without white edging along the gray bands. Even more unusual was a single specimen whose background color was an overall gunmetal blue.

Two other areas of southern Brewster County have also been identified as harboring colonies of curiously patterned gray-banded king snakes. According to Michael Forstner (pers. com.), the most bizarre and dramatic color pattern deviations to be found within the snake's range occur at Black Gap, where he found patternless, striped, speckled, and diamond-blotched individuals in addition to specimens exhibiting near-normal features of pattern and coloration. Equally unusual were king snakes he collected on Pepper's Hill, a moderately elevated ridge of harsh desert terrain that crosses Farm Road 170 near Villa de la Mina between Lajitas and Terlingua. While several adult specimens from the area displayed typical *alterna* phase coloration, some of their young were either dotted, speckled, or covered dorsally with squigglelike markings.

The snake's moderately wide head, narrow neck, and fairly large and slightly protruding eyes bear little resemblance to the cephalic features of other native species of king snakes. Its pale-colored belly is marked with irregularly shaped dark blotches that sometimes merge with one another. The dorsal scales are smooth and in 25 rows at midbody, and the anal plate is single.

COMPARABLE SNAKES The Texas coral snake has no gray in its pattern (only red, yellow, and black rings), nor does the gray-banded king snake exhibit bright yellow in its pattern. Furthermore, the coral snake's body markings completely encircle its body, whereas those of the gray-banded king snake fail to cross the snake's abdomen. In addition, the more slender coral snake has a small head, with black covering the front part and yellow crossing the back, tiny dark eyes, and a divided anal plate. Milk snakes also possess small heads and eyes, and their dorsal scales are in 21 rows at midbody. The pattern of the Texas long-nosed snake is heavily speckled with yellow, the dorsal scales are in 23 rows at midbody, and most of the scales under its tail are in a single row. Although rock rattlesnakes may resemble some specimens of the gray-banded king snake's *alterna* phase, their body scales are keeled and in 23 midbody rows, they have mostly small scales on top of the head (compared to large plates on the king snake's crown), and rattles.

SIZE Adults are usually 24 to 36 inches (61–91.4 cm) long but reach a maximum known length of 57¾ inches (116.7 cm).

HABITAT Long considered the rarest of Texas' serpents, the gray-banded king snake is now regarded as a relatively common, though highly elusive, dweller of the Trans-Pecos roughlands. Testimony to the reptile's abundance is the collection over the past 25 to 30 years of possibly as many as 1,500 specimens from the region by reptile hobbyists and commercial collectors, attracted to this snake by its beauty and color diversity and the relative ease with which it adapts to captivity. Indeed, few other native serpents arouse so much excitement among collectors. During the region's summer thunderstorms, when the gray-banded king snake is most active above ground, scores of reptile enthusiasts—some from as far away as Mexico, Canada, and Europe—flock to the snake's habitat for a chance to find one of these highly esteemed serpents.

In Texas, the species' known range extends from the Hueco Mountains of El Paso and Hudspeth counties in the west, eastward to Dunbar Cave in Edwards County (about 23 miles southwest of Rocksprings), north to the slopes of Guadalupe Peak (although it is apparently absent from the Franklin Mountains of El Paso County), then south to the Chisos Mountains and the Del Rio area. Outside Texas, it is known in the United States so far only from a single documented New Mexico specimen collected recently at the southern end of Eddy County, a Guadalupe Mountains locality near the Texas border, where the elevation is about 3,800 feet (1,156 m)(Painter, Hyder, and Swinford 1992).

Most of this region lies within the northern portion of the Chihuahuan Desert, that part of southwestern Texas characterized largely by great expanses of barren limestone hills and canyons interspersed with flat basins, where sotol and lechuguilla grow on rock-strewn hills and the lower elevations support the growth of desert scrub plants, primarily mesquite trees and creosote bush. At the eastern end of its geographic range, the reptile's habitat consists of acacia-lechuguilla plant associations.

Zoologists familiar with the gray-banded king snake say it occurs most commonly on the summits of steep-sided rocky hills, particularly where arroyos have their origins. Of approximately 85 specimens collected by Miller within a nine-mile radius of Langtry, about 82 percent were found in such situations. In Val Verde County, according to Miller, the snake is most frequently encountered near the Rio Grande, Pecos, and Devil's rivers and their tributaries; few have been found more than five miles from these waterways. Especially productive collecting areas within those boundaries have been located on or adjacent to road cuts dug through rocky hills.

A more detailed account of the species' typical habitat (except for *alterna* phase mountain populations) is provided by Michael Forstner (pers. com.), who described the snake's environment as open, fissured limestone hills with a surface accumulation of small or broken stones but without the sizable expanses of large, monolithic outcroppings and boulders usually inhabited by rock rattlesnakes. Throughout its range, it occurs

at elevations of 1,200 to 7,500 feet (670–2,286 m).

BEHAVIOR Noted for its gentle disposition and unhurried movements, this snake rarely attempts to bite when handled, although it has more subtle ways to discourage its enemies. At times it may twitch its body spasmodically when picked up and also discharge feces over its captor's hands; the offensive smell and feel of the voided material usually results in its quick release. On rare occasions it may even hiss and vibrate its tail. Tanzer (1970) suggested that hemorrhaging from the cloaca of females may be another seldom-used defensive tactic, just as it is in female long-nosed and speckled king snakes.

The gray-banded king snake is rarely encountered above ground except late in the evening and at night, when the hot daytime temperatures have diminished enough to make surface activity bearable. Among the few individuals collected during daylight hours, most were found in the open on overcast mornings or after moderate to heavy rains; two were discovered under flat limestone rocks lying in the shade of an oak tree, and a juvenile was found coiled under a dead sotol plant.

Although the snake has no particular fondness for water, the approach of a thunderstorm, signaled by a dramatic drop in barometric pressure, causes it to become surface-active. This was convincingly demonstrated one June night when Miller and several other collectors found 11 specimens crawling about on the surface 45 minutes after sundown as a mass of thunderstorms approached the Langtry area from the west. This probably represents the greatest number of gray-banded king snakes ever taken by collectors in a single night. Curiously, Miller and the others found no specimens while the storms were in progress or immediately thereafter, when the ground was still wet from the cooling showers.

According to Miller, the best collecting nights usually are those in May and June when the barometric pressure reaches approximately 29.3 psi. Although still nights are favored by many desert reptiles as ideal times for foraging, Turner (1977) believes that this king snake prefers windy nights for its nocturnal wanderings. The earliest recorded collecting dates are in mid-April, although the period of greatest activity, at least in Val Verde County, occurs from June to mid-July, coinciding somewhat with the advent of the limited desert rainy season. During the unbearably hot and dry weeks that normally follow the rains, the snakes seldom leave their subterranean shelters to venture above ground, keeping instead to the cool recesses of their underground passageways. That some of them become active again in the fall is evident from the October 15 collecting date reported by Miller. *Alterna* phase specimens from moderate elevations of the Davis and Chisos mountains, unlike those from the eastern end of the snake's range, can occasionally be found above ground throughout the summer months.

FEEDING Lizards apparently are the chief prey of this snake, with mammals a not-too-distant second choice. Although Michael Forstner (pers. com.) found a large number of small mammals in road-killed specimens he examined in far West Texas, the snake's choice food items proved to be lizards, most of them southwestern earless lizards and some crevice spiny, desert side-blotched, and Big Bend tree lizards. Natural food items mentioned by others include a canyon tree frog, Merriam's canyon and southern prairie lizards, whiptail lizards, a skink, lizard eggs, and a pocket mouse.

Lizards, which ordinarily are much too swift and elusive to be overtaken and captured by this slow-paced serpent, are no doubt captured as they sleep in rock crevices, beneath stones, or in the burrows of small animals. When first captured, they are seldom ever tightly constricted in the serpent's coils —a killing strategy used routinely by most other king snakes—but are held tightly in the snake's jaws. To subdue a struggling mammal or lizard, the gray-banded king snake is more likely to press its victim firmly to the ground with a single loop of its muscular body.

REPRODUCTION So secretive is this reptile that little is known about its reproductive biology in the wild; therefore, the following information comes from captive breeding reports.

Like the adult males of certain other snake species, those of the gray-banded king snake often engage in ritualized combat in which each contestant tries to assert physical dominance over the other for the right to mate with a nearby female. Such an encounter, called a combat dance, is more like a wrestling match than a mortal struggle, although the participants may engage in biting episodes, perhaps as a way to facilitate body alignment. According to Murphy, Tryon, and Brecke (1978), it begins with the snakes moving forward together, their bodies more or less aligned and their heads an inch or two apart. The most dramatic aspect of the encounter is the acute vertical body bridging they perform as each male tries to attain a higher body loop than his rival, whereupon the snake with the taller body bridge pushes firmly downward against the other, who then pushes back in response. Such body loops are sometimes elevated as high as 14 or 15 inches (38.1 cm) above the ground. When one of the participants is forced out of position, he tends to move forward to effect a realignment. Meanwhile, the prevailing animal applies body pressure against the other's body bridges, resulting in the rear portions of their trunks eventually being twisted together like a giant corkscrew. At the same time, their forebodies engage in a side-to-side pushing contest as each snake tries to maintain his head and forebody in an upright position. The ultimate goal of the entire episode seems to be for the dominant male to force the rival onto his back so that he is totally immobile. Once this has been achieved, the subdued snake attempts to leave.

For both male and female gray-banded king snakes, sexual maturity usually begins at 18 to 20 months of age. The females apparently are receptive to the males only after their first skin shedding of the season. Courtship and copulation, which occur in May, June, or July, can be somewhat violent affairs, according to Tryon and Murphy (1982), during which the male may seize his mate by the back of the neck and chew vigorously, each bite lasting about five seconds. When the eggs are laid, sometime in May or June (for second annual clutches, July to late August), each of the 3 to 14 eggs per clutch is $1\frac{1}{4}$ to $1\frac{5}{8}$ inches (2.8–4.1 cm) long. After an incubation that normally lasts 54 to 68 days, the infants usually hatch from their eggs during September and are $8\frac{1}{2}$ to 11 inches (21.6–27.9 cm) long.

PRAIRIE KING SNAKE

Lampropeltis calligaster
calligaster
PLATE 76

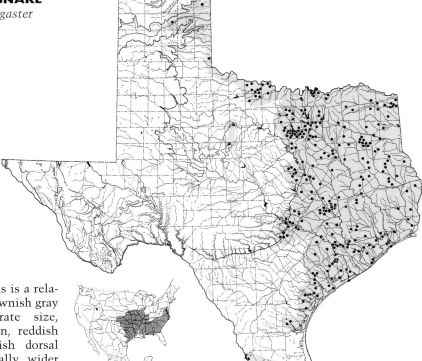

DESCRIPTION This is a relatively slender, brownish gray snake of moderate size, whose dark brown, reddish brown, or greenish dorsal blotches are usually wider than long and narrowly edged in black. As a rule, these markings are slightly concave at front and back and sometimes divided down the midline of the back to form two smaller blotches, one on either side of the spine. Flanking the primary markings on each side of the body is another row of smaller dark spots. In juveniles, the blotches not only are more reddish, but they also show greater contrast with the ground color. The ground color of older specimens may be so dark that the snake's dorsal markings are scarcely visible. In addition, such individuals may develop an indefinite pattern of four wide, dark stripes, one on either side of the spine and another low along each side of the body. Squarish dark spots mark the yellowish belly. The head pattern, when clearly defined, consists of a dark, backward-pointing V-shaped mark on the crown and a dark stripe from the eye to the end of the mouthline. The dorsal scales, in 25 to 27 rows at midbody, are smooth, and the anal plate is single.

COMPARABLE SNAKES The Great Plains rat, southwestern rat, and corn snakes, all of which closely resemble the prairie king snake, have weakly keeled scales on the back, a divided anal plate, and a prominent dark V that points forward instead of backward on top of the head. Furthermore, the underside of their tails bear two dark, lengthwise stripes or bold squarish spots. Glossy snakes have white, unmarked undertails and 29 or more rows of midbody dorsal scales.

SIZE While it is known to reach a maximum length of 54 inches (137.2 cm), the adult prairie king snake is generally 28 to 42 inches (71.1–106.7 cm) long.

HABITAT Primarily an inhabitant of open grassland, this snake prefers prairies, pastures, cultivated farmland, and coastal saltgrass savannah, although it is also found in open woodland and among rock ledges, especially those associated with clearings. In south-central Kansas, Fitch (1978) found it in a variety of grassland habitats as well as in areas of open woodland and along woodland edges. He also frequently encountered it in areas that once were shortgrass prairie but, having lain fallow over time, had become overgrown with tall grass and heavy brush. Although Fitch found that certain other reptile species ultimately abandoned such densely weed-covered places, the prairie king snake continued to thrive there. He also found it in virgin tallgrass prairie and on rolling sand prairies covered chiefly with big bluestem grass.

BEHAVIOR Although this generally mild-mannered serpent seldom bites when first handled, it may assume an aggressive posture and vibrate its tail when annoyed. An unusual defensive behavior noted in several species of native serpents—one not previously reported for the prairie king snake—is that of death-feigning. Through the courtesy of John A. Jones, we observed this phenomenon in a juvenile *L. c. calligaster* collected on the grounds of the Caldwell Zoo in Tyler, Texas. When intimidated by a nearby moving finger, the snake raised its forebody slightly above the ground, assumed the lateral, S-shaped defensive coil typically employed by most snakes when they are unable to escape a predator, and launched two or three vigorous strikes at the source of its annoyance. Almost immediately after being tapped lightly on the head, it twisted and turned violently, its frenzied body contortions accompanied by spasmodic head twitching, until, less than 20 seconds later, it turned partly onto its back, ceased all movement, and became rigid with its mouth held partly open. By this time, the serpent's body was so severely misshapen that we were convinced the reptile must be close to death. Numerous sharp kinks had appeared along its length, as if the spine were broken in many places. The middle part of the abdomen was flattened horizontally, and the snake's neck formed a sharp ∪-bend, causing the head to double back against the snake's body. At this point, the serpent had assumed the dehydrated appearance one often sees in snakes that have been dead for some time. Even the remarkable death-feigning behavior of hog-nosed snakes was not as believable as this transformation. Less than two minutes later, the snake's crooked form slowly returned to its customary supple shape, and the reptile again behaved normally.

Because the prairie king snake is an elusive serpent that spends most of the daylight hours hidden in small mammal burrows, under stones, or in vegetative debris such as grass clumps, haystacks, and shocks of grain, we know little about its life history. Most of the information we have about it comes from the work of Fitch, who for 30 years studied its ecology and behavior on 158 acres of prime grassland habitat in northeastern Kansas. During that time, he captured 1,414 eastern yellow-bellied racers on the site but saw only 166 prairie king snakes. In most years, the zoologist collected 1 to 4 prairie king snakes in a season, but in some years he found no specimens at all or, during the best seasons, as many as 32. The picture is similar in southern Illinois near the northernmost edge of the species' range, where Klimstra (1959) reported the capture of only 140 specimens of this species in 8 years, noting the following distribution of captures per month: March (6), April (21), May (37), June (27), July (12), August (16), September (13), and October (8).

Like most native snakes, this one does not travel great distances. Fitch found that males generally ranged over an area of approximately 54 acres (21.6 ha), whereas the less active females usually spent their entire lives on a parcel of land not exceeding 22 acres (8.8 ha). On average, both sexes considered, they moved approximately 58 feet (17.7 m) a day. In traveling each fall from their summer grassland habitats to their winter dens among rocky ledges in moderately wooded areas, some of the prairie king snakes at the Kansas study site moved even greater distances. In the southern part of the snake's range, however, where such rock formations are often absent, these serpents simply hibernate in burrows within the boundaries of their summer territories; in Illinois, according to P. W. Smith (1961), they occasionally overwintered in road embankments.

FEEDING The food of this reptile consists chiefly of small burrowing and surface-dwelling mammals, with reptiles, amphibians, birds and their eggs, and occasionally insects constituting the rest. Most of what we know about the snake's feeding habits has been revealed in just two studies, the one made in Kansas by Fitch and another conducted in southern Illinois by Klimstra. In the Kansas study, the following prey items, tabulated by frequency of occurrence, were reported: prairie voles (30), eastern moles (5), six-lined race runners (5), northern short-tailed shrews (4), white-footed mice (3), pine voles (2), least shrews (2), racers (2), slender glass lizards (2), five-lined skink eggs (2), eastern cottontail rabbit (1), hispid cotton rat (1), house mouse (1), southern bog lemming (1), timber rattlesnake (1), ring-necked snake (1), and Great Plains skink (1). Based on the calculated total weight of each prey species, the data also show that the prairie vole made up 48 percent of the consumed food and the eastern mole another 24 percent, whereas each of the remaining prey species involved less than 3.2 percent of the diet. Like the Kansas survey, the Illinois study showed mammals to be the prairie king snake's principal food, constituting 68.6 percent of the total amount consumed. Surprisingly, however, amphibians were more important in the Illinois sample, making up 11.2 percent by volume, reptiles 6.8 percent, and birds another 6.8 percent. One specimen contained 16 quail eggs. Insects, missing in the Kansas survey, were found in the stomachs of the Illinois king snakes, constituting 6.4 percent of the total volume.

REPRODUCTION Sexual maturity in this species occurs at about three years of age. Mating, which normally takes place in the spring soon after the snakes emerge from their winter shelters, is sometimes preceded by a stereotyped combat routine between two male suitors vying for the attention of a single nearby female. Such a fight between two male prairie king snakes was observed by Moehn (1967) one spring day at Nevada, Missouri. With their trunks closely intertwined like two symmetrically twisted ropes, the combatants lay horizontally on the ground, their forebodies separated and their heads raised a couple of inches above the substrate. Apparently it was the neck, held in a tense loop, that most affected the eventual outcome of the conflict, since it appeared that each snake, pushing that part of his body forcefully against the other's neck, sought to throw his rival off balance. Despite the vigorous nature of such contests, never do the participants suffer any serious bodily injury.

Sometime during late June or July, the female deposits 7 to 21 smooth-shelled, adherent eggs several inches below ground in loose soil or in an abandoned mammal burrow. Approximately 1⅓ to 2 inches (3.4–5.1 cm) long when laid, they incubate for the next 45 to 78 days (in captivity), producing hatchlings 9½ to 12⅕ inches (24.2–31 cm) long in August or early September. One zoologist has suggested that in the wild the females may lay eggs only every other year, or that their reproductive cycle is variable, being affected by weather, food availability, and other environmental factors.

SPECKLED KING SNAKE
Lampropeltis getula holbrooki
PLATES 77, 78

DESCRIPTION More uniformly cylindrical than most snakes, the relatively stout body of this serpent seems to be the same thickness for its entire length. Even the snake's head and neck are nearly the same diameter as the body. Blaney (1977), who studied in detail the taxonomy of this species, identified two distinctly different pattern types in East Texas speckled king snakes, one of which he regarded as a microgeographic race.

The predominant type, which ranges over most of the region from the Red River nearly to the upper Texas coast, is glossy black or dark brown with a single small, yellowish spot at the center of nearly every dorsal scale. The snake's head, like its body, is also black and covered with scattered yellow spots, and its yellow underside is checkered with large, squarish black blotches, or else each light-colored belly scale has a black margin along its posterior edge. The second type, confined to the state's coastal marshes from near Corpus Christi to the Louisiana border, is characterized by a pattern of irregular, pale-colored dorsal bands and by the expansion and intermingling of many of the remaining spots, resulting in the formation of small splotches of diverse shapes and sizes. In both

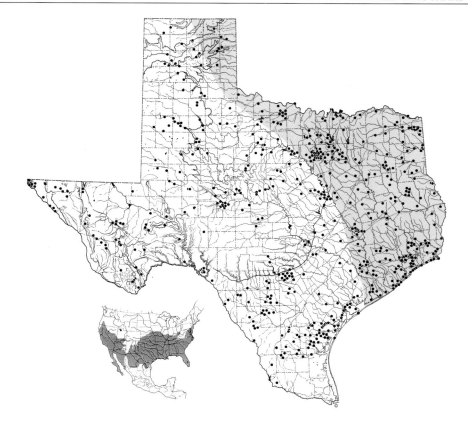

types, the dark ventral markings become progressively more prevalent toward the rear of the snake's body. The dorsal spots of very young speckled king snakes coalesce at regular intervals along the back to form numerous narrow, pale dorsal crossbars with little evidence of pale spotting between them, while the sides of the body are heavily speckled. The dorsal scales are smooth and shiny and arranged in 21 rows at midbody. The anal plate is single.

Intergradation between this subspecies and the desert king snake occurs in Texas along a broad band extending from the Panhandle and the western two-thirds of the Red River southward to the mid-Texas coast. In this region, where the two subspecies meet and intermingle, specimens are apt to be intermediate in pattern. Those near the middle of the zone of intergradation are likely to display almost equally the features of both subspecies, whereas snakes along either side of this zone more closely resemble the nearest subspecies.

COMPARABLE SNAKES The buttermilk racer of East Texas also has an abundance of pale-colored spots covering its generally dark-hued body and tail, but its markings are scattered indiscriminately over the dorsum. Furthermore, instead of each pale spot being confined just to the center of a scale, as it is in the speckled king snake, each of the racer's spots covers an entire scale. In addition, the racer's abdomen is not boldly checkered or otherwise decorated with black pigmentation, its neck is distinctly narrower than its head, and its anal plate is divided.

SIZE Three to 4 feet (91.4–121.9 cm) is the usual adult length of the speckled king snake, but this subspecies is reported to attain a maximum length of 6 feet (183 cm).

HABITAT Although it shows a strong preference for moist environments such as those near swamps, marshes, and grassy waterways, the speckled king snake occupies a wide variety of other habitats that include dry woodlands, rocky hillsides, mixed prairies, and overgrown pastures. Along the Texas Gulf

A.

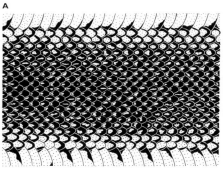

B.

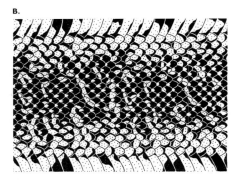

C.

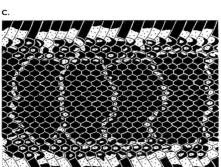

Figure 32. *Dorsal patterns of (a) typical phase of the speckled king snake, (b) coastal phase of the speckled king snake, and (c) typical desert king snake. (After Blaney 1977.)*

Coast and on the state's offshore barrier islands it occurs commonly along the edges of saltwater marshes, where local populations frequently exceed in numbers those found in drier inland environments.

BEHAVIOR This rather heavy-bodied, slow-moving serpent is more likely to stand its ground and face danger than to flee. When confronted by a large adversary, it draws its forebody into a tight, elevated S-coil, pulls its head back to face the threat, and often nervously vibrates its tail. In most cases it strikes out vigorously if closely approached, sometimes emitting a short hiss as it does so. One that is picked up or otherwise restrained is quick to bite, usually holding onto its captor as it chews viciously, meanwhile expelling the foul-smelling contents of its tail-based scent glands and voiding feces from its cloaca—covert actions meant to turn away an opponent.

Scent-gland emissions may have other uses as well. Brisbin (1968) suggested that a disturbed king snake uses them as a chemical alarm to alert its nearby companions to the potential danger, in much the same way

other vertebrate animals warn their fellow creatures of peril by emitting audible sounds and visual signals. Volsoe (in Klauber 1956) believed that scent-gland emissions may be used by female snakes to attract mates, but such a function has not been documented.

Over the northern part of its range, this snake remains active from April to October. In the mild climate of southeastern Texas its activity period is usually longer: it is often encountered above ground as early in the year as March and as late as November. During especially mild winters, when the temperature rises above 75 degrees F for two or three successive days, it may be encountered in any month. Its spring and fall surface forays are confined primarily to the hours of daylight, but it becomes largely nocturnal when midday temperatures are uncomfortably high in the summer.

When not on the prowl, the speckled king snake stays out of sight, hidden beneath any of a variety of surface objects including logs, piles of driftwood, mats of vegetative debris, loose tree bark, flat stones, and, when available, even pieces of tin, boards, and other man-made trash. Often when collectors find it under a board or piece of tin, the exposed reptile immediately crawls into a hole where the sheltering object had lain. Since it occasionally enters animal burrows to avoid temperature extremes or to escape its enemies, it is sometimes brought to the surface by farmers tilling their land. In the suburbs, the speckled king snake hides in piles of discarded construction rubble and under the scattered, weed-covered ruins of old farmhouses. Although chiefly a terrestrial serpent, it sometimes crawls into bushes or onto tree stumps.

In winter it hibernates in mammal burrows, decaying logs, rotting tree stumps, or piles of decaying vegetation. Smaller specimens occasionally hide under the loose bark of dead trees or tree stumps.

FEEDING Although its chief claim to fame is that it methodically devours rattlesnakes and other dangerous pit vipers, the speckled king snake eats a variety of vertebrate animals that includes small mammals, birds, lizards, baby turtles, and frogs, as well as the eggs of birds and reptiles. According to legend, the king snake chooses venomous serpents over all other kinds of prey, either from some compulsion to benefit mankind or because these particular prey species are more appetizing to its palate. Neither assumption is correct.

In fact, the king snake consumes an assortment of small animals, including other snakes, harmless as well as venomous. It is not known to focus its predatory attacks just on rattlesnakes, or on any other pit viper for that matter. What is not a myth, however, is that the king snake is aptly named for its capacity to overpower and consume other serpents, even those larger than itself. It can do so because it is endowed with an exceptionally muscular body, which it uses to constrict its prey. This commanding attribute, plus a high degree of immunity to the toxins of our local venomous snakes, makes it a formidable adversary when it attacks such dangerous opponents.

Unlike the slender, agile racers and whipsnakes that pursue their elusive quarry at full speed, the heavier, more slothful king snake locates prey by crawling slowly through its habitat, meticulously exploring every likely nook in an effort to ambush a concealed prey animal. It quickens its pace when it detects the odor of a potential morsel or when it sees the quarry in motion.

A rattlesnake can also detect the approaching king snake, for the king snake emits a scent from its skin that warns the rattler of the imminent danger. If the apprehensive rattlesnake retreats quickly enough, it may be able to avoid a confrontation; if it is unable or unwilling to do so, it usually reacts to the predator's approach by assuming a defensive posture just for the occasion. In this case, it does not assume the same aggressive S-loop and raised-head posture normally adopted when confronted by a large adversary such as man, but instead it presses its head and neck to the ground as it attempts to back away from its foe. At the close approach of the king snake, it raises its midsection off the substrate in an inverted ∪ and, with considerable force, whacks it sideways or downward against the assailant's approaching head, causing the attacker to pull back momentarily. But the king snake is a persistent aggressor. It quickly takes the offensive, seizing the victim's body in its jaws and instantly wrapping several powerful coils around the rattler's trunk. So overwhelming is the relentless pressure of the king snake's constricting coils that despite the rattler's repeated attempts to bite back in self-defense, it is rarely able to free itself. A victim of circulatory arrest, it soon becomes nearly motionless. Hardy (1994) recently suggested that as a result of the prey's severely compressed heart during constriction, death may actually be caused by a critically reduced flow of blood to certain vital organs. Before the swallowing process begins, the king snake may grab the victim's head and, with its coils still wrapped tightly around the rattler's midsection, almost vengefully pull the victim's forebody away from the rest of its trunk, stretching and twisting the prey's head and neck while chewing savagely on its head. It has been speculated that such violent stretching, twisting, and chewing may serve to subdue a still-resisting victim or somehow facilitate the swallowing process.

R. F. Clark's (1949) study of the speckled king snake's feeding habits in northern Louisiana shows that this serpent consumes other prey animals as eagerly as it does rattlesnakes. His investigations revealed that mice were the snake's chief prey, followed in decreasing order of frequency by rats, southern (broad-banded) water snakes, diamondbacked water snakes, eastern coachwhips, eastern hog-nosed snakes, southern copperheads, birds, unidentified snakes, western cottonmouths, rough green snakes, eastern garter snakes, canebrake rattlesnakes, and coral snakes. From his study and others conducted elsewhere, it is clear that venomous serpents are not the speckled king snake's chief food. Other prey reported for this species include the ground skink, green anole, mud turtle, snapping turtle, and cardinal.

Howell (1954) gives an account of a large speckled king snake that climbed a small hackberry tree to reach a bird's nest lodged in a clump of Spanish moss 6 or 7 feet above the ground. Although the nest was empty at the time, the snake had in its mouth a young cardinal not fully fledged, demonstrating the serpent's willingness to leave the ground when food is available overhead.

Some king snakes of the species *getula*, including this one, devour eggs of other reptiles, especially those of turtles, which they apparently find through their acute sense of smell. In fact, during the turtle nesting season in parts of South Carolina, certain local king snake populations (or at least some individuals of such populations) methodically raided chelonian nests; sometimes a single snake consumed an entire clutch of eggs or even the entire clutches of several different nests and of more than one species. For example, Knight and Loraine (1986) collected a king snake at Ellenton Bay in Aiken County, South Carolina, that regurgitated nine turtle eggs of at least three different species.

Even more remarkable is the probability that after locating nesting turtles, these serpents actually wait nearby for them to lay their eggs. In one such instance, Knight and Loraine encountered a female eastern king snake along a sandy road in Barnwell County, South Carolina. The snake, its head raised some 4 inches off the ground, watched and waited as a nearby box turtle excavated a hole in the earth and laid her eggs in it. Before the king snake could consume any of the eggs, however, it was captured by the biologists. That day it disgorged four eggs of several unidentified water turtle species and three days later defecated the remains of 13 others. Curiously, three of the eggs passed through the snake's digestive system unbroken and apparently unaffected by the snake's powerful digestive fluids, for they hatched and produced three common musk turtles after a 50-day incubation.

The king snake's propensity to search out and devour turtle eggs is also mentioned by other zoologists. According to Wright and Bishop (1915), the native inhabitants of Florida's Okefenokee Swamp believed the local king snakes to be habituated to turtle-egg depredations during the nesting season; they regularly saw the snakes waiting at the turtle nests in anticipation of egg-laying. They went on to say that of all the wild creatures in the swamp, only the Florida bear was more predisposed to pillage chelonian nests.

A more recent incident of turtle-egg predation by the speckled king snake is reported by Brauman and Fiorillo (1995), who saw a 54-inch-long female raid the nest of a yellowblotched map turtle, a threatened species inhabiting Mississippi's Pascagula River drainage system. Just after midday on July 6, they encountered the snake on a sandbar along the east bank of the river near Vancleave, its head and forebody inserted in a hole 1 foot (30.5 cm) in diameter and about $2\frac{1}{2}$ inches (6.3 cm) deep, which it had excavated in the loose leaf and sand substrate to reach the chelonian's nest. After the snake was removed from the hole, a single turtle egg was found in the bottom of the cavity. Six more were regurgitated by the serpent 20 minutes later, and six others three days after that. Since the maximum known clutch size for this turtle species is nine eggs, the snake probably had raided more than just one nest.

REPRODUCTION It is not uncommon for the males of some snake species, including the speckled king snake, to engage in lively combat during the breeding season or when they are competing for food, social dominance, or territory. Carpenter (1986), who summarized the numerous reports of combat behavior among snakes worldwide, documented it in no less than 77 species, both venomous and nonvenomous, and in serpents ranging in size from the tiny ground snake of the United States and Mexico to the huge king cobra of southeastern Asia, which at over 18 feet (5.5 m) in length is the earth's longest venomous serpent.

Although not as dramatic as that noted in some venomous snake species (see reproduction section for the western diamond-backed rattlesnake), the ritualized combat between rival male speckled king snakes is nevertheless spirited and equally intense. As observed by Carpenter and Gillingham (1977), it begins when the two snakes lie stretched out with the rear portions of their bodies closely entwined and the rest of their trunks in almost uninterrupted contact, though less tightly twisted. At the height of the confrontation, there is a constant flow of changing movement as each snake struggles to gain a dominant position. It is generally the larger male that triumphs. He asserts his supremacy by crawling on top of his smaller rival, maintaining this superior position until he is finally able to force his adversary's head and forebody to the ground with his own. During all of this, the smaller male sometimes responds by trying to crawl away, but he is relentlessly pursued by his antagonist. When the two make contact again, the subservient snake jerks his body spasmodically, and the dominant male responds with even more violent wrenching of his own. Meanwhile, there are back-and-forth movements of one body against the other, more jerking, and sometimes body bridging (the sudden thrust of a midbody loop directed at the adversary) as the combatants seek to gain a postural advantage. Throughout the entire ritual, which

may last more than an hour, these actions are repeated over and over again until one of the opponents (almost invariably the smaller one) accepts defeat. It is also during the latter stages of battle that biting may occur. Finally, to acknowledge his capitulation, the defeated snake usually withdraws from the area of contention, but he may also signal his surrender by assuming a submissive position with his head held flat against the ground. In one instance of combat between two captive speckled king snakes, the loser quickly disappeared beneath the sand of their enclosure, the only way he could escape the victor in such a confined space.

Both male and female speckled king snakes are capable of mating successfully when they are about two years and 10 months of age. Although mating in this subspecies generally occurs in April or May, soon after the snakes leave their hibernacula, late March copulations have been reported for populations in the southern states. Sometime between early June and mid-July, the female lays a clutch of 2 to 17 eggs in a decaying log or stump, a pile of rotting vegetation, a sawdust pile, or an abandoned animal burrow, though in a more unusual site, Penn (1943) discovered 7 eggs in a muskrat den. Speckled king snake eggs normally hatch in 60 to 75 days, revealing pencil-thick young that measure 9 to 11 inches (22.9–27.9 cm) long. Although they are speckled with light-colored spots low on the sides, virtually the only pale dorsal markings are the narrow, slightly crooked lines formed by the merging light spots at regular intervals across the snake's back.

DESERT KING SNAKE
Lampropeltis getula splendida
PLATE 79

DESCRIPTION This moderately large, dark brown to black serpent is similar in most respects to the speckled king snake, but its yellow-centered scales are confined chiefly to the sides of the body, whereas those on the middle of the back are arranged primarily as regularly spaced, narrow crosslines. (See illustration in speckled king snake account.)

In certain specimens, some of the scales between the crosslines are also light centered; in others the crosslines are absent. The abdomen of this subspecies is mostly black, except for the pale-hued, undivided anal scale and the yellow pigmentation irregularly distributed on the outer edges of the belly plates. The snake's dorsal scales are glossy

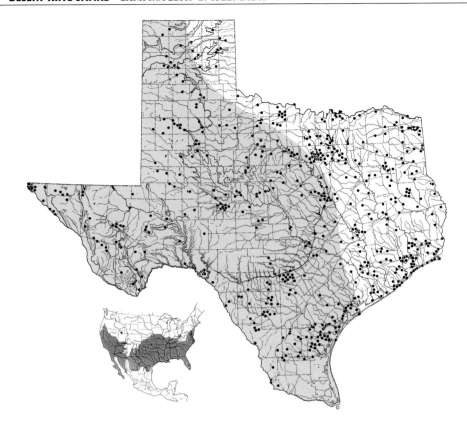

and unkeeled, those at midbody arranged in 23 or 25 rows.

In Texas, this subspecies intergrades with the speckled king snake over a wide band stretching from the Panhandle and the western two-thirds of the Red River southward to the mid-Texas coast. Specimens from near the middle of this zone may appear intermediate in pattern between the two races, whereas those from either side of the intergrade region will tend to look more like the nearest subspecies.

COMPARABLE SNAKES Each of the speckled racer's small dorsal spots consists of three colors—yellow, blue, and black—whereas those of the desert king snake are solid yellow or whitish. Unlike the light-colored dots of *L. g. splendida*, which on the snake's back are usually restricted to thin, yellow crosslines, those of the speckled racer occupy almost every scale on the snake's body. In addition, the racer has a conspicuous dark mask behind each eye, only 17 rows of mid-

body scales (the upper rows weakly keeled), a pale-colored belly, and a divided anal plate.

SIZE Most adults are between 36 and 45 inches (91.4–114.3 cm) long, although a specimen of record size measured 60 inches (152.4 cm) in length.

HABITAT Although the desert king snake occupies a wide range of habitats throughout the semiarid and desert regions of South and West Texas, it seldom wanders far from moisture. Vermersch and Kuntz (1986) stated that in south-central Texas it favors scattered woodlands near streams, especially those in which small mammal and tortoise burrows abound, providing the snakes adequate refuge from the hot summer sun. Other habitats mentioned included savannah-woodland interface and blackland prairie, where vertical, underground, drought-caused fissures also offer cool daytime retreats. In the arid Sierra Vieja Mountains of southwestern Texas, Jameson and Flury (1949) collected two specimens in the yucca-tobosa plant association of the Valentine Plain. In southeastern Arizona, Fowlie (1965) found it near streamside homes and along the margins of temporary bodies of water formed by torrential midsummer rains.

BEHAVIOR We have found this subspecies to be less irritable than its eastern counterpart, the speckled king snake, and therefore not as quick to bite when handled. Indeed, most specimens that we captured in the wild never attempted to bite in self-defense. An occasional irascible individual assumed an aggressive posture when confronted at close range, raising its head several inches off the ground and pulling it back above the middle of its tightly drawn coils as it gathered its forebody into a tight S configuration. At the same time it often rapidly vibrated its tail. A closer approach can bring a quick, open-mouthed thrust accompanied by a sharp, abbreviated hiss. In spite of this pugnacious defense, the desert king snake does not strike far; its intention is only to frighten off the interloper with its bold stance. Perhaps more disagreeable than the serpent's bite is the emission of feces from its cloacal opening and the discharge of musk from two glands at the base of its tail, actions initiated when the snake is first handled.

Based on a close examination of these scent glands and the results of laboratory experiments, Price and LaPointe (1981) concluded that the secretions are employed to repulse some of the desert king snake's natural predators. Their studies showed that spotted skunks, badgers, bobcats, and gray foxes (all potential consumers of king snakes) either refused food altogether when snake musk was applied to it or ate it only reluctantly; those that consumed the tainted morsels frantically wiped their snouts after eating it. It follows, therefore, that a king snake captured by a predator may reduce the risk of being eaten if it discharges musk during such an encounter.

The king snake survives in a hostile desert environment by carefully adjusting its activity pattern to avoid extremes of heat and cold, foraging on the surface only when the air temperature is moderate and remaining in animal burrows or deep rock crevices during scorching days and frigid nights. In regions with less severe temperature extremes, it simply hides by day under available surface objects such as rocks, logs, piles of organic litter, or human-generated debris, restricting its prowling activities mostly to nighttime hours and to dawn and dusk. In rural areas, a likely place to find it is among the scattered rubble of old farmhouses, many of which are near a permanent source of water—a desirable location for this moisture-loving serpent. The king snake can survive in waterless areas as well. For example, just across the international border on the dry, dusty outskirts of Nuevo Laredo, we encountered several specimens at night, crawling through trash heaps along the edge of the city's sprawling garbage dumps.

FEEDING Perhaps the most prevalent myth concerning the king snake's life history is that it preys almost exclusively on rattlesnakes. While it is true that the desert king snake, like other subspecies of *L. getula*, exhibits a preference for reptilian prey, including venomous as well as harmless species, it clearly does not limit its snake-eating habits to the relentless pursuit of rattlesnakes. Although there is ample evidence to show that it occasionally devours venomous serpents, the desert king snake does not dine solely on such prey but consumes a wide variety of snake species. The list of other animals on its menu ranges from frogs, lizards, and baby turtles to small mammals and birds, and even includes reptile and bird eggs.

Larger animals are constricted before being swallowed; smaller ones are simply seized and ingested with little preliminary maneuvering. The method used by this slow-moving, nonvenomous snake to overpower and kill a large rattlesnake is described in the speckled king snake account. Although it is unknown if the king snake's immune system also protects it from the nerve-damaging effects of coral snake venom, it must surely provide some degree of resistance to such toxins, since coral snakes have several times been reported as king-snake prey.

REPRODUCTION The breeding habits of this snake are similar to those of the closely related speckled king snake. Mating normally takes place in April and May, resulting in the deposition during June or July of egg clutches containing 5 to 12 eggs each. In south-central Texas, according to Vermersch and Kuntz (1986), they are laid in loose, damp soil or leaf mold, although a clutch of 8 eggs was found in the moist interior of a decaying log beside a streambed in southern Texas. Between 1⅛ and 1¾ inches (2.9–4.4 cm) long

when laid, they are white, sometimes with a yellowish wash, and covered with a wet substance that after drying causes them to stick to one another. They hatch sometime during August, September, or early October, producing young that measure 9 or 10 inches (22.9–25.4 cm) long.

LOUISIANA MILK SNAKE
Lampropeltis triangulum amaura
PLATE 80

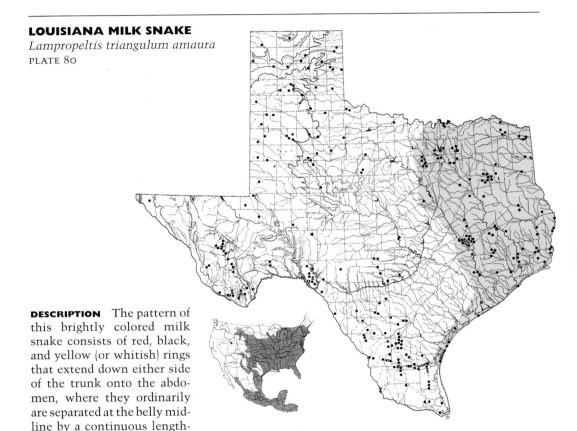

DESCRIPTION The pattern of this brightly colored milk snake consists of red, black, and yellow (or whitish) rings that extend down either side of the trunk onto the abdomen, where they ordinarily are separated at the belly midline by a continuous lengthwise band of the pale ground color. The two narrow black rings that border each wide red one usually do not continue horizontally across the bottom of the red ring to enclose it, but typically the red band extends across the belly, where a lengthwise row of irregular black spots replaces the lowermost portion of dark edging. Each yellow ring continues uninterrupted across the belly. The snout is normally speckled with black and white or may even be mostly black, and the rest of the head is black except for a yellow or whitish band just forward of the neckline. The dorsal scales, all smooth, are usually arranged in 21 rows at midbody, and the anal plate is single.

COMPARABLE SNAKES The red and yellow rings of the Texas coral snake are always in contact with one another, whereas in the milk snakes the two colors are invariably separated by a black ring. Furthermore, the coral snake's black rings, which are as wide as its red ones, are much broader than those of the milk snake, and all of the coral's rings cross the belly uninterrupted. Except for small, discreet spots on the very outside edges of some belly plates, the abdomen of the northern scarlet and the Texas scarlet snake is white and unmarked. The belly of the Texas long-nosed snake also is unmarked white; the sides of its black dorsal blotches

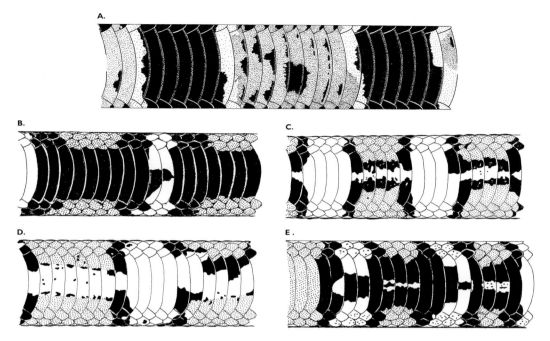

Figure 33. *Dorsal rings continue essentially uninterrupted across (a) the belly of the coral snake, compared to the broken belly patterns of the four native milk snakes: (b) Mexican milk snake, (c) New Mexico milk snake, (d) Louisiana milk snake, and (e) Central Plains milk snake.*

are prominently speckled with yellow, and the red interspaces are spotted with black. Moreover, it has 23 midbody rows of dorsal scales, and most of the scales under its tail are in a single row (double in milk snakes).

Assigning a particular specimen of *L. triangulum* to the correct subspecies may at times be difficult. Not only are the four Texas races generally similar to each other in color and pattern, but also wherever two subspecies converge geographically individual specimens normally carry the genes of both races, compounding the difficulty of assigning the specimen to either one. The simplest recourse in such cases is to assign the doubtful specimen to the nearest race, based on its collecting locality.

SIZE Adults usually range in length from 16 to 22 inches (40.6–55.9 cm), but a record specimen measured 31 inches (78.7 cm) long.

HABITAT Generally distributed over the eastern third of the state, this snake is most frequently encountered in the low-lying oak-cypress-tupelo forests of southeastern Texas and the pine-hardwood forests that occur in the east-central part of the state. In such re-

gions it is most prevalent in moist, sandy situations where trees and shrubs provide adequate shade, although under less typical circumstances it has been found at a few isolated localities on the treeless, grass-covered sand dunes of the Gulf Coast barrier islands.

BEHAVIOR Not prone to strike in self-defense, the milk snake is a relatively even-tempered reptile whose gentle disposition and brilliant coloration make it a prized commodity among snake hobbyists. But a specimen handled for the first time may react unexpectedly. When picked up, it sometimes turns its head slowly to one side, opens its mouth, and with calm deliberation clamps its jaws over a finger or some other part of the hand, maintaining its grip as it chews. Such vigorous chewing results in nothing more than a cluster of superficial puncture marks, which, while they may bleed slightly, are not serious.

Seldom encountered on the move above ground, the Louisiana milk snake is a secretive, burrowing serpent that is content to spend most of its life hidden in loose, sandy soil or snugly concealed under some surface object. The decaying interiors of stumps and logs are favorite aboveground shelters, as are the spaces between the trunks of trees and their loose bark. Guidry (1953), for example, found 18 of these elusive snakes in one spring afternoon by peeling the loose bark from pine stumps in a single square-mile tract of heavy forest about a mile north of Dewey-ville in Newton County. All of his previous collecting efforts in the same area had yielded only 4 specimens, all encountered at night along sandy roads.

Others have discovered this milk snake in similar circumstances. Along the eastern edge of Louisiana's Atchafalaya Basin and in an area close to the Bonnet Carré Spillway in St. Charles Parish, for instance, Dundee and Rossman (1989) frequently found it in both winter and early spring, hidden either beneath the bark of dead trees or deep inside their decaying interiors, some as high as 8 feet (2.6 m) above the ground. It just so happens that when the snakes were encountered, most of the trees in this bottomland hardwood forest were standing in several feet of water. Extensive flooding presented no serious, long-term obstacle to the serpents' customary wanderings, for like most snakes, these little reptiles have the capacity to swim. The same zoologists reported the sighting of a specimen of this subspecies swimming in Lake Maurepas, Louisiana, 2 or 3 miles (3.2–4.8 km) from the closest land; in Texas we observed one in the waters of Lake Livingston, no more than 3 feet (91 cm) from shore.

Although it ordinarily hides in and under logs and stumps as well as in the pithy centers of standing dead trees, it has also been taken in the decaying root system of a large dead tree, in the crevices of hardwood logs, in piles of coastal driftwood, under boards and tin, and beneath a brick pile. When not nestled in some aboveground shelter, the Louisiana milk snake is likely to stay out of sight by digging into sandy soil, where it is occasionally uncovered by farmers tilling their fields.

FEEDING Small snakes, lizards, and young mice appear to be its chief prey. Dundee and Rossman reported that captive *L. t. amaura* from Louisiana proved oddly discriminating in their choice of food, their selection of prey being based solely on where the serpents were captured. Milk snakes from the northern part of the state accepted only baby mice and consistently rejected green anoles, but those from southern Louisiana would eat only anoles.

REPRODUCTION What little information we have about this snake's reproductive biology indicates that the female ordinarily lays a clutch of 3 to 9 eggs sometime between early June and mid-July, though Tryon and Murphy (1982) reported one clutch that was laid on January 26 and hatched on March 11 and 12. The eggs measure $1^{3}/_{5}$ to $1^{3}/_{4}$ inches (4.1–4.4 cm) long. After incubating for about six weeks, they hatch during August or the first half of September, producing baby snakes that are 7 to 8 inches (17.8–20.3 cm) long.

MEXICAN MILK SNAKE
Lampropeltis triangulum annulata
PLATE 81

DESCRIPTION Like other native subspecies of milk snake, this race is marked with red, black, and yellow (or whitish) bands, but its pattern contains more dark pigmentation than the others. The broad, dark red bands, which in some specimens appear slightly orange, reach downward only to the lower edge of the first row of dorsal scales or the outer edges of the belly plates. They are flanked on either side by a moderately wide black ring

that is slightly narrower at the belly line and whose dark pigment not only continues under the red band but completely crosses the abdomen. The narrow yellow ring that separates each pair of black ones circles the body without interruption. The snout is entirely black or nearly so; the top of the head as far back as the parietals (the largest paired scales on the crown) is also black, as are the sides of the head down to and including the lower

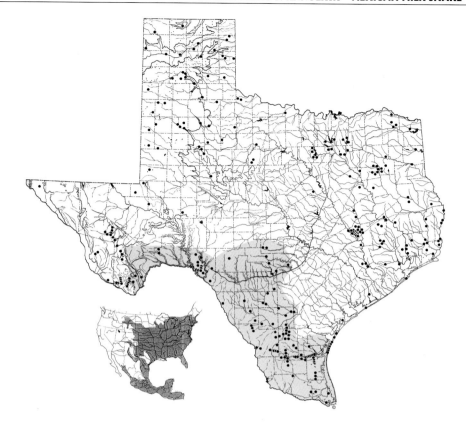

lip scales. A yellow collar crosses the back of the head. The dorsal scales, all smooth, are in 21 rows at midbody, and the anal plate is single.

COMPARABLE SNAKES *See Louisiana milk snake account and illustration.*

SIZE This is the largest subspecies of milk snake in Texas; adult specimens usually range from 24 to 30 inches (61–76.2 cm) long. The largest known Mexican milk snake measured 41½ inches (105.4 cm) in length.

HABITAT Primarily an inhabitant of the South Texas thornbrush savannah, where caliche and sandy soils support such arid-land vegetation as mesquite, catclaw, prickly pear cactus, lotebush, white thorn, black-brush, and granjeno, this milk snake sub-species ranges north to the southern portion of the Edwards Plateau, where it occurs chiefly in the vicinity of the region's lime-stone creekbeds and arroyos to an elevation of about 2,350 feet. Snakes from Del Rio to the Davis Mountains all appear to be inter-grades between this subspecies and the New Mexico milk snake. On the barrier islands just off the Texas Gulf Coast it can be found at sea level.

BEHAVIOR The Mexican milk snake ordinarily is mild-mannered and not inclined to bite, though if sufficiently provoked by rough handling it may seize a restraining finger and hang on doggedly as it repeatedly embeds its small teeth. The puncture wounds created by the serpent's teeth will bleed slightly, but the bite is not serious.

The milk snake is a shy creature that finds safety by staying out of sight. As a result, it is seldom encountered by the layperson unfamiliar with its habits. When not nestled in a rodent tunnel or hiding in loose soil, a milk snake is likely to spend the daylight hours concealed beneath some suitable surface object, for this is primarily a nocturnal reptile. It engages in late evening or nighttime forays mostly from early April to November, according to museum specimen collection records, though it is rarely seen during the hottest part of summer, when it probably retires to a moist underground refuge. There it generally remains until early autumn rains refresh the ground and bring the ambient temperatures down to a moderate level, at which time the snake resumes its nocturnal wanderings. No one has determined the extent of the snake's movements or the size of its home range, but its frequent appearance as a victim of vehicular traffic suggests that it travels some distance during its nighttime forays.

Although the best time to see it in the open is at night when the ground is still damp from recent rains, particularly in the spring, it is often found during the day by turning over objects under which it has taken shelter. Where they are available, stones and logs provide good shelter, but trash heaps and other kinds of man-made debris are sometimes also used by the snake.

Unlike the small springtime concentrations of Louisiana milk snakes that are sometimes encountered in the pine forests of East Texas, the Mexican milk snake is nearly always found one specimen at a time. An unusual exception involves the population of milk snakes (believed to be intergrades between *L. t. annulata* and *L. t. amaura*) living on Matagorda Island, a long ribbon of mostly sand that lies a couple of miles off the Gulf Coast. During the 1950s, in company with a collecting team from Chicago's Lincoln Park Zoo, Werler twice journeyed to the island to assemble a live collection of reptiles; each two- or three-day trip yielded more than a dozen of these attractive snakes. We know of no other place where so many Mexican milk snakes have been found in such a brief span of time.

Similar collecting results are reported by David E. Johnson, an amateur herpetologist who, as an airman assigned to the Air Force base on Matagorda Island, collected 33 milk snakes on the northern third of the island from February through May of 1953. He encountered most of the specimens on the middle or lower slopes of oceanside sand dunes situated 100 or more yards west of the Gulf, where they were found hiding beneath logs, boards, and other forms of driftwood as well as under dilapidated boat hulls and discarded materials such as plywood sheets, wooden signs, and aerial gunnery targets. A few were discovered a foot or two below the surface, nestled under large driftwood tree trunks or stumps that had washed ashore and become firmly embedded in the sand. Such heavy flotsam was pulled out of the ground only with the aid of a block and tackle secured to a truck. In spite of the large number of specimens he encountered there, it is Johnson's experience, as well as our own, that the island's milk snakes carefully avoided sharing their shelters with one another, for never was more than a single individual found in the same hiding place.

FEEDING Although captive Mexican milk snakes have regularly taken offerings of lizards and mice, almost nothing is known about the subspecies' food preferences in the wild. Lizards no doubt constitute a major source of prey for this mostly nocturnal predator, but except for the night-wandering geckos, the other day-active lizards are asleep in their shelters when the milk snake is busily foraging for a meal after dark. This may be to the serpent's advantage, however. Lacking the speed of certain day-active, lizard-eating competitors such as patch-nosed snakes and whipsnakes in the same habitat, it needs to search out and snatch the lizards from their nighttime sanctuaries without having to chase them. According to David E. Johnson (pers. com.), some of the milk snakes he collected on Matagorda Island regurgitated small glass lizards or their tails. Not surprisingly, the milk snake, like its larger kingsnake relatives, often uses its muscular coils to constrict prey that is either too large to subdue and swallow outright (other snakes) or that has the potential to inflict a serious bite on its captor (adult rodents).

Like the adult males of a number of other snake species, those of the Mexican milk snake sometimes engage in ritualistic combat. Most such encounters are carried out between males of the same species to decide which one will court and mate with a nearby female. Shaw (1951) observed such an encounter between captive male Mexican milk snakes that was not sex-related but was a contest over food. In a typical skirmish, performed on several different occasions, the dominant serpent pursued his cagemate, crawled over its back, and engaged it in a contest of neck flexing and body twisting.

REPRODUCTION See Louisiana milk snake account. The few reported accounts of egg-laying by this snake indicate that after an early spring mating the female usually lays a clutch of 4 to 12 eggs that are 1½ inches (3.8 cm) long sometime between late April and mid-July. The eggs generally hatch during June or July after an incubation period typically lasting 47 to 61 days, producing young that normally measure between 9 and 10 inches (22.9–25.4 cm) long. In a curious ex-

ception to the snake's usual pattern, according to Jack Joy (in Tryon and Murphy 1982), a female milk snake from South Texas laid only 2 eggs (the smallest number reported) on August 21 (the latest known deposition date), which hatched between October 31 and November 3 (the latest documented hatching date).

NEW MEXICO MILK SNAKE
Lampropeltis triangulum celaenops
PLATE 82

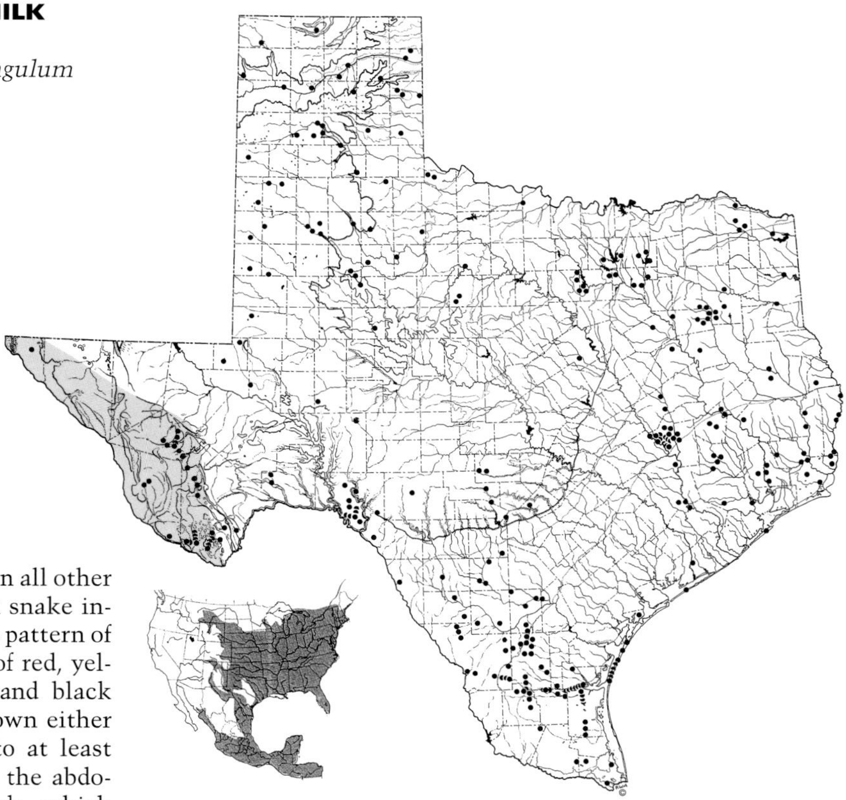

DESCRIPTION As in all other subspecies of milk snake inhabiting Texas, the pattern of this race consists of red, yellow (or whitish), and black rings that reach down either side of the body to at least the outer edges of the abdomen. The red bands, which extend well onto the belly, are bordered on each side by a narrow black one that continues around the bottom of the red color to enclose it. The black rings are generally widest along the midline of the back. Between each pair of black rings is a yellowish one that not only crosses the belly but also forms a narrow band of pale abdominal color separating the black-edged red rings along the entire length of the belly midline. The dark snout, usually speckled with white, may be nearly or entirely black in some specimens; the rest of the head is black, except for a yellowish collar near the neckline. The dorsal scales,

all smooth, are in 21 rows at midbody, and the anal plate is single.

COMPARABLE SNAKES *See Louisiana milk snake account and illustration.*

SIZE Adults are generally between 18 and 22 inches (45.7–55.9 cm) long, but the subspecies is reported to reach a maximum length of 25 inches (63.5 cm).

HABITAT This milk snake occurs in a variety of habitats ranging from 2,500 to 7,000 feet (762–2,134 m) elevation, including open woodland as well as rocky grassland. Generally avoiding the intolerably arid desert floor of West Texas, it does inhabit both the dry grasslands and the pinyon-oak zones of the desert mountains, as well as the grass–shin oak prairie of the Llano Estacado region in the western Panhandle. Snakes from Del Rio to the Davis Mountains all appear to be intergrades between this subspecies and the Mexican milk snake.

BEHAVIOR A relatively gentle creature, the milk snake usually shows little temper when annoyed, its first response being to crawl away to safety. When handled for the first time, a wild-caught specimen will probably expel fecal matter from its cloaca. It may also turn its head toward a restraining hand and in a matter-of-fact, almost casual way, seize it, embedding its small teeth repeatedly as it chews. The resulting punctures are superficial and cause no serious consequences.

Like most other milk snakes, it rarely ventures out into the open. Its nocturnal wanderings are usually restricted to cool, wet nights. Otherwise it occasionally takes shelter beneath surface objects such as rocks, logs, or recumbent desert plants, though most of its active season (lasting from late March into November) is spent at rest in some underground nook where it can avoid the dual hazards of perilously high temperatures and low humidity.

FEEDING Since little detailed information has been published concerning the life history of this reptile (including its feeding habits), we can only speculate about its dietary preferences. Based on the prey known to be taken by other races of milk snake, we can reasonably assume that it eats mostly lizards, other snakes, and very small mammals, which in some instances are killed by constriction before being swallowed. Like most of its kin, the New Mexico milk snake is a nocturnal hunter, active when most lizards are asleep in some sheltered refuge. It is likely, therefore, that after dark the snake finds such prey by poking into rock piles, underground crevices, and plant debris where the lacertilians spend the night.

REPRODUCTION *See Louisiana milk snake account.* The few documented incidents of egg-laying by the New Mexico milk snake do not differ in any essential detail from those of other native milk snake subspecies.

When first laid, milk-snake eggs are coated with a wet substance that dries and causes them to stick together so firmly that they cannot later be separated from each other without the risk of rupturing their leathery shells. Of course, the effectiveness of this mechanism depends on the eggs' being laid one against the other (which is the usual condition), for any egg that is remote from the rest cannot become part of the consolidated egg mass unless the female intervenes. That she evidently does so is reported by Green and Pauley (1987), who saw an eastern milk snake maneuver her clutch of recently laid eggs into the middle of her body coils, pulling them close together where they would bind solidly into a single bundle as their tacky surfaces dried. The advantage of such an egg mass is obvious. Single eggs are small enough to be easily devoured by certain common reptilian predators, which ordinarily swallow them whole. When they are cemented together with several others, the cluster is too large to be ingested by the marauding reptiles, and so it becomes much less vulnerable to such attacks. At least two reports note that female milk snakes were found coiled around their recently laid clutches of eggs, suggesting that they were either protecting them or trying to pull them closer together for the reason just mentioned.

CENTRAL PLAINS MILK SNAKE
Lampropeltis triangulum gentilis
PLATE 83

DESCRIPTION Although banded in red, black, and yellow, like all Texas milk snake subspecies, this race often appears more faded than the others. Its red markings sometimes assume an orange hue, and the yellow bands frequently take on a subdued greenish yellow or even whitish tone. The red bands (the longest of all measured from front to back) seldom cross the belly, for they are normally separated there by the lengthwise expansion

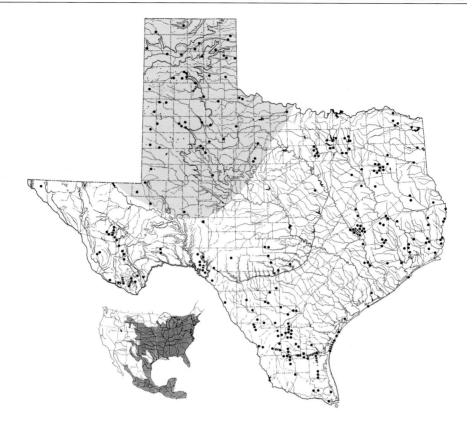

of the black rings, which flank them on either side. In addition, the black rings frequently become wider along the spine, particularly on the rear part of the body and also along midbelly, encroaching on the red bands in both places. The yellowish or white band that separates each pair of black-margined red ones frequently is peppered with dark pigment along its sides and may be mottled with large black blotches at the midline of the belly. The snout ordinarily is mottled with light and dark pigment (often as far back on the crown as the eyes), though occasionally it is mostly black. It may also be completely white, except for a few scattered black spots. From the eyes to the back of the parietals (the largest paired scales on the crown) the top of the head is black, as are the sides of the face down to and including the upper edges of the lower lip scales. Thereafter, a pale yellow or whitish collar crosses the back of the head. The dorsal scales are smooth and usually in 21 rows, and the anal plate is single.

COMPARABLE SNAKES *See Louisiana milk snake account and illustration.*

SIZE Adults attain a modest length of 16 to 24 inches (40.6–61 cm), but the largest documented specimen measured 36 inches (91.4 cm) long.

HABITAT Stone-covered grassland prairie, particularly in the vicinity of rocky ledges, is the preferred habitat of this uncommon milk snake, though it also occurs in wooded streambed valleys and along sparsely forested mountain slopes. In a long-term study of the red milk snake, a subspecies closely related to *L. t. gentilis*, Fitch and Fleet (1970) found that it preferred low, sparse ground cover to taller, denser vegetation, a condition seemingly favored as well by the Central Plains milk snake.

BEHAVIOR Not likely to strike out at the close approach of a large adversary such as man, this timid snake does its best to avoid a confrontation by crawling, not always rapidly, under a rock or some other nearby surface shelter. There are exceptions, however.

One concerns an irritable female, collected in Colorado by H. M. Smith (1978), who raised her forebody in a defensive posture and struck repeatedly whenever she was closely approached, a behavior that continued even after ten weeks of daily handling. Her progeny, perhaps because of genetic influence, displayed the same contentious behavior. They reacted to movement in the same way, rapidly vibrating their tails and lashing out at the source of their displeasure. Seldom, however, is a milk snake so impetuous. One that is seized may turn its head to one side and with almost casual deliberation clamp its jaws onto its captor's hand, chewing obstinately until forcibly removed.

Although *L. triangulum* is one of the most widely distributed of all snake species, ranging from southeastern Canada to Ecuador, little is recorded about the life history details of its 25 subspecies. It is not hard to understand why, since with few exceptions these are timid, retiring snakes whose mostly subterranean and nocturnal life frustrates most efforts by zoologists to observe their behavior in the wild. A notable exception is the long-term study conducted by Fitch and Fleet of the red milk snake's natural history in northeastern Kansas. Because this subspecies intergrades with the Central Plains race not far to the west, it seems likely that the two will not differ greatly, if at all, in their respective behaviors. We therefore include below some of the information from that report.

Optimum milk snake habitat at the study site consisted of open woodland or woodland edge, with a ground cover of short grass and low-growing, sparse vegetation, where the soil surface was generously littered with flat rocks under which the snakes could take refuge when they were not hiding below ground. Such rocky environments provide choice temporary shelter for both the red and Central Plains milk snakes, not only in Kansas but also throughout their collective geographic ranges. Elsewhere the snakes have been closely associated with the rocky environs of canyons, quarries, river bluffs, ledges, and hillsides, although where large stones are scarce or absent they will take shelter in or under logs and tree stumps or beneath boards, pieces of sheet metal, tarpaper, and other man-made trash.

Red milk snakes that were marked, released, and later recaptured during the Kansas study had moved distances of 250 to 1,300 feet (76–396 m), suggesting a home range area for this subspecies of about 50 acres (20 ha), although only 11 of 58 specimens involved in the survey were ever seen again. A hatchling released on August 25 was subsequently found at the same place on three different occasions over a span of 9 months, and a juvenile captured on June 11 was discovered about a month later under the same shelter where it was originally encountered. The greatest distance traveled was the 1,300 feet (396 m) traversed by a young adult male during the 2½ months that it wandered over its home territory.

Active from April into November, the Central Plains milk snake is a nocturnal reptile whose aboveground forays are most frequent after the soil has been dampened by recent showers. Otherwise it is likely to be found under a flat rock, where, particularly during the cool days of early spring, it will rest with the length of its back pressed gently against the rock's underside to absorb its solar-generated heat. This is a much safer way for the cold-blooded milk snake to raise its body temperature than basking conspicuously in the direct sun where it may be exposed to surface predators. With the arrival of the hot, dry midsummer, when it tends to move down into the cooler, moister soil, farmers frequently bring it to light when they plow their fields, dig postholes, or perform excavation work in general. Milk snakes have also been dug out of sand or gravel pits, both in summer and winter; one was found hibernating in a sand pit 6 feet (189 cm) below the surface.

FEEDING Only one significant study of the species' natural diet has been conducted; it is summarized in Fitch and Fleet's survey of the red milk snake in Douglas County, Kansas. In it the zoologists found that only small vertebrates were consumed by this subspecies. Of 20 prey animals identified in the study, there were 12 five-lined skinks, 2 ring-necked snakes, 4 least shrews, 1 Great Plains skink (tail only), 1 worm snake, and 1 deer mouse. This composition of prey species generally agrees with the food categories mentioned in anecdotal reports detailing the dietary habits of other native milk snake sub-species. Since the five-lined skink, the snake's principal quarry in eastern Kansas, is absent from the north-central part of Texas where the Central Plains milk snake occurs, *L. t. gentilis* no doubt preys to a large extent on other local ground-dwelling lizards. Equipped with a relatively small head and delicate jaws, the milk snake is no match for any but the smallest mammals and moderate-sized lizards; the more defiant ones are killed by constriction before being swallowed.

The milk snake got its name not from some chromatic resemblance to that nourishing liquid but from a myth fabricated during colonial times concerning the eastern milk snake, *L. t. triangulum.* That race, the largest of all U.S. milk snake subspecies, inhabits the northeastern part of the country, where it is often found in and near farm buildings, including dairy barns. Its tendency to enter such structures is easily explained by the abundance of mice and rats that are attracted to the stores of grain used to feed farm animals; small rodents, especially their nestlings, are the milk snake's chief prey. Those who perpetuate the myth would have us believe otherwise; they conclude that cows are the attraction. According to them, the snake twines its slender body about a cow's leg, takes a teat in its mouth, and sucks enough milk from the udder to satisfy its hunger. The reduction in yield, they say, is enough to be noticed. Although the farmer has not witnessed the act just described, he is convinced of its reality, for he sees no accidental coincidence between the snake's presence and a decline in the cow's milk produc-tion. After all, he has heard the story of the marauding milk snake all his life. The story begins to lose its credibility when one realizes that a milk snake, even a large one, can hold no more than a few tablespoonsful of liquid in its stomach, hardly enough to be noticed at milking time. Furthermore, it is inconceivable that a cow would tolerate the discomfort of having a snake sink several rows of needle-sharp little teeth into a teat while it drinks its fill. Finally, considering the structure of the snake's neck musculature, there is no way the reptile can create enough suction to draw milk from the cow's udder.

Stories like this are interesting examples of early American folklore, but to the degree that they are embraced as fact, they make the task of changing public attitudes about the relentlessly vilified serpent more difficult.

REPRODUCTION Breeding in this milk snake subspecies, which occurs in the spring, is accompanied by aggressive overtures from the male, who seizes his mate by the neck (or on the head, as illustrated in Markel 1990) to hold her in position during copulation. Noting eight recorded incidents of egg-laying by the Central Plains milk snake, none of which involved Texas specimens, Tryon and Murphy (1982) summarized all that was then known about the reproductive biology of this subspecies. Altogether, their accounts revealed that the females lay 4 to 12 eggs per clutch sometime between June 19 and July 15, each egg measuring 1 to $1^3/_4$ inches (2.5–4.4 cm) long. After incubating 42 to 56 days (hatching between August 11 and September 1), they produced babies that were 7 to $9^1/_3$ inches (17.6–23.9 cm) long.

NORTHERN CAT-EYED SNAKE

Leptodeira septentrionalis septentrionalis
PLATE 84

DESCRIPTION This is a slender, narrow-necked serpent whose relatively wide head supports a pair of large, bronze-colored eyes with vertical pupils. Its broad, dark brown or black, saddle-shaped dorsal blotches extend across the back to about the first row of scales on either side of the body, contrasting boldly with the snake's much lighter cream to apricot-buff ground color. These markings gradually narrow as they approach the belly, and occasionally two of them merge to form a single, large H-shaped blotch. The snake's pale orange abdomen is especially vivid on the underside of the tail, and the rear edge of

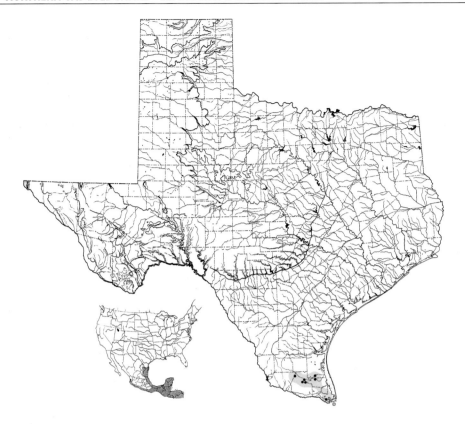

each belly scale is margined with dark pigment. The head markings are variable but usually consist of a nearly horizontal dark streak on each cheek and two or more randomly shaped dark spots on the crown that often terminate in a rearward-pointing, arrowlike mark close to the neck. The smooth dorsal scales are in 21 or 23 rows at midbody, and the anal plate is divided.

COMPARABLE SNAKES The ground snake may occur in a crossbanded phase with dark brown or black markings set against a pale ground color, but its head is only a little if any wider than its neck, and its dorsal scales are in 13 or 15 midbody rows. In the southwestern rat snake the dorsal blotches reach only halfway down the sides of the body, and a lateral row of dark blotches occupies the spaces below them. The belly is patterned with some dark pigmentation. The snake's head markings consist of a bold and well-defined dark transverse band across the forecrown and a large, forward-pointing, spear-point mark that dominates the rest of the head. In addition, its midbody dorsal scales are in 27 or 29 rows. Like the cat-eyed snake, the Texas night snake has relatively large eyes with vertical pupils, but its dorsal blotches are small and bordered by a lateral row of smaller spots.

Figure 34. *Broad head and elliptical eye pupil of the northern cat-eyed snake.*

SIZE Adults of this subspecies generally are 18 to 24 inches (45.7–61 cm) long, but the largest known specimen measured 38¾ inches (98.4 cm) in length.

HABITAT Essentially an inhabitant of semiarid scrub forest and tropical deciduous woodland, this subspecies of cat-eyed snake ranges northward from east-central Mexico to the southern tip of Texas, generally occupying areas of low to moderate elevation. In some parts of Mexico, where it occasionally occurs as high as 6,500 feet (1,981 m), the northern cat-eyed snake has been taken in cloud-forest clearings. In the South Texas chaparral, however, it usually keeps to thick brush near ponds, streams, and resacas where there is apt to be anuran prey. Such prime habitat is scarce in the lower Rio Grande Valley, largely because of the region's expanding urban and agricultural development. Thus, to insure the survival of this alien rarity in extreme southern Texas, it is important to preserve the region's wildlife refuges, both governmental and private. Such protected parcels of remnant subtropical forest, although scattered and few, may well be the only hope to conserve the northern cat-eyed snake and the host of other rare animal species found there with it.

BEHAVIOR When first approached, this timid serpent typically tries to escape, but one that is suddenly threatened may draw its body into a series of compact coils, beneath which it may even try to hide its head. If unable to flee, it may simply flatten its head in an intimidating gesture. Although it has a mildly toxic venom (used to subdue small prey animals) and short rear-set fangs to aid in its delivery, the snake rarely if ever attempts to use these resources defensively.

An exclusively nocturnal reptile, the northern cat-eyed snake spends the daylight hours coiled under a log, leaf litter, or pile of vegetative debris as it awaits the arrival of dusk to begin its foraging activities. Although it cannot be considered an arboreal species, it is an agile climber; its slender body easily takes it up into bushes and low tree limbs, where it searches for tree frogs, one of its preferred foods.

FEEDING Like all members of the genus *Leptodeira*, the northern cat-eyed snake is a nocturnal hunter. Although its chief prey consists of frogs and their tadpoles, other animals small enough to be overpowered, such as lizards, toads, salamanders, and even fish are occasionally attacked and eaten. One of the few reports of a cat-eyed snake feeding on warm-blooded prey is Ditmars' (1936) account of a *Leptodeira* that took mice in captivity.

Writing about the feeding habits of cat-eyed snakes in general, Duellman (1958) noted that during the dry season, when many frog species retreat to obscure, damp niches to avoid desiccation, lizards become the snake's most available prey. Covered with a less permeable skin than amphibians, the lizards are seldom restricted in their movements by a lack of moisture.

Just as water snakes are often attracted to concentrations of frogs and fish that have become trapped in drying bodies of water during periods of drought, *L. s. polystictus*, a Mexican subspecies closely related to the northern cat-eyed snake, is drawn to aggregations of frogs during the amphibians' mating season. For a brief time, such anuran gatherings present the snakes with an abundance of prey, and it is likely that similar breeding concentrations of frogs may attract the northern cat-eyed snake as well. Another closely related Mexican subspecies sometimes feeds on the eggs of certain tropical frogs, an unusual and unexpected prey item not known to be consumed by any other serpent. Deposited on the underside of leaves or branches suspended over water, the small, gelatinous eggs are plucked from the vegetation by the snake's needle-sharp teeth and swallowed. Armed with short, grooved fangs at the rear of the upper jaw and a venom of low toxicity, this snake is capable of disabling only small prey. Duellman's observations of the species' feeding behavior revealed that when it seized small frogs, it did not inject them with venom but swallowed them rather quickly and without much fanfare, usually still alive. When larger frogs were attacked, they were maneuvered to the back of the snake's mouth, where they could be pierced by the predator's rear-set fangs. This was followed by chewing motions as the serpent inflicted numerous shallow puncture wounds to the victim's skin, through which the venom was then ab-

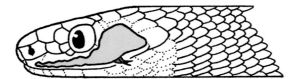

Figure 35. *Side of head of the northern cat-eyed snake, with position of modified venom gland and enlarged posterior grooved teeth shaded.*

sorbed. Considering the snake's primitive poisoning apparatus and the comparatively benign nature of its venom when injected into a human, it is easy to understand why this serpent is not regarded as a serious threat to man. Symptoms noted in the case of a zoo worker bitten by a 26-inch (66 cm) cat-eyed snake included minimal swelling, reddish discoloration, and a slight pain at the site of the bite, manifestations no more seri-

ous than those normally produced by a bee sting.

REPRODUCTION Surprisingly little detailed information has been recorded about the breeding habits of this common snake. The few published reports about its reproduction have disclosed that early spring mating is the rule; gravid females have been collected between February 11 and May 14. The eggs, 6 to 12 in a clutch, hatched 79 to 90 days after deposition. The young are 8½ to 9½ inches (21.6–24.1 cm) long and look essentially like the parents, but with more vivid patterns. As in certain other snakes, delayed egg fertilization occurs in this species. This was documented by Haines (1940), who reported the laying of fertile eggs by a captive female cat-eyed snake in each of three years of her confinement during which she had no contact with a male. She had obviously been inseminated in the wild before her capture.

WESTERN SMOOTH GREEN SNAKE
Liochlorophis vernalis blanchardi
PLATE 85

DESCRIPTION Except for a wash of yellow or whitish color around its mouth, this moderately small, smooth-scaled snake is uniformly bright green above and pale yellow or whitish on the belly. It should be noted, however, that recently killed specimens soon undergo a radical color change, from pea green to blue. Live adults occasionally have an olive-green dorsal color, and very young examples are bluish gray or olive brown. The body scales are in 15 middorsal rows, and the anal plate is divided.

COMPARABLE SNAKES The only Texas serpent closely resembling this remarkably distinct species is the rough green snake. It shares with its smaller cousin a similar, though slightly darker, shade of green on the back and sides and a whitish, yellow, or sometimes pale green underside—a hue that in both snakes extends as far up onto the snake's head as the upper lips. Its dorsal scales are prominently keeled and in 17 instead of 15 rows at midbody. Though most adult Mexican and eastern yellow-bellied

racers are completely dark green or dull brown above, they are longer than green snakes and more heavy-bodied. Juvenile racers, though similar in size to young green snakes, are easily distinguished from them by their boldly blotched patterns.

SIZE Throughout its range, 14 to 20 inches (35.6–50.8 cm) is the usual adult length of this snake, although it is reported to reach a maximum length of 26 inches (66 cm). The largest Texas specimen found so far measured just over 15 inches (38.1 cm) long.

HABITAT In Texas this snake occurs as a relict population along the Gulf Coast. The few specimens discovered there, almost 500 miles from the nearest populations to the north and northwest, have been found near sea level in habitats described as open shortgrass prairie or meadow. Known from fewer than 10 specimens, collected in Austin, Chambers, Harris, and Matagorda counties, it is one of our rarest serpents. Davis (1953) suggested that by moving along prairie corridors, such as those represented by the north-to-south-

trending blackland prairies of Central Texas, this snake long ago made its way southward from the mainstream midwestern populations to the Texas Gulf Coast.

Elsewhere it is essentially a cool-climate, upland snake that sometimes ranges to elevations of more than 9,000 feet (2,743 m). It has also been reported from open country bordering forest edge and from pine barren clearings, especially those in which grass fills the spaces between the scattered rocks and boulders. In Indiana, Minton (1972) found it most often in both moist, sandy places and on muck prairie, though in more unusual circumstances he discovered two examples in dry, sandy oak woods. Even more out of the ordinary is its occurrence in relatively dry vacant lots on the outskirts of Chicago, Illinois, where Seibert (1950) found it in surprisingly large numbers; an estimated 185 snakes per hectare were taken in such urban habitats in the late 1940s. In nearby Missouri, however, this ordinarily abundant species is in danger of being exterminated. There, se-

vere habitat destruction and the lavish use of agricultural pesticides have caused such a dramatic decline in its numbers that it is now regarded as one of that state's endangered reptiles.

BEHAVIOR   Because this is such a rare snake in Texas, our knowledge about its natural history comes primarily from studies and observations made outside the state. A gentle and delicate little serpent, it rarely bites in self-defense. When challenged, it sometimes snaps open its mouth in a menacing way, as if preparing to strike, but this benign gesture is never followed by biting. When handled, its most likely reaction is to discharge a combination of repugnant fluids from its cloaca and scent glands at the base of its tail, which when smeared over a captor's hands by the snake's writhing body may result in the creature's immediate release.

The western smooth green snake's normal active season is from the middle of April to mid-October, when average daytime temperatures range between 70 and 85 degrees F, though at the far northern end of its range this cycle may be shortened by several weeks to as much as a month. In Texas, where winters are often mild, it probably moves above ground as early in the year as March and as late as November, which is also true of many other reptile species living in the region.

Most smooth green snakes found in Texas were discovered during late April and early June, usually following rain showers. An opportune time to find these elusive snakes is immediately after a hurricane or severe storm, when the rising waters have inundated the low-lying coastal prairies, forcing many of the local terrestrial snakes from their hiding places. It was after such a hurricane that two smooth green snakes were discovered near Angleton, crawling over clumps of grass on one of the few available spits of high ground.

Although essentially terrestrial, the smooth green snake sometimes crawls up into the limbs of bushes and low trees. Its nighttime shelters consist of logs, piles of dead vegetation, rocks, and such man-made objects as boards, tin, and tarpaper.

Cochran (1987) was the first to describe an unusual behavior in the smooth green snake called rhythmic lateral head movement, an action previously reported in several other serpents including our native rough green snake and the super-slender vine snakes of Latin America and extreme southern Arizona, all essentially bush- and tree-dwelling species. When Cochran returned two captive *L. vernalis* to their cage, each swayed its head and neck slowly from side to side at a rate of 1 cycle per second; the movements were repeated 2 to more than 20 times during a single episode. The behavior, while still a matter of conjecture, has two possible explanations. One is that the subtle movement enhances the serpent's binocular vision as it stalks its prey; the other, that the gentle swaying of the snake's forebody simulates a twig or plant stalk moving slowly in the breeze, helping the snake to blend with its herbaceous surroundings and to confound its enemies.

In winter this species hibernates under logs and rocks as well as in gravel banks, anthills, and underground burrows. Large numbers of individuals sometimes spend the frigid months together in a common shelter.

In mid-autumn 1934, a Canadian farmer accidentally discovered a serpent hibernaculum on his property in Manitoba; to this day his story remains one of the most incredible accounts ever reported of a large-scale communal overwintering site for snakes. It began on September 25, when the farmer encountered two smooth green snakes as they crawled over the dome of an abandoned anthill measuring approximately 6 inches high and 3 feet across at the base. The hill, situated less than a mile from the swamp-bordered Assiniboine River, stood at the edge of a small clearing in a woodland of hazel trees and hawthorn scrub surrounded by oak and aspen trees. His curiosity thus aroused, the man examined the anthill more carefully. On its surface he found that some of the ant-made tunnel entrances were a bit larger than the others. Digging into the mound, he saw only a few ants, but there were 6 red-bellied snakes inside the upper portion of the hill. Four more snakes were excavated the following day. No further digging was attempted until October 6, when in just 40 minutes the farmer unearthed 75 additional snakes from the lower galleries, including green snakes. Four days later, after the entire anthill had been removed, the total number of snakes collected stood at 257, including 148 smooth green snakes, 101 red-bellied snakes, and 8 plains garter snakes. Five feet below the surface, where ground water was revealed at the bottom of the structure, rested most of the larger smooth green snakes, some with parts of their bodies submerged but with their heads out of the water and pointed upward. The majority of the smaller specimens were in the upper galleries, though unlike their larger counterparts, they had assumed no particular body position. Such vertical partitioning by size suggests that the older serpents in the mound were the first to arrive at the communal den, followed later by the juveniles.

FEEDING Food consists chiefly of insects and their larvae but also includes spiders, centipedes, millipedes, other arthropods, snails, slugs, and even an occasional salamander.

REPRODUCTION Over most of its range the smooth green snake mates in the spring, although in Ontario, Canada, late summer copulation is reported as well. It has also been shown that the more northerly populations lay their eggs later in the year than those to the south. In the Chicago area, for example, most eggs are deposited during June and July, whereas female smooth green snakes living in Michigan and southern Canada lay their eggs in late July to early September, about a month later on average. The thin-shelled, white eggs, 3 to 15 per clutch and measuring just less than 1 inch (2.5 cm) long, are deposited inside piles of decaying vegetation, rotting logs, sawdust piles, and animal burrows, or under boards, railroad ties, and even rusting cans, usually near damp grassy areas. As with certain other snakes, two or more females may deposit their eggs in the same place. One such communal nest site, representing three separate clutches, contained 27 eggs.

The most interesting thing about the breeding habits of the smooth green snake is the relatively short time it takes for the eggs to hatch, particularly those laid by females inhabiting northern Michigan, where colder temperatures and a short season of activity tend to slow egg development at the nest. As an example, eggs laid that far north are already in an advanced stage of development when deposited, usually around August 21, for they have previously been exposed to a period of internal incubation before leaving the mother's body. Although they may hatch in about 10 days, the actual out-of-body incubation can be as brief as 4 days. In the Chicago region the eggs hatch around August 10, after minimum incubation of about a month. It seems that the western smooth green snake, particularly its northernmost populations, represents an intermediate condition between egg-laying and live-bearing snakes. This appears to be a consequence both of the region's colder temperatures and the snake's limited active season, resulting in the egg's longer period of embryonic growth within the female's body, followed by a shorter-than-usual incubation period after deposition.

Approximately 4¾ to 6 inches (12.1–15.2 cm) long at hatching, the young are not the same bright green of most adults but instead display a grayish or brownish upper body color and a whitish belly. After just one year of growth they may be triple their original length and, after experiencing their second hibernation, may be sexually mature.

EASTERN COACHWHIP
Masticophis flagellum flagellum
PLATES 86–89

DESCRIPTION This long, slender serpent is the only Texas snake with one color on the forebody and another on the rear part of the trunk. In most specimens, the head and forward one-third or more of the body are nearly uniformly dark brown to black, fading gradually toward the tail, where it is light brown or tan. The extent of the dark pigmentation can vary, however. It can be confined to the head and neck, involve the entire forward half of the body, or cover the snake's full length. Frequently observed among East Texas coachwhips are nearly all-black specimens with a reddish tail, as well as those with small, widely spaced, light-colored blotches or banding across the back. Whatever the dorsal body coloration, all eastern coachwhips exhibit dusky scale margins on the tail, giving this part of the snake the appearance of a braided whip, which is probably the reason for the serpent's common name. The dorsal scales, arranged in 17 rows at midbody and in 13 rows just in front of the anal plate, are all smooth. The anal plate is divided. In contrast to the adult, the hatchling coachwhip is an overall tan or brown, with indistinct and somewhat jagged, narrow, dark crossbars on the back, which disappear altogether before they reach the tail, and a double row of dark spots on the forward part of the abdomen. In addition, the pronounced cream-colored spots and white-margined scales on the young snake's head are scarce or absent in the adult.

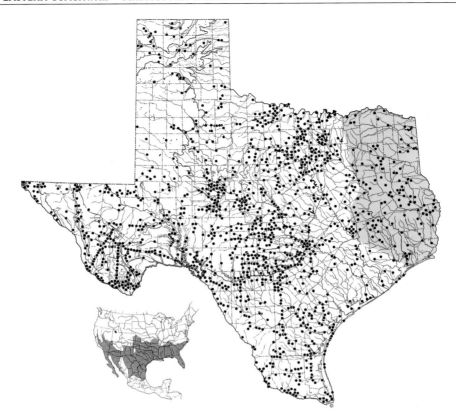

COMPARABLE SNAKES Except for the buttermilk and tan racers, which usually have some dorsal spotting, adult racers have a uniformly colored dorsum from head to tail tip and the number of dorsal scale rows is 15 just ahead of the anal plate (13 in the coachwhip). Furthermore, the tail of racers lacks the braided look of the eastern coachwhip.

SIZE Although the largest known eastern coachwhip measured nearly 8½ feet (259.1 cm) in length, most adults of this subspecies are between 3½ and 5 feet (106.7–152.4 cm) long.

HABITAT It inhabits a wide variety of dry, open places, including pine flatwoods, rocky hillsides, open or broken prairie, fields, pastures, and coastal plain grasslands in the southeastern corner of the state (Jefferson, Orange, Newton, and Hardin counties). Guidry (1953) also encountered it in woodland habitats.

BEHAVIOR Among the fastest moving of our local serpents, the slender, agile coachwhip eludes a predator with a sudden burst of speed that leaves the pursuer momentarily bewildered, giving the snake enough of a head start to make good its escape. In fact, this surprisingly nimble reptilian sprinter can easily outmaneuver most snake collectors. Just when it appears the elusive quarry is within easy reach, it may suddenly turn and, without slowing, streak off in another direction. It is probably safe to say that for every coachwhip placed in a collector's bag, several others get away. The snake does not limit its evasive tactics to ground-level maneuvers, for it sometimes eludes a pursuer by climbing into bushes or the lower limbs of trees, where it can watch the intruder, or disappear into the burrows of small animals, particularly those of gophers.

If escape is impossible, an aroused coachwhip puts up a furious defense, striking out savagely for as long as it is cornered, sometimes even directing its thrusts at the opponent's face. After embedding its needle-sharp teeth, the snake typically jerks its head back and to one side, inflicting numerous drawn-out lacerations that tend to bleed freely but cause no serious injury, unless they impact an eye. A coachwhip that is picked up not only bites viciously but also twists and thrashes wildly and in doing so may wrap part of its long, slender tail around its captor's arm or wrist in a desperate effort to free itself. It is in this behavior that we see yet another reason for the long-held myth that the coachwhip is capable of whipping a human antagonist.

In Texas, the snake's active period is a long one. Depending on latitude and the length of the winter season, it begins in March or April and usually continues at least through October, but may last even longer. This is strictly a daytime serpent; by night it hides in animal burrows and rock crevices or crawls beneath some type of surface shelter. Such retreats, according to Neill (1948), are also used as winter quarters, as are the tunnels left by decaying pine roots on dry hillsides.

FEEDING The eastern coachwhip eats a variety of prey including rats, mice, shrews, bats, birds and their eggs, snakes, small turtles, lizards and their eggs, and larger insects such as grasshoppers and cicadas. The kind of food consumed depends, of course, on the species of prey available in any given locality. Of 30 eastern coachwhip snakes from north-central Louisiana with food in their stomachs, R. F. Clark (1949) found mammals in 18 and birds in 12. A similar survey conducted at Fort Benning, Georgia, by Hamilton and Pollack (1956) revealed that 45 eastern coachwhips had eaten the following animals, listed by frequency of occurrence: lizards 68.9 percent, mammals 17.8 percent, snakes 8.9 percent, insects 8.9 percent, birds 2.2 percent, and one turtle at 2.2 percent. In certain arid regions where race runner and scaly lizards are particularly abundant, they may constitute a large part of the snake's diet.

Prowling its habitat for prey, the coachwhip glides effortlessly through the brush and grass, its head raised high to scan the immediate surroundings. The reptile's strategy is to flush from hiding any potential quarry, which is then pursued until it is overtaken or escapes. Lizards in particular are elusive targets; their explosive starts and excellent maneuverability make them difficult to catch, but the keenly alert snake, well endowed with its own attributes of speed and agility, immediately dashes in pursuit at the first hint of movement, matching the lizard's every turn until the prey is overtaken or finds a safe haven. Prey that is moving but not in flight may be approached cautiously, then quickly seized before it can flee.

An adult rodent, though not as fast as most lizards, is equipped with long incisor teeth, making it better able to defend itself against a coachwhip's attack. When seized by the snake, it can inflict serious bodily injury to its captor. To restrict the struggles of such prey, the serpent, although not a constrictor, may use a loop of its body to press the rodent firmly against the ground until it can be maneuvered into a favorable position to be swallowed.

REPRODUCTION Coachwhips mate in April or May. The females lay 4 to 24 (usually 12 or 13) eggs with granular shells sometime in June or July. Nest sites have included loose soil, piles of leaf litter, the inner core of decomposing logs and tree stumps, and the abandoned burrows of small animals. The eggs, 1 to 1½ inches (2.5–3.8 cm) long, hatch in August or September about 6 to 12 weeks after they are laid, producing young that measure 11 to 14 inches (27.9–35.6 cm) long.

WESTERN COACHWHIP
Masticophis flagellum testaceus
PLATES 90–94

DESCRIPTION Like the eastern subspecies, the western coachwhip is long and slender, with 17 rows of smooth dorsal scales on the forebody and 13 in front of the divided anal plate. Instead of showing *M. f. flagellum*'s distinct but gradual color change from front to rear, the western coachwhip typically is light tan or yellowish brown over its entire body and tail, though several other color and pattern variations occur within the state,

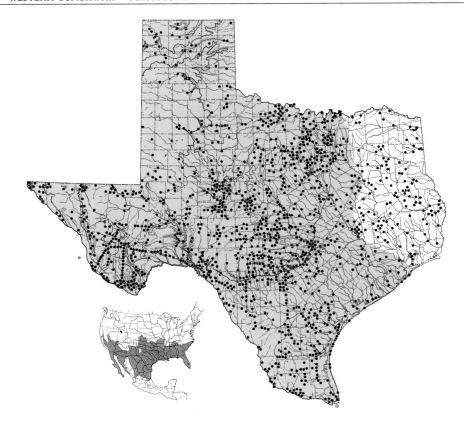

none of which is restricted to any particular part of the snake's range. They were defined in a study by L. D. Wilson (1970a), from which we have drawn freely to prepare the following descriptions.

The most common is the narrow-banded variety, whose slender, dark dorsal cross-bands, each only 1½ to 2 scales wide (measured front to back), occupy much of the body. About 94 percent of the specimens from throughout the serpent's range are so marked, but little more than half the individuals from Trans-Pecos Texas are of this type. About one-third of the coachwhips from this region are essentially unpatterned, particularly those with a light tan coloration. Less common are the boldly broad-banded individuals, whose distinctive markings consist of wide, dark crossbands 10 to 15 scales wide (measured front to back) that are separated from one another by a light tan space of equal width. This particular pattern type is not found in the Texas Panhandle and, in fact,

is so uncommon that it never represents more than 20 percent of any regional population. Another color phase consists of the pinkish, sometimes brick-red individuals found in Presidio and Brewster counties, particularly in the deserts that circle the Chisos Mountains, as well as in Big Bend National Park and the Black Gap Wildlife Management Area. Such specimens are among the most strikingly colored of all West Texas serpents. The often black-tipped head and body scales stand out sharply against the serpent's wine-red body, making it one of the most elegant serpents found in the desert. Whatever the snake's color or pattern, the tan or yellowish throat and underside of the serpent's forebody ordinarily are marked with two longitudinal rows of dark spots. The hatchling coachwhip, which displays little of the variation seen among the adults, is consistently tan to yellowish brown and marked by dark crossbars that are most prominent on the forward part of the body.

In El Paso County, where it is extremely uncommon, the western coachwhip apparently intergrades with the lined coachwhip, a more westerly tan or gray subspecies of *M. flagellum* whose tail is salmon pink underneath. Each of its forebody dorsal scales bears a horizontal dark streak through its center. **COMPARABLE SNAKES** The several subspecies of racer occurring within the Texas range of the western coachwhip have 15 dorsal scale rows just in front of the anal plate (the coachwhip has only 13), and the juveniles are boldly blotched, not finely crossbanded. Ruthven's whipsnake, which has 15 midbody rows of dorsal scales (17 in the coachwhip), also shows some lengthwise striping on the neck.

SIZE Among the longest of Texas snakes, the adults are generally 4 to 5½ feet (121.9–167.6 cm) in length, with a reported record size of 6 feet 8 inches (203.2 cm).

HABITAT The western coachwhip is widely distributed in a variety of open, arid, or semiarid habitats throughout the western three-quarters of the state, usually where there is sandy or rocky terrain. They include the Chihuahuan Desert scrub, the gently rolling High Plains, the grass-covered North Central Plains, the rock-strewn Edwards Plateau, the western edge of the Post Oak Savannah, and the scrubby Rio Grande Plain together with its grass-covered coastal prairie.

A good example of the snake's habitat diversity is reported by Milstead, Mecham, and McClintock (1950), who captured 3 western coachwhips in cedar savannah, 15 in mesquite-creosote, 3 in mesquite-sumac-condalia, and 2 in live oak, all within the boundaries of Terrell County. Jameson and Flury (1949) likewise found this serpent in a range of plant associations. Of 10 specimens they collected in the Sierra Vieja Mountains of southwestern Texas, 4 came from catclaw-tobosa, 1 from creosote-catclaw-blackbrush, 1 from mesquite-huisache-blackbrush, and 1 from yucca-tobosa, all in the plains belt. Two others were taken in the roughland belt, 1 from a streambed at the bottom of a canyon and the other in the lechuguilla-beargrass plant association on top of a mesa. Axtell (1959) encountered 7 western coachwhips in the Black Gap Wildlife Management Area of Brewster County, where he found 5 specimens in the floodplain, 1 in a dry streambed, and another in low limestone gravel hills, all in terrain with little vertical relief. When all of these records are considered, it is clear that the coachwhip favors relatively flat, semiopen situations rather than steep, uneven terrain.

BEHAVIOR The coachwhip, like all other snakes, prefers to avoid an encounter with man. In a brushy environment, this agile, fast-moving reptile can easily outmaneuver a collector's efforts to catch it, although its top speed is probably no more than 4 miles per hour, slower than a human running at a leisurely pace. The snake's advantage lies in its ability to thread its slim body through vegetation and to slip around rocks and other obstacles without reducing its speed. It may finally elude its pursuer by taking refuge in a patch of shrubbery, a clump of cactus, or an animal burrow, though it also avoids capture by climbing into bushes or the lower limbs of trees.

When sufficiently provoked, a coachwhip often rapidly vibrates its tail. In dry vegetation, the vibration produces a sound not much different from the whir of a rattlesnake's rattle. If it is unable to flee, the snake defends itself vigorously. With its forebody sometimes raised off the ground as high as a person's knee, the aroused serpent strikes savagely as it tries to drive away its foe. Despite the reptile's long, frantic thrusts, the assault is intended more to frighten and intimidate than to cause injury. If picked up, a coachwhip generally employs all of its offensive capabilities in an effort to get away, thrashing its body vigorously as it tries to free itself, biting repeatedly and with a vengeance, and expelling the foul-smelling contents of its cloacal sack, including feces, over the captor's hands.

An unusual defensive behavior observed by Gehlbach (1970) in several adult coachwhips is that of playing dead. A specimen he seized near the middle of the body at first twisted wildly and discharged a liberal amount of a watery substance from its partly open mouth, after which about 8 inches of the snake's forebody became rigid while the entire rear part became limp. At the same time, a sharp upward curve appeared in the neck, causing the serpent's head to be directed downward, and the lower jaw was spread out on both sides. Although prodded and moved, the snake steadfastly maintained this lifeless posture, its only response being to twist its head to one side.

Adapted to survive in a hot, dry climate, the western coachwhip is an active daytime serpent that moves about even during some of the hottest summer days when most other snakes seek to reduce their body temperatures by taking refuge under a bush or in the cool darkness of an animal burrow. During the hottest part of the day it does not hesitate to dart across the scorching pavement when going from one side of a road to the other, a practice avoided by most other serpents. Even a coachwhip cannot withstand prolonged exposure to the midday summer sun, although its heat tolerance, calculated by Bogert and Cowles (1947) to be near 108 degrees F, was greater than that of several other serpent species they tested.

The western coachwhip is active above ground only during the daylight hours. It almost invariably retires to the depths of an animal burrow before sundown, presumably only one snake to a tunnel, where it spends the night. The next morning, according to Jones and Whitford (1989) and Secor (1995), the snake begins its day by crawling to the burrow entrance and poking its head outside, exposing it to the sun's first warming rays, probably as a way to stimulate the core of its central nervous system, the brain. Later it exits the burrow to bathe its entire trunk in the solar heat. Only when the surface temperature exceeds 86 degrees F does the coachwhip's body warm sufficiently for the serpent to leave the site and begin its daily hunting routine. For the rest of the day the snake maintains a comfortable body temperature by moving in and out of burrows and clumps of vegetation, although in midsummer, whenever its body temperature rises above 100 degrees F, at least in more open habitats, the reptile takes refuge in any available animal burrow. Later in the afternoon, when the ground surface has cooled, the coachwhip resumes its hunting activities.

FEEDING The western coachwhip consumes a wide variety of prey species that includes small mammals, birds and their eggs, snakes, lizards, baby turtles, frogs, and occasionally even large insects such as lubber grasshoppers and cicadas. For coachwhips living near caves, weak or injured bats that have fallen from their ceiling roosts constitute an unusual food source.

In its typical hunting mode, this widely foraging snake is on the move almost constantly, its long, slender body moving easily across the hot, arid terrain, usually with the forebody raised to a considerable height and its head held horizontally. From this elevated position, the snake's alert eyes scan the immediate surroundings for any sign of prey movement. Incidentally, Ruben (1977) believes it is the coachwhip's unusual skeletal muscles that allow the creature's head to swivel so freely, even as the neck remains stationary. The head turns easily in any direction—up, down, or sideways—a decided advantage for an agile, hyperactive hunter of lizards.

For the wide-ranging coachwhip, active foraging not only consumes most of its waking hours but also involves cruising over a surprisingly extensive activity range, among the largest known for snakes. Secor determined that in San Bernardino County, California, the red coachwhip, *M. f. piceus*, regularly traveled about $3/5$ mile in a 24-hour period and maintained an overall activity range of nearly 145 acres.

In its search for prey, according to Secor, the snake does not stay out in the open continuously but moves from one patch of vegetation to another, stopping to investigate animal burrows along the way. From time to time, it interrupts this search pattern to linger for a few minutes in the shade of a thicket, where it can lower its body temperature or survey the immediate area for prey movement, sometimes enhancing its view of the surroundings even more by crawling into a bush and elevating its head and forebody above the top of the shrub like a periscope. The moment a lizard (its chief prey) is spotted, the snake's reaction is immediate. With a sudden burst of speed, it darts forward to give chase, maintaining visual contact with the fleeing lizard, whose own speed and agility often closely match the snake's. For some lizards, escape is achieved by running under a rock, into a rock crevice, or into an animal burrow. Indeed, many more lizards ordinarily escape than are captured.

When finally apprehended, the prey is held firmly in the snake's jaws while the coachwhip turns its head and neck perpendicular to the ground and presses downward, pinning its victim to the substrate. Although the snake's capture rate is influenced by a variety of factors, Jones and Whitford (1989) reported that on their southwestern New Mexico study site, coachwhips successfully caught 25 percent of the side-blotched lizards they pursued, 15 percent of the greater earless lizards, and only 13 percent of the western whiptail lizards.

Long considered an active predator whose hunting strategy is limited strictly to finding and chasing its prey (which in the desert Southwest consists primarily of lizards), this species has recently been observed by Jones and Whitford also to ambush such prey by lying in wait for it in the shade of mesquite thickets. This sit-and-wait hunting style, apparently practiced only in the mesquite sand dune habitats of the New Mexico study area during the hot summer months between late morning and midafternoon, resulted in a greater capture rate (80 percent) than active foraging in the more open creosote-bush habitats (17 percent). Several factors, it seems, were responsible for the superior success rate. In the first place, two of the local lizards (western whiptail and greater earless) that were most often captured in the dunes regulated their body temperatures by frequently darting in and out of the thicket. Thus, when they suddenly entered the shade after having been out in the bright daylight, their sight may have been briefly compromised, making them momentarily more vulnerable to attack. Since the coachwhip is coiled motionless around the base of the mesquite tree, its form blending with the surroundings, it is probably difficult to detect. When the lizard is within reach, the serpent lashes out at its quarry, seizes it in its mouth, and, in a behavior unusual for a nonconstricting snake, hangs on to the tree base with its tail. The coachwhip then retracts its forebody, and with its tail still anchored in place proceeds to manipulate the victim with its jaws so it

can be swallowed. Jones and Whitford concluded that such tail-anchoring during the sit-and-wait feeding episodes reduced prey escapes and generally improved the serpent's prey-handling efficiency.

Another unexpected feeding strategy not previously reported for the coachwhip—that of locating prey by chemical scent trailing—was observed by Secor in the red coachwhip, *M. f. piceus*. On one occasion, he saw a specimen enter a burrow, drag out a sidewinder rattlesnake, and swallow it head first. Following this episode, a close examination of the area showed the coachwhip's tracks in the sand to be overlapping those of the rattler, indicating that the aggressor had probably come across the pit viper's scent trail laid down the night before, which it then tracked to the rattler's underground daytime refuge.

In another apparent demonstration of chemical scent trailing, Secor encountered a red coachwhip that after flicking its tongue for 20 minutes to investigate a particular area of desert sand, used its head and forebody to excavate the spot. At this point, the zoologist left the area. Returning to the scene several hours later, he found the coachwhip holding a partly buried glossy snake in its mouth. From all indications, the predator had successfully located its prey by chemical scent, even as its quarry lay hidden under the sand, and was now in the process of digging it out of the substrate. The evidence for this conclusion, although circumstantial, is nevertheless strong, leaving little room for another interpretation.

REPRODUCTION Despite the western coachwhip's abundance and wide distribution throughout the state, little specific information is available about its breeding habits in Texas. Like the eastern subspecies, it mates in April or May. The female deposits her eggs sometime in May to July, probably in loose soil, under vegetative debris, or in decaying logs or tree stumps. One to 2 inches (2.5–5.1 cm) long when laid, the granular-surfaced eggs incubate for 6 to 12 weeks before they hatch in August or September, producing baby snakes that measure 12 to 14 inches (30.5–35.6 cm) long.

SCHOTT'S WHIPSNAKE

Masticophis schotti schotti

PLATE 95

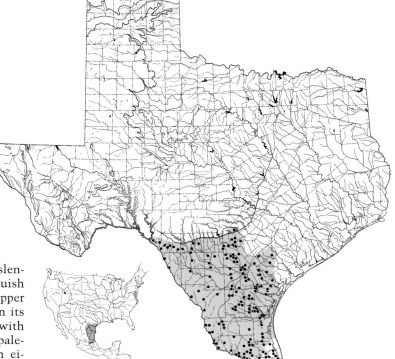

DESCRIPTION This long, slender, grayish green or bluish gray serpent, whose upper body is a bit darker than its lower sides, is marked with a prominent, narrow, pale-colored lateral stripe on either side of the trunk, usually edged below and sometimes above by a narrow dark seam. Along the middle of the back between the two pale stripes, the forward edges of the individual scales are tipped with white or pale yellow. A second light stripe, bordered above by a fine black or dark gray seam, occurs below the first, occupying the lower half of the first scale row and the outer edges of the belly plates. The abdomen, which is whitish or cream-colored behind the chin, becomes pastel blue, then pale salmon toward the rear, with bluish gray stippling at midbody. The most vivid coloring is usually under the tail, where it is most often salmon or coral pink but occasionally yellow.

The top of the head is uniformly olive or dark gray, with no white edging on the head plates. Beginning at the end of the mouth-line, several rows of reddish orange scales extend backward several inches onto the neck and the edge of the abdomen. The dorsal scales, all smooth, are arranged in 15 rows at midbody, and the anal plate is divided.

The body pattern of the hatchling is different from that of the adult, primarily in lacking both the paired white or cream-colored dashes on the forward edges of the individual dorsal scales and the bright pink or coral hue under the tail. The body is also darker, being dark olive-green or blackish brown instead of gray-green, and bears two white or cream-colored lateral stripes on either side of the body.

COMPARABLE SNAKES The Central Texas whipsnake is an overall darker serpent with paired, narrow, longitudinal white bars along the upper back, at least on the forebody, and a light-hued collar or two pale neck blotches at the back of its head. There are no white or cream-colored dashed margins on the forward edges of its upper body scales and no white borders on the large plates of its crown.

Other lengthwise-striped snakes occurring within the range of Schott's whipsnake include patch-nosed as well as garter and ribbon snakes, all of which have a pale-colored spinal stripe. The patch-nosed snakes have 17 rows of dorsal scales at midbody and an enlarged nose shield, and the garter snakes' body scales are keeled, with 19 or more rows of dorsal scales at the middle of the trunk and a single anal plate.

SIZE The adults ordinarily are between 40 and 56 inches (101.6–142.2 cm) long, but a record specimen of this subspecies measured 66 inches (167.6 cm) in length.

HABITAT The geographic range of Schott's whipsnake is restricted to the Rio Grande Plain of South Texas, a region embracing the dry, rocky, and often sandy mesquite savannah and thornbrush woodland between the southern edge of the Edwards Plateau (the Balcones Escarpment) and the southernmost tip of the state. Vermersch and Kuntz (1986) noted that in south-central Texas, where it occupies a variety of aridland habitats, the

snake favors those associated with streambeds and ponds.

BEHAVIOR A whipsnake is designed for speed. Its long, slim body glides effortlessly across the ground in a nearly straight line, seeming to flow with ease over rocks and other surface obstacles, almost as if they were not there. Given the chance, this reptile is perfectly willing to avoid a confrontation with man by dashing for the nearest cover— a tangle of thorny vegetation, a bush, or the burrow of some large animal. On the ground the snake is elusive and difficult to catch. Even former professional collectors, whose income depended on selling live snakes to clients, simply did not bother to chase one down, for it was not worth the effort; other species were more easily captured.

Besides being an expert escape artist on land, *M. s. schotti* is also an accomplished

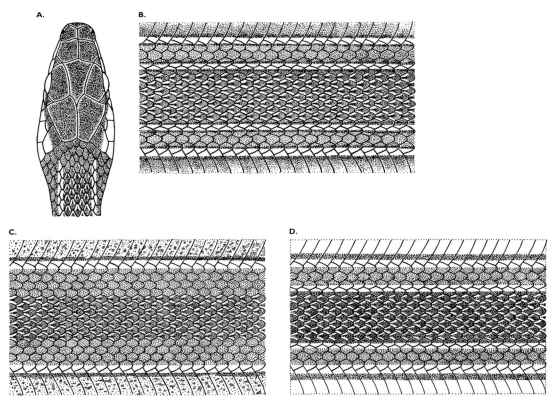

Figure 36. *Markings on (a) crown of Schott's whipsnake, (b) dorsal pattern of Schott's whipsnake, and (c and d) common dorsal pattern variations in Ruthven's whipsnake.*

climber that occasionally scrambles into a bush or tree to elude an assailant, then freezes. There its slender, unmoving form blends closely with the maze of narrow branches, making it difficult to detect.

When held at bay, this pugnacious reptile bravely defends itself by unleashing repeated vigorous strikes at its adversary, even as it looks for a way to escape. If it is picked up, it will thrash its body about while reaching back to bite the hand that holds it. The freely bleeding puncture wounds inflicted by its needle-sharp teeth are only superficial.

FEEDING Although Schott's whipsnake probably consumes primarily lizards and birds (the same prey species that constitute the chief diet of other native whipsnakes), documented observations of its feeding habits are lacking. Vermersch and Kuntz identified both whiptail and scaly lizards as prey items, and we once watched a young adult *M. s. schotti* in the wild devour a Texas earless lizard. A number of whipsnakes maintained in captivity by Gloyd and Conant (1934), some for nearly a year, ate a variety of small vertebrates that included mice, rats, fledgling English sparrows, garter snakes, leopard and green frogs, and bird eggs.

This is strictly a day-active reptile that depends on its acute eyesight to locate prey. The eyes of a whipsnake, although large and keen-sighted, are positioned on the sides of its head, just as they are in nearly all snakes; therefore they fail to provide the depth perception available to animals with forward-facing eyes. Imagine the challenge to such a foraging serpent as it pursues an erratic, swiftly moving lizard that darts quickly from rock to rock, changes course instantly, and stops and starts unexpectedly. To compensate for the absence of stereoscopic vision, this and other whipsnakes are equipped with a novel sighting device, a facial groove on either side of the head between the eye and nostril. According to Ficken, Matthiae, and Horwich (1971), these facial grooves, which nearly come together at the snout, most probably perform the same function as gun sights on a rifle. They allow the reptile to pinpoint its elusive target, thus increasing the serpent's chances of completing a successful attack. In the same way that whipsnakes direct their aim via such facial grooves, certain other snakes presumably line up rapidly moving prey with dark sight lines in precisely the same place.

In an active foraging mode, the snake glides slowly over the ground, its head held high for a better view of the immediate surroundings, its tense body stopping and starting erratically, sometimes poking into a patch of vegetation or a rock crevice as it tries to flush a potential morsel. At the first sign of movement, the whipsnake dashes to investigate; now its superior eyesight and fast reactions come into play. Even a lizard running at full speed has trouble eluding this reptilian sprinter, for the snake is so agile and quick that it frequently matches the lizard's every turn with one of its own, relentlessly pursuing its target until it is captured or escapes into a retreat inaccessible to the snake. When finally overtaken, any small animal is quickly seized and soon swallowed. A large victim, whose desperate struggles make it difficult to control, is still held in the serpent's jaws but is often pushed firmly against the ground by a segment of the snake's muscular body, to be manipulated into position for swallowing.

REPRODUCTION Gloyd and Conant, the first herpetologists to report on the egg-laying habits of this subspecies, described three sets of captive-laid eggs. In clutches of 3 to 6 eggs, the individual eggs were about 1½ inches (3.8 cm) long. They were deposited between May 16 and June 6, and although artificially incubated for a time, they failed to hatch. A more recent report by McCrystal and Dixon (1983) described the eggs and young of a female Schott's whipsnake from the Mexican state of Nuevo Leon. She laid 5 eggs on June 17, their surfaces covered with small, hard granules like fine sandpaper. The eggs in this clutch were about 2⅗ inches (4.1 cm) long but only ¾ inch (1.9 cm) in diameter. After incubating for 80 to 81 days, 3 of them hatched, producing babies that measured 14⅘ to 16 inches (37.6–40.6 cm) long.

RUTHVEN'S WHIPSNAKE
Masticophis schotti ruthveni
PLATE 96

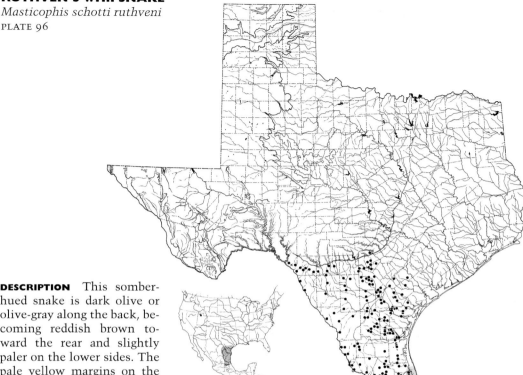

DESCRIPTION This somber-hued snake is dark olive or olive-gray along the back, becoming reddish brown toward the rear and slightly paler on the lower sides. The pale yellow margins on the forward edges of the 7 or 8 scale rows across the middle of the snake's back are characteristic not only of this subspecies but also of its closest relative, Schott's whipsnake. In Texas, its indistinctly striped pattern occurs in two basic variations. (See illustration in Schott's whipsnake account.) The first, which includes about two-thirds of all specimens, consists of a single vague, light-hued stripe low on either side of the body near the abdomen. The other has two pale stripes on each side: one along the outer margin of the belly, plus an obscure lateral stripe along the upper edge of scale row 3 and the lower edge of scale row 4. The belly is either heavily speckled on its outer edges or only lightly so along its midline. The bright yellow on the forebody gradually changes to pale blue-gray or olive at midbody, then to pink toward the rear, and finally to red under the tail.

The crown is uniformly dark olive without white margins on the head plates. From near the end of the mouthline on either side of the head, a few rows of reddish orange scales ex-tend several inches backward onto the neck and abdomen. The dorsal scales, all smooth, are arranged in 15 rows at midbody, and the anal plate is divided.

In color and pattern, the hatchling is probably similar to a baby Schott's whipsnake, which has two conspicuous light-hued stripes on each side of the body but lacks both the paired white or cream-colored dashes on the front edges of individual dorsal scales and the reddish undertail that characterize the adult.

COMPARABLE SNAKES The Mexican racer has dorsal scales in 17 midbody rows, none of which has pale margins on its forward edges. Neither does it have any pink or red coloration on its belly or under its tail. The rough green snake, which is completely green above and yellow on the belly, shows no sign of body striping.

SIZE The usual length of an adult is 40 to 56 inches (101.6–142.2 cm), although the record for this subspecies is 66⅛ inches (168 cm).

HABITAT This is chiefly a Mexican subspecies that ranges northward from central Veracruz to the southern tip of Texas, where it is known to occur in Cameron, Hidalgo, Starr, Willacy, and south-central Kenedy counties. In this region of semiarid brushland, where continuing urban and agricultural development is assimilating ever more natural landscape, its specific microhabitats have not been documented.

BEHAVIOR Today, more than 70 years after Arthur Ortenburger stated (in his 1928 monograph on the genera *Masticophis* and *Coluber*) that nothing much was known about this snake's natural history, we have little more information about it than he did then. Like other native whipsnakes, this high-strung serpent is easily aroused. Quick to defend itself when cornered or handled, it shows no hesitation before lashing out at its antagonist, repeatedly and vigorously. Often during a strike, it will increase the damage to its foe by momentarily relaxing its forebody to form a single sagging loop, which when suddenly straightened pulls the head back violently. This causes the embedded teeth to rake across the victim's skin and even deeper, tearing and lacerating as they go.

Gliding easily over the ground, the slender, agile whipsnake is difficult to catch. It is quick and elusive, sometimes changing direction abruptly without ever slowing down or, if unable to flee, darting into a mammal burrow or a tangle of brush. To avoid capture, it is also known to climb up into bushes or trees.

FEEDING Although details of this subspecies' feeding habits are unknown, it is likely that the snake eats essentially the same prey items consumed by other native whipsnakes. Such a diet would have lizards and birds high on the menu, followed in order of importance by snakes and small mammals.

REPRODUCTION Nothing is documented about this snake's breeding habits, though it presumably lays eggs. See Schott's whipsnake account.

CENTRAL TEXAS WHIPSNAKE
Masticophis taeniatus girardi
PLATE 97

DESCRIPTION The overall dorsal coloration of individual specimens can vary from velvety reddish brown to dull purplish black, but all Central Texas whipsnakes have an irregularly shaped, pale-hued collar across the back of the head, which in some snakes is separated by dark pigmentation into two pale neck blotches, one on either side of the spine. Except in the darkest specimens, most of the large plates on top of the head are pale-edged.

Two basic body pattern types occur in Texas: a paler one encountered most frequently in the Trans-Pecos region and a darker one that is more common on the Edwards Plateau. Both types consist of light and dark lengthwise stripes. In the light variety, a wide alternating light and dark band runs down the middle of the back, flanked by four narrow, dark stripes that stand out against a pale background color. In the other type, a narrow light stripe occupies the outer edges of the belly plates and part of the first row of dorsal scales, and each of the upper light stripes is reduced to a series of intermittent, long, whitish bars. Actually composed of two closely adjacent light stripes separated by a fine black seam, they ordinarily occur only on the forward one-quarter to one-half of the snake's trunk, becoming progressively less distinct toward the rear. Conant and Collins (1991) aptly compared them to the successively weaker imprints made on the pavement by an automobile tire after it has crossed a freshly painted center stripe. Moderate to heavy dark splotching covers the gray belly. On the undertail, where the hue is a striking bright pink or coral red, such dark pigment is confined to the lateral edges of the scales. The dorsal scales are smooth and arranged in 15 rows at midbody, and the anal plate is divided.

Except for the pale crossband on the back of the head, which is also present in the adult, the color pattern of a hatchling differs mark-

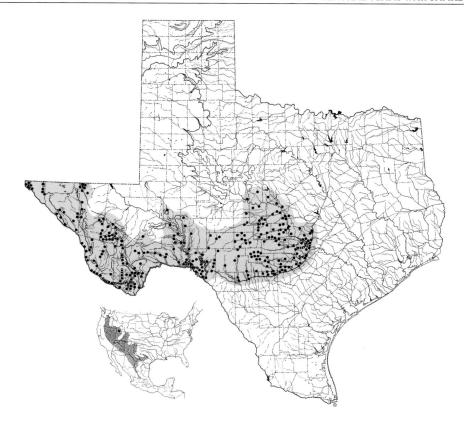

edly from that of a full-grown specimen. The young snake's most prominent features are its bold lengthwise stripes; unlike those of a mature individual, they are never interrupted along their length. Each side of its olive-green body is marked by a pair of distinct white or cream-colored stripes. The first one occupies the lowermost row of dorsal scales and the outer edges of the belly plates, where a diffuse dark line defines its lower margin. The yellow to pale orange abdomen is otherwise unmarked. The other stripe, which occurs on the upper half of scale row 3 and the lower half of scale row 4, is more pronounced.

COMPARABLE SNAKES The closely related Schott's and Ruthven's whipsnakes both have paired, pale, dashed spots on the front corners of their individual dorsal scales and reddish orange scales on each side of the neck just behind the end of the mouthline. Absent, however, are the light margins on the scales of the crown, a distinguishing feature of the adult Central Texas whipsnake.

SIZE The adult length of this slender serpent is 40 to 60 inches (101.6–152.4 cm). A record specimen measured 72 inches (182.9 cm) long.

HABITAT In Texas, this aridland snake lives in the desert-dominated Trans-Pecos region of the state, then ranges eastward across the Edwards Plateau, where the southernmost limit of its distribution is defined almost precisely by the Balcones Escarpment. Although habituated to dry environments, it ordinarily does not stray far from moisture; most specimens are found near some form of surface water such as rivers, streams, or springs. It likewise shows a clear predilection for rock-encumbered canyons, especially those containing streambeds, either dry or water-filled.

Typical Central Texas environments include cedar brakes and the oak-juniper woodlands that unevenly cover rocky limestone hills and canyons, as well as arid, brush-covered valleys. In the Hill Country just north of San Antonio, for example, Quillan (in Wright and Wright 1957) frequently found it

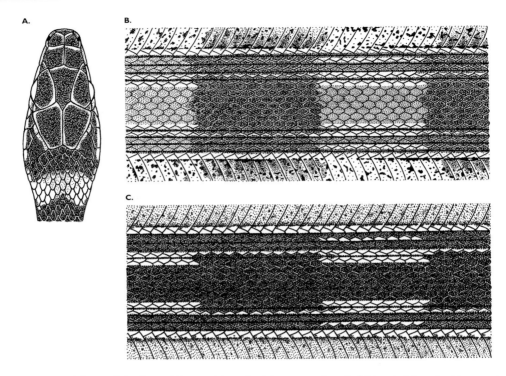

Figure 37. *Markings of the Central Texas whipsnake: (a) crown and neck, (b) banded dorsal pattern, and (c) darker, broken-stripe dorsal pattern.*

along rock-covered limestone ridges. It also occurs on the Llano Uplift, where some flood-plains, with their jumble of large and small granite boulders, provide ideal shelter for this rather common indigenous serpent. Along the rock-strewn shores of Lake Marble Falls, for example, we encountered three specimens in one day. Farther west, in northern Terrell County, Milstead and his colleagues (1950) observed it in a variety of habitats: the cedar savannah of mesa tops, the cedar-ocotillo plant community characteristic of sparsely vegetated mesa slopes, dense mesquite-sumac-condalia thickets, the streamside en-vironment of walnut and desert willow, and the persimmon–shin oak plant association of the steep rimrock, as well as the narrow strip of ground along the base of each lime-stone outcropping.

Throughout the Trans-Pecos region of Texas the snake occupies habitats that range from Chihuahuan Desert scrub vegetation—such as occurs in the limestone Hill Country around Amistad Reservoir at about 1,200 feet (366 m) elevation—to the higher and slightly

wetter montane evergreen woodland below about 6,000 feet (1,829 m), which covers the upper reaches of the taller desert mountains. Murray (1939) described it as one of the most common snakes he encountered in the Chi-sos Mountains above 4,000 feet. In Brewster County, Minton (1959) found it mostly in rocky desert foothills. In the Sierra Vieja Mountains of Presidio County, Jameson and Flury (1949) encountered six of seven speci-mens in rocky canyon streambed micro-habitats, another in a plant association of catclaw and grama grass, and one in an ocotillo–creosote bush association.

BEHAVIOR This whipsnake is seldom en-countered in the open, probably because it is alert, has good vision, and darts out of sight before being discovered. Nevertheless, when coiled under a bush it sometimes remains perfectly still if approached, relying on its concealing pattern for protection. If it makes any movement at all in such circumstances, it is merely a single flick of the head as the snake turns to face the disturbance. Even when a person steps to within two feet of the reptile, the snake may not give itself away by moving if it is well concealed.

Slender-bodied and agile, the snake easily climbs up into bushes or trees, where it is difficult to detect among the interlacing branches, particularly if it remains motionless. One that is chased into shrubbery, however, is apt to poke its head out defiantly from under the vegetation and, if approached too closely, may bite its tormentor, often maintaining a firm grip with its small, needle-sharp teeth as it chews. If picked up, it will savagely defend itself, biting viciously until released or its head is restrained. Should it be seized by the tail, the whipsnake employs a more drastic escape technique. If it cannot quickly pull itself free, it suddenly rotates the body on its long axis so vigorously that the caught portion of its tail twists free from the rest, leaving the snake with a shortened caudal member but a good chance to escape.

Minton, who discovered most of his Chisos Mountain specimens in March and April, encountered them primarily in rocky or brushy places. There they have been found in low bushes growing among boulders, in brush piles and under rubbish, and in rocky crevices (where only the snake's head was protruding when the snake was first discovered and into which the reptile withdrew when threatened).

Since the life history of the Central Texas whipsnake is little known, we include below some field observations made in Utah by Parker and Brown (1980) of the closely related and geographically adjacent subspecies, the desert striped whipsnake. We believe there is probably little difference in their behavior.

Like the majority of whipsnake species, this one shows a greater tolerance for heat than most other serpents, including the prairie rattler and bull snake, with which it often shares the same general habitat. As might be expected, it is also less resistant to cold than either of the others. Parker and Brown found that during early spring, the desert striped whipsnake typically spent most of each day basking in the sun. Crawling out from under a rock pile, generally between 8 and 10 in the morning, it nestled under the east side of a nearby bush (usually a sagebrush or rabbitbrush plant), where it was partially concealed from predators yet still exposed to the sunlight that filtered through gaps in the branches. As the angle of the sunlight changed, the snake periodically shifted its position clockwise around the bush to maintain its exposure to the sun's rays. In midafternoon, when its body temperature exceeded 90 degrees F, the whipsnake sometimes crawled to a shady spot to cool down, although by late afternoon, when the air temperature began to moderate, the snake would again be basking, this time on the west or southwest side of the bush, which was now in full sunlight.

During the hottest days of summer, the reptile spent little time in the open. Instead, it left its nighttime retreat between 6 and 7:30 in the morning, briefly lying in the sun to raise its body temperature, then either went underground again or spent the rest of the day in the shade. If it chose to retreat below ground, it often came to the surface once more around 4 or 5 in the afternoon.

FEEDING This active forager does not restrict its diet to any particular group of vertebrate animals. It attacks birds and their eggs as readily as lizards, and snakes as well as small mammals. Vermersch and Kuntz (1986) stated that around Hill Country caves it sometimes captures Mexican free-tailed bats, probably those that have fallen from their roosts.

Parker and Brown's study of the closely related desert striped whipsnake shows that lizards, which were preferred over all other kinds of animals, constituted 64.2 percent of the prey consumed. Half the lizards were side-blotched lizards; the other 50 percent included western whiptail, short-horned, desert horned, and sagebrush lizards. Also devoured were a western yellow-bellied racer and another desert striped whipsnake. The remaining 28.6 percent of the snake's diet consisted of mammals.

Holding its head several inches above the ground to survey its surroundings, the Central Texas whipsnake glides slowly over the ground, watching intently for a lizard to dart across its path or a smaller snake to make its presence known by moving. Occasionally it stops to turn its head from side to side so as to broaden its field of view. Ground-dwelling lizards on which the whipsnake is reported to feed—whiptails, race runners, and side-blotched—are alert, fast-moving species, whose evasive actions make them difficult targets. As a matter of fact, most human attempts to catch these agile lizards by hand usually prove unsuccessful. Bewildering as they may be, a lizard's evasive tactics are brilliantly matched at every turn by the rapid maneuvers of its ophidian pursuer. Once the whipsnake spots its moving prey, it instantly gives chase, neither slowing down nor deviating from its course, no matter how erratic, until it overtakes its victim or the lizard reaches a safe refuge. Prey is usually swallowed alive, but if the quarry is large enough to struggle free or if it is a mammal that can inflict a retaliatory bite, the snake may press it to the ground with a segment of its muscular body until the victim has been subdued enough to be safely ingested.

Equipped with a slender, light-weight body, the Central Texas whipsnake is also a proficient climber. It readily crawls into trees and bushes to rest, bask, or escape terrestrial pursuers, and it sometimes climbs into the uppermost tree limbs in search of avian prey. Quillan (in Wright and Wright 1957) mentions one he encountered 25 feet (7.6 m) above the ground in a sycamore tree near San Antonio, where it may have intended to pillage a summer tanager's nest. That this serpent is particularly destructive to birds and their eggs was also pointed out by Davenport (1943).

REPRODUCTION   After mating with a male, usually in May, the female lays a clutch of 4 to 9 (normally 6 to 8) eggs in June. They are $1\frac{5}{8}$ inches (4.4 cm) long and hatch sometime in August or early September, producing babies between $13\frac{3}{4}$ and 17 inches (34.9–43.2 cm) long. Little else is known about this subspecies' breeding habits.

Information discovered during Parker and Brown's study of the desert striped whipsnake in Utah may apply, at least in part, to the reproductive behavior of the Central Texas whipsnake, its closest relative to the east. Male desert striped whipsnakes reach sexual maturity at about one year of age, females at three. In the colder parts of the snake's range, copulation takes place at the den during the first few weeks after the reptile's emergence from hibernation in late April and May. Courtship involves a generally passive female but an actively protective male. For example, when approached by the zoologists, a male whipsnake courting a female hidden in a nearby clump of bushes responded by moving excitedly around the shrubs, apparently attempting to draw attention away from its mate. When confronted by another male whipsnake, however, the first suitor reacted more pugnaciously, trying to drive away its competitor with a sudden aggressive rush. Because there was no evidence that direct contact between the contestants occurred during this event, and since a larger male usually displaced a smaller one, such a contest may very well be decided on the basis of size alone. When it was time for the female to lay her eggs, she often traveled relatively long distances to find just the right nesting place. Most such locations apparently were abandoned rodent burrows on open, south-facing slopes with a gentle grade. One gravid female observed by the zoologists moved more than 1,640 feet (500 m) during her search, investigating five burrow systems in four days before choosing one in which to lay her eggs. Her 100-percent hatching rate demonstrates the female's ability to recognize an optimum nesting location. Since the same ideal nest site may be discovered by more than one female, it was not unusual for two or more whipsnakes to use the same tunnel for egg deposition.

GULF SALT MARSH SNAKE
Nerodia clarki clarki
PLATE 98

DESCRIPTION   A pattern of four longitudinal dark stripes on a gray to reddish brown background color and a single (sometimes triple) row of large, prominent yellow or cream-colored oval spots down the center of the dark brown to maroon belly separate this species from all other Texas snakes. The stripes are located one on either side of the spine and one low on each side of the body near the belly, their edges often irregularly shaped. In

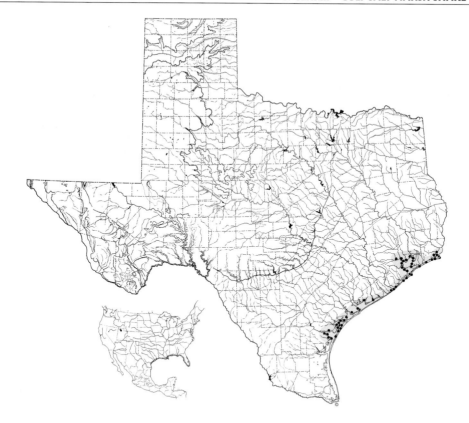

some snakes the lateral stripes are interrupted in several places along their lengths by the lighter ground color. A dark stripe on the side of the head passes from the eye to the back of the mouthline. The body scales are keeled and in 21 or 23 middorsal rows; the anal plate is divided.

COMPARABLE SNAKES Gulf and Graham's crayfish snakes have striped patterns but are less boldly marked and possess only 19 midbody scale rows. Garter and ribbon snakes, whose bodies are also longitudinally striped, lack the conspicuous pale belly spots of *Nerodia clarki*, and their anal plates are single.

SIZE The largest known specimen of this species measured just 3 feet (91.4 cm) in length. Most adults are between 2 and 2½ feet (61–76.2 cm) long.

HABITAT In Texas, this species is restricted almost entirely to the brackish coastal marshes stretching from the Sabine River southwestward to the vicinity of Corpus Christi Bay on the lower Texas coast. At least along the upper Texas coast, much of this salt marsh habitat is dominated by seashore saltgrass; marshy, smooth, and Gulf cordgrass; and annual seepweed. As Pettus (1963) pointed out, the snake's striped pattern and grayish background color closely match the ground cover of these slender-bladed grasses. A bit farther inland, the snake also occurs in shallow, freshwater marshes, though they are the snake's second choice for a home. Here we find a different set of aquatic plants; the most common are arrowhead, sedge, and naiad. On nearby dry land grow yaupon bushes and such trees as sweet gum, white ash, and loblolly pine.

Before the postwar building boom of the

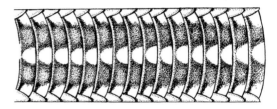

Figure 38. *Belly pattern of the Gulf salt marsh snake.*

1950s visibly accelerated development of the coastal marshlands, *N. c. clarki* was still an abundant snake along the Texas coast. Then collectors could capture a dozen or more specimens in a single day. During one afternoon in July 1946, for example, we captured 23 Gulf salt marsh snakes on Bolivar Peninsula near Gilchrist, where they had aggregated along a series of levees constructed into the salt marshes of East Bay. Since then, alteration of the habitat by dredging, construction, and chemical pollution has seriously reduced the snake's numbers in many parts of its historical range. Nevertheless, Gulf salt marsh snakes can still be found in the vicinity of Freeport and along certain coastal areas to the southwest, though in fewer numbers than before. It is probable that in relatively undisturbed marshlands, such as those just west of the Louisiana-Texas border, the snake still exists in moderate numbers.

BEHAVIOR More gentle than many other water snakes, *N. c. clarki* rarely bites when picked up, nor does it usually thrash about when handled, as do most *Nerodia.*

To survive in its saltwater environment, the salt marsh snake avoids drinking the saline water in which it lives, for to do so would soon result in dehydration and death. Instead, it apparently maintains an acceptable internal water balance by utilizing moisture obtained from ingested prey and perhaps also by drinking rainwater from onshore puddles following local showers.

Although it has been reported as typically nocturnal, we have often encountered it during the day basking, swimming, or feeding. **FEEDING** Small fish constitute the bulk of this snake's diet, but crayfish and crabs are also consumed. Reports that frogs are this species' natural prey in areas where it enters fresh or only slightly brackish water requires confirmation. In the late 1940s, specimens often were seen during daylight hours in the railroad yards of Galveston Island feeding in the shallows of an artificially created riffle; the water passed through a narrow channel from one side of a local marsh to the other, carrying with it many small fish.

REPRODUCTION Like all North American water snakes, this one bears live young. Born in August or September, they number 2 to 14 per litter and measure $7\frac{3}{4}$ to 10 inches (19.7–25.4 cm) long at birth.

MISSISSIPPI GREEN WATER SNAKE
Nerodia cyclopion
PLATE 99

DESCRIPTION Except for its large size, heavy body, and relatively wide head, nothing about the snake's general appearance is especially impressive or distinctive. Its drab olive-green to olive-brown dorsal color is marked with numerous obscure, narrow black crossbars along the back that are closely spaced and often slightly wavy in outline. Along each side of the body, a series of similar black bars alternates with the row above. The snake's most conspicuous markings are on the abdomen. Consisting of numerous yellowish halfmoons, they cover most of the belly, which is typically yellowish white on the forward third and grayish or brownish at midbody and the rear. In addition to the distinctive belly pattern, the species' most diagnostic feature is the arrangement of scales under the eyes, for no other native water snake has a row of small scales separating the orbit from the upper lip scales. The dorsal scales are keeled and in 27 or 29 rows at midbody. The anal plate is divided.

COMPARABLE SNAKES No other Texas water snake has scales between the eyes and the upper lip plates, and none exhibits a belly pattern of randomly distributed, pale halfmoons. The western cottonmouth, Texas' only semiaquatic venomous serpent, has a pit on each side of its head between the eye and nostril and a vertically elliptical eye pupil; the scales under its tail are arranged mostly in a double row (single in water snakes). It should also be mentioned that water snakes tend to flee quickly from an intruder, whereas the cottonmouth will retreat at a leisurely pace or not at all, often maintaining its position with the head pulled back and its mouth held wide open.

SIZE The adult Mississippi green water snake is generally 30 to 40 inches (76.2–101.6 cm) long. The largest specimen for which there is a confirmed record measured 50 inches (127 cm) in length.

HABITAT Despite being one of Louisiana's most abundant water snakes, this serpent occurs only sparingly in Texas. Most Texas records represent scattered localities along the state's coastal marshes from the Sabine River south to Nueces County, yet Guidry (1953) described it as extremely plentiful in both Jefferson and Orange counties, where he found it as often in brackish water as in fresh water, and moderately abundant just to the north in Hardin and Newton counties. Dundee and Rossman (1989) stated that in areas of prime southern Louisiana habitat it can be exceedingly common, citing as an example the spectacular congregation of more than 80 Mississippi green water snakes ob-

served by herpetologist Percy Viosca as they basked along a canal within the city limits of New Orleans during the early morning hours of April 7, 1915. Even more remarkable is Viosca's disclosure that in a single mid-June day in 1922, he collected 119 specimens from Delacroix Island in St. Bernard Parish.

Occupying a variety of habitats ranging from woodland swamp to grassy coastal prairie, it prefers environments characterized by quiet waters with some shoreline vegetation. Such habitats include lakes and ponds, rivers and bayous, swamps and marshes, flooded

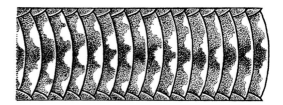

Figure 39. *Belly pattern of the Mississippi green water snake.*

woodland, sloughs and oxbows, as well as canals, ditches, and rice fields. In Alabama, Mount (1975) described it as a common reptile in the tupelo gum and cypress swamps of the Tensaw and Mobile river systems, the same kind of habitat it occupies in the wooded swamplands of south-central Louisiana. In Louisiana's Atchafalaya River basin, one of this country's largest freshwater swamps, Kofron (1978) found it to be the second most abundant of several water-snake species. In this area of mixed hardwood forest and swamp containing widespread stands of cypress, he captured a large number of specimens in the following environments: bayou canal (33), tidal ditch (32), grasses (21), swamp bottomland forest (18), flooded bottomland forest (10), freshwater marsh (10), flooded field (10), miscellaneous areas (7), bottomland forest (6), river (5), bay inlet (5), and freshwater bay (1). He seldom saw one in the Atchafalaya River itself, and he collected only a single specimen in a freshwater bay, where it rested among water hyacinths near shore.

Its occurrence in some brackish marshes has been reported by several zoologists. Indeed, over the years we have observed more than 20 Mississippi green water snakes in the brackish marshes along the west side of Bolivar Peninsula, some swimming with Gulf salt marsh snakes through aquatic vegetation near shore and others crawling across State Highway 87, which runs northeast to the mainland.

BEHAVIOR Ordinarily not as quick-tempered as either the diamond-backed or yellow-bellied water snakes with which it shares the same habitat, the Mississippi green water snake nevertheless exhibits the typical *Nerodia* temperament, striking out and biting when provoked and, like the others, expelling musk and feces when restrained. Though seldom found far from water, this essentially aquatic species frequently crosses roads when moving from one body of water to another. Dundee and Rossman (1989) commented that in the marshes of Cameron and Vermilian parishes of Louisiana, green water snakes frequently are seen on roads, especially during or after rains. Kofron (1978) also found them crossing such thoroughfares at

his Atchafalaya River basin study site, mostly in areas of grassy habitat and usually late in the evening or at night; the majority of specimens were encountered more than 260 feet from the nearest water, with a few as far away as 328 feet. Of several water-snake species inhabiting southern Louisiana's mixed cypress swamps and wet bottomland forests, this one alone was found to be active throughout the year, reaching its maximum abundance in June and July. From November to March, nearly all of the green water snakes observed by Mushinsky and his colleagues (1980) during a four-year study in southern Louisiana were active during the day, spending much of that time basking on tree limbs, logs, and other objects to increase their body temperature. Like most other water snakes of the region, they avoided the oppressive summer heat by becoming mostly nocturnal and spending much of their time in the water.

In winter the Mississippi green water snake was the most arboreal of all the local water snakes, and in summer the most aquatic. It was also the region's most day-active *Nerodia*. Although green water snakes encountered by Kofron in the Atchafalaya River basin during the summer seldom used logs and debris as a refuge, they frequently did so in cool weather. In the moderate and sometimes even frostless Gulf Coast winters, this species may temporarily seek shelter beneath logs and piles of vegetative debris, just as it does in the spring and fall, although in the more northern parts of its range the snake's hibernacula are generally more cold-resistant, consisting of mammal burrows, the decayed root systems of dead trees, rotting tree stumps, and deep rock crevices. Ernst and Barbour (1989) suggested it may also overwinter in muskrat and beaver lodges, as well as in the rubble of earthen or rock dams.

FEEDING Like the larger diamond-backed water snake, with which it shares much of the same Mississippi River floodplain, the green water snake consumes fish almost exclusively, a preference confirmed by several comprehensive field studies. The most detailed of these, conducted by Kofron in Louisiana's Atchafalaya River basin, revealed that of 42 green water snakes with food in their digestive systems, by far the greatest number contained fish (98.4 percent of the total by volume), mostly mosquito fish and sailfin mollies—small, abundant, nongame species. Prey items, by number, mentioned in the survey included 20 mosquito fish, 13 sailfin mollies, 13 unidentified fish, 9 other unidentified prey items, 7 striped mullet, 4 golden shiners, 2 sheepshead minnows, 2 bayou killifish, 1 three-toed amphiuma (a large aquatic salamander), and 1 unidentified frog. Catfish, often eaten by the largely nocturnal diamond-backed water snake, were conspicuously absent from the green water snake's diet (except for one blue catfish), perhaps because the snake is chiefly day-active and the catfish primarily nocturnal. The presence of marine and brackish water fish in the stomachs of some coastal-dwelling green water snakes is further evidence that this species occasionally inhabits brackish marshes.

Mushinsky and Hebrard (1977) also studied the feeding habits of the Mississippi green water snake in Louisiana. The results of their survey, conducted in Ascension Parish, were similar to Kofron's, indicating that by far the greatest volume of prey consumed by this reptile consisted of fish (98.4 percent of the total). From the 28 specimens examined, they removed food items in the following percentages by volume for these categories: 11.8 percent small fish, 86.6 percent larger fish, 1.0 percent tadpoles, and 0.6 percent frogs. When ranked according to the number of prey items consumed, killifish accounted for 77.6 percent of the total. In a departure from the snake's typical fish diet, Garton, Harris, and Brandon (1970) found an adult lesser siren (a large, aquatic, eellike salamander) in each of three southern Illinois specimens.

In its foraging behavior, the green water snake is little different from most other *Nerodia.* It readily captures fish by stalking them in shallow water or, preferably, by finding them in some small inlet or impoundment where they can be easily corralled. It is also reported to swim through the water with an open mouth, moving its head from side to side as it tries to snare its aquatic prey.

REPRODUCTION In the Gulf Coast states, mating usually takes place during the first three weeks in April, producing 9 to 34 young per litter sometime between mid-July and mid-September. Each newborn is 9 to 10½ inches (22.9–26.7 cm) long and more prominently patterned than the adult.

YELLOW-BELLIED WATER SNAKE
Nerodia erythrogaster flavigaster
PLATE 100

DESCRIPTION A large, rather heavy-bodied water snake with a somber, uniformly gray or greenish gray background coloration, this subspecies sometimes displays a row of indistinct, abbreviated crossbars along the middle of its back, markings that are narrowly dark-edged at both front and back. The belly is usually bright yellow, with or without some discreet dark pigmentation on the outer edges of the belly scales. The same yellow color extends upward onto the sides of the head, covering the upper and lower lip plates, which bear dark vertical sutures. The body scales are keeled, in 23 (occasionally 27) rows at midbody, and the anal plate is divided.

The infant bears little resemblance to the adult. It is patterned with large, dark, clearly defined middorsal blotches and a lateral row of similar but smaller markings that alternate with the larger ones. Spaces between the markings typically are pinkish or reddish.

COMPARABLE SNAKES Some other adult water snakes are dark-colored with little trace of dorsal markings and may be mistaken for this one, but their prominently patterned bellies make them easily recognizable. The sometimes patternless cottonmouth, which closely resembles this harmless water snake, can be recognized by the heat-sensing facial pits, elliptical eye pupils, and the mostly single row of scales under its tail (double in water snakes).

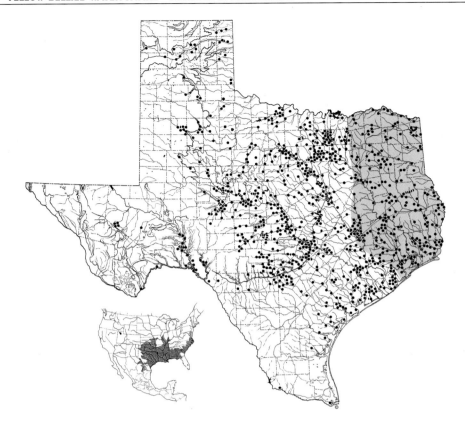

SIZE Although a specimen 53⅛ inches (134.9 cm) long represents the record for this subspecies, the usual adult length is between 2 and 3 feet (61–91.4 cm).

HABITAT In the Atchafalaya River basin of south-central Louisiana (a vast ecosystem involving one of the country's largest expanses of freshwater swampland), Kofron (1978) studied the habits and feeding behavior of the region's aquatic snakes. Much of the following information is from that survey and from three similar studies: one conducted in southern Louisiana by Mushinsky and Hebrard (1977), a second by Mushinsky, Hebrard, and Walley (1980) in Ascension Parish, and the other by Diener (1957) in parts of four central and south-central states, including Texas, where the yellow-bellied water snake is abundant.

Those studies reveal that the yellowbelly prefers aquatic environments with still or slow-moving water, including the sluggish portions of streams and rivers, small isolated ponds, lakes, swamps, bayous, wet bottomland forest, and even rice fields and muddy ditches. So habituated is it to quiet waters that streams flowing faster than 50 feet per minute are normally avoided, as are clear streams with rocky bottoms. It is also partial to waterways with brush and trees growing near or at the water's edge and supporting emergent aquatic vegetation, the kind of plant growth characteristic of shorelines adjacent to still or slow-moving currents.

In the south-central Louisiana study, 16 yellow-bellied water snakes were encountered in the following places: bottomland forest (6), river (4), grasses (3), swamp bottomland forest (1), flooded bottomland forest (1), and miscellaneous habitat (1). Those collected in swamp-bayou systems of southern Louisiana were taken in an area broadly described as partly cypress swamp and partly bottomland hardwood forest, although in this study habitat niches were not specifically identified.

BEHAVIOR When provoked, the yellow-bellied water snake shows the same quick temper displayed by most other members of the genus *Nerodia*. Its first reaction to the approach of man is to scramble for cover in the nearest expanse of underbrush or, failing that, to plunge immediately into the nearest body of water. Although it seldom does so, it can remain submerged for as long as an hour at a time as it waits for its foe to depart. When approached by boat, most Louisiana specimens observed in the wild by Mushinsky and Hebrard did not try to avoid capture by sliding into the water but instead rushed inland to the cover of shoreline vegetation. If denied the opportunity to escape, it resorts to another tactic—intimidation. When confronted at close range by a potential predator, it flattens its head and the entire body against the ground, presenting a larger, more forbidding image than before, its visibly tense body conveying the impression of a taut spring ready to unwind.

If restrained, the snake bites viciously and repeatedly, its numerous needle-sharp teeth producing freely bleeding puncture wounds and lacerations; although they are momentarily rather painful, they are only superficial and normally heal in just a few days. With the determined striking and biting come both musk from glands at the base of the snake's tail and fecal material from its cloacal opening. These foul-smelling substances, liberally smeared over the assailant by the serpent's frantic thrashing, are often so offensive that the reptile is set free, which is exactly what the snake intended.

Less aquatic than the diamond-backed or broad-banded water snakes with which it coexists, this subspecies may use the water primarily for feeding purposes but perform other functions on land. Most specimens in Diener's study were found approximately 13.7 feet on average from the nearest body of water, but one was observed as far away as 150 feet. In Ohio, Conant (1934) discovered a specimen of this species a surprising 200 yards from the closest pond. Diamond-backed water snakes, on the other hand, were usually encountered only 2.1 feet from water.

Although in most other parts of its geographic range the yellow-bellied water snake is first seen no earlier in the year than March or April, along the Gulf Coast it may occasionally move about during periods of warm winter weather. On early spring midafternoons, with temperatures holding near 60 degrees F, Diener observed limited numbers of specimens sunning on logs, driftwood, and matted vegetation, though by nightfall they were no longer to be seen. As the days became progressively longer and the temperatures warmer, the snakes were visible in greater numbers, basking or hiding by day and searching for prey during the evening and through much of the night. With the return of cooler late-summer temperatures, and through autumn, the snakes reversed their activity cycle again so that both sunning and hunting occurred in the warmer daylight hours; they were seldom active when the ambient air temperature dropped below 56 degrees F and not at all if the temperature stayed that low for at least two consecutive days. Then they could be found hiding beneath decomposing logs, boards, accumulations of driftwood, piles of vegetative debris, and rocks. During winter, the snakes took refuge under some of the same objects they employed as temporary shelter, as well as in abandoned animal burrows (especially those of muskrat and beaver), decaying stumps, and in the bases of rock or earthen dams.

FEEDING This subspecies and the closely related broad-banded water snake consume far more frogs and toads than any other Texas water snake. Fish normally represent their second choice of food, and salamanders a distant third. In fact, anurans (including their tadpoles) generally make up more than 60 percent of the snake's diet, although prey selection can vary according to region. Prey preference apparently also depends on the snake's age, according to Mushinsky and Lotz (1980), who determined that young snakes ate chiefly fish until they reached maturity, after which they consumed amphibians almost exclusively. In northern Louisiana, R. F. Clark (1949) listed fish as the chief food in the yellowbelly's diet, with crayfish and leopard frogs of secondary importance.

Based on analysis of the stomach contents of 34 specimens from several central and south-central states, Diener discovered that this species (including both Texas subspecies) devoured amphibians almost exclusively (91.8 percent of the total by volume). Those amphibians were 51.3 percent leopard frogs, 29.7 percent bullfrogs, and 10.8 percent unidentified anurans. The remaining stomach contents consisted of 5.5 percent fish and 2.7 percent unidentified prey animals.

Frogs, toads, and tadpoles also represented the principal food of the yellow-bellied water snake in the swamp-bayou environment of southern Louisiana's Ascension Parish, where the total food volume consumed by this subspecies was nearly 88 percent anurans and their tadpoles, 2.8 percent small fish, and 9.2 percent larger fish. The amphibians were mostly green frogs, with toads next in importance, and tadpoles the last. Small fish eaten by the snake were chiefly mosquito fish and killifish, and to a much lesser extent pygmy sunfish, sailfin mollies, topminnows, and typical sunfish.

In another, more limited survey conducted by Kofron in the Atchafalaya basin, five specimens were examined and found to have eaten only anurans, including 1 unidentified frog, 1 toad, 3 toad tadpoles, and 1 unidentified animal.

Although relatively heavy-bodied, the yellow-bellied water snake does not sit and wait for its prey. Primarily an active forager, it usually enters the water to search for food, swimming slowly along a shoreline or through the shallow waters of marshes and bogs as it seeks to flush out a meal, though it also looks for frogs and toads in damp woodlands. Once sighted, particularly if it is a terrestrial animal, the prey is pursued or quickly seized before it can begin its escape. To increase its success rate when foraging for fish, this and certain other water snakes sometimes employ a peculiar hunting strategy, often when there is a gentle current. With its tail securely wrapped around a stone, aquatic plant, or partially submerged tree limb and the rest of its body extended out into the water, the snake slowly sweeps its submerged head and forebody back and forth until its open jaws encounter a fish. After the prey is seized and swallowed, the snake repeats the process several times until its appetite is satisfied. The tactic is especially useful in murky water where the reptile's sight is of little value for locating prey.

A similar strategy, used near shore in shallow water, is that of swimming slowly in figure-8 profiles with its mouth agape, seizing any fish its open jaws may encounter. During this endeavor the snake may briefly entrap a fish within the closing loop of its shifting body coils, allowing just enough time for the reptile to snare its active quarry before it can escape.

Changing climatic conditions may provide the snake with additional feeding opportunities. For example, when a prolonged summer drought has severely reduced the size of already small, shallow pools, large numbers of fish and amphibians are often bunched together in the remaining puddles, making them easy targets for predators. It is then that the yellow-bellied water snake, together with other species of *Nerodia*, will congregate at the ponds, often for days at a time, voraciously gulping down the vulnerable prey for as long as they last. Similar water-snake feeding aggregations occur near narrow channels that serve as avenues between two large bodies of water, for example, between a bayou and an adjacent swamp. Such channels may function continuously; others only during periods of high water. When water passes through one of them, the flow often funnels a migration of small fish into the narrow corridor, attracting the attention of the snakes by their brief surfacing. In a somewhat similar situation, reported by Ernst and Barbour (1989), specimens of this species captured fish that were being washed over a dam spillway.

REPRODUCTION Mating usually takes place in April or May. The young snakes, 10 to 30 per litter, are usually born sometime in August or September, although the females have also been reported to give birth in October, somewhat later in the year than would be expected. The infants are $9\frac{1}{2}$ to 12 inches (24.2–30.5 cm) long and marked with a bold pattern of dark dorsal and lateral blotches set against a pinkish ground color. They bear little resemblance to their bland-looking parents.

BLOTCHED WATER SNAKE

*Nerodia erythrogaster
transversa*
PLATES 101, 102

DESCRIPTION Like the yellow-bellied water snake, its nearest relative to the east, this large, heavy-bodied water snake has a dark dorsal coloration and an unmarked belly, though it shows more variation in its upper body color than that subspecies, ranging from light brown to dark gray. The main difference between the two is the loss in the full-grown yellow-bellied water snake of the strongly blotched juvenile pattern and the continued presence of such a pattern in mature *N. e. transversa*. The black-edged, dark brown dorsal markings of this subspecies alternate with smaller lateral spots of the same color, although in some older individuals (those with an overall dark brown or olive coloration) the pattern has all but disappeared. If there are any markings at all in such specimens, they consist of abbreviated light-colored crossbars along the spine, each one edged in black, both front and back. Narrow dark spots are usually present on the outer edges of the snake's yellow or sometimes orange belly, but no markings occur on the underside of its pale orange or reddish tail. Although most specimens fit the overall description portrayed above, those from the arid western end of the snake's range ordinarily are much lighter in hue. The body scales,

23 to 27 in a row at midbody, are keeled, and the anal plate is divided.

The juvenile is prominently blotched on the back and sides, the belly is whitish, and a pair of tiny, pale spots normally marks the top of its head.

COMPARABLE SNAKES Other adult water snakes living within the range of this subspecies, though also dark-colored and dorsally marked, possess boldly patterned bellies. The cottonmouth has elliptical pupils and heat-sensing facial cavities, and the scales under its tail are arranged mostly in a single row, features not seen in our harmless water snakes.

SIZE The usual adult length is 30 inches to nearly 4 feet (76.2–120.7 cm), although this subspecies is reported to reach an extreme length of 58 inches (147.3 cm).

HABITAT In the eastern end of its range, the snake's typical habitat is little different from that of the yellow-bellied water snake. It includes most bodies of water with slow-moving currents supporting a growth of emergent vegetation. There it intergrades with the yellow-bellied water snake, producing some serpents intermediate in pattern and coloration. By moving upstream along the major river systems that penetrate into far West Texas, it has managed to invade the drier, more hostile environment of the Edwards Plateau and the Trans-Pecos region. Reliable evidence shows that it once ascended the Rio Grande drainage system at least to Calamity Creek in Brewster County, to Balmorhea in Reeves County, and to the Black River system in southeastern New Mexico, but today it is no longer found farther up the Rio Grande than the town of Boquillas in Big Bend National Park. Besides serving as convenient aquatic highways, such watercourses contain the prey the snakes must have to survive. In this inhospitable land, where stream levels can fluctuate dramatically according to seasonal periods of severe flooding and extreme drying, the blotched water snake manages to persevere, though its continued existence within some parts of its Chihuahuan Desert range is in doubt.

Even more harmful to the snake's welfare than natural calamities are the effects of human agricultural practices, specifically deep well drilling and excessive long-term pumping of underground water. The implications are obvious. We know that water from aquifers has been so grievously depleted in parts of southwestern Texas that in many places the snake's spring-fed microhabitats have been severely diminished or have disappeared altogether. Despite such losses, *N. e. transversa* continues to hang on in many areas where major sources of surface water have been eliminated. Obviously it does not need large watercourses to endure, since even under ordinary circumstances it often survives in irrigation ditches, small ponds, and cattle tanks; during extended dry periods it likewise can be found in rain-filled pools and roadside ditches at a considerable distance from permanent water. It is inclined to wander farther from its aquatic haunts than any of the other races of its species—out of bare necessity, for in this parched land the watercourses on which it depends for its survival are sometimes transitory.

Curiously, the blotched water snake has not been discovered in the Rio Grande Valley south of Kingsville. The reason is not clear, although Conant (1955) speculated that the presence of eolian sand deposits and sand dunes in Kenedy County and in much of the area to the west may thwart its southward movement into the Valley.

BEHAVIOR When provoked and unable to escape, most water snakes respond in a similar way. This one is no exception. See yellow-bellied water snake account.

The snake's activity cycle is influenced mostly by prevailing temperatures. Thus, in early spring, particularly after a cold front has moved through the snake's habitat, and again in the fall, this serpent is active chiefly during the early morning hours. Otherwise it is on the prowl in the evening and at night, scrupulously avoiding the hot midday sun. In the San Antonio area, Vermersch and Kuntz (1986) described it as day-active in winter, even in January and February, two of the coldest months in the year, provided the air is warmer than 71 degrees F and the water is above 64 degrees F. At that time of year the snake could be found during the day, basking on branches along the banks of the San Antonio River. Several times the two biologists observed large numbers of these snakes moving about in March, just before the arrival of a cold front. In spring it often basks in the sun, lying quietly on logs, driftwood, shrubs, or matted vegetation in or near the water; at other times it hides under logs and rocks that are partly submerged in shallow moving streams. It also spends a lot of time in the water. In the more arid parts of its range, the blotched water snake can be seen swimming along the edge of shallow, rock-encumbered streams or lying wholly submerged in the aquatic vegetation with only its head above water.

FEEDING Food consists chiefly of amphibians and fish. Leopard frogs and bullfrogs are its principal anuran prey, with toads, tadpoles, salamanders, and crayfish constituting less important dietary items.

Like some other water snakes, this one may catch fish by wrapping its tail and the rear part of its body around a limb, rock, or plant in or along the bank of a flowing stream, while it slowly sweeps its open mouth back and forth through the water. When a fish is encountered, it is immediately seized and swallowed.

REPRODUCTION   Mating occurs in April and May, after which litters of 5 to 27 babies per female are born sometime in late July, August, or September. The young measure 7½ to 12 inches (19–30.5 cm) long.

BROAD-BANDED WATER SNAKE
Nerodia fasciata confluens
PLATE 103

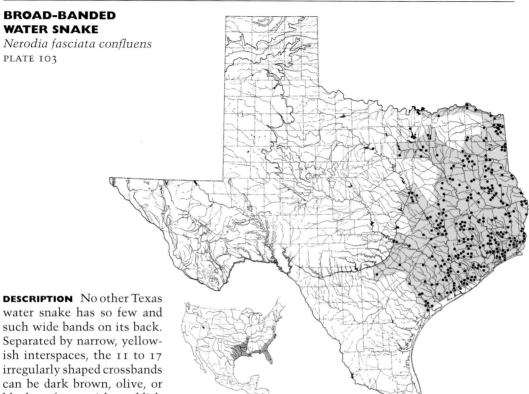

DESCRIPTION   No other Texas water snake has so few and such wide bands on its back. Separated by narrow, yellowish interspaces, the 11 to 17 irregularly shaped crossbands can be dark brown, olive, or black, often with reddish brown patches along their sides. There is considerable color variation within local colonies or among geographically separated populations, so some snakes display more red along the sides than others. For the same reason, the black pigment may so dominate a snake's pattern that its dorsal markings are barely evident. In all specimens the belly is tan or yellowish with large, rectangular, dark brown or black spots. On either side of the snake's head, a bold, dark cheek stripe usually runs from the eye through the end of the mouthline. The dorsal scales are keeled and arranged in 21 to 25 rows at midbody. The anal plate is divided.

The young broad-banded water snake is more vividly colored than the adult, its bright yellow interspaces standing out conspicuously between the dark crossbands, and each side of its head is covered with a pale orange hue.

COMPARABLE SNAKES   Other adult unstriped water snakes inhabiting the broad-banded's range lack its prominent facial mask and its large, dark, rectangular belly spots. The

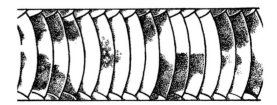

Figure 40. *Belly pattern of the broad-banded water snake.*

cottonmouth's elliptical pupils, facial pits, more angular head profile, and single row of scales under its tail distinguish it from the broad-banded water snake.

SIZE Most adults of this subspecies measure 20 to 30 inches (50.8–76.2 cm) long; the record length is 45 inches (114.3 cm).

HABITAT This moderately large water snake prefers the quiet, shallow waters of swamps, marshes, bayous, sloughs, ponds, and lakes, where shorelines are bordered by woodland or vegetation of some sort. It also occupies rice fields, canals, and slow-moving streams. Although it inhabits coastal prairie marshland near brackish water, it cannot live permanently in a saltwater environment, for to survive it must have access to fresh drinking water. This was convincingly demonstrated by Pettus (1958), whose laboratory experiments showed that when the broad-banded water snake was deprived of fresh water and was forced by circumstances to drink salt water instead, it invariably died.

No comprehensive study has examined the serpent's habitat preferences in Texas, but Kofron (1978) initiated such a survey to determine the snake's preferred haunts in the floodplains of south-central Louisiana. In the vast wetlands and waterways of the Atchafalaya River delta, a region covering 2,100 square miles of mixed hardwood forest and swampland, he collected 48 specimens in the following habitats: grassy areas (16), bottomland forest (8), flooded bottomland forest (7), disturbed swamp–bottomland forest (6), river (2), freshwater marsh (2), bayou canal (2), tidal ditch (2), miscellaneous habitat (2), and flooded field (1).

BEHAVIOR Like most water snakes, this serpent shows little restraint when threatened or handled. Its first reaction to the sight of an approaching human is to flee, into water if possible. If its escape is thwarted, the snake may flatten its head and body to the ground so that it appears larger and more fearsome and perhaps also as a way to mimic the broad, flat-headed configuration of the venomous cottonmouth. This form of intimidation, a common tactic among water snakes, is meant to frighten away the enemy. If the snake is further provoked, it strikes out savagely and repeatedly, though seldom hitting its mark, for this too is a bluff. If picked up or stepped on, however, the reptile's response is even more vigorous. Striking out furiously, it also emits twin jets of a foul-smelling liquid from scent glands at the base of its tail, often accompanied by the release of fecal material from the cloaca, the two together creating a strong, malodorous mixture that frequently turns away an opponent. If that fails, the snake will continue to bite for as long as it is restrained. The serpent's small, needlelike teeth, although capable of causing numerous freely bleeding lacerations and punctures, do not produce any serious injury to mankind.

In southern Louisiana, according to Mushinsky, Hebrard, and Walley (1980), the broad-banded water snake first becomes active as early in the year as late January (though normally not before late March), but a spell of chilly weather at this time of year will force it to seek temporary refuge under piles of vegetation near water or to enter the burrows of animals such as crayfish or muskrats. For the next couple of months it moves about by day, often basking on logs, stumps, or tree limbs close to the ground, something it does more frequently than the diamond-backed or yellow-bellied water snakes with which it shares the same habitat. It is not until summer that the broad-banded becomes nocturnal. Unable to tolerate the extreme daytime heat of midsummer, it forages at night, returning to a cool refuge before sunup, a pattern that usually continues through October.

A strong swimmer, the snake spends about 60 percent of its time in the water. Jacob and McDonald (1976) determined that it could remain submerged for up to 24 minutes at a time, in large part because it could conserve oxygen by dramatically reducing its heart beat from a normal 33.2 beats a minute on the water's surface to only 6.77 beats per minute when submerged.

With the approach of cold weather, usually by early December along the coast, the snake retires to a winter refuge consisting largely of plant debris near water, decaying logs or stumps, and probably also crayfish and muskrat burrows. During moderate winters in southern Louisiana, according to Tinkle (1959), hibernation may last only three months, from early December to late February.

FEEDING Fish and frogs (including tadpoles) are the snake's principal food. In southern Louisiana, Mushinsky and Hebrard (1977) found that among their sample specimens, fish were the chief prey by volume, constituting more than 75 percent of the total food consumed. Mosquito fish and killifish, by far the most important species, made up 30.6 percent and 29.0 percent, respectively, of the snake's piscine fare. Other prey fish reported by the zoologists included gizzard shad, sunfish, American eel, pygmy sunfish, and other fish. Frogs and toads, which did not represent an especially large volume of prey, nevertheless were the second most notable food category, constituting 21.8 percent of the total. They included frogs (13.6 percent), toads (3.3), and tadpoles (4.9). Tree frogs, although abundant in the snake's habitat, were rarely consumed. Crayfish represented another 0.3 percent of the overall total.

Another, less exhaustive food study conducted in south-central Louisiana by Kofron produced results similar to the Mushinsky and Hebrard survey. It verified that fish were the prey of choice (especially mosquito fish and killifish) and that frogs and toads together represented the reptile's second most popular food item. In an earlier study, R. F. Clark (1949) mentioned frogs and fish as the snake's principal quarry, but he also reported that squirrels and birds had been consumed by this essentially aquatic serpent. The last two items have not been mentioned by other zoologists, before or since Clark's survey, and their listing as legitimate prey needs confirmation.

In its quest for food, the broad-banded water snake moves busily through its aquatic environment, poking its head into piles of debris and aquatic vegetation where prey is apt to be found.

REPRODUCTION Following courtship in April or May, a single female gives birth to 7 to 40 young at a time, usually from mid-July to mid-September. In a departure from the norm, Guidry (1953) reported on a female of this subspecies from southeastern Texas that gave birth to 22 young on October 20. The newborn water snakes typically measure 7 to 9½ inches (17.8–24.2 cm) long.

FLORIDA WATER SNAKE
Nerodia fasciata pictiventris
PLATE 104

DESCRIPTION Except for all-black specimens whose body pattern is obscured by a preponderance of dark pigmentation, the snake's broad crossbands (which may be black, brown, or reddish) stand out conspicuously against a paler ground color. Extending down to the belly, they are typically broader (front to rear) at midback than along the sides and often edged with widely scattered, single, pale scales. Usually a large, dark spot occupies the pale interspace between each pair of adjacent bands. The snake's head, which is distinctly wider than its neck, generally is dark on top and lighter on the sides, where a dark stripe extends from the eye to the end of the mouthline. The vertical margins of both upper and lower lip scales are edged in black. The belly markings are distinctive, consisting of black, red, or dark brown wormlike markings that cross the yellowish abdomen along the edges of the abdominal plates. The dorsal scales are keeled and in 25 rows at midbody. The anal plate is divided.

COMPARABLE SNAKES The moderately stout-bodied Florida water snake can be mistaken for the venomous cottonmouth, but the cottonmouth does not range as far south in the state as Cameron County. The large,

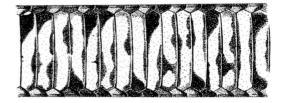

Figure 41. *Belly pattern of the Florida water snake.*

heavy-bodied diamond-backed water snake, a semiaquatic serpent living side by side with *N. f. pictiventris* in the Brownsville area, can be distinguished by the dark brown chainlike markings on its back, the dark half-moons on its belly, and the absence of a dark bar running backward from each eye.

SIZE Adults are generally 24 to 42 inches (61–106.7 cm) long, although the maximum size recorded for this subspecies is 62½ inches (158.7 cm) in length.

HABITAT The snake's natural range includes the extreme southeastern edge of Georgia and nearly all of peninsular Florida, where it inhabits a wide variety of freshwater environments, particularly those characterized by small or shallow bodies of water.

Not a native Texas subspecies, it was introduced here accidentally by the South Texas animal dealer known as Snake King, whose wild-animal compound in Brownsville held a constant succession of reptiles, both local and extralimital. Among them were various species of water snakes commonly sold to circuses, sideshows, and zoos. When a severe hurricane devastated the animal compound on September 5, 1933, an untold number of Florida water snakes escaped from their flimsy cages and eventually established a breeding colony in the area. It is also believed that over the years others were intentionally released into local resacas, to be recaptured later as needed. Since then this alien subspecies has become an established part of the South Texas snake fauna.

Three factors in particular may have favored the Florida water snake's successful colonization in Texas. One, of course, is the semitropical South Texas climate; its high average annual temperature and high relative humidity are not markedly different from those in peninsular Florida. Another is the abundance of resacas in the Brownsville region, which replicate the snake's choice Florida habitats of small, shallow waterways. Finally, the snake's large number of offspring—up to 57 per litter—no doubt gave it an edge when it was first liberated into its new habitation.

BEHAVIOR On land, a provoked individual, especially if it is unable to flee, responds by greatly flattening its head and body in an apparent attempt to intimidate its foe; it then strikes out vigorously when approached too closely. Like most other members of the genus *Nerodia*, it generally bites fiercely when picked up, at the same time voiding a noxious musk from glands at the base of its tail.

Encountered along the bank of a stream, pond, or resaca, where it is apt to be seen basking on a log, stump, or brush pile along the shore, it quickly slips into the water at the slightest disturbance and either dives below the surface or tries to hide in the emergent vegetation. Jacob and McDonald (1976) found that this species of water snake can stay submerged for as long as 24 minutes at a time and that when submerged, its heart rate slows to a mere 6.77 beats per minute compared to 33.2 beats per minute when it is at the surface.

In Florida it is primarily nocturnal, being particularly active after heavy nighttime showers have coaxed an abundance of frogs (its preferred prey) out of hiding, although sometimes it can be encountered during the day as it basks in the sun.

FEEDING In Florida, according to Carr (1940), the principal food of this snake is frogs, especially young bullfrogs, although others list toads, fish, and aquatic invertebrates as prey. Carr also points out that spring breeding aggregations of barking tree frogs provide the snake with a bountiful food supply, for at such times the anurans float unprotected on top of the water, making easy targets for the fast-moving and voracious water snakes. This active forager, which probes the shoreline vegetation for prey, locates its quarry by odor and movement. When it flushes a frog from hiding, the snake quickly pursues its victim, which when overtaken is promptly swallowed whole and alive.

REPRODUCTION According to Carr, the Florida water snake mates in the spring (March 11 to May 14), although Ashton and Ashton (1981) claim that breeding may occur anytime between fall and the following early spring. Born sometime from May to August, the baby snakes, 25 to 57 per litter and 7½ to 10½ inches (19–26.7 cm) long, do not all look alike, not even those from the same litter. A newborn individual may resemble either the dark phase or the pale variety, or it may look like something in-between.

1. PLAINS BLIND SNAKE.
Leptotyphlops dulcis dulcis.
Adult from Bexar County.

2. NEW MEXICO BLIND SNAKE.
Leptotyphlops dulcis dissectus.
Adult from Payne County,
Oklahoma.
PHOTO BY R. W. VAN DEVENDER.

3. TRANS-PECOS BLIND SNAKE.
Leptotyphlops humilis segregus.
Adult from Presidio County.

4. KANSAS GLOSSY SNAKE.
Arizona elegans elegans.
Adult.

5. TEXAS GLOSSY SNAKE.
Arizona elegans arenicola.
Adult.

6. TEXAS GLOSSY SNAKE.
Arizona elegans arenicola.
Lateral head pattern of an adult.

7. PAINTED DESERT GLOSSY SNAKE.
Arizona elegans philipi.
Adult from Presidio County.

8. TRANS-PECOS RAT SNAKE.
Bogertophis subocularis subocularis.
Orange adult.

9. TRANS-PECOS RAT SNAKE.
Bogertophis subocularis subocularis.
Yellowish adult from Brewster
County.
PHOTO BY J. E. WERLER.

10. TRANS-PECOS RAT SNAKE.
Bogertophis subocularis subocularis.
Blotched pattern phase adult from
Brewster County.

11. TRANS-PECOS RAT SNAKE.
Bogertophis subocularis subocularis.
Unhatched specimen in eggshell.

12. TRANS-PECOS RAT SNAKE.
Bogertophis subocularis subocularis.
Hatchling and spent eggshell.

13. WESTERN WORM SNAKE.
Carphophis vermis.
Adult from Titus County.

14. NORTHERN SCARLET SNAKE.
Cemophora coccinea copei.
Adult from Newton County.

15. TEXAS SCARLET SNAKE.
Cemophora coccinea lineri.
Adult from Aransas County.

16. BUTTERMILK RACER.
Coluber constrictor anthicus.
Adult from Liberty County.

17. TAN RACER.
Coluber constrictor etheridgei.
Adult from Hardin County.

**18. EASTERN YELLOW-BELLIED
RACER.**
Coluber constrictor flaviventris.
Adult from McLennan County.

19. MEXICAN RACER.
Coluber constrictor oaxaca.
Adult from Cameron County.

20. MEXICAN RACER.
Coluber constrictor oaxaca.
Juvenile from Cameron County.

21. SOUTHERN BLACK RACER.
Coluber constrictor priapus.
Adult from Lamar County.

22. SOUTHERN BLACK RACER.
Coluber constrictor priapus.
Juvenile from Florida.
PHOTO BY R. W. VAN DEVENDER.

23. BLACK-STRIPED SNAKE.
*Coniophanes imperialis
imperialis.*
Adult from Cameron County.
PHOTO BY P. FREED.

24. PRAIRIE RING-NECKED SNAKE.
Diadophis punctatus arnyi.
Adult from Dallas County.

25. PRAIRIE RING-NECKED SNAKE.
Diadophis punctatus arnyi.
Underside of body and tail of adult
from Dallas County.

26. REGAL RING-NECKED SNAKE.
Diadophis punctatus regalis.
Adult from El Paso County.

27. MISSISSIPPI RING-NECKED SNAKE.
Diadophis punctatus stictogenys.
Adult from Polk County, Arkansas.
PHOTO BY J. A. CAMPBELL, COURTESY OF THE
UNIVERSITY OF TEXAS AT ARLINGTON.

28. TEXAS INDIGO SNAKE.
Drymarchon corais erebennus.
Adult.
PHOTO BY R. A. ODUM.

29. TEXAS INDIGO SNAKE.
Drymarchon corais erebennus.
Juvenile.
PHOTO BY R. A. ODUM.

30. SPECKLED RACER.
Drymobius margaritiferus margaritiferus.
Adult from Cameron County.

31. BAIRD'S RAT SNAKE.
Elaphe bairdi.
Adult.

32. BAIRD'S RAT SNAKE.
Elaphe bairdi.
Olive-gray adult from Jeff Davis County.
PHOTO BY R. W. VAN DEVENDER.

33. BAIRD'S RAT SNAKE.
Elaphe bairdi.
Juvenile.

34. CORN SNAKE.
Elaphe guttata guttata.
Dark adult from Brazos County.
PHOTO BY P. FREED.

35. CORN SNAKE *(detail)*.
Elaphe guttata guttata.
Undertail markings of adult
from Brazos County.
PHOTO BY P. FREED.

36. CORN SNAKE.
Elaphe guttata guttata.
Pale adult from Brazos County.
PHOTO BY J. E. WERLER.

37. GREAT PLAINS RAT SNAKE.
Elaphe guttata emoryi.
Dark adult from Parker County.
PHOTO BY W. W. LAMAR, COURTESY OF THE
UNIVERSITY OF TEXAS AT ARLINGTON.

38. GREAT PLAINS RAT SNAKE.
Elaphe guttata emoryi.
Adult from Terrell County.
PHOTO BY J. E. WERLER.

39. SOUTHWESTERN RAT SNAKE.
Elaphe guttata meahllmorum.
Adult from South Texas.

40. TEXAS RAT SNAKE.
Elaphe obsoleta lindheimeri.
Adult from Harris County.

41. TEXAS RAT SNAKE.
Elaphe obsoleta lindheimeri.
Reddish adult from McLennan
County.
PHOTO BY J. E. WERLER.

42.TEXAS RAT SNAKE.
Elaphe obsoleta lindheimeri.
Juvenile from Dallas County.

43.TEXAS RAT SNAKE.
Elaphe obsoleta lindheimeri.
Young adult in open-mouth threat.
PHOTO BY P. FREED.

44. TEXAS RAT SNAKE.
Elaphe obsoleta lindheimeri.
Young swallowing a mouse.
PHOTO BY P. FREED.

45. WESTERN MUD SNAKE.
Farancia abacura reinwardti.
Adult from Liberty County.

46. WESTERN MUD SNAKE.
Farancia abacura reinwardti.
Adult from Liberty County
showing belly and undertail
markings.

47. MEXICAN HOOK-NOSED SNAKE.
Ficimia streckeri.
Adult from Duval County.

48. WESTERN HOOK-NOSED SNAKE.
Gyalopion canum.
Adult from Brewster County.

49. PLAINS HOG-NOSED SNAKE.
Heterodon nasicus nasicus.
Adult from Jackson County, Oklahoma.
PHOTO BY R. W. VAN DEVENDER.

50. PLAINS HOG-NOSED SNAKE.
Heterodon nasicus nasicus.
Head of adult from Jackson County, Oklahoma.
PHOTO BY R. W. VAN DEVENDER.

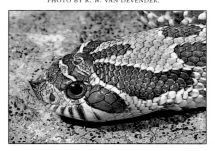

51. DUSTY HOG-NOSED SNAKE.
Heterodon nasicus gloydi.
Adult.

52. MEXICAN HOG-NOSED SNAKE.
Heterodon nasicus kennerlyi.
Adult from Cameron County.

53. EASTERN HOG-NOSED SNAKE.
Heterodon platirhinos.
Typical adult color phase from
Harris County.

54. EASTERN HOG-NOSED SNAKE.
Heterodon platirhinos.
Pale brown adult.

55. EASTERN HOG-NOSED SNAKE.
Heterodon platirhinos.
Dark brown adult.

56. EASTERN HOG-NOSED SNAKE.
Heterodon platirhinos.
Red adult.

57. EASTERN HOG-NOSED SNAKE.
Heterodon platirhinos.
Pinkish adult.
PHOTO BY R. A. ODUM.

58. EASTERN HOG-NOSED SNAKE.
Heterodon platirhinos.
Black adult.
PHOTO BY R. A. ODUM.

59. EASTERN HOG-NOSED SNAKE.
Heterodon platirhinos.
First stage in defensive behavior:
open-mouth threat display.

60. EASTERN HOG-NOSED SNAKE.
Heterodon platirhinos.
Second stage in defensive behavior:
neck-spreading and tail-curling.

**61. EASTERN HOG-NOSED
SNAKE.**
Heterodon platirhinos.
Third stage in defensive behavior:
body-writhing.

62. EASTERN HOG-NOSED SNAKE.
Heterodon platirhinos.
Fourth stage in defensive behavior:
death-feigning.

63. TEXAS NIGHT SNAKE.
Hypsiglena torquata jani.
Dark adult from Pecos County.

64. TEXAS NIGHT SNAKE.
Hypsiglena torquata jani.
Pale adult from South Texas.

65. TEXAS NIGHT SNAKE.
Hypsiglena torquata jani.
Head of adult.
PHOTO BY R. W. VAN DEVENDER.

66. GRAY-BANDED KING SNAKE.
Lampropeltis alterna.
Adult *blairi* color phase from
Val Verde County.
PHOTO BY J. E. WERLER.

67. GRAY-BANDED KING SNAKE.
Lampropeltis alterna.
Adult pale *blairi* color phase.
PHOTO BY J. E. WERLER.

68. GRAY-BANDED KING SNAKE.
Lampropeltis alterna.
Typical adult *blairi* color phase.
PHOTO BY J.E. WERLER.

69. GRAY-BANDED KING SNAKE.
Lampropeltis alterna.
Adult dark *blairi* color phase from
Val Verde County.

70. GRAY-BANDED KING SNAKE.
Lampropeltis alterna.
Adult dark *blairi* color phase.

71. GRAY-BANDED KING SNAKE.
Lampropeltis alterna.
Adult dark *blairi* color phase.

72. GRAY-BANDED KING SNAKE.
Lampropeltis alterna.
Adult *alterna* color phase from
Terrell County.
PHOTO BY J. E. WERLER.

73. GRAY-BANDED KING SNAKE.
Lampropeltis alterna.
Adult pale *alterna* color phase.

74. GRAY-BANDED KING SNAKE.
Lampropeltis alterna.
Brown adult from Val Verde County.
PHOTO BY J. E. WERLER.

75. GRAY-BANDED KING SNAKE.
Lampropeltis alterna.
Speckled adult from Jeff Davis
County.
PHOTO BY J. E. WERLER.

76. PRAIRIE KING SNAKE.
Lampropeltis calligaster calligaster.
Adult from Harris County.

77. SPECKLED KING SNAKE.
Lampropeltis getula holbrooki.
Adult from Jefferson County.
PHOTO BY R. W. VAN DEVENDER.

78. SPECKLED KING SNAKE.
Lampropeltis getula holbrooki.
Adult from Galveston County
showing pale orange belly of
some Gulf Coast specimens.

79. DESERT KING SNAKE.
Lampropeltis getula splendida.
Adult.

80. LOUISIANA MILK SNAKE.
Lampropeltis triangulum amaura.
Adult from Liberty County.

81. MEXICAN MILK SNAKE.
Lampropeltis triangulum annulata.
Adult from Duval County.
PHOTO BY J.E. WERLER.

82. NEW MEXICO MILK SNAKE.
Lampropeltis triangulum celaenops.
Adult from Lubbock County.

83. CENTRAL PLAINS MILK SNAKE.
Lampropeltis triangulum gentilis.
Adult from Colorado.
PHOTO BY R. W. VAN DEVENDER.

84. NORTHERN CAT-EYED SNAKE.
Leptodeira septentrionalis septentrionalis.
Adult from Cameron County.

85. WESTERN SMOOTH GREEN SNAKE.
Liochlorophis vernalis blanchardi.
Adult from Arkansas.

86. EASTERN COACHWHIP.
Masticophis flagellum flagellum.
Adult from Tyler County.
PHOTO BY T. J. HIBBITTS.

87. EASTERN COACHWHIP.
Masticophis flagellum flagellum.
Black adult from Angelina County.

88. EASTERN COACHWHIP.
Masticophis flagellum flagellum.
Head of black adult from Angelina County.

89. EASTERN COACHWHIP.
Masticophis flagellum flagellum.
Juvenile from Cherokee County,
Oklahoma.
PHOTO BY R. W. VAN DEVENDER.

90. WESTERN COACHWHIP.
Masticophis flagellum testaceus.
Uniformly tan adult from Bexar
County.

91. WESTERN COACHWHIP.
Masticophis flagellum testaceus.
Banded phase from Denton County.
PHOTO BY W. W. LAMAR, COURTESY OF THE
UNIVERSITY OF TEXAS AT ARLINGTON.

92. WESTERN COACHWHIP.
Masticophis flagellum testaceus.
Adult reddish color phase from
Terrell County.

93. WESTERN COACHWHIP.
Masticophis flagellum testaceus.
Head of adult reddish color phase
from Terrell County.

94. WESTERN COACHWHIP.
Masticophis flagellum testaceus.
Juvenile.

95. SCHOTT'S WHIPSNAKE.
Masticophis schotti schotti.
Adult from Atascosa County.

96. RUTHVEN'S WHIPSNAKE.
Masticophis schotti ruthveni.
Adult from Cameron County.

97. CENTRAL TEXAS WHIPSNAKE.
Masticophis taeniatus girardi.
Adult from Burnet County. ·

98. GULF SALT MARSH SNAKE.
Nerodia clarki clarki.
Adult from Brazoria County.

99. MISSISSIPPI GREEN WATER SNAKE.
Nerodia cyclopion.
Adult from Brazoria County.

100. YELLOW-BELLIED WATER SNAKE.
Nerodia erythrogaster flavigaster.
Adult from Jasper County.

101. BLOTCHED WATER SNAKE.
Nerodia erythrogaster transversa.
Adult from Bexar County.

102. BLOTCHED WATER SNAKE.
Nerodia erythrogaster transversa.
Juvenile from Bexar County.

103. BROAD-BANDED WATER SNAKE.
Nerodia fasciata confluens.
Young adult from Liberty County.

104. FLORIDA WATER SNAKE.
Nerodia fasciata pictiventris.
Dark adult from Florida.

105. BRAZOS WATER SNAKE.
Nerodia harteri harteri.
Adult from Palo Pinto County.

106. CONCHO WATER SNAKE.
Nerodia harteri paucimaculata.
Adult from Coleman County.

107. DIAMOND-BACKED WATER SNAKE.
Nerodia rhombifer rhombifer.
Adult.
PHOTO BY R. A. ODUM.

108. DIAMOND-BACKED WATER SNAKE.
Nerodia rhombifer rhombifer.
Head of adult.
PHOTO BY R. A. ODUM.

109. MIDLAND WATER SNAKE.
Nerodia sipedon pleuralis.
Adult from Missouri.
PHOTO BY SUZANNE L. COLLINS, THE CENTER FOR
NORTH AMERICAN AMPHIBIANS AND REPTILES.

110. ROUGH GREEN SNAKE.
Opheodrys aestivus.
Adult from Harris County.

111. SONORAN GOPHER SNAKE.
Pituophis catenifer affinis.
Adult from Luna County, New
Mexico.
PHOTO BY J. E. WERLER.

112. BULL SNAKE.
Pituophis catenifer sayi.
Adult from Atascosa County.

113. LOUISIANA PINE SNAKE.
Pituophis ruthveni.
Adult from Angelina County.

114. GRAHAM'S CRAYFISH SNAKE.
Regina grahami.
Dark adult.
PHOTO BY R. A. ODUM.

115. GRAHAM'S CRAYFISH SNAKE.
Regina grahami.
Pale adult from Liberty County
on crayfish chimney.

116. GRAHAM'S CRAYFISH SNAKE.
Regina grahami.
Belly of an adult.
PHOTO BY P. FREED.

117. GRAHAM'S CRAYFISH SNAKE.
Regina grahami.
Head of an adult.
PHOTO BY R. A. ODUM.

118. GULF CRAYFISH SNAKE.
Regina rigida sinicola.
Adult from Harris County.
PHOTO BY J. E. WERLER.

119. TEXAS LONG-NOSED SNAKE.
Rhinocheilus lecontei tessellatus.
Adult.
PHOTO BY J. E. WERLER.

120. TEXAS LONG-NOSED SNAKE.
Rhinocheilus lecontei tessellatus.
Head and forebody of adult from
Starr County.
PHOTO BY R. W. VAN DEVENDER.

121. TEXAS LONG-NOSED SNAKE.
Rhinocheilus lecontei tessellatus.
Pale adult from Brewster County.

122.TEXAS LONG-NOSED SNAKE.
Rhinocheilus lecontei tessellatus.
Juvenile.

123.TEXAS LONG-NOSED SNAKE.
Rhinocheilus lecontei tessellatus.
Head of a juvenile.

124. BIG BEND PATCH-NOSED SNAKE.
Salvadora deserticola.
Adult from Brewster County.

125. MOUNTAIN PATCH-NOSED SNAKE.
Salvadora grahamiae grahamiae.
Adult from Brewster County.

126. TEXAS PATCH-NOSED SNAKE.
Salvadora grahamiae lineata.
Adult from Cameron County.

127. GREAT PLAINS GROUND SNAKE.
Sonora semiannulata semiannulata.
Unpatterned adult from Jeff Davis County.

128. GREAT PLAINS GROUND SNAKE.
Sonora semiannulata semiannulata.
Collared adult from Noble County, Oklahoma.
PHOTO BY R. W. VAN DEVENDER.

129. GREAT PLAINS GROUND SNAKE.
Sonora semiannulata semiannulata.
Adult with abbreviated crossbands from Brewster County.

130. GREAT PLAINS GROUND SNAKE.
Sonora semiannulata semiannulata.
Adult with abbreviated crossbands from Garvin County, Oklahoma.
PHOTO BY R. W. VAN DEVENDER.

131. GREAT PLAINS GROUND SNAKE.
Sonora semiannulata semiannulata.
Fully banded adult from Nevada.
PHOTO BY P. FREED.

132. GREAT PLAINS GROUND SNAKE.
Sonora semiannulata semiannulata.
Fully banded adult from Travis County.

133. TAYLOR'S GROUND SNAKE.
Sonora semiannulata taylori.
Gray adult from South Texas.
PHOTO BY R. A. ODUM.

134. TAYLOR'S GROUND SNAKE.
Sonora semiannulata taylori.
Brown adult from South Texas.
PHOTO BY R. A. ODUM.

135. MARSH BROWN SNAKE.
Storeria dekayi limnetes.
Adult from Galveston County.

136. TEXAS BROWN SNAKE.
Storeria dekayi texana.
Adult from McLennan County.

137. TEXAS BROWN SNAKE.
Storeria dekayi texana.
Juvenile from Harris County.

138. FLORIDA RED-BELLIED SNAKE.
Storeria occipitomaculata obscura.
Grayish brown adult from San
Jacinto County.

139. FLORIDA RED-BELLIED SNAKE.
Storeria occipitomaculata obscura.
Yellowish adult from Anderson
County.

140. MEXICAN BLACK-HEADED SNAKE.
Tantilla atriceps.
Adult. (Since no live specimen of this species was available, we have used a photo of a southwestern black-headed snake. Outwardly, the two species are identical.)

141. TRANS-PECOS BLACK-HEADED SNAKE.
Tantilla cucullata.
Adult from Brewster County with complete white collar.

142. TRANS-PECOS BLACK-HEADED SNAKE.
Tantilla cucullata.
Adult from Brewster County with interrupted white collar.

143. TRANS-PECOS BLACK-HEADED SNAKE.
Tantilla cucullata.
Adult from Brewster County without white collar.
PHOTO BY R. A. ODUM.

144. TRANS-PECOS BLACK-HEADED SNAKE.
Tantilla cucullata.
Head of adult from Brewster County without white collar.
PHOTO BY R. A. ODUM.

145. FLAT-HEADED SNAKE.
Tantilla gracilis.
Adult from Chase County, Kansas.
PHOTO BY SUZANNE L. COLLINS, THE CENTER FOR NORTH AMERICAN AMPHIBIANS AND REPTILES.

146. SOUTHWESTERN BLACK-HEADED SNAKE.
Tantilla hobartsmithi.
Adult from Graham County, Arizona.
PHOTO BY R. W. VAN DEVENDER.

147. PLAINS BLACK-HEADED SNAKE.
Tantilla nigriceps.
Adult from Cameron County.

148. WESTERN BLACK-NECKED GARTER SNAKE.
Thamnophis cyrtopsis cyrtopsis.
Adult.
PHOTO BY P. FREED.

149. EASTERN BLACK-NECKED GARTER SNAKE.
Thamnophis cyrtopsis ocellatus.
Adult from Bexar County.

150. EASTERN BLACK-NECKED GARTER SNAKE.
Thamnophis cyrtopsis ocellatus.
Head of adult from Bexar County.

151. CHECKERED GARTER SNAKE.
Thamnophis marcianus marcianus.
Adult.

152. CHECKERED GARTER SNAKE.
Thamnophis marcianus marcianus.
Head of adult.

153. WESTERN RIBBON SNAKE.
Thamnophis proximus proximus.
Adult.

154. WESTERN RIBBON SNAKE.
Thamnophis proximus proximus.
Bluish adult.

155. WESTERN RIBBON SNAKE.
Thamnophis proximus proximus.
Courting pair of bluish specimens
from Titus County.
PHOTO BY JIM YANTIS.

156. ARID LAND RIBBON SNAKE.
*Thamnophis proximus
diabolicus.*
Adult from Terrell County.

157. GULF COAST RIBBON SNAKE.
Thamnophis proximus orarius.
Adult.

158. RED-STRIPED RIBBON SNAKE.
Thamnophis proximus rubrilineatus.
Adult from Bexar County.

159. WESTERN PLAINS GARTER SNAKE.
Thamnophis radix haydeni.
Adult from Oklahoma.

160. EASTERN GARTER SNAKE.
Thamnophis sirtalis sirtalis.
Adult from Brazoria County.

161. EASTERN GARTER SNAKE.
Thamnophis sirtalis sirtalis.
Reddish adult from Harris County.

162. TEXAS GARTER SNAKE.
Thamnophis sirtalis annectens.
Adult from Dallas County.

163. RED-SIDED GARTER SNAKE.
Thamnophis sirtalis parietalis.
Adult from Polk County, Iowa.
PHOTO BY R. W. VAN DEVENDER.

164. TEXAS LYRE SNAKE.
Trimorphodon lambda vilkinsoni.
Dark adult.

165. TEXAS LYRE SNAKE.
Trimorphodon lambda vilkinsoni.
Pale adult.

166. LINED SNAKE.
Tropidoclonion lineatum.
Dark adult from La Salle County.
PHOTO BY D. G. BARKER, COURTESY OF THE
UNIVERSITY OF TEXAS AT ARLINGTON.

167. LINED SNAKE.
Tropidoclonion lineatum.
Pale adult from Val Verde County.

168. ROUGH EARTH SNAKE.
Virginia striatula.
Adult from Harris County.

169. WESTERN EARTH SNAKE.
Virginia valeriae elegans.
Dark adult from Latimer County,
Oklahoma.
PHOTO BY SUZANNE L. COLLINS, THE CENTER FOR
NORTH AMERICAN AMPHIBIANS AND REPTILES.

170. WESTERN EARTH SNAKE.
Virginia valeriae elegans.
Pale adult from Arkansas.
PHOTO BY SUZANNE L. COLLINS, THE CENTER FOR NORTH AMERICAN AMPHIBIANS AND REPTILES.

171. TEXAS CORAL SNAKE.
Micrurus fulvius tener.
Adult from Harris County.

172. TEXAS CORAL SNAKE.
Micrurus fulvius tener.
Adult eating a rough earth snake.
PHOTO BY P. FREED.

173. SOUTHERN COPPERHEAD.
Agkistrodon contortrix contortrix.
Adult from Liberty County.

174. SOUTHERN COPPERHEAD.
Agkistrodon contortrix contortrix.
Adult from Harris County engaged in mouth-gaping.
PHOTO BY E. P. HADDON.

175. BROAD-BANDED COPPERHEAD.
Agkistrodon contortrix laticinctus.
Adult from McLennan County.

176. TRANS-PECOS COPPERHEAD.
Agkistrodon contortrix pictigaster.
Adult from Val Verde County.

177. TRANS-PECOS COPPERHEAD.
Agkistrodon contortrix pictigaster.
Head and forebody of an adult from
Val Verde County.

178. WESTERN COTTONMOUTH.
Agkistrodon piscivorus leucostoma.
Adult from Liberty County.

179.WESTERN COTTONMOUTH.
Agkistrodon piscivorus leucostoma.
Young specimen.
PHOTO BY R. A. ODUM.

180.WESTERN COTTONMOUTH.
Agkistrodon piscivorus leucostoma.
Harris County juvenile striking.

181.WESTERN DIAMOND-BACKED RATTLESNAKE.
Crotalus atrox.
Adult from Atascosa County.

182. WESTERN DIAMOND-BACKED RATTLESNAKE.
Crotalus atrox.
Dark adult from Jeff Davis County.
PHOTO BY J. E. WERLER.

183. WESTERN DIAMOND-BACKED RATTLESNAKE.
Crotalus atrox.
Reddish adult.

184. WESTERN DIAMOND-BACKED RATTLESNAKE.
Crotalus atrox.
Combat behavior, males separated.
PHOTO BY R. L. STANLEY.

185. WESTERN DIAMOND-BACKED RATTLESNAKE.
Crotalus atrox.
Combat behavior, males entwined.
PHOTO BY R. L. STANLEY.

186. CANEBRAKE RATTLESNAKE.
Crotalus horridus atricaudatus.
Adult from Polk County.

187. MOTTLED ROCK RATTLE-SNAKE.
Crotalus lepidus lepidus.
Adult from Jeff Davis County.

**188. MOTTLED ROCK RATTLE-
SNAKE.**
Crotalus lepidus lepidus.
Pale adult from Val Verde County.
PHOTO BY J. E. WERLER.

**189. MOTTLED ROCK RATTLE-
SNAKE.**
Crotalus lepidus lepidus.
Pinkish adult.

**190. MOTTLED ROCK RATTLE-
SNAKE.**
Crotalus lepidus lepidus.
Tan adult from the Hueco
Mountains, Hudspeth County.

191. BANDED ROCK RATTLE-SNAKE.
Crotalus lepidus klauberi.
Adult from Franklin Mountains, El Paso County.

192. BANDED ROCK RATTLE-SNAKE.
Crotalus lepidus klauberi.
Juvenile showing yellowish tail.

193. BANDED ROCK RATTLE-SNAKE.
Crotalus lepidus klauberi.
Head of adult.

**194. NORTHERN BLACK-TAILED
RATTLESNAKE.**
Crotalus molossus molossus.
Adult from Brewster County.

195. MOJAVE RATTLESNAKE.
Crotalus scutulatus scutulatus.
Dark adult from Jeff Davis County.
PHOTO BY J. E. WERLER.

196. MOJAVE RATTLESNAKE.
Crotalus scutulatus scutulatus.
Pale adult from Brewster County.

197. PRAIRIE RATTLESNAKE.
Crotalus viridis viridis.
Adult.

198. DESERT MASSASAUGA.
Sistrurus catenatus edwardsi.
Adult.
PHOTO BY R. A. ODUM.

199.WESTERN MASSASAUGA.
Sistrurus catenatus tergeminus.
Adult from McLennan County.

**200.WESTERN PYGMY RATTLE-
SNAKE.**
Sistrurus miliarius streckeri.
Adult from Polk County.

BRAZOS WATER SNAKE
Nerodia harteri harteri
PLATE 105

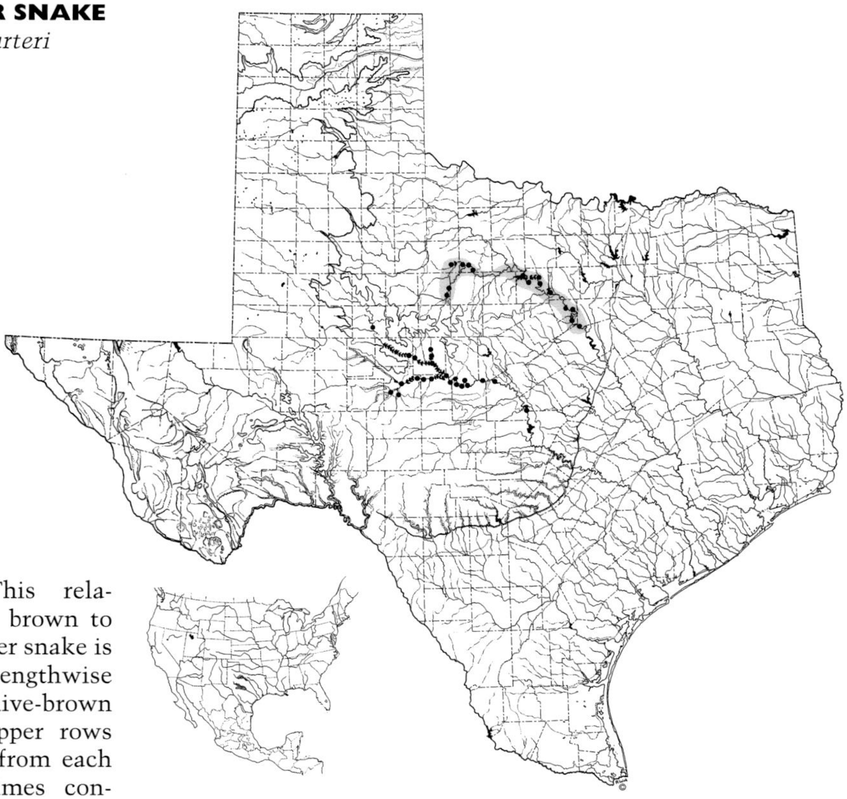

DESCRIPTION This relatively small, light brown to grayish brown water snake is marked by four lengthwise rows of large, olive-brown spots, the two upper rows usually separated from each other but sometimes connected along the spine by a continuous dark median stripe. The spots of each lateral row alternate with the adjacent dorsal series, as the two upper rows frequently do with each other. The snake's greenish or yellowish abdomen, whose rear half is pink or rose-colored down the middle, is conspicuously marked with a row of dark spots near the outer edges of the belly plates. Normally the rear pair of chin shields is separated by two rows of small scales. The dorsal scales, all keeled, are arranged in 21 or 23 rows at midbody, and the anal plate is divided.

COMPARABLE SNAKES Other native water snakes have fewer than four distinct rows of large, dark spots on the back, numbering fewer than 52 in a single longitudinal row. Furthermore, the primary markings of the juvenile blotched water snake (adults are essentially one color above) are four or five times the size of the lateral spots, whereas those of the Brazos water snake in both juveniles and adults are nearly the same size as the lateral spots. The diamond-backed water snake is less likely to be mistaken for the Brazos water snake, for its dorsal pattern consists not of spots but of a chainlike network of dark markings with lateral bars reaching down the sides to the edge of the belly.

SIZE More slender than most other Texas water snakes of the genus *Nerodia*, the adults of this subspecies are usually 20 to 30 inches (50.8–76.2 cm) long. The largest known specimen measured 35½ inches (90.2 cm) in length.

HABITAT Found only in a limited section of Central Texas, the Brazos water snake has evolved to fill a distinct niche, one not ordi-

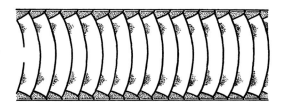

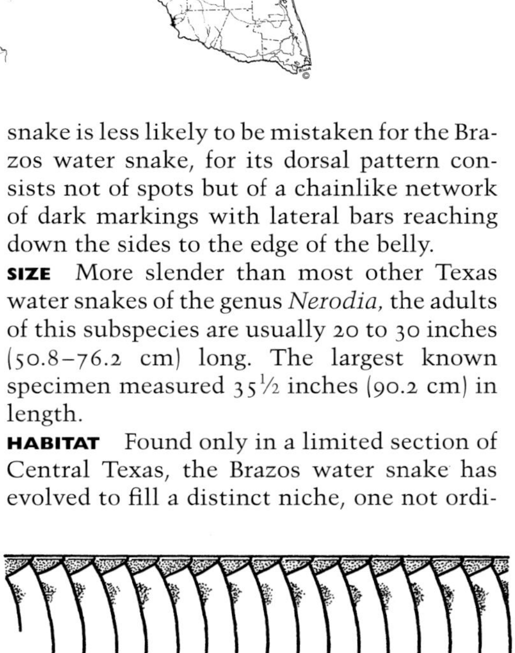

Figure 42. *Belly pattern of the Brazos water snake.*

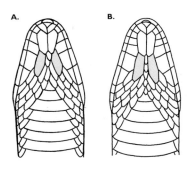

Figure 43. *Rear chin shields separated by (a) two rows of small scales in the Brazos water snake and (b) none or only one row in the Concho water snake.*

narily exploited by the two other water snakes living in the region. That niche is typified by certain shallow, fast-flowing portions of the upper Brazos River and two of its tributaries.

Inhabiting swift, rocky stream riffles along approximately 182 miles of the upper Brazos River drainage, in addition to the shorelines of Lake Granbury and the upper portion of Possum Kingdom Lake, the Brazos water snake occurs as far upstream as Paint Creek in Throckmorton County and Deadman's Creek, another tributary of the Clear Fork of the Brazos, approximately 15½ miles by stream above the town of Lueders in Jones County. Downstream it ranges as far south on the Brazos as the bridge crossing at FM 1118, east of Brazos Point in Bosque County. The snake's preferred microhabitat is a shallow riffle where the water is usually no more than a foot deep. Among the underwater stone fragments, infant snakes can find a good supply of easily accessible small fish. It is further characterized by a rocky shoreline of unshaded, loose, flat stones under which the young snakes can find shelter from predators and, in cool weather, a reliable source of solar-generated heat. Finally, it must have gently sloping stream banks and be free of dense vegetation close to the water's edge. This subspecies and the Concho water snake are races of a single species, *N. harteri*, which, together with the Trans-Pecos black-headed snake, are the only snake species endemic to the state. Few other serpent species in the United States occupy such a restricted geographic range.

BEHAVIOR At the approach of man, the first response of this alert, fast-moving serpent is not to seek shelter beneath a rock or some other surface object but to streak directly for the nearest water. Plunging into a stream or river, it swims with vigorous lateral undulations of its strong, slender body, often underwater, until it reaches the opposite shore. Once there, it is apt to remain submerged for a time before rising to the surface, or it may swim along the shoreline with only its head above water. Not as vicious in its self-defense as most other members of the genus *Nerodia*, the Brazos water snake usually bites when first captured. It may even briefly chew on its assailant's hand, but with little effect, for its teeth, although numerous and sharp, are not long enough to cause any noticeable damage.

In their riverine habitat, most specimens were observed either in the water or on land within 10 feet of the shoreline. The infant snakes, which restricted their activities primarily to the shallow parts of the riffles, seldom mingled with the adults, whose preferred sites included the deeper middle parts of the riffles, the edges of the deeper river pools, piles of plant debris near the water, and the low limbs of salt cedar overhanging the riffles. When not foraging, the infant snakes were most likely to be found coiled under small flat rocks along the shoreline or on a gravel bank, whereas the larger snakes hid under large rocks, in holes along the sides of the steeper stream banks, or in dense grass.

Along the shorelines of reservoirs, where riprap has been dumped to stabilize the lakefront, most specimens were found beneath large or small slabs of rock less than 4 feet from the water's edge. Others were discovered as they coiled under beached boats and boat sheds. The smaller snakes usually selected hiding places adjacent to shallow portions of the lakes; in the absence of rocky riffles, they somehow met the requirements for suitable nursery areas.

FEEDING The dietary habits of this subspecies, although not well known, are probably similar to those of the Concho water snake, whose diet and feeding strategies have been carefully studied. The two closely related snakes occupy similar restricted habitats containing essentially the same piscine prey species. In the case of the Concho water snake, the diet consists almost entirely of fish, which are somewhat partitioned according to snake size. For example, the infant water snakes consume only minnows, whereas the juveniles and adult males take mostly minnows but also small catfish, and the generally larger females devour primarily bigger prey such as catfish, sunfish, and gizzard shad. See also the Concho water snake account.

REPRODUCTION What little information is recorded about the reproductive biology of this subspecies comes from observations of captive specimens. Carl (1981) witnessed courtship activity during the first two weeks of May but did not say precisely when copulation took place; presumably it occurred soon after courtship. All other reports mention birth in September or October, but one of Carl's female Brazos water snakes deposited her young on July 25. Litter size varies from 7 to 23 young. The newborn snakes, between 6¾ and 10 inches (17.1–25.4 cm) long, look much like the adults, except that their dorsal spots are more prominent and their overall coloration is more vivid, particularly on the abdomen.

CONCHO WATER SNAKE
Nerodia harteri paucimaculata
PLATE 106

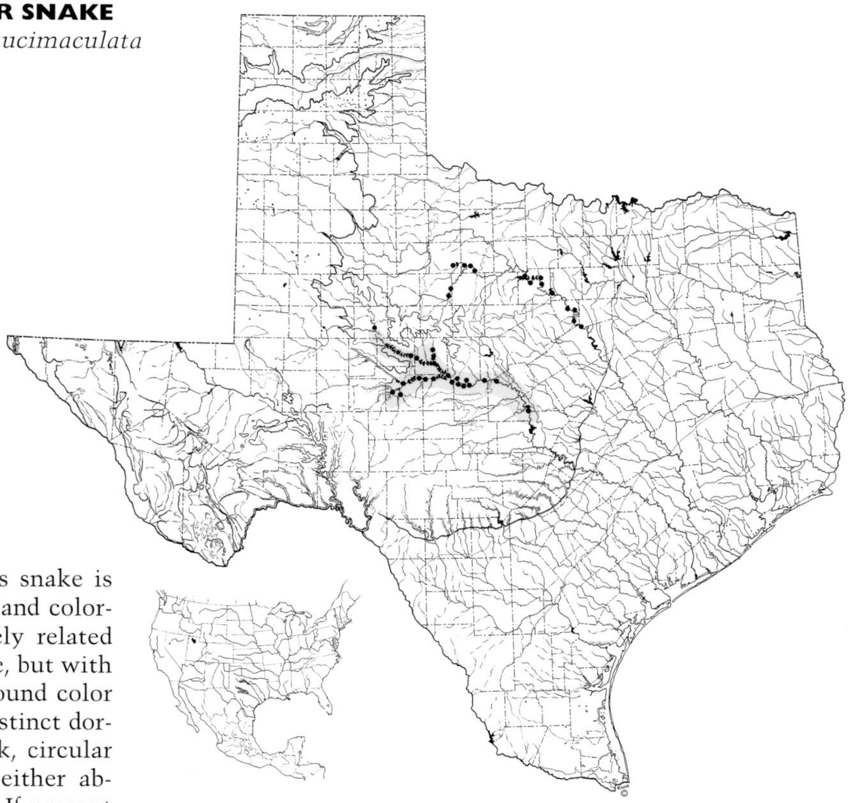

DESCRIPTION This snake is similar in pattern and coloration to the closely related Brazos water snake, but with a slightly paler ground color and usually less distinct dorsal spots. The dark, circular ventral spots are either absent or indistinct. If present and distinct, they are ordinarily confined to the lateral edges of the belly plates. Normally there is only one row of small scales between the rear pair of chin shields instead of two. (See illustration in Brazos water snake account.)

The snake's pale brown to grayish brown back is marked with a longitudinal row of somewhat circular dark brown spots on either side of the spine, flanked below by an alternating row of similar but slightly smaller dark spots or vertical bars. The two adjacent rows of primary spots may alternate with one another or they may meet across the middle of the back. Extending down the center of the abdomen is a band of pale orange or rose-colored pigment, which is most distinct on the rear portion of the body. The dorsal scales, all keeled, are arranged in 21 or 23 rows at midbody, and the anal plate is divided.

COMPARABLE SNAKES Two other species of *Nerodia* frequently share the Concho water snake's aquatic habitat. One is the diamond-backed water snake, whose pale brown or yellowish back is marked by a dark brown chain-like dorsal pattern; the other, the blotched water snake, has but a single row of large dark blotches down the middle of its back.

SIZE One of Texas' smallest water snakes, the adults of this relatively slender species are usually 16 to 26 inches (40.6–66 cm) long but reach a known maximum length of nearly 42 (106.7 cm) inches.

HABITAT Until recently, this snake was among the least understood of all Texas serpents. Several comprehensive field studies made over the last few years have yielded a surprising wealth of information about its distribution, habitat, and behavior, making it one of the best chronicled of all snakes. These reports, from which we have drawn freely in this account, include those by Dixon, Greene, and Mueller (1988, 1989); Dixon, Greene, and Whiting (1990); B. D. Greene (1993); Greene et al. (1994); Mueller (1990); Scott et al. (1989); Whiting (1993); and N. R. Williams (1969). The natural habitat of the Concho water snake, according to Scott and his colleagues, is confined chiefly to the numerous riffle areas scattered along approximately 238 miles of the upper Colorado and Concho river drainage systems in Central Texas. Plus, more than 40 miles of usable artificial shoreline habitat occurs at E. V. Spence Reservoir, Ivie Reservoir, and Ballinger Municipal Lake (also known as Moonen Lake). Even when the limited distribution of this subspecies is added to the equally small range of the Brazos water snake (both races of a single species, *N. harteri*), their combined geographic ranges are relatively meager. Few other snake species in the United States have such a restricted distribution. Surprisingly, considering the overall richness of Texas' serpent fauna, this and the Trans-Pecos black-headed snake are the only species endemic to the state. Occupying the warm, semiarid central part of Texas, a region characterized by relatively dry summers and rather mild winters, the Concho water snake is strictly confined to water and to a narrow ribbon of shoreline on either or both sides of such waterways. Its principal habitat is the riffle, a rock-filled section of streambed or riverbed 30 feet to over a mile long, where a drop in elevation, usually over a short distance, causes the water to rush over and through the layers of rocks before collecting in a shallow pool at the downstream end of the riffle. The riffle may consist chiefly of large stones, all small stones, or most frequently a mixture of both sizes.

Not all riffles are inhabited equally. The best ones, it is believed, have several features in common, one of which is an abundance of flat, unshaded rocks of various sizes close to the water's edge. Those on the riffle floor also vary in size but are generally smaller. In addition, the stream banks along the preferred sites are gently sloping and free of aquatic and shoreline vegetation, a condition that allows periodic turbulent flooding to prevent the buildup of silt around and under the rock bases and so insures the maintenance of adequate under-rock cover for young snakes during times of low water. Poor-quality riffles, by contrast, are those where silt covers the bases of the rocks and dense grass grows down to the water's edge. Moreover, the steep stream bank usually present at either end of each riffle supports the growth of trees and shrubbery on which adult serpents can bask by day and find refuge during times of flooding. They sometimes also provide resting spots for young snakes. Finally, the water in the riffles harboring the largest concentrations of Concho water snakes is usually only 4 to 12 inches (10.1–30.5 cm) deep.

The principal vegetation in the general area of the rivers consists of mesquite, pecan, cedar, elm, western soapberry, hackberry, buttonbush, salt cedar, willow, agarita, prickly pear and slender stem cactus, spiny aster, greenbrier, poison ivy, Johnson grass, and switchgrass, but the streams themselves are relatively free of aquatic plants.

Although the snake is intimately associated with riffles over most of its range, there are at least three locations where, instead of occupying a riffle environment, it survives along a natural rocky shoreline and at artificial sites created by the distribution of riprap along a portion of the lakeshore: Ballinger Municipal Lake in Runnels County; Ivie Reservoir in Concho, Coleman, and Runnels counties; and the E. V. Spence Reservoir in Coke County. A large population of Concho water snakes has also managed to survive for several decades in an artificial riffle site at Cervenka Dam, a man-made structure built nearly 30 years ago along the Colorado River in Coke County.

BEHAVIOR Because of its modest size, flight is this serpent's only effective defense against a large adversary, although when provoked and unable to flee, the snake may flatten its body vertically, making itself appear larger and perhaps more menacing. A moderately pugnacious reptile, it usually nips when picked up, maintaining its hold and briefly chewing in retaliation, although the results of such a bite are inconsequential.

Like most species of the genus *Nerodia*, this one, when alarmed, invariably seeks to escape in the water. If surprised on a bush or a tree limb overhanging the water, it plunges into the stream below and often swims to the opposite bank, sometimes remaining submerged there for a time, or it may swim slowly at the surface with only its head above the water. Despite the rushing and often turbulent waters into which it retreats, the Concho water snake, employing strong lateral undulations of its slender body, displays a remarkable ability to swim against the racing currents of such fast-flowing streams, often moving along the channel bottoms to avoid the more rigorous surface currents. Even when disturbed under a rock or trash pile, it does not seek shelter beneath a similar nearby object; instead it streaks for the nearest body of water. So closely is this snake associated with water that of thousands of specimens observed during a five-year study of its natural history, all were either swimming in rivers, streams, or reservoirs or were discovered on land within 10 feet of water, but usually no more than 3½ feet from the shoreline. The adults and infants often occupied the same section of a stream or river.

The larger snakes, which in most cases were difficult to observe in the riffles of flowing rivers, also inhabited a relatively wide range of other microhabitats, particularly the margins of deeper pools and reservoirs associated with such rivers, where they were sometimes seen basking on low tree limbs, debris piles, or large rocks. Adult females, on the other hand, were especially attracted to stacks of flood-deposited organic debris such as those formed by tree branches and remnants of prickly pear cactus. They also utilized dense piles of herbaceous vegetation created by the matted tangles of live greenbrier and spiny aster. In any case, the site was always in partial contact with water. Seldom was an adult male Concho water snake observed at such basking locations. Despite the greater size of the adults, which would ordinarily make them more conspicuous than the young, they were not often observed in the open, for they tended to spend a considerable part of each day under large rocks, in crevices and holes in dirt banks near shore, or in dense grass.

Very young snakes confined their activities chiefly to the shallow riffles, where they were usually more noticeable, especially when actively searching for prey. When not foraging, the infant snakes withdrew to the gently sloping stream banks, where they almost invariably took shelter under small, flat rocks, which they ordinarily chose as refuges over the larger ones. The smaller rocks, it has been suggested, absorb solar radiation more quickly, providing the young serpents with the higher daytime temperatures they require to promote rapid growth. Unlike the adults, which almost always hid singly under large solitary rocks, the infants tended to congregate in small groups beneath common sheltering objects. As many as five very young Concho water snakes were found under one small stone. As they grew, the snakes selected progressively larger rocks as refuges.

The Concho water snake's active season, which usually lasts about 28 weeks, normally begins sometime in April and ends during the first week of November. With the late arrival of autumn or the advent of an early spring, this season can last even longer. Whatever its length, the level of activity was not constant, reaching a peak in late April and early May, dropping to its lowest level in July and early August, then gradually increasing again into October. Just as the serpent's activity cycle varied with the season, it also depended on the snake's sex and age. The adult males, for example, were most active in late April and early May; like the males of most snake species, they are then evidently searching for mates. Gravid females, on the other hand, like the gestating females of many other snake species, wander little while they are heavy with young. Being less mobile at such times, they remained sedentary, probably as a way to reduce their exposure to predators who might find the sluggish snakes easy targets. Immediately after giving birth, they exhibited a remarkable increase in activity. Having eaten little or no food during the latter stages of pregnancy, the females, now somewhat emaciated, were ready to engage in a renewed period of foraging, during which they would regain their normal body weight. The juvenile water snakes, although active in all seasons, were most evident in September, soon after the females had given birth to their young.

A day-active serpent whose daily movements typically occurred between 6 AM and 10 PM, the Concho water snake was seldom seen in the open later than an hour after sunset, except when the river ceased to flow during extreme drought conditions. Then it was frequently found at night in residual pools within the otherwise dry river channels, for at such times the midday water temperature of the pools often soared to uncomfortably high levels. During the more moderate daytime temperatures of spring, the adult water snake was often encountered as it basked on a tree limb, rock, dirt bank, or pile of debris, but during the hot daylight hours of midsummer it was more apt to be seen in the water or coiled in the shade of a grass clump, bush, or tree and, in the case of males, also in the cool recesses of animal burrows.

The tracking of overall activity ranges of nine adult Concho water snakes (fitted with miniature radio transmitters and monitored continuously for 45 to 107 days) showed that they had moved linear distances ranging from 693 to 2,244 feet. Over its lifetime, this snake may travel even farther, although such lengthy movements are considered exceptional. Several specimens marked as juveniles and later captured as adults at distant locations along the same river system had moved 4 to 12 miles from their original home sites,

the farthest-ranging individual having traveled this distance in four years. Since most Concho water snakes demonstrated a strong fidelity to their home sites (one female remained sedentary at precisely the same place for 30 days), it is unclear why these particular serpents made such long journeys. Neither a marked reduction in the available prey nor a drastic environmental change (factors that ordinarily prompt snakes to make substantial shifts in their home territories) was evident.

On average, the adult males moved approximately 167 feet in a day, and the adult females traveled about 111 feet a day. For males, the maximum recorded single daily movement was 1,307 feet; for females, 1,287 feet. Such daily travels, it should be noted, were not all made in one direction but were divided nearly equally between upstream and downstream excursions. The home range of infant water snakes, which proved to be relatively small and limited primarily to specific riffle areas, increased gradually as the snakes grew.

Unlike the river-dwelling snakes just mentioned, those inhabiting Ballinger Lake were more far-ranging. One specimen traveled a full mile along the lakeshore in just one season. Considering the uninterrupted 8,580-foot-long rocky shoreline habitat of the lake, including 1,098 feet of dam riprap, the snakes' greater vagility there is not surprising.

Although the Concho water snake is known to overwinter in rock ledges, debris piles, cracks in eroded banks, and within the understructures of low-water crossings, it is likely, judging from the available evidence, that most adult specimens hibernate in the tunnels of small burrowing animals, particularly those of crayfish. Such tunnels, which riddled the slopes of the higher stream banks, usually occurred in the vicinity of the denser salt cedar thickets. It is to these sections of the river that many of the adult water snakes moved with the arrival of cool autumnal weather. There they remained until mid-November of one year (1988), when two bouts of cold weather—on November 18 and again on November 20—finally prompted the snakes to enter hibernation.

To locate the serpents' hibernacula, which had not previously been described, several specimens implanted with miniature radio transmitters were tracked to their winter quarters. Excavation of the sites disclosed that most of the snakes were hibernating 18 inches to 3 feet below the surface of the ground, 5 to 23 inches above water level, and 10 to 26 feet from the nearest shoreline. In these underground retreats the snakes' body temperatures ranged from approximately 43⅓ to 47¾ degrees F, even when the outside air temperature had dropped to near freezing. At more northern latitudes, where winter temperatures are severe and adequate reptile denning sites sometimes scarce, the local snakes frequently find themselves compelled to congregate in moderate to large numbers in the few available refuges deep enough to provide suitable thermal protection. Such is not the case with the Concho water snake, whose Central Texas environment has a relatively mild climate and a prevalence of small, near-surface animal burrows. It is in these somewhat shallow refuges that it normally overwinters, singly or in small groups.

One solitary Concho water snake was found hibernating on the northwestern side of Ballinger Lake, where it had taken refuge in a crayfish burrow dug into a dirt bank under the partly exposed roots of a small hackberry tree. In the bottom part of a vertical washout beneath the base of the tree was an open entranceway that connected with two main tunnel arteries. One extended upward 14½ inches, where it ended in a plugged opening at the surface. It also took a downward course for nearly 22 inches before veering away in a perpendicular direction. The other, a horizontal extension of the open entranceway, traveled about 16½ inches before turning downward and reaching a dead end some 3 feet below the top of the cutbank. At the bottom of this passageway was the adult male water snake, coiled in a loose ball with its head directed upward. A hibernaculum discovered along the riprap shoreline of Ballinger Lake on January 10, 1989, proved of particular interest, for it was occupied not only by two Concho water snakes but also by specimens of two other snake species. Consisting of an 8-foot-long crayfish burrow with an entrance under several layers of surface rock, the tunnel was an L-shaped structure with two unequal arms, the first one 3 feet long and the second 5 feet in length. At its

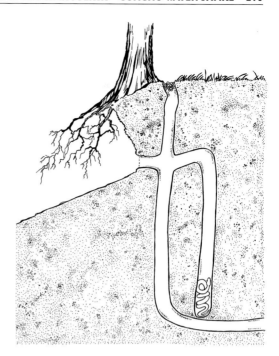

Figure 44. *Cross section of a Concho water snake hibernaculum in a crayfish burrow dug into a dirt bank at Ballinger Municipal Lake.*

deepest part, the tunnel was 9⅗ inches below ground level. In the first section of the burrow was an adult Concho water snake with its body in an extended position. Next to it, in the longer part of the tunnel, lay two entwined adult serpents, a Concho water snake and a blotched water snake. Directly behind them was a large eastern yellow-bellied racer, its body also in an extended position but with part of its forebody turned back toward its tail. Finally, at the end of the burrow, resting in damp sand and laden with eggs, was the tunnel's original tenant, a large female swamp crayfish.

The most curious aspect of this hibernaculum, besides the two entwined snakes, was the complete or partial wall of debris that separated each animal (or pair of animals, if found together) from its neighbor along the length of the burrow. Were they the unwitting result of head and tail movements against the tunnel wall made by the snakes as they attempted postural adjustments? Or did the reptiles deliberately create their own isolated chambers for purposes of security?

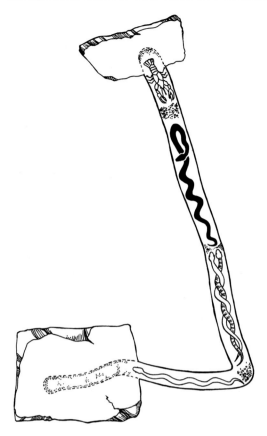

Figure 45. *Top view of a communal Concho water snake hibernaculum in a crayfish burrow in the riprap facing of Ballinger Municipal Lake.*

The reason for their presence is still open to speculation.

Another site (possibly an actual winter den but more likely a temporary refuge used by four Concho water snakes during a brief cold spell after they had already emerged from hibernation) was discovered on March 11, 1989, along the west bank of the Colorado River at a place called Turkey Bend. On a rather steep slope directly above a large pecan tree, it consisted of a nearly foot-high pile of debris containing a mixture of packed leaves, stems, stones, bark, and other decomposing vegetation. The site was 19 feet from the river and about 13 feet above its surface. Beneath this mound of debris were two male and two female water snakes, all adults, whose individual body temperatures at the time of their

discovery ranged between 56½ degrees and nearly 65 degrees F.

Very small Concho water snakes apparently do not share winter dens with their adult counterparts, for never were they found in the same hibernaculum with grown specimens. In fact, only once during four years of fieldwork were hibernating infants located in their winter den. The single site, discovered on November 26, 1990, along the Colorado River just below Freese Dam, represented one of several piles of riffle rocks dredged from the river and deposited on shore during construction of a low-water crossing. Twenty-eight inches high and 9 feet in diameter, it consisted of loosely aggregated particles ranging in size from soil to rocks more than 2 feet long. At the bottom of the pile, clustered together near its center, were nine infant Concho water snakes resting on wet substrate a couple of inches above seeping ground water; the temperature was about 64 degrees F, the same as the river's. No adult Concho water snake observed in a hibernaculum was so intimately associated with moisture, and perhaps for good reason. As a result of their reduced body size, infant snakes generally are more susceptible to dehydration during hibernation than are the adults, and since water contributes a greater degree of thermal stability to the surrounding area than dry substrate, the presence of nearby moisture would tend to enhance the quality of a winter refuge for the less cold-tolerant young. Despite the artificial nature of this rock-pile hibernaculum, there is a distinct similarity between it and the naturally occurring gravel bars associated with riffles. They share the same particulate rock sizes and resemble one another in general configuration. It is probable, therefore, that young Concho water snakes overwinter primarily in the gravel bars, for such shelters are readily available, and they apparently meet the requirements of infant snakes for satisfactory hibernacula.

In severe winter weather, many young Concho water snakes (and perhaps some adults as well), whose hibernacula are inadequate to protect them from exceptionally cold temperatures, perish during winter dormancy. As an example, the snake's 1987 and 1988 mortality rate during hibernation in the study area is estimated to have been about 50 to 53 percent each year.

Perhaps an even greater threat to the water snake than subfreezing temperatures is a wide range of predators that live in or near the serpent's habitat and consider it an easy target. Included in this category are king snakes, coachwhip snakes, yellow-bellied racers, raccoons, great blue herons, and a variety of hawks and owls, not to mention such potential enemies as bullfrogs, bass, channel catfish, and cottonmouths, known predators of other water snakes. The degree to which some of these streamside carnivores reduce Concho water snake populations is reflected in the report of one local fisherman who saw a great blue heron snatch four of the serpents from one riffle in just 15 minutes. Another account—by a field biologist working in the Concho water snake study area—stated that roughly 30 percent of the great blue heron carcasses he found on the ground beneath the birds' rookery contained snake skeletons. Although the reptilian remains were not identified by species, they were probably those of the Concho water snake, by far the most abundant and readily available riverine serpent in the area. Other causes of death noted during the study included juvenile snakes crushed under small rocks that were trampled by humans or livestock and water snakes deliberately killed by shooting and bashing. Such malicious destruction of Concho water snakes, although illegal as well as regrettable, probably does not constitute a major cause of mortality in this subspecies. In some instances, human activity may even benefit the water snakes by discouraging the presence of herons and other voracious predators in the serpent's habitat.

FEEDING A comprehensive study of the Concho water snake's feeding habits, conducted by B. D. Greene and his colleagues from 1987 to 1992, shows that these snakes feed almost exclusively on fish, with a minor exception noted only on the rare occasions when infant water snakes consumed cricket frogs. Included in the list of piscine prey eaten by the river-dwelling population were carp, flathead minnow, red shiner, mosquito fish, green sunfish, bluegill sunfish, longear sunfish, spotted bass, bigscale log perch, greenthroat darter, freshwater drum, gizzard shad, channel catfish, flathead catfish, variegated pupfish, and brook silverside.

As expected, the infant snakes, obviously too small to swallow large prey, subsisted almost exclusively on minnows, particularly the redhorse shiner (41.8 percent) and flathead minnow (32.9 percent). As the snakes grew, their diets changed gradually. Juveniles and adult males, while continuing to take mostly minnows, also consumed small catfish, whereas adult females, whose diet included the greatest array of fish species (13 of the 16 recorded), devoured primarily the larger prey such as catfish, sunfish, and gizzard shad, almost all of them fingerlings. Since the adult females are generally bigger than adult males, it is no surprise that they consumed the largest fish, occasionally even capturing prey the size of adult sunfish.

The diet of Concho water snakes inhabiting Ballinger Lake differed significantly from that of the river-dwelling population, with the bigscale log perch (35.4 percent of the total diet) representing the reptile's chief prey, both by number and volume, followed by variegated pupfish (28.1 percent), flathead minnows (12.5 percent), and redhorse shiners (9.1 percent).

Riverine Concho water snakes in the study area confined their foraging activities almost entirely to the riffles. The juveniles concentrated their efforts chiefly on the shallow riffle margins, whereas the adults hunted primarily in the deeper riffle parts of the stream. When examined for food contents, none of the snakes in either size category contained bass, crappie, or black bullheads, prey fish known to inhabit the deeper river pools.

When actively seeking food, the Concho water snake was observed to employ two different foraging strategies. In the first, used mostly by the adults, the serpent moved slowly along the riffle bottom in a random search pattern, frequently pausing to investigate under-rock cavities with probing thrusts of its head as it sought to locate hidden prey, particularly the more sedentary young catfish. In the other approach, employed more often by the juvenile snakes, the motionless serpent, partly or completely submerged in the riffle with its tail anchored to a rock, snapped at passing schools of minnows as they swam within range of its jaws. This tactic proved especially productive around waterfalls and bridge abutments, where underwater structures provided good cover for schools of red shiner and flathead minnows, the young snakes' principal quarry. Using this hunting method in such surroundings, one juvenile water snake captured five minnows within 15 minutes. In more exceptional circumstances, when unusually heavy rains produced flooding along the upper Colorado River on June 10, 1989, many fish, debilitated by the silty water, found their way to shallow pools along the riverbanks, where they were easily scooped up by the hungry snakes without regard to any particular feeding style. At such times the serpents fully exploited the feeding bonanzas by gorging themselves with fish. Similar foraging opportunities presented themselves during periods of prolonged drought, when parts of drying streams and rivers were reduced to isolated pools laden with fish.

REPRODUCTION A five-year field study of the Concho water snake's natural history conducted by a team of Texas A&M University and Colorado River Municipal Water District biologists revealed no significant differences between the general pattern of the snake's reproductive biology and that of other North American water snakes of the genus *Nerodia*, but it did provide considerable new information about the snake's breeding behavior. Like the other water snakes, this one ordinarily mates in the spring and the female gives birth in late summer.

Male Concho water snakes attain sexual maturity when they are only 11 or 12 months old, but they usually first mate at 20 or 21 months of age. The females produce their first litters when they are either 24 or 25 months old or 36 or 37 months of age, depending on their reproductive development. Although courtship and mating have not been observed in nature, based on the recorded testicular activity of the males, the breeding season in this snake probably occurs early in the year, from March 15 to May 15. Two females discovered with sperm in their oviducts in October were too small to have bred earlier in the year, suggesting the probability of an uncommon secondary mating period in the fall, when a few males become sexually active.

Available evidence indicates that like many other snake species, female Concho water snakes severely restrict their movements during pregnancy, when, heavy with young, they are less able to escape predators. Instead, they spend their days and nights hiding in some secure refuge, such as the space beneath a boulder, under a low-water crossing, and, most often, in piles of herbaceous vegetation and stacks of decaying plant material in contact with water, which is where they were observed 70 percent of the time during the latter stages of pregnancy. It is in these mounds of vegetation, with their dense cover and the right mix of moisture and temperature, that the pregnant snakes apparently find the best conditions for the proper development of their growing embryos. When they do venture out into the open, it is usually just to bask in the sun, for females seldom if ever engage in feeding activities when they are gestating.

Between July 27 and September 22, after a gestation of 3 to 3½ months, the females give birth to their young on or near the rocky riffles of a river. Individual litters consist of 4 to 29 young (average 11), measuring 7½ to 9 inches (19.1–22.9 cm) long. Based on information derived from the movements of several gravid females implanted with miniature radio transmitters, there is circumstantial but convincing evidence that when birthing is imminent, Concho water snakes living close to one another redistribute themselves along the river so that their young will not be compelled to compete for food in the same riffle. The case in point involves four radio-monitored snakes, all near-term females that occupied the same general area of a low-water crossing several miles north of Ballinger. Three of them moved downstream from this location (all in one day) and stationed themselves at separate riffles 99 feet (30 m), 231 feet (70.4 m), and 990 feet (302 m) away. The fourth remained at the low-water crossing. Although this event by itself was curious enough, even more remarkable was the discovery 36 hours later that all the females, including the one that remained in place, had given birth.

DIAMOND-BACKED WATER SNAKE

Nerodia rhombifer rhombifer
PLATES 107, 108

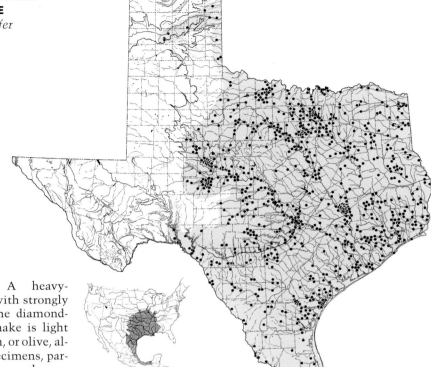

DESCRIPTION A heavy-bodied serpent with strongly keeled scales, the diamond-backed water snake is light brown, yellowish, or olive, although some specimens, particularly those from the upper Texas coast, often are dark orange or dark brown. Short, dark crossbars along the middle of the back alternate with vertical lateral bars; the two sets of markings are connected by dark diagonal lines, resulting in a pattern resembling a section of chain-link fencing. Scattered dark spots, usually crescent-shaped, mark the yellowish belly and underside of the tail, the spots increasing toward the rear of the abdomen. Specimens living in murky water may be covered with a thin film of silt or algae, obscuring their markings and making identification of such snakes difficult.

The head of an adult diamond-backed water snake is large, somewhat flattened, and distinctly wider than the neck. Its yellowish lip scales are usually margined with vertical black bars. Under the chin of older males are many small, prominent tubercles, a feature that distinguishes such diamond-backed water snakes from all other Texas serpents. Although the purpose of these papillae is still unknown, they are probably related to courtship. The strongly keeled dorsal scales are in 25 to 31 rows at midbody,

and the anal plate is divided. The dorsal ground color of infants is paler than that of adults and the pattern darker and more pronounced; the abdomen is generally bright yellow, often with an orange tinge.

COMPARABLE SNAKES The cottonmouth has a pit on each side of the face between the eye and nostril, elliptical pupils, and a more angular facial profile. The scales under its tail are mostly in a single row, whereas those of the diamond-backed water snake are arranged in a double row. Other Texas water snakes that may be confused with the diamond-

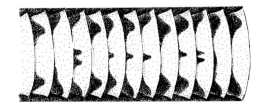

Figure 46. *Belly pattern of the diamond-backed water snake.*

backed water snake have little or no distinct dorsal pattern or are marked with spots, solid blotches, or crossbands; none has the distinctive chainlike markings of *N. rhombifer*.

SIZE Although the yellow-bellied water snake may approach this species in length, large diamond-backed water snakes, because of their greater girth, are Texas' largest *Nerodia*. Mature individuals are usually 30 to 48 inches (76.2–121.9 cm) long, with a maximum known length of 68$\frac{1}{3}$ inches (173.5 cm), according to Betz (1963).

HABITAT Occasionally found along fast-flowing streams and rivers, this snake prefers the calmer waters associated with swamps, marshes, bayous, lakes, ponds, stock tanks, drainage ditches, and water holes. Studying this species in Louisiana's Atchafalaya River basin, one of North America's largest swamps, Kofron (1978) encountered the snake in a wide variety of wetland niches. The 308 specimens captured during his two-year survey came from the following habitats: bayous and canals (68), tidal ditches (48), grassy locations (28), swamp–bottomland forest (26), freshwater bays (26), freshwater marshes (25), flooded fields (23), rivers (21), flooded bottomland forest (18), bay inlets (12), unflooded bottomland forest (4), and various other locations (9). In western Texas, where suitable water-snake habitat is scarce, it has made its way into the otherwise inhospitable arid terrain by following the Rio Grande upstream to the Devil's River, the westernmost outpost of its geographic range. Several biologists have commented on the diamond-backed water snake's tendency to explore new territory by moving considerable distances overland from its usual home range, which allows it to establish its presence in more and more aquatic locations.

BEHAVIOR Few other native snakes are as pugnacious as this one. Without warning, it strikes out viciously when cornered, its needlelike teeth creating a series of freely bleeding punctures or scratches. When handled, it not only bites savagely but also discharges from its cloacal opening a liberal amount of foul-smelling, glutinous material that it smears over its captor's hands by twisting and thrashing. This often results in the snake's quick release.

Some of the following information is based on studies of the snake made in south-central Louisiana by Kofron (1978) and by Mushinsky, Hebrard, and Walley (1980). Since their coastal study area is similar in most respects to the neighboring Texas marshlands and swamps, what is reported for the Louisiana water snakes should apply as well to snakes living along the upper Texas coast.

Although essentially nocturnal, particularly during the warmer summer months, the snake frequently basks in the sun during a part of each day, coiled or with the body extended along a tree limb or sloping tree trunk overhanging the water, or sometimes just resting on logs or brush at the water's edge. From such stations it quickly drops or slips into the water when alarmed. As daytime temperatures gradually increase from May to June, the snake becomes more active at night and more arboreal. As the weather cools again in September and October, it prowls instead from noon to approximately six in the evening.

Diamond-backed water snakes captured by Kofron on land were found within 25 feet (7.6 m) of the shoreline, although some specimens were observed swimming amid whitecapped waves in the deeper parts of East Cote Blanche Bay. Others were taken from among rocks piled along the water's edge and some from beside roadways constructed through marsh habitats, especially where unpaved shoulders were liberally covered with grasses. In August and September they could also be found among floating mats of hyacinth plants clustered near the bayou banks. Along the shores of Tennessee's Reelfoot Lake, the diamond-backed water snake frequently lay coiled by day in the moist, dark spaces created by the wandering root systems of large cypress trees.

Specimens in Kofron's study were never found beneath vegetative debris during hot weather, but in winter they sought shelter in or under such material, provided it was no more than 50 yards from water. Elsewhere, the snake often takes refuge beneath logs or plant litter in summer, especially when the debris is partly submerged in water. Like many other semiaquatic serpents, it often utilizes crayfish burrows for both summer and winter retreats.

This is one of the first snakes to make its appearance in the spring. In southern Louisiana it has been seen moving about on the surface of the ground as early as January 24. In south-central Texas Vermersch and Kuntz (1986) encountered it on warm days during every month, even in winter, when it moved about or sunned itself on tree limbs overhanging the water. Those living farther north are obligated to spend the colder months in hibernation, for if exposed to the subfreezing temperatures that commonly occur at such latitudes, they would soon die. According to Ernst and Barbour (1989), this snake hibernates in muskrat or beaver lodges, bankside animal burrows, and perhaps also in the mud bottoms of swamps.

FEEDING The food habits of this species have been well documented. In a majority of studies, fish were the chief prey, although the kinds of fish eaten often varied from one study site to another, no doubt depending on species availability. In Reelfoot Lake, Tennessee, for example, where fish constituted 98.5 percent of the snake's diet by volume, the inland silverside was the food of choice. In the Atchafalaya River basin of Louisiana, where piscine prey represented 97 percent of the serpent's diet by frequency, the mosquito fish was the species most often consumed. In his study of the diamond-backed water snake's feeding habits in Bowie and Red River counties, Texas, Bowers (1966) found that fish (50 percent) and anurans (44.6 percent) were nearly equally represented as prey when measured by volume of food ingested, but frogs and toads were eaten in greater numbers. Prey animals mentioned by others include large insects, crayfish, eellike salamanders called amphiumas, baby turtles, and even birds. Since catfish are armed with long, sharply pointed dorsal and pectoral spines, it would seem logical to conclude that water snakes generally avoid them. That seems not to be the case, however, for these fish are indeed often consumed by diamond-backed water snakes. Although such prey is sometimes ingested without difficulty, there are reported incidents in which the spines of swallowed catfish penetrated the snake's body wall. In some cases the spines eventually separated from the fish's body and dropped off after the rest of the animal had been digested; at other times the consumed catfish remained firmly lodged in the predator's throat, ultimately resulting in the snake's death.

Generally regarded as a marauder of game fish, this snake often takes the blame for any reduction in the local populations of such species, no matter what the reason for their decline. This reputation is based at least in part on sightings of diamond-backed water snakes near fishing piers, to which they are attracted by the dead fish, fish innards, and baits routinely discarded by anglers. Actually, game fish represent only a small percentage of the serpent's total diet. Kofron, for example, found that in south-central Louisiana it fed primarily on mosquito fish, sheepshead minnow, golden shiner, and sailfin molly and only occasionally on such sport fish as largemouth bass and catfish. This heavy-bodied snake is rather lethargic; its plodding movements cannot be compared, for example, with the speed and agility of such fast-moving terrestrial serpents as racers and coachwhips. Even in the water it is no match for a lively bass or sunfish, but what it lacks in speed, it makes up for in its novel foraging tactics. With its tail wrapped firmly around a branch or some other solid object on shore and its forebody extended out into the water, the snake sweeps its submerged head and neck from side to side until its mouth encounters a fish, a tactic that works especially well in murky water where the snake cannot see its prey. It sometimes employs a similar strategy in shallow water near shore, moving slowly in figure-8 profiles, snapping up any fish its open mouth touches.

The green water snake, a large species that coexists with the diamond-backed water snake over much of its range, would be a serious competitor for the same piscine prey except for two things. First, each snake has a different activity period; the former is essentially a daytime prowler and the latter hunts mostly at night, reducing the probability that the two will encounter one another during foraging. Furthermore, since the diamond-backed water snake is mostly nocturnal, it is more apt to come in contact with night-active prey such as frogs and catfish. The green water snake, on the other hand, is a day-active hunter more likely to find day-active prey.

REPRODUCTION Mating normally takes place in April, May, or June, although there is evidence to suggest that copulation may sometimes also occur in summer or fall, in which case the sperm remains viable in the female's oviducts until the following spring. The female diamond-backed water snake, one of Texas' most prolific serpents, gives birth to 8 to 62 young sometime in late August, September, or early October. An even later birth date was reported by Kennedy (1964), who collected a specimen in Polk County that produced 25 young (plus 1 dead infant and 4 underdeveloped embryos) on November 3. The newborn infants are 9 to 12 inches (22.9–30.5 cm) long.

MIDLAND WATER SNAKE
Nerodia sipedon pleuralis
PLATE 109

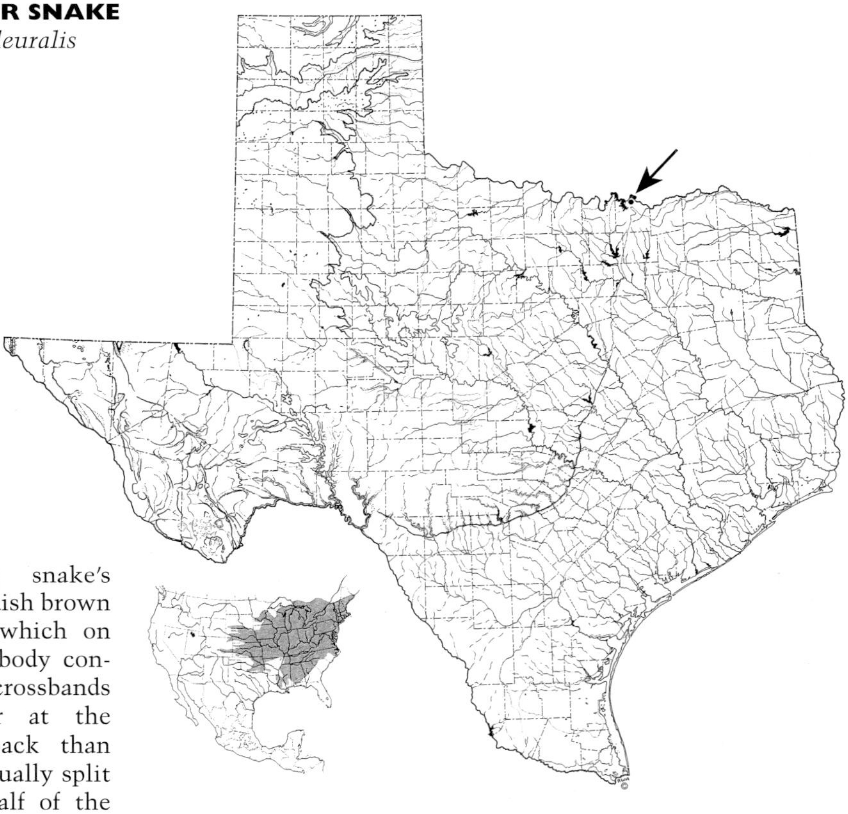

DESCRIPTION The snake's dark brown or reddish brown dorsal markings, which on the neck and forebody consist of complete crossbands that are broader at the middle of the back than along the sides, usually split up on the rear half of the body into smaller dorsal blotches and alternating lateral bars. Along the sides they are separated from one another by wider tan, gray-brown, or reddish brown (sometimes almost light orange) interspaces wider than themselves. Not every specimen is so boldly patterned, however. A large individual whose upper body markings have become indistinct with age may appear as a uniformly dark gray snake. Especially distinctive is the pattern of red or reddish brown half-moons that extend longitudinally along the serpent's abdomen in two somewhat uneven, parallel rows. Irregular dark spotting is usually also present on the outer edges of the belly plates.

The snake's head, which is relatively large and distinct from the neck, is brown on top and essentially unmarked except for dark sutures along the lateral edges of the upper and lower lip scales, which are paler than the crown. Ordinarily there is no dark line from the eye to the back of the mouthline. The dorsal scales are keeled and usually in 23 rows at midbody. The anal plate is divided.

COMPARABLE SNAKES The dorsal crossbands of the blotched water snake are neither clearly defined nor do the bands on the forebody extend down either side of the trunk to the edge of the abdomen. Its obscure abdominal spots are not half-moons, and they are confined to the outer edges of the belly plates. Unlike the midland water snake's wide, dark crossbands, the dark brown dorsal pattern of the diamond-backed water snake resembles the interwoven strands of chain-link fencing, and the small, blackish half-moons on its abdomen are not arranged in a double, longitudinal row but are randomly scattered down the belly, mostly along the sides. The western cottonmouth also shows some resemblance to the midland water snake, but it is stouter, its head is chunkier and more angular, its pupils are vertical, and it has a pit on either side of the head between the eye and nostril. Furthermore, the bold black-and-white (or yellowish) mottling on its abdomen is unlike the half-moon belly pattern of the midland water snake.

SIZE Adults are generally 22 to 40 inches (55.9–101.6 cm) long. The largest known specimen measured 59 inches (149.9 cm) in length.

HABITAT We include this snake in our list of Texas serpents based on two specimens in the Carnegie Museum collected in Grayson County five miles north of Sherman. They may, however, actually represent an intergrade population between northern and midland water snakes (Conant and Collins 1991). Over most of its geographic range, the snake seems to prefer clear, slow-moving streams with sand, gravel, or rock bottoms, but it also lives in a wide variety of other aquatic environments including rivers, lakes, ponds, swamps, and marshes. It is less attracted to mud-bottomed watercourses with poorly defined shorelines (where broad-banded, yellow-bellied, and diamond-backed water snakes are more at home), and it usually avoids swift-flowing rivers and streams. Yet even ditches, if they are wet for most of the year, can support small numbers of midland water snakes.

BEHAVIOR Extremely wary of approaching enemies, the snake's first line of defense against a predator is to dart immediately into the nearest body of water and swim submerged or at the surface until it believes it is out of harm's way. When caught unawares on land without an avenue of escape, like most water snakes of the genus *Nerodia*, it threatens its foe by radically flattening its head and body to make itself appear wider and more sinister. It is this fearsome posture in particular that causes a water snake to be mistaken for the venomous cottonmouth. If the reptile is approached too closely it will take the offensive, lunging with quick, vicious strikes at the source of its annoyance, though such assaults are intended more to drive away an opponent than to injure it. When picked up, the same snake responds with even greater frenzy, biting at the restraining hand and often maintaining a tenacious grip on its captor as it chews. The serpent's saliva contains a cogent anticoagulant, so the wounds will bleed freely, though they are not serious. Biting is not the snake's only method of defense. To discourage those who would seize it, the water snake, like many other serpent species, discharges a foul-smelling musk from glands at the base of its tail and equally offensive feces from its cloaca, both of which the snake tries to smear over its captor by vigorously thrashing about.

During the still-mild days of spring and perhaps also into early summer, the midland water snake is most likely to be encountered idly basking on a log, tree stump, or rock at the water's edge, where it can immediately slip into its aquatic sanctuary. Even more convenient for such purposes are the limbs of trees and bushes that extend some distance out over the water.

An accomplished swimmer, this species is as much at home under the water as it is on the surface. According to Ferguson and Thornton (1984), it has the capacity to remain submerged for more than an hour at a time without showing signs of stress. The researchers determined that during such lengthy underwater forays the snake's heart rate dropped to 5 beats per minute, a mere 9 percent of its at-rest rate. For its size, this is a relatively sedentary serpent that usually does not stray far during its active season. As long as there is a plentiful food supply, it is satisfied to linger indefinitely along the bank of a particular stream, pond, or lake. Fitch and Shirer (1971), who tracked several Kansas specimens of this species fitted with miniature radio transmitters, discovered that their daily movements averaged only 12.2 feet (3.7 m) a day. As further evidence of the snake's ordinarily limited home range, Stickel and Cope (1947) recaptured the same specimen just 383 feet (117 m) from the spot where it was first found two years earlier.

More cold-tolerant than many snake species with which it coexists, the midland water snake has a longer active season than most other *Nerodia* species. In Missouri, according to Johnson (1987), the species normally is active from April to October, but several other zoologists state that in some parts of its range it is occasionally encountered in every month. This snake is either day- or night-active, depending on the season. In the spring and fall, when nighttime temperatures are rather cool, it is most likely to be seen during the day, feeding or warming itself in the sun's rays. In midsummer, particularly in the southern portions of its range, it limits its foraging activities chiefly to the hours of late evening and night; by day it usually seeks refuge under rocks, logs, and other available surface objects near the water.

During the winter the snake shelters in a wide range of natural sites that have included upland rock crevices, hollow logs, decaying tree stumps, small mammal and crayfish burrows, and ant mounds, though it frequently also hibernates in man-made earth or stone structures near its summer home. Its winter inactivity is sometimes interrupted by brief periods of abnormally high temperatures, during which the torpid snake leaves its refuge to bask at the surface in the warm midday sun.

FEEDING By far the most important item in the diet of *N. sipedon* is fish, which by most accounts, according to Ernst and Barbour (1989), constitute 50 to 96 percent of the snake's food by volume and 59 to 90 percent by frequency of occurrence. Amphibians (frogs, toads, tadpoles, and salamanders) are next in importance, making up 4 to 52 percent of the menu by volume and 17 percent by frequency of occurrence. Other prey species include small mammals, birds, juvenile turtles, lizards, and a variety of invertebrates, especially crayfish.

The midland water snake hunts its prey either by day or at night; its feeding schedule depends largely on the time of year. Although this opportunistic hunter will not hesitate to take a meal whenever it is readily available, nighttime foraging is the rule, except during early spring and late fall when after-dark temperatures are too cool for aquatic prowling. To find its piscine prey, the snake actively searches the shallow water near the edge of a stream or pond, poking its head into the large and small recesses where the fish often take shelter from predators. When conditions are right, it will occasionally drive groups of small fish or tadpoles against a bank with a loop of its body, for when such prey are forced into a tighter space, they can be more easily captured. In another foraging tactic it swims slowly in shallow water with its mouth wide open. Moving its head from side to side, the snake tries to entrap in its jaws any small fish it encounters. This is especially effective in midsummer after a serious drought has reduced larger bodies of water to remnant pools and puddles crowded with fish.

REPRODUCTION Mating, which occurs sometime between April and early June, may involve the simultaneous courtship of a single female by several males. Born during August or September after 3 to 4 months of gestation, the young snakes, 8 to 46 (usually 15 to 30) per litter, measure $7\frac{1}{2}$ to 12 inches (19.1–30.5 cm) long.

ROUGH GREEN SNAKE

Opheodrys aestivus
PLATE 110

DESCRIPTION Like a number of other arboreal serpents, the rough green snake has a long, emerald-hued, pencil-thin body and an elongated, gradually tapering tail of the same color. This unpatterned dorsal tone extends down either side of the body nearly to the abdomen, where it fades to yellow or yellowish green, the same pale color that marks the snake's immaculate belly, throat, and lips. Correctly identifying a dead specimen is an-

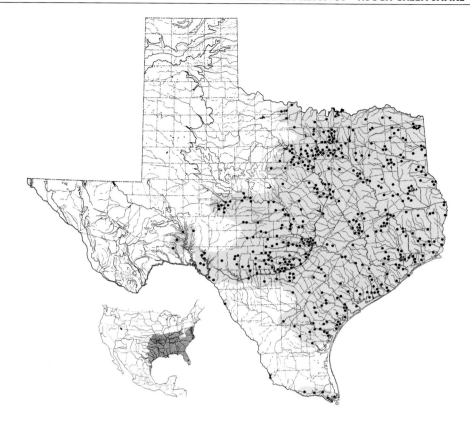

other matter, for soon after it dies, the reptile's normal coloration turns to deep blue. Its dorsal scales are keeled and arranged in 17 rows at midbody. The anal plate is divided.

COMPARABLE SNAKES The only native serpent species likely to be confused with the rough green snake is the smaller and extremely rare (in Texas) smooth green snake, whose dorsal scales, arranged in only 15 rows at midbody, lack keels.

SIZE Although adults are generally 22 to 32 inches (55.9–81.3 cm) long, a specimen of record size measured 45⅝ inches (115.9 cm) in length.

HABITAT The rough green snake is probably the most arboreal of all Texas serpents. Sometimes encountered in partially wooded meadows, pastures, and even suburban gardens, this typically brush- and tree-dwelling creature is found most frequently along the edges of deciduous or evergreen woodland adjoining a lake, pond, stream, marsh, swamp, or other open terrain. For example, in central and eastern Oklahoma, Goldsmith (1984)

found that among 98 sightings of this species, 84 were associated with a watercourse of some kind: 38 near lakeshores, 22 near creeks or dry creekbeds, 17 in upland ravines, and 7 along rivers. Of the rest, 10 were encountered on upland roads and 4 in wooded areas of somewhat higher elevation away from water. Cook (1954) says that in June, Mississippi youngsters often discovered it in fruiting plum trees growing in open fields. Although she gave no reason for the serpent's abundance in such places at that particular time of year, a possible explanation may have been the concentrations of insect prey that are sometimes drawn to the trees by the ambrosia of overripe fruit, which in turn may have attracted the snakes.

At the western edge of its Texas range, the rough green snake has made its way into the easternmost parts of the arid Trans-Pecos region and the barren southern plains—both formidable barriers to the serpent's continued westward expansion—by clinging to the moist corridors of wooded gulches and canyons that transect these areas. Such vegetated corridors, according to Bailey (1905), occur near Kerrville and at Rocksprings, where the rough green snake is found in brush-covered gulches lined with stands of pecan, sycamore, elm, cherry, and oak. Nowhere does the snake appear to be attracted to any particular tree species, though it favors those with limbs growing more nearly horizontal than vertical, like willow and ironwood; apparently their boughs provide a more convenient perching angle than many of the others.

Even city parkland devoid of trees will support populations of this adaptable little serpent, as long as the area is not too dry and provided it contains plenty of leafy brush in which the snake can hide and forage. Similarly, Webb (1970) found that in the grasslands of Oklahoma, where trees are scarce or absent, it attains moderate perching heights by climbing into bushes. In such habitat he also discovered it hiding in animal burrows, with only its head protruding from the tunnel openings.

BEHAVIOR It seems strange that despite the snake's large geographic range and its relative abundance (an estimated 430 individuals occupied 1 hectare [2.47 acres] of a central Arkansas study site), detailed information about its ecology and behavior remained a mystery until the 1970s. Much of what has been learned since then comes from the field studies of Michael V. Plummer (1976, 1981, 1985, 1989, 1990a,b), conducted mostly in central Arkansas. In presenting the following material, we have drawn freely from his data. Additional information for this account is taken from the reports of Steven K. Goldsmith's investigations of the species in Oklahoma (1984, 1986).

Except for its superbly cryptic coloration, this species is poorly designed to defend itself. Although it has been known to bite, its attempts to foil an aggressor's attack are usually nonviolent. Thus, it may seem odd at first to watch such a mild-mannered little snake threaten with its jaws agape; the exposed dark purple color of its mouth cavity looks strangely unlike the pinkish hue that typically lines the mouths of most other serpents. This menacing posture, all bluff, is intended to startle an opponent and perhaps delay its attack just long enough for the snake to

make an escape. When it does flee, its movements are agile and sure, its slender form seeming to flow through the leafy canopy.

Under some circumstances the reptile's retreat is anything but graceful. For example, if the snake is touched or jostled while on a limb, it is likely to react with a sudden jerk of its entire body, sometimes so violently that the creature flips off its perch and onto the ground below, where it immediately crawls to freedom. Such a vigorous response may well serve as a defensive reaction, both to startle a predator and to catapult the potential victim to another, perhaps less vulnerable spot. In a more controlled escape, an individual that is frightened as it rests on a bush or tree limb may simply launch itself into space, landing on the grass below and quickly disappearing into the underbrush. It then travels only a short distance before stopping.

One that is handled for the first time occasionally reacts by frantically twisting and thrashing about to escape, simultaneously discharging a musky liquid from its caudal scent glands and fecal-laden fluid from its cloacal opening. Smeared over a captor's hands, these pungent substances can so overpower the senses of touch and smell that the captor will release the serpent immediately.

Depending on where they live, rough green snakes leave hibernation in March, April, or May, those from southern Texas and southern Louisiana appearing at the surface a month to a month and a half earlier than specimens from states farther north. In and around San Antonio, Texas, according to Vermersch and Kuntz (1986), they emerge from winter dormancy in March or early April when the air temperature is consistently above 70 degrees F for several days. Thereafter they are encountered most frequently from April to July and again in September and October, at least in southern Illinois, according to Morris (1982). It is in the spring and fall that they are most likely to be seen on the ground, perhaps because the arboreal foliage, then more sparse than during midsummer, is somewhat less effective as background camouflage. When moving across a road or trail, the snakes are especially noticeable, their bright green bodies standing out prominently against the dark-hued corridors.

Strictly a day-active serpent, the rough green snake moves about from sunup to 30 minutes before dark, usually confining its travels to narrow zones of heavy vegetation adjoining sizable bodies of water or other open spaces. Most specimens in a central Arkansas study area restricted their daily movements to the foliage along the edge of a lake. Their longest horizontal journey in a single day was less than 200 feet (61 m), although specimens captured at least four times over the course of an entire season had moved, on average, a total of 203½ feet (62 m) for males and 223 feet (68 m) for females.

A rough green snake coiled motionless against a leafy background is so well camouflaged that it becomes invisible to the human eye, even when close enough to be touched. Knowing this instinctively, the perfectly disguised serpent does not move when first approached. In response to the motion of vegetation waving gently in the breeze, it may sway its forebody back and forth, apparently to blend even more into the essence of its arboreal surroundings.

To spot one of these dainty little reptiles in its completely green environment takes practice, though a specimen resting on a tree branch is easily detected when seen from below. Its pale belly stands out conspicuously against an umbrella of dark green foliage. It was Ditmars (1936) who devised a novel way to locate green snakes hidden in their shrubby roadside habitats. He would shake small bushes in which the camouflaged reptiles might be concealed, causing the serpents to give away their presence by suddenly moving. Although this approach was simple, and for Ditmars moderately effective, Conant (1951) found it unproductive, considering the few specimens collected in relation to the large number of shrubs investigated.

This reptilian gymnast is remarkably well adapted for a life in arboreal vegetation. Its long, slender form is easily supported by even the most delicate tree limb extremity, for an adult of average size weighs only a few ounces. Despite the creature's slender build, its strong, wiry body serves to move it effortlessly through the dense vegetation, while the prehensile tail sometimes helps to hold it firmly on a limb. Even bridging open spaces is not difficult. In crossing the gap between one tree branch and another, it may extend half its body vertically or horizontally in midair, its muscular trunk held as rigid as a pencil.

As it moves slowly forward, it often pauses, the head and several inches of its forebody raised upward between 30 and 90 degrees for a better view of its surroundings, a posture frequently used during feeding and courtship activities. Goldsmith reported another, more curious behavior in which the snake moved several inches of its neck and forebody in rhythmic S-like waves; the undulations traveled from back to front and ended at the serpent's head, which remained motionless throughout the event. Averaging 3.9 seconds each, the undulations occurred in uninterrupted clusters, each cluster lasting a full 20 to 30 seconds. At this time there is no clear explanation for the reptile's unusual behavior. It sometimes took place when the green snake encountered another serpent or a potential prey animal, or even when the serpent was simply crawling. It also occurred in the absence of such activities. Goldsmith believed that since the reptiles elevated their forebodies whenever they performed such undulations, the behavior may be a remedial action to correct the lowered arterial pressure caused by the snake's raised anterior trunk. He remarked that a similar motor pattern has also been observed in certain other kinds of terrestrial and arboreal serpents.

When it comes to perching locations, this snake has some well-defined preferences. Choice spots are along the outer edges of leafy branches where stems, usually no more than ⅜ inch (1 cm) in diameter, are generally situated less than 10 feet (3.3 m) above the ground—averaging 7½ feet (2.3 m)—and no more than 10 feet from water. The more horizontal the limb, the better the perch. Although one was discovered in a tree nearly 46 feet (14 m) from the ground, it is equally at home in the tops of vines and bushes.

At night the snake roosts along the outermost parts of the same branches it used by day, for the slender terminal portions of the limbs, no more than ⅙ inch (0.4 cm) thick, easily hold this lightweight serpent but will not support most of its nocturnal enemies. The delicate boughs thus provide a relatively safe haven from predators. Most of the time, a rough green snake at rest drapes its body evenly across the branches in loose S configurations, its head generally placed somewhere near the outermost body loops. A snake in hiding will pull itself together in a more tightly coiled, circular posture and rest its head just about in the middle of its body mass.

Rough green snakes are decidedly arboreal, but they do not spend all of their time above the ground. Of 76 specimens Goldsmith observed during a central Oklahoma field study, for example, 43 were spotted in arboreal vegetation, 19 crawling on the ground, 10 on roads (some dead, apparently killed by vehicular traffic), and 4 in natural shelters (3 under logs and 1 in a tree root hole). In other places they have also been found occasionally under stones, boards, cardboard, and piles of dead leaves.

Though it is not an aquatic reptile, the rough green snake readily enters the water. It not only inhabits shallow waters along the shorelines of rivers, streams, and ponds but also seems at ease in deeper water some distance from land. In Virginia, for example, Richmond (1952) saw one resting on a water lily leaf growing in a river marsh some 200 yards (182.6 m) from the nearest bank, with no other vegetation in between, and another swimming calmly in the middle of the Chickahominy River approximately 200 feet (61 m) from shore. His most surprising discovery, though, was not a snake in the water but one underwater. On the first day of April 1944, as he surveyed some temporary rain pools, Richmond noticed a rough green snake in one of them, resting on a submerged bush, its head and body completely underwater. Astonished at finding the snake in such unusual circumstances, he lifted the creature from the pool to examine it. Judging the snake to be active and in apparent good health, he placed it back into the pool, whereupon it swam 15 or 20 feet (4.6–6.1 m) away, coming to rest on another submerged bush, where it stayed with only its head out of the water. This behavior has not been reported by others, so it could be simply an example of aberrant defensive behavior by a single snake. Or is it perhaps a more widespread but rarely observed reaction by the species to the presence of an intruder?

Before the arrival of disagreeably cold weather, usually in early and mid-November in most places and sometimes as late as mid-December across the southern end of the serpent's range, the rough green snake enters hibernation. Its cold-weather retreat usually consists of an underground burrow, a deep pile of leaf litter, or the inner core of decomposing logs and tree stumps. In a more unusual circumstance, Coast Guard telephone linemen working near Virginia Beach, Virginia, removed two specimens from hibernacula 2 feet underground, each coiled in the rotting base of a separate uncreosoted telephone pole. The possibility that the rough green snake spends the winter in crayfish burrows, as do many other small serpents, has been suggested by Vermersch and Kuntz (1986), although this has yet to be documented.

FEEDING The majority of snake species dine almost exclusively on small vertebrate animals, but this arboreal hunter eats a variety of adult and larval insects, spiders, slugs, snails, and on rare occasions even very small frogs. In order of preference, the foremost prey species are caterpillars, spiders, grasshoppers, crickets, and dragonflies; together they represent about 90 percent of the diet in most areas.

The rough green snake is an active forager. In searching for prey it moves slowly through the vegetation with its tongue flicking, hoping to flush its quarry. Since there is strong evidence that the snake detects prey by sight alone, the value of such rapid tongue movements during foraging is not clear. In fact, Goldsmith found that captive specimens were unable to detect motionless insects placed in their cages. So acute is the reptile's vision that even the slightest movement of an insect's leg or antennae, if not more than a foot away, gets its attention. Also of possible importance during stalking is the slow, rhythmic, side-to-side waving of the head observed in this species, a behavior some believe enhances the snake's binocular vision when it is scrutinizing its prey.

When exploring a limb, the reptile usually travels outward from the base, methodically investigating leaves and branches along the way, occasionally raising its head for a better look around. At the sight of a nearby insect, the snake pauses briefly, fixes its eyes on the quarry, then advances again, its quick forward progress interrupted once more by similar brief stops. No longer is the tongue busily flicking. It now protrudes stiffly from the snake's mouth, straight out, the tips neither widely spread nor waving up and down in the usual exploratory mode. This tactic, some believe, helps the predator focus on its prey, like sighting a target down a gun barrel. Moreover, rapid tongue flicking would tend to alert the quarry to the serpent's stealthy advance. As the serpent approaches the prey, its movements become slow and steady, the forward progress of its body barely noticeable. At the same time, it slowly pulls its forebody into several lateral S-shaped flexures, which, when the snake is less than half an inch from its target, are suddenly straightened, driving the predator's head swiftly toward the target. In one study, 75 percent of all such strike attempts proved successful. If an insect flees before it can be seized, it is generally pursued and often captured. To prevent a sizable insect such as a large grasshopper from using its strong legs to pull or push itself from the serpent's grasp, the snake sometimes lifts its victim off the ground or away from a limb.

REPRODUCTION Mating in this species generally takes place in the spring, but in some parts of the snake's range it may occur in the fall. The males engage in their first sexual encounters when they are 21 months old, the females either at the same age or at 33 months.

An egg-layer, the rough green snake has most frequently been reported to deposit its clutch on or near the ground in decaying tree stumps and logs, in moss, within piles of dead leaves, beneath flat rocks, under old cardboard, and on one occasion even in the rockwool insulation of a discarded refrigerator panel. Despite such reports, Plummer's recent field research indicates rather convincingly that nesting sites on or near the ground are the exception, at least at his Arkansas study sites. His observations (enhanced by first installing tiny radio transmitters in a number of green snakes to monitor their movements) revealed that the reptiles invariably deposited their eggs in the elevated hollows of live trees, a type of nest site so far unreported for any other Texas snake species except the Texas rat snake.

The study area, a 52-acre (20.8 ha) lake in White County, Arkansas, was margined by a brushy band of shoreline vegetation 3¼ to 13½ feet (1–4.1 m) wide, dominated by a stand of alder trees 5 to 13 feet (1.5–4 m) tall. This in turn was surrounded by oak-hickory forest typical of the region. During their active season, the female green snakes inhabited the narrow belt of alder that rims the lakeshore, each occupying a strip of vegetation approximately 50 feet (15.2 m) wide. As the time for egg-laying drew near, the gravid serpents left their arboreal shelters and traveled along the ground, directly away from the lakeshore and into the surrounding oak-hickory forest, making no deviations along the way. They usually reached the nest site in one or two days.

The tree of choice generally had several features in common: it was an oak or hickory 5 or 6 inches (12.7–15.2 cm) in diameter, it contained a partly hollow interior about 4 feet above the ground, and it was accessible from the outside through a small opening in the tree's exterior. Such a tree, on average, was 183 feet (55.8 m) away from the lakeshore. The nest chamber itself, a narrow slit inside the tree trunk, typically not much wider than the diameter of a green-snake egg but sometimes larger, was usually only big enough to accommodate a single egg laid horizontally on the cavity floor, thus limiting the way the eggs could be arranged within the meager space. As a result, the eggs frequently ended up in a single vertical layer, like cans stacked in an automatic soft-drink dispenser, each egg resting on its side, one on top of the other.

It is unknown how the female initially finds a suitable nest tree. One possibility suggested by Plummer is that she has a remarkable instinctive ability to do so, though it seems more probable that her first success is the result of trial and error. There is little doubt that when a female green snake finds her first decent nest tree, she will have little difficulty locating it again for subsequent egg depositions.

Why do the females travel so far to lay their eggs in one particular tree while along the way they pass so many others that appear just as suitable? So far the question remains unanswered. One case documented by Plummer demonstrates the determined effort made by a gravid female to nest in a specific tree. From her home site along the lakeshore, she traveled 179 feet (54.6 m) directly to a small oak tree, where she tried unsuccessfully to enter a small opening high up on the trunk, twisting and prodding with her snout to enlarge the tight hole. This went on for over an hour. Finally, unable to get through, the creature discontinued her efforts and crawled into a nearby bush to rest. Three hours later she returned to the hole, renewed her efforts, and finally forced her way into the tree cavity, where she then laid her eggs.

In some cases, the tree cavity where the female deposited her eggs already contained the old shells of eggs hatched there in previous years by her or by other female green snakes. This suggests two possibilities: a single female regularly used the same nest site year after year, or several different females together used the site as a communal hatchery.

Evidence of communal nesting comes from several different sources. In one instance, a gravid female observed by Plummer in central Arkansas traveled directly to a nest tree, climbed its trunk, and tried to enter the hollow interior through a small opening 9 feet above the ground, the same hole she presumably had used in a previous nesting episode. The tree's steady growth, however, apparently had reduced the size of the hole until it was no longer large enough to admit the snake's body. Unable to enter, the female left the tree and went elsewhere. When the zoologist later opened the cavity, he found 16 spent green-snake eggshells from past years: an older group of 11 and a more recently hatched group of 5. In yet another example of communal nesting in this species, Palmer and Braswell (1976) discovered a batch of viable keeled green-snake eggs in the rock-wool insulation of a narrow metal refrigerator panel discarded in sandy woodland. Leaning undisturbed against an oak tree for several years, the dilapidated panel contained 74 eggs, all of which eventually hatched. In Plummer's view, the choice of this object as a nest site is not surprising. Artificial as it may have been, the panel contained two basic ingredients necessary for the successful development of green-snake eggs, an elevated hollow core insulated from temperature extremes and an exterior opening narrow enough to prevent entry by most predators.

Such tiny nest-cavity entryways cannot prevent the intrusion of certain small reptilian marauders. A prime example is that of a female *O. aestivus* that deposited her eggs in the hollow of a hickory tree. When Plummer opened the nest cavity the next day he found three green-snake eggs, recently broken into, their contents gone. In the same space was a female broad-headed skink, a carnivorous tree-climbing lizard with an apparent appetite for other reptiles' eggs, which had previously entered the tree hollow to lay and brood her own clutch of eggs.

It is not known if predators devour many green-snake eggs in the nest, but there is every reason to believe that overland travel is an especially hazardous venture for *O. aestivus*, particularly when the female, heavy with eggs, begins her summer migration to a distant nesting site. Then her movements may be a bit slower than usual. In addition, she can be detected more easily by ground-dwelling adversaries, those not likely to inhabit elevated foliage, particularly king snakes and racers. Even after the deposition of her eggs, the female's journey back to her home site, often across open ground, puts her at greater risk than when she is traveling above ground. Although she may not be burdened with the added weight of her eggs, the same terrestrial predators that challenged her on the first leg of her journey are still lurking at the surface to confront her again on the return trip. Plummer's research dramatically demonstrated just how dangerous such overland travel can be, for during his studies of rough green snake nesting movements, four of nine (and possibly two other) gravid females fitted with miniature radio transmitters were lost to predators, most of them as they traveled on the ground. That raises the question, How much, if at all, does the added weight of a tiny radio transmitter restrict the locomotor ability of a snake already heavy with eggs, thus compromising her ability to avoid a predator? So far there is no clear-cut answer. What is certain, however, is that when a green snake makes a long trip on the ground, with or without the added burden of eggs, its risk of being devoured by a predator becomes much greater than when it remains aloft.

Across the snake's geographic range the females lay clutches of 2 to 14 (usually 4–6) elongate, leathery-shelled eggs, each one approximately 1 to 1½ inches (2.5–3.8 cm) long. In at least some parts of Texas, clutch size may be greater on average. From two southeastern Texas locations, Guidry (1953) mentioned a group of 8 eggs laid by one female green snake on June 17 that hatched July 20, and a clutch of 10 eggs laid by another on August 28 that emerged October 20. Once they are deposited at the nest site, sometime between mid-June and late Au-

gust, the eggs are left to incubate, grow, and hatch, all without parental care. The young emerge from the eggs 30 to 50 days later. At least in the laboratory, eggs incubated in dry conditions produced smaller young than those kept under conditions of ample moisture. The olive-green hatchlings, which generally measure between 6⅛ and 7⅝ inches (15.6–19.4 cm) long, take on the bright green hue of the adults after their first molt.

SONORAN GOPHER SNAKE
Pituophis catenifer affinis
PLATE III

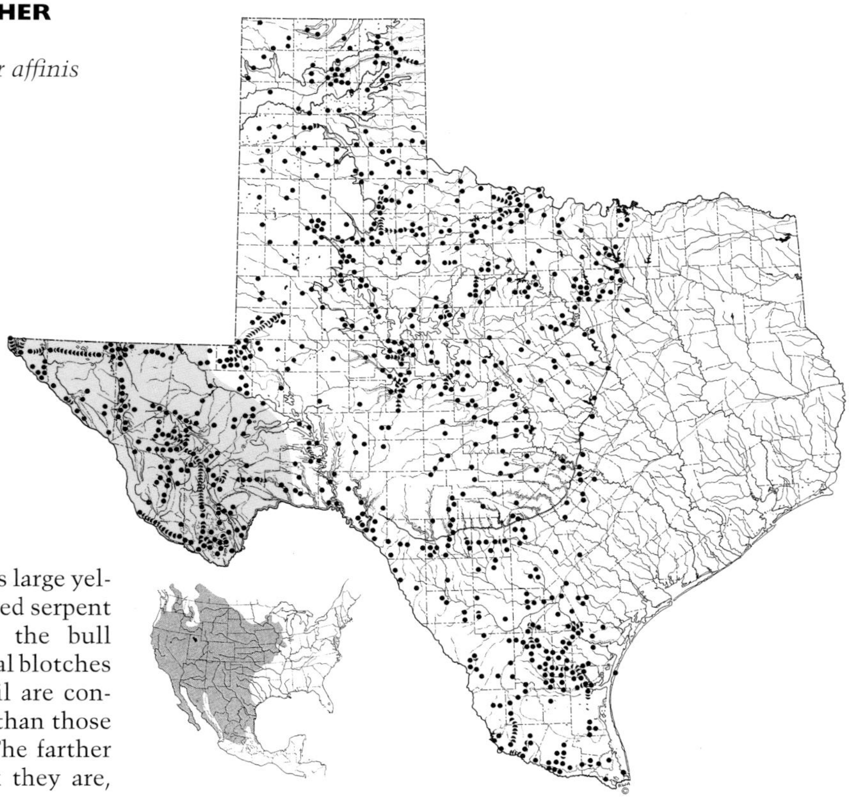

DESCRIPTION This large yellow to cream-colored serpent closely resembles the bull snake, but the dorsal blotches on and near its tail are conspicuously darker than those on the forebody. The farther back on the trunk they are, the darker they become; on the tail they are nearly black. Below and alternating with the dorsal markings is a row of smaller dark spots, with yet another, even smaller series below them. In the pale areas between blotches, each scale may display a dark streak along its keel. The head markings, which consist of a dark bar across the head just forward of the eyes and another on each side of the head from the eye to the back of the mouthline, are like those of the bull snake, though ordinarily not as well defined.

Black spots usually mark the snake's white or yellowish belly, particularly along the outer edges.

A distinctive feature of this and other Texas *Pituophis* is the usual presence on the forehead of four prefrontal scales instead of the two found in other native colubrid species. Typically arranged in 31 or 33 rows at midbody, the Sonoran gopher snake's dorsal scales are strongly keeled, except for those on the lower rows. The anal plate is single.

COMPARABLE SNAKES The rostral plate of the bull snake is about twice as high as it is wide, standing out in bold relief above the adjacent scales; the same scale in the Sonoran gopher snake is barely higher than wide and not raised above its neighbors. See the bull snake account.

SIZE This subspecies is reported to reach a maximum length of 7 feet 8 inches (233.7 cm), although the usual adult is 4½ to 5½ feet (137.2–167.6 cm) long.

HABITAT The bull snake has managed to adapt to some extremely dry conditions at the lower end of its U.S. range, but it is the Sonoran gopher snake that often occupies the Southwest's most inhospitable desert habitats. Despite their tendency to inhabit dry environments, gopher snakes will nearly always choose irrigated farmlands over the adjacent deserts, no doubt attracted by the abundance of crop-eating rodents found there. Otherwise, gopher snakes are remarkably adaptable, occurring in nearly every type of major habitat encountered across the Southwest. In a census made by Klauber (1939) in southern California, for example, this subspecies was found in these diverse environments: cultivated fields (104 specimens), brushy desert (54), grass (42), rocky desert (17), orchards or vineyards (7), sandy desert (6), and barren desert (4). In the vicinity of Alamogordo, New Mexico, it was encountered in a variety of habitats including the mesquite plains association, the creosote association of the alluvial slopes, and the high pine-spruce forests at elevations exceeding 8,000 feet. In Texas it is generally restricted to the desert benches and sand dunes along the east side of the Rio Grande near El Paso, where the vegetation is primarily mesquite, creosote bush, and desert grasses.

BEHAVIOR The closely related gopher and bull snakes practice many of the same behaviors. Both are accomplished diggers that use their modified snouts to penetrate and loosen sand or soil, after which they pull the dislodged material away from the excavation site in a sharp bend of the neck. Because the gopher snake's nose has a less prominent profile, it is not as well suited for digging as that of the bull snake; in fact, the gopher snake does not display its larger relative's general tendency to burrow. Nevertheless, it is not unusual for it to penetrate a gopher nest by tunneling down through the dirt mound marking the entrance to the rodent's burrow system.

Tree climbing is another activity shared by both serpents, although the gopher snake is not as likely to ascend bushes and trees, except when seeking avian prey. Another conspicuous similarity is the way they cope with a potential threat. A close encounter with either of these pugnacious reptiles usually brings a quick and vigorous response. It begins when the snake assumes a typical defensive pose, with its forebody drawn into a tight S posture while the head, held high off the ground, is flattened to appear large and triangular. To make an even greater impression, the snake forcefully expels air from its lung, past a flap of cartilage at the opening of the air duct in the floor of its mouth. This results in a loud, vibrating hiss that can sometimes be heard as far away as 50 feet (15.2 m). At the same time, the serpent rapidly shakes its tail.

This dramatic performance is surprisingly like that of an angry western diamond-backed rattlesnake preparing to strike: the pit viper's triangular head is elevated, the forebody drawn into an S configuration, and the rattle set into whirring motion by the rapidly vibrating tail. Anyone who has ever been suddenly confronted up close by a large, agitated rattler will agree that the experience elicits a spine-tingling fright. The gopher snake's behavior could be another case of a harmless snake mimicking to its own advantage a venomous one. Some herpetologists believe it is, for the similarity between the two in physical appearance and defensive behavior must surely benefit bull snakes and gopher snakes alike by at least briefly discouraging their adversaries. The one notable exception, of course, is man, whose mortal fear of rattlesnakes compels him to destroy them all and anything that looks and acts like them, bull snakes and gopher snakes in particular.

When given the opportunity, however, the gopher snake will move slowly away from an intruder, for big as it is, it has little real defense against a large foe. At best, it will strike sharply at the threat, often directing its thrust upward, but usually with little damaging effect, for its several rows of sharp but relatively small teeth produce only minor puncture wounds. It seems, too, that young gopher snakes are more inclined than the adults to defend themselves by biting.

Although the serpent's choice refuge is a hole in the ground excavated by some small animal, the gopher snake also hides under rocks and logs. In Arizona, where Fowlie (1965) stated it was the most frequently encountered serpent, it often crawled into wood-rat homes dug beneath the jointed sections of dead cholla plants. Those inhabiting low-lying deserts are generally active early in the morning or late in the evening, for the daytime temperatures there are much too high to be tolerated by most reptiles, though specimens living at moderately high elevations are mostly day-active.

FEEDING   The gopher snake's diet is similar to that of the bull snake, consisting mostly of mice, rats, gophers, rabbits, and ground squirrels, along with birds and their eggs. Lizards are also eaten, but mostly by the smaller snakes.

It often traps burrowing mammals in their underground homes and suffocates them by pressing them firmly against a tunnel wall with a segment of the snake's body. Above ground the larger prey animals are wrapped in the snake's muscular body coils and squeezed until dead, but small ones may be seized and simply swallowed alive.

REPRODUCTION   The breeding habits, number of eggs laid, and size of hatchlings are very much like those of the bull snake. Ritualistic

combat behavior, which has been observed in a number of different serpent species, both harmless and venomous, nearly always occurs when one male encounters another male as they both court the same female. Such behavior, however, is sometimes also initiated when food, not sex, is the issue. It does not involve the kind of physical violence that results in broken bones, torn flesh, or even serious bruising; it is actually a bloodless event perhaps best described as a no-holds-barred wrestling match.

Such a contest, involving two large male Sonoran gopher snakes, was described in detail by Bogert and Roth (1966). In this particular encounter, the two snakes were observed in combat for approximately an hour, during which the momentum of their lively gyrations carried them nearly 30 feet (9.2 m) from the spot where they were first seen. With their bodies and tails closely intertwined horizontally, like the turns of a giant corkscrew, only their heads and forebodies remained free to move about unrestrained. Although the head and neck positions changed periodically, the heads were nearly always oriented in the same direction. The main goal of the struggle apparently is to attain physical superiority over the opponent by bringing the head and neck slightly upright and, with that advantage gained, pressing the competitor's head to the ground. In such skirmishes, which may last more than an hour, one of the combatants finally wins when the other gives up and crawls away.

BULL SNAKE
Pituophis catenifer sayi
PLATE 112

DESCRIPTION   The markings of this long, moderately stout-bodied serpent consist of a row of large, squarish black, brown, or reddish brown blotches down the center of the back, which contrast conspicuously with the snake's tan to yellowish ground color, especially on the front and rear thirds of the body. The less distinct lateral markings, composed of smaller blotches and spots of variable shape and size, frequently intermingle to cre-

ate a haphazard mosaic. The tail blotches, which are reduced to narrow rings of deep reddish brown and separated from one another by contrasting interspaces of tan or yellow, are the most prominent. Dark spots randomly mark the yellow belly, mostly along its outer edges. The snake's relatively small head is somewhat pointed at the snout, often lightly speckled with black above, and may have a dark-bordered pale band across the

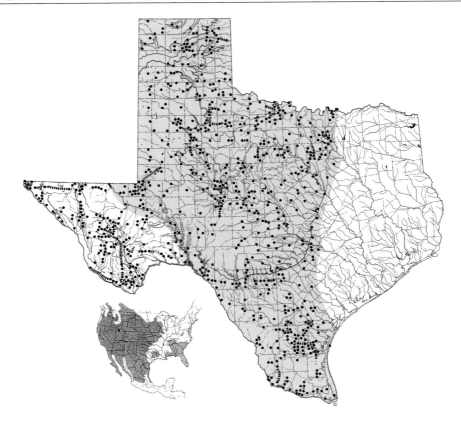

crown just ahead of the eyes. A dark band usually extends from each eye to the end of the mouthline.

Texas snakes of the genus *Pituophis* possess four prefrontal scales instead of the usual two, and the large scale on the end of the nose is vertically longer than in most other snakes. In the bull snake it is about twice as high as it is broad, reaching upward between the internasal scales. Moreover, it rises conspicuously above the adjacent scales, producing a distinct elevated vertical ridge on an otherwise smooth plane. The dorsal scales, usually in 33 rows at midbody but ranging from 28 to 37, are strongly keeled, except for those in the first several rows on either side of the belly. The anal plate is single.

COMPARABLE SNAKES Only in the genus *Pituophis* do we normally find four prefrontal scales on the forehead; all other Texas snakes ordinarily have but two. In the adult Texas rat snake the top of the head is uniformly dark, and that of the Great Plains and southwestern rat snakes bears a forward-directed spearpoint marking. In addition, all of these look-alikes have a divided anal plate. Glossy snakes have smooth dorsal scales and an unmarked belly. The prairie king snake also possesses smooth body scales but has fewer than 28 rows of midbody dorsal scales and dark markings on top of the head, which typically resemble a backward-pointing V.

Despite certain physical features that characterize the western diamond-backed rattlesnake (a heavy body and the presence of rattles on the end of its tail), the bull snake is often mistaken for that venomous pit viper. To the uninitiated, the two snakes may look alike, for broadly considered they have several features in common. One is the similarity in color and pattern, since both display a row of large, dark brown middorsal markings on a ground color of paler brown. In addition, both species are clad in strongly keeled scales. As a defensive response, each in its own way is able to produce a loud, menacing sound, the rattler by vibrating its noise-making caudal appendage and the bull snake by expelling air forcefully past a modified epiglottis in the bottom of its mouth. The similarity does not end there. Sufficiently provoked, the bull snake sometimes rears its forebody high off the ground and, like the rattler, flattens its head ominously before delivering a vigorous strike. Finally, the bull snake may rapidly shake its tail when threatened, a behavior sure to contribute to a mistaken identification.

Probably the best way to recognize a diamond-backed rattlesnake (in addition to its characteristic rattle) is to look for a boldly black-and-white-banded tail, the hallmark of this species. The bull snake, on the other hand, has a long, pointed, yellowish tail bearing reddish brown, ringlike blotches.

SIZE This is one of Texas' longest snakes, reaching a maximum known length of nearly 9 feet (274 cm). Average adults are usually between 4 and 5 feet (121.9–152.4 cm) long.

HABITAT This wide-ranging serpent typically inhabits sandy plains and prairies but is also abundant in other kinds of dry, open spaces, including the rocky, tree-studded country that dominates the Edwards Plateau, the gently rolling thorn scrub of the Rio Grande Plain, and the rocky hills and canyons of the Trans-Pecos, at both high and low elevations. In the Guadalupe Mountains, where some bull snakes live at exceptionally high elevations, a large specimen was captured in pine forest at an elevation of 9,000 feet (2,752 m) near the eastern rim of the plateau. Many more, however, live at or near sea level. Throughout its range, this serpent is decidedly partial to cultivated fields, where it finds an abundance of small mammals, its most important prey.

BEHAVIOR A sudden encounter with a large, angry bull snake in the wild can be an awesome, even frightening experience for the uninitiated. Almost everything about the reptile's defensive behavior looks or sounds menacing. As the snake raises its forebody a foot or more above the ground and draws it back into a sinister S-shaped striking posture, it may also flatten its head or inflate its neck with air. At the same time, it rapidly vibrates its tail, and if the motion occurs in dry vegetation, it often produces a rattlerlike buzzing noise. The most fearsome thing of all is the loud hissing that accompanies the

reptile's posturing. Created when the snake forces air through its windpipe and past a small vertical fin of cartilage near its opening, the vibrating noise is sustained through the partially open mouth with each prolonged exhalation. Surprisingly, the sound is loud enough to be heard up to 50 feet away. Another kind of hiss accompanies each strike. It is a sharper, more explosive sound than the other, and of brief duration; it has been compared to the hiss of a red-hot chunk of metal being dunked into cold water.

Despite the bull snake's remarkable capacity to create fear among the inexperienced, it is a rather slow-moving reptile whose first choice is to avoid man. Its threatening behavior, however frightening, is mostly bluff. Even the snake's energetic strike is intended more to intimidate than to cause physical harm. Although indeed large and capable of inflicting a nasty bite, the bull snake surely has never seriously injured a human.

It is without doubt one of the most proficient of all snake excavators. Its digging ability is matched by few other native serpent species. Even its close relative, the Sonoran gopher snake, is not as good a digger, although another close ally, the Louisiana pine snake, is. One of the reasons is revealed in a study by Knight (1986) comparing the skulls of some eastern and western subspecies of the genus *Pituophis* native to the United States. His results show that the skulls of the bull snake and the pine snakes (collectively the eastern group) are better structured to withstand the rigors of digging than are those of the western group, including the Sonoran gopher snake of western Texas. Simply stated, in bull snakes and pine snakes the bones in the snout region are shaped and arranged to form a butt joint, a configuration that increases skull rigidity, thereby reducing the stress on the delicate premaxillary and nasal bones, those most directly impacted by burrowing.

Just how a snake can dig up soil and move it more than a foot away from the excavation site without benefit of limbs is one of the more fascinating bits of serpent lore. A bull snake possesses a rather subtle but effective adaptation to deal with the task: a modified nose scale, tall and laterally compressed, that extends forward beyond the surrounding scales like a miniature shovel blade turned

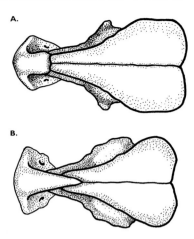

Figure 47. *Snout bone configurations of gopher snake species: (a) the more rigidly constructed butt joint of the bull and pine snakes, which is better adapted for burrowing than (b) the snout of the Sonoran gopher snake and its allies.*

sideways. Its function, like that of a spade or scraping tool, is to loosen and move sand and dirt.

As described by Carpenter (1982), the process begins when the snake pokes its head forcefully into the substrate a number of times to loosen the soil with a side-to-side rocking motion. When enough soil has been freed, the snake turns its head sharply to one side and gathers up the material in this neck flexure before pulling its body backward or sideward from the excavation site. During all of this, the rear two-thirds of the reptile's body remains in place to serve as an anchor. After the soil has been moved and deposited and the snake's neck is straightened again, the serpent returns to the hole to repeat the cycle. More digging is followed by more scooping, until the job is done. The entire process, which in a typical case took 23 minutes to complete, moved about 478 cubic inches (7,710 cubic cm) of sand from the excavation site to the dump pile, quite an achievement for an animal without arms or legs.

For its large size, this species travels only moderate distances when foraging. After tracking bull snakes fitted with miniature radio transmitters, Fitch and Shirer (1971) determined that in Kansas the serpents' daily movements averaged about 468½ feet. At

Crescent Lake National Wildlife Refuge in Nebraska, Fox (1986) reported home ranges of 10 to 42½ acres (4–17.2 ha).

Except on the hottest summer days, when it moves about after sundown, the bull snake is usually a day-active reptile. Relatively thick-bodied, it crawls rather slowly, reaching a top speed equal to that of a man walking at a brisk pace. Such a lethargic gait, together with its large size, makes the bull snake an easy target for its enemies, including man. Not only is it readily detected by humans in the wide-open spaces of its plains habitat, but because it tends to cross roads, it is also a frequent victim of vehicular traffic, suffering more casualties from this cause than most other West Texas serpents, with the possible exception of the western diamondbacked rattlesnake.

As would be expected, bull snakes living in South Texas have a longer active season than those inhabiting the more northern parts of the state. During especially mild days in midwinter they can sometimes be found above ground, basking in the sun. No matter where they reside, however, when temperatures drop to below freezing, bull snakes must find adequate shelter to survive. Those living in the vicinity of rocky hillsides usually hibernate in deep crevices below ground, often in company with other serpents, especially large species such as rattlesnakes and whipsnakes. In flatland prairies and other regions devoid of rocks, they generally spend the winter in the burrows of other animals. For example, in the Nebraska Sandhills, according to Fox, bull snakes are known to hibernate individually in pocket gopher burrows, usually in the chambers at the end of the tunnels at depths of 3.3 to 7.5 feet (average 5 feet). At this site, Fox found a bull snake and a yellow-bellied racer at each of four such winter dens and two bull snakes at a fifth. Three others contained only a single bull snake.

FEEDING The bull snake eats a wide variety of small mammals, including mice, rats, gophers, ground squirrels, and rabbits, although other prey species such as lizards and other snakes are occasionally consumed as well. Unlike most large serpents, this one apparently finds and catches most of its prey not by searching for it above ground but by actively raiding the subterranean tunnel systems and nests of burrowing mammals, a task for which it is eminently adapted. That this is the bull snake's preferred foraging style was underscored by Reynolds and Scott (1982). Working in northeastern Coahuila, Mexico, they found the reptile's principal food to be deer mice and Merriam's kangaroo rats, both active digging species. Surprisingly, the hispid cotton rat, another small rodent common in the study area, was never consumed by the snake, perhaps because it typically spends most of the daylight hours moving through the network of crisscrossing trails it makes above ground in its grassy habitat. Other small animals also occasionally devoured in the area included spotted ground squirrels, nestling and immature desert cottontail rabbits, and black-tailed jackrabbits.

Chiefly a destroyer of rodents, the bull snake also often demonstrates a keen appetite for birds and their eggs. Some specimens become so partial to an egg diet during the avian nesting season that they eat little else. Nowhere has this been documented more dramatically than in a report by Imler (1945) in which he described bull snake activities at Nebraska's Crescent Lake National Wildlife Refuge. During one year alone, bull snakes ate all of the eggs from 114 of 274 duck nests in the area and depleted the clutches of others. Similar depredations were reported by Glup and McDaniel (1988) at another wildlife refuge in the north-central portion of the Nebraska Sandhills. In 1985 and 1986 these snakes took 12.5 percent of the eggs from 249 mallard nests, 34 percent of the eggs from 426 blue-winged teal nests, and 33 percent of the eggs from 114 gadwall nests, sometimes even while the hens were still on the nest.

At another time and place, a bull snake is reported to have swallowed the entire clutch of eggs being laid by a box turtle, even before the female chelonian could finish the task of covering up her nest. Because of this egg-eating propensity, *P. c. sayi* is not often championed by man. Yet for every egg consumed, these efficient predators eat hundreds of rodents harmful to our interests. From the perspective of agricultural economics, its size and feeding habits make the bull snake one of man's best friends.

In its hunting endeavors, this reptile employs two methods to kill prey, both of which make use of the snake's muscular body. In one strategy, which can be applied most effectively above ground, the serpent seizes a large animal in its mouth before wrapping one or more powerful coils around its unfortunate victim. Thereafter, every movement of the struggling prey, however feeble, results in a further tightening of the snake's vicelike hold; in a very few minutes, death comes from circulatory arrest. Even for this strong predator, subduing large rodent prey is not entirely without risk. Armed with long, sharp incisor teeth, such victims, when given the opportunity, are quite capable of inflicting serious or even fatal injuries to their assailants. Bull snakes with unsightly scars or wounds on their bodies bear this out. On the other hand, smaller prey such as mice are usually held in the serpent's jaws without being constricted and are simply swallowed alive.

A different strategy is used to subdue prey encountered in animal burrows, since such confining underground spaces are generally much too narrow to permit the bull snake to coil about its prey. When a rodent is located inside a tunnel, the snake presses the mammal forcefully against the tunnel wall with a segment of its strong body; the unrelenting pressure finally causes death by circulatory arrest. The interesting thing is that more than one victim at a time may be dealt with in this way. Keenly sensitive to external stimuli, the serpent reacts instinctively whenever anything brushes against it, making it possible for the snake to subdue two or more rodents with as many separate flexures of its body.

REPRODUCTION Sexual maturity in this subspecies occurs at approximately 3 years of age. Thereafter, bull snakes mate annually sometime in late April or May, soon after they leave hibernation. About two months later, usually in June or July, the female lays her clutch of 3 to 22 adherent, granular-shelled eggs in loose soil beneath a rock or log, under leaf litter, or beneath piles of other vegetative debris. Approximately $2\frac{1}{4}$ inches (5.7 cm) long and among the largest eggs of any North American serpent, they incubate over the next 50 to 80 days, hatching in August or September. The hatchlings range in length from 11 to 19 inches (27.9–48.3 cm), but the average is about 15 inches (38.1 cm).

LOUISIANA PINE SNAKE

Pituophis ruthveni
PLATE 113

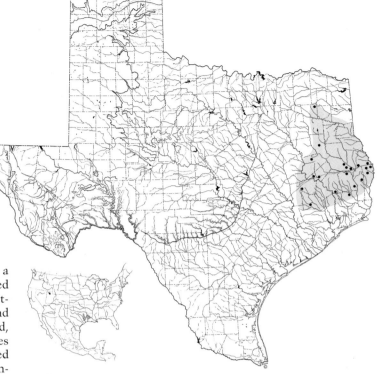

DESCRIPTION This is a large, relatively heavy-bodied snake with a brown, whitish, or even yellowish ground color. The closely spaced, dark brown dorsal blotches on its forebody are obscured by dark background pigmentation and are poorly defined. By contrast, the deep reddish brown blotches on the rear part of the body and on the tail are bolder and more widely separated, standing out conspicuously against the yellowish ground color. The smaller lateral blotches, at least in the neck region, tend to intermingle, often creating a continuous horizontal band or a series of intermittent dark streaks, whereas those on approximately the rear half of the body are large, well-defined, and broadly separated. Numerous small dark spots or splotches cover the crown, and in some specimens a narrow, usually indistinct dark bar crosses the head between the eyes. Marking the snake's belly are small, irregularly placed black splotches. The snake's rostral scale is longer than it is wide and raised slightly above the surrounding scales. Like all Texas snakes of the genus *Pituophis*, the Louisiana pine snake normally has four prefrontal scales on the forecrown. The dorsal scales are keeled and arranged in 27 to 33 rows at midbody. The anal plate is single.

COMPARABLE SNAKES The Texas rat snake, the only other large, blotched East Texas ser-

pent, has a uniformly dark crown and a divided anal plate. The corn snake, whose anal plate is also divided, has a dark forward-directed spearpoint mark on top of its head, a bold dark lengthwise stripe behind each eye, and two conspicuous parallel dark stripes under the tail. The prairie king snake, which is covered with smooth scales, likewise carries a bold, dark longitudinal stripe behind each eye. In none of these look-alikes are there more than two prefrontal scales on the forecrown.

SIZE Adults of this subspecies ordinarily are 4 to 5 feet (121.9–152.4 cm) long, but a specimen of maximum length measured 70½ inches (179.1 cm) long.

HABITAT A forest-dwelling *Pituophis*, the Louisiana pine snake is restricted largely to open longleaf pine–oak sandhills interspersed with moist bottomlands. It is sometimes also encountered in adjacent blackjack oak woodlands and in sandy areas of short-leaf pine–post oak forest. Unfortunately, intensive lumbering is eliminating large tracts of this reptile's habitat. Even before destruction of the serpent's prime habitat began in earnest during the 1920s, logging operations had already severely reduced significant portions of the original forests. What was happening in Louisiana was also occurring in Texas, where many areas of the native indigenous forest were being clear-cut and replaced with tree farms. This practice, which continues even today, has proved calamitous for the pine snake. Wherever such slash pine monoculture is substituted for the original longleaf pine forest, the newly created environment is unsuitable pine snake habitat, in spite of its natural woodland appearance. Indeed, such managed forests are of little use to many native wildlife species that once lived in the original woodland settings.

Additional reasons for the pine snake's decline include the frequent torching of grasslands within the snake's habitat and the expanding human population, with its attendant increase in snake-killing episodes, especially those directed at large, conspicuous species such as this one. There is no doubt that the ever-expanding vehicular traffic moving over more and more new highways and rural roads in East Texas is responsible as well for a reduction in pine snake numbers. Some alteration of the land, if it is not too severe, may actually improve the serpent's habitat. We know, for example, that the Louisiana pine snake prefers disturbed woodland over dense forest, for specimens have frequently been discovered in fields, farmland, and tracts of second-growth timber. Little else is known about its ecology.

The closely related northern pine snake, *P. melanoleucus*, whose ecology and behavior have been carefully studied by several herpetologists in the northernmost part of its geographic range, also exhibits a distinct preference for open woodlands. Although only 20 percent of the southern New Jersey study region examined by Zappalorti and Burger (1985) represented open, man-disturbed areas within the pine and pine-oak forests, a remarkable 88 percent of the Pine Barrens specimens were found there.

BEHAVIOR Like its close relative the bull snake, it often hisses loudly, spreads its head, and sometimes vibrates its tail when angry. Being a somewhat nervous creature, in the wild it may also strike when closely approached and perhaps even bite when first handled, although most specimens refrain from biting unless unduly provoked. To free itself from its captor, a large, wild-caught pine snake ordinarily thrashes about frantically. Under such circumstances, the strenuous writhing of its muscular body can be constrained only by gripping the reptile firmly with both hands.

Except for reports that Louisiana pine snakes have been found on dry, sandy ridges (usually near the entrances of animal burrows where they retreated when disturbed), almost nothing is known about the natural history of this rare *Pituophis*.

The northern pine snake, a species closely related to the Louisiana pine snake, ranges from the east-central part of the United States to as far north as the New Jersey Pine Barrens, where its ecology and behavior have been studied in detail by Burger and Zappalorti (1986, 1988, 1989, 1991, 1992), Zappalorti and Burger (1985), Zappalorti, Johnson, and Lesczynski (1983), and Zappalorti and Reinert (1994). Much of what they have learned about the natural history of that snake probably applies as well to the Louisiana pine snake, for the two serpents are morphologically very similar and their habitats much alike. We have therefore drawn freely from these reports to present a picture of pine snake ecology and life history, mindful that future field studies of *P. ruthveni* may reveal life history differences between these two closely related but geographically widely separated species.

This is a capable burrower, whose large and slightly protruding nose scale, like that of the Louisiana pine snake, is adapted for digging in sand and loose soil. With it the northern pine snake normally excavates its own summer retreats, hibernacula, and nest sites. The summer den, typically about 4 feet long, is a relatively simple structure. Usually located near a rotting log, its entryway initially follows an old decaying tree root into the ground. It normally consists of only one surface entrance and one or two underground chambers. In the New Jersey Pine Barrens study area, the accumulation of sand at the burrow entrance, called a dump pile, was evident in nearly half the serpents' observed summer refuges. Most snakes hibernate in a variety of natural sites, such as deep rock crevices, rock piles, abandoned animal burrows, ant mounds, and the decaying interiors of rotting logs and tree stumps, to mention just a few. Pine snakes, unlike other native serpent species (with the possible exception of the hog-nosed snake), apparently excavate their own underground winter dens in the sandy soil. The snake's hibernaculum is usually more complex than its summer den, though both are normally near an old rotting log or tree stump with at least one of the burrow entryways tracking a decomposed root shaft down into the soil. Not only is the winter refuge usually longer (average length 21 feet) than the summer shelter, but it also contains more side chambers (1 to 14, average 8) and its burrow entrances are more heavily shaded by plants and closer to trees. Northern pine snakes have been seen excavating tunnels in the sandy soil, but not often. Further confirmation of the serpent's burrowing behavior is provided by the frequency with which specimens have been dug from underground chambers whose entrance tunnels were too small in diameter to have been excavated by large animals; the structures also consisted of too many side tunnels to have been made by small mammals. It is significant that sand piles marking the entrances were similar to those left by female pine snakes after they had finished digging in sandy substrate. In addition, the burrow systems used by these reptiles contained neither the stored food nor the nesting debris usually deposited by small mammals in their underground shelters.

Except for hatchlings (which usually occupied winter den chambers with snakes their own size), most specimens were located individually in chambers off the main tunnel. When not secluded in an underground burrow, the northern pine snake was most frequently seen basking on dry, level surfaces like roadways, bare ground, or layers of pine needles, but it avoided wet surface material such as damp moss and moist decaying wood, just as it did dense vegetation. Its preference was for cleared fields and natural open areas within woodlands. Never was it observed above ground before 8:55 AM or after 8:20 PM.

FEEDING Almost nothing has been recorded about the feeding habits of this seldom seen species, but its diet probably is similar to that of other pine snakes, whose chief prey is small mammals. Birds and their eggs probably are also consumed by this reptile, and lizards may be a source of food for the young snakes. After seizing the animal in its jaws, the well-muscled serpent wraps one or more coils around its victim, applying ever greater pressure until its prey is dead.

REPRODUCTION Field observations of natural nest sites and egg-laying in the wild have not been reported for the Louisiana pine snake. The only bits of information we have about its reproductive biology are those provided by Gordon Henley (pers. com.) of Lufkin's Ellen Trout Zoo and Steven B. Reichling (1988, 1990) of the Memphis Zoo and Aquarium, both of whom recorded the results of captive breeding in this species.

Henley apparently was the first to breed this species in captivity. His initial success followed the observed mating of a pair of pine snakes on March 19, 1984, which resulted in

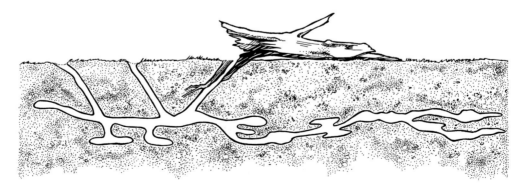

Figure 48. *Cross section of a winter den excavated by a northern pine snake in the New Jersey Pine Barrens. (After Burger et al. 1988)*

the female's laying of 4 eggs on May 18, one of which hatched on July 18 and another on July 24. During the next five years, pine snake matings at the Ellen Trout Zoo yielded 12 more eggs but produced only one viable hatchling. Despite this low hatching rate, Henley's efforts generated previously undocumented baseline reproductive data for this rare Texas species. His information shows that captive mating occurred from March 19 to March 26 and egg-laying from April 29 to May 18. The number of eggs per clutch ranged from 1 to 5, with an average of 4, and they measured a remarkable $4\frac{2}{3}$ inches (11.8 cm) long and nearly $1\frac{1}{3}$ inches (3.4 cm) in diameter. Incubation, which lasted 58 to 66 days, resulted in the hatching of young that measured $17\frac{1}{3}$ to 22 inches (44–55.9 cm) long, except for one abnormal hatchling whose length was only $12\frac{4}{5}$ inches (32.5 cm).

Reichling described ritualistic combat between two male Louisiana pine snakes placed together in the same enclosure, one of which later courted a female. Although no mating was witnessed between the two, the female laid 4 large eggs on May 26, 3 of which were infertile. The fourth egg hatched on July 15. Four more eggs were laid the following year, all of which hatched. The fertile eggs ranged in length from 4 to $5\frac{1}{2}$ inches (10.1–14 cm) and in width from $1\frac{1}{6}$ to $1\frac{1}{5}$ inches (2.9–3.1 cm). The hatchlings measured $20\frac{4}{5}$ to $22\frac{1}{5}$ inches (52.8–56.4 cm) long. According to Reichling, these figures indicate that Louisiana pine snake eggs are the largest of any U.S. serpent, but they represent the smallest number per clutch of any large snake found in this country.

Most egg-laying snake species simply deposit their eggs in or under decaying logs, under piles of plant debris, or in abandoned animal burrows. The female northern pine snake, at least in the New Jersey Pine Barrens, is the only serpent known to construct an underground chamber in which to lay her eggs. Such a chamber, at the end of a tunnel usually 5 to 6 feet (152.4–182.9 cm) long but sometimes nearly 8 feet (2.9 m) in length, normally is only 5 to 6 inches (12.7–15.2 cm) below the surface of the ground. In most cases, the tunnel first slants downward for a third to half of its length before sloping upward again, a design possibly calculated to prevent flooding of the chamber during heavy rainfall. Soon after the gravid female moves to the nest area in mid-June, she begins the search for a suitable spot in which to dig. The preferred location—a sandy or grassy clearing generally devoid of trees—guarantees that a maximum amount of sunlight reaches the ground each day, providing the necessary warmth for the developing eggs just below the surface.

Covered with moist, soft sand and containing few if any tree roots, such a site also offers suitable conditions for digging. Curiously, Burger and Zappalorti found most of the snake's egg-laying sites in man-made clearings, many near roads, railroad beds, and human habitations. One was discovered approximately 165 feet (50.5 m) from an occupied home, 3 others were within 330 feet (100 m) of heavily traveled paved roads, and 10 were less than 106 feet (32.3 m) from secondary roads, many of which were unpaved and infrequently used. To the degree that forest clearing is limited to small, fragmented sections of woodland, man's alteration of the northern pine snake's habitat may improve the serpents' chances of survival.

GRAHAM'S CRAYFISH SNAKE
Regina grahami
PLATES 114–117

DESCRIPTION Featuring a relatively small head that is but little wider than its neck, this small to medium-sized snake is olive, dark brown, or yellowish brown above. The most prominent features of coloration are the broad cream or yellowish stripes, one on either side of the body near the abdomen. Occupying the three lowest rows of dorsal scales, each is margined below by a narrow, zigzag pinstripe where it and the outer edges of the belly scales meet and often by a thread-like upper margin as well. Sometimes also

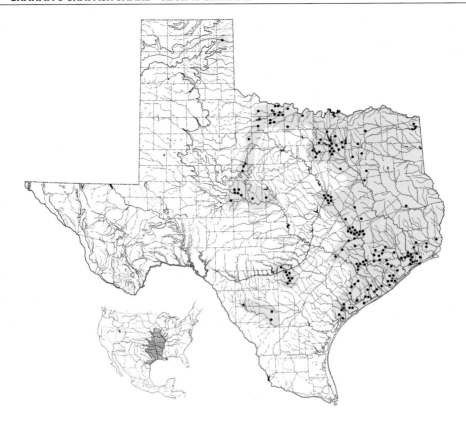

present along the midline of the back is a pale, often indistinct, dark-edged band. On the snake's cream or yellow abdomen may be a median row of very small black spots or, less often, none at all. When present, such spots sometimes unite to form a narrow, discontinuous, dark line. The top and sides of the head are the same dark hue as the upper body; the upper and lower lip scales and throat are the same color as the rest of the belly. The dorsal scales are keeled and in 19 rows at midbody; the anal plate is divided.

COMPARABLE SNAKES The Gulf crayfish snake has glossy instead of dull scales; a broad, light-colored band on each side of the body involving the first, or at most only the first and second, rows of dorsal scales above the belly; and a double row of large, dark, half-moon abdominal spots. The Gulf salt marsh snake, the only striped water snake of the genus *Nerodia* in Texas, is boldly patterned with a dark gray stripe on either side of the spine and another low on each side of the body. Furthermore, its dark-hued abdomen displays a central row of large, pale, oval spots

that may be flanked by two rows of darker ones, the lip scales are dark-edged, and the body scales are in more than 19 rows at midbody. Garter, ribbon, and lined snakes are also longitudinally striped, but they have a distinct, narrow, median light stripe, no row of dark spots down the middle of the abdomen, and a single anal plate.

SIZE Adults are usually between 18 inches and 28 inches (45.7–71 cm) long, but the species has a maximum known length of 47 inches (119.4 cm).

HABITAT Although generally distributed over much of central and eastern Texas, this

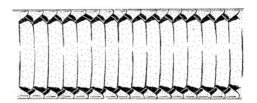

Figure 49. *Belly pattern of Graham's crayfish snake.*

serpent occurs primarily in isolated colonies throughout its geographic range. It favors still or slow-moving bodies of water such as ponds, sluggish streams, lakes, wet meadows, prairie marshes, swamps, and the still backwaters of floodplains, especially those with muddy bottoms and abundant aquatic shoreline vegetation where embankments support sizable crayfish colonies. Exceptions are the Graham's crayfish snakes found by R. F. Clark (1949) in northern Louisiana in and near small, fast-moving streams. In the more typical habitats of Louisiana's Atchafalaya River basin, Kofron (1978) collected 10 specimens in grassy areas, 2 in freshwater marshes, and 1 each in a bayou canal and in a bottomland forest.

Often prospering in the face of expanding human development, this adaptable serpent inhabits not only rice fields and freshwater canals but in the midst of large human populations also maintains its numbers by keeping to the natural shelter of sprawling urban parklands. One such concentration of crayfish snakes thrives to this day in Missouri's Forest Park, even though the park is encircled by extensive urban development. Another endures in San Antonio's Brackenridge Park, where the snake can still be found along that section of the San Antonio River and in one or two of the park's isolated ponds. Perhaps one reason the reptile so successfully avoids the throngs of visitors who constantly use its parkland habitat is the snake's secretive behavior.

BEHAVIOR Unlike most water snakes of the genus *Nerodia*, which strike out viciously and often unexpectedly when closely approached, Graham's crayfish snake is an inoffensive serpent that rarely bites, even when restrained. Without ever using its teeth defensively, it manages to discourage a human adversary by twisting its tail and the rear part of its body around a restraining hand while releasing feces from its cloacal opening. The offensive odor, plus the feel of the slimy substance on one's skin, is often enough to gain the serpent its release.

At the northern end of its geographic range, it generally moves about from mid-April to late September or early October. In the coastal regions of Texas and Louisiana, provided winter temperatures remain moderate, it can sometimes be found above ground even

in December, January, and February, basking in the warm midday sun. In their study of water snake behavior in southern Louisiana, Mushinsky, Hebrard, and Walley (1980) found that in March, when this species reached its greatest abundance, it was primarily a day-active, basking reptile, but in April and May it was out in the open both by day and at night. During the rest of the year, it was seldom encountered.

Since a snake maintains almost no metabolic control over its own body temperature and because it cannot generate its own internal heat through physiological activity, it must receive such heat from its surroundings. Thus in spring and again in the fall when nighttime temperatures are cool, Graham's crayfish snake is day-active, basking in the sun to elevate its body temperature to a comfortable level. This it does by crawling into bushes or low tree branches overhanging the water, where, in addition to exposing itself to the radiant solar heat, it also takes advantage of the elevated station to watch for intruders. Piles of plant debris, logs, and rock piles are used for the same purpose. In this regard, Mushinsky and his coworkers found Graham's crayfish snake to be the most arboreal of the five water-dwelling snake species inhabiting a southern Louisiana swamp.

For the snake to maintain an acceptable comfort level year-round, it must alter its daily routine in response to the changing seasons. During midsummer, when direct exposure to the midday sun can elevate the reptile's body temperature to critically high levels, the snake spends most of the daylight hours under logs, rocks, and brush piles or in crayfish burrows. It has also been discovered in the depressions of rotting logs and in aquatic vegetation raked out of small ponds. Near Waco, Strecker (1926a) found young specimens among piles of drift material or beneath stones and boards at water's edge, where up to four or five snakes were sometimes encountered together under a single sheltering object. In the evening, when the daytime summer heat has subsided, the snake leaves the thermal protection of its shelter to begin its nocturnal wanderings. In the fall, the return of cool evenings prompts the serpent to return to a daytime mode of basking and prowling. Soon after the first chill of autumn, the snake ceases all surface activity

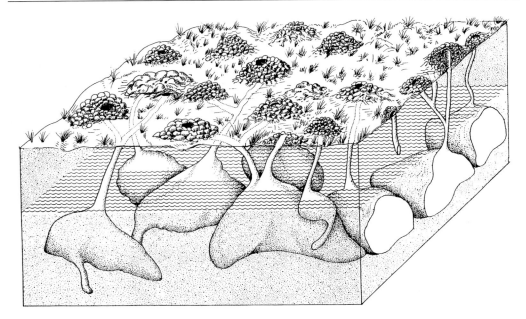

Figure 50. *Crayfish burrow system of* Fallicambarus (F.) devastator. *(After Hobbs and Whiteman 1991.)*

and moves into its winter shelter, which usually consists of decaying logs and stumps, thick masses of vegetative debris, and probably also crayfish burrows.

Just as mammal and tortoise burrows provide convenient summer and winter shelters for many snake species in arid regions, crayfish domiciles serve a similar function for a number of small to moderate-sized serpents in more moist environments. Documented reports of snakes inhabiting such burrows are numerous, suggesting that the tunnel systems make excellent ophidian retreats. According to Hobbs and Whiteman (1991), most of the underground crayfish dwellings they observed in east-central Texas were excavated by the species *Fallicambarus devastator*, whose subterranean chambers were the largest of several kinds of crayfish inhabiting the region, making them choice retreats for all but the biggest snakes. Not only are these subterranean galleries spacious, but they also contain sufficient moisture to prevent desiccation of the serpents during hibernation.

Nothing is known about the snake's daily movements. The only available bit of information about the subject comes from a study by R. J. Hall (1969), who after marking and releasing 14 Graham's crayfish snakes back to

the wild recaptured only 3. One was found three days later in the same pool where it had first been released, and eight or nine months after they had been set free two others were located in a pond adjacent to the one originally inhabited. In any case, none of the snakes had wandered more than 1,940 feet (591 m) from the spot where it was first liberated, suggesting that this species ordinarily does not travel great distances.

That the snake is an efficient burrower was confirmed by Kofron and Dixon (1980), who observed a captive specimen excavating tunnels in the loose soil of its enclosure, both in and out of the water; the burrows ended in a chamber beneath the water's surface. While it lay coiled in the submerged chamber, the snake breathed by occasionally poking just the tip of its head out of the water, with only its eyes and nostrils showing. Between breathing episodes, the snake remained submerged for 5 to 46 minutes.

FEEDING Unlike water snakes of the genus *Nerodia*, whose diet consists largely of fish and amphibians, this species eats primarily crayfish. Fish, small frogs, prawns, snails, and slugs are also consumed but usually only when its preferred prey is unavailable. Among the earliest feeding observations are those of Strecker (1926a), who saw Gulf crayfish snakes in a Texas lagoon feeding exclusively on crayfish, which were abundant in the waterway. In another stream habitat containing no crayfish, the snakes ate only minnows and cricket frogs. Likewise, R. F. Clark (1949) and Liner (1954), reporting on two widely separated regions of Louisiana, found that this species consumed only fish. On rare occasions it may deviate even further in its prey selection, as noted by Strecker, who observed crayfish snakes near Waco eating a species of small freshwater prawn. Although most zoologists have reported crayfish as the sole or predominant item in the snake's diet, Behler and King (1979) also mentioned snails and slugs as prey.

Burghardt (1968) conducted a study that clearly demonstrated the snake's fondness for crayfish. Placing several different potential prey animals (fish, earthworms, amphibians, slugs, crickets, baby mice, and crayfish) in separate containers of distilled water for a short time, he produced a liquid extract from each that was applied to a cotton swab and placed close to the test snakes. Though showing only a cursory interest in several of the sample odors, the snakes reacted strongly only to the crayfish extract, particularly to that of the newly molted crustaceans, which incidentally was the only one physically attacked in a feeding response. It is worth noting that since the snakes used in the experiment were all newborn individuals, which prior to the test had never experienced a meal, they could not have been familiar with any of the test odors. Although crayfish are ordinarily abundant in most areas inhabited by Graham's crayfish snake, the soft-shelled individuals preferred by this species are not always readily available. As explained by Godley, McDiarmid, and Rojas (1984), the various species of crayfish (of which there are many) molt 1 to 12 times annually. Of the three species living within the range of the snake and included in the study, all molted at about the same time, indicating that on average for the year less than 15 percent of any crayfish population consists of freshly molted specimens, those forming the bulk of the snake's diet.

To locate its prey, the serpent uses several different foraging strategies. According to Strecker, one is to lie in wait in a crayfish tunnel, with only its head and part of its forebody outside the chimney, until the unsuspecting prey comes close enough to be seized. In another, the snake simply crawls into a burrow to find and devour the crayfish hiding within. In a third strategy, the reptile prowls out in the open until it encounters its prey. It has also been suggested by Godley and his coworkers that most crayfish are attacked within six hours of their early molt stage, while they are still soft-shelled, defenseless, and easy to manipulate. Once seized, the victim is quickly swallowed, either head first or tail first (unlike the tail-first-only ingestion strategy practiced by the striped crayfish snake, a closely related serpent from Florida and southern Georgia). One to four crayfish were found in the stomachs of individual Graham's. In two instances, only a single large pincer was discovered in a snake's stomach, suggesting that in such cases the victim was probably too big to subdue, and during the ensuing struggle the pincer was wrenched from the crustacean's body.

REPRODUCTION The male of this species is believed to become sexually mature after his first year of life, whereas the female is capable of breeding only after her third year. Courtship can be an unusual affair. On occasion it involves not one but two or more males, all of whom swim about excitedly as they search for a mate. If there is just one female in the immediate vicinity, all the males will seek her out, attracted to the chemical odor she emits during the breeding season. When they finally come together, the males intertwine their bodies with that of the female, forming a rather compact bundle of coils as each male attempts copulation.

Mating usually occurs in April or May and generally produces young between late July and mid-August, although we have a record of a female from Elm Creek in Runnels County that gave birth to 10 young on September 3. The newborn snakes, 6 to 39 per litter (average 16 to 18), are between 7 and 10 inches (17.8–25.4 cm) long. They are similar to the adults in coloration, but with more distinct stripes.

Along a small tributary of the Brazos River near Waco, Strecker observed so many gravid females in dry, abandoned crayfish chimneys that he concluded such tunnels were a normal hideaway for Graham's crayfish snakes heavy with young. As a matter of fact, the snake's entire life history is intimately associated with the crustacean domiciles. Not only do the gravid females utilize them as a refuge from predators, but also individuals of both sexes enter the tunnels for protection from summer heat and winter frost and as a place to search for crayfish, their chief prey.

GULF CRAYFISH SNAKE
Regina rigida sinicola
PLATE 118

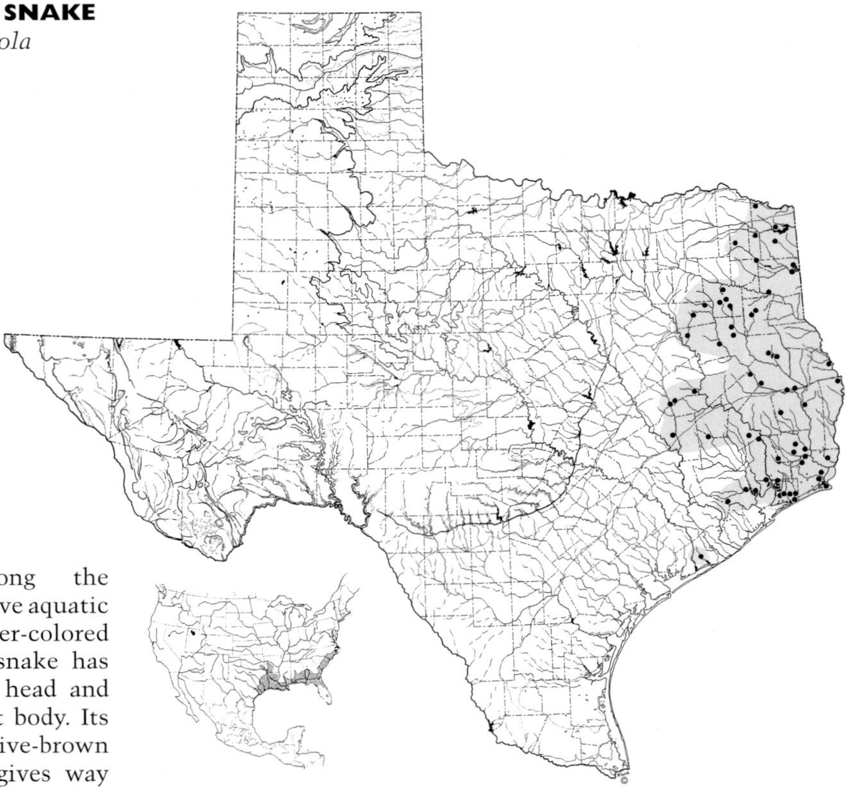

DESCRIPTION Among the smallest of our native aquatic serpents, this somber-colored but glossy water snake has a relatively small head and a moderately stout body. Its overall brown or olive-brown dorsal coloration gives way to a tan hue low on the sides. An inconspicuous dark stripe is frequently visible on either side of the spine, and along the first or first and second rows of dorsal scales above the abdomen, a tan stripe extends the length of the snake's body. Below it, a zigzag pinstripe creates a delicate black seam between the lowest row of dorsal scales and the belly plates. Some Texas specimens are so dark that not even the ordinarily discernible lateral bands are visible; even in such dingy snakes the most conspicuous markings are those on the belly, consisting of two lengthwise rows of bold, blackish spots, large and half-moon shaped, which extend down the center of the cream-colored abdomen to the base of the tail. Occasionally such crescents are so closely spaced that they appear as two parallel dark stripes with scalloped edges. The tail is usually marked with a single median, sometimes discontinuous, narrow dark stripe. The top and sides of the head are the same dark tone as the body, but the upper and lower lip scales are yellowish and unmarked. The dorsal scales, of which all but the lowest rows are keeled, occur in 19 rows at midbody, and the anal plate is divided.

COMPARABLE SNAKES This species and Graham's crayfish snake look much alike. They are approximately the same size, with small heads and a brownish dorsal coloration. Although both exhibit a pale-colored stripe on either side of the body near the belly, that of Graham's crayfish snake involves the first three scale rows above the abdomen, whereas in the Gulf crayfish snake it covers only the first or first and second rows. The most conspicuous difference between them is in their belly markings. In Graham's crayfish snake the abdomen is either unspotted or (most often) patterned with a single median row of small black spots. The Gulf crayfish snake's belly is marked with two parallel rows of large dark spots, usually half-moons, which extend down the length of the abdomen. In the lengthwise-striped Gulf salt marsh snake, a single median row of large, pale oval spots, often sandwiched between two rows of darker ones, marks the length of the snake's dark brown or reddish brown belly, and the dorsal scales are in more than 19 rows at midbody. Garter, ribbon, and lined snakes, although also longitudinally striped, have a distinct narrow pale stripe along the spine, and their anal plate is single.

SIZE Adults of this subspecies are usually under 2 feet (61 cm) long. The largest recorded specimen measured $31\frac{3}{8}$ inches (79.7 cm) in length.

HABITAT One of Texas' most elusive and little-known serpents, this highly aquatic reptile generally inhabits the margins of swamps, marshes, lakes, ponds, streams, sloughs, and freshwater tidal marshes, but most any quiet body of water will do, provided it has a muddy bottom and supports some form of vegetative shoreline debris in or under which the snake can hide. Sometimes it even occupies canals, ditches, and rice fields. In a departure from its usual preference for low-lying habitats, specimens collected by R. F. Clark (1949) in north-central Louisiana were found in small streams in upland sandjack oak woodland. Kofron (1978), on the other hand, encountered it in the following central Louisiana habitats: five in grasses, one in a bayou canal, one in bottomland forest, and one in a miscellaneous unidentified habitat.

BEHAVIOR If approached as it perches on a limb overhanging a pond or stream, the snake

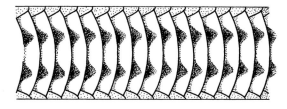

Figure 51. *Belly pattern of the Gulf crayfish snake.*

immediately drops into the water and swims to the bottom, where it conceals itself in the accumulation of decaying plant debris. When confronted on land and unable to escape, the same snake is likely to flatten its head and body in a threatening gesture, relying on its intimidating behavior to forestall an opponent's attack. It seldom bites, even if picked up or otherwise restrained. Its typical response to being handled is to discharge the offensive-smelling contents of its scent glands while evacuating a considerable amount of excreta from its cloacal opening, which it then tries to smear over its captor's hand by squirming—reason enough to give the snake its freedom.

The Gulf crayfish snake spends the daylight hours hiding in stumps and fallen tree trunks, under loose tree bark near the ground, in crayfish chimneys, or in emergent aquatic vegetation. It has also been found under logs, stones, or other debris, natural and man-made, that rests in or near the water. When the snake is uncovered by turning over such an object, it may not be immediately visible, since it often remains partly or completely concealed in the soft mud on which the sheltering object rested. Strecker (1926a), one of Texas' pioneer herpetologists, probably was the first naturalist to report this particular habitat niche. In De Soto Parish, Louisiana, some 20 miles from the Texas border, he located seven Gulf crayfish snakes under boards lying partly in water and partly in mud, but it was only after he used a stick to stir the muck beneath the boards that the serpents became visible. R. F. Clark found it in somewhat similar circumstances. All of the 18 specimens he collected in north-central Louisiana were discovered in small, flowing streams, the majority as they lay partially concealed beneath submerged logs or tree bark. The space between the trunk and the bark of dead trees or stumps, especially those standing in water near shore, represents one of the snake's preferred shelters. In Louisiana's Atchafalaya River basin, Kofron discovered a young specimen under wooden debris at the base of a levee, another under general debris, a third as it rested among water hyacinths by day, and a fourth in the grass of a levee. Three more were captured on a June night crossing a highway, and one was collected after dark in a bayou. Wright and

Wright (1957), using a fish seine, collected it in rice fields and open marshes. In Georgia, Neill (in Wright and Wright 1957) found it in layers of pine needles that had accumulated in the water near the shoreline of shallow pools.

Reported as active from March through October, it may also be encountered along the Gulf Coast in midwinter whenever the temperature is moderate enough. Except late in the evening and at night, when it may be seen crossing roads that pass through appropriate habitat, particularly after drenching rains, it is seldom observed out in the open. Indeed, the greatest number of specimens ever observed at one time, according to Wright and Wright, were the several dozen individuals (perhaps as many as 70 or 80) collected by E. B. Chamberlain in an area of South Carolina following a severe flood.

FEEDING Although the Gulf crayfish snake occasionally consumes fish, sirens, frogs, dragonfly nymphs, and other aquatic insect larvae, its chief prey consists of crayfish, which it seizes and ingests with the aid of sturdy, chisellike teeth that apparently are specially adapted for dealing with hard-shelled invertebrates. Rojas and Godley (1979) concluded that besides being sturdy, the snake's teeth are hinged at the base and operate in a ratchetlike fashion to assist in pulling prey into the mouth.

Kofron found that of 37 Gulf crayfish snakes from south-central Louisiana with food in their stomachs, all but 2 contained crayfish. Three of the ingested crustaceans were hard-shelled individuals, dispelling the notion held by some that only recently molted crayfish, with their more vulnerable soft exoskeletons, are devoured. Being too small to eat such prey, the infant snakes apparently limit their diet to dragonfly nymphs and similar aquatic insect larvae.

REPRODUCTION Not much information is available about the reproductive biology of this species, except that in the southern part of the snake's range the female ovulates in May or early June, mates in the spring, and gives birth to 6 to 14 young per litter in August or September. The newborn snakes, between $7\frac{1}{4}$ and 8 inches (18.4–20.3 cm) long, are generally patterned and colored like the adults, except for a more pinkish hue on the belly.

TEXAS LONG-NOSED SNAKE
Rhinocheilus lecontei tessellatus
PLATES 119–123

DESCRIPTION This is an attractive snake with a colorful and complex pattern: its black, yellow-edged, dorsal saddles alternate with bright red or orange interspaces, the lateral extensions of the saddles becoming progressively narrower until they end in blunt points near the belly. The snake's distinctly speckled look results from the liberal distribution of small spots, both cream-colored and black, that dominate the sides of the body and obscure the main pattern elements. Pale dots center the black scales, and dark spots occupy the red ones. Only along the middle of the back are the saddles unicolored. An irregular, vertical black spot usually occurs low on the sides of the body between the dark saddles, occasionally reaching the outer edge of the white or yellowish belly, though the snake's underside is generally unmarked. The serpent's predominately black head, tipped with a long, pointed, slightly upward-tilting red or pink snout, is speckled with small yellow spots.

In South Texas specimens the black and red dorsal markings generally take the form of squarish blotches that fail to reach the heavily black-spotted, yellow lower sides of the body. A variation has been reported from several scattered West Texas locations, including southwest Irion County and the Rio Grande region of the Big Bend. In this faded version, the ground color is white or pale gray, and the red markings, which in most other populations take on a vivid scarlet hue, are reduced to pale orange speckles or to long, pale orange blotches. In addition, the small, black dorsal saddles are often hour-glass shapes confined to the middorsal region.

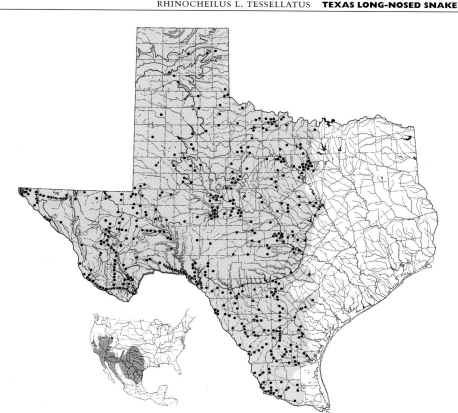

The smooth dorsal scales are arranged in 23 rows at midbody, and the anal plate is single. The long-nosed snake's most distinctive feature of scalation occurs on the underside of its tail; among Texas nonvenomous snakes, this is the only species with most of its undertail scales in a single row.

COMPARABLE SNAKES The coral snake can be distinguished from the long-nosed snake by the extension of the well-defined dorsal pattern across the belly, the solid black nose, the 15 rows of dorsal scales, and the divided anal plate. The Texas scarlet snake's red, black-edged saddles are essentially devoid of yellow speckling, as are the black rings of milk snakes. Finally, in none of these mimics are the scales on the underside of the tail mostly in a single row.

SIZE Although the snake's maximum known length is 41 inches (104.1 cm), the usual adult size is between 20 and 30 inches (50.8–76.2 cm) long.

HABITAT Found over the entire western two-thirds of Texas, this subspecies occupies a variety of dry habitats with sandy to grav-elly soils in prairie grassland, thornbrush, or desert. It also occurs on rocky slopes at low to moderate elevations. Specific habitat descriptions include those of Fouquette and Lindsay (1955), who collected it from the area of deep sands in Hutchinson County (the northern Panhandle), in both the floodplain and rocky slopes, and above the rimrock in Dawson County (the southern Panhandle), where the dominant flora were mesquite, grama and buffalo grass, plus some other small woody plant species. In Bexar and adjacent counties, Vermersch and Kuntz (1986) remarked that it generally occupies areas dominated by mesquite, acacia, prickly pear cactus, and low thornbrush; that it occasionally inhabits oak-hackberry woodland where the soil is sandy; and that it prefers loamy, organically fortified soils. In an early survey of Stockton Plateau amphibians and reptiles, Milstead and his colleagues (1950) described the snake's Terrell County habitat as the mesquite-creosote association. Jameson and Flury (1949) encountered it in southwestern Texas in the catclaw-grama and catclaw-tobosa associations within the Sierra Vieja Mountains of northwestern Presidio County.

Only occasionally is the long-nosed snake found in barren desert. Aside from its burrowing ability, it apparently is poorly equipped to survive in a harsh desert environment unless the land has first been made permeable by irrigation farming.

BEHAVIOR This shy, docile snake rarely bites in self-defense. Armed with small teeth, it is ill-equipped to fight off a larger adversary, especially one the size of man. So its chief defense lies in a repertoire of deceptive tactics that when used separately or together during a single encounter may cause its foe to halt an attack, at least momentarily, thus allowing the snake a brief opportunity to seek shelter. Some of these actions are also intended to misdirect the aggressor's assault.

One approach is for the snake to tuck its head beneath its own body coils, as its tail, held slightly elevated and perhaps even curled, is moved slowly about to attract the enemy's attention. Conceivably this can serve two purposes. On the one hand, a timid predator, unsure of the raised caudal member, may mistake it for the serpent's head primed to strike. A more likely explanation is that it directs the enemy's attack to the animated tail and away from the snake's more vital head. Another tactic involves a continuous, rapid coiling and uncoiling, twisting, or even thrashing of the body. When performed by banded snakes like this one, it gives the illusion of a larger-than-life serpent while also unnerving the opponent with its intensity. Some long-nosed snakes (probably the more nervous ones) vibrate their tails when danger threatens, creating a brief but steady cadence that sounds like a buzzing rattlesnake if the tail beats against ground litter. The value of such behavior is self-evident.

A long-nosed snake held in the hand for the first time has a surprise for its captor. As it twists and turns to escape, its cloaca and the paired scent glands at the base of its tail release a disgusting mixture of feces and musk, which the snake's writhing smears over itself and the restraining hand. Some long-nosed snakes add a discharge of blood from the nostrils as well as from the cloacal opening, apparently in much the same way that a severely stressed horned lizard squirts blood from the corner of its eye. Zoologists have not interpreted such behavior, but a possible explanation is that the sight of blood increases the apprehension and confusion in a captor already confounded by the snake's complex suite of deceptive tactics. Curiously, McCoy and Gehlbach (1967), the first herpetologists to report this bizarre behavior in long-nosed snakes, observed it only in females.

More cold-tolerant than many other local snake species, it normally makes its first appearance sometime in late April, at least in the southern half of the state, although following an unusually mild winter it will emerge a week or two earlier. Klauber (1941) noted that in southern California individuals of this species could be found in the open when the air temperature was as low as 59 degrees F. On one cool night when it was apparently too cold for any other snakes to be out, he watched as a gusty wind blew a long-nosed snake completely across a desert highway. Nevertheless, most individuals of this species were encountered from 7:00 PM to 11:30 PM, usually in May, when temperatures ranged between 62 degrees and 87 degrees F.

Except for infrequent daytime trips above ground, it hides below the soil surface until dusk. It is sometimes accidentally uncovered there during the day by farmers and others who plow up the land. In its underground movements, the snake's burrowing efforts are aided by its sharply pointed snout, while its countersunk lower jaw prevents loose sand from entering the mouth. It may likewise pass the day in the burrows of other animals, in crevices below the ground, and even among rocks or in deep layers of surface debris. By late September, the end of its active season, the long-nosed snake will have retreated to an underground shelter to hibernate.

FEEDING Like so many other aridland serpents, the long-nosed snake preys on a variety of terrestrial lizards that abound in its semidesert environment, ones that can be easily detected at night by their scent as they sleep beneath the sand or within a rock crevice. With its sharp snout, the snake digs into the substrate to reach its unsuspecting victim, or simply pulls it from a fissure. Since its lacertilian prey (earless, race runner, whiptail, desert side-blotched, and spiny lizards) are keenly alert and remarkably fast, daytime lizard hunting is not a reasonable alternative for this relatively lethargic serpent. Lizard eggs are consumed as well, and one report confirms that a female long-nosed snake ingested some of her own eggs. This opportunistic feeder devours small snakes as well and sometimes also insects and centipedes. Despite its modest size, it does not hesitate to scoop up small mammals, wrapping them tightly in its coils until they are subdued enough to be swallowed. Fouquette and Lindsay reported that in the Texas Panhandle one of these snakes ate a pocket mouse and another consumed a kangaroo rat.

REPRODUCTION Mating, which occurs in the spring, results in the deposition of egg clutches anytime during a span of more than two months, leading Fitch (1970) to conclude that a single female may produce more than one clutch per season. Laid below the soil surface sometime between mid-June and mid-August, the 4 to 9 eggs (average 6 per clutch) are $1^{3}/_{8}$ inches (3.5 cm) long. Hatching 2 to $2^{1}/_{2}$ months later, the young are 7 to 10 inches (17.8–25.4 cm) long. They do not have the extensive lateral speckling of the adult, nor is there much if any red in their overall coloration. Instead, the infant, which is generally paler than the adult, is crossed dorsally with more or less solid, black and yellow (or whitish) banding. The end of its snout is yellow and the neck collar is orange.

BIG BEND PATCH-NOSED SNAKE
Salvadora deserticola
PLATE 124

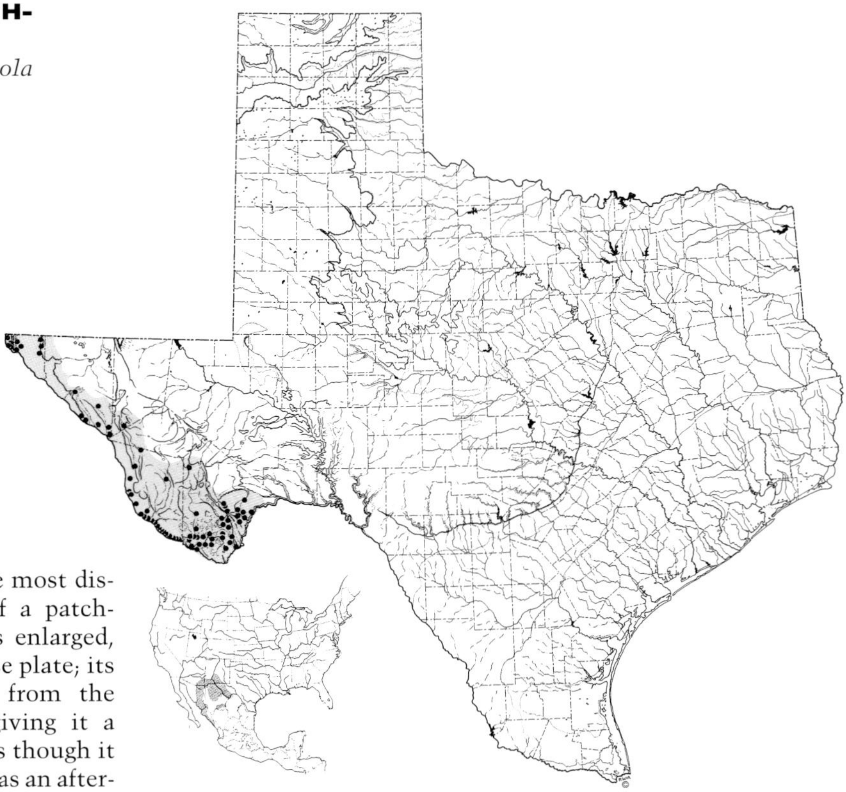

DESCRIPTION The most distinctive feature of a patch-nosed snake is its enlarged, laterally flared nose plate; its edges stand free from the adjacent scales, giving it a patchwork look, as though it had been attached as an afterthought. All snakes of this genus in the United States are longitudinally striped. In this species, a tan, yellowish, or brownish orange band about three scale rows wide extends down the center of the snake's back and is flanked by slightly narrower black or dark brown stripes on scale rows 6 and 7, whose upper and lower edges often form zigzag borders. Below these markings, where the body hue changes to light gray, a dark line, barely one scale wide, runs along

A.

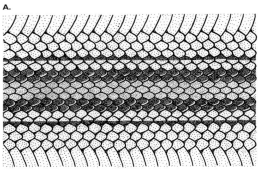

C.

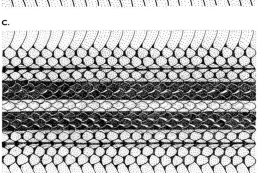

B.

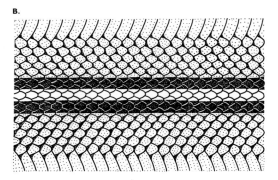

Figure 52. *Dorsal body patterns of (a) the Big Bend patch-nosed snake, (b) the mountain patch-nosed snake, and (c) the Texas patch-nosed snake.*

the fourth scale row above the abdomen, at least at midbody. The belly, which may be plain off-white, is usually tinted with a pale orange blush, especially toward the tail. The dorsal scales are smooth and in 17 midbody rows. The anal plate is divided. Two or three small scales separate the rear pair of chin shields, and there are usually nine upper lip plates on either side of the head.

COMPARABLE SNAKES   The mountain patch-nosed snake rarely has a thin dark line on each side of its body, but when such a stripe is present, it lies along the third row of dorsal scales and not the fourth. Its rear chin shields are separated by only a single small scale. Besides the absence of an enlarged nose plate, all garter and ribbon snakes within the range of the Big Bend patch-nosed snake can be distinguished by their keeled body scales, single anal plate, and greater number of dorsal scale rows (19 or 21). The Central Texas whipsnake has a dark instead of pale mid-dorsal band (which is flanked by broken, pale stripes), a pale crossband or two pale blotches on the back of its head, and 15 (not 17) rows of dorsal scales at midbody. Furthermore, its nose scale is not enlarged.

SIZE   Adults are usually between 24 and 32 inches (61–81.3 cm) in length. The largest known specimen measured 40 inches (101.6 cm) long.

HABITAT   Essentially a serpent of desert scrub flatlands, desert valley hillsides, and the lower, rocky slopes of foothills and mesas, the Big Bend patch-nosed snake also commonly occupies the dry, mesquite-lined washes and rocky gorges that cut through such habitats at higher elevations. It is frequently encountered as well along terraces just above the Rio Grande. Jameson and Flury (1949), whose pioneer studies in Presidio County provided the first meaningful ecological picture of the reptile and amphibian fauna of the Sierra Vieja Mountains, collected this species mainly in the plains belt, where one was taken from the catclaw-tobosa plant association, one from the tobosa-grama grassland community, and two from the creosote-catclaw-blackbrush association. Of two others found in the roughland belt, one was discovered in a streambed and the other in a huisache-lechuguilla plant community. Whatever the habitat, the snake occupies areas with sandy or gravelly soils.

BEHAVIOR Like its close relatives the racers and whipsnakes, this nimble, fast-moving reptile is capable of exerting a sudden burst of speed that can quickly take it out of harm's reach. It can also elude a pursuer by dodging and turning or by suddenly changing direction, even as it glides forward at top speed. A captured patch-nosed snake does not always submit gracefully. An occasional specimen will refrain from biting under such circumstances, but chances are the snake will respond by nipping the handler, although it clearly does not react with the same hostility as its racer and whipsnake cousins, whose vicious response to being picked up is well known to snake collectors.

Spurred by an unusual tolerance for hot weather, the snake frequently remains active during the middle of the day when the high temperatures have become unbearable for most other desert-dwelling serpents. Such thermal tolerance has its limits, however, for like all snakes, the patch-nosed snake cannot endure prolonged exposure to extreme solar radiation. During midsummer, when daytime temperatures regularly soar past 100 degrees F, it is compelled to seek relief in some shady spot, limiting its foraging activities chiefly to the hours of early morning and late evening. Large rocks, animal burrows, and the decayed root channels of desert plants provide satisfactory daytime refuges, the same kinds of shelter it uses to guard against the chill of night. Texas specimens have been collected in every month but February, their midwinter appearances being limited to unseasonably warm days.

Although it is adapted to scooping loose sand with its curiously enlarged and flared nose scale, the patch-nosed snake is not considered a true tunneling species in the same class as such accomplished excavators as bull, glossy, and hog-nosed snakes, with which it coexists in the same arid environment. Just how proficient it may be as a burrower is still open to question. According to Schmidt and Davis (1941), the patch-nosed snake has been observed to poke its head into the sand to loosen the substrate, and then, using a crook of its neck as a scoop, pull a small quantity of the material away from the new cavity. Repeated many times, this digging action can result in the excavation of a shallow depression in the loose ground, but there is no confirmation, borne out by direct observation, that the snake can dig deep tunnels in the soil such as those created by certain other burrowing desert serpents. In its usual daytime pursuits it is chiefly a ground-dweller, although it can sometimes be found in the branches of low-lying desert shrubs.

FEEDING In typical patchnose fashion, this snake subsists to a large extent on the abundant lizard prey that inhabits the desert, pursuing such quarry on days when other lacertilian-eating serpents, unable to endure the high temperatures, lie hidden in some shady nook until the midday heat has abated. Since no detailed study of its food habits has been made, it is not known which lizard species rank highest on its menu. Those that are most numerous, provided they are also of suitable size and easily captured, are probably the ones most commonly devoured. Dunham (1981) suggests that *S. deserticola*, a common resident of the Grapevine Hills in Big Bend National Park, represents one of the area's important predators of tree and canyon lizards, both abundant lacertilian species in the region's lechuguilla-creosote-cactus plant community.

The serpent is also adept at finding and uprooting lizard and snake eggs from nest chambers in sand or soil a few inches below the surface (they are uncovered by the reptile's previously described digging behavior). Indeed, there are those who contend that the snake's enlarged and laterally flared nose scale is specifically adapted to this task and is not used as a tunneling device. Curiously, the Big Bend patch-nosed snake does not generally eat the eggs of its own kind; according to Shaw and Campbell (1974), they are accompanied by a special pheromone, deposited by the laying female, which discourages other patch-nosed snakes from consuming them. Small mammals are frequently eaten as well, and even small snakes are not safe from this predator.

REPRODUCTION Actual breeding dates are unknown, though mating probably occurs in spring and early summer, after which 5 to 10 eggs per clutch are laid in June, July, or August. Hatching in late summer, the young are patterned like the adults and measure between 9 and 10 inches (22.9–25.4 cm) long.

MOUNTAIN PATCH-NOSED SNAKE

Salvadora grahamiae grahamiae

PLATE 125

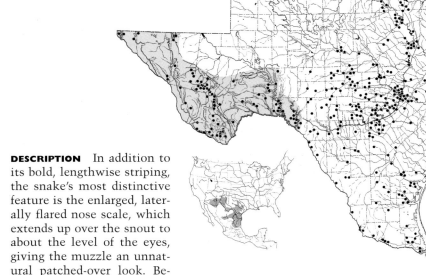

DESCRIPTION In addition to its bold, lengthwise striping, the snake's most distinctive feature is the enlarged, laterally flared nose scale, which extends up over the snout to about the level of the eyes, giving the muzzle an unnatural patched-over look. Between two dark brown to nearly black stripes on either side of the spine (each two or three scales wide) lies a slightly broader pale gray to pale yellow vertebral band. Below the dark stripes the body is a bit darker, generally assuming a tan or olive hue. Only occasionally is a narrow dark line faintly indicated along the third row of scales above the belly plates. The head is usually pale gray, except for a brown mask behind each eye, which marks the beginning of each dark body stripe. The snake's underside is an immaculate white or yellow. The dorsal scales are smooth and arranged in 17 midbody rows, the anal plate is divided, there are usually eight upper lip scales, and the rearmost chin shields either touch one another or are separated by only a single scale.

COMPARABLE SNAKES The Big Bend patch-nosed snake has a narrow dark stripe, usually zigzag in outline, on the fourth row of scales above the belly, nine upper lip scales, and two or three small scales between the rearmost chin shields. (See the illustration in the Big Bend patch-nosed snake account.) Garter and ribbon snakes living within the range of the mountain patch-nosed snake are distinguished by their lack of an enlarged nose plate, their keeled body scales, a single anal plate, and a greater number of dorsal scale rows (19 or 21). The Central Texas whipsnake has a dark center stripe bordered on either side by broken white stripes, a white collar or two pale patches on the back of its head, and 15 midbody rows of dorsal scales, and it lacks an enlarged nose plate.

SIZE Adults of this subspecies normally are between 22 and 30 inches (55.9–76.2 cm) long. A record specimen measured 37½ inches (95.2 cm) in length.

HABITAT In Texas this snake inhabits the more humid, wooded mountain slopes and mesas of the Trans-Pecos region at elevations between 4,000 feet (1,219 m) and at least 6,000 feet (1,829 m). Although it may occasionally occupy the lower elevations of desert grassland, where it sometimes coexists with its cousin the Big Bend patch-nosed snake, it is more likely to be encountered in evergreen pine-juniper woodland, along the rocky slopes of canyons and hillsides, and in upland streambeds. At the Black Gap Wildlife Management Area in Brewster County, Axtell (1959) observed both species living side by side, finding one Big Bend patch-nosed snake at approximately 2,000 feet (610 m) and a specimen of the mountain patch-nosed snake on a nearby hillside no more than 300 feet (91 m) higher. Other examples of cohabitation of the two species are not rare where their geographic ranges overlap, but apparently the mountain species has an aversion to the low desert elevations inhabited by *S. deserticola,* for it seldom establishes permanent residence below 4,000 feet. It seems also to favor craggy mountain slopes and rock-laden ravines over the less severely tilted alluvial plains and lowland deserts. Within its Texas range it has been recorded from a variety of plant communities, including cedar-savannah and cedar-ocotillo associations on the Blackstone Ranch in Terrell County. In the Sierra Vieja Mountains of northwestern Presidio County, it has been reported by Jameson and Flury (1949) from the following plant communities: catclaw-cedar, lechuguilla-beargrass, catclaw-grama, and grama-bluestem.

BEHAVIOR Fast and elusive like its close relatives the racers and whipsnakes, the mountain patch-nosed snake easily avoids capture by gliding swiftly for cover, sometimes changing direction so suddenly and unexpectedly that it is momentarily lost from sight. When the graceful body flows forward through the underbrush, its boldly striped pattern creates an optical illusion that increases its chances of avoiding the enemy. As one's attention is focused on a single visible segment of the snake's trunk sliding through a portal in the undergrowth, the reptile appears to be stationary, for the eye cannot detect any difference between one bit of stripe and the next. When the snake's tail tip finally slips through the brushy window, the bewildered predator, having waited too long to attack, will have missed its opportunity. In the absence of such protective undergrowth, the fleeing reptile may dart into the nearest animal burrow or rock pile. Although not particularly savage in its efforts at de-

fense, the mountain patch-nosed snake often bites when picked up, its small teeth inflicting only superficial punctures on its captor's hands.

Active mainly early in the morning and again from late afternoon until dusk, it may be found basking in the first rays of the rising sun, especially on cool spring or autumn mornings. Its active season generally lasts from late March to mid-October, though it can be drawn out of hibernation even earlier by a spell of unseasonably warm winter weather, as reported, for example, by Minton (1959), who encountered one of these snakes in Big Bend National Park on February 26.

FEEDING Lizards are by far the most important single item in any patch-nosed snake's diet. Those most often consumed are the plentiful whiptails, slender lacertilians with long tails and slim heads represented within the snake's Texas range by 9 or 10 species and subspecies. Most are alert, swift, and elusive, able to evade a human pursuer easily, but the snake is itself a fast, nimble predator whose speed and uncommon agility confront such lizards with a real challenge. With its head raised above the ground for a better view of its surroundings, the snake glides slowly over the rough terrain as it tries to startle some unseen basking lizard to flee or, by poking its nose into the undergrowth, attempts to flush one from hiding. Once the prey is in motion, the serpent instantly dashes after it in eager pursuit. As long as the lizard keeps going and remains in sight, the chase continues, but if it stops suddenly before the snake has sufficiently closed the gap between them, the snake may be unable to locate it. Even when the serpent has come to a halt just a few inches from the lizard, chances are it will not detect its motionless quarry, for it depends on its acute eyesight to spot the movement of a potential victim. Apparently in this case, neither the snake's sense of smell nor its tongue and associated Jacobson's organ (both highly developed organs of prey detection) help it to locate the unhidden lacertilian; at this point, only the lizard's renewed movement will again alert the bewildered predator, at which time the chase will be resumed.

Less important items on the snake's menu include small rodents, other serpents, and the eggs of both lizards and snakes. The patch-nosed snake uses its head, with its peculiarly enlarged nose scale, to excavate eggs from their sandy underground chambers.

REPRODUCTION Little detailed information is available about the snake's breeding habits. Mating takes place in spring or early summer, after which the females lay individ-

ual clutches of 6 to 10 eggs. The long, white eggs, each about 1 to 1¼ inches (2.5–3.2 cm) in length, hatch sometime in August or September, producing babies that are near-replicas of the parents and 8½ to 10 inches (21.5–25.4 cm) long.

TEXAS PATCH-NOSED SNAKE

Salvadora grahamiae lineata

PLATE 126

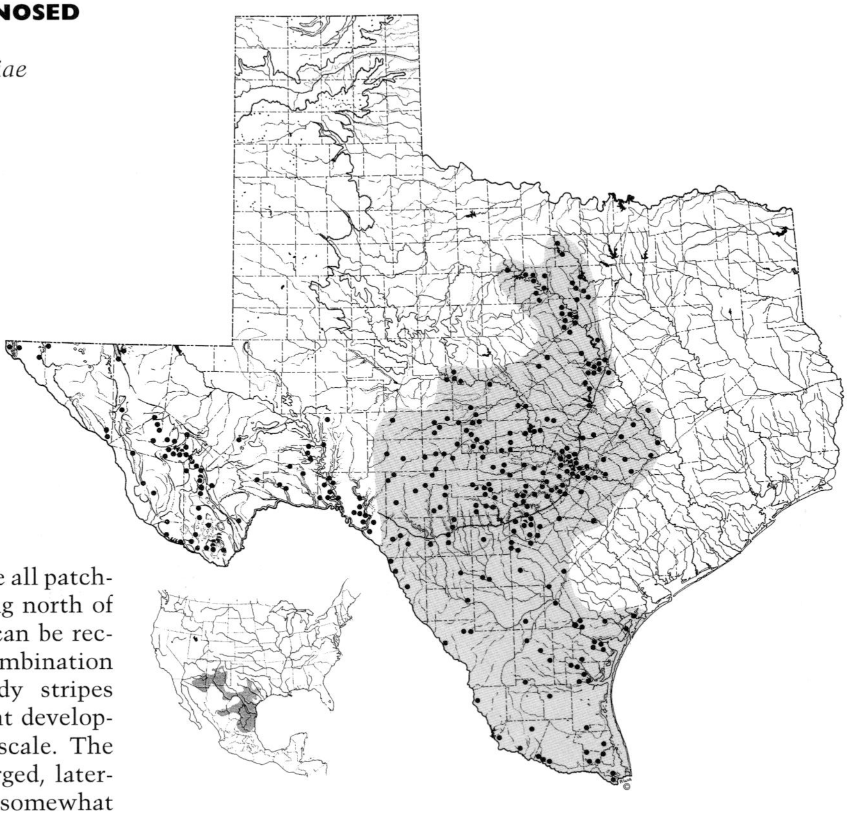

DESCRIPTION Like all patch-nosed snakes living north of Mexico, this one can be recognized by the combination of lengthwise body stripes and the extravagant development of its nose scale. The nose scale is enlarged, laterally flared, and somewhat free-standing along the edges. The cream, yellow, or pastel orange center stripe, one and two half scales wide, is bordered on either side by a broader (2 and 2 half scales wide) dark brown to blackish stripe that continues along the body as far forward as the eye. Below the dark stripes, where the color of the snake's trunk is considerably paler, a thin, well-defined dark line runs along the third row of scales above the belly on the forebody and on the second row toward the tail (it is this feature that distinguishes the Texas patch-nosed snake from the mountain subspecies). The top of the snake's relatively small head is gray-brown to yellow-olive, and

its upper and lower lip scales are white or pastel yellow. The color of its unmarked belly can be olive-buff or pale green. Smooth dorsal scales are arranged in 17 rows at midbody, and there are usually eight upper lip scales on either side of the mouth, of which two touch the eye. The anal plate is divided.

COMPARABLE SNAKES The narrow, dark lateral stripe of the Big Bend patch-nosed snake occupies the fourth scale row above the belly (see illustration in Big Bend patch-nosed snake account), its rearmost chin shields are separated from one another by two or three small scales, and typically nine upper lip scales occur on either side of the mouth. Ribbon and garter snakes living within the range of the Texas patch-nosed snake lack its enlarged nose plate; they also possess keeled body scales, an undivided anal plate, and 19 or 21 rows of midbody dorsal scales. The modestly striped Schott's and Ruthven's whipsnakes both have a wide, dark center stripe, 15 rows of smooth dorsal scales at midbody, and a nose scale of average size.

SIZE Although this slender serpent is known to reach a maximum length of 47 inches (119.4 cm), the adults are usually between 26 and 40 inches (66–102 cm) long.

HABITAT Occupying a variety of habitats from sea level to nearly 2,000 feet (610 m) elevation, this snake is found as far north in the state as Throckmorton and Young counties and as far south as Brownsville. This region of Central Texas includes the northern prairies and Cross Timbers, the scrubby cedar-oak savannah of the Edwards Plateau, the brushland dominated by mesquite and prickly pear cactus on the Rio Grande Plain (including the intensely cultivated farmlands of the Valley), and to a limited extent the blackland prairies just east and northeast of San Antonio. It favors rocky hillsides, particularly those supporting rock ledges, but Vermersch and Kuntz (1986) noted that in south-central Texas it also frequents river and creek floodplains, replete with rotting logs and decaying plant debris.

BEHAVIOR An alert serpent with fast reflexes, the Texas patch-nosed snake is quick to flee when approached. Endowed with a slender body that glides easily over the ground, it instantly darts into the nearest clump of vegetation when disturbed or takes shelter under surface debris, natural or manmade, that may include rocks, boards, fallen tree limbs, corrugated sheet metal, and trash heaps (the same kinds of objects it uses for temporary shelter to avoid inclement weather). For instance, near Stinson Field in South San Antonio, in a single season Vermersch and Kuntz found 35 specimens of this subspecies beneath tar paper, wooden shingles, and other kinds of discarded building materials. In more remote areas where such artificial shelters are not always available, the snake exploits other retreats. For example, the land north and west of San Antonio is basically limestone, with exposed horizontal surface layers of rock often separated by narrow spaces, particularly along canyon walls and on higher ridges, that create unlimited shelters for a myriad of small creatures. It is in these that the snake frequently seeks refuge when frightened. Where neither man-made debris nor rock crevices are handy, it slips into animal burrows to escape its enemies.

A frightened patch-nosed snake, especially if it is cornered, may do nothing more than stand its ground and vibrate its tail; only rarely will it strike out at its antagonist. One that is seized usually responds more aggressively, for this is an excitable snake that often thrashes about frantically when handled, sometimes even biting as it tries to gain its freedom. Another strategy used by the snake to free itself from a collector's grasp is reported by Wright and Wright (1957). If grabbed by the head, a patch-nosed snake tries to liberate itself by first wrapping its tail around some accessible part of its captor's hand before looping the end of its tail over its own trunk. With the tail thus firmly anchored, it pulls backward doggedly in an effort to free its entrapped head. In South Texas this is one of the first snakes to leave its winter refuge in the spring. Occasionally it emerges from hibernation as early in the year as late February or the beginning of March, though during particularly mild winters specimens may be encountered above ground even earlier. One was found at the surface in mid-December, another on January 5. Strictly a day-active serpent whose daily wanderings are limited only by the extreme afternoon midsummer heat, it spends much of its time busily searching for prey.

FEEDING Without benefit of field studies to ascertain in detail the food preferences of the Texas patchnose, we can only speculate concerning the snake's favorite prey. For the most part, documented reports dealing with its diet list the various prey items it has accepted in captivity, leaving largely unresolved the question of the serpent's natural diet. Some of the items may indeed be the same as those consumed in nature, although others may not; unfamiliar prey may be devoured as a last resort to avoid starvation.

Lizards probably represent the favorite quarry of this subspecies. Whiptail, race runner, and spiny lizards no doubt rank high on the list of preferred prey. Reptile eggs may also be included, for it is believed that the snake's strangely enlarged and flared nose scale, slightly protruding along the edges, is specifically adapted for scraping away the 2 or 3 inches (5–7.6 cm) of sand that ordinarily cover the buried eggs. That such concealed food items are detected by their odor alone seems likely, for otherwise how could the snake be aware of their presence? It is generally agreed that since hungry patch-nosed snakes completely ignore nearby unmoving lizards, these serpents cannot identify lacertilian prey by smell or through the function of the tongue and associated Jacobson's organ (typically important sources of prey recognition in serpents). Like most of its kin, the Texas patch-nosed snake sometimes includes small rodents in its diet, as well as an occasional frog or young snake. McCallion (1945) saw one eat a small Brazos water snake and observed the struggles of another as it tried unsuccessfully to devour a small Great Plains rat snake.

REPRODUCTION Most details about the courtship and mating behavior of this relatively abundant serpent are still a mystery. Like almost all snakes of temperate latitudes, it probably breeds in the spring, an assumption verified by Davenport (1943), who observed a mating pair in Bexar County during May. From the scant information available, we know that sometime between the first of April and the end of June, the female lays 4 to 10 eggs in a cluster, each egg measuring 1 to 1¼ inches (2.5–3.2 cm) long.

The first naturalist to document the details of egg-laying and hatching in this subspecies was Conant (1942), whose account was based on the maternal activities of a captive female collected in the fall of 1940, some 8 miles (13 km) north of Palo Pinto township. On April 1 of the following year, the snake laid 10 eggs. What is unusual about this event is the early laying date. According to published records, Texas snakes seldom deposit their eggs in months other than June or July, and certainly never as early in the year as April 1, a time when most species are only beginning to think about mating. Several reasons for this anomaly have been suggested. One attributes the early deposition to a previous fall mating. Others suggest that the female mated with a cagemate from the same area or that sperm from an earlier mating remained viable in the female's oviducts until it fertilized her most recent batch of eggs. In this case, the hatchlings, which measured between 8 and nearly 10½ inches (20.3–26.7 cm) long, emerged from their eggs during the span of a week, from August 4 to August 10. In features of coloration and pattern, the infants were similar to the adults but showed a greater tendency than mature individuals to strike and vibrate the tail when annoyed.

GREAT PLAINS GROUND SNAKE
Sonora semiannulata semiannulata
PLATES 127–132

DESCRIPTION So varied are the snake's background color and pattern—ranging from olive brown to bright orange or reddish and from no markings to bold crossbands—that even specimens from the same locality can look like entirely different species, a circumstance responsible in part for the long-standing confusion over the snake's proper classification.

Based on an examination of more than 500 ground snakes from Texas, we believe there are two different subspecies of the Great Plains ground snake in the state, each distinguished by the number of dorsal scale rows on its body. Generally, 15 midbody rows of scales occur in the Great Plains ground snake, but if this number is only 14, then the number of rows near the anus is also 14. In Taylor's ground snake, only 13 rows of scales normally are present at midbody. In the few instances in which this number is 14, then 13 rows occur near the anus. Moreover, the broad range of color and pattern variation displayed by the Great Plains ground snake is not duplicated in Taylor's subspecies, which is essentially a unicolored serpent. In both races, a more or less distinct dark spot or horizontal dash usually occupies the forward or middle portion of each dorsal scale, giving the

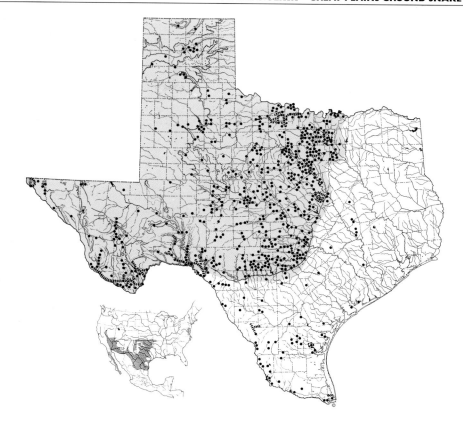

snake the appearance of being longitudinally striped with numerous thin, dotted lines.

The array of color and pattern variation displayed in the Great Plains ground snake is enough to bewilder the layman, for not only does this subspecies come in collared, cross-banded, blotched, striped, and unicolored phases, but individual snakes can also exhibit any combination of such elements. Adding to the confusion is the possibility of finding specimens representing all of those pattern phases together in a single local community. Among the most colorful of all Great Plains ground snakes are those inhabiting West Texas, where some individuals are both black-crossbanded and marked with a rela-tively wide red-orange stripe down the middle of the back. In others, either of these pattern elements is missing. Central Texas specimens, however, tend to have heads somewhat darker than the body, and their dorsal markings may consist of several dark crossbands, one, or none. There are also Great Plains ground snakes whose only marking is an abbreviated dark collar across the neck.

Whatever the snake's upper body pattern, its underside is off-white to orange-yellow, usu-ally unmarked but occasionally crossed by one or more of the dark dorsal crossbands, es-pecially beneath the tail. The snake's small, blunt head, only a little wider than its neck, is followed by a relatively thick body. The dorsal scales are smooth, a loreal scale is present, and the anal plate is divided.

COMPARABLE SNAKES The lack of a loreal scale and the absence of crossbanding or lon-gitudinal striping on the body distinguish flat-headed and black-headed snakes from this ground snake. Ring-necked snakes have bold black spots on a red-orange or yellowish belly, and the only dorsal marking, if pres-ent, is a pale neck ring. Both species of earth snakes possess at least some keeled dorsal scales, which are arranged in 17 rows at mid-body. The Texas brown snake, also with 17 midbody rows of keeled dorsal scales, lacks a loreal scale and has a prominent dark spot on the lip scales directly below the eye. Blind snakes are much more slender than a ground snake, their sightless eyes are visible only as black dots beneath the overlying scales, and their belly scales are no larger than the dorsal scales.

SIZE Adults are generally 8½ to 12 inches (21.6–30.5 cm) in length. A record specimen measured 18 inches (45.7 cm) long.

HABITAT This snake has a wide distribution in Texas, including roughly the western two-thirds of the state, exclusive of the East Texas woodlands, the middle and upper coastal plain, and the South Texas thornbrush savannah. In such dry country, dominated by sandy or rocky terrain, it is most likely to be encountered in grassy plains, open desert grasslands, mesquite thickets, and oak-juniper savannahs, including those in the Guadalupe Mountains at slightly over 6,000 feet elevation (the greatest height at which this snake has been reported). In the Panhandle region of northwestern Texas, Fouquette and Lindsay (1955) found 52 of 55 Hutchinson County specimens on rocky limestone slopes where the primary vegetation was sparse bluestem, grama grass, and sumac. Two others were collected on sandy hillsides, and only 1 came from the floodplain. Along the southern edge of the subspecies' range in Bandera, Medina, Kendall, Comal, and Bexar counties, the majority of 38 specimens encountered by Vermersch and Kuntz (1986) came from rocky hillsides in oak-juniper habitat. Not far to the west, on the Stockton Plateau, a series of 21 Great Plains ground snakes collected by Milstead, Mecham, and McClintock (1950) in northern Terrell County was taken in a variety of plant associations that included cedar-ocotillo (9), cedar-savannah (3), cedar-oak (3), persimmon–shin oak (2), mesquite-creosote (2), and walnut–desert willow (2). Like a number of other small snake species whose presence is not easily detected, this one is attracted to suburban environments where it can readily hide beneath the myriad of human-generated trash items that normally occur in such places.

BEHAVIOR Small and inoffensive, the ground snake is no threat to man. Its tiny teeth and limited mouth gape, combined with a gentle disposition, make it an utterly harmless creature. Like so many other small serpents of desert and open prairie, it avoids daytime predators by hiding underground by day, either in the burrows of other animals or in tunnels of its own making. Or it may simply spend the day under a variety of surface objects such as stones, fallen cactus plants, or other debris. So comfortable is it below the surface that a released captive almost invariably and without hesitation digs straight down into the ground if the substrate consists of loose soil or sand. In plain sight above ground, this slow-moving little snake is extremely vulnerable. When threatened in the open, its chief recourse is to find cover, for considering its small size and lack of defensive resources, the snake has no other way to protect itself from an aggressive adversary.

Despite the serpent's inability to retaliate, it may use a peculiar death-feigning tactic in an effort to deter its foe. In one of the few observations of this defensive behavior, Hillis (1977) described how a Great Plains ground snake, when picked up, bent and twisted its body as though seriously injured and, with its jaws agape and its tongue hanging loosely from its mouth, rolled over repeatedly. After some 30 seconds of such animated writhing, nearly all motion ceased and the snake came to rest, belly up. When the subject was turned right side up, it promptly turned over again, just like a death-feigning hog-nosed snake, ostensibly to convince its tormentor that it was indeed dead. After maintaining this apparent moribund position for about 10 minutes without being further molested, the snake finally righted itself and crawled away. Gehlbach (1970) noted a similar reaction by a captive ground snake that was seized by a hungry milk snake.

In Texas, the Great Plains ground snake ordinarily is active from the end of February through December, although reports of specimens observed above ground during unseasonably warm weather in January are not rare. From Vermersch and Kuntz we learn that the ground snake is most often encountered from March through May, at least in south-central Texas. Around the Central Texas town of Palo Pinto, Philip Harter (according to Kassing 1961) discovered the largest number of individuals in March. In Tulsa County, Oklahoma, and vicinity (some 250 miles to the north of Palo Pinto), Kassing found it in greatest abundance a full month later. In fact, 40.5 percent of the total number of ground snakes encountered there during the year were taken in April, and only 3 percent in July and August, when the drying effects of midsummer's sparse rainfall and high temperatures probably forced the snakes deeper into the moister soil. At such times, according to Kassing, they retreated to depths of more than 10 inches (25.4 cm) or crawled into the labyrinth of multilayered rock ledges. The best time to find them wandering above ground, however, is in the spring, especially after the topsoil has been soaked by a pouring rain.

By the end of October or early November, depending on the latitude, the snake will have retired to its hibernaculum, normally an animal burrow or a tunnel of its own making. In a departure from the norm, two hibernating specimens were discovered near Drumright, Oklahoma, 2 feet (61 cm) below ground, nestled together with a king snake in a hole at the base of an uprooted telephone pole.

FEEDING This snake consumes a variety of invertebrate prey, including spiders, centipedes, scorpions, and both soft- and hard-bodied insects, in addition to the eggs of ants and spiders. Kassing (1961), the only zoologist to have studied its feeding habits in any detail, found the species' chief prey in the Tulsa, Oklahoma, area to be spiders and their eggs, followed in descending order of preference by centipedes, scorpions, and finally insects, particularly those living in moist microhabitats under rocks. Because some of these creatures are capable of inflicting incapacitating stings or bites on their captors, it would seem that the ground snake must somehow be adapted to deal with them. According to the late Philip Harter (in Kassing 1961), of Palo Pinto, Texas, the snake skillfully avoided a scorpion's venomous caudal stinger by seizing the arachnid by the tail, thereby preventing serious injury to itself. Just how the little serpent managed to maneuver the scorpion into its mouth to be swallowed, without first subduing it or giving up its grasp of the prey's lethal weapon, was not explained.

REPRODUCTION Kroll (1971) was the first to report male combat behavior in this species. He described an encounter between two captive male ground snakes, one of which was mating with a female when it was challenged by an interloper, a specimen smaller than it-

self. Momentarily abandoning its mate, the larger male promptly attacked the intruder, biting it on two different parts of the trunk before the snakes came together and intertwined their bodies. Stubbornly maintaining this position, they rolled over several times on the floor of their cage. Five minutes later, after separating briefly, the larger male inflicted bites on the body of his challenger before the pair once again braided their trunks together in a corkscrew embrace, a position they held for another 10 minutes. With the ritualized combat over, the larger specimen, deemed to be the victor, returned to the female, and the two resumed their mating. Kroll observed two similar sex-related bouts between captive male ground snakes, one of which involved a single male challenged by two different contenders in succession, each of which lost its contest and with it the right to mate with the female.

Copulation, which usually occurs in May or early June, may also occasionally take place in the fall, although sperm from the late matings, having successfully overwintered in the female, does not fertilize the eggs until the following spring. Mating begins with aggressive overtures by the male, which includes biting her behind the neck. This is followed by the intertwining of their entire bodies in a corkscrew configuration as the two rub each other with the sides of their heads. Finally the male curls his tail beneath that of the female, bringing their cloacal openings into alignment to permit intromission.

Dates on which the females laid eggs (at least in captivity) varied in two parts of the snake's geographic range; as would be expected, those living at more southern latitudes experienced an earlier mating season than those of their more northern counterparts. Accordingly, specimens from the vicinity of Palo Pinto, Texas, deposited eggs from May 28 to June 16 (most from June 3 to June 5), and those from around Tulsa, Oklahoma, laid from June 14 to July 4 (most from June 19 to June 21). Although the species' natural nest site has not yet been discovered, it probably consists of a chamber at the end of a tunnel dug by the snake itself. Kassing suggested that in the serpent's oak-hickory habitat around Tulsa, where limestone escarpments are prevalent, the eggs may be deposited under the second or deeper layers of overlapping limestone ledges a foot (30.5 cm) or more below the surface. To reach such depths, the snake follows a burrow (probably made by itself) that typically begins as an opening at the surface of the soil beneath a rock or first-level rock ledge, then continues downward along the spaces sandwiched between successive layers of limestone. Despite many attempts to track an escaping ground snake to the end of its tunnel, she was never able to do so.

The 3 to 6 eggs in a clutch, each about ¾ inch (1.9 cm) long, ordinarily hatch sometime during August, after an incubation of 53 to 67 days. Between 3⅛ to 4¾ inches (7.9–12.1 cm) in length at hatching, they are close replicas of the adults.

Although the normal hatching rate of ground-snake eggs in nature is unknown, it must far exceed the success rate of eggs laid in captivity and incubated under artificial conditions. Attempts by Kassing to incubate such eggs in the laboratory, including careful efforts to duplicate natural conditions, resulted in a surprisingly low success rate. Only 23 of 148 eggs hatched, most of the others having become hard and either greasy-looking or moldy about halfway through their normal incubation. The reason for this dismal failure was not determined.

TAYLOR'S GROUND SNAKE
Sonora semiannulata taylori
PLATES 133, 134

DESCRIPTION The overall color of this somewhat thick-bodied little snake is gray to medium brown above, usually with a more or less distinct dark spot or horizontal dash on the forward or middle part of each dorsal scale. Such markings, when viewed together, create the impression of numerous subtle, lengthwise stripes, giving the snake a delicately textured appearance. The extraordinary color and pattern variations of the Great Plains ground snake are not observed in this subspecies, an essentially unicolored serpent. In some specimens, all or part of the head is slightly darker than the rest of the body. The belly has a pale yellowish hue and is unmarked. The snake's small head is barely wider than its neck, and its body is relatively thick. The dorsal scales are smooth, a loreal scale is present, and the anal plate is divided.

A subspecies of the Great Plains ground snake, it differs from that race in normally having only 13 (sometimes 14) midbody dorsal scale rows instead of the 15 (occasionally 14) that characterize the Great Plains ground snake. Those with the unconventional 14 rows at midbody will have 13 rows near the anus (14 in *S. s. semiannulata*).

COMPARABLE SNAKES See the Great Plains ground snake account.

SIZE Adults are generally 10 to 16 inches (25.4–40.6 cm) long but are known to reach a maximum length of about 17 inches (43.2 cm).

HABITAT For the most part, this subspecies inhabits the South Texas thornbrush savannah, but it is also found in the live oak and post oak savannahs to the northeast, where it has so far been reported in Austin, Bastrop, Brazos, Freestone, Harris, Robertson, and Wilson counties. Like other small, secretive snake species, it is sometimes encountered as often in the suburbs of towns and cities as in wilderness areas.

BEHAVIOR *See the Great Plains ground snake account.* The life history of *S. s. taylori* is not known in any detail; however, much of what has been written about the behavior of the closely related Great Plains ground snake may apply to Taylor's subspecies as well. In some areas of South Texas, where rock formations are scarce or absent, the snake turns up beneath a variety of plant debris, such as recumbent desert plants (particularly prickly pear cactus), fallen tree limbs, and pack rat nests. This is especially true in the brush country extending from Falfurrias to Edinburg, where sandy soils probably support as large a Taylor's ground snake population as occurs anywhere else across the Rio Grande Plain. In such places, where surface shelter is sometimes scarce, it may even take refuge under dry cattle dung.

Collecting records for this subspecies point to an active season that begins in early February and ends by the end of October, although it is likely that during mild winters, following several consecutive days of unseasonally high temperatures, the snake will make a brief appearance at the surface in any of the other months.

FEEDING Since no comprehensive study of this subspecies' feeding habits has been performed, we can only assume that the snake's selection of prey is similar to that of the Great Plains ground snake, consisting chiefly of spiders and their eggs, centipedes, scorpions, and insects.

REPRODUCTION Mulaik and Mulaik (1941) report that a female of this subspecies laid 6 eggs on May 2; each egg measured over ³⁄₄ inch (1.9 cm) long. The hatchlings were about 3 inches (7.6 cm) in length.

MARSH BROWN SNAKE
Storeria dekayi limnetes
PLATE 135

DESCRIPTION This drab little pale brown to grayish brown snake displays a broad, pale stripe down the middle of its back, which is margined along each outer edge by a row of widely spaced, often obscure, small black spots. Individual scales along the sides of the body are usually edged with horizontal white and black dashlike flecks that are most visible after the snake has eaten a large meal or when a female is heavy with young. The belly color can be yellowish tan to pastel pink, often with a row of dark dots along the outer edges of the ventral plates. The subspecies' most distinctive features are the horizontal black bar behind each eye and the absence of large, dark neck blotches and dark markings on the upper and lower lip scales. Unlike the adults, young of the year have a yellowish tan collar across the neck and a dark dorsal coloration with virtually no markings. The dor-

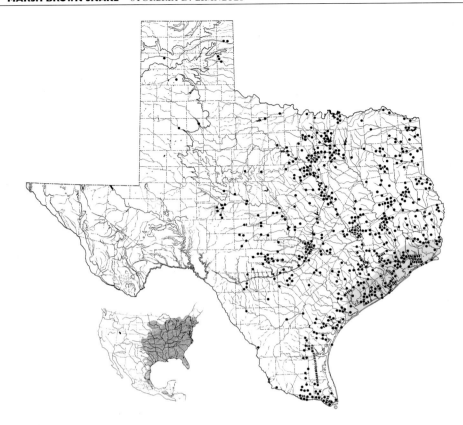

sal scales are keeled and arranged in 17 mid-body rows, a loreal scale is absent, and the anal plate is divided.

COMPARABLE SNAKES *See the Texas brown snake account.*

SIZE Adults are generally 9 to 13 inches (22.9–33 cm) long, with a maximum known length of nearly 17 inches (43 cm), according to Boundy (1995).

HABITAT Confined chiefly to the narrow strip of coastal brackish and freshwater marshes and wet prairies between the Louisiana border and Eagle Lake in Texas, this snake also occurs in the region's scattered hardwood savannahs. Though it prefers a salt marsh habitat, a specimen from outside this zone was reported by Sabath and Sabath (1969); it was found on dry prairie in Colorado County 75 miles (121 km) inland from the nearest marsh.

BEHAVIOR At the first sign of danger, as when the cover to its shelter has been removed, the brown snake may momentarily freeze, then crawl slowly away as it seeks an-

other refuge. If provoked, however, it is apt to flatten its body in a harmless bluff, making itself appear larger and more threatening. This causes the skin to stretch and the body scales to separate, exposing numerous small horizontal streaks of color, both pale and dark, that ordinarily lie concealed between the snake's closely spaced scales. Apparently this is a diversionary display meant to startle an adversary into inaction. A gentle, inoffensive creature, it rarely bites in self-defense, even when roughly handled. It relies instead on the discharge of musk from its scent glands and feces from its cloaca. Should it bite a hand or finger, the serpent's tiny teeth are too small to be effective as weapons and will scarcely puncture human skin. When all else fails, the marsh brown snake is capable of perpetrating a hoax that conceivably could thwart an assailant. The subterfuge, infrequently observed in this species, is also practiced occasionally by several other kinds of snakes, and it is commonly performed by hog-nosed snakes. Called letisimulation, or

A. 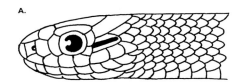 B.

Figure 53. *Lateral head patterns of brown snakes: (a) the dark streak behind the eye of the marsh brown snake and (b) the large dark neck patch and upper lip markings of the Texas brown snake.*

death-feigning, it generally occurs when the snake is touched or jostled. In this case, reported by Liner (1977), the serpent writhed briefly upon being touched, then turned over onto its back with its body contorted by a number of unnatural kinks that gave the snake a desiccated appearance. Attempts to straighten the bizarre twists forcibly were unsuccessful. The first time Liner saw the snake in this condition, he was sure it was dead, so convincingly did it play its role. Then he observed several similar episodes the same day, confirming that the first such incident was not merely a chance event. Compared to the habitual stereotypic death-feigning behavior of hog-nosed snakes, letisimulation occurs so infrequently in several small species of native snakes, including this one, that it cannot be considered normal behavior.

Several comprehensive studies have been conducted on the behavior of other races of *S. dekayi,* but even basic information about the marsh brown snake's natural history is scarce. Like the other subspecies, it has a long active season; specimens have been reported on the surface of the ground from late February through late November, though in the relatively temperate climate of the Gulf Coast it probably also comes out of hiding on mild midwinter days in any month. It is often day-active in the spring and fall but nocturnal during most of the summer. When not moving about on the surface, the marsh brown snake coils under boards, logs, brush piles, and other debris on both natural and artificial levees, as well as in the beach debris that accumulates above the storm-tide zone. Among the more unusual shelters used by this snake in the open marsh are abandoned alligator nests and muskrat houses.

FEEDING In the absence of specific documented details about this subspecies' diet preferences, it is probably safe to conclude that its menu is similar to that of the other races of brown snake, whose prey consists chiefly of snails, slugs, earthworms, and insect larvae.

REPRODUCTION Since information about the breeding habits of the marsh brown snake is usually included in the literature dealing with the Texas brown snake, such data are not readily separable according to subspecies. However, the two are probably very similar in their reproductive biology. A female collected in Galveston County by the late Tom Dieckow (pers. com.) gave birth on June 28 to 6 young, which were 3½ to 4½ inches (8.9–11.4 cm) long. See also the Texas brown snake account.

TEXAS BROWN SNAKE
Storeria dekayi texana
PLATES 136, 137

DESCRIPTION The dorsal color of this plain-looking little snake is usually grayish brown to dark brown (sometimes tan or chestnut), except for a wide, indistinct, paler band extending down the middle of the snake's back. The band's outer edges are generally lined with a row of evenly placed small dark spots. In some cases the spots in each row are connected by a narrow dark line, like rosary beads on a string. Other specimens do not quite match this description. For example, brown snakes that have recently eaten large meals

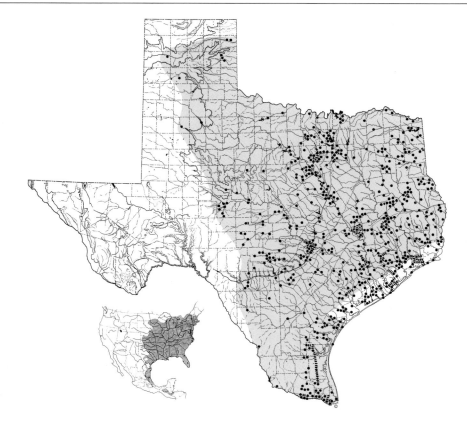

or females heavy with young often appear to be liberally speckled over the entire body with small horizontal .flecks, both pale and dark. Such conspicuous specks of color, ordinarily concealed between the dorsal scales, become visible only when the snake's skin is stretched. The only markings on the pale yellow, white, or pinkish white abdomen are one or two minute black dots near the outer edges of each belly plate or, less often, none at all.

A dark blotch of moderate to large size occurs on each side of the neck directly behind the head, often reaching down the sides as far as the belly line; another small, dark mark usually occupies the pale upper lip scales below each eye. (See illustration in marsh brown snake account.) No such dark nuchal blotch occurs in the newborn Texas brown snake, however; instead, the almost uniformly dark gray to dark brown juvenile enters the world with a distinct yellowish collar across its neck. The dorsal scales are keeled and arranged in 17 midbody rows, there are

seven upper lip scales on each side of the face, a loreal scale is absent, and the anal plate is divided.

COMPARABLE SNAKES The Florida red-bellied snake has 15 rows of dorsal scales at midbody and a distinct white, circular patch below and behind each eye. The dorsal pattern of rough and western earth snakes, when present, is not clearly defined, and both serpents possess a long horizontal loreal scale. Ground snakes lack a loreal scale, their dorsal scales are smooth and in 13, 14, or 15 rows at midbody, and usually each of the snake's pale upper body scales contains a central dark spot. In ring-necked snakes, whose dorsal scales are smooth, the only upper body marking is a distinct pale collar (sometimes interrupted at the middle of the back), and the bright yellow or orange-red belly is punctuated with bold black spots. The worm snake can be recognized by its smooth scales and by the deep pink color of its belly, which extends up along either side of its body to the third row of dorsal scales. The lined snake and the several kinds of garter snakes coexisting with the Texas brown snake all have a single anal plate and a pale lateral stripe on each side of the body.

SIZE Adults, which are usually 9 to 13 inches (22.9–33 cm) long, are known to reach a maximum length of 18 inches (45.7 cm).

HABITAT The Texas brown snake occupies a variety of environments ranging from mixed pine-oak woodland and pine forest to juniper brakes, grasslands, and thorn scrub. Regardless of habitat, it shows a preference for wet, shaded places that offer some ground cover and enough surface litter where hiding places, earthworms, and other favored prey abound. Such habitations include river and creek floodplains and their slopes, swamps, freshwater marshes, damp woods, and even water-filled ditches. Excluded, however, is the narrow coastal strip of mostly brackish marshland and prairie extending from the Louisiana border to Port Lavaca, where the Texas brown snake is replaced by its close relative, the marsh brown snake. Like several other kinds of small secretive serpents that thrive around human habitations, the Texas brown snake is abundant in large metropolitan areas. Klemens (1993) says of the northern brown snake in southern New England that it favors such disturbed sites over undisturbed habitats. To support this conclusion, he points out that approximately 93 percent of the specimens he collected in the region over 17 years came from the following modified natural areas: rural-agricultural 31 percent, suburban 13 percent, urban 18 percent, and radically disturbed 31 percent.

BEHAVIOR This inoffensive little snake is no threat to man, for it rarely bites, even when provoked. One that is discovered under surface debris remains still for an instant when first exposed, then tries to escape. When further provoked but unable to flee, the snake may flatten its body in a threatening gesture, causing the body scales to separate. This reveals rows of pale and dark flecks of skin color that were not visible before. Such a sudden and unexpected transformation—from a somber-hued serpent to one covered with a mosaic of bold new colors—may have the effect of startling the onlooker. Only rarely will the disturbed snake strike. If picked up, it is apt to squirm vigorously as it tries to free

itself, at the same time expelling musk from scent glands in its tail and feces from its cloacal opening.

When present in small groups, it may respond to rough handling in a more unusual way. According to Noble and Clausen (1936), several captive northern brown snakes maintained in the same enclosure came together and immediately intertwined their bodies when their cage was shaken. The resulting single large cluster of snakes was so cohesive that it could be picked up and supported by any one exposed part. The researchers repeatedly elicited the ball formation, but always in the presence of certain conditions: the cage floor had to be free of cover, and the temperature at the time of the experiment had to stand between approximately 64 and 79 degrees F.

The active season of this cold-tolerant species is relatively long, normally lasting from March into November over most of its geographic range. An even longer period of activity is reported in Texas, where specimens have frequently been found at the surface in every month, with collecting records beginning as early in the year as January 30 and ending as late as December 27. Except on the coolest spring and fall days, when it is likely to be encountered above ground after sunup, the Texas brown snake is primarily a night-active serpent, spending the days hidden in a carpet of leaf litter or concealed beneath surface objects. Among its most commonly used shelters are logs, rocks, brush piles, and loose tree bark. Within the boundaries of large metropolitan areas, where it is often abundant, it typically hides beneath mulch piles, cardboard, shingles, boards, roofing paper, and other types of discarded building materials. Suburban yards littered with such rubbish often attract this snake like a magnet. It can also be found in the dense mats of grass growing along the foundations of houses. Though such a diminutive snake might be expected to occupy a small home range, this is not necessarily the case. Most individuals of this species travel only 10 to 15 feet (3–4.6 m) every few days and less than 200 feet (61 m) in the course of a summer season, but Freedman and Catling (1979) noted that a specimen of the northern subspecies moved 1,234 feet (376 m) in 30 days. Even more remarkable are the results of studies by Noble and Clausen in which northern brown snakes were shown to have wandered nearly ¾ mile.

The same zoologists found that this subspecies exhibits a strong tendency to associate closely with others of its own kind, especially during times of unsatisfactory environmental conditions, such as when the humidity is low (ranging between 20 and 45 percent) and temperatures are between 70 and 98 degrees F, for aggregating at such times helps to reduce the serpents' rate of body water loss. To demonstrate just how much moisture can be lost from the snake's body when it is subjected to dry heat, the researchers exposed several northern brown snakes to a temperature of 86 degrees F, first as isolated individuals and then in aggregations. After six hours in the experimental chamber, the average loss of body weight per individual was 7 percent for isolated snakes but only 1.5 percent for each clustered snake. At 95 degrees F, the average isolated specimen had lost 17 percent of its body weight, the average clustered snake only 4.5 percent.

Except when winter temperatures drop to near freezing, the Texas brown snake waits out the cold weather by coiling under surface debris. With the approach of a severe cold front, its survival depends on getting below the frost line, where regardless of the outside temperature, that of the den generally stays around 35 to 40 degrees F. Such hibernacula have included animal burrows, deep rock crevices, and anthills, though decaying logs, rotting tree stumps, and compost heaps are also used, their interiors kept warm by the heat generated by organic decomposition. In contrast to the large winter aggregations of brown snakes discovered by Noble and Clausen near Flushing, New York, in which more than 350 specimens of the northern subspecies *S. d. dekayi* were uncovered on two 30-square-foot (2.8 m²) plots of ground, the Texas brown snake apparently hibernates singly or in small groups, at least in the southern end of its range. Unlike many other serpents that only hibernate with their own kind, the larger northern aggregations of *S. dekayi* are known to share their dens with other snake species. One such communal den held 76 northern brown snakes, 10 eastern garter snakes, and one northern water snake. These winter gatherings, whether they contain one species or several, evidently benefit the serpents by reducing their body water loss during long periods of winter dormancy.

Despite the Texas brown snake's continued abundance within many of the state's large metropolitan areas, over the last 20 years it seems to have been on the decline. Where formerly half a dozen or more specimens could be found in one day beneath surface objects in certain Houston parklands, some of the same sites now yield only one or two specimens or none at all. Pesticides, fertilizers, and other chemicals may be responsible for their decline (through poisoning of the snakes' prey), though that has yet to be proved. Another peril that no doubt also threatens them are the hordes of ferocious imported fire ants, whose bold attacks on all kinds of animal life, both domestic and wild, are well documented.

FEEDING No comprehensive study has been conducted to determine the precise nature of the snake's feeding habits in Texas, but such surveys have been completed in other parts of the species' range. They reveal that in varying proportions, earthworms and slugs make up the serpent's chief prey. Seigel (in Johnson 1987) found that in northwestern Missouri the Texas brown snake consumed 75 percent slugs and 25 percent earthworms. In Pennsylvania, Surface (1906) determined the diet of the northern subspecies to be 67 percent slugs and snails, 17 percent earthworms, and 16 percent insect larvae. Other items on the snake's menu have included sowbugs, spiders, small fish, small frogs, and amphibian eggs.

While studying the skulls of brown and red-bellied snakes, Douglas A. Rossman, of Louisiana State University's Museum of Natural Science, first noted that snakes of the genus *Storeria* possess teeth proportionately longer and more slender than those of most other closely related serpents and similar to those of certain Latin American snail-eating snakes (Rossman and Myer 1990). He also found published reports listing snails in the diet of brown snakes. Intrigued by these clues and wishing to investigate the issue, Rossman and Myer performed a series of feeding experiments using brown and red-bellied snakes as predators and snails as prey. The results, while not unexpected, were revealing. The snakes did, indeed, consume the gastropods, and their feeding behavior when dealing with such prey followed an orderly sequence of events.

First was the assault phase, in which the serpent, without lunging at its prey, simply seized it by the exposed soft body part, then shoved it forward along the ground until the shell became lodged against some firm object, in this case a rock in its cage. A snail with its body partly or completely withdrawn inside its shell was not attacked. With its prey firmly pressed against the rock, the snake twisted its head and forebody in a half to three-quarter rotation and held it there, while maintaining its grip on the victim's soft body. This resulted in considerable torsion, as the snail's body was held in a severely rotated position within its rigidly braced shell. Finally, after more than 10 minutes in such a strenuous mode, the gastropod, too fatigued to resist any longer, relaxed the large columellar muscle that held it to the shell and was then easily pulled free from its protective casing.

If the brown snake, as has been established, is uniquely adapted for extracting snails from their shells, why have not more snails been found in the stomachs of dissected wild-caught specimens? Such gastropods are reported to represent only a small percentage of the snake's overall diet. One explanation might be that some of the food items removed from the stomach tracts during studies of the snake's feeding habits and identified as slugs were actually snails that had first been extracted from their shells.

REPRODUCTION Both spring and fall matings have been observed in this species, with the birth of young ordinarily taking place from mid-June through August following a gestation period of about 75 days. Most Texas birth records are for July, but Guidry (1953) documented one that occurred in the southeastern corner of the state as late in the year as September 12. Over the snake's entire range, females of this species are reported to have 3 to 41 young per litter (average about 14), but the three Texas litters reported by Sabath and Worthington (1959) were somewhat smaller, numbering 8, 10, and 12 infants. At birth, each Texas brown snake is 3½ to 4½ inches (8.9–11.4 cm) long. The only marking on its overall dark brown to blackish dorsal coloration is a narrow, pale yellow collar, which disappears during the infant's first year of life.

Unlike the gravid females of many other snake species that regularly congregate at some open, unshaded spot to absorb the sun's radiant heat as a way to aid the growth of their developing embryos, female brown snakes do not mingle. Instead, during the last three or four weeks of their gestation, they go into hiding, each one separately, isolating themselves both from the males and from one another.

FLORIDA RED-BELLIED SNAKE
Storeria occipitomaculata obscura
PLATES 138, 139

DESCRIPTION The upper body color of this dark little snake varies from slate gray to some shade of brown, and the underside of the body ordinarily is tan, yellow, or pale orange, at least in Texas specimens. Dorsal markings consist of two, or sometimes four, longitudinal rows of ill-defined small dark spots, one on either side of the spine, and occasionally a lateral row on each side.

Three pale-colored nuchal spots are often present; they may be absent or may connect with one another to form a collar that extends down either side of the neck to intercept the light color of the belly. In some individuals, particularly those from Anderson County, the light nuchal markings are scarcely visible. The snake's head, which normally is darker than the body, displays one of the serpent's most distinctive markings, a white spot under the eye that involves all of the fifth upper lip scale and usually the edge of the fourth. There are two preoculars, the keeled dorsal scales are in 15 rows, and the anal plate is divided.

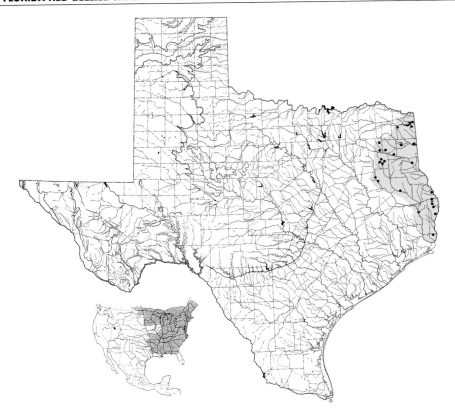

COMPARABLE SNAKES Brown snakes, in which the dorsal scale rows are in 17 rows at midbody, either have dark markings on the upper lips or lack a single prominent light spot on the fifth upper lip scale. (See illustration in marsh brown snake account.) Earth snakes possess a horizontal loreal scale that touches the eye (the red-bellied snake lacks a loreal), and they have no prominent pale spot on the fifth upper labial. The worm snake is covered with 13 rows of smooth scales and is without a single pale spot on the upper lips. Ring-necked snakes have small black spots on the lips, a double row of bold black spots on the belly, and smooth body scales.

SIZE Adults are generally 8 to 10 inches (20.3–25.4 cm) long; the maximum known size for this species is 16 inches (40.6 cm).

HABITAT Primarily an inhabitant of moist woodland containing plenty of logs and ample leaf litter, this serpent also occupies open places adjacent to such shaded forest, including bogs, swamp edges, old fields, and sometimes even roadside ditches.

A good account of the snake's habitat pref-erence is given by Semlitsch and Moran (1984), who found this subspecies (actually intergrades between the northern and Florida races) to be moderately common within two natural aquatic depressions in the U.S. Department of Energy's Savannah River Plant along the Atlantic Coastal Plain below Aiken, South Carolina. Here, surrounded by relatively dry slash and loblolly pine plantations, prime red-bellied snake habitats contained sweet gum, black gum, water oak, and wax myrtle trees, as well as bulrush, rush, cattail, and spike rush plants. Between the two zones were thick tangles of blackberry, honeysuckle, and greenbrier. The snake was also discovered in fair numbers at an abandoned borrow pit covered with secondary plant growth not much different from that at the other two locations. The zoologists captured 137 red-bellied snakes at the first two sites in approximately four years and another 39 at the borrow pit in just two years. This is in sharp contrast to the several dozen specimens reported thus far from all of East Texas.

Although not necessarily restricted to the

immediate vicinity of water, in Texas, as elsewhere, the Florida red-bellied snake shows a strong preference for damp situations. During drying conditions, it seems compelled to seek places of greater moisture.

BEHAVIOR Nearly all who encounter this little snake are struck with its shyness. A totally inoffensive species, it refuses to bite in self-defense, although when provoked it makes good use of several other tactics to thwart an opponent. Often its initial reaction to a threat is to flatten its head and body in order to appear larger and more sinister, although such behavior is not likely to discourage a determined predator. If picked up, the red-bellied snake is apt to engage in a form of intimidation perhaps unique among our native snakes. Turning the upper jawbones outward while also curling back the lip scales to reveal its upper jaw teeth, it gives the impression of a snarling serpent. At the same time, the snake may push one side of its head against the restraining hand, causing the exposed teeth to snag the skin. The slight pricking sensation of the snake's tiny teeth probably has little effect on a large adversary, but the same maneuver directed at a smaller assailant may actually penetrate the skin, perhaps startling a predator into releasing its captive.

In a more common reaction to being handled, the red-bellied snake discharges musk from its scent glands and fecal matter from its cloaca, smearing the slimy, foul-smelling substance over its captor by thrashing about.

Occasionally the snake engages in an elaborate death feint that begins as it twists convulsively on its long body axis, its mouth wide open, its tongue hanging limply from the mouth. Soon its belly-up body becomes rigid and contorted, and several places along the length of its body are laterally compressed

as if severely injured. If turned over during the display, the snake again assumes the original belly-up position, for it instinctively knows this is how a dead snake should look.

Owing to its small size, secretive habits, and overall scarcity, the natural history of the Florida red-bellied snake received little attention from zoologists until Semlitsch and Moran conducted a long-term field study of the serpent's habits and ecology at the South Carolina coastal plain locations mentioned above. Their research disclosed that the snake was active in every month, but its peak season of activity occurred in September and October. That was when the water level of its aquatic basin habitat began to drop in response to the drying effects of late summer heat and reduced rainfall, prompting it to follow the soil moisture gradient into lower, wetter portions of the basins. Aside from the dehydrating effects such drying conditions might have on the snake, they present an even greater dilemma for the reptile's invertebrate prey, which is primarily slugs. Being even more dependent on moisture for their survival than the red-bellied snakes themselves, the slugs also move into the receding wetness of the basins, soon to be followed by the hungry serpents. To the zoologists, these seem the most logical reasons for the snake's large-scale movements.

Learning anything about the snake's movements over any length of time proved difficult. For reasons not clear, few specimens that were marked and released again to the wild were ever recaptured. Of 61 South Carolina examples marked by Semlitsch and Moran, only 4 were captured again during the next 12 months (using drift fences with pitfall traps, a normally effective technique for sampling populations of small species such as this). A similar failure to recapture thwarted Blanchard (1937), whose studies of

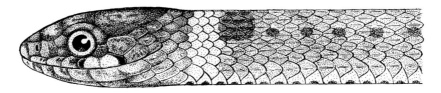

Figure 54. *Profile of the Florida red-bellied snake, with white spot on the upper lip scales below and behind the eye.*

the northern red-bellied snake in Michigan resulted in the retaking of only 2 of 157 marked and liberated specimens.

Several explanations for this phenomenon have been proposed. One is that since this species has a short life span, it seldom lives long enough to be recaptured during the course of a long-term field study. Another suggests that because the snake's local populations are large, the odds of retaking the same individual twice are greatly diminished. A third speculates that the redbelly moves about frequently, probably leaving a local study area before a researcher can recapture it. Since none of these possibilities is supported by evidence, the issue of the elusive snakes remains a puzzle.

There is surprisingly little specific information about the distances usually traveled by the red-bellied snake, but one record noted by Blanchard for the northern race may give us a clue. A female wandered more than 1,300 feet (396 m) in 24 hours, and another specimen covered less than 100 feet (30 m) over seven days. Although Semlitsch and Moran believe that Florida red-bellied snakes occupying their South Carolina study sites were more sedentary, they gave no indication of actual home range sizes.

Primarily a nocturnal species, the red-bellied snake nevertheless occasionally basks in the sun during cool weather or makes daytime forays up into the underbrush. When not on the move, this secretive reptile passes the daylight hours under logs, boards, flat stones, leaf litter, or other surface objects under which there is some degree of moisture. In Florida, two specimens were discovered in piles of debris that had accumulated at the bases of magnolia trees. Sometimes it

even leaves its customary refuge to crawl onto a paved roadway, either at night or during the day.

At the northern end of its geographic range, where it is often locally abundant, this species may aggregate in large numbers during winter dormancy. In southern Manitoba, Canada, for example, 101 northern red-bellied snakes, 148 smooth green snakes, and 8 plains garter snakes spent the winter together in a large anthill; the reptiles were dispersed through the mound from near the top to a depth of 57 inches (146 cm). Such large communal dens are probably not duplicated in the South, where the Florida red-bellied snake most likely hibernates singly or only in small groups. Preferred overwintering sites include gravel banks, ant mounds, logs, tree stumps, piles of vegetative debris, the space under loose tree bark, and rock crevices.

FEEDING Studies show that slugs are the snake's chief prey. In South Carolina, Semlitsch and Moran found nothing but slugs in the digestive tracts of 10 specimens. Other reports mention snails, isopods, earthworms, soft-bodied insects, and insect larvae. Some suggest that this snake may also eat small frogs and salamanders, but no hard evidence exists that it does.

REPRODUCTION By the time they are two years old, both male and female red-bellied snakes are biologically prepared to breed. Mating, which usually occurs in the spring but may also take place in summer or fall, produces litters of young as early in the year as June and as late as August in South Carolina populations. Numbering 1 to 21 per litter (usually 4 to 9), the newborn snakes are 2¾ to 4 inches (7–10.2 cm) long.

MEXICAN BLACK-HEADED SNAKE
Tantilla atriceps
PLATE 140

DESCRIPTION This small, slender serpent, with a dark brown or black skullcap that stands out conspicuously against its tan to pale brown body, is indistinguishable from *Tantilla hobartsmithi* except under magnification. Beginning on the snout, the dark

head pigmentation reaches backward along the dorsal midline to a point one to two scale lengths behind the parietals (the rearmost large scales on top of the head), where it ends in a straight or only slightly convex line of demarcation. It does not extend as far down

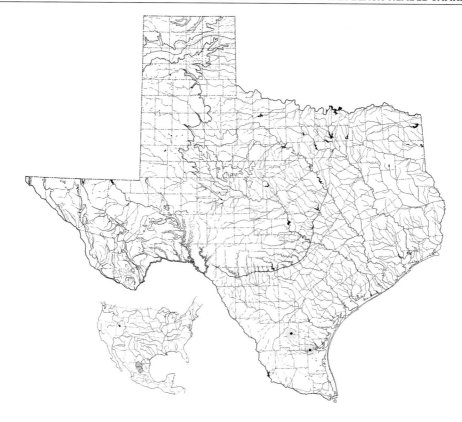

either side of the head as the end of the mouthline, reaching only to the top edges of the upper lip scales. An indistinct pale collar may separate the back edge of the dark cap from the soft brown body color. Except for the cream or white outer edges of the belly scales, the abdomen is pink to coral red. On either side of the snake's small head, which is no wider than the neck, are seven upper lip plates. The first pair of lower lip scales usually meets beneath the chin. The dorsal scales, all smooth, are in 15 midbody rows, and the anal plate is divided.

COMPARABLE SNAKES *See southwestern black-headed snake account;* because the geographic ranges of the two snakes are not known to overlap, the only practical way to identify a specimen is to assign it to one species or the other based on its collecting locality.

The plains black-headed snake has a longer cap, which extends backward three to five scale rows past the parietal plates; its rear margin is either convex or pointed. Its first pair of lower lip scales usually meet beneath the chin. The flat-headed snake's crown is normally only a bit darker than its body and it lacks a well-defined rear margin, but in the occasional specimen whose nearly solid cap is darker than usual, the back edge forms a distinct concave border. In addition, it has only six upper lip scales on each side of the head. Instead of a dark brown or black cap, ring-necked snakes have a pale collar on the neck (in the prairie ring-necked snake) or usually none at all (in the regal ring-necked snake), and distinct but random black spotting on their bright yellow bellies.

SIZE Adults are generally 5 to 8 inches (13–20.2 cm) long. They are known to reach a maximum length of $9\frac{1}{8}$ inches (23.2 cm).

HABITAT Primarily an inhabitant of the vast Chihuahuan Desert of north-central Mexico, this snake ranges northeast across the border into South Texas. There it has been found so far only in Duval and Kleberg counties, where the predominately caliche and clay soils support mostly brushy plants

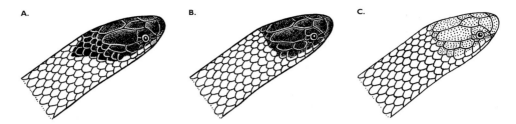

Figure 55. *Head markings of black-headed and flat-headed snake species: (a) long, pointed cap of the plains black-headed snake, (b) straight-edged cap of Mexican and southwestern black-headed snakes, and (c) faint cap of the flat-headed snake.*

and cactus. South of the border, according to Conant and Collins (1991), it is more liberal in its choice of environments, occupying not only desert flats and forested mountain canyons but also other habitats in between.

BEHAVIOR The Mexican black-headed snake probably does not bite when handled. Even if it were persuaded to do so, it is doubtful that the serpent's tiny teeth could pierce a man's skin. Like others of its clan, it is equipped with a pair of modestly enlarged, grooved teeth at the back of each upper jawbone. These primitive fangs, it is believed, aid the delivery of a weak venom from glands in the serpent's cheeks, down the dentary canals, and into the snake's small invertebrate prey, thus stunning the victim for easier handling. In no case are these toxins dangerous to man.

Nothing is known about the life history of this species, although based on information gleaned about the behavior of other species of black-headed snakes, it is probably safe to say that it is secretive, nocturnal, and can be found during the day concealed beneath rocks, limbs, and recumbent desert plants. Like other *Tantilla* species, it is likely to favor damp microhabitats, which in hot, dry weather afford a measure of protection against dehydration.

FEEDING Judging from the known feeding habits of other black-headed snakes, the prey of this species probably consist primarily of spiders, centipedes, and millipedes.

REPRODUCTION Nothing has been reported about the Mexican black-headed snake's breeding behavior, but based on information about reproduction in related species, the female is likely to lay only 1 or 2 eggs per clutch.

TRANS-PECOS BLACK-HEADED SNAKE

Tantilla cucullata
PLATES 141–144

DESCRIPTION Formerly regarded as two different races of the same species, the black-hooded snake (*T. rubra cucullata*) and the Devil's River black-headed snake (*T. r. diabola*) are now considered to represent pattern phases of the same species, here called the Trans-Pecos black-headed snake (*T. cucullata*).

Three different types of head pattern are normally found in this seldom-encountered serpent. One is distinguished by its all-black head. The second resembles the former Devil's River race in that it has a pale collar on the back of the head. The black on the rear of the head usually encroaches a short distance (one scale or less) onto the middle scale row of the pale collar. In the third pattern, the pale collar is completely interrupted by black along its dorsal midline, separating it into two whitish patches. Also present in this variety are a pale snout, small white spots on the upper lip scales, and usually a large white spot behind each eye. A single odd specimen, collected near Volcanic Dike Overlook in the Basin–Panther Pass area of Big Bend National Park by Easterla

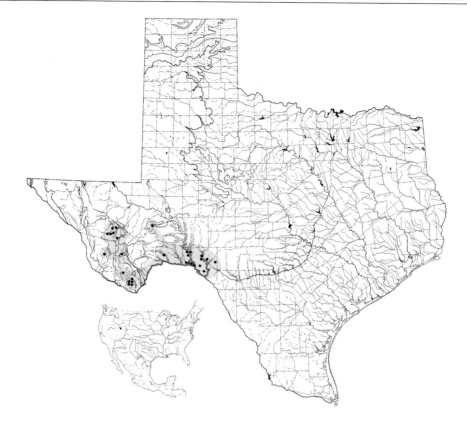

(1975), represents an intermediate condition. In this snake, the longitudinal black line that normally interrupts the white collar at mid-neck is replaced by a broken black × that emerges from the dark cap and is followed by a diagonal row of three small, widely spaced black spots (the lower two arms of the ×). Whatever the character of the head pattern, all of them have an unmarked pale brown or grayish brown upper body and a white abdomen. The dorsal scales, all smooth, are arranged in 15 rows at midbody, and the anal plate is divided.

COMPARABLE SNAKES The dark cap of the plains black-headed snake fails to reach the lower jaw, its rear edge is either convex or pointed, and it is not followed by a pale collar. It also has a pinkish to pink-red belly. The black skullcap of the southwestern black-headed snake is short, extending only one scale width behind the end of the parietal scales, and it does not reach as far down along the sides of the face as the end of the mouthline. The yellow belly of the regal ring-necked snake, which gradually becomes orange toward the rear and then red under the tail, is irregularly marked with bold, black spots.

SIZE Most adults of this large *Tantilla* are 8 to 15 inches (20.3–38.1 cm) long. A record specimen measured $25\frac{5}{8}$ inches (65.1 cm) in length.

HABITAT The Trans-Pecos black-headed snake has so far been found only in Trans-Pecos Texas, its known distribution extending for the most part along a north-south axis beginning at the Davis Mountains in the north and ending in the Chisos Mountains at Big Bend National Park, and from the Cuesta del Burro Mountains in the west to the vicinity of the Pecos and Devil's Rivers in the east and northeast. Most specimens have been encountered in steep-sided rocky canyons of Big Bend National Park at elevations between 5,400 and 5,600 feet (1,651–1,712 m), where the dominant vegetation consisted of pinyon pine, juniper, and oak. The lowest park-site record is for one specimen found near Vol-

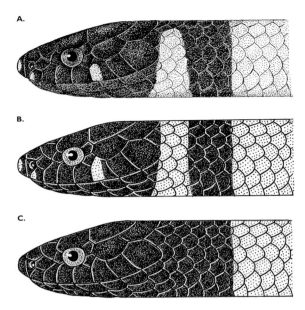

Figure 56. *Three head patterns of the Trans-Pecos black-headed snake: (a) divided white collar, (b) complete white collar (formerly the Devil's River black-headed snake), and (c) completely black hood.*

canic Dike Overlook, outside the Chisos Mountains at only 3,871 feet (1,180 m). The first specimen to be discovered was not taken in Big Bend National Park but was found by Minton (1956) 6 miles (9.7 km) south-southeast of Alpine in hilly grassland at an altitude of about 5,000 feet (1,520 m), where the reddish lava soil supported scattered stands of juniper and cholla. Another specimen was collected in a streamside oak-woodland habitat at an elevation of 4,125 feet (1,257 m) in a pass between the Big Aguja and the Little Aguja mountains. At this Jeff Davis County site the dominant plant species were creosote bush, acacia, yucca, and grasses of several kinds. The westernmost locality at which this snake has been found is the one in the Cuesta del Burro Mountains of Presidio County, where, at 5,115 feet (1,559 m), the low hills of arid grassland were vegetated chiefly with creosote bush, yucca, ocotillo, and agave. Curiously, all of the *T. cucullata* so far reported from northern Brewster, Jeff Davis, and Presidio counties have been of the black-hooded variety, whereas in the Chisos Mountains nearly half the specimens displayed white collars and the rest were marked with the solid dark hoods that characterize the more northern and western populations.

All of the specimens (21) from the lower elevations of the Chihuahuan Desert east of the Pecos River (from Langtry to the Del Rio area) have a pale collar. Of these, 5 have a black row of scales completely dividing the collar, 2 have partial separation of the collar by black, and 16 individuals show no division of the collar.

BEHAVIOR This snake has two slightly enlarged, grooved teeth at the end of each upper jawbone, which, combined with specialized salivary toxins, help to impede the struggles of its arthropod prey. It is harmless to man, however, and rarely ever bites when handled. A highly secretive species, it spends nearly its entire existence below ground in the region's vast labyrinth of subterranean spaces and rarely comes to the surface. As a result, its habits above ground are largely unknown, and what it does under the ground is still a complete mystery. The best time to look for it is during the desert's limited rainy season in July and August. According to Easterla (1975) and other naturalists who have had the most field experience with it, the snake is usually encountered early at night when the air temperature is between 68 and 76 degrees F and the ground is still cool and damp from a recent shower. Easterla goes on to say that it is never encountered on nights after heavy rains have drenched the area and left the soil muddy, but only when the ground has partly dried a day or two later. He also suggests that the best collecting results occur when the night sky is overcast or the moon is no more than half full. Of all the weather conditions that encourage the snake's emergence, surface moisture is clearly the most important. This was convincingly demonstrated by Easterla, whose collecting efforts on Big Bend National Park's Basin road resulted in the discovery of three specimens in two nights of a normally wet summer season, but none at all over the next three, presumably dry, summers. In like manner, the diligent attempts of Degenhardt and coworkers (1976) to locate this snake during eight dry summers by driving over basically the same route failed to disclose a single specimen. Incidentally, this seldom-seen snake is almost invariably discovered by driving slowly over paved roads through its habitat; practically all of the nearly two dozen reported specimens have been taken as they crawled across the pavement.

FEEDING Because of the general inaccessibility of live specimens, no detailed study of the snake's feeding habits has been undertaken. Its natural food is probably similar to that of other black-headed snakes, consisting chiefly of centipedes and millipedes and perhaps also scorpions. That centipedes constitute one of the serpent's natural prey items is confirmed by at least one field observation. When discovered by John McClain (pers. com.) under a canyon ledge along a small tributary of the Devil's River, one of these snakes was busily trying to subdue a struggling centipede.

To one captive specimen, Degenhardt and his colleagues offered a variety of small animals that included centipedes, millipedes, scorpions, adult and larval moths, spiders, small lizards, and chirping frogs, none of which was eaten. Another was tempted with some of the same fare plus adult ants and their pupae, but only centipedes were devoured. For an entire season one other snake was successfully maintained in the laboratory, where it readily consumed Big Bend centipedes, taking even the largest arthropods (6 to 7 inches, or 15 to 18 cm, long) if their heads were first removed.

REPRODUCTION All that is known about the reproductive biology of the Trans-Pecos black-headed snake is that it lays 1 or 2 eggs, probably in July or early August. At the time of laying, each egg is nearly $1\frac{4}{5}$ inches (4.6 cm) long. Details about the snake's mating behavior, nest location, egg incubation period, size of young, and description of the hatchlings remain to be discovered.

FLAT-HEADED SNAKE
Tantilla gracilis
PLATE 145

DESCRIPTION Among Texas snakes of the genus *Tantilla*, this is the only one normally lacking a well-defined, solid-black cap. (See illustration in Mexican black-headed snake account.) The dorsal color is tan, yellowish brown, or even reddish brown, gradually becoming a bit darker on the head. Only seldom is the crown uniformly dark enough to have a clearly delineated rear border, in which case the back edge of the cap is concave. The snake's belly is usually whitish with a pale salmon-pink to coral-red hue down its middle; the underside of its tail is colored like the abdomen, but more vividly. The moderately flattened head is about the same width as the neck. On either side of the head are six upper lip scales and one postocular, but there is no loreal scale. The smooth dorsal scales are in 15 midbody rows, and the anal plate is divided.

COMPARABLE SNAKES Native black-headed snakes share with the flat-headed snake an unpatterned, brownish body but differ from it in having a distinct black cap whose sharply delineated rear margin may be convex, pointed, or straight, but never concave. They normally possess seven instead of six upper lip scales on either side of the head. Earth snakes have a loreal scale, 17 midbody rows of dorsal scales (at least some of which

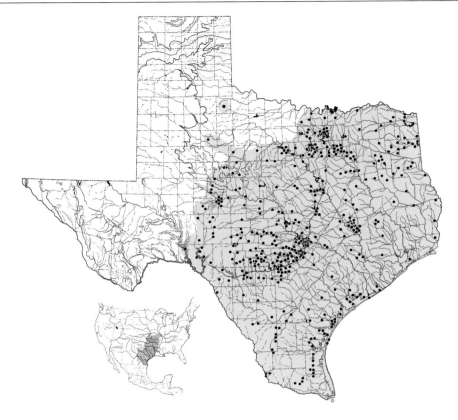

are keeled), and a whitish instead of pinkish belly. Brown snakes, whose strongly keeled body scales occur in 17 midbody rows, typically have a pale, broad stripe down the middle of the back and one or more dark spots on each side of the head and neck. Some Florida red-bellied snakes possess a pale, reddish brown upper body, but their strongly keeled dorsal scales are arranged in 17 midbody rows, and they have a prominent circular white spot on each side of the head directly below the eye. The more heavy-bodied ground snakes, which may or may not be patterned with black crossbands or a reddish stripe down the center of the back, ordinarily lack a pink belly and usually have a loreal scale. The bright yellow or orange ring normally present on the nape of ring-necked snakes, together with their black-spotted bellies, will distinguish them from the flat-headed snake. The very slender blind snakes have tiny blunt-snouted heads, degenerate scale-covered eyes, and belly plates no larger than the dorsal scales.

SIZE Most adults of this small, slender species are between 7 and 8 inches (17.8–20.3 cm) in length. The largest specimen on record measured $9\frac{7}{8}$ inches (25 cm) long.

HABITAT Widely distributed across the state, this snake inhabits every natural region in Texas except the High Plains and the Chihuahuan Desert region of the Trans-Pecos. It can be found in both the hardwood bottomlands and the pine-oak uplands of eastern Texas, the oak-hickory forests of the Cross Timbers, the oak-juniper brakes of the Edwards Plateau, the southeastern coastal prairies, and the South Texas thorn woodland. It has been reported to favor habitats with loose, damp soil, into which it can easily tunnel. Experiments performed by D. R. Clark (1967), however, revealed no preference for any particular soil type he investigated, probably because the flat-headed snake is only a modest burrower. It chose a sand substrate nearly as often as clay-loam or a mixture of sand and clay-loam. This helps to explain the snake's high degree of adaptability.

BEHAVIOR Like several other small burrowing serpents in Texas (including blind, worm, brown, ground, and earth snakes), this is an altogether harmless species that rarely, if ever, bites when handled. Lacking any effective means to protect itself, its first line of defense is to stay out of sight, a strategy it employs with exceptional skill. This helps to explain why, during a 5½-year study of this species in northeastern Kansas, Force (1935) never found a specimen out in the open, even though she captured nearly 500 specimens in the course of her work.

The flat-headed snake's year-round activity, at least in Texas, is reflected in the wide range of collecting dates reported for museum specimens of this species; the records begin as early in the year as January 3 and end as late as October 10. It probably can be found at the surface during any time of the year so long as both the temperature and humidity are high enough for its comfort. The term "active" in this case is not intended to convey wandering movement in the typical sense, for except when it is drawn out of hiding by warm spring or late summer rains, this secretive species is rarely encountered in the open. It is considered to be active when it comes to the surface to coil beneath a rock, log, or some other form of shelter. Only by turning over such surface objects is a collector apt to find it. Even then, the odds are against locating more than one specimen under a single object, and rarely do more than two snakes occupy the same retreat (unlike earth and brown snakes, this species is not gregarious). In wooded areas it hides beneath or within rotting logs, stumps, and tree limbs or finds its way under the loose bark at the base of dead or dying trees; others are found in leaf litter. Some turn up regularly in yards, gardens, and vacant lots of residential areas, as well as around abandoned buildings where clutter and dilapidated structures, often partly strewn over the landscape, provide the snakes with plenty of ground shelter. Throughout its range it inhabits mostly grassy or partly wooded, rock-strewn hillsides, especially those littered with flat stones, which the snake uses routinely as a refuge. Whatever its choice of cover, an essential requirement is that the soil beneath the sheltering object be damp; anything resting on a dry substrate is routinely avoided. In midsummer, when the ground surface has become dry from continual high temperatures and lack of rain, the flat-headed snake becomes relatively scarce, having probably moved deeper into the ground via animal burrows, ant mounds, and rock crevices to reach a more satisfactory level of moisture. Such underground spaces may also be used as winter retreats.

FEEDING As reported in some detail by Force, the food of this species in nature consists largely of centipedes and such soft-bodied, ground-inhabiting insect larvae as cutworms, wireworms, and leatherjackets (larvae of the crane fly). She also mentioned that young flat-headed snakes contained fungus grubs. Other prey items consumed by it, either in nature or in captivity, include scorpions, spiders, sowbugs, slugs, earthworms, and the larvae of scarab and darkling beetles. Ants, termites, or their brood are never mentioned in studies of its feeding habits, a surprising void considering the results of pheromone-trail studies by Gehlbach and colleagues (1971). A flat-headed snake readily followed the vacated trails of both army ants and termites, suggesting that these insects may be one of its natural prey species. It has been convincingly demonstrated that a snake's strong tracking propensity for specific prey species generally indicates a natural preference for such prey.

Considering the flat-headed snake's small size, one wonders how it can possibly subdue a violently writhing centipede, whose agile body, equipped with many pairs of constantly groping legs, makes it a formidable foe. Part of the answer may lie in the snake's venom-delivery system, primitive though it may be. Like all other species of the genus *Tantilla*, the flat-headed snake is endowed with a pair of moderately enlarged teeth at the very end of each upper jawbone. Each fang has an exposed channel that runs down the length of its lateral surface. Associated with this modified dentition is a weak toxin, contained in rudimentary venom glands, one at the base of each cheek. Unlike the highly proficient venom-delivery apparatus of the pit vipers, which forces the lethal toxins under pressure through the snake's hollow fangs and into its victim, the flat-headed snake's mode of in-

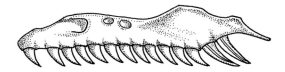

Figure 57. *Upper jawbone of the flat-headed snake, with enlarged grooved teeth at the rear of the maxillary.*

jection is less sophisticated and relatively inefficient. In this case the toxins flow down the fangs' grooves by the force of gravity alone, after which they mingle with the snake's saliva, permeating the victim's tissues through the puncture wounds inflicted by the serpent's constantly chewing teeth. The venom is believed to numb the snake's invertebrate prey, but tests have shown that it has no effect on warm-blooded animals such as humans and mice.

REPRODUCTION Sexual maturity occurs in females when they are between 1 and 1½ years old and in males between 1½ and 2½ years of age. Mating, which generally takes place sometime from late April to early May, results in the deposition of 1 to 4 (usu-

ally 2 or 3) eggs per female, typically during the second two weeks of June but occasionally as late as mid-July. The eggs vary in length from ½ to 1 inch (1.3–2.5 cm) long. They are laid where there is an adequate source of moisture, usually in damp soil under a rock, in a decaying log, or in decomposing vegetation. One clutch of eggs was even found in slightly damp sand between two layers of limestone.

Cobb (1990) discovered two natural nests of this species in northeastern Texas, each under a surface rock 4½ to 5 inches (11.4–12.7 cm) below the surface of the ground. The eggs were resting in underground chambers 1½ and 2½ inches (3.8–6.3 cm) in diameter, respectively, that were believed to be the remains of abandoned carpenter-ant tunnels. Moreover, several egg clutches he obtained from Smith and Henderson county specimens were laid between June 10 and July 26; their incubations lasted 50 or 51 days, somewhat less than for eggs laid by flat-headed snakes from Oklahoma, which, according to Force, required 83 or 84 days to hatch.

SOUTHWESTERN BLACK-HEADED SNAKE
Tantilla hobartsmithi
PLATE 146

DESCRIPTION The snake's dark brown or black skullcap stands out conspicuously against its tan to pale brown body color, reaching backward along the dorsal midline from the snout to a point one to three scale lengths behind the parietals (the rearmost large scales on top of the head), where it ends in a straight or only slightly convex line of demarcation. The dark pigment continues down either side of the head to the edges of the upper lip scales but ordinarily fails to cross the end of the mouthline. A narrow, sometimes indistinct, pale collar often margins the back edge of the dark cap, with no dark pigment separating it from the soft brown body color. The abdomen is pink to coral red down the center, cream or white along the outer edges. On either side of the snake's small head, which is no wider than the neck, are one preocular scale, usually two

postocular scales, and seven upper lip scales, but no loreal scale. The first pair of lower lip scales usually fails to meet beneath the chin. The dorsal scales, all smooth, are arranged in 15 midbody rows, and the anal plate is divided.

COMPARABLE SNAKES In color and pattern, as well as in nearly all diagnostic features of scalation, the Mexican black-headed snake is identical to the southwestern black-headed snake. As far as we know, the two differ solely in the structure of the male hemipenes. They can therefore be distinguished only by carefully examining such organs under magnification, a difficult assignment for the nonprofessional and an impossible task if the snake is female. Two features of scalation, while also useful in helping to separate the two snakes, are not consistent enough to be reliable. One is the number of scales directly

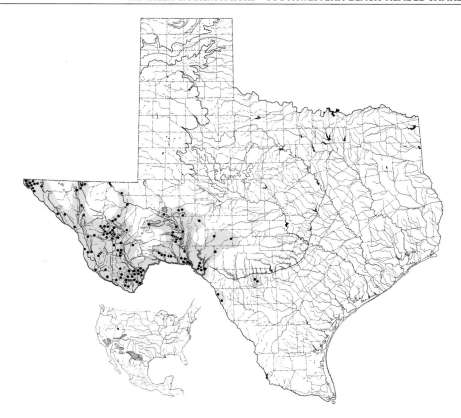

behind the eye (the postoculars): normally there is but one in the Mexican black-headed snake and usually two in the southwestern black-headed snake. Another is the arrangement of the first pair of lower lip scales in relation to the mental shield on the chin: the two lip scales of the Mexican black-headed snake ordinarily meet beneath the chin, whereas in the southwestern black-headed snake they are usually separated by the mental scale. Since the two species' geographical ranges are not known to overlap, the only practical solution to the dilemma is to assign the specimen to one or the other species based on its collecting locality.

The dark cap of the plains black-headed snake, which is longer than that of the southwestern black-headed snake, extends backward three to five scale rows beyond the parietal plates and is either convex or somewhat pointed along its rear margin. (See illustration in Mexican black-headed snake account.) Also, the first pair of lower lip scales ordinarily meet beneath the chin. The head of the Trans-Pecos black-headed snake is en-

tirely black as far back as the neck (occasionally there are some pale freckles on its nose) or is separated behind the parietal scales (the last pair of large plates on the crown) by a prominent white collar, the dark pigment in either case extending down to the lower lip scales. Furthermore, its belly is uniformly white. The flat-headed snake's crown is typically only a bit darker than its body, and it lacks a well-defined rear margin, but in the occasional specimen whose nearly solid cap is darker than normal, the back edge forms a distinct concave border. The flat-headed snake has only six upper lip scales on each side of the head. Instead of a dark brown or black cap, ring-necked snakes have a pale collar on the neck (in the prairie ring-necked snake) or usually none at all (in the regal ring-necked snake), and distinct but random black spotting on the belly.

SIZE Adults usually measure 7 to 9 inches (17.8–22.9 cm) long. The record length for this species is 12⁵⁄₁₆ inches (31.3 cm).

HABITAT Although essentially a desert species, it usually lives in areas containing some source of moisture, such as along riverbeds, streams, and arroyos. It shows a strong preference for rocky situations (where it commonly occurs beneath surface stones), but it occupies a wide variety of habitats ranging from low and midlevel desert grasslands to relatively moist mountain woodlands. In Presidio County's Sierra Vieja Mountains, Jameson and Flury (1949) found it in tobosagrama grasslands. In southeastern Brewster County, Axtell (1959) collected it in the sotol-lechuguilla plant association. On the Stockton Plateau in northern Terrell County, Milstead and his coworkers (1950) reported taking it in the following plant communities: cedar-ocotillo, persimmon–shin oak, mesquite-creosote, and the cedar savannah association. In the Chisos Mountains of Big Bend National Park, where it occurs at much higher elevations, at least to 6,000 feet (1,962 m), Degenhardt and his colleagues (1976) described it as common on the precipitous inclines and rocky gullies of Green Gulch, where the higher slopes are heavily vegetated with pinyon pines, juniper, oaks, and grasses.

BEHAVIOR When first picked up, this inoffensive little snake does not bite but, like most species of the genus *Tantilla*, may thrust its small head forcefully between the fingers or into a fold of skin as it tries to burrow out of sight. Such intense poking is startling and can easily be mistaken for biting, unnerving the captor and often causing it to drop its quarry.

The serpent's best protection is to stay out of sight, which it does by hiding underground in rock crevices and animal burrows or nestling into the decayed root systems of desert plants. Above ground it avoids detection by coiling under whatever surface objects are available. To find it, one must turn rocks,

limbs, and boards, as well as dead cacti and other desert plants (especially yucca, agave, and sotol). In Texas its active season usually lasts from early March to mid-November. In Big Bend National Park it is often found under leaf litter scattered over the slopes and gullies of Green Gulch and the Basin. In Arizona, according to Fowlie (1965), it is not uncommon for this snake to crawl under dried cow dung during unusually hot weather, drawn there by the condensation that has dampened the underlying soil. Not all of its time is spent in hiding, for it is occasionally found on roads at night, particularly when the asphalt is still wet from a recent rain.

FEEDING Most reports mention centipedes, millipedes, and insect larvae as the usual prey of this species. Lindner (1962), however, examined the digestive tracts of 37 specimens and found that they contained only butterfly, moth, and beetle larvae. Fowlie, on the other hand, believed that his Arizona specimens fed largely or altogether on spiders, though he gave no evidence to support this conclusion.

In common with other native serpents of the genus *Tantilla*, this species has a pair of slightly enlarged, grooved teeth on the back end of each upper jawbone, which, together with a weak venom, the snake apparently uses to subdue its struggling prey. (See illustration in flat-headed snake account.) Despite its potential to thus stun small invertebrate animals, this diminutive snake is not dangerous to man.

REPRODUCTION Each of three females of this species collected by Easterla (1975) in Big Bend National Park laid a single egg on the following dates: June 23, July 28, and August 4. When laid, each egg was about 1 inch (2.5 cm) long. Since the eggs apparently failed to hatch, we have no information about the size of the infants.

PLAINS BLACK-HEADED SNAKE
Tantilla nigriceps
PLATE 147

DESCRIPTION The dark cap of this small, slender serpent stands out in sharp contrast to its pale body, a characteristic shared by nearly all other native species of the genus *Tantilla*. In this species the dark brown to

black cephalic pigmentation begins at the snout and extends backward to a point along the dorsal midline two to five scales behind the last pair of large plates on the crown (the parietals), ending in a distinctly convex or

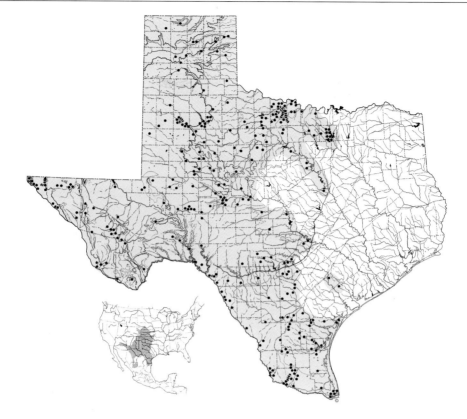

even pointed line of demarcation where it meets the light brown to brownish gray body color. The dark cap is not followed by a pale collar, nor does it reach down along the sides as far as the end of the mouthline, though it extends down either side of the head to the top edges of the upper lip scales. The abdomen is pink to reddish along the midline, whitish along the outer edges. On either side of the snake's small head, which is no wider than the neck, are seven upper lip scales. The first pair of lower lip scales normally meet beneath the chin. The dorsal scales, all smooth, are in 15 midbody rows, the loreal scale is absent, and the anal plate is divided.

COMPARABLE SNAKES The crown of the flat-headed snake, ordinarily just a bit darker than the serpent's upper body, is sometimes covered by a solid blackish cap, in which case its well-defined rear margin is concave. In both the Mexican and southwestern black-headed snakes, the dark cap is shorter than in the plains black-headed snake (usually ending one to three scales beyond the parietal plates), and its rear margin is normally straight across

the nape and bordered behind by an indistinct pale collar. The Trans-Pecos black-headed snake's head and throat are completely black, or the black forecrown is followed by a distinct white collar, interrupted by a median black line or not, and then by a dark bar. It also has a sizable white spot on its snout and another below and behind each eye, and the black pigmentation on top of its head reaches down below the end of the mouthline. Its belly is white. Ring-necked snakes have a yellow or orange collar (in the prairie subspecies) or usually none at all (in the regal subspecies), but each has a loreal scale and distinct but random black spotting on its yellow to yellowish orange belly. The Great Plains ground snake has a loreal scale and lacks a distinct black cap.

SIZE Adults are generally 7 to 10 inches (17.8–25.4 cm) long. A record specimen measured 15¹/₁₆ inches (38.3 cm) in length.

HABITAT Primarily a resident of rocky grassland prairies and desert grassland, it also occurs in such diverse habitats as thorn scrub and open elevated woodlands, usually where there is at least a small amount of moisture. Despite the snake's broad distribution across the western two-thirds of the state, few accounts detail its habitat preferences.

One such habitat profile was reported by Fouquette and Lindsay (1955) for a northwestern Texas study site. Of 12 plains black-headed snakes the zoologists collected in Hutchinson County, 6 were discovered on sandy limestone slopes that rose rather abruptly from a nearby creekbed, where the vegetation was chiefly sparse bluestem, grama grasses, and sumac; on the hilltops it consisted of buffalo and grama grasses. Three others were found along the ordinarily dry, wide creekbed, in which water could be found only at night and following heavy rains. Three more were encountered in the deep, gradually rising sands above the creek, an area of rather dense vegetation consisting of a heavy growth of sage, scattered clumps of sumac, and a ground cover of grasses. Two specimens came from Wet Tobacco Creek, a floodplain location in Dawson County, where the soil was less sandy than in the previously described floodplain; the dominant plant growth was mesquite.

BEHAVIOR In spite of the two small fangs on the back of each upper jawbone and the presence of weak toxins in its primitive venom glands, this timid little snake is harmless to man. Its venom resources are used only to help subdue the snake's tiny invertebrate prey.

Like most species of the genus *Tantilla*, it is seldom seen actively crawling about in the open; such infrequent aboveground forays usually take place after warm evening or nighttime showers. If it is encountered at all, chances are it will be discovered hiding beneath any of a variety of surface objects that include flat rocks (its preferred shelter), boards, and even dried cattle dung. It also occurs beneath human debris scattered along roadways. In the mesquite chaparral of the lower Rio Grande Valley, B. C. Brown (1950) found four specimens in junkyards (two under old pieces of cardboard, one beneath a piece of gypsum wallboard, and one in the soil under a cactus plant), all during warm, sunny winter days. Other objects under which the snake has been reported to take refuge include logs, compost piles, and pieces of sheet metal.

A moderately cold-resistant species, the plains black-headed snake is generally active from February to November in South Texas and from April to October in the northern part of the state, where during severe winter weather it moves several feet down into the ground to avoid the lethal effects of subfreezing temperatures.

FEEDING Although various authors have mentioned a wide range of invertebrate animals as the natural prey of this species, no comprehensive study has been conducted to verify such reports. Even anecdotal information about the snake's diet is scarce. Items said to be eaten by the plains black-headed snake include centipedes, millipedes, spiders, worms, and both insects and their larvae.

REPRODUCTION Nothing has been reported about the reproductive biology of this species, except the statement by Tennant (1984) that a captive specimen maintained by Jim Stout laid 2 eggs on June 11. The eggs, which hatched on July 25, produced babies 2½ inches (6.1 cm) long.

WESTERN BLACK-NECKED GARTER SNAKE

Thamnophis cyrtopsis cyrtopsis
PLATE 148

DESCRIPTION Like other Texas garter snakes, this one is marked with three pale lengthwise stripes on a dark body. In the western black-necked garter the center stripe is typically orange close to the head, fading to off-white or pale yellow on the rest of the trunk; each side stripe, generally positioned on scale rows 2 and 3 above the belly plates, is pale yellow at the front of the body but becomes whitish or pale brown farther back on the trunk. In addition, each lateral stripe is often flanked below by another, less distinct stripe

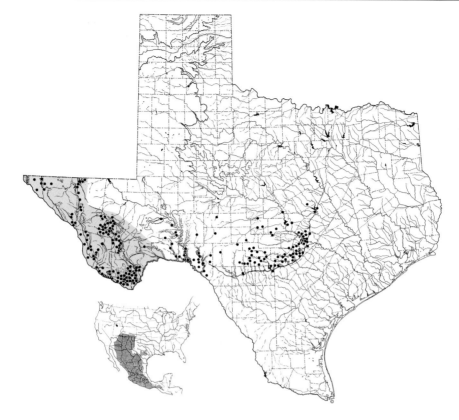

of slightly darker hue, whose bottom edge may be lined with a continuous row of regularly spaced, small black spots. These spots are either singular or arranged in vertical pairs. Between the center stripe and each side stripe are two alternating rows of larger black spots, indistinct in some specimens, prominent in others (particularly on the forebody). For example, black-necked garter snakes from the Big Bend region display a uniformly black or dark brown ground color between the stripes, whereas individuals from the western end of the state tend to be light brown along the sides, with dusky spotting. Whatever its coloration, a specimen that has flattened or inflated its body as a threat gesture, or whose skin has been tightly stretched after a heavy meal, takes on a strangely speckled look as the light-colored, dashlike spots, ordinarily concealed by the overlapping scales, are exposed.

Another conspicuous hallmark is the pair of large, black blotches directly behind the snake's gray or bluish gray–topped head.

Sometimes each blotch is preceded by an abbreviated white crescent near the end of the mouthline. Also prominent on the head are vertical black margins along some or all of the light-colored upper lip scales, a standard feature of all Texas garter snake species. The chin, throat, and belly normally are white, but in some specimens they have a greenish or bluish tint. The body scales are keeled and usually in 19 rows at midbody. The anal plate is single.

COMPARABLE SNAKES *See eastern black-necked garter snake account.* In the checkered garter snake, the white or yellowish crescent near the end of the mouthline is tall, reaching nearly to the top of the snake's head; each light side stripe occupies only the third row of scales above the belly, at least on the forebody (both second and third rows in the western black-necked garter snake); and the dorsal scales are in 21 rows at midbody. The arid land ribbon snake, which is more slender than the garter snake, has an unblotched dorsum and unmarked upper lip

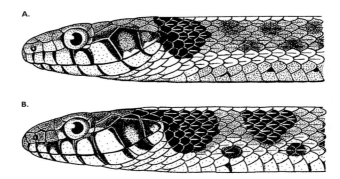

Figure 58. *Lateral body marks of black-necked garter snake subspecies: (a) double row of black spots on the side of the western black-necked garter snake and (b) a single row on the eastern black-necked garter snake.*

scales, and there are no large black blotches on its neck. Patch-nosed snakes, which lack bold head and neck markings as well as dark body blotches, have smooth dorsal scales and a divided anal plate.

SIZE Adults are generally between 16 and 28 inches (40.6–71.1 cm) in length. A record specimen measured 42³⁄₁₆ inches (107.2 cm) long.

HABITAT Restricted to the Trans-Pecos region of the state, this serpent occupies a variety of habitats ranging from arid desert flats near sea level to the forested slopes of the Davis Mountains 5,700 feet (1,737 m) high, though it seems to prefer rocky canyon streams and small permanent bodies of water situated in foothills and on mountains. Otherwise it is remarkably adaptable, living in areas containing abundant ground cover or in rocky places devoid of vegetation. At the same time, it generally avoids the sandy lowland environments, those more likely to be inhabited by its close neighbor, the checkered garter snake. Whenever it has a choice, it selects rocky situations over those with a soil substrate. For example, of 15 specimens collected in the Black Gap region of southeastern Brewster County by Axtell and his colleagues (1959) during a five-week field study, 8 were discovered near limestone streambeds and their associated pools, and only 2 were found around the area's manmade earthen stock tanks. Some of its other haunts include desert grassland, chaparral woodland, talus slopes, oak forest, and pine-fir woodland. It may also be found in remote desert areas, but its presence in such seemingly untenable places usually indicates the presence of springs or some other form of permanent moisture, however scant, for water and its associated amphibian prey are critical to the snake's survival.

Just how much this aridland serpent depends on moisture is revealed by Jameson and Flury (1949). Their field studies in the Sierra Vieja Mountains of southwestern Texas showed that of 102 specimens collected on the Miller Ranch in 1948, all but 3 came from the vicinity of streambeds, 1 was taken from a lake in the tobosa-grama association, and 2 others from the catclaw-cedar vegetation at the mouth of a canyon. Even more detailed is Mosauer's (1932) description of the snake's microhabitat in a portion of the Guadalupe Mountains. Three specimens he observed there routinely basked in the sunshine of a grassy streamside bank that was moistened by the spray from a nearby small riffle.

This species may directly benefit from man's alteration of the landscape. A day-active reptile, it tends to lose body water more rapidly than nocturnal snakes, and since it is not a true desert-adapted species, it depends more on surface moisture than typical aridland serpents. Wherever agricultural irrigation or the damming of transient streams or springs occurs in the desert, the western black-necked garter snake exploits the new source of water, for such an artificial niche frequently provides a more dependable water supply and a greater source of amphibian prey than many natural bodies of water in the Trans-Pecos. As long ago as 1939, Klauber reported this phenomenon in southern California's Imperial Valley. He discovered that irrigated sections of land within this chiefly desert environment attracted sizable numbers of several snake species, those known to be more widely scattered in the drier neighboring regions. One species in particular, the checkered garter snake, did not previously inhabit the valley. This moisture-dependent reptile invaded the area only after agricultural development provided the water necessary to sustain it and its amphibian prey. To reach these farmlands from distant rivers, it migrated along the vast network of freeflowing irrigation canals that connected the two, much as the western black-necked garter has done in West Texas. Meanwhile, the sidewinder rattler, a true desert dweller and a historical inhabitant of California's Imperial Valley, regularly avoided the wet cultivated fields, apparently unable to adapt to the area's high humidity.

BEHAVIOR   Like most other garter snakes, the western black-necked is relatively mild-mannered, normally biting only if roughly handled or severely provoked. Even then, most specimens refuse to use their teeth defensively. One that is intimidated may respond by flattening its forebody and its head, which it widens into an ominous triangle, apparently to mimic the broad cephalic configuration of a pit viper. For additional emphasis, the snake may even add a menacing hiss to this brazen but innocuous display. Unlike individuals in other parts of the subspecies' range, specimens of *T. c. cyrtopsis* collected by Fleharty (1967) in Catron County, New Mexico, proved less submissive following this stereotyped bluff, frequently striking out at their opponents when unable to flee.

It is not unusual for a captured black-necked garter snake to retaliate by spewing an odorous musk from its scent glands and a vile discharge of fecal matter from its cloacal opening, the smell and feel of which can be offensive enough to encourage its prompt release. This behavior is widespread among the various species of garter and water snakes and is used as well by many other ophidian species.

Field collecting records in Texas point to an annual activity cycle that begins sometime in March and lasts through most of October. Chiefly a daytime prowler when temperatures are not too high, the western black-necked garter snake forages mostly during the morning and late afternoon, spending the intervening hours settled along the shoreline of a stream or pond or basking atop a rock jutting out of the water. From such a perch it quickly enters the water if alarmed, swimming across the surface to the safest refuge, usually the shoreline farthest from the disturbance. At night it finds sanctuary in the spaces where tree roots are exposed along streambanks, as well as in rodent burrows, rock and streambank crevices, and in piles of dead vegetation.

In the Trans-Pecos, the dry season normally occurs in late spring and early summer. During this period of hot weather, when temperatures regularly soar past 100 degrees F, the already meager supply of surface water is often reduced to mere pockets of riverbed pools and puddles of muddy water. It is then that the garter snake becomes more sedentary and nocturnal. At such times it aggregates around these limited reserves of moisture, both to help conserve its own body fluids and to feed on the large concentrations of amphibian prey that are also compelled by drought conditions to gather there. Once the rains of midsummer arrive, however, it moves out into the damp countryside, making the most of the scattered puddles created by passing showers. At other times it can be found a mile or more from the nearest surface water, though such far-reaching excursions away from moisture are unusual. To learn something about the serpent's natural wanderings, Fleharty marked, released, and then recaptured a number of black-necked garter snakes. Of these, only 18 percent were recovered more than once, and very few were seen again as long as two years later, many presumably having been destroyed by local fishermen during the course of the study. Despite the low retrieval rate, certain useful information was obtained. For instance, the greatest distance traveled by one of these snakes (780 feet) was recorded over a period of less than one year, and during the course of a single day a specimen moving overland traveled just 34 feet from the original point of release. Another snake, which was swimming across a lake, covered a distance of 150 feet in the journey from one side to the other.

FEEDING   Most of what we know about the feeding habits of this reptile is contained in three studies. One, conducted in Central and West Texas by Fouquette (1954), explored the effects of food competition among three kinds of garter snakes and a ribbon snake living in the same region of the state. Another, performed by Fleharty (1967), examined the results of competition among three species of *Thamnophis* inhabiting a New Mexico study site. The third, conducted by Jones (1990), investigated habitat use and the predatory behavior of the black-necked garter snake along two desert streams in western Arizona.

One fact to emerge from these studies was that the adult snake feeds almost exclusively on amphibian prey (chiefly frogs, toads, and their tadpoles), whereas the newborn western black-necked garter snake, too small to consume adult anurans, eats mostly very small fish and some young tadpoles. Specific food items mentioned in the studies included Great Plains and red-spotted toads, canyon tree frog, Great Plains narrowmouth toad, plains spadefoot, lowland and Rio Grande leopard frogs, bullfrog, and minnows.

Fouquette's results showed that of 40 specimens with identifiable food in their stomachs, 39 had consumed amphibians: 61 percent of the snakes had taken tadpoles, 36 percent adult frogs and toads, and 5 percent salamanders. More than half the snakes with tadpoles in their stomachs had eaten those of the canyon tree frog, and a third contained those of the Great Plains narrowmouth toad. Only 2 had devoured leopard frog tadpoles. The study also revealed that the serpents had eaten a greater variety of adult than larval anuran species, including, in order of importance, the leopard frog, red-spotted toad, Great Plains toad, plains spadefoot, canyon tree frog, and cliff chirping frog. Up to this point, the data provide an overall picture of the *T. cyrtopsis* menu, combining the diets of both the eastern and western subspecies, yet their diets are not always the same. Some species of amphibian prey living within the range of one snake subspecies do not necessarily inhabit that of the other. The menus of both subspecies change seasonally, with tadpoles making up a significant part of the snakes' diet in June and July, whereas during spring and again in late summer, adult frogs and toads constitute the primary source of food.

In the spring, for example, when adult frogs and toads are widely scattered through the re-gion's plentiful and diverse aquatic habitats, the snake actively searches for them along streambeds and their associated riffles and secondarily around the shorelines of creeks and lakes. At this time of year the snake preys mainly on leopard frogs. So gregarious are these abundant amphibians that frequently as many as 75 individuals will gather along a streambank, the mass of bodies so closely packed that some frogs are obliged to perch on the backs of others. This tendency to congregate makes them especially vulnerable to garter snake predation. The canyon tree frog, common along boulder-strewn waterways, also falls victim to this snake, but the amphibian's inclination to hide in rock crevices during daylight hours when the reptile is actively foraging significantly reduces its exposure to predation.

Later in the season, when the scorching sun has reduced many such bodies of water to remnant pools and puddles and eliminated others altogether, the serpent's amphibian prey are confined to increasingly fewer water holes, where adult and larval frogs can sometimes be astonishingly abundant. During this annual period of drought, the black-necked garter snake gives up its wandering habits to concentrate instead on the cornucopia of prey available in the area's few remnant puddles and pools. To catch the actively moving tadpoles and adult frogs in such bodies of water, particularly in the deeper pools, the snake employs a sit-and-wait, or ambush, strategy. Jones discovered that in this mode the garter snake floats partially submerged and motionless in the water, its head effectively concealed in the mats of surface algae. In this posture the serpent waited for its prey. When an unsuspecting adult leopard frog (the chief prey item in the study) swam within striking range, it was quickly seized and swallowed. Not all such attempts were successful. Of 29 initial strikes observed by Jones, only 17 produced results. When a snake failed to make a catch on its first lunge, it often chased its target for a short distance, staying on the surface of the pond or pursuing the frog underwater briefly (never for more than 10 seconds).

It is evident from these observations that the black-necked garter snake submerges for only a relatively short time. Fleharty suggested that since the snake's specific gravity is lower than that of certain other, more aquatic garter snake species, its greater degree of natural buoyancy makes it better adapted for surface hunting than for deep diving. This may also explain why fish are seldom included in the adult snake's diet.

Drummond (1983) also expressed the view that diving serpents, which routinely forage along the bottom of ponds, are equipped with a specialized eye lens that enhances underwater vision and thereby improves the serpent's ability to detect prey, a feature presumably absent in surface-floating species such as *T. c. cyrtopsis.*

Newborn western black-necked garter snakes, too small to consume adult anurans, feed chiefly on small fish and transforming tadpoles. Both prey items represent a highly vulnerable source of food for the tiny serpents. Transforming tadpoles are at an awkward stage of development, being unable either to swim very well or to hop effectively, and tiny fish have a tendency to become trapped in small, isolated pools during the dry season, where they can be readily captured by the young snakes. It is probably no coincidence, therefore, that among the only reported observations of western black-necked garter snake births in nature, each of four females gave birth to her young while partly submerged in a landlocked pool filled with appropriately sized prey, ostensibly to give the babies direct and immediate access to food. That the newborn serpents consume dead as well as live fish is documented by Jones, who watched four individuals take such prey from nearly dry pools.

REPRODUCTION Although no information is available concerning the mating period or breeding behavior of this subspecies, it has been suggested that copulation may actually occur in the fall. The young, born sometime during June, July, or August, consist of 7 to 25 babies per litter, each newborn snake measuring between 8 and 10 inches (20.3–25.4 cm) long. At birth their colors are brighter and more contrasting than those of adults.

One Arizona herpetologist reported seeing four females give birth to their young while partly submerged in pools. This report, combined with the observations of other naturalists who witnessed newborn-size western black-necked garter snakes swimming in shallow bodies of water, suggests that birthing in water may be the normal mode for this snake.

EASTERN BLACK-NECKED GARTER SNAKE
Thamnophis cyrtopsis ocellatus
PLATES 149, 150

DESCRIPTION The standard character used to identify this garter snake is the single row of large dark spots on either side of the serpent's neck, in addition to a large, black blotch at the back of the head. In typical garter snake fashion, three light-colored stripes run the length of the body, one down the middle of the back and another low on either side. The one along the spine is orange or orange-yellow; the other two, on scale rows 2 and 3 above the belly plates, are pale yellow or off-white. Farther back on the yellowish to olive-green trunk, the lateral dark spots form a double row, the lowest series infringing onto the lateral stripe from above. This, together with a similar encroachment of smaller black spots from below, gives the stripe a distinctly wavy look. Toward the tail the two rows of larger black spots merge to form a broad black band that continues to the end of the tail. (See illustration in western black-necked garter snake account.)

The snake's gray or bluish gray crown is generally unmarked, but as in other Texas garter snakes, the whitish upper lip scales bear prominent black streaks along their vertical sutures. The chin, throat, and abdomen usually are white but in some individuals may have a greenish tint. The keeled dorsal scales are arranged in 19 rows at midbody, and the anal plate is single.

COMPARABLE SNAKES No other Texas garter snake species is marked with a single row of large, black spots on either side of its neck. In the checkered garter snake each of the pale side stripes involves only the third row of

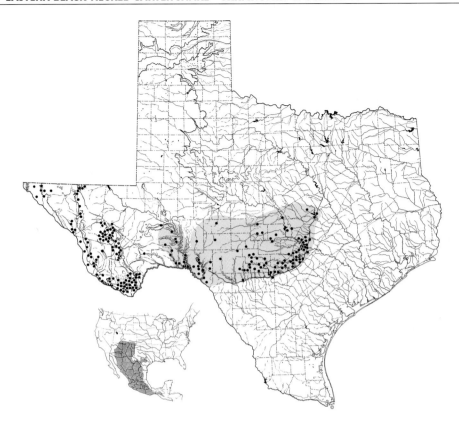

scales above the belly, at least on the fore-body (both the second and third rows in the eastern black-necked garter snake), and the dorsal scale rows are in 21 rows at midbody. In the Texas garter snake, the bright orange center stripe is wider, occupying one full scale row plus half of each adjacent row, and each lateral stripe involves the third row of scales above the belly plates in addition to parts of rows 2 and 4. The red-striped ribbon snake is longer and more slender; it has an unblotched body and unmarked white upper lip scales. Patch-nosed snakes, which lack prominent head and neck markings, have smooth dorsal scales and a single anal plate.

SIZE The usual adult length is between 16 and 20 inches (40.6–50.8 cm); a specimen of record size measured 43 inches (109.2 cm) long.

HABITAT This snake occurs sporadically across the Edwards Plateau, one of the state's most arid natural regions. It exists in such a hostile environment by staying close to the countless springs, streams, and seeps that emanate from the plateau's vast underground aquifers, providing the moisture indispensable to the serpent's survival. Where natural watercourses are in short supply, it frequently resides near stock tanks, though rockier places are usually preferred. As a result, it is most likely to be found in rocky canyons, on stone-covered hillsides, and among limestone outcroppings.

BEHAVIOR A reasonably mild-mannered reptile, the eastern black-necked garter snake seldom defends itself by biting. Instead, it often flattens its head and forebody in a bold attempt to frighten away its foe, although the effect of such a bluff on a determined opponent is probably negligible. One that is picked up usually employs the typical garter snake tactic of expelling a noxious-smelling musk from its scent glands, at the same time defecating on the handler. The offensive odor of these substances, plus the feel of the slimy discharge on a captor's hand, often gains the snake its immediate release.

According to Vermersch and Kuntz (1986), this snake emerges from hibernation sometime in April, although following a mild winter it probably comes to the surface even earlier. It is essentially a day-active serpent, which may become nocturnal during the hottest season of the year when prolonged exposure to the torrid sun would be unbearable. Otherwise it tends to bask comfortably in the warm sun of spring and fall, spending the cool nights coiled under rocks, logs, and piles of dead vegetation or in the spaces where tree roots grow out of streambanks.

Seasonal rainfall markedly influences its movements. During the early part of the year, for example, when precipitation is scant, many of the region's sources of flowing water eventually dry up or are reduced to remnant pools and puddles. At such times the serpent fastidiously limits its travels, confining itself instead to the scattered pockets of water that contain the moisture and amphibian food necessary for its survival. When summer rains sweep across the plateau and refresh the parched earth, the garter snake resumes its frequent wanderings, for the moisture and prey once narrowly concentrated are again widely available.

FEEDING In the only comprehensive study ever undertaken of the feeding habits of this species in Texas (including both subspecies), Fouquette (1954) determined that frogs, toads, and their tadpoles were by far the most important items in the serpent's diet.

Although the diet of the eastern black-necked garter snake has not been as well investigated as that of its close relative, the western black-necked, Fouquette lists prey items taken in nature specifically by *T. c. ocellatus.* They include Great Plains and red-spotted toads, canyon tree frog, cliff chirping frog, leopard frog, slimy salamander, and ground skink. The kinds of food items consumed by the very young snakes in a natural state have not been reported but are probably restricted to tiny fish and small tadpoles, the same sort of prey eaten by babies of the western subspecies. Worms, which were rarely accepted by Fouquette's captive specimens, cannot be considered this snake's natural food, nor can mice, crickets, beetles, and caterpillars, all of which were offered to the snakes but consistently refused.

See also western black-necked garter snake account.

REPRODUCTION Surprisingly little has been recorded about the reproductive biology of this subspecies. According to Vermersch and Kuntz (1986), breeding occurs in April or May, resulting in litters of 7 to 25 young. Born between late June and the end of August, the baby snakes are more vividly colored than the adults. Each measures 7 to $10\frac{1}{2}$ inches (17.8–26.7 cm) long.

CHECKERED GARTER SNAKE
Thamnophis marcianus marcianus
PLATES 151, 152

DESCRIPTION The ground color of this snake varies from yellow to dark gray, though most specimens are tan or pale gray. Besides the typical garter snake pattern of three pale-colored longitudinal stripes on the body, the snake's most distinctive pattern element is the bold checkerboard design of squarish dark spots lying in two rows on either side of the trunk between the narrow white or yellowish center stripe and the less well-defined lateral stripe, with a third row under the last stripe. The pale center stripe may be the width of just a single scale row, or it can involve part of each adjacent row as well. Its edges are either straight and sharply delineated or slightly jagged where the adjacent

dark blotches encroach upon them. Near the head, each pale side stripe occupies only the third row of dorsal scales, counting up from the edge of the belly; farther back on the trunk, it widens to include both the second and third rows. The only dark pigmentation on the whitish or cream-colored abdomen consists of small dark spots on the outer edges of each belly plate.

The head is somewhat wide at the back and distinct from the neck. On top it is either uniformly olive (in olive-gray specimens) or light brown (in straw-colored individuals), except for a pair of small, black-edged white or yellowish spots near its center. The most distinctive cephalic markings, however, are

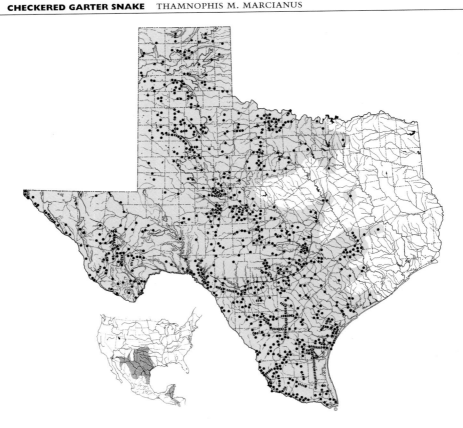

those on either side of the head, where a whitish or bright yellow crescent, preceded by a black border and followed by a large black collar, reaches upward onto the head from near the end of the mouthline. The color of the last two upper lip plates matches that of the crown, and the remaining labial scales above the mouth are off-white or vivid cream. Several are vertically edged in black, the lines bordering the back edges of the fifth and sixth upper lip scales being the most prominent. The last line, which is by far the longest, extends upward nearly to the top of the snake's head. The dorsal body scales are keeled and arranged in 21 rows at midbody. The anal plate is entire.

COMPARABLE SNAKES Among the several cohabiting garter snakes with which it may be confused, the eastern black-necked and western plains garter snakes most nearly resemble *T. m. marcianus*. The eastern black-necked garter has a single horizontal row of large black blotches on either side of its neck, a center stripe that frequently is orange, a wavy pale stripe low on each side, only 19 rows of midbody dorsal scales, and no well-defined yellowish crescent near the back of its head. Furthermore, the large black spots that dominate the body create the impression of an overall dark snake (the checkered garter is basically pale-toned). Likewise in the western black-necked garter there is

Figure 59. *Head markings of the checkered garter snake, including the distinct pale-colored crescent near the end of the mouthline.*

no clear-cut yellowish crescent at the back of the head; the center body stripe is generally orange, at least on the forebody; each side of the neck is marked with a large black blotch; and the dorsal scales are in 19 rows at midbody. Although the plains garter snake may have a yellow crescent behind the end of the mouthline and two lateral rows of alternating dark spots, it lacks a wide, dark collar. In addition, its dorsal stripe is usually orange, and each side stripe, at least on the forebody, occupies dorsal rows 3 and 4 above the belly. The Texas garter snake, whose overall dorsal ground color is much darker than that of the checkered garter, is marked along the spine by a wide orange center stripe. It has neither a yellow crescent on the side of its head nor a black collar; each of its yellowish side stripes is on the third dorsal scale row and on most of the second and fourth rows, at least on the forebody; and only 19 dorsal scale rows circle the trunk at midbody. The red-sided garter snake is adorned with red or orange bars along the sides of its body and lacks both the yellow crescent and the dark collar. In sharp contrast to the checkered garter snake, ribbon snakes are long, slender serpents with unblotched backs and unmarked upper lip scales; they have no dark collar and no yellowish crescent. The small lined snake, which has no distinctive marks on its head or neck, has two parallel rows of bold half-moons down the center of its belly. The lengthwise-striped patch-nosed snakes, which also lack bold head and neck markings, possess smooth dorsal scales and a divided anal plate.

SIZE The usual adult length varies from 18 to 24 inches (45.7–61 cm). At 42½ inches (107.9 cm) long, the largest known specimen is a veritable giant for its kind.

HABITAT Better suited to a dry environment than most other Texas garter snakes, this abundant serpent is widely distributed across the arid and semiarid western three-quarters of the state. It occurs in a variety of habitats at low to midlevel elevations, extending from the dry grasslands of the Panhandle to the South Texas thornbrush savanna. It avoids the higher mountain elevations, usually ascending no higher than about 3,000 feet (912 m). In the vicinity of the Guadalupe Mountains, for instance, Mecham (1979) says the checkered garter snake occurs along

the lower eastern and northeastern slopes, staying close to permanent sources of water, just as in Big Bend National Park, according to Easterla (1989), it does not live high in the Chisos Mountains but remains close to fixed bodies of water, however large or small, along the Rio Grande floodplain and its principle tributaries, Tornillo and Terlingua creeks. Nevertheless, the snake is occasionally discovered a considerable distance from permanent water. A specimen collected in Hutchinson County by Fouquette and Lindsay (1955) was about 1,000 yards (917 m) from the nearest surface water. Where moisture is scarce, particularly in desert regions, the checkered garter snake is often attracted to temporary bodies of water that include mud puddles, roadside ditches, and flooded fields, and it can be unusually abundant along the permanent irrigation canals that have turned some of this barren landscape into productive farmland. Though it is sometimes found in open woodland, it prefers treeless terrain over heavily shaded habitats.

BEHAVIOR Unless seriously provoked, the checkered garter snake seldom strikes or bites. This is a relatively gentle creature whose first line of defense upon being handled is to expel musk from its scent glands and a dose of slimy fecal material from its cloaca, a strategy that often succeeds in gaining its release.

As with other serpent species whose north to south distribution encompasses the entire state of Texas, the length of the checkered garter snake's seasonal activity cycle varies with latitude. In Kansas, for example, and probably across the Texas Panhandle as well, the serpent first leaves its winter den sometime in April; in South Texas it comes out of hibernation as early as March. When roused from winter lethargy by an interlude of unusually warm weather, it may emerge even earlier. For example, on February 19, 1949, during a mild winter in the San Antonio area, we discovered a large adult checkered garter snake crawling along the shore of Olmos Creek, and another the following day near the same place.

For the next several months of balmy weather the snake is strictly day-active, but with the arrival of midsummer's hot, cloudless days, it will probably not be seen abroad in daylight, choosing instead to hide in some cool, shaded nook until late evening. Such a retreat can take the form of a rock, log, board, discarded tin, rock crevice, animal burrow, or pile of decaying plant litter. In Barber County, Kansas, one was found just inside the opening of a gypsum cave (Collins 1993).

After leaving its temporary refuge, the checkered garter snake forages through the night. Once comfortable daytime temperatures return in late summer, it resumes its diurnal activities, for this species is essentially a daylight wanderer. Even then, it is sometimes seen foraging at the surface after a warm evening or following a nighttime shower, often in large numbers, perhaps to avail itself of the abundant amphibian prey that also become surface-active when the ground has been soaked by a sudden heavy rain. This can occur at any time during its active season. By October, checkered garter snakes living in Kansas (the upper end of their geographic range) will crawl into an animal burrow or find a deep crevice on some rocky hillside in which to spend the winter; those in South Texas will do so much later, in November or even December, depending on local weather conditions.

FEEDING Where adequate moisture exists in the form of springs, streams, ponds, roadside ditches or irrigation canals, this species feeds chiefly on adult frogs and toads as well as on their tadpoles. In a diverse list of anuran prey found in the stomachs of wild-caught checkered garter snakes from Texas, Fouquette (1954) included Woodhouse's, Great Plains, and green toads; leopard and spotted chorus frogs; and both Couch's and plains spadefoots.

At times, such prey can be remarkably abundant. When they come together for their annual breeding aggregations, the anurans present the snake with a short-term feeding bonanza, for during these few days the frogs and toads are confined to a relatively small area and, being totally preoccupied with mating and egg-laying, become easy targets for a variety of predators. In due time, when the amphibian eggs hatch, the tadpoles in turn become a bountiful source of food for the foraging reptiles. Fouquette, for example, discovered more than 40 leopard frog tadpoles in the stomach of one checkered garter snake from Presidio County. Salamanders are eaten as well, but they apparently constitute only a small part of the snake's diet. A checkered garter snake collected near Austin contained a large smallmouth salamander.

Earthworms are the second most significant item on the snake's menu, with lizards ranking next in importance, particularly in arid regions where earthworms and amphibians are unlikely to thrive. In such places, earless lizards are especially vulnerable to predation by this species. Fish and slugs are also mentioned as occasional prey items, as are small rodents, although such animals are probably consumed only rarely. Carrion may also be eaten. One checkered garter snake, for instance, was observed swallowing a large toad that had been crushed on a highway by passing vehicular traffic.

REPRODUCTION It is early spring, and the male garter snake, having endured months of forced inactivity and now stirred by the sun's warmth, leaves his winter den. Spring has arrived, and with it his desire to find a mate. For most species of garter snakes living far to the north, where males and females overwinter together in large numbers within a single communal hibernaculum, copulation simply occurs as both sexes leave the den, the males generally emerging first, followed by the females. For the male checkered garter snake, which probably hibernates alone, finding a mate is not so simple. To locate a female and consummate a mating, he may have to travel some distance from the den. But wandering about aimlessly without some clue to her whereabouts would expend a great deal of energy and increase his risk of being spotted by a predator. The solution is a species-specific chemical scent, called a pheromone, produced by the female during the breeding season, which allows the male to track her, sight unseen. This substance might loosely be compared to the perfume used by humans of one sex to attract those of the other. Such chemicals, carried in the blood of the female garter snake and secreted through her structurally adapted skin, leave an uninterrupted trail on the substrate as she moves over the ground. This pheromone, produced only by the female checkered garter snake, is never followed by other females of the same species and rarely by males of other species.

Copulation occurs sometime between late

March and the end of May, producing individual litters of 3 to 30 young sometime from June to early October. In a sample group of gravid females from South Texas and northeastern Mexico, Ford and Karges (1987) found the average litter size to be 13.2 infants. The same zoologists demonstrated that some details of the snake's breeding behavior did not conform to the general reproductive patterns exhibited by the vast majority of our native serpents. Their data showed that in South Texas the female often produced two litters of young in the same year and, as she grew larger over time, the size of her young at birth increased accordingly. Overall, the length of the newborn checkered garter snake varies from 6¼ to 9¼ inches (15.9–23.5 cm).

WESTERN RIBBON SNAKE
Thamnophis proximus proximus
PLATES 153–155

DESCRIPTION This slender, medium-sized black or dark brown snake is longitudinally marked with three conspicuous light stripes. The one along the middle of the back is usually bright yellow or pale orange. The lateral stripe on each side of the body, which always occurs on the third and fourth scale rows above the belly, is pale yellow. Some northeastern Texas specimens are curiously different in displaying a peculiar overall bluish green hue that even pervades the serpent's pale-colored stripes.

The snake's head, which is distinctly wider than the neck, is black or dark brown on top, where it is marked only by a pair of small, prominent pale spots that closely adjoin one another or actually come together. The same dark pigmentation that occurs on the crown extends down each side of the head, stopping above the upper lip scales, which (together with the lower lips and chin) are an immaculate white, cream, or pale greenish color, as is the snake's belly. The other obvious facial marking is a pale vertical bar directly in front of each eye. The heavily keeled dorsal scales are arranged in 19 (rarely 21) rows at midbody, and the anal plate is single.

COMPARABLE SNAKES Although garter snakes are also longitudinally striped, they are stockier and have relatively shorter tails (occupying less than a quarter of the garter snake's total length but nearly a third in the

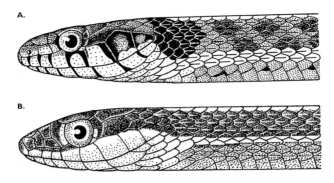

Figure 60. *Head markings of (a) garter snake, including vertical black lines along the sutures of the lip scales, and (b) ribbon snake, with no marks on lip scales.*

ribbon snake). Distinct dark pigmentation marks their upper lip scales and the outer edges of their abdominal plates. Lined snakes, whose bodies also bear three longitudinal pale stripes, have small heads and a double row of bold, black spots down the middle of the abdomen. The bellies of crayfish snakes normally show some dark spotting, and their anal plates are divided.

SIZE Although their slim bodies appear longer than they really are, adult ribbon snakes are usually between 20 and 30 inches (50.8–76.2 cm) long. The maximum known size is nearly 42 inches (107 cm), according to Minton (1972).

HABITAT Although well adapted to a wide variety of habitats, this moisture-loving serpent typically lives along the brushy or grassy margins of still and moving bodies of water ranging from ditches, wallows, cattle tanks, and even water-filled vehicle tracks to marshes, damp meadows, swamps, sloughs, rice fields, ponds, lakes, springs, streams, and rivers. It sometimes invades the edges of soggy woodlands, but it is not considered a forest dweller. It may also inhabit areas disturbed by human development, provided such places are not continually occupied by man.

A notable example of such habitat is an abandoned two-acre housing project in the post oak belt near Bryan, where D. R. Clark (1974) conducted a 31-month study of this subspecies. On this deserted tract, covered with old concrete building foundations, the ribbon snake was abundant, especially along several interconnecting drainage ditches that provided the only choice microhabitats

within a ¾-mile radius of the study site. Minton (1972) pointed out that in Indiana, ribbon snakes are much more sensitive to drastic man-made alterations to their habitat than any of the local garter snakes, noting that disruptive activities such as land cultivation or the elimination of wet lowlands results in their speedy disappearance. Garter snakes, on the other hand, are so adaptable to man-modified habitats that they survive in many inner-city parks long after most other moderate- to large-sized serpents have been eliminated there.

BEHAVIOR The ribbon snake is usually sighted near a pond, stream, or marsh, its long, slender body slipping through the grass or draped gracefully across the limbs of a shrub overhanging the water. At the first approach of a human, it is apt to slide quickly into the water and hide in the aquatic shoreline vegetation or swim rapidly away on the surface. Some naturalists tell of alarmed ribbon snakes diving to the bottom of a stream and hiding there until they perceive the danger has passed (a tactic often used by water snakes), but most observers say that such behavior is unusual for this species. Not every ribbon snake retreats at the first sign of danger. An exceptionally bold individual may stand fast, threaten with a wide-open mouth, and even flatten its body before striking out at its adversary, though usually with little effect, for this snake seldom bites unless picked up. Even then it is reluctant to use its teeth. Instead, it does what countless other snakes do to defend themselves: it releases a strongly scented liquid from the anal glands at the base of its tail and a slimy goo from the cloaca, smearing them over the captor's hand with its frantic writhing. Unlike the musk discharged by most other snake species, that expelled by the ribbon snake has a sweet smell, compared by one zoologist to overripe fruit.

Over most of its vast north-south geographic range, the western ribbon snake remains active from April through October, although at times it has been seen in the open as early in the year as March 9 (in Kansas) and as late as November 30 (in Arkansas). Guidry (1953) reports that its southeastern Texas period of activity lasts from March into November, but he gives no specific dates, though as in the case of many other South Texas snake species, this one probably comes to the surface even earlier than that during mild winters and remains active longer. Because it prefers plenty of solar radiation, the ribbon snake spends the early part of the year in open areas where it can bask in direct sunlight, provided daytime temperatures do not rise excessively. As the vegetation grows and becomes more dense, transforming the sunlit areas into shaded ones, the snake seeks other, more open spaces. Later in the year, with the advent of high summer temperatures, it returns again to its cool, shaded retreats. There is no doubt that this is primarily a daytime serpent, its daily activity cycle divided into morning and afternoon periods, except on warm nights, when it is also likely to be on the prowl. Long-term field studies show that during these excursions, males moved approximately 8 feet (2.4 m) per day and females about 3½ feet (1.1 m); the maximum distance covered between captures was more than 690 feet (211 m) for males and about 318 feet (97 m) for females. According to Ernst and Barbour (1989), this species is inclined to crawl about during light summer rains, perhaps to feed on the amphibians that are often drawn out of hiding by the passing showers.

Moisture, in fact, is of considerable importance to the western ribbon snake. In studying a Brazos County population of this subspecies, D. R. Clark (1974) found that adequate moisture at the surface and in the upper layers of the soil is critical to the serpent's well-being; without it a significant number of snakes might die in a single season. In 1969, for example, when the preceding winter had produced a normal level of rainfall of nearly 15 inches, he collected 104 ribbon snakes in wire-mesh funnel traps. In 1971, following a winter of severely reduced rainfall that measured just under 3½ inches, the zoologist captured only 28 snakes at the same study site. From this, Clark concluded that after an especially dry winter the snakes are deprived of the moisture necessary to prevent desiccation of their bodies and to sustain their amphibian prey, most of which need water to begin the successful development of their progeny. This led him to believe that because of the serious 1971–1972 winter drought, many of the snakes, particularly the young, may have died from desiccation during hibernation and that others probably succumbed to starvation.

When not on the move, the ribbon snake occasionally hides in or under decaying logs or beneath various forms of ground cover, including boards, discarded sheet metal, and sometimes even rocks. It may also crawl into rotting logs or tree stumps to avoid winter's subfreezing temperatures or hibernate in anthills, mammal burrows, springs, or gravelly banks close to water. In Arkansas, six juvenile specimens were once dug from small chambers hollowed out of rocky soil two feet beneath the surface, and in southern Illinois, P. W. Smith (1961) often observed it in the fall at the base of rock bluffs where, he believed, it overwintered in deep underground crevices with northern copperheads and timber rattlers.

FEEDING Frogs and toads (including their tadpoles) are the snake's chief prey, with fish and salamanders representing less important elements in the diet. Lizards, insects, and snakes are eaten only rarely.

One survey, conducted by D. R. Clark in Brazos County, revealed that nearly 92 percent of the local ribbon snakes with food in their stomachs contained frogs and toads (including the tadpoles of leopard frogs, eaten by 25 percent). Each of two others had consumed a lizard and one a fish. Rossman (1963) found a similar feeding pattern among published and unpublished accounts of the species' feeding habits throughout its range. In a table of prey items prepared from those data, he listed 17 different frogs and toads, 2 species of salamanders, and 4 kinds of fish. From all indications, small mammals, lizards, earthworms, and other invertebrates routinely eaten by certain garter snakes are rarely, if ever, devoured by the western ribbon snake.

Since they produce skin secretions harmful to most predators, large toads are generally also avoided, though small ones are not. The few serpent species able to ingest these amphibians safely are those with oversized adrenal glands, although not all snakes so equipped enjoy equal protection from anuran skin-gland toxins. Among our native serpents, the eastern hog-nosed snake, which eats chiefly toads, is endowed with the largest adrenals in relation to its size, whereas those of the ribbon snake are only moderately oversized. Thus, since the digitaloid poisons produced by the well-developed skin glands of adult toads are more toxic than those of immature individuals, the smaller toads are the preferred choice of the ribbon snake. One report stated, for example, that a single western ribbon snake consumed 64 metamorphosing toads at one time, but accounts of this species eating large toads are rare.

To apprehend its prey, the ribbon snake depends on stealth, speed, and maneuverability. Observations made in the wild by Wendelken (1978) help to explain how the ribbon snake hunts the elusive cricket frog, one of its favorite foods, whose small size and erratic escape behavior make it troublesome to find and difficult to catch. Gliding at a leisurely pace over the ground, the reptile pokes its head into places likely to harbor prey. Moving ahead slowly, it often makes a series of three quick, forward thrusts into the surrounding vegetation as it tries to flush its prey from hiding, each probe aimed at a different area across a semicircular arc. Until a frog is driven from shelter, the tactic is repeated many times. When a frog hops into the open, the waiting serpent rushes forward to seize it; the snake's quick, supple body matches the prey's every evasive maneuver. If the fleeing prey is captured, it is promptly swallowed, whole and alive. If it manages to get away, the ribbon snake raises its head a couple of inches above the ground and becomes motionless, apparently anticipating further movement by the now out of sight quarry. After several minutes of fruitless

waiting, the stereotyped probing behavior begins again.

A less sophisticated approach is used to catch prey confined to small bodies of water. When summer droughts have reduced ponds or creeks to mere puddles, ribbon snakes (together with a variety of water snakes and even cottonmouths) frequently gather at such wallows to feast on the impounded aggregations of fish, frogs, and sometimes tadpoles by moving through the shallow water with their mouths wide open, snapping up their victims as they come in contact with the serpent's jaws.

Other ribbon snake feeding bonanzas are the spring or summer breeding choruses of frogs. During such an event, when hundreds of anurans come together at an appropriate body of water to mate and lay their eggs, the serpents find a concentration of prey that is seldom matched elsewhere or at any other time of year. Fouquette (in Rossman 1963) noted that a western ribbon snake stalking a Mexican tree frog on such an occasion advanced whenever the amphibian inflated its balloonlike vocal sac to call but remained motionless when the call was discontinued. Unable to hear airborne sound, the snake evidently took its cue from the rising and falling rhythm of the frog's throat sac, apparently sensing that during such vocalizations the amphibian's body movements would briefly compromise its ordinarily acute vision. When fully inflated, the large vocal sac probably also was a factor in hampering the frog's line of sight.

REPRODUCTION In east-central Texas, male ribbon snakes were found to be sexually mature when less than one year old, but the females reached maturity at approximately two years of age. Although Dundee and Rossman (1989) reported finding gravid females in Louisiana as early in the year as February 28, throughout the subspecies' geographic range copulation typically occurs in April or May. Young may be born as early as the end of June or as late as October (one captive Texas female produced a litter on October 13), but ordinarily births are from mid-July through September, yielding litters of 4 to 27 (average 10–15). Field studies of two western ribbon snake populations revealed that litter size averaged 13 in Louisiana and only 8.4 in Texas, despite similar dimensions in the respective females. At birth the young measure between 9 and 11¾ inches (22.9–29.8 cm) long.

In Illinois, a female ribbon snake about to give birth was discovered beneath a stone lying in pastureland containing only a few su-

mac, coralberry, and mullein plants, suggesting that gravid female ribbon snakes give birth some distance from water, a key element in their usually moist environment.

ARID LAND RIBBON SNAKE
Thamnophis proximus diabolicus
PLATE 156

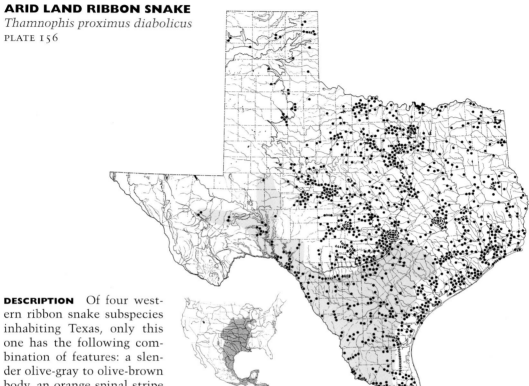

DESCRIPTION Of four western ribbon snake subspecies inhabiting Texas, only this one has the following combination of features: a slender olive-gray to olive-brown body, an orange spinal stripe of moderate width, a pale yellow lateral stripe on either side of the body that often narrows toward the tail and is frequently bordered above by a line of discreet horizontal black dashes, and sometimes a narrow dark stripe along each side just above the belly. Uncommonly dark specimens from tributaries of the Canadian River in the northwestern part of the Texas Panhandle, although geographically much closer to populations of the western ribbon snake than to other arid land ribbon snake colonies far to the south, are nevertheless considered *T. p. diabolicus.*

As in other ribbon snake subspecies, a pair of small, pale, dashlike spots marks the top of the head, both the upper and lower lip scales are pale-colored and immaculate, each yellowish lateral stripe is on scale rows 3 and

4 above the belly, the keeled dorsal scales are arranged in 19 rows at midbody, the pale abdomen displays no dark markings, and the anal plate is single.

COMPARABLE SNAKES Garter snakes are heavier-bodied and have proportionately shorter tails (occupying less than a quarter of the garter snake's total length but nearly a third in the ribbon snake). In addition, they have black markings on the edges of their upper lip scales and some dark pigmentation on the outer edges of their belly plates. Lined snakes have relatively small heads and a double row of bold, black spots down the middle of the abdomen. The dorsal scales of patch-nosed snakes are smooth, the anal plate is divided, and there is no pair of small, pale spots on top of the head.

SIZE Most arid land ribbon snakes are between 2 and 3 feet (61–91.4 cm) long. The largest known example measured 48½ inches (123.2 cm) in length.

HABITAT Across the dry Trans-Pecos region of Texas, in a land that once was more damp and where ribbon snakes no doubt were then more generously distributed, this semiaquatic reptile manages to survive the oppressive aridity by clinging to the margins of major waterways and their tributaries, to ponds and streams, springs and seeps, and even to permanent and semipermanent cattle tanks and irrigation canals. Water, in fact, is a primary environmental factor limiting the ribbon snake's distribution, for it sustains both the serpent's physiological and dietary needs. It is still unclear whether a separate population of this subspecies occurs about 250 miles (403 km) north of the Trans-Pecos along the tributaries of the Canadian River system that wind through flat shortgrass prairie in the northern Panhandle counties of Hartley and Oldham.

BEHAVIOR A denizen of shoreline vegetation, this snake is often seen resting atop a bush or low tree limb overhanging a stream, pond, or marsh. If closely approached, it quickly drops from its perch into the water, swimming to the opposite side or taking cover in the emergent vegetation near shore, but seldom retreating inland.

A provoked ribbon snake is unlikely to bite; its best defense lies in its alertness (enhanced by keen eyesight), speed, and agility. One that is unable to escape may face the enemy, then flatten its head and body in a harmless bluff, hoping to intimidate its foe into a standoff. Once seized, the reptile uses its chemical defenses in an effort to gain its release. Like many other snake species, it emits a pungent musk from a pair of glands at the base of its tail, at the same time expelling a distinctly offensive liquid from its cloacal opening. By vigorously twisting and turning its body, the snake smears the loathsome fluids over its captor, frequently with good results. Repulsed by the slimy, foul-smelling goo, the aggressor is often prompted to release its struggling victim.

In the nearly subtropical Trans-Pecos environment, this serpent may be seen above ground during every month of the year. Even in winter, after several consecutive days of uncommonly high temperatures have warmed the subsurface soil, it may briefly bask in the midday sun. A day-active species in spring and fall, it tends to reverse its daily activity cycle during midsummer when daytime temperatures are unbearably hot. Then it spends the daylight hours concealed in the shade of brushy vegetation near the water's edge or hidden under logs, boards, rocks, or other surface objects. At dusk, when temperatures have moderated, it emerges from its daytime refuge to search for food. It is especially active after warm showers, apparently attracted by the numerous frogs and toads that are themselves stimulated to move about at such times.

FEEDING *See the western ribbon snake account.*

REPRODUCTION Detailed information about the snake's breeding behavior is lacking. Mating in this species generally occurs in April or May, producing litters of 4 to 27 young sometime between late June and mid-September. The newborn snakes measure 9 to 10 inches (22.9–25.4 cm) long.

GULF COAST RIBBON SNAKE

Thamnophis proximus orarius
PLATE 157

DESCRIPTION Of the four subspecies of the western ribbon snake in Texas, this one is characterized by an olive-brown dorsal coloration, a relatively broad stripe of pale gold along its spine, and the absence of a dark stripe below each of its yellowish lateral stripes. The upper lip scales normally are pale yellowish green, except for the first three, which are tan. The belly, also pale green down the middle, is usually faded orange along the outer edges. In common with the other subspecies of *T. proximus*, the Gulf Coast ribbon snake displays a pair of small, pale spots on top of the head, pale upper and

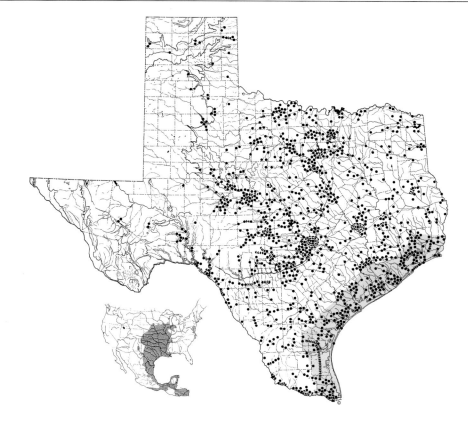

lower lip scales devoid of dark pigmentation, and an unmarked abdomen. Like them, it always has the side stripes on scale rows 3 and 4 above the belly, the keeled dorsal scales in 19 midbody rows, and a single anal plate.

Rossman (1963) mentioned specimens from southeastern Texas (including the Channelview area) and from Refugio, San Patricio, and Victoria counties whose usually all-brown dorsal scales contained varying amounts of black pigmentation. He believed some of them to be intergrades between the Gulf Coast and western ribbon snake subspecies, whereas others may have merely been the result of abnormal chromatic variation.

COMPARABLE SNAKES Garter snakes are heavier-bodied and have relatively shorter tails (occupying less than a quarter of the garter snake's total length but nearly a third in the ribbon snake); some distinct, dark pigmentation marks the upper lip scales and the outer edges of the belly scales. The Texas lined snake, also striped lengthwise, has a small head and carries a double row of bold, black spots down the middle of its belly.

Graham's crayfish snake usually has a row of small, often indistinct dark spots down the middle of its abdomen; the closely related Gulf crayfish snake has the length of its belly punctuated by a double row of prominent black crescents. Neither has a bold, gold spinal stripe, and in both species the anal plate is divided. The Texas patch-nosed snake's dorsal scales are smooth, and its anal plate is divided. Schott's whipsnake, whose anal plate is also divided, has no light spinal stripe; its dorsal scales are smooth and arranged in only 15 rows at midbody.

SIZE The usual adult length for the species is 20 to 30 inches (50.8–76.2 cm), and the record length is 48½ (123.2 cm) inches. It is likely, however, that this subspecies does not attain as great a length as the others.

HABITAT Although this snake occurs abundantly along the entire coastal plain of Texas and Louisiana, little detailed information is available about its ecology. The most comprehensive field study of its habitat and life history is the 13-month survey conducted by Tinkle (1957) at Tulane University's Sarpy

Wildlife Refuge, a largely swampy region in the Mississippi Delta near Lake Pontchartrain, Louisiana. The area, supporting a diversity of ideal microhabitats, harbored a sizable population of ribbon snakes; 221 specimens were encountered there during the study, along with only 73 cottonmouths, 60 broad-banded water snakes, 18 speckled king snakes, 16 eastern yellow-bellied racers, 5 western mud snakes, 4 Texas rat snakes, 3 rough green snakes, and 2 delta crayfish snakes. The others together represented less than the number of *T. p. orarius* observed on the same tract of land.

Situated in a cypress-gum swamp, the area's basic habitats were described as (1) the swamp itself, where less waterlogged expanses supported an abundant palmetto growth, (2) the dry ridges, where predominant plants were willow, maple, and buckrush and where wild blackberry bushes covered much of the open ground, (3) the permanent deep pools, and (4) the extensive shallow-water flats that fluctuated seasonally between being wet and dry and where principal emergent plants in spring and summer consisted of thick clumps of cattail and cutgrass. Areas harboring the most ribbon snakes were the main ridge, a 600-yard-long earthen crest through the swamp, and the shoulders of roadside ditches in the flats.

In Texas, where it is abundant along the Gulf coastal plain from the Louisiana border to Brownsville, the snake occupies a broad range of wet, open habitats including lakes, ponds, streams, marshes, swamps, wet meadows, rice fields, cattle tanks, and ditches. It also inhabits partially open woodland, provided such places contain the moisture necessary to sustain the serpent's amphibian prey. In the southeastern corner of the state, Guidry (1953) found it in a wide variety of terrain, including suburban areas.

BEHAVIOR   For the most part, this active, alert species avoids predators by fleeing. At the Sarpy Wildlife Refuge, ribbon snakes discovered basking on roadside cattail mats generally slid down among the bases of such plants when approached, but a few took refuge in the water. When confronted on the ridges, they invariably escaped into the dense umbrella of blackberry vines that blanketed the area or quickly disappeared into some nearby underground refuge.

More gently disposed than most serpents its size, this species seldom bites when provoked. It may try to unnerve its foe by spreading its head and body in a threat posture, but it has no real defensive authority to back it up, for its teeth are too small to injure a human seriously. Held in the hand, a ribbon snake is likely to discharge fecal matter from its cloacal opening and a sweet-smelling musk from scent glands at the base of its tail. These substances are intentionally spread over the restraining hand by the reptile's frantic writhing. The feel of this slimy, foul-smelling goo is often so offensive that it results in the snake's quick release.

During mild winters, the Gulf Coast ribbon snake can be found above ground at almost any time; its activity cycles conform closely to favorable conditions of temperature and rainfall. Even those already in hibernation can be drawn out of their winter quarters by brief periods of warm weather. In 1954, for example, Tinkle found them moving about in fair numbers at the Sarpy Wildlife Refuge both in January (at 59 degrees F) and in December (at 74 degrees F), following three consecutive days of warm weather on each occasion. With the return of chilly weather, the snakes went back into hibernation. At other times, they found temporary shelter under loose tree bark, in or under decaying logs, and beneath large boards, always in sites above the maximum high-water level. Along the main ridge of the refuge, deep earthen crevices provided adequate winter shelter, not only for the ribbon snakes but also for the area's speckled king snakes, Texas rat snakes, and western cottonmouths.

In early spring, with daytime temperatures still cool, ribbon snakes were commonly observed all along the main ridge, either searching for food at ground level or basking on top of the blackberry vines. Later in the season, as the growing foliage shrouded most of the area in shade, the serpents were no longer found there. Between mid-March and May 30, these sun-loving reptiles left the gloomy parts of the ridge in favor of more open spaces. In early June, when direct, prolonged exposure to the summer sun can be unbearable for the reptiles, they returned to the shaded ridge, remaining there the entire summer and through the fall.

The other important climate influence on

the snake's activity is rainfall. Tinkle described an event that aptly illustrated this. On a warm June day between 9:30 and 10:30 in the morning, he captured only 6 ribbon snakes in the grass and cattails that bordered the water-filled borrow ditches, but in the next hour and a half, during which a light rain fell in the area, he succeeded in collecting 31, about five times the number found earlier. After the rains had stopped, only 6 more were taken at a nearby similar site between noon and 3:15. The presence of so many wandering ribbon snakes during periods of warm rain probably can be explained by the great numbers of frogs and toads (the snakes' chief prey) that also come out of hiding at such times.

Of 23 ribbon snakes marked and released at the refuge, Tinkle recaptured only 5, suggesting that their home ranges probably extended beyond the study site, or that in the absence of sufficient ideal habitat, the area could not support many resident individuals. Apparently their travels were relatively far-ranging. Recaptured six days to nearly five months after their release, they had moved between 50 feet (15.2 m) and 300 feet (91.2 m).

FEEDING The diet of this snake is similar to that of the other ribbon snake subspecies, consisting primarily of frogs, tadpoles, and fish. Salamanders are sometimes eaten as well, but lizards, insects, and snakes are taken only rarely.

To find its elusive prey, a ribbon snake depends primarily on its superbly keen eyesight. Ditmars' (1936) detailed account of how one of these serpents pursued and eventually captured a fleeing frog is a perfect example of the snake's remarkable ability to detect movement, however slight. Having just seized, then lost, a wood frog it was hoping to take as a meal, the snake eagerly chased its quarry as it frantically scampered away. Apparently tiring after a dozen leaps, the frog came to a sudden halt. Losing sight of its prey, the bewildered snake also stopped, its head raised, its tongue flicking, and its gaze focused in the frog's direction. For a few moments both remained motionless. Then, sensing no further danger, the frog, in a move typical for its kind, settled down to rest by pulling its limbs against its body and almost imperceptibly pressed itself to the ground. The movement was enough to catch the snake's eye. Instantly the waiting predator darted forward to seize its unsuspecting victim before it could make an escape. From this and similar accounts, it is evident that the ribbon snake is incapable of recognizing motionless prey by sight alone, although it can easily detect even subtle movements of such animals up to a distance several times its own length.

REPRODUCTION Most Gulf Coast ribbon snakes at the Sarpy Wildlife Refuge, both male and female, reached sexual maturity when two years old (some not until the third spring of their lives). No detailed observations have been made of their breeding habits, nor is there information about the precise time of copulation. The breeding period probably begins a bit earlier in this subspecies than it does for the species as a whole; pregnant females have been collected in southern Louisiana as early in the year as April. Tinkle found 6 to 17 (average 13) ovarian embryos in females from the Sarpy Wildlife Refuge. He observed that like the gravid females of many other serpent species, ribbon snakes on the refuge tended to congregate in open areas where exposure to the heat of solar radiation presumably helped to promote the development of the growing embryos.

RED-STRIPED RIBBON SNAKE
Thamnophis proximus rubrilineatus
PLATE 158

DESCRIPTION This and the three other kinds of ribbon snake inhabiting Texas are all races of a single species, differing only in details of coloration. In the red-striped ribbon snake the overall coloration varies from olive-brown to olive-gray. The relatively narrow stripe along the middle of the back normally is bright red (rarely orange), and a pale lateral stripe occupies each side of the body. In some specimens a narrow dark line occurs below each side stripe. As in all other Texas ribbon snakes, a pair of small whitish spots marks

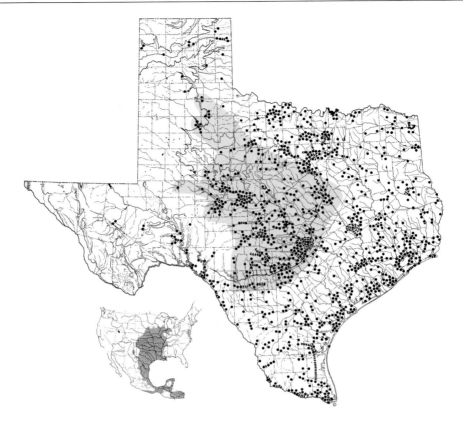

the top of the head, the upper and lower lip scales are pale and immaculate, the lateral stripes are always on scale rows 3 and 4 above the belly, the keeled dorsal scales occur in 19 midbody rows, the abdomen is without markings, and the anal plate is single.

COMPARABLE SNAKES   Several kinds of garter snakes occur within the red-striped ribbon's range; they are stouter than *T. p. rubrilineatus* and possess relatively shorter tails. In addition, they have some dark pigmentation on their upper lip scales and along the outer edges of their belly plates. Lined snakes possess small heads and a double row of prominent black spots down the middle of the abdomen. Schott's whipsnake, though relatively slender (but much longer than the ribbon snake) and striped lengthwise, has no pale spinal stripe. Its dorsal scales are smooth and arranged in only 15 rows at midbody, and its anal plate is divided. The Texas patch-nosed snake's spinal stripe is wide, its dorsal scales smooth, and its anal plate divided. Graham's crayfish snake, although displaying a faintly striped pattern, has no distinct,

light middorsal stripe, and its abdomen is marked with bold, black spots. Its anal plate is divided.

SIZE   The usual adult length is between 20 and 30 inches (50.8–76.2 cm). The largest known specimen measured 48 inches (121.9 cm) long.

HABITAT   This locally abundant ribbon snake, which occupies the Edwards Plateau and some of the surrounding regions, normally is restricted to the margins of watercourses, particularly those with open, grassy borders. Included in this category are streams, ponds, rivers, marshes, and cattle tanks. Davenport (1943) noted that in Bexar County the greatest numbers occurred near clear, spring-fed rivers; in certain remote wooded canyons, the serpent's presence was attributed to the permanent springs or seeps that provided the reptiles with moisture and amphibian prey.

BEHAVIOR   In water as on land, this is an agile, fast-moving serpent whose best defense is a quick retreat from danger. Often found lying quietly on branches overhanging a stream or pond, it immediately drops into the water if closely approached and swims quickly to the opposite bank, where it disappears into the shoreline vegetation. Some say that like most water snakes, it will occasionally dive to the bottom of a stream or pond to hide in the submerged vegetation, reappearing again when it decides the danger is past. One that is cornered on land is usually reluctant to bite in self-defense, although a spirited individual sometimes flattens its head and body in a threatening posture and even strikes at its foe. A captured ribbon snake trying to free itself may do no more than rotate its body deftly in one's hand, though most react with more determination. In a typical response, the snake discharges foul-smelling fecal material from the cloacal opening at the base of its tail and emits an odorous liquid from its scent glands. Both substances are then generously spread over the captor's hand by the serpent's vigorous writhing.

The snake generally ventures out into the open by day, dividing its daily activity cycle into morning and afternoon periods, but when temperatures are high, it also engages in nocturnal wanderings. Warm rains, which tend to bring out frogs and toads, also lure the ribbon snake into the open, where such prey can be found more abundantly than at most other times. Throughout its range, this species normally remains active from April through October. In Bexar County, Vermersch and Kuntz (1986) discovered it in the open during winter, basking on sun-warmed limestone rocks and on branches overhanging streams.

Few other serpents move with such flowing rhythm. As the slender-bodied reptile glides sinuously over land or through water, the delicate, pale stripes that run the full length of its body enhance its graceful movements. Davenport appropriately described the sight of a red-striped ribbon snake swimming in crystal-clear water above a backdrop of bright green aquatic vegetation as a symphony of color and movement.

The lengthwise striping serves a useful function as well. For all its apparent speed, the ribbon snake moves at a slow pace of less than 3 miles an hour. The illusion of swiftness comes from the long stripes, which, like the racing stripes on a sports car, convey rapid forward movement. It also results from

the serpent's ability to thread its way through dense underbrush and to change direction without slowing.

The striped body can also make a snake seem to be at rest when in fact it is in motion. Anyone who has ever tried to capture a ribbon snake (or any other striped snake, for that matter) as it moved through the brush knows the frustration of grabbing at a visible segment of the reptile's body only to settle for a handful of grass and twigs. To understand why this happens, we should remember that when we see only a fraction of the creature's length at a time sliding through the underbrush, each passing segment of the striped pattern precisely follows every preceding segment, so there appears to be no movement at all (like watching just a single rail of train track through a hole in the floor of a moving railroad car). Thus, by the time a catch is attempted, the snake's tail has often passed through the portal and the reptile is gone. Seen through the same limited brushy space, the motion of a moving blotched or banded snake becomes immediately obvious, for the serpent's alternating light and dark pattern elements produce a modulating image that quickly catches the eye. Here, an apt analogy might be that of looking through the same hole as before, but this time keeping an eye on the passing railroad ties instead of on the rail. This is one reason that ribbon snakes are often more easily caught in the open than when crawling through weeds or underbrush.

FEEDING The diet is similar to that of other ribbon snakes, consisting mainly of frogs and toads, including their tadpoles. Fish and salamanders are eaten less often, and lizards, insects, and snakes are captured only rarely.

Among the snake's chief prey is the cricket frog, an abundant little anuran found almost year-round in nearly every kind of freshwater environment. Like the ribbon snake, it favors shallow water containing aquatic or emergent vegetation, grassy shorelines, and plenty of sunlight. How the ribbon snake finds and captures such an elusive quarry was explained by Wendelken (1978), who watched as an example of the red-striped subspecies searched for cricket frogs along Onion Creek near Austin.

Moving slowly over an area of mudflats containing a scattering of sticks, small stones, and short clumps of vegetation, it repeatedly thrust its head at the bases of such objects. Often three forward jabs were made in quick succession, each directed at a different point across a semicircular arc. The goal of such a sweep obviously was to flush from hiding any concealed frogs. The serpent was clearly successful in its efforts, for 10 cricket frogs were driven into the open during these observations, though the actual capture rate in this particular case was disappointing.

Perhaps contributing to the snake's poor showing is its inability to recognize still prey by sight alone (although it can easily detect even slight movement at a distance equal to several times its own length). In a typical encounter, a cricket frog leaped several feet away from the approaching predator, usually in two or more erratic bounds, then became motionless, often with the snake already in pursuit. If, after a series of quick searching probes near the spot where the frog came to rest, the snake failed to find its quarry, it raised its head several inches off the ground and became completely still, apparently waiting and watching for renewed activity. It maintained this posture for a few minutes before repeating the entire foraging cycle. There is no doubt that despite its relatively high escape rate, the tiny cricket frog, difficult to see when at rest, is successfully disclosed by the characteristic search-and-flush technique described by Wendelken.

REPRODUCTION Males become sexually mature when less than 12 months old, females when they are approximately two years of age. Mating, which normally occurs in April or May, results in the birth of 4 to 27 young during July or August, although some *T. proximus* have been born as early in the year as late June and as late as October. According to Davenport, about 10 young constitute the normal litter size of Bexar County red-striped ribbon snakes. The spaghetti-thin young are 9 to 10 inches (22.9–25.4 cm) long at birth.

WESTERN PLAINS GARTER SNAKE

Thamnophis radix haydeni
PLATE 159

DESCRIPTION This moderate-sized, greenish gray to olive-brown garter snake is marked with a distinct bright yellow or orange stripe down the middle of its back, a pale yellow or greenish stripe on either side of the trunk along scale rows 3 and 4, and two alternating rows of squarish black spots between the middorsal and lateral stripes. Another row of black spots is located below each side stripe, and a row of prominent but smaller black spots, sometimes crescent-shaped, occurs on the outer edges of the whitish to greenish belly scales. An overall darkening of the snake's ground color, which occurs in some older individuals, may obscure the dorsal markings and make such snakes difficult to identify. The lips are boldly marked with vertical black bars. The dorsal scales are keeled and in 19 or 21 rows at midbody. The anal plate is single.

COMPARABLE SNAKES All native garter snakes except the checkered garter snake and this one possess fewer than 19 middorsal scale rows, but the checkered garter snake's center stripe is narrower than that of the western plains subspecies and its lower stripes never occupy the fourth row of scales. Since there is evidence that hybrids between checkered and plains garter snakes occur in Hutchinson County, certain specimens there may not be clearly assignable to either species. Like some western plains garter snakes, the Texas garter snake has a broad, pale-orange center stripe and lateral stripes that reach the fourth row of body scales, but there is no double row of black spots between them. Ribbon snakes, on the other hand, are more slender and longer-tailed than garter snakes and have no black markings on their lips or abdomen. Lined snakes, which also lack black lip sutures, have two distinct rows of large, black, half-moons down the middle of the belly.

SIZE Adult specimens are generally 22 to 28 inches (55.9–71.1 cm) long. The maximum reported length is 42⅗ inches (108.2 cm).

HABITAT Although surprisingly abundant over much of its broad geographic range, this is one of Texas' rarest garter snakes, entering the state only along the northern edge of the Panhandle, where it has been found sparingly in Dallam, Hartley, Hemphill, and Hutchinson counties. Typical habitats include grassy plains, prairies, and farmlands, where it usually lives along the vegetated margins of streams, rivers, ponds, lakes, sloughs, and marshes. In Ohio, Reichenbach and Dalrymple (1986) described one such habitat as an area of prairie slough ponds in poorly drained clay soils surrounded by big bluestem, little bluestem, blazing star, and prairie dock. According to Webb (1970), garter snakes from Cimarron County, Oklahoma (close to the Texas border), were captured in and near a shallow pond bordered with sunflowers, grasses, and other herbaceous plants; in the next county to the east, specimens were collected among small rocks lying near a sandy riverbed, in a dry tumbleweed plant not far from water, and in tall sedges.

Despite the snake's fondness for water, it does not entirely restrict itself to wet environments. For example, in eastern Colorado it has been encountered both in dry grasslands and in sand hills a considerable distance from standing water. Elsewhere it has even been seen occasionally in cultivated fields. At one time it could also be found in and near large metropolitan areas, sometimes in surprisingly large numbers. Until at least the late 1960s, its close relative the eastern plains garter snake was common in parks, gardens, and vacant lots of Chicago's populated suburbs, sometimes even hibernating beneath inner-city sidewalks. It was once so abundant there that in 1950, from a single 320-acre (129.5 ha) parcel of land near the city, one herpetologist collected 298 specimens of this prolific species in just six months. Because of expanding land development and perhaps also as a result of long-term pesticide use, some of these urban populations have been severely reduced and others have been completely eliminated. That populations of even greater density occurred in natural open prairie environments was illustrated by Seibert (1950), who concluded that at least 845 plains garter snakes occupied a single hectare of prime habitat at his Illinois field study site, and by Reichenbach and Dalrymple, who estimated a density of at least 114 garter snakes per hectare at their Ohio study location.

BEHAVIOR Herpetologists disagree about the disposition of this garter snake. Some describe it as aggressive and quick to bite when handled; others say it is quite docile and not likely to use its teeth in self-defense. Whatever its temperament, one strategy used by the plains garter snake remains fairly constant—that of evacuating a considerable amount of excreta from its cloacal opening while discharging the offensive-smelling contents of its anal scent glands. Whether or not this tactic actually protects the snake from its natural predators, there is no doubt that it has the desired effect on humans, for a person whose hand is suddenly covered with the repugnant fluids does not hesitate to release the reptile.

Studying young plains garter snakes in the laboratory, Arnold and Bennett (1984) cataloged a whole suite of antipredator responses that involved a succession of behaviors ranging from defensive to offensive displays. The serpent's first course of action is to flee, but if it is unable to do so (especially when its escape efforts have resulted in physical exhaustion), the snake may respond to further intimidation by rolling into a loose ball, hiding its head beneath one or more loops of its body, and waving or wiggling its elevated tail. By attracting the predator's attention to the animated tail, this tactic probably helps protect the snake's head from attack. Tail-waving was also sometimes performed when the garter snake was uncoiled and its head fully exposed. If further provoked at this stage, the serpent often assumed a more aggressive role, striking out repeatedly at the source of annoyance from a coiled or partly extended position and with its body sometimes flattened against the ground, apparently to make itself look larger and more foreboding. The zoologists observed that although vigorous, such attacks were often executed with the mouth closed; even when

the jaws were open, the snake seldom made an effort to bite. It is clear, therefore, that such bluffing is merely an attempt to intimidate and frighten its foe, for the serpent's relatively small teeth (its only offensive resource) are incapable of injuring a large adversary.

More tolerant of cooler temperatures than of uncommonly hot ones, the plains garter snake has been found at the surface as early in the year as March and as late as November. One specimen was found crawling out in the open in mid-October, despite recent episodes of snow and below-freezing weather. Even in midwinter, during interludes of unseasonably warm weather, the snake may leave its lair to briefly bask in the midday sun. It is one of the first snakes encountered in the spring and one of the last to enter hibernation. As with reptiles generally, the snake's annual activity cycle depends largely on prevailing temperatures. During the mild days of spring and autumn it is normally day-active, and in midsummer, when daytime temperatures are often unbearably hot, the snake is more apt to prowl at night or at other times of the day when the solar radiation is less oppressive. From March to May, for example, and again from September to November, Reichenbach and Dalrymple found it in the open mostly between 11 AM and 4 PM; in the summer they encountered it primarily during the early morning and late afternoon hours, the warmest part of each day having been spent in a crayfish burrow. Such tunnels not only protect the snakes from temperature extremes but also serve as convenient shelters from surface predators. In Colorado these reptiles sometimes avoided the daytime summer heat by spending the mornings in wet gullies and the afternoons beneath assorted pieces of debris, though during midday they submerged themselves in small streams with their heads resting out of the water on the nearest streambank.

Seibert and Hagen (1947) observed Ohio specimens out in the open when the air temperature ranged from 70 to 85 degrees F, but they saw none when it dropped below 45 degrees F. During cool weather, they found the snakes under pieces of metallic debris, presumably because the discarded metal readily absorbed the solar radiation and quickly warmed the snakes coiled underneath, though on hot days the reptiles sought shelter under tarpaper and rocks.

Plains garter snakes are not usually inclined to move great distances in their daily wanderings. Most of those studied in Illinois by Seibert and Hagen traveled less than 6½ feet (198 cm) in a single day. On an Ohio study site, however, some specimens recaptured by Reichenbach and Dalrymple several months to as long as a year after being marked and released had wandered nearly 3,000 feet (912 m).

To survive the severe winters common across the unsheltered northern Great Plains, the garter snake must find a suitable hibernaculum that will protect it from subfreezing temperatures. Most frequently used are the burrows of small mammals, although post holes, rock crevices, old wells, and building foundations are also known to serve as winter dens. In addition, Dalrymple and Reichenbach (1981) believed this species may also hibernate in crayfish holes. In parts of Nebraska the snake is known to wait out the winter in the fallen logs of woodlands bordering the area's streams and marshes. Elsewhere it has been reported to hibernate in anthills, sometimes in association with large numbers of other snake species. In southern Manitoba, Canada, for example, 8 plains garter snakes, 101 northern red-bellied snakes, and 148 smooth green snakes spent the winter together in a large anthill, according to Criddle (1937), where they were dispersed throughout the mound from near the top to a depth of 57 inches (145 cm).

FEEDING Studies of this species' food habits in Illinois, Minnesota, Missouri, and Ohio indicate that the snake has a varied diet, consisting chiefly of frogs and their tadpoles, earthworms, and occasionally toads, but it also consumes fish, salamanders, snails, slugs, leeches, rodents, birds, and carrion. Seigel (1984) demonstrated that in Missouri its diet changed according to season, for in the spring and fall the snake consumed chiefly earthworms, and in summer it ate mostly ranid frogs.

Although the plains garter snake usually forages by day, Ernst (in Ernst and Barbour 1989) several times encountered specimens feeding at night on chorus frogs that had congregated in large numbers during the anurans' spring breeding season.

REPRODUCTION Courtship and copulation usually take place in April or May, not long after the snakes have left their winter quarters, although mating may also occur in the fall. In common with many other serpent species, the male normally finds a mate by locating and following the scent trail she unwittingly leaves behind during the breeding season as she crawls over the ground. As might be expected in such circumstances, more than one male may discover the same chemical trail, resulting in several males converging on a single female, all of whom court her at the same time. The infant snakes, 5 to 92 per litter, are born sometime from July through September, when they are 7 to 8 inches (17.8–20.3 cm) long.

EASTERN GARTER SNAKE
Thamnophis sirtalis sirtalis
PLATES 160, 161

DESCRIPTION Like most garter snakes, this olive to nearly black subspecies is marked by three pale stripes extending from the neck to nearly the end of the tail. The straw-colored stripe that traces the spine is the most conspicuous, being the width of one complete scale row plus half of an adjacent row on either side. Less clearly defined are the lateral stripes, one on either side of the body, which ordinarily occur only on dorsal scale rows 2 and 3 above the belly plates but may occasionally involve the edge of row 1 as well. Between the upper and lower stripes are two alternating rows of rectangular or oval black spots, with yet another row of vertical black marks situated below the lateral stripe. The

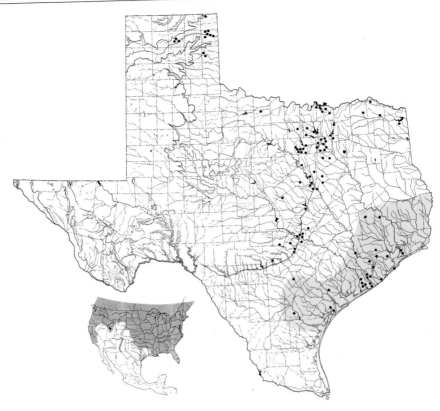

skin of most eastern garter snakes (usually concealed by the body's overlapping scales) normally is greenish or some shade of olive, yet in the majority of specimens we have seen from the southeastern part of the state, it was reddish or reddish orange, as were the edges of some dorsal scales. Also present on the skin are pairs of small, white, nearly horizontal dashlike marks, best seen when the body is distended, as when the snake is heavy with food or young or when it flattens itself in a threat posture. Its whitish abdomen is marked only with one or two rows of small black spots along the outer edge of each belly plate. The head is dark on top and pale greenish white on the cheeks and underside of the jaw. Prominent dark vertical bars edge the upper lip scales, and a parallel pair of tiny white or yellowish dashlike spots marks the top of the crown. The dorsal scales are keeled and arranged in 19 rows at midbody. The anal plate is single.

COMPARABLE SNAKES On the checkered garter snake each lateral stripe is narrower and situated just on the third row of dorsal scales (except on the forebody, where it may occupy the fourth row as well), the dorsal scales are arranged in 21 rows at midbody, and a large black mark on each side of the neck directly behind the head is preceded by a cream-colored crescent. The more slender ribbon snakes lack prominent dark spots between the longitudinal stripes, and they have neither vertical black sutures on the lips nor distinct dark markings on the outer edges of the abdomen. Lined snakes closely resemble garter snakes, but their bellies and the underside of their tails are decorated with two longitudinal rows of prominent, dark half-moons. Brown snakes have 17 rows of dorsal scales at midbody and a divided anal plate. The Gulf salt marsh snake has no black spots along its sides, its belly is vividly marked with a central row of large yellowish oval spots on a dark abdomen, its midbody dorsal scales are in 21 to 25 rows, and its anal plate is divided. Both Graham's and gulf crayfish snakes (which lack a distinct, light middorsal stripe) have either one indistinct or two prominent rows of dark oval-shaped spots down the center of the belly, and their anal plates are divided.

SIZE Although the eastern garter snake is reported by Froom (1972) to reach an extreme length of 54 inches (137 cm), its usual adult length is 18 to 26 inches (45.7–66 cm). The largest specimen reported from Texas is one from Harris County that measured 32½ inches (82.6 cm) long.

HABITAT Although abundant over much of its vast geographic range, which includes the eastern third of the United States as well as parts of central and eastern Canada, this snake is infrequently encountered in Texas. In some midwestern and northeastern states it often occurs in such large numbers close to urban centers that it has been referred to as the sparrow of the snake world. At one site in Wyandot County, Ohio, for example, Reichenbach and Dalrymple (1986) counted 45 to 89 specimens per hectare.

A moisture-loving serpent, it can be found in almost any area containing damp soil and some natural or man-made debris under which it can find shelter. Such habitats include the vicinity of streams and ponds, meadows, marshes, wet grasslands, drainage ditches, and even the suburbs of large cities where it occupies seldom-disturbed vacant lots, gardens, and parklands. Being decidedly partial to more open spaces, it is unlikely to inhabit dense woodland.

Most specimens we observed in the past were encountered in moist, grassy areas within the city limits of Houston, where scattered weeds and shrubs were the dominant plants and ground debris was abundant. From the 1950s through the early 1970s, the garter snake was frequently encountered in and around MacGregor Park not far from downtown Houston, where it could be found crawling along the boggy edges of small, sluggish canals or hidden beneath debris near some source of moisture. We also observed individuals sunning along the banks of drainage canals in Freeport. Today, because of commercial and residential development around the park, it appears to have been eliminated from the area, for no specimens have been reported from this part of the city in at least 20 years. Despite its disappearance from var-

ious parks and previously undeveloped areas in and around the city, probably due in part to the long-term use of agricultural and industrial chemicals, the snake has been collected recently in western Harris County and near several Galveston County communities including Alta Loma, Arcadia, Webster, and La Marque. One specimen was collected along the edge of a salt marsh near Sargent in Matagorda County.

BEHAVIOR Most garter snakes quickly glide away when approached, but one that is unable to escape usually responds by greatly flattening its head and body to make itself appear larger and more sinister. This action, which stretches the snake's scaly integument and suddenly reveals numerous flecks of pale skin where a moment ago there were only dark scales, is enough to startle some adversaries. In addition, the reptile's flared head may be slightly raised and pulled in close to its body coils, its widespread jaws now somewhat resembling the broad cephalic configuration of a pit viper. The aroused garter snake may then suddenly strike vigorously, although such an attack is intended as a bluff, for the reptile's array of sharp but small teeth are incapable of inflicting any serious bodily injury to a large adversary. Potentially, the most harmful thing about the bite is a mildly toxic ingredient of the snake's saliva (which is also present in the salivas of some other garter and water snakes), whose most likely function is to immobilize its small prey. The unidentified component may account for the excessive bleeding reported in some garter snake bites inflicted on humans and for the hyperallergic reaction suffered by Carl E. Ernst (Ernst and Barbour 1989) following repeated bites by this species. Aside from such uncommon reactions, it should be emphasized that the bite of the eastern garter snake is otherwise quite harmless to man.

Some individuals, it turns out, may not even bite. The vast majority of the garter snakes we captured in southeastern Texas over the years made no attempt to strike or bite, seeming quite agreeable to being picked up. Despite its unusual tolerance to being handled, when seized this snake usually discharges a combination of offensive-smelling fluids from its cloaca and the scent glands at the base of its tail, which it then tries to smear over the restraining hand by vigorously squirming.

Ordinarily attracted to water, it finds the bulk of its moisture-dependent prey there, and when danger threatens, it darts into a nearby stream, pond, or canal to escape its enemies, sometimes diving to the muddy bottom to hide. Otherwise it may seek shelter beneath any of a wide variety of objects including stones, logs, piles of plant debris, the loose bark of trees, boards, and sheet metal or in rock crevices, rock walls, mammal burrows, rotting logs, and old sawdust piles, to name just a few. When on the prowl, it occasionally climbs into shrubs and tree branches close to the ground.

Except when moving to or from its winter quarters, the distance traveled by this garter snake ordinarily is negligible. In Illinois, for example, Seibert and Hagen (1947) reported daily movements of less than 3½ feet (106.7 cm) for females and about 2⅓ feet (61.9 cm) for males, although in most parts of its range the serpent's home area is about two to five acres.

In midsummer, when the temperature is oppressively high, the snake restricts its prowling activity to the more pleasant early morning and evening hours, whereas in the spring and fall it usually becomes active from 1 PM to 3 PM.

More tolerant of cold than most other snakes living so far north, this subspecies enjoys a lengthy active season that typically extends from March or April to November, making it one of the last serpents of the colder regions to enter hibernation in the fall and among the first to become active again in the spring. At the beginning of March and sometimes even earlier (before the arrival of sustained warm weather prompts it to leave its hibernaculum), the reptile often basks in the sun's warm rays for a couple of hours each day, returning to the recesses of its winter den before dusk. During these brief forays, it ignores the sometimes frozen surface soil and scattered patches of snow that linger in the nearby woodlands.

Finally, with the arrival of uninterrupted mild weather, the garter snake begins the journey to its summer foraging territory, which can be either nearby or a considerable distance away. Near the northern limits of the snake's geographic range, suitable hibernacula often are far from the serpent's summer feeding grounds, but in the warmer southern end of its range, the snake's prey and winter quarters frequently occur together in the same area.

Winter shelters can be rocky hillsides, rock fissures, gravel banks, earthen dams, stone causeways, abandoned wells, ant mounds, crayfish tunnels, mammal burrows, or decaying logs or tree stumps. Near Minneapolis, Minnesota, Breckenridge (1944) described a series of deep dens situated along the wooded, east-facing bluffs of the Mississippi River where subterranean layers of rocky and sandy soils were accessible through rotting stumps and the attendant tunnels created by the gradual disintegration of their dendritic root systems. Whatever the nature of the refuge, to be a safe winter haven it must be deep enough or sufficiently insulated from the cold to protect the snake from prolonged freezing temperatures, and it must contain sufficient moisture to prevent dehydration of the serpent's body tissues.

At more northern latitudes the dens tend to be located in rocky, south-facing hillsides, where they receive maximum daily exposure to solar radiation and some protection from winter's chilling north winds. In such deep-crevice shelters, large numbers of garter snakes spend the winter together, often in the company of other snake species of the same or smaller size than themselves. In southeastern Texas, the eastern garter snake does not typically hibernate in deep, rocky dens, for not only are such geological formations scarce or missing from the pine-oak forest and Gulf Coast environments, but also winters there are usually mild enough for the reptiles to pass the coldest days in mammal burrows, decaying logs, and perhaps also in streamside crayfish burrows. On a cold day in early February, near the town of Alvin, we found an adult specimen, apparently in hibernation, under a log partially buried in the mud of a small stream. Like other serpents of the area, the eastern garter snake may be active even in midwinter as the result of a transitory warm spell.

FEEDING The diet of this wide-ranging garter snake includes a variety of both invertebrate and vertebrate animals. Consisting chiefly of frogs and their tadpoles, toads and their tadpoles, or earthworms but more often involving a combination of such prey, it may also include leeches, slugs, snails, millipedes, spiders, insects, crayfish, fish, salamanders, snakes, small birds, chipmunks, mice, voles, moles, and shrews. The principal item in the diet of a given local garter snake population depends largely on prey availability, which in turn is influenced by such factors as micro-habitat, season, and, in the case of earth-worm prey, permeability of the soil. Thus we find that earthworms may represent the most important diet item in one place, and amphibian prey species in another.

An enlightening example of the snake's diet diversity was reported by E. E. Brown (1979), who compared the food habits of this subspecies in two widely separated regions of the country, Michigan and New York. In the first state, amphibians constituted 83.7 percent of the serpent's food, followed by 5.46 percent earthworms, 5.46 percent birds, 3.6 percent fish, and 1.8 percent mammals. The New York garter snakes, however, con-sumed quite a different diet. Although they also devoured a fairly significant number of amphibians (16.5 percent of the total), they had eaten a much larger number of earth-worms than the other group (82.5 percent) and only a single fish. Other studies reviewed by Brown not only supported the conclusion that the snake's choice of prey can vary significantly from region to region but some-times also according to season. When con-sidered together, the data showed that am-phibians represented anywhere from 15 to 97 percent, by volume, of the snake's total diet and earthworms from 3 to 80 percent.

Birds captured by this garter snake are gen-erally helpless nestlings. In one case, two young yellowthroats (a species smaller than a house sparrow) were snatched from their nest by a 31-inch female garter snake; in another, a large garter snake boldly pulled a 9-day-old hermit thrush from its nest, even as an interested naturalist stood nearby and watched. In addition to living prey, this sub-species occasionally eats carrion, a behavior underscored by reports of individual garter snakes swallowing the carcasses of a vole and a fish, as well as the foreleg of a pocket go-pher and discarded fish parts.

Gliding slowly and almost unnoticed along a streambank or through a wet meadow, its tongue darting in and out of its mouth in rapid, deliberate spurts, the foraging reptile attempts to pick up the scent of potential prey. Together, the tongue and the Jacobson's organ (a remarkable chemical-detecting ap-paratus in the roof of the snake's mouth) serve to identify microscopic airborne particles or those left on the ground by moving prey. With these devices, a relatively fresh trail is easily followed. When prey is sighted, usually as a result of its own movement, the preda-tor, with its head elevated for better visibil-ity, relies on sight alone to pursue and cap-ture its quarry. Smaller animals are quickly seized, pulled into the serpent's mouth, and gulped down without hesitation. In response to the struggles of larger prey such as adult mice, frogs, and toads, the snake may vig-orously chew on its victim, embedding its moderately enlarged rear teeth. Some zoolo-gists believe this action introduces the ser-pent's slightly toxic saliva into the tissues of its prey, which helps to immobilize it.

In water, where its tracking ability is ren-dered useless, the garter snake employs a dif-ferent hunting strategy. Generally avoiding swift currents and large, open bodies of water in favor of shallow pools and quiet streams (especially those in which drying conditions have created a concentration of tadpoles or fish), it attacks prey both at the surface and underwater. It frequently swims slowly along the shoreline, quickly seizing fish that hap-pen to break the surface nearby. At other times, diving briefly, it may sweep its open mouth from side to side through the water as it tries to snare any fish that happen to swim close to its jaws.

REPRODUCTION At northern latitudes, early spring breeding aggregations immediately follow the snakes' emergence from hiberna-tion. Representing one of the most unusual ophidian mating behaviors found among our native serpents, these gatherings usually oc-cur near the entrance to a winter den, where scores of males and females engage in fren-zied courtship and mating.

In one such assemblage, discovered on March 15 near Huntington, West Virginia, Green (in Green and Pauley 1987) observed a large mass of garter snakes at the base of a shale bank. Consisting of several dozen specimens entwined together in a loosely consolidated ball approximately 2 feet (61 cm) in diameter, the participants constantly moved in and out of the sphere of bodies without ever losing the basic shape of the mass. Although copulation was not observed, Green believed the snakes were engaged in courtship behavior.

A similar event was observed by Gardner (1955) in Connecticut. In this case, what began as a small group of 4 or 5 entangled, writhing garter snakes soon became 15 or 20 as additional specimens joined from as far away as 20 to 25 feet (6.1–7.6 m) from several different directions. Upon entering the tangled mass, the newcomers aligned their heads and necks somewhat parallel to those already present, which, held relatively motionless, extended out from one side of the ball while their back ends were an animated tangle of bodies and tails. So tumultuous was this flurry of snakes that the ball of serpents slid several feet down an embankment without any interruption in the action. Eventually three of the snakes (apparently two males and a female) left the group and attempted copulation.

Some courtship and mating aggregations, unlike the one just described, do not necessarily take the shape of a spherical mass. One of the earliest accounts of a great sexual gathering comes from as long ago as 1880 (related by an anonymous witness in McCauley 1945). It describes a scene in which hundreds of eastern garter snakes lay in a heap in a sunny glen along the stony banks of the Patapsco River in Howard County, Maryland. Instead of bundling up into a ball, the snakes merely piled on top of one another in layers.

In the South, where winters usually are not as severe as in the north and where underground shelters are plentiful, eastern garter snakes, as far as we know, do not hibernate together in large numbers. Having probably overwintered individually or in small groups in some decaying log or stump, mammal burrow, or crayfish domicile, the male emerging from hibernation may find himself at a considerable distance from the nearest female. How he manages to locate her is one of the more curious aspects of ophidian biology. After all, being deaf to airborne sounds, snakes cannot communicate by auditory signals, nor is the male's eyesight acute enough to spot a female at any great distance. To find her, he depends instead on his tongue and Jacobson's organ.

During the breeding season, the female unwittingly leaves a continuous chemical trail on the ground wherever she goes, allowing the male to track her once he has crossed her path. Such chemical markers, called pheromones, are carried in the female's blood and released through her skin, but apparently only during the mating season. The pheromone released by the female attracts only males of the same species, contributing to the effectiveness of the male garter snake's trailing ability. Once the male encounters such a trail, he employs both his tongue and Jacobson's organ to follow it, the tongue serving as the antenna that receives and delivers the chemical particulates to the Jacobson's organ in the roof of the snake's mouth, which instantly processes and identifies them.

Merely locating a trail does not necessarily bring success, for the trail leads in two directions: back to where the female has been and forward in the direction she is going. Following the trail in the wrong direction (a 50 percent probability) will lead the male away from his target. To learn how the snake solves this dilemma, Ford and Lowe (1984) used a test arena that was perfectly flat. After a sexually receptive female crossed this unobstructed plane, a male placed in the arena was unable to detect her direction of travel. Only when the same area was studded with wooden pegs and the experiment repeated did the male consistently track in the right direction. From this the zoologists concluded that as the female pushed sideward and backward against the pegs to aid her forward movement, the pheromone-bearing sides of her body marked such areas with chemical scent. They noted that if she were traveling in an easterly direction, for example, her side touched only the southeastern face of each peg, leaving a bit of pheromone wherever it made contact. When the searching male first encountered the trail, he quickly investigated both sides of the nearest peg with flicks of his tongue to orient himself in the right direction, after which he again followed the substrate trail. Although

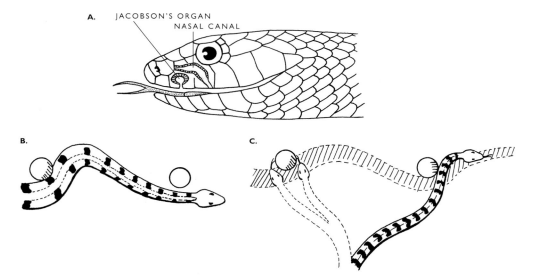

Figure 61. *Tracking of female garter snake trails: During the breeding season, a male garter snake uses (a) his tongue and Jacobson's organ to detect the pheromone trail left by a female of the same species. (b) The female deposits her scent when she brushes against the leading edges of objects along her path, in this case pegs. (c) By investigating both sides of the pegs, the male can determine which direction the female is traveling along the pheromone trail (shaded area). (After Ford and Lowe 1984.)*

there are no such manufactured pegs in nature, all sorts of natural objects occur in the snake's uneven habitat that when dabbed with pheromone can serve as directional markers to help guide an amorous male to a previously unseen mate.

Male garter snakes even follow pheromone trails into bushes and small trees. Once, two male garter snakes traced such a trail up the trunk of a small hemlock tree and out onto one of its branches, where a female garter snake lay stretched out on a limb. In their vigorous efforts to court her, the trio lost their balance and together fell to the ground. Soon the female climbed back into the hemlock, leaving her suitors behind. Before long, like male dogs pursuing a bitch in heat, the two male garter snakes once again made their way up the tree trunk, precisely tracing her path. Surprisingly, when two or more males simultaneously court the same female, a common occurrence in this species, they apparently display no antagonism toward one another; the successful competitor seems to win out over his rival almost by chance.

It is reported by Devine (1975) and others that after mating, a kind of enforced chastity is imposed on the female by her mate in the form of a copulatory plug, a gelatinous substance composed of male kidney secretions that forms and congeals in her cloaca as the mating act ends. Effectively blocking copulation by other males for the next few days, the plug is eventually expelled, at which time another male may breed with her. Mating, incidentally, does not always occur in the spring. When it takes place in the fall, the sperm remains viable in the female's oviducts until the next spring.

We can find only a few records of reproduction for this subspecies in Texas. A female from Old Ocean, Brazoria County, having a snout-to-vent length of $18\frac{1}{3}$ inches (46.6 cm), gave birth to 12 young on July 8. The newborn snakes averaged $6\frac{4}{5}$ inches (17.3 cm) long and ranged from $6\frac{1}{2}$ to $7\frac{1}{5}$ inches (16.5–19 cm) in length. A second specimen from the same locality, collected on March 28, contained 7 embryos. Another female eastern garter snake, from near Arcadia in Galveston County, which was $25\frac{1}{3}$ inches (64.3 cm) long, gave birth to 21 young on July 14. They averaged $7\frac{1}{8}$ inches (18.1 cm) in length, ranging from $6\frac{3}{5}$ to $7\frac{4}{5}$ inches (16.8–19.8 cm).

TEXAS GARTER SNAKE

*Thamnophis sirtalis
annectens*

PLATE 162

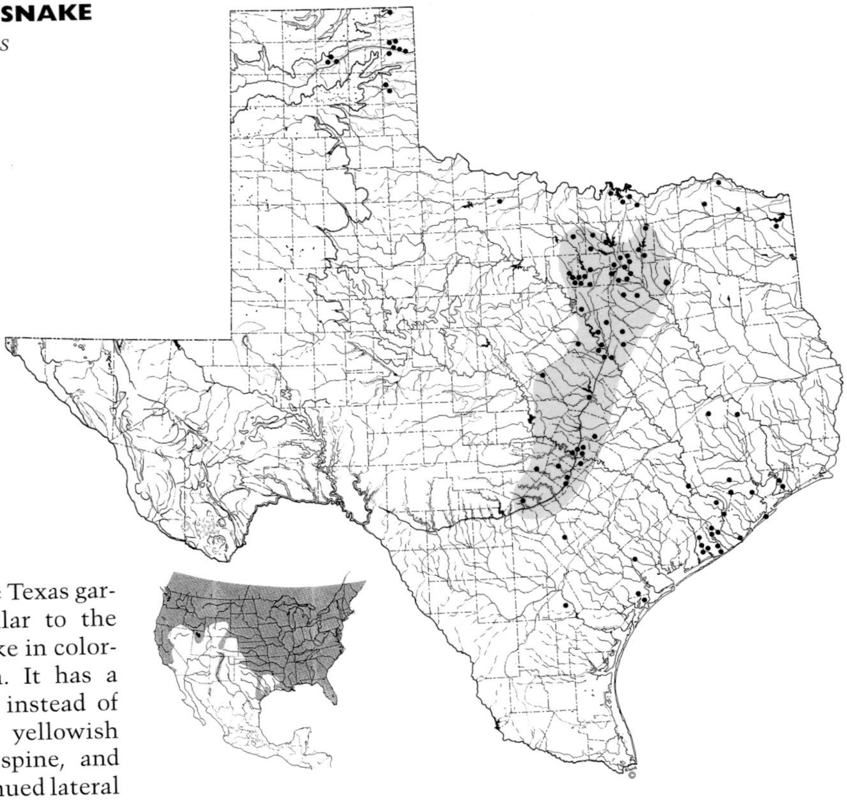

DESCRIPTION The Texas garter snake is similar to the eastern garter snake in coloration and pattern. It has a wide deep-orange instead of slightly narrower yellowish stripe along the spine, and the distinct light-hued lateral stripe on each side of its body involves not only the third row of scales above the belly plates but also the adjacent parts of rows 2 and 4, at least on the forward third of the trunk. Between the upper and lower stripes on either side of the grayish brown trunk are two alternating rows of squarish dark spots, which in some individuals are obscured by an overall darkening of the ground color. As in most other *Thamnophis*, paired dashlike flecks of light color are present on the skin between the dorsal scales. Ordinarily hidden by the overlapping scales, they are most conspicuous when the skin has been distended after a heavy meal or when the snake menacingly flattens its body. The white or light-greenish abdomen is unmarked except for the encroachment of some dark dorsal ground color onto the outer edges of the belly plates. The top of the head is the same dark hue as the ground color of the body, its only markings being a pair of small, side-by-side, yellowish dashlike spots near the back of the crown. As in other na-

tive garter snakes, the pale upper lip scales bear black streaks along their vertical sutures. The dorsal scales are keeled and arranged in 19 rows at midbody. The anal plate is undivided.

COMPARABLE SNAKES No other native *Thamnophis* has the pale lateral stripes on the second, third, and fourth rows of scales above the belly plates. The western plains garter snake, whose middle stripe may also be orange, at least on the forebody, is patterned with a row of distinct large black spots below its light lateral stripe. The eastern black-necked garter snake has a *single* row of large, black, roundish spots on each side of its neck and a curved black mark behind the end of the mouthline. In addition to its three light stripes, the pale body of the checkered garter snake is adorned with a bold pattern of dark checkerboard spots and a pale crescent behind the end of the mouthline, which is followed by an even larger dark blotch. The more slender ribbon snakes have neither dark vertical seams on their upper lip scales nor distinct rows of dark spots between their light stripes. The lined snake also has three pale stripes on its body, but the double row of bold, black half-moons down the middle of its belly is absent in the Texas garter snake. Patch-nosed snakes have smooth dorsal scales and a divided anal plate.

SIZE Adults of this subspecies range from 15 to 28 inches (38–71 cm) long. A record specimen is said to have measured 42¾ inches (108.6 cm) in length.

HABITAT Uncommon throughout most of its Central Texas range, the Texas garter snake is seldom encountered in large numbers. Most specimens that formed the basis for B. C. Brown's (1950) original description of this subspecies were collected along a small tributary of Boggy Creek, about 1 mile east of Austin (21 snakes) and from Waco and vicinity (10 specimens). Eleven others came from various scattered localities throughout the reptile's range, with no more than 2 specimens represented from any single location.

Like most other garter snakes, this one is found in a wide range of habitats, though nearly always in the vicinity of moisture, whether along the margins of streams, rivers, ponds, lakes, or marshes or around damp soil some distance from such bodies of water. Although even drainage ditches and irrigation canals relatively free of plant life sometimes attract this moisture-dependent serpent, its most typical haunts include a ground cover of grass, weeds, or other brushy streamside vegetation. The Dallas County specimens collected by Curtis (1949) were encountered along small creeks in the hilly southwestern part of the county, though one was discovered at the south end of White Rock Lake near a fish hatchery pond. In many years of local collecting, Tim Jones (pers. com.) encountered only three specimens in the Waco area, none of which was found near a permanent source of surface water.

BEHAVIOR When approached in the field, this snake quickly escapes into brush or evades its foe by entering the nearest body of water, where it swims to the opposite bank and disappears into the emergent vegetation.

When cornered, it reacts like most other garter snakes in similar circumstances, gathering its forebody into a defensive, lateral S posture, its slightly uplifted head pulled back and readied for a strike. To this is added the serpent's tendency to flatten its head and body, making itself look larger and more threatening. If this harmless bluffing fails to deter its foe and the snake is further provoked, it may strike out energetically but with little effect, for the vigorous lunge is just another way to make itself appear dangerous. Most Texas garter snakes, even when handled for the first time, are reluctant to bite. When they do, the reptile's small, needle-sharp teeth produce only shallow puncture wounds on the skin, which except in the largest specimens are neither painful nor serious. A more effective defensive behavior is to discharge feces from its cloacal opening and musk from paired glands at the base of its tail. These substances are then liberally smeared over the handler's skin by the snake's vigorous struggles.

Although the Central Texas range of *T. s. annectens* includes some of the most populous metropolitan areas in the state, little has been recorded about the snake's natural history. Like most other native garter snakes, it is primarily day-active; by night it generally hides under logs, piles of plant debris, or rocks and probably in animal burrows as well. Two were found near Austin beneath boards in the back yard of an old abandoned farmhouse close to a creek.

FEEDING Documented records detailing the Texas garter snake's food preferences are unknown. In common with other subspecies of *T. sirtalis*, it undoubtedly feeds chiefly on worms and amphibians, which are readily available in its moist leaf-litter habitat. When the opportunity arises, like its kin, it probably also consumes a variety of other animal species such as small mammals, birds and their eggs, and other snakes.

REPRODUCTION Aside from the report of a brood of 11 young born to a Dallas County female on July 29 (Curtis 1949), there are no documented records of reproduction in this subspecies.

RED-SIDED GARTER SNAKE

Thamnophis sirtalis parietalis

PLATE 163

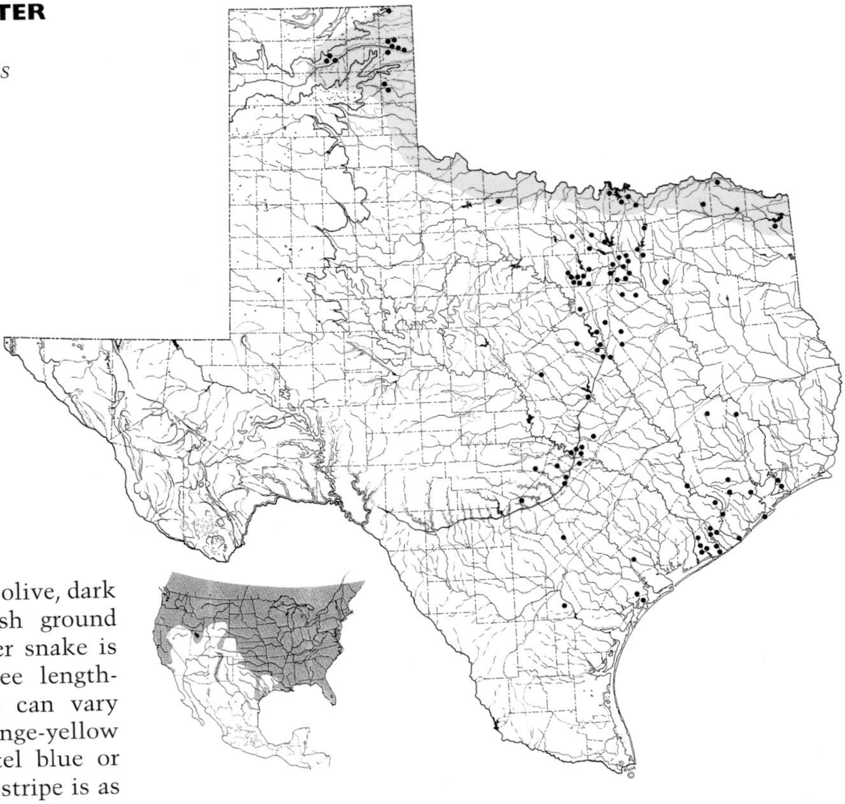

DESCRIPTION The olive, dark brown, or blackish ground color of this garter snake is marked with three lengthwise stripes that can vary from yellow or orange-yellow to shades of pastel blue or green. The spinal stripe is as wide as one entire scale row and the two adjacent half scale rows; each of the less clearly defined lateral stripes (one on either side of the body) occupies parts of dorsal scale rows 2 and 3 above the belly. Between the stripes on each side of the body are two alternating rows of small, black, oval blotches, not always clearly defined, between which are vertical red or rust-colored bars. The reddish hue, which is largely confined to the skin between the scales but may also be present on the scale edges, is most conspicuous when the dorsal scutes are separated, as when the snake flattens its body in threat or when the skin is stretched after the snake has swallowed a large meal. Also visible on the skin at such times are numerous pale, dashlike marks. The dark spots below the lateral stripes may or may not extend onto the belly. Narrow, dark vertical bars usually margin some or all of the pale upper lip scales. The dorsal scales are keeled and in 19 rows at midbody. The anal plate is single.

COMPARABLE SNAKES Besides lacking vertical red bars on the sides of the body, other Texas garter snakes living within the range of *T. s. parietalis* can be distinguished as follows: In the checkered garter snake the lateral stripe is narrow and occupies only the third scale row above the abdomen (on the forebody it may also occupy the fourth), and its dorsal scales are in 21 rows at midbody. In addition, a large black blotch occurs on each side of the neck immediately behind the snake's head and is preceded by a pale crescent. In the western plains garter snake the lateral stripe involves the fourth row of scales above the belly, and the dorsal scales are arranged in 21 midbody rows. Ribbon snakes are more slender, have neither red color nor dark spots between the lengthwise stripes, lack vertical dark sutures on the upper lips, and have no obvious dark markings on the abdomen. The lined snake, which also lacks any red coloration, displays a double row of bold, dark half-moons on the belly.

SIZE Sixteen to 26 inches (40.6–66 cm) is considered the usual adult length for this subspecies. The largest known specimen was 48⅞ inches (124.2 cm) long.

HABITAT No other snake lives as far north on our continent as this one. With a vast north-south geographic range that extends 1,700 miles, this cold-tolerant subspecies is found from the southern end of great Slave Lake in Canada's Northwest Territories (approximately 400 airline miles south of the Arctic Circle) to extreme northern Texas. As expected in such a broad-ranging reptile, it occupies a wide variety of habitats, most of them near moisture. In spring and summer it is likely to be found in brushy or grassy areas close to moist or aquatic environments, including lakes, ponds, rivers, streams, wet ditches, swamps, and prairie swales, although it sometimes inhabits relatively dry places such as arid fields, vacant suburban lots, rocky slopes, and upland prairies. As the first chill of fall settles over its summer home, the red-sided garter snake moves to the vicinity of its winter den, usually a deep sinkhole or rocky, wooded hilltop into which it can later retire to escape the lethal effects of prolonged subfreezing weather.

BEHAVIOR Considering its relatively small size, it is no wonder this defenseless reptile prefers to avoid an encounter with an adversary the size of man. When approached, it usually disappears into the underbrush. If it finds itself clearly in danger and with no avenue of escape, it may resort to a simple form of intimidation in a bold attempt to startle its foe. All at once the snake flattens its entire body so that the taut red skin (most of it normally concealed between the overlapping scales) suddenly pops into view, creating a bold, new image of large reddish patches speckled with horizontal white flecks. Ominous as it may appear to some adversaries, this defensive posturing does not deter them all. It works well with animals unfamiliar with the serpent's bluff but is of no real value against an aggressive foe. Nor is the snake's strike a serious deterrent to its larger enemies. Some garter snakes, especially the older females, bite viciously when picked up, but their small teeth, including the somewhat enlarged rear ones, are capable of causing no more serious injury to man than a cluster of tiny puncture wounds. Perhaps even more unpleasant than the creature's superficial nip

is the way it tries to discourage its captor. Voiding foul-smelling fecal material from its cloaca and musk from scent glands at the base of its tail, the snake thrashes its body about in an effort to smear the repulsive material over the restraining hand.

If seized by the tail, the snake may rotate its body, like a spinning top, until part of that caudal appendage breaks away, leaving a relatively bloodless stump at the point of separation. Meanwhile, the dismembered segment takes on an animated life of its own. Twisting and jumping about, it may briefly draw attention to itself and away from the snake, just as do the tails of many lizard species under similar circumstances, giving the victim a few seconds to escape. In his study of red-sided garter snakes in Kansas, Fitch (1965) discovered that of 940 specimens he examined, 17.9 percent had incomplete tails, due, he believed, to the serpent's fragile tail anatomy and the tail-twirling escape behavior.

In common with most garter snakes, this one favors moist environments, though it does not always confine itself to the margins of ponds or streams. Fitch was surprised to find that during dry weather, when amphibian prey was abundant along the water's edge, red-sided garter snakes at his Kansas site did not congregate along the shoreline of the area's two large ponds but chose instead to occupy the drier surrounding terrain.

In Kansas, Fitch determined that male red-sided garter snakes occupied a summer range of 35 acres, and the females inhabited only 22.7 acres. He also found that most of them traveled less than 700 feet between captures in a month, and they moved less than 1,110 feet in a single year. For the most part, they covered greater distances when migrating between their summer meadowland homes and winter dens, usually the deep crevices of partly wooded hilltop outcroppings. In Kansas such trips averaged 1,745 feet (534 m) for females and 1,138 feet (356 m) for males. For one Manitoba garter snake the excursion involved an extraordinarily long journey of 10 miles (16 km). Not all red-sided garter snakes migrate to a distant communal hibernaculum; some, particularly the very young, spend the winter in mammal burrows near their summer feeding grounds.

Apparently more tolerant of cold than any other North American serpent, the red-sided manages to survive low temperatures that prompt most cohabiting reptiles to seek refuge underground. After most other snake species have already retired to their winter dens, the red-sided garter snake lingers at the entrance to its hibernaculum. Having arrived there sometime between late August and September, it subsequently spends the midday hours basking in the sun but at night and on cloudy days withdraws into the den's warmer recesses. Sometime between late October and early November, when daytime temperatures have consistently dropped below the freezing mark and the upper soil level has just started to freeze, the snake finally retires to its winter refuge. It remains in hibernation for the next five to seven months, depending on the length of the winter season, generally reappearing above ground again between late March and May.

In some parts of Canada, the snake's choice dens are large sinkholes. Such geological formations apparently result when underground water gradually erodes the relatively soft limestone bedrock, causing it to collapse inward. What remains at the surface is a large, rubble-filled hole or sizable depression, usually pocked with numerous openings that lead to a labyrinth of subterranean galleries. In such places, the local garter snakes come together each fall, sometimes by the thousands, to take advantage of the spacious network of underground spaces that they will later share as winter refuges. Most individuals retire to the same dens year after year. One such den, reported by Aleksiuk and Stewart (1971) near the town of Inwood in Manitoba, contained an estimated 8,000 red-sided garter snakes, a number that probably has not been matched by any other serpent hibernaculum anywhere else in the world. To be effective as winter havens, these underground spaces must be deep enough to shelter the snakes from severe subfreezing temperatures, which in central Canada can plummet to minus 40 degrees F.

Perhaps contributing to the red-sided garter's ability to survive such harsh winter conditions, according to Aleksiuk and Stewart, is the snake's abstinence from late fall feeding. Unlike certain northern mammals and many reptiles that eat heavily during late fall to increase their fat reserves just prior to entering hibernation, the red-sided garter snake eats no food at all during this period, resulting in a reduced accumulation of body fat and a reduction in the percentage of water in body tissues. It therefore enters winter dormancy hungry and somewhat dehydrated but better prepared to avoid crystallization of its body tissues during subfreezing temperatures.

FEEDING This snake is a generalized feeder whose diet consists chiefly of frogs, toads, and earthworms but also includes small mammals, birds, fish, reptiles, and perhaps spiders and insects.

In his Kansas study, which included two distinctly different sites, Fitch found the snake's diet to vary somewhat according to habitat. At the lowland location, an area characterized by patches of marsh and an abundance of shallow pools, the red-sided garter devoured leopard frogs almost exclusively (91 percent of the total diet), but at the upland site, where less than 1 percent of the area was open water, it consumed only 41.4 percent frogs, the rest of the menu consisting of voles, mice, one snake, and one bird (all eaten by the adults), as well as earthworms (consumed by the juveniles). When both sites were considered together, however, the 200 prey items contained in the stomachs of these Kansas red-sided garter snakes were distributed as follows: 120 leopard frogs, 7 bullfrogs, 25 unidentified frogs, 12 juvenile American toads, 8 gray tree frogs, 6 cricket frogs, 5 earthworms, 5 wood mice, 5 western narrowmouth toads, 2 prairie voles, 1 harvest mouse, 1 garden toad, 1 striped chorus frog, 1 unidentified bird, and 1 juvenile copperhead. Able to ingest only the smallest prey, the diminutive newborn garter snake obviously is limited in its feeding opportunities; earthworms, therefore, may represent a major part of its diet. Fitch suggested that in places where earthworms are absent or not available to the newborn garter snakes in late summer, the infant reptiles may not be able to find other suitably sized prey to sustain them during the beginning stages of their lives. He noted, too, that even the smallest rodents and shrews (vertebrate animals commonly available to the adult snakes) are too large for the tiny garter snake to ingest, as are the adult frogs consumed by the larger serpents. Recently metamorphosed frogs and toads, however, are small enough to be eaten by the newborn garter snakes, although in some places like Fitch's northeastern Kansas study site, these anurans have already grown into sizable amphibians before the snakes are even born, making earthworms the infant snake's chief source of food.

REPRODUCTION Although famished after spending the long winter in hibernation, the male garter snake's first notion after leaving his den is not to satisfy his hunger but to find a mate. His amorous quest begins soon after he has emerged from winter dormancy sometime between late March and early May, when the sun has warmed the soil and the air temperature has climbed to around 60 degrees F. The males are usually the first to appear, followed in one to several days by the females.

These annual spring courtship and mating events are dramatic affairs that caught the attention of several field biologists. One of them, Michael Aleksiuk, then a herpetologist at the University of Manitoba, described in some detail (in Aleksiuk and Stewart 1971) such extraordinary garter snake breeding aggregations. At a large sinkhole 60 miles (97 km) north of Winnipeg, he watched in awe as thousands of red-sided garter snakes emerged from the rock rubble capping their winter den. Before long, they had covered the ground like a huge living carpet, most of them in constant motion, slithering over one another and climbing onto rocks and into nearby bushes. A closer examination soon revealed the reason for this writhing mass of serpents—it was their mating season.

During the next week or two, many if not most individuals in the emerging horde would eventually participate in this zealous breeding activity. These were not, however, normal sexual encounters between a male and a female but more like one great sex orgy, in which as many as 100 (but generally 30 or fewer) males at a time vigorously courted a single female in hopes of being the one to mate with her. In such a squirming mass of reptile bodies, called a mating ball, the closely packed gob of males so completely covered the single female that she was of-

ten invisible. The impassioned group usually maintained their cohesiveness for 5 to 10 minutes before copulation was achieved and the snakes dispersed.

To prevent other males from breeding with an already inseminated female, the successful male will deposit a mating plug in her cloaca before copulation is completed. Composed of a gelatinous, semen-associated substance that quickly congeals after being implanted, the plug presumably blocks any subsequent penal insertion for a period lasting four days to at least a couple of weeks, depending in part on the prevailing temperature. This time span coincides approximately with the length of the usual spring mating season. Not only does the plug physically bar copulation by other males, but it also emits a pheromone (a chemical odor) that makes such females sexually unattractive. Unlike the perfumes worn by humans as a source of sexual attraction, the snake's plug-derived pheromone acts instead as a sexual repellent.

For the inseminated female, the mating season apparently is now over. A few days after copulation, she moves away from the den site and back to her summer feeding grounds, where she remains until fall. For the male, the mating season does not end there. He remains near the hibernaculum for the next week or so, waiting for more females to appear, whereupon he again competes with the other males for the opportunity to copulate with more unbred females. Although it is believed that females carrying a mating plug do not breed again while at the den site, recent evidence suggests either that they do or that they are inseminated a second time at another time and place in the same spring. Using electrophoretic tests, Schwartz and his colleagues (1989) demonstrated convincingly that multiple paternity occurred in 50 percent of 32 litters they examined. In addition, Whittier and Crews (1986) found that about a third of the females in a group of free-living garter snakes mated with more than one male. It is not clear, therefore, just how effective such mating plugs may be in limiting multiple paternity. During the latter part of their pregnancy, small numbers of gravid female garter snakes (usually fewer than eight in a group) sometimes come together at some open place where they bask daily in the direct sunlight as a way to aid the growth of their developing embryos by raising their own body temperatures. Typically such gatherings occur near a choice refuge where the gravid snakes can promptly seek shelter from predators.

Few other North American snake species are as prolific as this one. Although single litters of red-sided garter snakes have contained more than 70 young, Fitch's Kansas records show the usual number to be 7 to 20, with an average of 13 or 14. Elsewhere within its geographic range an average litter may consist of about 30 young. The female ordinarily gives birth during late July or early August, sometimes as late as September or early October. Newborn red-sided garter snakes are 5 to 9 inches (12.7–22.9 cm) long.

TEXAS LYRE SNAKE
Trimorphodon lambda
vilkinsoni
PLATES 164, 165

DESCRIPTION The snake's conspicuous features include a relatively wide head, large vertically slit eye pupils, and a rather narrow neck—features more typical of the dangerously venomous pit vipers than of the generally harmless family of colubrids to which it belongs. The dorsal pattern consists of dark brown, saddle-shaped blotches, each accented with a pale center and an even paler outer margin; a blotch is considerably wider along the middle of the back than it is low on the sides, where it narrows almost to a point. Along the midline, the pale brown or gray ground color between such markings is twice the length (measured front to back) of a single blotch. Near the abdomen, a series of dark, rounded spots, which alternate with the primary markings or are aligned with them, intrudes onto the outer edges of the belly. Otherwise, the pale abdomen is immaculate. The name "lyre snake" is appropriate for most races of *T. lambda*, but it does not accurately describe this one. Instead of the large, chevron marking that typically appears on the crown of other subspecies, the upper head pattern of the Texas lyre snake usually consists of one to three ill-defined spots or, less frequently, none at all. Occasionally, a small, dark V appears on the rear part of the head as well. If present, the dark crossbar on the forecrown between the eyes is indistinct.

A scale called the lorilabial, on the side of the snake's head between the loreal and the upper lip scales, is found in no other Texas serpent. The dorsal scales are smooth and usually arranged in 23 rows at midbody; the anal plate is divided.

COMPARABLE SNAKES The nearly solid, dark brown crossbands of the Trans-Pecos copperhead, which do not become narrower laterally, are wider than the light interspaces that separate them. There is also a pale, delicately dark-edged ∨ on either side of the copperhead's face and a facial pit on each side of its head between the eye and nostril. Its anal plate is single. Gray-banded king snakes from the Big Bend region resemble to some extent the Texas lyre snake, even to their relatively large eyes, but the king snake's pupils are round, and its anal plate is single. The small night snake, whose elliptical pupils resemble those of the Texas lyre snake, is spotted dorsally and has distinct large, dark blotches on the top and sides of its neck.

SIZE Most adults of this rather slender snake are 18 to 30 inches (45.7–76.2 cm) in length. A record specimen measured 41 inches (104.1 cm) long.

HABITAT Seldom observed in the wild except by naturalists familiar with its habits and habitat, the Texas lyre snake is probably more abundant than the few published records of its capture suggest. This is demonstrated by the experience of McCrystal (1991), who found 35 to 40 specimens of this subspecies each year in the Big Bend region of Texas. Primarily a resident of arid, rocky terrain, particularly in hilly country, it is intimately associated with rock piles, rock outcroppings, and talus slopes in which it finds an endless network of underground hiding places.

Aside from the lyre snakes encountered in the Big Bend by McCrystal, most Texas specimens have been discovered in El Paso County's Franklin Mountains, where from 1961 through 1975 Banicki and Webb (1982) found 22 examples of this elusive serpent, primarily along Trans-Mountain Road; some of them were found while the highway was still under construction. According to the zoologists, the Franklin mountain range is approximately 15 miles long and 3 miles wide, with the greatest elevation represented by

7,192-foot (2,199 m) North Franklin Peak. The highest point in these mountains at which they found a lyre snake was along the summit of Trans-Mountain Road at an elevation of 5,280 feet (1,615 m). Another specimen was collected by Medica (1962) at 5,500 feet (1,682 m), near the base of the Organ Mountains, a site 30 miles (48 km) north of the Franklins and not far from Las Cruces, New Mexico. According to Banicki and Webb, the snake's preferred habitat in the arid Franklin Mountains contains a variety of desert plants; the dominant species include ocotillo, catclaw mimosa, white thorn, Torrey yucca, lechuguilla, prickly pear cactus, cholla, and grasses. In the region's deeper, more protected canyons it is found among stands of ash, hackberry, juniper, and oak. The snake is sometimes also encountered on desert flats where creosote bush is the dominant large plant and in the area's shallow canyons where the prevailing tree is mesquite. At the opposite end of its Texas range in Big Bend National Park, the lyre snake has been collected in the Grapevine Hills at 3,135 feet (859 m) and in the Chisos Mountains as high as 5,940 feet (1,856 m).

BEHAVIOR The Texas lyre snakes in our care did not bite when first handled, but one specimen invariably cocked back the forward quarter of its body whenever it was provoked, drawing it into a tight S-shaped defensive posture without ever launching a strike. During such threat posturing, the reptile may rapidly vibrate its tail. Describing the actions of a California lyre snake, a closely related subspecies from the West Coast, Klauber (1940b) noted that the serpent readily struck at nearby moving objects but with more accuracy at night than by day. This is expected, for the lyre snake's elliptical pupils are specifically adapted for night vision. According to McCrystal, the Texas lyre snake can be spotted at a distance by the way it crawls with its head held high, much like a racer when searching for prey. The lyre snake endures moderately cold weather better than most other local serpents; Klauber encountered a specimen of the California subspecies crossing a road at 9:15 PM when a strong wind was blowing and the temperature stood at a brisk 66 degrees F. Although the area ordinarily was one of the most productive for collecting desert reptiles, that night he found no other serpents at the surface during 2½ hours of driving. In a similar encounter (this one along the base of the Little San Bernardino Mountains in Riverside County, California), he discovered a lyre snake at 7:25 PM as it crossed the road in an open wash. A gale was blowing at the time and the temperature registered a chilly 64 degrees F. To a temperature-sensitive reptile, extreme heat can be as devastating as severe cold. Thus, like most desert dwellers, this nocturnal creature prudently avoids the sweltering daytime sun by crawling into the labyrinth of underground spaces commonly found in the rocky soils of the arid Southwest, or into the deep crevice of some large boulder. On cool days, however, the lyre snake may spend the day at the surface coiled in the space between two large boulders, the narrow gap creating a safe haven for its slender body. Or it may coil under the loose, slightly raised flake of a granite boulder. In a natural process called exfoliation, thin layers of the boulder's curved surface eventually break loose after the rock has been exposed repeatedly to the desert's relentless cycle of alternating torrid days and chilly nights; wind and rain also play a part in the process. The resulting convex stone flakes, some measuring several feet across, often remain in place with much of their surface slightly elevated above the parent rock. Beneath these rock slivers a number of lizard and snake species find ideal cool-weather retreats. Although Klauber never discovered a California lyre snake under such granite flakes, Lowe, Schwalbe, and Johnson (1986) noted that in Arizona the Sonoran lyre snake is often found there, but it is unknown if the Texas lyre snake hides under similar sheets of exfoliated rock.

FEEDING Although no detailed studies are available describing the food habits of the Texas lyre snake, this subspecies is known to prey chiefly on lizards, many of which it is believed are detected in their nighttime rock-crevice shelters, asleep and easy targets for the foraging serpents. Even mice, bats, birds, and other small snakes are not safe from this night prowler.

When it finds its quarry, the lyre snake seizes its victim and hangs on, for its primitive venom delivery system does not quickly kill the prey but slowly immobilizes it, until it is incapacitated enough to be swallowed. In common with several other native colubrid species that independently evolved a similar envenomation apparatus, this snake has a small fang at the rear of each side of its upper jaw. Slightly curved and slanting backward at an angle greater than 45 degrees from the vertical, they are not hollow like those of pit vipers but carry a deep groove down their front face. To engage them, the snake must first manipulate the prey to the back of its mouth, where it can be stabbed by the rear-positioned fangs. With slow chewing movements, the snake releases venom from a small gland at the base of each fang, which then flows sluggishly down the enlarged tooth to find its way, almost fortuitously, into the puncture wounds created by the fangs and teeth. Klauber noted that the California lyre snake often grasped a lizard so that the predator's fangs engaged the underside of its victim, where small, thin belly scales offer less resistance to fang penetration than the larger, more heavily armored dorsal scales.

Lethal primarily to the lizards that constitute its usual diet, the Texas lyre snake's venom is not considered dangerous to man. Primarily hemorrhagic, in a human victim it causes redness, itching, and usually some numbness. Even small mammals show considerable resistance to its effects. In a series of experiments, Cowles and Bogert (1935) found that a rat and a mouse, each bitten by a large California lyre snake, suffered only modest symptoms of envenomation; both easily survived the experience. Such potentially dangerous prey animals are sometimes subdued by constriction.

Though most North American rear-fanged snakes are small and pose no real threat to human health, two large African arboreal species in particular are dangerous to man and have been implicated in human fatalities. One is the six-foot-long boomslang, *Dispholidus typus*, a specimen of which killed Karl P. Schmidt, a leading herpetologist of his time. The other is the equally large bird snake, *Thelotornis kirtlandi*. The venoms of both species contain a powerful, slow-acting toxic component that in serious cases of poisoning causes extensive internal hemorrhaging and kidney damage.

REPRODUCTION Apparently the only published information about the Texas lyre snake's breeding behavior in the state comes from Gus Rentfro (in Tennant 1984), whose captive 28-inch (71.1 cm) female laid 6 adhesive-shelled eggs late in June. The eggs, 1⅛ inches (2.9 cm) long, hatched after a 77-day incubation. The young measured about 8½ inches (21.6 cm) in length. Except for a more pronounced dorsal pattern and a dark line connecting the outer edges of the head spots, they were described as near-replicas of the adults.

LINED SNAKE
Tropidoclonion lineatum
PLATES 166, 167

DESCRIPTION Except for its small, pointed head, thick neck, and the double row of bold, black half-moons down the middle of its belly, the little lined snake closely resembles a small garter snake. It has the same dark trunk, ranging in hue from gray-brown to olive-brown, and three narrow longitudinal stripes on its body. The stripe along the midline of the back is whitish, pale gray, or yellow and usually flanked by a row of minute black spots. Below it, along each side of the body on scale rows 2 and 3 above the belly, lies another light stripe, often less conspicuous than the first and edged above and below by a horizontal row of small black spots. Two parallel rows of rather large black spots adorn the snake's white or yellowish abdomen, one pair on each belly plate. To a greater or lesser extent, dark flecks cover the top of its head. The upper and lower lip scales are pale and immaculate. The keeled body scales are arranged in 19 rows at midbody, and the anal plate is single.

COMPARABLE SNAKES In color and markings, garter snakes bear a strong resemblance to the lined snake, although their black belly spots, when present at all, are neither large half-moons nor arranged in a uniform double row down the middle of the belly. Instead, such markings are small, often irregularly shaped, and somewhat randomly distributed over the ventral plates, usually near their outer edges. Besides, a garter snake's large head, which is followed by its much narrower neck (as seen from above), stands out prominently compared to that of the lined

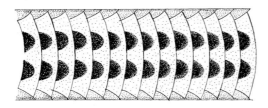

Figure 62. *Belly pattern of the lined snake.*

snake, and black edging marks the vertical sutures of at least some of the garter snake's upper lip scales. The abdomen of the gulf crayfish snake, like that of the lined snake, is boldly patterned with two rows of black half-moons down its middle, but the lengthwise stripes on its back and sides are dark and obscure, and its anal plate is divided. The most conspicuous marking of Graham's crayfish snake is not a light middorsal stripe but a pale band of color that runs along each side of the trunk at the belly line. In addition, a row of small black spots extends down each side of the abdomen, and a single row of dark dots typically runs down its middle. As in all crayfish snakes, the anal plate is divided. Besides its distinct dark mark on the upper lip below the eye and another just back of the head, the Texas brown snake differs from the lined snake in having only 17 rows of dorsal scales at midbody and a divided anal plate.

SIZE Although the record length for this snake is 21½ inches (54.6 cm), most adults measure between 8¾ and 15 inches (22–38.1 cm).

HABITAT Essentially a snake of open grassland prairie and sparsely wooded flatlands where the limestone substrate and its decomposing surface debris provide an abundance of sheltering rock, this species generally avoids dense woods (there are a few curious records from the timbered northeastern corner of the state). It also shuns constantly wet places. Writing about the lined snake in the Waco area, Strecker (1926a) commented that during the many years he collected reptiles near the old lagoon along east Waco's railroad tracks and in the Brazos River bottoms, he found only two specimens of this species, both from the dry part of Gurley Park, about ½ mile from the river. Nevertheless, *T. lineatum* was then, and still is, remarkably abundant throughout the drier parts of the Waco area.

To many Texans living within its range, this little garden snake is a familiar sight, for apparently it is encountered more often in some urban neighborhoods than in many remote areas. With only a bit of dry land on which to live, some shelter to protect it from enemies and adverse weather, and a steady supply of earthworm prey, this adaptable little creature survives within some of the state's largest metropolitan areas. There it can be found by poking around litter-strewn vacant lots, flower beds, and abandoned wooden buildings or by looking under trash and leaf piles, rocks, boards, fallen tree limbs, tin, paper, and other surface debris. Strecker, for example, collected 15 lined snakes from under loose paving stones near an old house and noted the discovery of dozens more that were driven from their underground shelters when fire hoses were used to extinguish a warehouse blaze. Others have been found in ground-level utility meter boxes. Away from urban centers, the lined snake is found in greatest numbers along open, rock-strewn prairies and hillsides where surface shelter is plentiful. In such prime habitat it is sometimes surprisingly abundant. For instance, in one day alone Taggart (1992) captured 47 specimens of this species from under rocks scattered over a single hillside in Hodgeman County, Kansas, and in just three hours he collected another 72 from under flat rocks in Ellis County, Kansas.

BEHAVIOR Except for its readiness when picked up to discharge the vile contents of the scent glands at the base of its tail, this is certainly one of the most indulgent of Texas snakes, rarely offering to bite, even when roughly handled. When prodded, it may do little more than tuck its head under one of its own body coils. Upon being provoked, one female of this species flattened her head, body, and part of her tail in a startling display, then struck at her tormentor, a defensive behavior that may be employed by this snake only on rare occasions. Otherwise this timid little serpent is quite defenseless. The lined snake tries to avoid its enemies by hiding peaceably beneath some form of surface shelter or by passing the daylight hours underground. By nightfall and sometimes even sooner (especially in spring and fall when daytime temperatures are more moderate), it leaves the safety of its lair in search of food, often spurred by warm rains, for at such times earthworms, its chief prey, are to be found crawling on top of the ground in large numbers. More tolerant of cold weather than many other Texas serpents, the lined snake ordinarily stays active from March to some time in October or November. Even in midwinter, when the temperature has sufficiently warmed, it may briefly bask in the sun, though at such times it is more apt to coil under some form of aboveground cover to avoid predators, at the same time enjoying the heat transmitted to it by the underside of the sun-warmed object. Despite its considerable tolerance for cool weather, the lined snake, like other serpents, is not immune to the fatal effects of below-freezing temperatures. Sooner or later it must find shelter from the bitter chill of winter. Where the soil is soft enough, the snake will dig its way several inches into the ground. In one such hibernaculum, discovered in a Dallas suburb in January, Hamilton (1947) found seven lined snakes buried 6 to 8 inches deep in the black gumbo soil of a small garden. Four of them occupied an area the size of a dining table, suggesting that this was a communal overwintering site, whereas the others were dispersed more randomly throughout the 1,200 square feet (110 m²) of the plot. In every case, they were coiled with one complete circle of body coil stacked directly on the other, much as dead snakes are preserved in small jars. For lined snakes living in hard soil, crawling into existing holes probably is the answer, particularly the narrow tunnels excavated under large stones by other burrowing creatures.

FEEDING For a snake like this, whose small head and narrow-gaped mouth prevent the ingestion of large prey, earthworms represent the ideal food, an item it devours almost exclusively. Observing captive lined snakes for two years, Ramsey (1947) found that when attacking an earthworm, the snake nearly always seized it near midbody, then pulled back its own head half an inch or so before it began to ingest its prey. From there the process did not conform to the usual snake practice of swallowing the prey head first. Instead of manipulating a worm in its mouth until it found the front (or back) end, the serpent held it by the middle, bent it into a hairpin configuration, and, with both sides of the worm dangling free, proceeded to swallow it. Frantically twisting, wriggling, and discharging lots of slime, the victim tried unceasingly to escape. A worm that exerted too much pressure after wrapping itself around the snake's neck was scraped free by rubbing it against the ground as the serpent pulled its head backward. This brought it closer to the snake's jaws and placed it in a better position to be swallowed.

Small worms were easily devoured, though the struggles of a large one often presented the snake with a dilemma, especially if the annelid succeeded in slipping one end of its body into a burrow or some other opening in the ground where it could gain enough of a grip to pull itself free. In response to such a strategy, the snake reacted with a tactic of its own. Probing the ground with its tail, it cast about for some object around which it could wrap the rear part of its body and anchor itself against the struggling worm. When both predator and prey gained a sufficient grip to create an impasse, the struggle was sometimes resolved when the snake's sharp, rear-set teeth, aided by the worm's constant twisting and rolling, more or less sawed the victim in two. With that, the snake swallowed one part of its prey while the other part escaped underground. Seizing the earthworm by the tail as it enters its burrow head first is perhaps the least successful way to attack it; it then enjoys an added degree of leverage to pull its body deeper into its hole, and it can discharge feces into the snake's mouth. In two instances where Ramsey saw the worm release excrement into a snake's oral cavity, the prey was promptly released and not attacked again until the foul substance had been eliminated from the serpent's mouth.

REPRODUCTION Mating generally occurs in September or October but may also take place in the spring. Sperm from the fall copulations, which is held safely in the female's oviducts through the winter, fertilizes the eggs after ovulation the following spring. In either case, the female lined snake gives birth sometime in August to litters of 2 to 13 (usually 7 or 8). The young are 3¾ to 5 inches (7.6 – 12.1 cm) long and resemble slightly paler replicas of the adults. Thereafter, the males reach sexual maturity when they are about a year old, the females after their second year of life.

ROUGH EARTH SNAKE
Virginia striatula
PLATE 168

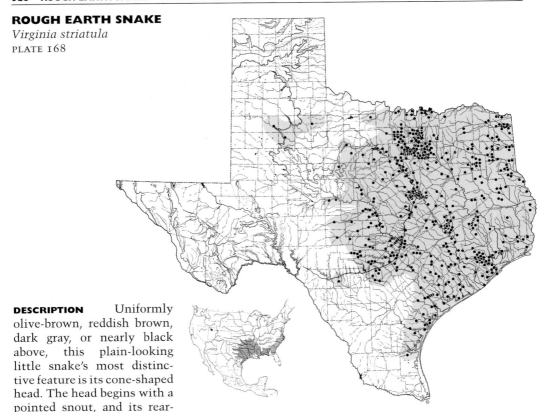

DESCRIPTION   Uniformly olive-brown, reddish brown, dark gray, or nearly black above, this plain-looking little snake's most distinctive feature is its cone-shaped head. The head begins with a pointed snout, and its rearmost part, although broad, is only slightly wider than the neck. Rarely is there an indistinct light marking across the back of the snake's head or two or more small, whitish spots (usually only in very young specimens). The rest of the crown varies in individual specimens from light brown to a deep olive or blackish hue. The belly is dirty white, cream, or pale yellow, although in some rough earth snakes it is grass-green or even pinkish.

In the absence of any explicit and consistent features of color or markings, the snake's identification can best be confirmed by examining certain details of scale arrangement, a task accomplished on such a small snake only under magnification. Beginning at the head, they include a single internasal scale, an elongated horizontal loreal plate that touches the eye, one postocular scale, and five upper lip scales on either side of the face. The body scales, arranged in 17 middorsal rows, are keeled only along the upper back part of the snake's trunk. The anal plate is nearly always divided.

COMPARABLE SNAKES   The earthy color of *V. striatula* is so like that of several other similar-sized local snakes that its pointed, cone-shaped snout is an important item of distinction. The western earth snake typically has a more reddish upper body, smooth dorsal scales (a few weakly keeled on the rear part of the trunk), two internasal scales, and usually six upper lip scales on either side of the head. The flat-headed snake has a lighter-hued upper trunk, smooth dorsal scales in only 15 rows at midbody, and no loreal scale. Ground snakes ordinarily look like they are striped lengthwise with numerous thin, dotted lines, whether or not they display other dorsal markings. Their smooth dorsal scales are arranged in 13 to 15 rows at midbody, and they possess a preocular scale that separates the eye from the loreal scale. The brown snake, which is somewhat thicker in body than the rough earth snake, typically possesses a pale band down the middle of the back, on either side of which is a row of discreet small black spots. In addition to having two internasal plates and seven scales lining each side of the upper lip, it lacks a loreal scale. The Florida red-bellied snake, rare in Texas, likewise lacks a loreal scale; it can be distinguished by the presence of six upper lip scales on each side of the mouth, by the conspicuous pale patch (or three separate spots) on the neck, and by the prominent circle of pale pigment on the upper lip below and behind each eye. Ring-necked snakes possess a distinct pale nuchal collar (sometimes interrupted at the middle of the back) and numerous small but bold black spots on the belly. In addition, their dorsal scales are smooth, and they have two internasals on the forecrown. Another potentially confusing species is the western worm snake, a smooth-scaled serpent whose deep-pink belly color extends up along the sides of the body to the third row of dorsal scales.

SIZE Among the smallest of Texas serpents, adult rough earth snakes are generally 7 to 10 inches (17.8–25.4 cm) in length. A record specimen measured 12¾ inches (32 cm) long.

HABITAT This abundant reptile inhabits the eastern half of the state, where it is likely to be encountered in almost any region with damp soil and debris for concealment. Suitable habitat includes pine woods, hardwood forest, sparsely wooded rocky hillsides, swamp edge, and grasslands. It usually avoids desert or semidesert habitats, invading such regions only along the wooded margins of rivers and streams that flow through them. A testament to the snake's adaptability is its continued abundance well within the borders of large metropolitan areas, where despite disruption by human activity, it continues to prosper.

BEHAVIOR Although we have never known the rough earth snake to bite (nor apparently has anyone else), this harmless little creature continues to be mistaken for a venomous copperhead by many urbanites. As the most abundant serpent species in many large metropolitan areas of the state, it often becomes a target for the naive city dweller who happens to find it in a vacant lot, compost heap, flower bed, or belowground utility meter box, a few of the preferred hiding places near the home. It seems that rough earth snakes are found in greater numbers in some residential neighborhoods than can ordinarily be discovered in many wilderness areas. The snake's typical first response when discovered on the ground is to lie motionless, then, after a few seconds, to crawl away into some nearby shelter. During its attempted escape it is easily caught, for this is a small and relatively slow-moving species. Although it does not defend itself by biting, a captured specimen will discharge an unpleasant-smelling musk from glands at the base of its tail and perhaps even feces from its cloaca, actions intended to repel a captor. In a most unusual case of self-preservation, reported by Kirk (1969), a rough earth snake that was being swallowed tail first by a larger serpent of another species avoided becoming a meal by turning its head to one side, seizing its captor by the glottis, and hanging on with determination until it was finally regurgitated. In another instance, reported by Thomas and Hendricks (1976), a specimen being handled by one of the zoologists demonstrated an unusual death feint, the kind of defensive behavior employed by several other native serpent species when they are physically disturbed, particularly if lightly tapped on the head. This behavior pattern, which involved an unvarying sequence of events, was repeated a number of times over a period of several weeks. Each incident began as the snake defecated, twisted and squirmed fitfully for about 45 seconds, then became still, sometimes coming to rest belly up. At this point, the snake's stiff and wretchedly contorted body, its tongue hanging awkwardly from its open mouth, gave the serpent every appearance of being dead. If left undisturbed for several minutes, the snake regained its normal demeanor and nonchalantly crawled away.

Despite the species' abundance, it is no surprise that specimens are seldom seen out in the open, for this is primarily a nocturnal reptile, though it occasionally leaves its daytime refuge during the hours of early morning and late evening, especially following drenching rains. When it comes to the surface it is apt to be found lurking beneath some sheltering object, such as a rock, log, or fallen branch, or hidden in a carpet of leaf litter. Another good place to find it is under the loose bark of either a dead tree or decaying tree stump. In Central Texas, Strecker (1927) frequently discovered small specimens in wooded creek and river bottoms, congregated next to dead vines partially buried in a bed of fallen leaves. Other herpetologists have also commented on the importance of ground leaf litter in the rough earth snake's microhabitat. Indeed, Edward H. Taylor (in Smith 1950) reported successfully collecting this species in large numbers simply by raking his hands through the layer of dead leaves that had accumulated along the banks of abandoned gravel pits. That is not an altogether safe practice, for copperheads and coral snakes frequently inhabit the same kind of ground litter.

In a comprehensive study of the snake's ecology, Clark and Fleet (1976) determined that at a particular Brazos County site the average size of the snake's territory, based on a circle-radius measurement, was about 268 feet (82 m) for males and 69 feet (21 m) for females. They also calculated that the species' population density varied during the nearly three-year study from 348 snakes per hectare (2.47 acres) in 1969 to 229 snakes per hectare in 1971. The marked difference in numbers was attributed to the greater amount of rainfall during the more successful year, which apparently resulted in a higher reproductive rate. The drying conditions in 1971, on the other hand, seemed to reduce the snake's reproductive rate, since on average, the number of young per litter born to the females during that year was less than in 1969.

Severe dehydration of the soil can present a real threat to the species' welfare, but cool temperatures do not. More tolerant of cold weather than most other local serpents, the rough earth snake is among the first species to emerge from hibernation in the spring and one of the last to seek refuge as winter begins. Its usual active season in Central and South Texas starts at the beginning of March and ordinarily lasts through November. According to Clark and Fleet, most activity at the Waco study site was recorded in March and April and again in September and December. In summer, however, when temperatures were high and rainfall negligible, the rough earth snake was seldom seen at the surface; it probably moved deeper into the soil where temperatures were cooler and the ground damper. During the winter, except when temperatures drop much below 50 degrees F,

this hardy reptile is sometimes discovered on top of the ground, sheltered under surface objects, or even venturing out into the open if the weather is warm enough. During an uncommonly mild winter in the Waco area, for example, Strecker found a rough earth snake on February 7, hidden under a stone; 7 active specimens on February 15, in a gully along a railroad bed; 10 more on February 19, nestled beneath the rotting remains of a large fallen tree; and 7 others on February 22, coiled under large decaying logs not far from the Brazos River. Our own experience with this snake in the Houston area over a span of more than three decades confirms the species' unusual tolerance for cool weather; we have observed it above ground in every month of the year, nearly always concealed under some form of surface debris but occasionally out in the open as well. Like all snake species, it must find a safe haven from the lethal effects of winter's subfreezing temperatures. This it does by digging down into soft soil, entering the burrows of other small creatures, or by crawling into the decaying heartwood of dead stumps and fallen tree trunks. In the Houston area we have several times found it overwintering in large piles of compost, where the mass of warm, loosely packed plant material apparently provided an ideal medium in which to pass the winter. Such a refuge, incidentally, may contain several specimens, even including examples of other small serpent species. In like manner, rough earth snakes have been discovered sharing their winter shelters with other hibernating reptiles and amphibians. In Victoria, one such den contained a mix of rough earth snakes, ribbon snakes, copperheads, lizards, frogs, and toads. Another, found in the Waco area, included essentially the same combination of species plus a Texas rat snake.

FEEDING As would be expected, the diet of such a small snake consists largely of invertebrate prey. In several comprehensive investigations of the species' feeding habits, including the Brazos County, Texas, study by Clark and Fleet, only earthworms were found in the sampled stomachs. Other naturalists report a wider range of menu items that includes slugs, snails, sowbugs, insects, small frogs, and young lizards, particularly the abundant little ground skinks. Circumstantial evidence also suggests that insect eggs and larvae may be eaten as well, for in Florida, Ashton and Ashton (1981) found several of these snakes along the edges of ant colonies very near their brood.

REPRODUCTION The females become sexually mature during the second fall of their lives, but some males reach maturity even earlier, engaging in copulation during the first spring of their existence. For the male rough earth snake, finding a female is not an altogether random affair. Instead of engaging in aimless searching for a mate, he merely locates the scent trail left on the ground by a receptive female and follows it to her lo-

cation. Although mating usually occurs in March or April (and occasionally in the fall), at least in Central and South Texas, the female does not ovulate until May or June, suggesting that the sperm remains viable in her cloaca until the eggs are ready for fertilization. Sometime between July and late September, after a gestation period of approximately 10 weeks, the young are born, each litter consisting of 2 to 13 young and each newborn measuring 3 to 4¾ inches (7.6–12.1 cm) long. At this time, and for the next year or so, the juvenile rough earth snake carries a distinctive light band across the back of its head.

WESTERN EARTH SNAKE
Virginia valeriae elegans
PLATES 169, 170

DESCRIPTION This ordinary-looking gray, medium brown, yellowish brown, or reddish brown little snake has no conspicuous markings by which it can be easily identified. Some specimens are plain-colored above; others have an obscure light stripe down the middle of the back, which is often bordered on either side by a longitudinal row of dark, widely spaced dots or flecks, and below it may be another row of similar spots. The color of the belly typically is off-white, dull gray, or pale yellow, but in some individuals it is cream, pastel green, or subdued

pink. Except for the small brown dots on the outer edges of the ventral plates in a few specimens, the snake's underside is unmarked. Its small, narrow head is only a bit wider than the neck and bluntly pointed. Its crown, generally a little darker than the upper body, often displays irregular dark speckling, as sometimes do the pale pink to coral-pink upper lip scales. There may also be a dark shadow-stripe on either side of the face between the eye and nostril.

Since the western earth snake displays considerable variation in its overall appearance and also closely resembles several other diminutive serpents living within its geographic range, trying to identify this nondescript little snake may be difficult. The best way to arrive at a positive identification is to examine certain details of scale structure and arrangement under magnification. In V. v. elegans, most of the dorsal scales are smooth, although some on the upper rear of the body may be weakly keeled. When examining the snake for this feature, it is important to distinguish between an actual keel and the faint horizontal pale line, present in some specimens, that extends through the center of individual scales and looks surprisingly like a ridge. These dorsal scales are arranged in 17 rows at midbody. On the head are two internasal scales, six upper lip scales on each side of the mouth, one elongated loreal scale in front of each eye (with no preoculars), and two scales directly behind each eye. The anal plate is divided.

COMPARABLE SNAKES The closely related rough earth snake has a more cone-shaped head, distinctly keeled dorsal scales on much of its body, a single internasal scale, only five upper lip plates on either side of its mouth, and a single scale immediately behind each eye. The flat-headed snake can be distinguished by its paler upper body, smooth dorsal scales in only 15 midbody rows, and the absence of a loreal scale. Ground snakes, whose 13 to 15 rows of middorsal scales are smooth over the entire body, have the appearance of being striped longitudinally with many thin dotted lines, and they have a preocular scale separating the eye from the loreal plate. Brown snakes, which also lack a loreal scale, possess seven upper lip scales on each side of the mouth. The Florida red-bellied snake lacks a loreal scale, its upper lip plates number six on either side of the mouth, there is a distinct pale collar (or three separate spots) on its neck, and a conspicuous whitish patch on the upper lip below and behind each eye. Ring-necked snakes are easily distinguished by their pale nuchal collars

(sometimes interrupted at the middle of the back) and the bold black spotting on their yellowish bellies. The western worm snake possesses only 13 midbody rows of dorsal scales, and the deep-pink color of its belly continues up the sides of its body to the third such row.

SIZE Adults of this subspecies generally measure between 7 and 10 inches (17.8–25.4 cm) long. Their maximum length according to Laposha and Powell (1982) is 15 inches (38 cm).

HABITAT This uncommon snake prefers moist, heavily shaded woodland, such as that found along creek and river floodplains, where the ground surface is covered with a bed of leaf litter and an abundance of rotting logs, though it also occurs in less densely timbered habitats and along woodland edges. In south-central Texas, according to Vermersch and Kuntz (1986), it occupies mixed oak, juniper, cedar elm, and hackberry woodlands and sometimes even wet lowland marshes. It does not limit itself to moist environments, for it has also been collected in dry deciduous forest, along the slopes of well-drained, partly wooded hillsides, and in abandoned fields, especially those adjoining woodlands. Despite the snake's sporadic occurrence in Texas and in most other parts of its range, it occurs with reasonable frequency near human habitations and in areas disturbed by man, particularly those supporting residual stands of timber or brush.

BEHAVIOR This is an inoffensive little snake whose small teeth are scarcely large enough to penetrate human skin. Perhaps that is why when picked up it does not even attempt to bite. Instead, it may try to repel its captor by discharging from its cloaca a slimy goo, smearing it over the restraining hand by writhing; it often proves offensive enough to gain the snake its release. When held captive, it has also been known to curl up the ends of its lips, though just what effect such a grimace might have on a predator is still unclear.

In another kind of defensive behavior, reported by Ernst and Barbour (1989), a V. valeriae collected in Pennsylvania was observed to feign death by turning over onto its back when disturbed, then cocking its head to one side to watch its adversary. When turned right side up, the snake promptly assumed the original belly-up position. It apparently sensed that to portray itself as dead, it must maintain the appropriate upside-down posture. As revealed in a single observation by Yeatman (1983), this defenseless little creature may take a more direct approach when actually attacked by a predator. A specimen of the eastern race, *V. v. valeriae*, which had been seized by a black racer, twisted a loop of its body into a knot, creating an obstruction that saved the smaller snake from being swallowed.

Texas locality records for this infrequently encountered serpent are scarce, and most of them are widely scattered, but there is presently no way to determine whether the western earth snake is actually as uncommon as the inventories reflect or merely so secretive that it remains unnoticed. Seldom is it encountered in groups. One exception, reported by Mount (1975) in Alabama, is the occasional sighting in late fall of several individuals, sometimes in company with rough earth snakes, congregating near their winter denning sites, which in this case happened to be natural cavities in the soil beneath large stones. When the western earth snake has not buried itself in loose earth or crawled into rock crevices, individual specimens are most likely to be found hiding in forest-floor leaf litter or coiled under almost any available surface object, including rocks (especially flat ones and those on wooded hillsides), logs, and human-generated trash such as boards, sheet metal, cardboard, and piles of organic debris. To find one crawling out in the open is an uncommon event, although warm, heavy rains apparently promote surface activity. In southern Illinois, according to P. W. Smith (1961), specimens were regularly discovered in the bottoms of ditches or other excavations into which they had fallen and were unable to escape. Although primarily a nocturnal hunter, the western earth snake occasionally comes out of hiding during the day. It maintains this basic daily schedule throughout the entire active season, which over most of its geographic range lasts from April to October. In Texas, where generally milder and shorter

winters result in a longer active season, this relatively cold-tolerant snake often remains above ground for most of the year, going underground only when temperatures drop to near freezing. Just how cold-resistant it is was discovered accidentally by Fitch (1956). A specimen he held in captivity crawled into its water vessel whenever the temperature dropped to near freezing, floating there with its body in a nearly vertical position, sometimes with its snout poking out of the water. On February 11, a very cold day, the snake was discovered in the container, its body frozen solid within the ice. Despite being found in such a seemingly life-threatening condition, it was not only alive after the ice melted but also apparently in good condition.

In nature, the snake survives winter's hard freezes by retiring into deep crevices on rocky hillsides; crawling into rotting logs, tree stumps, or piles of decaying vegetation; or working its way underground to depths known to vary from 10 to 30 inches. The western earth snake normally hibernates singly, but it sometimes shares its winter quarters with others of its own kind or with snakes of other species.

FEEDING No detailed study has been made to ascertain the snake's food preferences in Texas, although elsewhere it is known to feed chiefly, if not entirely, on earthworms. Secondary prey items listed in its diet include insects and their larvae, snails, and slugs.

REPRODUCTION Copulation generally occurs in the spring soon after the snakes leave their winter dens, though some western earth snakes do not mate until fall. Sometime in August or September, after a gestation lasting 11 to 14 weeks, the females give birth to their young, 2 to 14 (average 6 or 7) per litter. Even earlier birth dates are mentioned by Dundee and Rossman (1989), including one litter born to a female in Washington Parish, Louisiana, on June 30 and another litter born to a Mississippi female on July 4. The newborn snakes, measuring $3\frac{1}{8}$ to $4\frac{1}{2}$ inches (7.9–11.4 cm) long, are described as opalescent charcoal-gray, even when born to brownish females.

Family Elapidae
CORAL SNAKES AND THEIR ALLIES

Found primarily in tropical and subtropical regions of the world, this family of venomous snakes contains some of the earth's most feared and dangerous serpents, including the cobras and mambas of Africa; the tiger snake, black snake, death adder, and taipan of Australia; and the cobras, kraits, and coral snakes (not closely related to American corals) of Asia. Also included in this family are the venomous sea snakes, whose special adaptations (laterally compressed bodies, paddle-like tails, and nose valves, among others) allow them to exist in a marine environment. Comprising nearly 60 species in two subfamilies, they are widely distributed across the South China Sea and the Indian and Pacific oceans. The approximately 61 species of American coral snakes, included in the

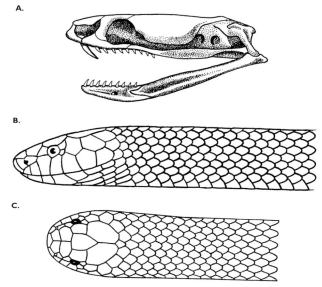

Figure 63. *Characteristics of the family Elapidae, the only dangerously venomous native snake species with (a) short, nonmovable fangs near the front of the upper jawbones, (b) smooth dorsal scales and a round pupil, and (c) a nontriangular head that is little if any wider than the neck.*

genera *Micrurus*, *Leptomicrurus*, and *Micruroidies*, and distributed from the southern United States to Argentina, are also members of the family Elapidae. Only one, the Texas coral snake, occurs in Texas. These long, slender-bodied serpents typically have smooth dorsal scales and nearly always lack a loreal scale between the nostril and eye. Their fangs, like those of other elapids, are relatively short and incapable of rotational movement, fitting into a groove in the lower jaw when the snake's mouth is closed.

TEXAS CORAL SNAKE
Micrurus fulvius tener
PLATES 171, 172

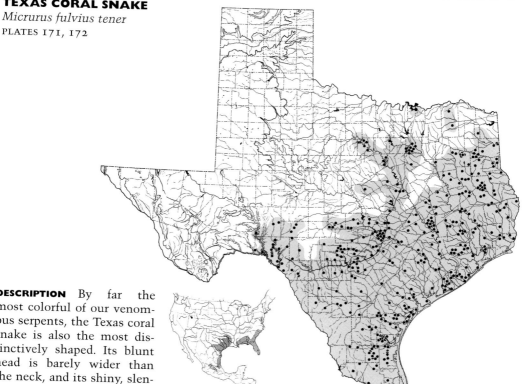

DESCRIPTION By far the most colorful of our venomous serpents, the Texas coral snake is also the most distinctively shaped. Its blunt head is barely wider than the neck, and its shiny, slender trunk, ordinarily only as thick as a ballpoint pen, maintains approximately the same diameter for its entire length. Narrow, sulphur-yellow rings separate the broad, alternating red and black body rings; the red rings are mottled unevenly with black. There is no trace of red on the snake's head or tail, only black and yellow. From the snout to just behind the eye, the head is black, followed by a broad yellow band across the back of the crown. Thereafter, the pattern follows the typical North American coral snake color sequence of black-yellow-red-yellow, black-yellow-red-yellow, etc. The red and yellow rings are always in direct contact with each other. These rings continue uninterrupted across the belly. The round pupils of the snake's small, black eyes are not easy to make out, for they are nearly as dark as the rest of the eye. The smooth, glossy dorsal scales are in 15 rows throughout the length of the body, and the scales under the tail are arranged in a double row, just as in most nonvenomous snakes. The loreal scale is absent, and the anal plate is divided.

COMPARABLE SNAKES Some kinds of harmless native snakes possess the same red, yellow (or whitish), and black colors in banded or seemingly banded patterns that mark the coral snake. A careful examination of these mimics shows, however, that their black bands invariably separate the red and yellow ones, whereas in the coral snake's sequence of colors the red and yellow are always in contact. Hence, the time-tested rhyme, "Red touch yellow, kill a fellow; red touch black, venom lack," remains the simplest way to separate them. Another way to remember the coral's color code is to visualize a traffic control signal with its red light always located next to the caution yellow, the same color arrangement as in the coral snake. Since the red and yellow rings of some Latin American coral snakes do not make direct contact with each other, it is important to recognize that these memory aids are useful only in the United States and northern Mexico. To rely on them in other parts of Mexico or in Central or South America can be dangerously misleading. Minton (pers. com.) mentioned three separate incidents of coral snake envenomation in Mexico and Costa Rica suffered by collectors who based their judgments on the North American rhyme and made serious errors in identification. Another distinction between the Texas coral snake and its harmless look-alikes concerns their dorsal markings. Those of the coral snake continue uninterrupted across the snake's belly, but the markings of some of the harmless mimics never reach the abdomen (scarlet and long-nosed snakes), or they are interrupted there (milk snakes). To the extent that it is marked with red, yellow, and black, the long-nosed snake also bears a resemblance to the coral, although its overall speckled appearance contrasts strikingly with the coral snake's bold, clear-cut pattern. Very young long-nosed snakes, however, show little, if any, such spotting. Unlike *Micrurus*, long-nosed snakes of all ages possess an immaculate belly or one marked with just a few small dark spots; a red, pinkish, or pale-colored snout; and an undivided anal plate. In addition, the scales under its tail are arranged mostly in a single row.

SIZE Most adult Texas coral snakes are about 2 feet (61 cm) long, but specimens up to 3 feet (91.4 cm) in length are occasionally found. An unusually large one, 46½ inches (118.1 cm) long, was collected by Don Mascarelli in Colorado County, and a record individual of 47¾ inches (121.3 cm) is said to have been taken in Brazoria County (Tennant 1984).

HABITAT Wherever it occurs—whether in the mixed hardwood and pine forests of East Texas, the tallgrass prairie and deciduous woodlands of north-central Texas, or the small parcels of remnant subtropical forest below Brownsville—the coral snake prefers partially wooded sites containing organic ground litter. Even in Terrell and Pecos counties, where the westernmost extension of its range crosses into the Chihuahuan Desert, the coral generally restricts itself to isolated stands of live oaks growing in or near moist canyons.

It also occurs with moderate frequency in and around some of our major Texas cities, living successfully in such populated areas by taking refuge in the vegetative debris of gardens, wooded lots, and undeveloped parklands. Also plentiful there are several kinds of small terrestrial snakes that constitute its most important prey species. Just how plentiful the coral snake was in at least one of our large urban areas is revealed in a three-month survey made by A. C. Stimson in the early 1960s (pers. com.). Aimed at determining the snake's abundance in the immediate Houston area, the study produced 113 verified coral snake sightings within a 12-mile radius of city hall, a surprisingly large number even for that time. Like most reptilian species, the coral snake is not nearly as common around the Houston metropolitan area today as it was then.

BEHAVIOR A disturbed coral snake usually tries to escape by crawling rapidly away from the source of its annoyance and, if possible, hiding beneath leaf litter or other surface debris. If touched, it may suddenly thrust the affected body segment forcefully against the source of contact to repel it, a behavior known as body-bridging. If further harassed, the snake frequently flattens its tail and the rear part of its body, while the black-and-yellow-banded tail, curled and raised back over its trunk, waves slowly back and forth like a menacing head. As part of the performance the illusory head may even strike backward or sideward in imitation of the real thing. At the same time, the snake often tucks its head beneath its body coils; thus, the tail and not the more vulnerable head becomes the focus of attention for a predator's attack. As if this unusual behavior were not disconcerting enough, the coral snake adds still another element to its charade, snapping its body back and forth in quick, jerky movements. Startled by such strange conduct, the bewildered interloper will probably delay an attack just long enough for the snake to make a successful escape. Not all predators are so easily confused. It is true, for example, that a bird of prey in flight attacks with such speed and suddenness that the snake has little or no time to anticipate the assault, in which case the reptile is seized before it can crawl to safety or mount an effective defense.

It is generally agreed that another function of the tail display is to alert a potential predator to the serpent's venomous qualities. In support of this theory, Gehlbach (1972) demonstrated that when exposed to rubber models painted to resemble real coral snakes and manipulated to simulate their defensive tail displays, javelinas and coatimundis generally were frightened by the imitation reptiles and usually made every effort to avoid them. Incidentally, such a tactic is practiced not only by eastern and Texas coral snakes but also, according to H. W. Greene (1973), by at least 15 other species of *Micrurus*. Greene believes that when the life histories of other coral snakes are finally known, this behavior will prove to be the rule among them. This tactic is not restricted to coral snakes; nearly 80 species of snakes worldwide, both harmless and venomous, when touched or stressed use this or a similar tail display in an attempt to thwart or misdirect a predator's attack.

Naturalists do not fully agree about when this secretive snake is most often found abroad. Some claim it is primarily nocturnal, others report diurnal habits, and still others describe it as active only during early morning and late evening. Judging from this diversity of opinion, we suspect that it may come to the surface at any time of the day or night, depending on the temperature, the humidity, and the kind of habitat it occupies. Neill (1957), for example, basing his information on more than 200 sightings, says that in Florida this species is nearly always observed in the open on bright, sunny mornings from just after sunrise to about 9 AM. Our own experience with the Texas subspecies is not much different from his for the Florida race. Like him, we have found that the snake moves about chiefly in the morning, although Houston-area residents also report seeing it late in the day, particularly after the ground has been cooled by showers. In the arid southern part of the state, it has been discovered crossing roads early at night when daytime temperatures were very high and the humidity low. Some 150 miles below the Texas border, we encountered them after sunset, usually between 9 PM and midnight, as they crawled over the relatively dry Tamaulipan landscape.

Whatever the moisture content of its habitat, this species shows little tolerance for prolonged high temperatures. Although no field studies exist that define the thermal preference of free-living coral snakes, herpetocul-turists have found by trial and error that for successful captive maintenance, the snake is best kept at temperatures not exceeding 85 degrees F, and a range between 74 and 78 degrees F is preferred. Long-term exposure to temperatures above 85 degrees F usually causes captive corals to languish and die.

MIMICRY Although bright colors occur in a wide variety of invertebrate animals, sometimes presumably to signal their noxious qualities and thus to discourage attacks on them by certain color-sighted predators, such conspicuous warning colors among back-boned species are rare. The brightly colored coral snakes are a notable exception among vertebrates. It is believed that following a hurtful but nonfatal encounter with one of these highly venomous reptiles, a predator learns to associate the unpleasant experience with the serpent's vivid color pattern and thereafter to avoid it. Whatever degree of protection may be afforded a coral snake by virtue of its bright warning colors, the same measure of security is presumably extended to the similarly hued harmless snakes and to the slightly venomous mimics living in the same region. To an experienced predator encountering such a harmless look-alike, the rationale may well be that whatever looks dangerous must in fact be dangerous and should therefore be avoided.

Not all biologists embrace the theory of coral snake mimicry. A long-standing objection to the theory has been that coral snakes, being nocturnal, are not out in the open when most day-active, color-visioned predators are searching for prey; logically, therefore, these diurnal serpents are never seen by such animals. This objection is not a valid one, however, for there is ample evidence to show that coral snakes do indeed move about in daylight. Even when they do not, we know they are likely to be discovered by coatimundis, javelinas, and other daytime foragers who search through the organic leaf litter where coral snakes are apt to hide. Other objections to the mimicry theory argue, for instance, that a pattern of bright, contrasting rings in both venomous and harmless species inhabiting one region simply reflects the result of convergent evolution among totally unrelated species. Such brilliant coloration, they theorize, by its visual impact, serves primarily to startle potential predators into temporary inaction. It probably does, especially when, as has been reported for coral snakes, the serpents occasionally snap and thrash their bodies erratically about, sometimes with such vigor that they actually leave the ground. This animated behavior also serves to make the contrastingly colored reptile appear nearly invisible against a leaf-covered forest floor. Although we can accept the premise that vivid color patterns in unrelated species from the same area developed independently as warning signals and perhaps also as a way to accomplish disruptive coloration, that does not explain why there is such a striking resemblance between so many species of coral snakes and their respective cohabiting mimics.

Some of the most compelling circumstantial evidence to date in support of the mimicry theory comes from a study by Greene and McDiarmid (1981). The zoologists show that in case after case, one or more harmless or only slightly venomous snake species living in a given local area of Latin America matches precisely the color pattern of the venomous coral snake with which it shares the same habitat. Of interest in this regard are the tropical coral snakes, which do not always come ringed in red, yellow, and black (unlike the native North American species). Some are banded with just two colors—red and black—and others are red with scattered black spots of irregular size and shape. At least one is black with speckled, narrow white rings. Other combinations also occur. Whatever combination of colors and markings adorn these snakes, most of them share their respective habitats with one or more harmless or only mildly venomous lookalikes. Those decorated with red, yellow, and black rings are often imitated almost exactly by their harmless cohabiting mimics, so that in both species the red and yellow colors are side by side. The mimicry theory gains even more credibility when we examine the color varieties of the milk snake, a single, widely distributed harmless species whose extensive distribution brings it in contact with several different kinds of Mexican and Central American coral snakes. Wherever it shares a common habitat with a particular coral snake species, its color pattern almost invariably

matches that of the venomous species in nearly every detail. In Oaxaca, Mexico, for example, it and a native coral snake both possess black bands that encroach into the red ones. On the Yucatan Peninsula, it is either uniformly red or red-spotted, like the local species of coral snake there. In southern Mexico, where it coexists with still another kind of coral characterized by a series of secondary black rings in addition to the primary ones, the milk snake shares a similar pattern. Farther south, in Honduras, we encounter the same milk snake species again, only this time, like its venomous neighbor, it is ringed with just two colors, black and reddish orange. Can we simply write off so many striking resemblances as mere coincidences of nature? Perhaps, but we believe Greene and McDiarmid cite enough similar examples to convince most skeptics that a functional mimicry system does indeed exist between coral snakes and certain colubrid snake species.

FEEDING According to Roze (1982), about 90 percent of the 120 or so known species and subspecies of New World coral snakes eat other snakes, sometimes including examples of their own kind, and approximately 60 percent of them also consume various slender amphibians and other reptiles. In a radical departure from the norm, we learn that several kinds of large corals from northern South America and the southern part of Central America confine their diets almost exclusively to *Synbranchus marmoratus*, a moderate-sized, freshwater eel abundant in the region's tropical ponds and marshes. It appears, however, that until they reach maturity, the juveniles of one of them reject the eels in favor of a serpentlike lizard, *Bachia trinasale*. The most extraordinary diet of all belongs to *Micrurus hemprichi ortoni*, a subspecies of coral snake found chiefly along the Amazonian slopes of Colombia, Ecuador, and Peru, whose prey consists exclusively of *Peripatus*, an arthropodlike invertebrate. Thus we find that to one degree or another, all coral snakes are specialized predators.

The Texas coral snake is no exception. Its diet consists almost entirely of small terrestrial snakes and elongate lizards. H. W. Greene (1984), who examined the stomachs of preserved museum specimens, found that

53 percent of the prey items in the sample represented a variety of colubrid serpents (ring-necked, ground, brown, red-bellied, flat-headed, lined, and rough earth snakes), as well as examples of the more slender blind snakes, all of them species that ordinarily live in ground litter or hide beneath logs, rocks, and other surface objects where coral snakes themselves are apt to be found. These snakes are small enough to be easily caught and consumed, and they apparently lack any particular defensive strategy that would effectively protect them from coral snake predation. Another 14 percent were ground skinks, and the rest were small specimens of larger ground-dwelling serpents such as rat, king, patch-nosed, and ribbon snakes. Even venomous snakes are occasionally eaten. For example, coral snakes cannibalized by other coral snakes made up about 1 percent of the consumed items, and copperheads another 2 percent. Certain other species, particularly water and garter snakes, were generally avoided, as were all kinds of amphibians. Very small coral snakes feed on some of the same prey consumed by the adults. Greene's records show that seven juveniles had eaten three ground skink tails, a complete skink of an unidentified species, a rough green snake, a brown snake, and a rough earth snake. The smallest individual for which there is a confirmed feeding observation was a captive-hatched specimen that first took ground skinks when it was approximately two months old.

Of 18 separate records of ground skink remains found in coral snake stomachs, 12 consisted of the tail only. Six of these had undoubtedly been wrenched from the skink's body before being swallowed; 5 others probably had been also. It should be mentioned here that a skink's tail is designed to break away from its body, leaving behind a nearly bloodless stump. Thus, when the snake seizes the lizard's tail, it is likely to come away with the appetizer while forfeiting the main course. Meanwhile, the liberated skink survives the encounter and eventually goes on to grow a new, though less perfect, caudal member. Incidentally, Greene's study shows that ground skinks were more often taken as food in the forested eastern part of Texas than they were anywhere else in the state,

for it is there that they occur in greatest abundance.

Certain other lizards, though also plentiful in some of the same regions occupied by the coral, are not always available to it as food. For instance, whiptail lizards seek hot, open spaces (a microhabitat usually avoided by the snake), and most scaly lizards and anoles are essentially arboreal and therefore not apt to be encountered by this ground-dwelling predator. Greene's study also adds much new information to our understanding of the coral snake's feeding behavior. In his review he describes how the coral snake, when foraging, crawls slowly over the ground, moving its head from side to side in a random search pattern, occasionally poking its nose into the organic surface litter as it attempts to locate or flush from hiding any small terrestrial snake or lizard. During these explorations, the slightest nearby movement caused the coral snake to point its head abruptly in the direction of the action, although not all motion elicited an attack. For example, if the potential target was large, and particularly if it moved suddenly, the snake promptly lowered its head and quickly turned away to avoid it. Small moving objects, on the other hand, were approached without hesitation, to be more closely scrutinized. Using intermittent series of tongue flicks to gather chemical samples from the immediate surroundings, the coral snake readily distinguished between choice prey species and those it considered unacceptable. Undesirable items such as large beetle larvae, cricket frogs, and newborn mice were all shunned after a brief tongue-flick examination, as were most small water snakes, especially if they had recently expelled the repugnant contents of their cloacal sacs. When moved rapidly near the coral snake, some of the same small animal species provoked a quick attack. Greene concluded from this that the sight of such fast-moving prey initially overrides any negative chemical cues the predator may perceive. Such attacks were brief; after being momentarily grasped, the unacceptable prey was soon released. The reason for this, Greene suggests, is that once seized, the prey continues to impart chemical signals that eventually are received and identified by sensory buds in the snake's mouth or, according to

Burghardt (1970), by the predator's Jacobson's organ.

In a curious foraging tactic observed by Neill (1951), an example of this species from Florida was seen to crawl rather quickly across the ground of a Clay County live oak hammock, turning its head from side to side as it moved along and constantly flicking its tongue in and out of its mouth. Up to this point, the reptile's feeding behavior fits the search pattern described by Greene. The odd thing about this specimen was the way it flipped its tail and the rear part of its body forward from one side to the other, sometimes nearly reaching to the snake's head. As it did, the tail tip was in constant motion, like an animated probe attempting to flush from hiding some concealed small snake or lizard, which under such circumstances would probably find itself very close to the coral snake's jaws. Since coral snakes possess relatively small eyes and apparently have poor vision, they do not strike with accuracy, especially when pursuing ground skinks, whose erratic behavior makes them difficult targets. In his feeding experiments with captive corals, Greene found that during 11 attempts to capture these active little lizards, the snake missed its target 8 times, making a successful catch just once and then only after trapping the skink in the corner of the cage. On each of 2 other tries, the snake seized the skink by the tail, which was subsequently snapped from the lizard's body. As a result, the lizard made a successful escape, essentially unharmed, as the snake proceeded to swallow the skink's separated caudal member. Small snakes, on the other hand, were more easily caught, since they move more slowly and generally less erratically than a skink, and their greatly elongated bodies present more of a target. This was demonstrated by Greene, whose feeding experiments showed that coral snakes succeeded in capturing live snakes in 100 percent of the trial feeding encounters; the success rate for skinks was an unremarkable 27 percent (including two tail-only captures). Whatever the prey, once seized, it is held firmly in the snake's jaws until immobilized by the predator's venom.

The victim is not always easily subdued. To control vigorously struggling prey, the coral snake may pull its victim a short distance backward or forward over the ground. This does two things. It frees the prey's writhing coils (if it is a snake) from around the coral snake's body, and it probably also causes the predator's fangs to penetrate the victim more deeply. An especially active and relatively large reptile whose intense resistance makes it difficult to hold is quickly released after being briefly attacked and poisoned. Such prey is soon followed and often successfully recaptured. This is sometimes accomplished visually, although when an escaped victim slips out of sight, the snake relies on its flicking tongue and the associated Jacobson's organ to track it down. When actively foraging for prey, the coral snake routinely employs the same receptors to locate, then follow, the chemical trails of certain commonly consumed prey species that cross its path.

REPRODUCTION Although the majority of Texas serpent species mate only in the spring, the coral snake does so at almost any time of the year. When breeding occurs as late in the season as August or September, the sperm remains viable in the female's oviducts until ovulation takes place the following summer. The white eggs, 1½ inches (3.8 cm) long, are laid 2 to 12 in a clutch in June or July in decomposing organic material such as loose soil or inside a rotting log. When they emerge from their eggshells about two months later, the hatchlings are 6½ to 8 inches (16.5–20.3 cm) long.

VENOM AND BITE This seemingly inoffensive snake, which may not even attempt to bite if handled carefully, usually crawls away at the first sign of danger. It should never be touched, however, for an aroused specimen becomes unpredictable, and considering the high lethal toxicity of its venom, this serpent is potentially very dangerous to man. Sometimes merely holding the snake gently causes it to turn its head, open its mouth, and, without any apparent provocation, bite the hand that supports it. Some say that because the coral snake is unable to open its mouth widely, it can effectively bite only a highly curved surface of the human body such as a finger, toe, or the loose skin between these digits. That, unfortunately, is not the case. Just as a bit of epidermis can be pinched out with the fingers, so too can a coral snake gather up a fold of skin between its biting jaws, allowing its fangs to penetrate the skin. The serpent may use other defensive tactics as well. A coral snake that is approached too closely may lash out wildly at the oncoming target, though this is not considered typical *Micrurus* behavior.

The snake is far more likely to bite only when touched. Most coral snake bites occur when the snake is willfully handled, usually by someone who is attracted to the reptile's bright colors and, deceived by its small slender head, considers the snake harmless. The snake usually reacts to such familiarity by abruptly swinging its forebody sideways to seize the restraining hand. Then, seeming to sense that its biting apparatus is an imperfect one, the coral snake maintains its grip as long as it can, chewing on the hand to embed its short fangs as it tries to inject as much as possible of its meager venom supply. The minute, rigidly attached fangs, barely $1/8$ inch long, are incapable of deep penetration, and the primary muscles responsible for the ejection of venom from the venom glands are not well developed in this species and are unable to drive the venom forcefully from the gland, down the fang canal, and into the victim.

Despite the snake's somewhat primitive method of venom delivery, its neurotoxically active venom is undoubtedly one of the most lethally potent of any U.S. serpent. The dose needed to kill a person of average stature is estimated by Minton and Minton (1969) at only 4 or 5 milligrams of dry weight, which, incidentally, represents nearly the entire pool of venom contained in the glands of most specimens 20 to 24 inches long. Larger snakes, of course, can be expected to deliver a greater quantity of venom. This was demonstrated by Fix and Minton (1976), whose studies of coral snake venom extraction, using the eastern coral snake as a model, yielded 20 mg or more from each of two especially large individuals measuring between $33^1/2$ and $35^1/2$ inches long. (Such large coral snakes are seldom encountered in Texas.) According to Russell and Puffer (1971), the venom is nearly 11 times as lethal as that of the copperhead, 5.26 times as toxic as that of the cottonmouth, and nearly 4 times as virulent as western diamond-backed rattler

venom. Because of the coral snake's highly toxic venom, it is often said that a victim bitten by this species has little or no chance to survive the experience. On the contrary, and in spite of frequently quoted mortality figures ranging anywhere from 10 to 75 percent, few human fatalities result from such poisoning. In the first place, not every bite is accompanied by the injection of venom. Although Russell (1980) found 17 human deaths among 82 published reports of coral snake bites nationwide, he could find no record of a fatality from such an accident since Wyeth coral snake antivenin was first developed and made available back in 1967. It is of particular interest to note that we are unable to find even one authentic record of a human fatality from coral snake envenomation in Texas since 2 deaths were mentioned by True in 1883, more than 100 years ago. Those cases, incidentally, are the first published records of coral snake bite fatalities for the United States and, at least until now, the last for Texas.

The severity of a coral snake bite is not easy to assess. Unlike the venoms of North American pit vipers, which typically cause severe local tissue damage and extensive hemorrhaging, that of the coral snake produces only minimal early signs of envenomation or none at all. Consequently, the victim often has no reason to believe he or she has been poisoned. Pain, if present, is usually minimal at first and confined to the area of the fang punctures. In a serious bite it may be moderate to severe, depending on the amount of venom delivered. The fang punctures, so small that they may scarcely bleed, are separated from each other by $1/4$ to $3/8$ inch; the presence of only scratch marks usually indicates an imperfect bite and the probability that no venom was injected. Swelling at the bite area is usually absent as well or, if present, is hardly noticeable. It is evident that the lack of conspicuous signs or symptoms soon after a bite belies the potentially serious consequences that may follow. Unfortunately, this can give the victim a false sense of security, resulting in his or her unwillingness to seek medical aid.

In most cases of coral snake poisoning the first alarming manifestations do not appear until several hours after the bite, at which time it may be too late to save a severely envenomed patient by the administration of appropriate snakebite serum. Prognostic symptoms, when they finally appear, include apprehension, giddiness and euphoria, thickening of speech, increased salivation, and tongue tremors. Nausea and vomiting may also occur, as well as pinpoint pupils, blurred vision, and drooping eyelids. The victim may later experience weakness, drowsiness, and a feeling of impending unconsciousness. In many respects the symptoms produced by coral snake poisoning are not much different from those observed in a seriously intoxicated person. In advanced cases of envenomation there is hypertension, and the pulse weakens and becomes irregular. Convulsions may also occur. This is followed by the sudden onset of facial and bulbar-center paralysis, after which limb paralysis occurs. Finally, death comes as a result of respiratory and cardiac failure. Fatalities generally occur when the snake has been given the opportunity to inject a lethal dose of venom, either by maintaining its grip for more than just a few seconds (most when they have hung on for longer than a minute) or by inflicting multiple bites.

Family Viperidae
VIPERS

This nearly worldwide family of venomous snakes is divided into three subfamilies, only one of which, the Crotalinae, commonly called pit vipers, is represented in Texas. Including about 144 species, the crotalids range throughout the Americas from southern Canada to Argentina, occurring as well in South and Central Asia, Malaysia, and the southeastern edge of Europe, but they are absent from Antarctica and Australia. Like the true vipers of the subfamily Viperinae, they have a wide, somewhat triangular head, vertically elliptical pupils, and a long, hollow fang on either side of the head near the front of the upper jaw. The fang is attached to a short, modified bone (the maxilla) and can be rotated through an arc of about 90 degrees, bringing it from a horizontal at-rest orientation against the roof of the mouth to an extended striking position. This venom delivery system is the most sophisticated among all venomous snakes.

The single important external feature that immediately distinguishes the pit vipers from the true vipers (and from all other Texas snake species) is the pair of infrared-sensing facial pits, one on either side of the head between the eye and nostril. With these organs, the serpent can locate warm-blooded prey even in total darkness, gauge its distance, and visualize its size and outline. This unique adaptation allows the snake to hit its mark without the benefit of its eyesight, a decisive advantage when hunting at night or deep inside a mammal burrow.

Texas snakes belonging to the subfamily Crotalinae, in the family Viperidae, include the southern copperhead, broad-banded copperhead, Trans-Pecos copperhead, western cottonmouth, western diamond-backed rattlesnake, canebrake rattlesnake, mottled rock rattlesnake, banded rock rattlesnake, northern black-tailed rattlesnake, Mojave rattlesnake, prairie rattlesnake, desert massasauga, western massasauga, and western pygmy rattlesnake.

A.

B.

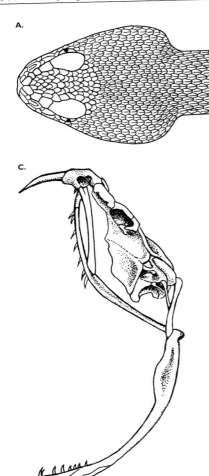

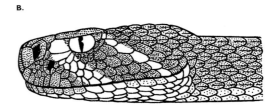

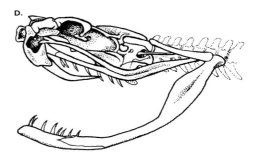

C.

D.

Figure 64. *Characteristic features of pit vipers: (a) a broad, triangular head followed by a relatively narrow neck, (b) elliptical pupils and temperature-sensing facial pits, and (c and d) large movable fangs.*

SOUTHERN COPPERHEAD

*Agkistrodon contortrix
contortrix*

PLATES 173, 174

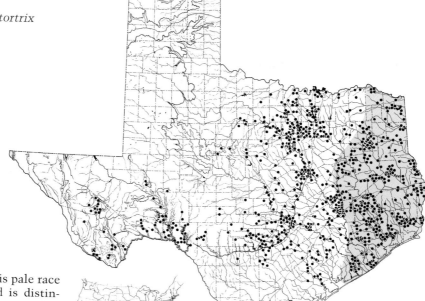

DESCRIPTION This pale race of the copperhead is distinguished from the two other Texas subspecies by the distinctly hour-glass configuration of its dark crossbands; each one, although wide and rounded at the base, is very narrow at the middle of the back, where it may occasionally divide and form two separate triangular markings, one on either side of the body. The crossbands are usually a lighter shade of brown at their centers than along their outer margins. The snake's ground color is pale brown or light tan, often with a pinkish cast. The large, oval, dark brown spots that mark the outer edges of the belly may extend upward between the crossbands onto the first one or two dorsal scale rows. The dorsal scales, arranged in 23 or 25 rows at midbody, are weakly keeled, and the anal plate is single. Most scales under the tail are arranged in a single row, except those near the end of the tail, which are paired.

COMPARABLE SNAKES The eastern hog-nosed snake, especially in its copper or reddish color phases, bears a superficial resemblance to the southern copperhead. The similarity is particularly evident in the juvenile hog-nosed snake, which, at least in southeastern Texas, frequently is pale orange on the head and forebody. The snake's markings, when present, are oval, rectangular, or irregular in shape, not hour-glass-shaped and never continuous across the snake's back from one side of the belly to the other. Its neck is not distinctly narrower than its head, its snout is upturned and pointed, its pupils are round instead of elliptical, and it lacks the facial cavities characteristic of the pit vipers. The dark dorsal crossbands and yellowish interspaces of the broad-banded water snake, especially those of the brightly colored young, may resemble the pattern of a copperhead, but in the water snake there are dark vertical sutures along the upper and lower lip scales, a divided anal plate, and no facial pits. The light and dark crossbanded pattern of the infant cottonmouth closely resembles that of the copperhead, but the dark bands are jagged along the edges instead of smooth and nearly as wide at the middle of the back as along the sides. In both the juvenile and adult cottonmouth, a wide, dark mask runs backward from the eye.

SIZE Adults are generally between 24 and 36 inches (61–91 cm) long, but a specimen of record length measured 52 inches (132.1 cm).

A.

B.
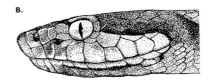

Figure 65. *Lateral head markings of (a) cottonmouth, with dark stripe, and (b) copperhead, with pale mark below and behind eye.*

HABITAT Generally distributed over the moist eastern third of the state, the southern copperhead inhabits primarily the wooded lowlands, most often in the vicinity of river bottoms, streams, and swamps, but it also ranges inland across the hilly northeastern part of the state to the Red River. Although it occurs in heavily shaded forest, the southern copperhead seems to prefer partially wooded areas where some sunlight filters through the trees to the forest floor. In such places it finds shelter under logs and boards, beneath the loose bark of fallen dead trees, within the decaying interiors of logs and stumps, and even in the accumulated leaf litter carpeting the forest floor. It is also attracted to dilapidated wooden buildings and to abandoned sawmill sites, where discarded sawdust piles and heaps of scrap lumber provide good shelter for the copperhead and for some of the prey species on which it feeds. Since it frequently hides beneath the boards of unused plank roadways, particularly those in forested areas, such boards should be carefully avoided. On one occasion, we discovered three copperheads under a large board lying in a partial woodland clearing in the Sabine National Forest and two others beneath a second nearby plank.

Although we have no precise information about the southern copperhead's population density in Texas, there is no doubt that in the wooded eastern third of the state it usually outnumbers all other venomous species. Ford, Cobb, and Stout (1991) found the copperhead to be the most abundant snake in Sheff's Wood, a relatively undisturbed second-growth forest of lowland floodplain, upland deciduous woodland, and upland pine forest in Smith County. In certain suitable areas around Houston it sometimes occurs in relatively large concentrations after the first prolonged warm spell in spring. During the first week of March 1988, for example, when day-time temperatures reached 80 degrees F, 20 copperheads were collected near Liberty in just a few hours, and a similar number was found a few days later not far from Arcola in Brazoria County. It was Guidry (1953) who encountered one of the largest nonhibernating concentrations of southern copperheads yet reported in southeastern Texas. In several hours of nighttime collecting, he captured 35 specimens in a small area of woodland in Newton County.

Such sporadic collecting efforts do not provide a true picture of the snake's population density. In a careful, long-term study of the Osage copperhead's natural history in Douglas County, Kansas, Fitch (1960) determined that this subspecies typically occurred in concentrations of about 5 individuals per acre, although in areas of prime habitat it increased to 10 or 20.

BEHAVIOR A copperhead at rest usually lies coiled and motionless, depending on its cryptic pattern and coloration to avoid detection. This constitutes its best defense against predators. Seen against a carpet of dead leaves dappled with sunlight, the snake's contrasting tones of pale and dark brown present one of the best examples of successful camouflage found among our native terrestrial serpents. Fitch described the snake's typical resting coil as flat and pancakelike, the body closely wound into one, two, or even more tight coils, with the tail terminating the outermost loop and the head, neck, and forebody in an S curve on top. From such a position an alert copperhead can survey the immediate surroundings and, if necessary, quickly prepare to launch a defensive strike. This it does with a single flick of the head, directing its gaze upward at the approaching foe. What happens next is up to the intruder, for the usually inoffensive copperhead ordinarily chooses to avoid detection by remaining completely still. The snake's other option is to retreat into the nearest refuge. If the threat does not appear too foreboding, and especially if shelter is unavailable, the snake is apt to move away slowly until it is out of sight. If approached too closely or too quickly, particularly by a large animal such as man, a disturbed copperhead usually responds by initiating a short though sometimes inaccurate strike (in a specimen of average length, it seldom exceeds 6 inches). Such an assault may be preceded by tail-shaking and, especially when the reptile is restrained, by the emission of fine jets of musk from a pair of glands at the base of its tail, which some say smells like cucumber. Sometimes a provoked copperhead strikes out wildly, even when its tormentor is still out of reach. A more unusual defensive response, for a snake that finds itself threatened while out in the open with no place to hide, is to protect its head by tucking it beneath the coils of its body, making no immediate active attempt to defend itself.

In southeastern Texas the copperhead usually makes its first appearance in early March and stays active until at least late October or early November. During mild winters, when unseasonably high temperatures exceeded 75 degrees F, we have observed basking specimens in December and February. Chiefly day-active during the cool days of spring and fall, the copperhead becomes largely nocturnal during the hot summer months.

Fitch determined that after leaving their winter refuge, Kansas copperheads engaged in three kinds of movement during their active season. The most frequent were short forays associated with the snake's routine activities, such as those involved with foraging. Longer movements, representing travels out of an original home territory and into a new one, were uncommon. The most routine long-distance forays were the seasonal migrations of most copperheads between their summer territories and their rocky, hilltop hibernacula, which were often ¼ to ½ mile apart. Otherwise, the copperheads did not travel great distances. Kansas specimens were often recaptured a few hundred feet from where they were first caught and released, even when the interval between captures was as much as several years. Still more surprising, some adult snakes were found again at nearly the same spot where they were born a number of years earlier.

FEEDING Although mammals generally constitute the bulk of the copperhead's diet, they are not the only class of animal eaten by this snake. In his exhaustive field study, Fitch found that of 512 food items consumed by this species in northeastern Kansas, the most frequently devoured, listed in order of preference (with number of prey items in parentheses), were prairie voles (90), cicadas (80), white-footed mice (66), short-tailed shrews (39), ring-necked snakes (35), little short-tailed shrews (33), five-lined skinks (30), caterpillars (29), pine voles (24), harvest mice (18), and narrowmouth toads (13). Prey types taken less than a dozen times each included frogs (8), jumping mice (6), slender glass lizards (6), cotton rats (6), worm snakes (4), house mice (4), brown skinks (3), common garter snakes (3), racers (2), eastern wood rats (2), eastern cottontail rabbits (2), brown snakes (2), unidentified birds (2), hatchling box turtle (1), Great Plains skink (1), six-lined race runner (1), black rat snake (1), and an unidentified snake.

In this survey, prairie voles accounted for more than twice the biomass of any other prey species, probably because they represented the most abundant small mammal in the study area. Contributing to the vole's vulnerability is its tendency to establish well-used trails when moving through grassy fields, where the snakes wait in ambush for their next meal. The pine vole, an uncommon prey species inhabiting the study area, proved surprisingly palatable to the local copperhead population, for it made up more than 10 percent by weight of the total prey consumed. Since its geographic distribution closely coincides with that of the copperhead, Fitch suggested that this mammal may be the reptile's principal source of food in all portions of the serpent's range.

In northern Louisiana, according to R. F. Clark (1949), the copperhead's diet differed significantly from that of the Kansas population, perhaps as the result of differing prey availability. Of 55 specimens with food in their stomachs, 22 contained southern leopard frogs, 7 had eaten green frogs, one contained a bullfrog, 15 had mice, and 10 had devoured birds.

Cicadas, another item high on the snake's list of foods, are mainly those recently transformed into adults and those still in the soft, defenseless nymph stage, which are especially vulnerable for a short time after they leave their underground habitations. In Dallas County, Curtis (1949) discovered a number of copperheads in bushes and small trees, all gorged with cicadas. A similar gathering of copperheads, also in the act of hunting cicadas, was observed in trees growing along the banks of the Colorado River at Wharton. Over a period of two weeks, dozens of the ordinarily terrestrial serpents were observed as they lay coiled or stretched out on branches of both large and small trees, to which they apparently had gained access by crawling along the tangles of wild grapevine stems growing up into the tree limbs. Others were seen nestled in the grapevines themselves. Studying the dietary composition of the southern copperhead in Smith and Anderson counties, Lagesse and Ford (1996) verified the importance of cicadas in the serpent's diet, at least during mid to late summer when these insects are particularly abundant in East Texas. Their survey showed that by number, such insects made up 36.9 percent of the food items consumed, with other arthropods constituting another 26.2 percent. Other prey items contained in the sample included lizards and snakes (21.4 percent), mammals (2.4 percent), and unidentified animal parts (13.1 percent).

Among the more unusual prey items have been hatchling box turtles and very small musk turtles, which because of their size and generally inflexible shells would be suitable fare only for the larger copperheads.

Somewhat surprisingly, adult moths are also captured and eaten. Considering their erratic flight patterns, such insects would appear to make impossible targets for a slow-moving serpent that ordinarily uses a sit-and-wait hunting style. A three-year-old copperhead raised by Fitch (one that had not previously consumed food voluntarily) immediately showed great interest in a hawk moth placed in its cage, following with apparent excitement the flying insect's every move. After striking unsuccessfully at the elusive target several times, the reptile finally managed to capture the moth and eat it. That moths were eventually devoured by other caged copperheads in Fitch's care suggests these insects may represent a preferred item in the snake's diet. Caterpillars are also commonly consumed. In their study of copper-

head food habits, Uhler and his colleagues (1939) found caterpillars of seven genera in 28 of 105 copperheads from Virginia, and Orth (1939) removed the larvae of shingid moths from the stomach of a wild-caught copperhead. Indeed, where insects are readily available, they may constitute the snake's chief prey.

This was illustrated in a study by E. V. Brown (1979), in which he summarized the prey items consumed by 35 copperheads collected in North Carolina and South Carolina. Although mammal remains in this survey accounted for a high percentage (59.2 percent) of the total volume of food consumed, insects represented the greatest percentage of prey by number (56.5 percent). (Insects ranked second by volume, at 24.9 percent.) Other invertebrates reported as food for this species include spiders and millipedes.

Very young Kansas copperheads limited their choice of prey mostly to shrews, narrowmouth toads, and small snakes, but they sometimes also ate voles and cicadas. In some parts of the species' range, where small frogs and lizards constitute part of the infant's diet, the juveniles lure such prey by elevating their yellowish-tipped tails and wriggling them slowly to imitate active insect larvae. When attracted by such movement, the would-be predator tries to seize the decoy worm but is quickly struck and held by the snake.

The adult copperhead usually obtains its food by ambush. Coiled motionless in leaf litter, it may wait in the same position for hours or even days until a prey animal comes within striking range. At other times it attempts to surprise its quarry by prowling slowly over the forest floor. The movement of a copperhead crawling over a carpet of dead leaves is difficult to detect; not only does the reptile's cryptic pattern blend well with the surrounding leaf litter, but also the snake's forward motion, interrupted by frequent intervals of rest, is so slow and smooth as to be almost imperceptible. Such a stealthy approach is nearly as likely to succeed in ambushing prey as the actual sit-and-wait ambush strategy.

Large rodents are usually struck and immediately released, for such prey, armed with long, sharp incisor teeth, are capable of inflicting serious injury to their captors. This tactic, executed in a fraction of a second, averts a potentially dangerous struggle between the snake and its quarry and allows the predator to track the envenomed rodent to its final resting place, where the lifeless mammal can then be safely seized and swallowed. Birds, amphibians, and insects, on the other hand, are not usually released after the initial bite but are firmly held in the snake's mouth until their struggles have diminished enough for them to be manipulated for swallowing.

REPRODUCTION Most male copperheads are sexually mature at two years of age, females at three. In Texas, mating occurs shortly after the snakes leave their winter quarters, usually in April and early May, with birth of the young occurring in August or September, approximately 105 to 110 days later. Copulation may also take place in the fall, in which case the male spermatozoa remain inactive but viable in the female's oviducts until the following spring, at which time they fertilize the mature ova. Five or six young constitute the average litter size for this subspecies; each infant measures 8 to 10 inches (20.3–25.4 cm) long at birth. The babies are near-replicas of the adults, but with a paler background color, more vivid crossbanding, and a bright sulphur-yellow tail tip.

In late summer, several weeks before the birth of their young, gravid copperheads may remain together in small groups (like the gravid females of many other snake species), at which time they may occupy common shelters that are secure from predators and near open spaces where the snakes can bask in direct sunlight. In Kansas, Fitch once found two such aggregations of Osage copperheads within 100 yards (91.2 m) of each other. One group contained three gravid females that had taken shelter in a cavity beneath a flat rock 2 feet (61 cm) in diameter; a week later he discovered four more gravid copperheads nestled closely together under another rock of similar size. Such reports of aggregating female copperheads are not unusual. At a Bradford, Connecticut, den, for example, Finneran (1948) encountered late summer gatherings of gravid female northern copperheads every year from 1940 to 1946, each group containing 5 to 11 snakes.

Like the males of a number of other snake species, those of the copperhead sometimes engage in ritualized combat when competing for the attention of a single nearby female.

Such an event was described by Joseph Ackroyd (in Gloyd 1947). With approximately two-thirds of their forebodies closely intertwined and raised vertically off the ground, the antagonists faced each other, their necks free and their heads held in a horizontal plane 3 or 4 inches apart. As they swayed slightly, the snakes gazed at one another intently, as if in a hypnotic state. At this time, the only other movement noted was the alternate winding and unwinding of a single turn of coil (presumably the one nearest the serpent's head), first clockwise, then counterclockwise; during these rhythmic movements, the distance separating the serpents' heads never changed. During the ritual, one or the other of the snakes thrust his head sharply at that of his opponent, but apparently with a closed mouth, for such stylized combat behavior (at least as it has so far been observed among the pit vipers) results in no injury to either contestant. The event lasted about 20 minutes before it was interrupted by the observer.

VENOM AND BITE Although most abundant in wilderness areas, the southern copperhead is frequently encountered in certain suburban parks and woodlots of our largest East Texas cities. In such places, where it can find shelter under brush and man-made debris such as boards, rock piles, roofing paper, and other construction rubble, it is generally the most abundant local venomous snake and the one responsible for the vast majority of human envenomations in and around the cities of Houston, Beaumont, and Port Arthur. In Harris County alone the number of people bitten each year by this snake and treated in local hospitals and clinics is probably between 20 and 30, yet we can find no record of a human fatality resulting from such injuries. This is no doubt a result of the copperhead venom's relatively low lethal toxicity compared with that of most other native venomous snakes, together with the modest quantity of venom carried in its venom glands. The total amount of venom contained in both glands of a copperhead is usually 40 to 70 mg of dry weight, according to Minton and Minton (1969), and the same authors estimate the minimum lethal dose required to kill an adult human at 100 or more milligrams. Another mitigating factor is the small size of the copperhead's fangs, each of which seldom measures more than $5/16$ inch, resulting in a shallow subcutaneous bite.

According to information assembled by Karant (in Wingert et al. 1980), only a single human death was discovered in his review of 2,000 cases of copperhead bite. He explained that this solitary fatality was probably not the direct result of copperhead poisoning but most likely was caused by certain side effects of envenomation that were never clearly defined. Despite these reassuring statistics, Amaral (1927) reported a human death from a copperhead bite involving a 14-year-old bitten on a finger. Likewise, P. Wilson (1908) recorded 5 deaths from copperhead envenomation, 3 of which he believed may have been exacerbated by the large amounts of whiskey consumed by the victims in their misguided attempts at treatment.

According to Sherman A. Minton (pers. com.), who over the years has been involved as a physician with approximately 50 copperhead bite cases, generalized symptoms of envenomation by this species include local pain and swelling, nausea, vomiting, sweating, and thirst. In addition, the victims usually experience enlargement and tenderness of local lymph nodes, and the presence of blood- or serum-filled blisters is not unusual. In only one case, involving a 5- or 6-year-old girl, did he note hypotension and other evidence of shock. Minton commented that tissue necrosis can be severe but corrective skin grafting is rarely necessary.

BROAD-BANDED COPPERHEAD

Agkistrodon contortrix laticinctus
PLATE 175

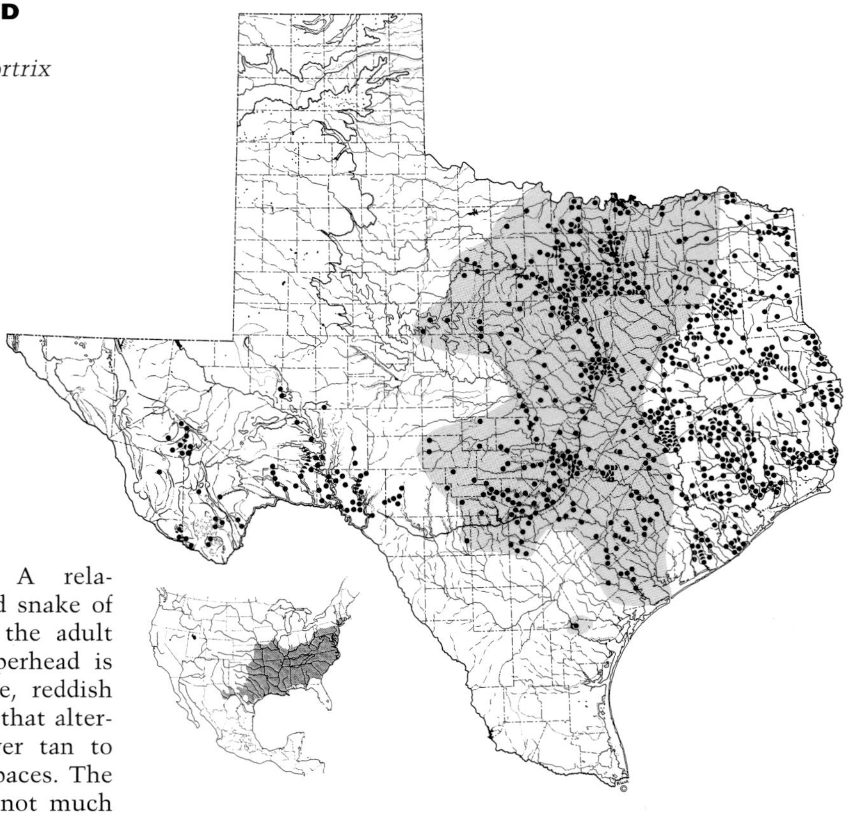

DESCRIPTION   A relatively stout-bodied snake of moderate length, the adult broad-banded copperhead is marked with wide, reddish brown crossbands that alternate with narrower tan to pale brown interspaces. The bands, which are not much wider on the sides of the body than along the spine, may be finely edged in white; the terminal portion of the tail is greenish gray, often crossed with subtle, thin white lines. A narrow, dark brown ∨ lies along each side of the head, its apex near the end of the mouthline, with one arm terminating behind the eye and the other tracing the lower lip. Very young specimens are clad in shades of gray instead of brown, and their tail tips are bright yellow.

The snake's body scales are only weakly keeled and usually in 23 middorsal rows. Most scales under the tail are arranged in a single row, except those near the end of the tail, which are paired. The anal plate is single.

COMPARABLE SNAKES Among our native serpents, the infant western cottonmouth most closely resembles the broad-banded copperhead. Although the two snakes share a similar dorsal pattern of wide, dark body crossbands and pale interspaces, the cottonmouth's head is mostly dusky and bears a broad, horizontal, mahogany cheek stripe behind each eye. In addition, its dorsal scales are in 25 rows at midbody. Both the eastern and dusty hog-nosed snakes are sometimes mistaken for the copperhead, but except for occasional unmarked specimens of the eastern species, their dorsal patterns consist of spots or blotches. Other distinguishing features of hog-nosed snakes are their sharply upturned snouts, round pupils, absence of heat-sensing facial pits, and divided anal plates. Although the wide, dark crossbands and yellow to reddish interspaces of the broad-banded water snake somewhat resemble those of the copperhead, they are seldom clearly defined. The water snake, which lacks facial pits, has a wide dark band extending backward from the eye to the end of the mouthline, round pupils, and a divided anal plate.

SIZE The usual length of adults is 22 to 30 inches (56–76.2 cm). The maximum length reported is 37¼ inches (95 cm).

HABITAT This Central Texas subspecies of the copperhead is most commonly associated with wooded areas extending from the Red River in the north to the Balcones Escarpment in the south, except that to the southwest its range continues to Frio County and to the southeast to Victoria County. The region encompasses primarily the post oak woodlands of the Cross Timbers and the live oak–cedar association of the Edwards Plateau, although the broad-banded copperhead occurs as well in the generally inhospitable Blackland Prairie, where it is confined to the margins of woodland streams that flow through the area. According to Gehlbach (in Gloyd and Conant 1990), the largest concentrations of copperheads found in the Waco area occur in the deciduous woodlands, containing primarily cedar elm and sugarberry but including some American elm, bur oak, and pecan. Elsewhere throughout its range it frequently occurs near some form of surface water such as streams, ponds, or lakes, often in the vicinity of ridges and rocky ledges and usually where the sandy or gravelly soils are blanketed with accumulations of leaf litter.

BEHAVIOR Like other subspecies of *A. contortrix*, the broad-banded copperhead relies heavily on its concealing coloration to protect it from its enemies. Coiled motionless on a layer of dead leaves, its cryptic pattern matching almost precisely the multihued browns of the forest floor, the reptile is invisible to the human eye, its body outline difficult to detect. It is generally recognized that fast-moving snakes or those known to move about a great deal are likely to be striped or to have no pattern (patch-nosed, garter, and ribbon snakes; coachwhips, whipsnakes, and racers), but slow, heavy-bodied species such as this are usually blotched or crossbanded.

The copperhead is not an aggressive animal. To avoid discovery, it normally remains motionless when approached, but if threatened it may vibrate its tail and, from scent glands at the base of its tail, spray two fine jets of a strong, unpleasant-smelling musk into the air. If this fails to deter its antagonist, the snake may try to crawl away to safety. One that is deliberately provoked and unable to escape is apt to strike out at its foe, the quick lunge of its head seldom spanning more than 5 or 6 inches.

In regions where rocky forested hilltops adjoin brush-covered flatlands, the copperhead remains in the woodlands the entire summer, moving randomly through the area as it seeks new hunting grounds. With the approach of cold weather, sometime in October or November (depending mostly on latitude) the snake leaves its home range and returns to its upland den area to prepare for winter. Such den sites are typically on rocky hilltop ledges where shelflike slabs of stone are separated by snug spaces. They reach far down into the ground, providing the snakes with good protection from subfreezing temperatures. Dundee and Burger (1948) found such a denning area along the Verdigris River in Rogers County, Oklahoma. Situated along a limestone and sandstone cliff, it stretched out for nearly 1½ miles, creating myriad winter havens not only for copperheads but for cottonmouths and coachwhips as well. Although the zoologists noted some mixing of the three species along the bluff, they determined that to satisfy its own species-specific requirements, each kind of snake usually segregated itself from the others. Thus, the copperheads confined themselves mostly to the drier east and southeast cliff exposures, the cottonmouths to the moist northeast-facing sides of the bluff, and the coachwhips to the more open sites.

Not all broad-banded copperheads spend the winter in hilltop hibernacula. Those living near the southernmost end of their geographic range, where underground rock formations are scarce or absent, frequently hibernate in decaying logs, tree stumps, or mammal burrows, singly or in small groups. In McLennan County, for example, Strecker (1935) found four specimens hibernating together in a hollow pin-oak log; three others, discovered near Waco by a high school science teacher, spent the winter in a large pile of partially buried decaying vegetation mixed with sawdust. In another instance, Johnny Binder (pers. com.) uncovered two hibernating copperheads from beneath an accumulation of drift material nestled along the banks of the Brazos River. Some of the same places the copperhead uses for winter shelter (decaying logs and tree stumps, piles of plant debris, mammal burrows, and rock piles) are also utilized as summer retreats.

In the spring and fall when nighttime temperatures are moderately cool, the broad-banded copperhead is most likely to be encountered in the open during the day, basking in the sun, but in midsummer when daytime temperatures are often unbearably hot, it confines its activities to the hours of early morning, evening, and night.

FEEDING The broad-banded copperhead is an opportunistic feeder that eats a wide variety of both vertebrate and invertebrate prey. Food items consumed by this subspecies have included small mammals (mostly rodents and shrews but also bats), ground-nesting birds, lizards, snakes, frogs, small toads, salamanders, insects (mostly cicadas and caterpillars), and spiders. Cicadas in the nymphal stage of their life cycle are sometimes quite abundant in some localities, presenting an easy mark for the slow-paced copperhead. Reports of

copperheads gorging on cicada nymphs and recently transformed, soft-bodied adults are fairly common. Consuming such insects is not entirely without risk. Conant (1951) reported the case of a northern copperhead from Washington County, Ohio, that swallowed a 17-year cicada only to have the insect burrow its way through the snake's neck, costing the reptile its life. Although adult broad-banded copperheads eat a large number of mammals, the very small ones probably consume young lizards and frogs, which they presumably lure to within striking range by wriggling their yellow-tipped, wormlike tails to imitate active larval insects.

REPRODUCTION The male broad-banded copperhead normally becomes sexually mature soon after reaching the second year of life, whereas the female does so in her third year. Thereafter, the snakes mate either in spring or late fall; spermatozoa from the later copulations remain viable in the female's oviduct until the following spring, when they fertilize the first ovulating eggs of the season. Although populations living at more northern latitudes apparently produce young only in alternate years, those from the southern end of the snake's range do so annually. The infant snakes, 3 to 11 per litter, are born between late July and the end of September. Eight to 10 inches (20.3–25.4 cm) long at birth, they bear the same crossbanded pattern as the adults, but the overall body hue of newborn snakes is more grayish than brown, the dark markings lacking the rich brown tones of mature individuals. Also distinctive in the infants are their yellowish tail tips.

VENOM AND BITE Although the bite of a large broad-banded copperhead may cause serious medical consequences in humans, especially when the victim is a small child, records of human fatalities from copperhead envenomation are rare (even though the incidence of copperhead poisoning in Texas ranks second only to the number of snakebites inflicted on humans by the more wide-ranging western diamond-backed rattlesnake). Such a low mortality rate can be attributed to the snake's relatively short fangs, its modest venom supply (40–70 mg of dry weight per snake when extracted by milking, according to Minton and Minton (1969), and the comparatively low lethal toxicity of its venom.

Symptoms of poisoning by this species are

generally not dramatic, consisting primarily of pain and swelling. A typical case history was reported by Fitch (1960), who, after being bitten on the middle finger of his right hand, carefully observed and recorded the signs and symptoms produced by the bite. Early manifestations included twitching muscles and a dull ache at the bite location, followed in about 10 minutes by noticeable swelling and discoloration in the same area. The pain, which at first was not severe, soon became intense as the swelling moved steadily up the hand; in a short time it was followed by throbbing pain in the palm at the base of the middle finger and numbness of the skin. At this point, Fitch made a ½-inch incision through one of the fang punctures, the one that was the primary source of venom injection. (The other fang struck a knuckle joint and apparently delivered little or no venom.)

Two hours after the bite, the swelling had reached 4 inches above the wrist and the throbbing pain was still present in the palm of the hand, at which time Fitch took a quarter-grain of codeine. Approximately 15 minutes later, when respiratory congestion became evident, he took an antihistamine in an effort to relieve the symptoms. By 10:15 PM the pain had reached its peak, prompting Fitch to take a second quarter-grain of codeine. Between 30 and 45 minutes later, the victim became nauseated and subsequently regurgitated, but he experienced no further deterioration in his condition after 12:45 AM. The systemic manifestations experienced earlier were gone by morning, although the affected hand eventually swelled to almost twice its usual size, and it was nearly a month before Fitch regained full use of his hand.

TRANS-PECOS COPPERHEAD
Agkistrodon contortrix pictigaster
PLATES 176, 177

DESCRIPTION Like the broad-banded copperhead, this subspecies is marked with straight-edged, squarish crossbands that are nearly as wide along the spine as they are on the sides, but it differs from that subspecies in its heavily mottled belly pattern of deep chestnut (sometimes almost solid black) and the pale inverted ∪ at the base of each crossband. The chestnut brown, cinnamon, or dark seal-brown crossbands, which are distinctly darker along their outer margins and also finely edged in white, are separated from one another by spaces of pale hazel brown or an even paler, almost off-white color. The crossbands of some specimens contain a few small, dark spots. The dorsal scales, arranged in 21 or 23 rows at midbody, are only lightly keeled, and the anal plate is single. Most scales under the tail are in a single row, except those near the end of the tail, which are paired.

COMPARABLE SNAKES The grayish Texas lyre snake is more slender than a copperhead, has a pale belly, and possesses a divided anal plate.

SIZE Slightly smaller on average than the other races of copperhead, adults of this subspecies are 20 to 30 inches (51–76 cm) long. The maximum known length is 32⅞ inches (83.5 cm).

HABITAT An inhabitant of the arid Trans-Pecos region of Texas, this copperhead occupies a variety of sites ranging from moist, tree-dominated mountain canyons to dry desert flats, which in some cases appear to be devoid of surface water. In his study of the copperhead's natural history, Fitch (1960) described the Trans-Pecos copperhead's typical Chisos Mountain habitat as the mouth of a canyon encompassing an area roughly 100 yards (91.2 m) long and 20 to 110 feet (6.1–33.5 m) wide, where the plant life consists of willow, walnut, hackberry, Mexican buckeye, persimmon, fragrant sumac, and grape, in addition to some typical desert plants such as catclaw and prickly pear cactus. The largest trees in this sheltered canyon grove have trunks about 2 feet (61 cm) in diameter, and the ground beneath them is mostly bare and rocky, but with scattered accumulations of leaf litter. When he gave this description, Fitch estimated that less than 1 square mile (2.59 km²) of such suitable habitat still existed in all of the Chisos Moun-

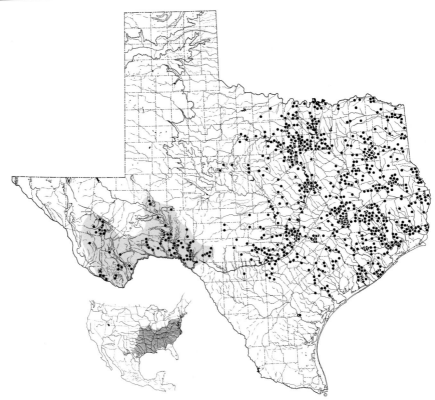

tains, although he painted a more optimistic picture for the Davis Mountains, where, he suggested, the remaining groves of live oak totaled at least several square miles.

In more arid circumstances, the Trans-Pecos copperhead may be found under bushes growing atop limestone outcroppings 100 feet (30.6 m) above canyon riverbeds. Others have been collected in arroyos lined with igneous boulders, and some in dense stands of river cane, a habitat that can harbor unusually large numbers of the serpents. The discovery of such a copperhead bonanza was described by William G. Degenhardt (in Gloyd and Conant 1990), who together with his wife, Paula, encountered a plethora of serpents on July 8, 1961, in a section of cane thicket growing along a trail leading into Santa Elena Canyon in Big Bend National Park. Many of the cane stalks, which an earlier flood had reduced to a foot-deep jumble of dried stems, carpeted much of the canyon floor and were partially covered with Bermuda grass. Off to one side, along the north wall of the canyon, were talus

slides and sizable boulders, places where the snakes probably sought refuge during times of river flooding and within whose recesses they may have found winter refuge. It was dusk when the Degenhardts encountered the first copperhead as it lay stretched out on the tangled heap of cane stems. More copperheads were discovered as they crawled up through the flattened stalks, and others as they moved across bare ground nearby. Altogether, the zoologists collected 15 specimens that evening and saw at least that many more.

Although the largest concentrations of Trans-Pecos copperheads have been reported in moist woodland canyons such as the one described by Milstead, Mecham, and McClintock (1950), where 90 specimens were collected in one month near Independence Creek on the Stockton Plateau, more recent reports show that the subspecies is widely distributed in some remarkably dry habitats far removed from surface water and trees, including some of the most arid creosote-bush and chaparral flats in Terrell and Brewster counties. In such dry environments, where daytime temperatures rise to periously high levels for cold-blooded creatures such as these, copperheads probably seek relief from the extreme daytime heat by crawling into rock crevices or animal burrows.

Until Milstead and his coworkers first surveyed the Independence Creek location in Terrell County, fewer than a dozen specimens of this snake had been found by experienced collectors. Since then, many have been taken from the wild, not only by professional and amateur herpetologists but by commercial collectors as well. Such collecting has no doubt contributed to the snake's decline, but there is growing evidence that a more serious threat to the Trans-Pecos copperhead (one that in time may eliminate it from certain West Texas canyons) is man's alteration of the serpent's environment. In some places, the relentless pumping of underground aquifers for crop irrigation is seriously diminishing the water flow to a number of the region's canyon springs, depriving the fragile microhabitats of the moisture necessary to sustain them and some of their attendant wildlife species, including the copperhead.

In spite of the snake's limited and highly discontinuous distribution, Gloyd and Conant express optimism for its long-term survival, citing the subspecies' ability to adapt to a relatively wide variety of habitats, often in remote and inaccessible locations, together with its secretive, nocturnal behavior.

BEHAVIOR This is one of Texas' least excitable venomous snakes. Although capable of delivering a poisonous bite, it rarely strikes out at an approaching foe. Minton (1959) described Big Bend specimens as inoffensive, intent on crawling away at the approach of a collector's light, and attempting to bite only when pinned to the ground. Like the other subspecies of A. contortrix, the Trans-Pecos copperhead depends on its remarkable cryptic coloration and sedentary behavior to avoid discovery. At night, however, when it is not otherwise easily detected, it unintentionally announces its presence by rustling dead leaves as it crawls through the dry ground litter.

Though primarily a terrestrial snake, it occasionally ascends bushes and trees to a height of at least 4 feet. Fitch encountered one

2 feet above ground, climbing over the exposed root system of an overturned live oak at Independence Creek in Terrell County. Another, reported by Englehardt (1932), was discovered as it lay coiled 4 feet above ground, also in a live oak.

Chiefly a nocturnal serpent whose daily activity cycle usually begins soon after dusk and continues until early the next morning, the Trans-Pecos copperhead is sometimes day-active, especially on overcast days or in places sheltered from the sun by the contour of the land or heavy vegetation.

FEEDING What little information is available suggests the snake's diet is not greatly different from that of the other subspecies of copperhead. It consists of a variety of both vertebrate and invertebrate animals, including small mammals, birds, snakes, insects, and perhaps also lizards and frogs. Based on circumstantial evidence, Seifert (1972) believed that frogs were consumed by this serpent, although he neither found these amphibians in the snakes' stomachs nor actually saw them captured. His conclusion was supported by the presence of specific parasites in the mouths of copperheads, which in all probability could only have arrived there by way of ingested frogs or tadpoles, the parasite's intermediate host.

Birds, when they are attacked, are probably the nestlings of ground-dwelling species or those that nest near the ground in trees and bushes. A more unusual avian prey species was reported by McCrystal and Green (1986). At 1:15 PM on June 20, 1983, they watched a Trans-Pecos copperhead eat an already dead baby cliff swallow that lay under a bush inside Santa Elena Canyon. What is noteworthy about this incident is the remote and inaccessible location of the cliff swallow nests, high on the sides of sheer limestone canyon walls on both sides of the Rio Grande where they ordinarily would be unavailable to the snakes. How the young bird, not yet able to fly, became a victim of copperhead predation in this instance was revealed the following morning when the zoologists observed Chihuahuan ravens raiding the swallow rookeries. After snatching the baby birds from their nests, the ravens sometimes dropped them in midair, apparently in an attempt to kill them as they hit the ground below. Sometimes the winged marauders could not locate the nestling swallows after their fatal fall some distance up on the riverbank, making them potential prey for the copperheads, which is probably how the snake encountered the young cliff swallow it consumed.

REPRODUCTION According to Gloyd and Conant, this subspecies of copperhead breeds either in April or during the fall (actual dates vary from September 11 to October 8). Described by Fitch (1985) as producing the smallest number of young of any copperhead subspecies, female Trans-Pecos copperheads give birth to 3 or 4 young per litter. Born sometime between late August and mid-September, the newborn serpents measure $8\frac{1}{3}$ to $10\frac{4}{5}$ inches (21.2–27.4 cm) long. Unlike the adults, their overall coloration is subdued, being more gray than rich brown, with less distinctive crossbanded markings and an almost black belly. As in other races of cop-

perhead, the infant's greenish yellow tail tip may be used as an animated lure to attract lizards and frogs to within striking distance of the young snake's jaws.

VENOM AND BITE Because it is confined largely to remote and often inaccessible areas of West Texas, and as a result of its primarily nocturnal habits, this copperhead subspecies is seldom encountered except by professional collectors who know where and when to find it. Considering its relatively small size and mild-mannered disposition, it can be ranked as one of our least offensive venomous serpents and one of the least dangerous to man. Although its venom has been described as less toxic than that of other copperhead races, in a worst-case scenario a bite by one of these snakes could prove extremely serious, and thus none should be treated with indifference.

WESTERN COTTONMOUTH

Agkistrodon piscivorus leucostoma
PLATES 178–180

DESCRIPTION Often the first thing one notices about the cottonmouth, besides its chunky body and stubby tail, is the snake's large, angular, flat-topped head, whose wide jaws stand out prominently against the relatively narrow neck. The head markings are not conspicuous in the adult snake, except for a broad, dark cheek stripe narrowly trimmed in white. Below this mask, which stretches from the eye to the back of the mouthline, is an area of yellowish brown that is often suffused with darker brown.

The overall appearance of this stout-bodied serpent is typically dark and lackluster, with little noticeable distinction between the snake's obscure markings and its dull ground color. As a rule, the adult pattern consists of broad, ill-defined crossbands of grayish brown, dark brown, or black, each band light-centered, dark-edged, and sometimes also narrowly trimmed in white on its jagged outer margins, especially along the sides. This pattern generally darkens with age, disappearing altogether in most older individuals. Patternless young snakes are also occa-

sionally found throughout the snake's range; such solid black or dark brown cottonmouths occur with the greatest frequency among Gulf Coast populations.

The newborn cottonmouth bears little resemblance to its parents. For the first year of its life, the boldly patterned juvenile looks remarkably like a young copperhead, its tan body marked with broad, jagged, mahogany crossbands, each containing a light brown, vertical inner core. Both the crossbands and the paler interspaces bear prominent, widely scattered dark spots. Equally pronounced are the white horizontal pinstripes bordering the dark mask and the narrow, pale-colored ones that edge the lower lip scales. The tail tip, like that of the baby copperhead, is sulphur-yellow.

Because of considerable color and pattern variation among individual western cottonmouths, the most useful diagnostic features are those found in the less conspicuous but more reliable details of scalation. Among the most important of these is the arrangement of the scales under the tail, called subcaudals,

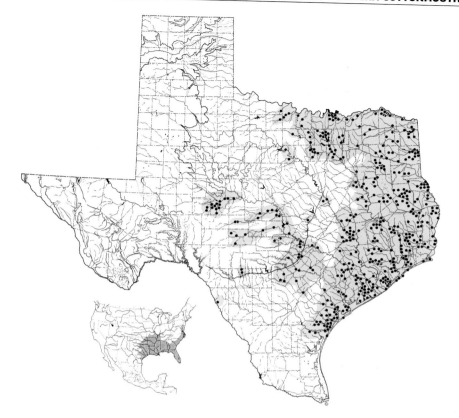

which in this species typically occur in a single row, except for a few divided ones near the end of the tail. The weakly keeled dorsal scales are arranged in 25 rows at midbody, and the anal plate is single.

COMPARABLE SNAKES Several harmless water snakes of the genus *Nerodia* resemble the cottonmouth by virtue of their relatively thick-set bodies, somewhat large, wide heads, and dark bodies. Unlike the cottonmouth, however, they have round pupils, no facial pits, a divided anal plate, and two rows of scales under the tail. Such details are helpful only when the snake is examined close up. A safer though perhaps less conclusive way to recognize a water snake is to observe its behavior in the water. In contrast to the cottonmouth, which swims with much of its body visible above the waterline and its head raised fully out of the water and held nearly parallel to the surface, a water snake moves with its head barely out of the water, its submerged body trailing behind, largely unseen.

There is also a close similarity between the very young cottonmouth and the juvenile copperhead; a notable difference between them is seen in their head markings. The pale cheek of the copperhead is bordered above by a narrow, dark line that extends rearward from the eye and curves around the end of the mouthline, whereas in the young cottonmouth the side of the head is dominated by a broad, dark mask thinly margined with white, both above and below. (See illustration in southern copperhead account.)

SIZE Although the western cottonmouth is known to reach a maximum length of slightly more than 5 feet (152 cm), most Texas specimens are 24 to 36 inches (61–91.4 cm) long. Several particularly large adults, measuring just over 4 feet (122 cm) long, were captured in the coastal marshes of Hall's Bayou along the upper Texas coast. As a rule, western cottonmouths inhabiting the inland forests of East Texas do not grow as large as those found elsewhere.

HABITAT The ubiquitous cottonmouth occurs over the entire eastern half of the state, occupying nearly every kind of stable aquatic habitat from brackish coastal marshes to cool, clear upland streams, and from sea level sites to elevations as high as 2,300 feet (703 m). It is especially abundant in the lowland swamps, marshes, and slow-moving streams of southeastern Texas as far down the coast as Corpus Christi but is surprisingly absent from the lower Rio Grande Valley, where much of the coastal environment seems equally suitable for its survival. That it also occurs on Texas' offshore barrier islands is well documented. One 2½-foot specimen was discovered under a clump of prickly pear cactus growing in sand dunes on the mainland side of San Jose Island, an unlikely microhabitat for this moisture-loving serpent. Despite its propensity for wet environments, this snake is occasionally found some distance from water. A few individuals have been observed at localities a mile or more from any permanent source of moisture.

The largest cottonmouth populations in Texas occur in the vast undisturbed coastal marshes of the state; in particularly favorable localities they may outnumber any other large local serpent, for these marshes support an abundance of cottonmouth prey and consist of immense areas of habitat often inaccessible to man. In such places a collector may catch a dozen or more specimens in a single night, given the right weather conditions and other favorable circumstances.

One of the greatest natural concentrations ever reported for this species was discovered not in Texas but in Hickman County, Kentucky, at a place called Murphy's Pond, an inland habitat hundreds of miles from the nearest coastal environment. Barbour (1956) estimated the density of cottonmouths in selected portions of the region at more than 300 individuals per acre, an incredibly high ratio that under ordinary circumstances is probably unequaled anywhere in Texas.

Occasionally, portentous weather conditions cause even larger concentrations of the western cottonmouth in Texas, although such aggregations are exceptional and generally of short duration. For example, when a major hurricane churns inland across the upper Texas coast, creating powerful storm surges, heavy downpours, and extensive flooding, cottonmouths are among the vertebrates most frequently observed seeking refuge from the rising waters. At such times, large numbers of the displaced pit vipers, along with other snakes and a variety of small mammals, gather on isolated patches of high ground. If they can find no dry land on which to escape, the cottonmouths will crawl onto almost any available object protruding above the floodwaters, including bushes, tree limbs, and floating debris. In the absence of more conventional shelter, the snakes do not hesitate to take refuge in boats, boat sheds, and beach homes, where their presence can pose a real danger to people returning to salvage flood-damaged property after a storm. One woman, upon entering her bayside trailer home after Hurricane Carla, discovered two adult cottonmouths on top of a partly submerged refrigerator and another on the kitchen counter. Similar experiences are not unusual following such great storms along the Texas coast.

In the East Texas pine and pine-oak forests, the cottonmouth confines itself mostly to large and small ponds scattered throughout the region, to palmetto and cypress swamps, and to broad river bottoms and their attendant sloughs. Ordinarily far less common in such sylvan habitats than it is in the vast coastal swamps and marshes, this serpent and the southern copperhead were reported by Burkett (1966) to be the two most abundant large snake species in the pine-oak forests of Nacogdoches County. There it successfully occupied a broad range of habitats, living in the neighborhood of swamps and ponds, near sluggish muddy streams, and also, somewhat unexpectedly, along clear, fast-moving streams with rocky bottoms. Farther inland in Texas, where aquatic environments are less prevalent, it is usually restricted to the woodland borders of sizable rivers and their tributaries and to lakes and ponds with shoreline vegetation. It has also managed to follow the Colorado and Brazos river systems westward across the semiarid and essentially inhospitable (to an aquatic serpent) Edwards Plateau to Crockett and Irion counties. In this austere land, where creeks and rivers cut through stone canyons and flow over solid bedrock, the cottonmouth is most apt to be found near cool, shallow springs a short distance from the main waterways.

Despite its affinity for natural wetlands, it sometimes also inhabits wet agricultural and suburban areas, particularly those supporting an abundant food supply. Such places can include rice fields, artificial fish ponds, and drainage ditches. This venomous serpent has even been found within the borders of some of the state's largest cities, but it is seldom encountered there. Far more likely to turn up in such urban wetlands are the quick-tempered but harmless water snakes of the genus *Nerodia*, whose heavy bodies and relatively wide heads convey the image of a dangerous serpent, causing them to be erroneously identified as cottonmouths and thus to be slaughtered, often in large numbers.

BEHAVIOR A cottonmouth surprised near the water's edge often tries to escape by swimming away, although one encountered some distance from water may simply remain motionless or, if outstretched, pull back its head and neck slightly. If discovered in a coiled position, especially when confronted out in the open by a human, it is likely to stand fast and merely flick its head back at a 45-degree angle so that its gaze is directed upward at its foe. When further provoked, the snake is apt to open its mouth widely and expose the white interior in a threat gesture. It may also nervously vibrate or twitch its tail. If the tail is in motion among dry leaves or if it strikes a nearby hard object, the resulting whir can sound like the buzz of a rattlesnake.

When approached too closely, the snake will usually strike, though not with the long, quick thrust typical of most adult rattlesnakes. Instead, a cottonmouth of moderate size is likely to deliver a short jab that spans a distance no greater than 10 or 12 inches. Not only can it strike while floating on the surface of the water, but it is also capable of delivering a venomous bite when completely submerged.

Another tactic used by the cottonmouth to avoid a direct confrontation is to squirt a foul-smelling liquid from two glands inside the base of its tail, which some say has the smell of a male goat, an odor that most people find quite offensive. Following the passage of Hur-

ricane Cindy across the upper Texas coast in mid-September 1963, during which 15 to 23 inches of torrential rains flooded the entire southeastern corner of the state, Ed Guidry, an amateur Port Arthur herpetologist, encountered scores of cottonmouths stranded together on a small promontory not far from his home (pers. com.). His presence so disturbed the already irritated snakes that many of them simultaneously expelled the musk from their scent glands, producing an overpowering odor that Guidry described as absolutely nauseating.

During the sweltering daylight hours of midsummer, when this semiaquatic serpent is largely inactive, it remains coiled in some shaded spot, taking refuge from the hot sun by hiding in hollow logs, rotting tree stumps, exposed tree root systems, streamside flotsam, and abandoned mammal burrows. Young specimens may even hide in crayfish holes. In wetland habitats altered by man, young as well as adult cottonmouths seek shelter under discarded building materials, rock piles, beached boats, and in the debris of dilapidated wooden structures near water. By evening, when the high temperatures have moderated, the snake leaves the comfort of its daytime refuge to begin its nightly foraging cycle. Like most other snakes, the cottonmouth reverses this activity pattern in the spring and fall, basking in the warm sun on cool days but seeking cover during the chill of night. At such times it often rests in shallow water or on a mudbank near the water's edge, and it does not hesitate to coil on a log, a tree stump, a pile of dead vegetation sticking out of the water, or a low, horizontal tree limb overhanging the water. Smaller ones sometimes climb onto cypress knees, where they blend with the dark wood.

This is a relatively cold-tolerant reptile whose period of winter inactivity varies with latitude. It may hibernate for several months of each year, only briefly, or not at all during mild South Texas winters. In the more northern parts of its range, probably including northeastern Texas, the cottonmouth often migrates each fall from its summer haunts in the wet bottomlands to nearby wooded hillsides where rock formations, with their deep holes and crevices, provide more suitable denning sites than are generally found in the lowlands.

One such location, containing 40 aggregating cottonmouths, was discovered in northern Oklahoma by Dundee and Burger (1948). In this rocky area, characterized by 150-foot-high (46 m) bluffs that more or less paralleled the east side of the Verdigris River, the snakes confined their denning activities mostly to the higher parts of the northeast-facing slopes. Not all of the serpents in the area chose to make the arduous climb to the elevated dens; some, it was thought, spent their winters in the nearby river valley, coiled comfortably in crayfish and rodent burrows until they emerged again sometime in March.

In southeastern Texas, where surface rock formations are uncommon, this relatively cold-tolerant snake seldom if ever congregates at specific communal dens, nor does it always spend the entire winter in hibernation. It often responds to cold weather by crawling into rotting logs, decaying tree stumps, or piles of dead vegetation. Since their decomposing interiors generate a certain amount of natural heat, such sanctuaries probably are better places in which to escape the cold than are most other aboveground shelters. Based on numerous field observations in Georgia and Florida, Neill (1947) expressed the opinion that cottonmouths in those states chose rotting pine stumps over all other kinds of winter refuge. On mild winter days he found many first-year young by peeling away the loose bark from such stumps, particularly those situated on hillsides next to sizable bodies of water. He failed to find them there in very cold weather, presumably because the snakes then moved deeper into the stumps' warmer recesses. The use of somewhat similar winter sites by cottonmouths was reported by Arny (1948), who found 112 such snakes in and beneath logs and piles of drift in southern Louisiana on November 21 and 22.

This species sometimes uses less conventional hibernacula. For example, near Addicks Dam, just west of Houston, Texas, an 18-inch (46 cm) cottonmouth managed to find its way to a large, leaf-filled knothole 10 feet above the ground in a large oak tree, where it was found in mid-December. It could only have reached this ordinarily inaccessible spot by crawling along the tangled stems of wild grapevine that grew up the side of the tree trunk. We found two other specimens near Livingston, Texas, in early January, coiled under a large pile of old newspaper and wooden debris in the unused garage of a lakeside cabin.

FEEDING The cottonmouth takes a wide variety of small vertebrate animals, some invertebrates, and occasionally even bird eggs, although it usually avoids bufonid toads and their tadpoles. As an example of the cottonmouth's indiscriminate appetite, Burkett (studying Texas, Oklahoma, and Louisiana populations of this subspecies; 1966) found that nearly 70 percent of the serpent's diet by volume consisted of fish, amphibians, and reptiles; less than 20 percent of birds; nearly 13 percent of mammals; and the rest of unidentifiable animal remains. Barbour (1956), on the other hand, determined that in western Kentucky the most frequently consumed prey was the siren, an aquatic eellike salamander, which together with a large number of ranid frogs accounted for nearly two-thirds of the snake's diet.

On the Welder Wildlife Refuge, approximately 30 miles (48 km) north of Corpus Christi, Texas, Cottom, Glazener, and Raun (1959) discovered that birds and not reptiles or fish were the chief item in the cottonmouth's diet, comprising nearly 37 percent by volume of the total amount of food consumed. Within the borders of this 7,800-acre (3,158 ha) cattle ranch and research preserve, the snake found an abundance of avian prey, much of it concentrated in tremendous numbers among the tall sedges growing along the margins of the region's numerous shallow ponds and lakes. According to the zoologists, red-winged blackbirds and cowbirds in particular frequently fed and drank at the bases of the aquatic tule plants, falling easy prey to the serpents, which were also plentiful in the area. They also found that in the more open marshes, other terrestrial wetland species became the principal avian victims, especially the area's more common coots, sora rails, and purple gallinules. They reported that even meadowlarks, sparrows, buntings, and cardinals (birds that spend considerable time feeding on relatively dry ground near the snake's habitat) were not safe from cottonmouth predation.

The investigators determined that after birds, snakes were the most important prey species on the refuge, representing more than 29 percent of the cottonmouth's total food consumption. The ubiquitous water snakes were chief among them. Also eaten were a ribbon snake and a western diamond-backed rattler. In one case, the field workers discovered that a 49-inch Great Plains rat snake had been devoured by a cottonmouth 8 inches shorter than its victim; the prey was considerably more slender than the predator, which allowed it to be folded into the pit viper's stomach like an accordion.

Amphibians, accounting for more than 14 percent of the food consumed, were next in importance. Each of three snakes had eaten a western lesser siren, and two had captured a frog apiece, one of which was identified as a green tree frog.

Mammals, representing 13.97 percent of the total food consumption, were taken nearly as often as amphibians, but the number of prey species in this category was limited to only three that were readily identifiable: pygmy mice were eaten by four snakes, hispid pocket mice by two, and least shrews by two others.

The most unexpected find to come out of the Welder Wildlife Refuge study was the cottonmouth's possible consumption of freshwater pond snails, as well as cicadas, butterfly larvae, grasshoppers, large water bugs, and large water beetles. Together they represented 5.61 percent of the serpent's diet at the refuge. Whether any, some, or all of these invertebrates were in the stomachs of insect-eating prey species before such animals were consumed by the snakes is debatable, although the authors of the study were certain most of them represented primary food items.

Fish, an important part of the snake's diet in most other parts of its range, were curiously not found in the refuge cottonmouths. Elsewhere the list of piscine prey species known to have been consumed by this snake is lengthy. Such a list recently compiled by Ernst (1992) from numerous published reports includes minnows, shiners, killifish, topminnows, catfish, drum, gizzard shad, goby, mullet, freshwater eel, bowfin, pirate perch, mudminnow, pickerel, sunfish, black bass, and crappie. In reality, the kinds of fish actually eaten by this serpent probably include all of the species available in any given locality.

In spite of its tendency to devour a wide assortment of fish, there is no evidence to suggest that the cottonmouth makes any serious reduction in native game species. Admittedly, a sick or injured bass, perch, or catfish too weak to avoid capture occasionally falls victim to this slow-moving pit viper, but few healthy, active fish are apprehended unless they have first become trapped within small, remnant pools created by long periods of summer drought. Under such circumstances, several cottonmouths may congregate along the water's edge for days at a time, gorging themselves on the abundant food supply for as long as it lasts.

Among the amphibian prey eaten by the cottonmouth throughout its widespread range, Ernst mentioned salamanders, frogs of the genus *Rana*, tree frogs, and narrowmouth, spadefoot, and bufonid toads. The list of reptilian prey included baby alligators, snapping turtles, mud and musk turtles, cooters and sliders, softshell turtles, box turtles, anoles, skinks, ground skinks, other cottonmouths, rattlesnakes, rat snakes, mud snakes, hognosed snakes, king snakes, whipsnakes, water and crayfish snakes, brown snakes, and garter and ribbon snakes. Their inventory of avian prey species included cormorants, sora rails, pied-billed grebes, glossy ibis (eggs), Louisiana herons (eggs), American egrets, domestic chickens (eggs), mourning doves, fish crows, chickadees, seaside sparrows, cardinals, towhees, and wood thrushes. Also mentioned are the mammal prey species, moles, shrews, bats, squirrels, muskrats, mice, rats, and cottontail rabbits. Finally, their summary of prey listed these invertebrates: snails, a variety of insects, and crayfish.

That carrion is also consumed is documented by frequent reports of dead fish from an angler's stringer or discarded innards taken from a recently gutted catch. An unusual report of carrion eating comes from Wharton

(1958), describing how some Florida cottonmouths waited in heron rookeries to feed on dead fish that the birds accidentally dropped from their nests. In one extreme case of carrion consumption, cottonmouths were seen to devour flattened, road-killed frogs, which the serpents had first pulled free from the pavement.

In contrast to the catholic diet of the adult cottonmouth, that of the juvenile snake probably consists almost entirely of small frogs and perhaps also of lizards, which it attracts to within striking range by an unusual form of deception, termed caudal luring. Lying motionless with its tail elevated an inch or more above its coiled body, the snake slowly undulates the yellow-tipped appendage so that it looks remarkably like a larval insect in motion. The ruse, according to those personally familiar with it, nearly always succeeds. Convinced that the wriggling form represents an easy meal, the hungry frog or lizard darts forward to snap up the quarry, only to find itself in the jaws of the waiting snake. Caudal luring, incidentally, is employed as well by the very young of several other North American pit vipers, including copperheads, rock rattlesnakes, and massasaugas; like the cottonmouth, they are born with a pale green or yellowish tail tip, colors fittingly adapted for caudal luring.

Although the adult cottonmouth may obtain its prey by waiting in ambush for it to move within striking distance, the snake is more likely to prowl through the surrounding habitat as it seeks to flush out its hidden quarry. The method of hunting is determined by the snake's age and the kind of prey involved. Just as this opportunistic serpent employs two different foraging strategies, so also does it engage in two tactics to subdue its prey. In the first approach the victim is released immediately after it has been struck and envenomed, a strategy designed to prevent retaliation by larger prey like squirrels, rats, and adult mice, whose teeth and claws present a serious risk to the predator. Executed in a mere fraction of a second, this tactic eliminates a direct, sustained struggle between the snake and its potentially dangerous quarry. The same precautionary behavior is employed by other pit vipers whose diets also include large rodents.

In most instances, the mortally wounded victim will have scurried some distance out of the snake's line of sight before succumbing to the venom's lethal effects, leaving the predator with the seemingly impossible task of finding a carcass that is no longer in view. The snake manages to solve this dilemma by bringing into play one of its more subliminal talents, chemosensory searching. It begins by accelerating its rate of tongue flicking to increase the chemical reception of its Jacobson's organ. The snake follows the odorous trail left on the ground unwittingly by the escaping prey, tracking the poisoned animal to its final resting place. Thus the more dangerous animals are safely dispatched before the actual swallowing process begins.

Live frogs and fish are handled differently. As a rule, they are not quickly released after the initial bite but are held firmly in the snake's jaws until dead or until their struggles have sufficiently diminished for them to be swallowed, still alive. Considering the highly active nature of such prey and their greater resistance to cottonmouth venom, it stands to reason that if bitten and suddenly released into the water, even after being poisoned, they would have an excellent chance to escape. A good example of this is reported by Burkett, who watched a large leopard frog, struck twice within an hour and a quarter by a feeding cottonmouth, survive for 45 minutes. Consequently, when dealing with cold-blooded prey, the snake's strike-and-hold tactic is not surprising.

In spite of this pit viper's local abundance over much of the southeastern United States, little detailed information was available about its feeding behavior until Savitsky (1992) published the results of her in-depth laboratory experiments with captive specimens of this species. Using a complex testing enclosure to simulate certain natural environmental conditions, she found that although the reptile often included a relatively large number of fish in its natural diet, it was neither particularly skillful in catching such live prey nor always strongly motivated to do so. Results of her observations, summarized below, reveal how the cottonmouth finds, catches, and manipulates piscine prey for swallowing.

The snakes in the study confined their foraging activities primarily to the shallow water along the edge of the pool and to the shoreline immediately adjacent to the water. Rarely did they seek prey in the deeper water. The snake's preference for the land-water interface, which reduces the likelihood that the reptile will encounter the greatest number of live fish, would tend to increase the serpent's chances of coming in contact with a variety of other small vertebrate animals such as frogs, water snakes, and baby turtles, as well as small mammals that come to the water to drink. This parallels the field notes of several zoologists who have observed the cottonmouth, especially at night, lying in the water near the bank of a pond or stream, or coiled onshore near the water, where they apparently foraged for food.

Cottonmouths attempting to locate dead fish by chemical trailing progressed with the head held low and parallel to the ground, but when the same snakes performed a more random search for live prey, the head was raised several inches above the ground and frequently moved from side to side, apparently to scan the area for signs of movement. In most cases the snakes moved forward at a slow steady pace. Despite its otherwise lethargic behavior, the cottonmouth proved unusually alert to any nearby movement, particularly that of jumping or surfacing fish. It reacted to such movement immediately by snapping its head to face the distraction, which it often hastened to investigate. Once there, it occasionally struck at the source of the commotion, although such capricious strikes were sometimes strangely misdirected at nearby inanimate objects, and even at itself. At times, pieces of wood were bitten and held momentarily, suggesting that some of these thrusts were temper-driven and not simply feeding responses.

Approximately 80 percent of all attempts to capture live fish were made from above the water's surface, either at the edge of the shore or in the shallow water close to shore; none was made in deep water. One explanation for the reptile's preference for surface foraging while in the water is the snake's unusual buoyancy, the result of its large functional lung (the other is small and degenerate, as it is in most snakes), which not only extends rearward nearly to the end of the body

cavity but also has a long, vascularized rear portion. Although this morphological adaptation inhibits the snake's diving ability, it no doubt facilitates its surface movement. So well suited is the cottonmouth for floating on top of the water that Savitsky aptly expressed the view that it does not venture into the water, but ventures onto it.

When attacking potentially dangerous fish (those with large, stiff dorsal fins), the cottonmouth avoided the sharp spines by directing its strike at the upper body of its prey, grabbing the victim just behind the head and forward of the dorsal fin. This approach was executed with more care when the target was a very large fish in the water. Then the cottonmouth was even more circumspect, taking additional time to track the prey with its head from above the surface until it was certain of an accurate strike. All live piscine prey were seized and held in the snake's jaws until they succumbed to the venom, and most (more than 70 percent) were taken to dry ground before any attempt was made to ingest them. Neither live nor dead fish were ever swallowed underwater. A more unusual prey-capture technique used by two of the serpents was that of swimming slowly on the surface with the mouth wide open at the waterline, apparently in an effort to scoop up any fish that might be in its path. Neither snake was successful, but such a tactic might prove useful when used in a shallow, drying pool crowded with small or medium-sized fish.

Curiously, seizing dead fish in the water seemed to be more difficult for the cottonmouth than catching live ones. Even when the reptile successfully grasped a dead fish underwater, it often had difficulty maintaining its hold, sometimes losing its prey before reaching the surface. Its success rate with floating dead fish was not much better. The cottonmouth was most successful when taking dead fish from dry sites, particularly those along the narrow strip of land just above the waterline, although the wet stump- and branch-covered area of the enclosure also became a favorite place from which to pick up dead fish, for there the arrangement of the natural wooden objects allowed the snake a reasonable degree of movement as it foraged in the water and prevented the dead fish from floating away.

The final stage of prey handling, that of prey manipulation in preparation for swallowing and the act of ingestion itself, proved somewhat lengthy and involved. The cottonmouth, which lacks the confidence and skill of water snakes of the genus *Nerodia* when they consume fish, seemed almost clumsy in its prey handling efforts. Before seizing the carcass in its jaws, the snake usually nudged the fish with its snout, lightly at first, then more forcefully, although the reason for this prodding is still not clear. During all of this, the serpent's tongue was in constant motion. In many cases picking up the dead fish proved troublesome for the cottonmouth, since the snake often made several attempts before successfully seizing its prey and even then sometimes dropped it again, only to repeat the cycle a second or third time. With the fish held securely in its mouth, the snake, its head raised and its snout pointed skyward, gradually forced the morsel down into its gullet with intermittent sinuous neck movements. All things considered, the cottonmouth's capture and handling of both live and dead fish was less than skillful.

This foraging style is in sharp contrast to the feeding behavior of the diamond-backed water snake, whose underwater agility, efficient prey handling, and greater number of teeth in its upper jaw give it a decided underwater foraging advantage.

REPRODUCTION At more northern latitudes (for example, in southern Illinois, where the western cottonmouth reaches the northern limit of its range), the female may bear young only every other year. In the South, where mild winters promote nearly year-round serpent activity, an annual reproductive cycle is the rule. The female is sexually mature at $2\frac{1}{2}$ to 3 years of age, the male after he has reached his second birthday. Mating usually takes place in the spring soon after the snakes leave their winter quarters, but it can occur at any time during the snake's active season, with specific copulation dates reported for January 21, March 10 and 11, August 31, and October 10 and 19. In Florida, mating has been observed in every month except January. Despite the wide range of mating dates, the young are ordinarily born in August or September, following an approximate 160 to 170 days of gestation, for the females of this species apparently retain viable sperm in their oviducts for extended periods, with ovulation occurring in spring or early summer. The number of young in a litter varies from 1 to 16; the newborn snakes average about $10\frac{1}{2}$ inches (26.7 cm) long.

Combat between male cottonmouths has been documented a number of times, just as it has been between the males of certain other North American pit viper species. Such stereotyped behavior has been reported for a variety of snakes belonging to several families worldwide, all of which display the same basic components in their male-to-male combat rituals, yet there are some marked differences in these rituals among the various genera and species. Pit vipers in particular are known to engage in the most spectacular contests. During the peak of their encounters they intertwine their trunks and vertically raise a third or more of their forebodies off the substrate as each opponent tries to gain a postural advantage that will allow him to pin his adversary's head to the ground. Once this is accomplished, the loser leaves the scene as quickly as possible. These strenuous physical encounters are not merely idle sparring matches between adult males; they are distinctive confrontations usually provoked by the presence of a receptive female or, at least in captivity, by the introduction of food into the snakes' enclosure. See also the western diamond-backed rattlesnake account.

VENOM AND BITE According to Parrish (1964), whose study provides the most recent survey of statewide snakebite statistics, only 7 percent of Texas' 461 hospitalizations for snake envenomation during 1958 and 1959 were caused by cottonmouths, despite the serpent's local abundance in many parts of southeastern Texas. The nationwide rate of approximately 10 percent was not much higher. Such a low incidence is not surprising, considering the snake's normally unaggressive behavior. Although very young cottonmouths often are quick to strike when approached, most adults of this subspecies we encountered in the field either tried to escape or simply pulled back their heads in a defensive stance without taking any aggressive action. Not only is the bite rate from this snake relatively low, but hospital records also show that few humans die from cottonmouth envenomation. Scarcely one human fatality a year can be attributed to this species nationwide.

Although not as lethally toxic as the venoms of most rattlesnake species, cottonmouth venom causes considerable local hemorrhaging, rupturing small blood vessels and allowing the blood to seep into the surrounding tissues, resulting in dark discoloration of the bite area and the oozing of bloody fluids from the injection site. Since the venom literally dissolves the affected tissues, the area at the site of the bite can become gangrenous, and in severe cases may even liquefy, complicating an already serious medical emergency. As evidence of the deleterious effects of cottonmouth venom, Allen and Swindell (1948) reported that in Florida approximately half of all bite victims suffered

gangrene-crippled fingers or toes. In spite of the high incidence of tissue necrosis in such cases, Findlay Russell, one of the country's leading snakebite practitioners, believes this condition can be largely prevented by the prompt intravenous injection (by a physician) of adequate amounts of antivenin. Sherman A. Minton (pers. com.), another of the nation's eminent snakebite experts, takes a different view. Based on the results of animal experiments he conducted in the laboratory, together with clinical evidence, he found antivenin to be of little value in preventing necrosis from pit viper venoms. Other symptoms of cottonmouth envenomation may include pain in the bite area, swelling, weakness, giddiness, rapid or reduced pulse, drop in blood pressure, some breathing difficulty, and nausea and vomiting.

WESTERN DIAMOND-BACKED RATTLESNAKE
Crotalus atrox
PLATES 181–185

DESCRIPTION Though showing considerable color diversity, ranging from chalky gray to dull red, this species is most easily recognized by its prominent black-and-white-banded tail, whose two differently colored rings are of nearly equal width (a, p. 376). The body, normally light brown, gray, or gray-brown, carries a row of dark, diamond markings down the middle of its back, each one edged first with black, then white. This pattern is not always conspicuous, since it may be obscured by the minute flecks and dots, both light and dark, that liberally cover the snake's body and give it an overall dusty appearance. In some specimens, particularly those from the Rio Grande Valley, the black diamonds contrast sharply with the yellowish ground color to create a bold, clearly defined pattern, whereas diamond-backed rattlesnakes from extreme southwestern Texas may be pinkish, with indistinct diamonds.

The lateral head markings of this species are also definitive. They consist of two parallel pale stripes on each side of the face, one of which passes diagonally downward from in front of the eye to the middle of the upper lip. The other extends from behind the eye to a

point just preceding the end of the mouthline (a, p. 376). The strongly keeled scales are in 25 or 27 midbody rows, and the anal plate is single.

COMPARABLE SNAKES The snake most likely to be mistaken for *C. atrox* is the Mojave rattler, whose diamondlike dorsal markings are similar to those of the diamond-backed rattlesnake but usually better defined. This species also has a black-and-white-banded tail, but its dark caudal rings are significantly narrower than its pale ones. The pale line extending downward diagonally from behind the eye does not intersect the mouthline but passes above and behind it. In addition, most of the pale scales that margin the dorsal markings are unicolored, and no more than three rows of scales lie between its supraoculars. The massasaugas and prairie rattlesnakes also show some resemblance to the western diamond-backed rattlesnake, but their rounded, nearly uniformly colored dorsal markings are unlike the angular, polychromatic diamonds of *C. atrox*, nor do they display the diamondback's boldly ringed, black-and-white-banded tail. The series of large plates on top of the massasauga's head

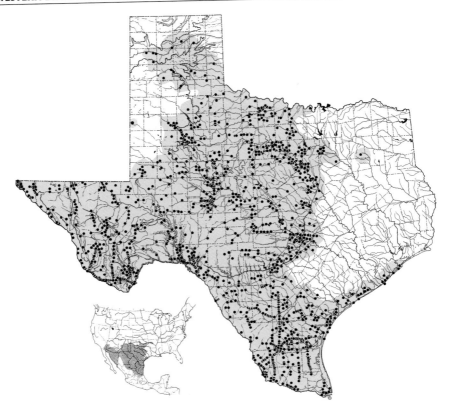

differs from the mostly small scales that cover the diamondback's crown. The black-tailed rattlesnake is uniquely marked with a combination of an all-black forecrown and a uniformly black tail (indistinctly banded in juveniles). The harmless bull snake may not precisely resemble the western diamond-backed rattlesnake, but the two snakes share enough physical features to cause them to be confused with one another. Moreover, both species respond in a similar way when threatened. See the bull snake account.

SIZE Among U.S. serpents, the western diamond-backed rattlesnake is exceeded in size only by the slightly heavier and longer eastern diamond-backed rattlesnake, *Crotalus adamanteus*, which inhabits the coastal lowlands of the southeastern states. On average, adult western diamond-backed rattlesnakes are between 3 and 4 feet (91.4–121.9 cm) long.

Historically, the largest *C. atrox* have come from Hidalgo and Starr counties in the lower Rio Grande Valley. Before the 1960s, speci-

mens 6 feet (182.9 cm) long were captured there by collectors for the Brownsville-based reptile dealer known as the Snake King, who shipped them for public display to zoos and circuses throughout the country. Having viewed several such giants closeup, we can attest to the sense of awe they inspire. Equipped with exceptionally long fangs, a large venom supply, and the body length to deliver a far-reaching strike, these brutes clearly convey their frightful ability to deliver a lethal blow. Such large rattlesnakes are seldom encountered today. The few that undoubtedly still survive in South Texas are probably confined to the handful of remote areas not yet severely altered by human hands. Although diamond-backed rattlesnakes of even greater size have been reported, there is no satisfactory documentation to establish the maximum length achieved by this species. One reason is that exceptionally large rattlers seldom find their way into scientific collections, where their size can later be verified by a tape measure. Instead, most presumably

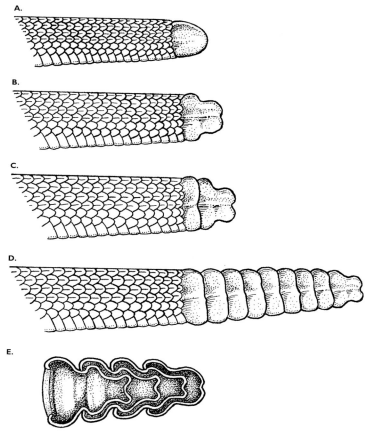

Figure 66. *Stages in the growth of the rattle: (a) the prebutton, which is shed along with the infant's first molt, (b) the button, which is the first permanent rattle segment, (c) the second functional segment, and (d) a mature string of nine segments. (e) Cross section of the loosely interconnected rattle segments.*

near-record or record individuals, if they are preserved at all, become tanned skins or mounted specimens whose true length can easily be stretched by as much as 35 percent in the tanning or mounting process. The most generally accepted maximum recorded length for this species is an imposing 7 feet 4 inches (223.5 cm).

THE RATTLE Representing one of nature's most unusual animal noise-making devices, the unique appendage we call the rattle consists of loosely connected, interlocking hollow parts called segments, which click against one another whenever the tail is vibrated. The term "rattle" more properly applies to the sum of the appendage's parts.

Composed of a horny material known as keratin (essentially the same substance that forms animal hair and nails), the rattle itself is actually quite lifeless, containing neither blood vessels nor nerve endings. Therefore, when any one part of this appendage is pulled away from another, the snake experiences no pain or discomfort, much like cutting hair or trimming fingernails, neither of which hurts.

Not all rattlesnakes have a functional rattle. The newborn rattler, for example, enters the world with only one segment on the tip of its tail. Called the prebutton, it is present only for a few days after birth and is then discarded with the first shedding of the snake's skin. Thereafter, the prebutton is replaced by the button, the first in a succession of segments that will form the functional rattle. So long as it remains intact, the button always constitutes the outermost end of the rattle. An additional segment is added with each skin shedding, the one most recently acquired making its appearance near the base of the tail and not at the terminal end of the string. It is only when a second segment is added to the button that the rattle acquires its noise-making capability.

Contrary to popular opinion, a rattlesnake does not add one segment to its rattle with each year of age; rather, it does so with each shedding of the skin, which ordinarily occurs three or four times annually. Under the most favorable conditions (when food is plentiful and short winters permit annual cycles of maximum growth), a rattlesnake may shed its skin five or more times a year, adding as many segments annually. It could be assumed then that a five-year-old rattlesnake that has shed five times each year would have developed a prodigiously long rattle string consisting of 25 segments. That is not likely to happen. Such excessively long strings are easily broken, as, for example, when the snake trails its caudal appendage through dense brush or between craggy rocks, where they become entangled and break off. They may likewise be pulled free when caught under one of the snake's own shifting body coils. Thus, most free-roaming rattlesnakes possess only moderate-sized rattle strings of 4 to 7 segments. Klauber (1956) mentions a large, wild-caught western diamond-backed rattlesnake from near Edinburg, Texas, that had 23 segments in its rattle. This, he believed, was a record string at the time, not only for Texas but for the country.

Captive-raised specimens, on the other hand, may grow even longer strings. The longest one known to Klauber, containing 29 segments, belonged to a captive-reared timber rattlesnake kept at the San Diego Zoo, although a prairie rattler with an even longer string was reported recently by Chiszar and Smith (1994). Captured in Weld County, Colorado, in 1985 and maintained at the University of Colorado biology laboratory until its death in 1993, the nearly 3-foot (91 cm) serpent had grown a record rattle string of 38 segments.

Captive-reared specimens are fed more often by their keepers, and they are usually offered food all year long, even in winter, resulting in more frequent skin sheddings and,

consequently, in longer rattle strings. Also, their cages are usually free of objects containing sharp irregularities and protuberances on which the rattle can become caught and break off. Finally, a long-term captive rattlesnake conditioned to cage life generally loses its apprehension. Not easily agitated by movement in such a setting, the snake may seldom sound its rattle, resulting in the retention of all or most of its caudal segments.

A very long rattle (12 or more segments) provides no real benefit to its owner. On the contrary, such a long string makes less noise than one of moderate length, for the longer string, by virtue of its additional length and weight, tends to dampen its own noise-making capacity. In this regard, Klauber expressed the opinion that the most efficient rattle is one bearing 6 to 8 segments.

The sound produced by this unusual device is as foreboding as it is startling. Ask someone who has heard the noise what it sounds like, and he or she will usually reply that it resembles the buzzing of a cicada or cricket, but with a more ominous overtone. Others compare it to the hiss of escaping steam. Whatever the nature of the sound, when made by a large snake, it can sometimes be heard at distances of more than 100 feet (30.5 m), depending of course on such factors as wind velocity and direction, land topography, and the acuity of the listener's hearing.

Not all rattlers will sound off when approached—something to remember when walking in rattlesnake country. A rattlesnake may occasionally refuse to rattle, even when prodded, though without ever making a sound, it may respond to such irritation by suddenly striking out at the source of its annoyance. Then there is the remarkably rare specimen whose entire tail end has been lost through some sort of accident, and with it the potential ever to grow a new rattle, for when the rattle-producing matrix is gone, so too is the snake's ability to form new rattle segments. This can happen when, as has been witnessed by others on several occasions, a hooved animal such as a deer responds to the threat of a nearby rattlesnake by bounding into the air before coming down on the snake with its sharp-edged hooves. Although the snake is sometimes killed in such an attack, it may only be wounded or just lose its tail.

More often, a rattlesnake will lose its noise-making appendage only temporarily. After snagging in a tangle of underbrush and pulling free from the snake's tail, the rattle is lost for only a relatively short time; it eventually grows back, a segment at a time, until it can once again sound its warning.

Why does the snake have a rattle in the first place? The most widely accepted theory holds that the noise of the rattle was developed chiefly to serve as a warning to large animals such as bison, which might otherwise accidentally or with intent trample the relatively defenseless serpent. More recently, Schuett and his coworkers (1984) offered a radically different, though seemingly plausible explanation for the rattle's origin. This appendage, they reasoned, may have evolved originally as a relatively small organ that served only as a caudal lure and was incapable of noise-making. They also suggested that the rattle's jointed form tended to resemble the segmented body of a larval insect, which when moved slowly, in peristaltic fashion, acted as a lure, drawing unsuspecting frogs and lizards to within striking distance of the snake's jaws. They believed, too, that the rattle's hard, lifeless composition protected the snake's tail tip from injury during such caudal attacks. Some infant rattlers do indeed lure small prey with their tail ends, although the western diamond-backed rattlesnake is not one of them. The species that have been observed to do so include the more primitive ones, those whose juvenile forms display sulphur-yellow on the end of the tail and on the adjacent base rattle segment.

HABITAT This snake is by far the most abundant and widespread venomous serpent in Texas. Nevertheless, it avoids the extensive pine and pine-hardwood forests covering the eastern quarter of the state, just as it does most densely wooded habitats within its range, for this is essentially a snake of sparsely vegetated, arid and semiarid terrain. It also occurs more commonly in the lowlands than at higher elevations, although in the moderately elevated hills and plateaus that spread out north and west of Austin, the western diamond-backed rattlesnake is locally plentiful. In some places outside Texas, this species ascends the mountains to considerable heights. Near Otowi, New Mexico,

for example, it is reported to range as high as 7,000 feet (2,134 m); in the Mexican state of San Luis Potosí near Alvarez, specimens have been found at an altitude of 8,000 feet (2,438 m), the greatest elevation at which it is known to occur. In the Chisos Mountains of Texas, on the other hand, the western diamond-backed rattler wanders up the slopes of Green Gulch only to 4,500 feet (1,371 m). Although one was collected on the Marine Ranch in the Eagle Mountains at 5,500 feet (1,672 m), in Texas it probably reaches its maximum elevation (approaching 6,000 feet [1,829 m]) on the slopes and canyons of the Davis Mountains in Jeff Davis County.

Within those limits, it lives in a wide variety of habitats, including desert flats, brush-covered plains, mesquite- and creosote-covered intermesa valleys, rolling hills, cedar-covered mesa tops, thorny thickets, rocky canyons, sandstone outcroppings, river bluffs, rocky mountain foothills, and plant-covered sand dunes, to mention just a few. Despite the snake's propensity for dry habitats, it frequently chooses to live near watercourses and dry arroyos that sometimes contain water. As every West Texas rancher knows, this precocious reptile is frequently seen around abandoned wooden buildings and trash heaps near human habitations.

One of our more familiar Texas stereotypes—the angry rattlesnake coiled defiantly in a prickly pear cactus thicket—is really not that far off the mark, particularly when the setting is the South Texas brush country where the diamond-backed rattlesnake undoubtedly reaches its greatest population density. Here, in the open mesquite-cactus-chaparral environment of the Rio Grande Plain, it is encountered most frequently in or near the impenetrable stands of prickly pear cactus that dot the gently rolling landscape. Since nothing else in this habitat provides the snake as much natural shelter (tree stumps, logs, and large stones are usually scarce or absent), there is a distinct correlation between the two. Several things make the thorny plants good cover for the diamond-backed rattlesnake. One is the variety of small animals that live in the cactus clusters and dig tunnels beneath the plants, thereby creating secure underground retreats for the snakes. The sizable nests of loosely stacked plant debris deposited by packrats near the centers of the prickly pear clumps furnish excellent aboveground shelter as well. Finally, the cactus plants themselves, with their spiny armament and clusters of broad, flat leaf pads, create a dense, thorny fortress that protects the snakes from the sun as well as from a variety of large predators, including man.

Testimony to the snake's abundance in such habitat are the Texas Highway Department signs that until recently were posted at certain roadside rest areas south of Falfurrias on U.S. Highway 281 and below Freer on State Highway 16. In a sober, matter-of-fact warning they read, "Beware of rattlesnakes."

On the low offshore islands where the rattlesnakes take refuge in the cactus and saltgrass that grow behind the sand dunes, they are equally abundant. They are also plentiful in the scrubby vegetation, cactus, and saltgrass clumps on the adjacent mainland, just as they are among the elevated piles of driftwood that line the more isolated beaches from Galveston to Brownsville. Clearly, the diamondback represents one of the most abundant of all Texas snake species.

That it was even more prevalent in years past is amply documented by numerous eyewitness accounts of earlier times, one of which described the killing by a West Texas rancher of 1,200 rattlesnakes on 10,000 acres (4,049 ha) of brushland that was cleared for cattle raising in Shackelford County. Another Texas rancher, engaged in similar work, destroyed 60 rattlers per square mile, and a third reportedly disposed of 77 rattlesnakes per square mile (2.59 km²). No reference about this snake's former abundance is as revealing as the statement by Crimmins (1927) that in the mid-1920s approximately five tons of snakes (mostly *C. atrox*) were purchased by reptile dealers during just one collecting season in South Texas alone.

BEHAVIOR This precocious rattlesnake has variously been called temperamental, short-tempered, aggressive, fearless, excitable, high-strung, brazen, and irascible—terms that accurately describe most individuals of this species. There is no doubt that *C. atrox* is easily provoked, and once provoked, it shows a zeal to protect itself that can justly be characterized as determined and vigorous and, in the extreme, even insolent.

When abruptly encountered in the wild, the diamond-backed rattlesnake can be expected to do one of several things. If not approached too closely, it may simply lie motionless, confident that it will be overlooked. If the snake feels intimidated, it may seek refuge beneath or behind some nearby object, where it remains until no longer threatened. When clearly harassed, its most likely course of action is to throw itself into a defensive posture, its rattle buzzing loudly and its forebody lifted into a tight, lateral S configuration with the rear part of its body arranged in a wide, circular base coil to support the momentum of a strike. It may also flatten the rear third or more of its body against the ground, adding to its already formidable appearance and creating a broader, firmer base from which to strike. The snake maintains this animated position for as long as the threat remains, facing the source of annoyance with its head elevated some 8 inches to more than a foot above the ground for better visibility. At the same time, it slowly backs away, if permitted to do so, while prepared to launch a strike. When it does come, the strike is usually executed with such speed and suddenness that the snake hits its mark, injects its venom, and returns to its original pre-strike position before the victim realizes he has been bitten.

Not every western diamond-backed rattler is so quick-tempered. Most specimens have a disposition that fits the typical species' mold, but some individuals respond quite differently when disturbed. An occasional diamond-backed rattlesnake is encountered that reacts to such an annoyance in a completely noncombative way. Instead of assuming the usual stand-and-fight position when confronted, it simply tries to escape by crawling rapidly away from its tormentor, never stopping long enough to initiate a strike and in some cases not even bothering to sound its rattle.

The snake's striking distance is generally considered to be one-third to one-half its own body length. Under certain circumstances, such as when the reptile strikes from a downhill slope, this distance can be substantially increased, just as it can if the snake, backed

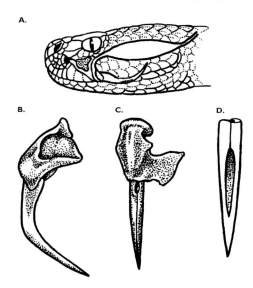

Figure 67. *The rattlesnake fang: (a) size and position of the venom gland, duct, and fang inside the rattler's head; the fang and its attachment to the short, movable maxillary bone seen from (b) the side and (c) the front; and (d) the slotted opening near the end of the fang through which the venom is delivered. (After Klauber 1956.)*

against a solid object, gains added momentum by virtue of such bracing. Then the span of its strike may even exceed the rattler's full length.

Completed in a fraction of a second, the strike is the result of the sudden straightening of the S-shaped forebody loop, propelling the serpent's head swiftly toward its target. Before the head reaches its objective, the mouth opens widely, the fangs rotate downward from the roof of the mouth, and just before hitting their mark are directed forward in a nearly horizontal plane. At the moment of impact, the venom, if it is indeed delivered (in an estimated 15 to 20 percent or more of native pit viper bites the snake injects no venom at all), is forced from the venom glands, through the fleshy ducts that connect them to the base of the fangs, then through each fang's hollow core into the victim, similar to the injection of liquid medicine via a syringe and hypodermic needle. During all of this, the snake's rattle is generally in motion.

Rattlesnakes can both climb and swim. Western diamond-backed rattlesnakes have been discovered in mesquite trees as high as

5 feet above the ground, and small specimens are occasionally found crawling over the tops of prickly pear clumps. Climbing is not typical behavior for such a heavy-bodied snake, yet at times it is forced to do so. Following the severe hurricanes that occasionally churn inland along the coast, many *C. atrox* climb out of the floodwaters to rest on tree limbs 6 or more feet above the ground, sometimes remaining there for several days until the water has receded. Under more normal circumstances the diamondback can occasionally be seen swimming in the coastal bays, often far from the nearest land. Davenport (1943), in an unconfirmed report, claims that one was observed out in the Gulf of Mexico 15 miles (24.2 km) from shore. The report, if true, can perhaps best be explained by the possibility that the snake was washed out to sea by a storm, carried there on a floating log or tree limb.

In Oklahoma, Landreth (1973) found the adult western diamond-backed rattlesnake's midsummer activity to be restricted chiefly to the cooler late-night hours centered around midnight, for daytime temperatures at that time of year are usually much too hot for the snake's comfort. Such late-night summer forays are even more mandatory for *C. atrox* living in South Texas; at least in July and August, midday temperatures there regularly exceed 90 degrees F and often surpass the 100-degree mark.

Just as it affects the snake's summer cycle of movement, temperature also dictates the serpent's degree of winter inactivity. To survive the cold winters, diamondbacks living in the central and northern parts of their range spend several months of each year in hibernation. Such populations generally use the same rocky hillside dens year after year, typically beginning the journey to their favorite hibernacula sometime in October when the temperature makes its first significant decline of the season. Moving from their summer habitations to the dens (usually a distance of less than a mile but sometimes more than two), the rattlesnakes take a relatively direct route, traveling only in the morning and evening. Once there, the serpents do not immediately retreat into the rock crevices they have traveled so far to find. Instead, during the middle of each day numbers of them coil out on the rock ledges near the den entrance to bask in the warm sun. By late afternoon, when the solar radiation has perceptibly diminished, they leave the open areas and crawl into the den openings to avoid the approaching chill of night. So long as the daytime temperatures remain comfortable, the cycle of alternate basking and refuge-seeking continues for the next couple of weeks until, as the days become progressively cooler, the snakes finally retire to the inner recesses of their hibernacula. They remain there until spring or until an unusual warm spell brings them to the surface for a brief period of sun bathing. Unlike Landreth's Oklahoma diamond-backed rattlesnakes, which invariably spent most of the winter in hibernation, in South Texas *C. atrox* moves about on at least some days in every month of the winter season, and during unusually mild winters it may retreat to the relative warmth of mammal burrows only on cold nights.

Although 200 or more western diamond-backed rattlesnakes sometimes occupy a single den, usually fewer than half that number do so. At certain winter dens in undisturbed areas of Texas, the species can still be found in large numbers, although some of the rattlesnake hibernacula made famous by the well-publicized and heavily attended rattlesnake roundups have for some time been decimated by the repeated removal of so many specimens. To perpetuate these commercially lucrative though ecologically harmful events, early in the year roundup supporters capture diamond-backed rattlesnakes in South Texas where they are still plentiful and later release them at the more depauperate northern dens in time for the annual spring hunting spectacles.

Such large aggregations of denning rattlesnakes are rare on the plains and across the gently rolling brush country of South Texas. It is easy to understand why, since rocky hillsides with deep internal crevices are normally absent there. In such places the snakes pass the cold days and nights, individually or in small groups, nestled comfortably in the burrows of small mammals, whose tunnels are often remarkably abundant in this environment. They have also been observed hibernating in holes and cracks near bayside cliffs.

A more unusual coastal hibernaculum, uncovered one fall in Nueces County by construction workers using heavy road-building machinery, consisted of deep earthen cracks produced after a long summer drought shrank the thick, black soil. The resulting fissures created just the right conditions for large groups of wintering diamondbacks. One such den contained more than 100 rattlers, an extraordinarily large number of pit vipers to be found in a single lowland hibernaculum.

Collecting reptiles on Blackjack Peninsula, just north of Rockport, Clay Touchstone (pers. com.) and his companions found 156 *C. atrox* in just three days, all of them as they coiled beside mammal burrows in early spring. The snakes, which apparently had spent the winter in the tunnels, preferred these particular burrows, with entrances situated on spoil banks several hundred feet long. Located near the Gulf Intracoastal Waterway, the mounds of sandy residue left over from past dredging activities in the channel provided the rattlesnakes with ideal winter homes, for they were higher than the surrounding landscape and therefore more secure than the others from winter flooding.

In spring, *C. atrox* follows basically the same pattern of movement as in the fall, but in reverse. It emerges from its winter shelter for short periods, moving progressively farther from its hibernaculum as the days become warmer. When it appears there is no further risk of dangerously cold weather, the snake finally leaves the vicinity of the den and heads for its summer home.

FEEDING This rattlesnake eats chiefly small mammals ranging in size from diminutive shrews and pygmy mice to full-grown wood rats, cottontail rabbits, and rock squirrels, the smaller prey falling victim to the juvenile rattlers and the bigger animals targeted by the larger snakes.

The most comprehensive study ever made of the western diamond-backed rattlesnake's food habits in Texas was conducted by Beavers (1976). Encompassing a broad spectrum of habitats, it revealed that mammals easily represented the major prey category by weight (94.8 percent), as well as by frequency of occurrence (86.7 percent). This matches rather closely the results of a survey made on the Welder Wildlife Refuge near Sinton by

Cottam and his colleagues (1959), in which small mammals constituted 82.36 percent of the snake's diet by volume. In his own study, Beavers found that by weight, wood rats were the serpent's most important single food item, with pocket mice representing a close second choice, although by raw numbers, the pocket mice were the most frequently consumed prey item of all. Pocket mice are among the most abundant of all West Texas rodents, and they occupy many of the same areas of sandy soil and sparse vegetation inhabited by *C. atrox.*

Other mammal prey mentioned by Beavers (and their percentage of the snake's diet by weight) were cottontail rabbits (13.71), plains pocket gophers (9.14), rock squirrels (9.14), hispid cotton rats (7.47), kangaroo rats (6.64), deer mice and white-footed mice (4.21), harvest mice (3.63), Old World rats (3.05), Mexican voles (1.16), and northern pygmy mice (0.49).

In their southeastern Texas study area, Cottom and his coworkers gave a similar picture of the diamond-backed rattlesnake's feeding habits. Although the snake was found to subsist there primarily on small mammals, just as it does everywhere else in its range, at the Welder Wildlife Refuge, a region of abundant vegetation, heavy grass cover, and a high relative humidity, the available prey species varied somewhat from those found in the rattler's drier, more typical haunts. The packrat, the single most important prey item on the snake's game list, represented 17.65 percent of the total food consumed at the refuge, followed by the cotton rat at 16.18 percent. The pocket mouse, which elsewhere was one of the snake's prime foods, constituted only 6.71 percent, and the pygmy mouse another 8.0 percent. Also consumed were a juvenile cottontail rabbit, a young plains pocket gopher, and a marsh rat, each representing just 5.88 percent of the total food eaten; the harvest mouse accounted for only 4.41 percent.

Surveying the diamond-backed rattlesnake's food habits in Mexico's northwestern Chihuahuan Desert, Reynolds and Scott (1982) found that the most abundant rodents in the snake's mesquite-grassland habitat (Merriam's kangaroo rat and deer mouse) were also the mammals most frequently consumed by *C. atrox,* representing, respectively,

18.4 percent and 14.3 percent of the snake's diet by frequency of occurrence. Other mammals devoured by this serpent included the silky pocket mouse (12.2 percent), desert pocket mouse (10.2 percent), spotted ground squirrel (8.2 percent), banner-tailed kangaroo rat (6.1 percent), hispid cotton rat (4.1 percent), desert cottontail rabbit (4.1 percent), rock pocket mouse (4.1 percent), rock squirrel (2.0 percent), and cactus mouse (2.0 percent). Other mammals cited elsewhere as items in the snake's diet include the fox squirrel, swamp rabbit, young jackrabbit, and grasshopper mouse.

Even birds are not safe from diamond-backed rattlesnake predation. Ground-dwelling species such as doves and bobwhite quail probably are those most easily ambushed, though one report of a laughing gull being partially swallowed by a large *C. atrox* is documented by King (1975). Mockingbirds and burrowing owls are also listed as prey. It would seem to us that wading birds, those that regularly nest in great colonies along the Texas coast, may fall victim to the diamond-backed rattlesnake more often than we know. Consider, for example, that in early summer hundreds of them nest together in trees and bushes on our offshore islands, some of the same places inhabited by the diamondback. As a result of the customary quarreling that occurs among the birds in these large rookeries, some of the young inevitably are pushed from the nest and fall to the ground. Unable to get back into the nest, they would become easy targets for the snakes.

Lizards, too, are occasionally consumed by this rattlesnake, but chiefly by the smaller serpents. A list of the lacertilian prey eaten by *C. atrox* includes Texas banded geckos, as well as spiny, race runner, desert side-blotched, earless, and horned lizards. Another species can be added to the list, for some years ago we encountered a 2½-foot western diamond-backed rattler in Starr County in the act of swallowing an adult reticulate collared lizard.

Klauber (1956) also mentions as prey bird eggs, amphibians, and, most surprising, lubber grasshoppers, all of which must be consumed only rarely by this large, essentially mammal-eating snake.

That some prey animals can gradually develop a resistance to their predator's venom is documented in an article by Perez and his colleagues (1978). According to these biologists, the southern plains wood rat, the sigmid cotton rat, and the Mexican ground squirrel all possess antihemorrhagic factors in their blood that endows them with a significant degree of resistance to western diamond-backed rattlesnake venom. As this protection slowly increases over time, so also do the toxic components of the snake's venom, which help to overcome the mammal's new defense. Like the swing of a pendulum, the critical advantage gradually shifts from one contender to the other, although it is unlikely that the rodents will ever develop sufficient resistance to the toxins to render them completely immune.

Without its remarkably efficient venom delivery system, this robust snake would have little chance to catch and subdue its active prey. Fast-moving serpents like coachwhips, racers, and patch-nosed snakes actively search for their quarry and, when necessary, overtake it by pursuit; the heavy-bodied diamond-backed rattlesnake usually employs a passive hunting strategy. Coiled beside a trail, under a bush, or near a clump of cactus, it patiently waits for its victim to pass within striking range. This is not its only hunting tactic. Like most rattlers, it occasionally employs a leisurely foraging mode, roaming an area and probing into burrows, crevices, and trash piles likely to harbor concealed prey.

It is not always the most abundant local animal that constitutes the greatest portion of the snake's diet. First of all, some prey species in the area may occupy a different microenvironment from the snake, effectively limiting physical contact between the two. Even when they live side by side, one may be active as the other remains in seclusion (day-active versus night-active), and because of its superior tactical behavior, one prey species may be more elusive than another and thus better able to avoid capture.

After being poisoned, the prey ordinarily travels only a short distance before succumbing to the lethal effects of the serpent's venom. The snake uses its tongue and Jacobson's organ to track the prey to its final resting place. In trial feeding encounters, for example, an average time of three minutes elapsed from the moment a diamond-backed rattlesnake struck a mouse to the time the victim was completely immobilized. During this period, the envenomed rodent typically traveled more than 6 feet before the venom stopped it.

Not only is prey selection a matter of species availability, but it is also influenced by quarry size in relation to predator size. Although Cottam and his colleagues saw rattlesnakes kill prey that was too large for them to swallow, others, including Reynolds and Scott, demonstrated that such attacks are unusual. This was based on food studies of wild-caught snakes and on behavioral experiments with captive specimens. Using captive individuals of several rattlesnake species, Reynolds and Scott tested the response of their serpents to variously sized mammals. The results showed that individual snakes did, indeed, select prey according to size. It seems obvious that small snakes, because of their small heads and slender body girth, are clearly limited to small food items. The larger rattlesnakes, although capable of swallowing both large and small prey, ignored the smaller animals and killed only those of moderate size. This was verified in the biologists' survey of the food habits of wild-caught specimens. Their field studies showed that when a wild-caught rattler attained a head length of 30 mm, it was large enough to swallow adult Merriam's kangaroo rats and deer mice, the most abundant mammal species in the area. Rattlesnakes with a head length shorter than this devoured mostly the smaller silky pocket mice.

They also found that the snakes avoided large mammals placed with them in the test arena and that the serpents made every effort to stay as far from the rodents as possible. In one case, a Mojave rattler used as a test predator tried to stay away from a rock squirrel placed with it in the arena but was unable to do so. Finally, after the squirrel walked on it several times, the snake struck and incapacitated the fearless mammal. Even then, the snake carefully maintained a maximum distance from its bothersome companion. Another snake showed a similar lack of interest when confronted by a large white-throated wood rat, although in this case the rodent had chewed off and eaten a significant portion of the reptile's tail before the experiment ended. Not once during the test did the snake strike at the offending rodent. The point is that a rattlesnake looking for food carefully selects its prey size, normally choosing an animal of moderate dimensions in relation to its own size. Animals too small to be worth the snake's expenditure of energy are ignored, and relatively large individuals are carefully avoided as too dangerous to handle and (perhaps equally important) too big to swallow.

REPRODUCTION In common with certain other serpents that occupy a rather extensive north-south geographic range, the western diamond-backed rattlesnake mates either every year or biennially, depending on latitude. We find that *C. atrox* from the Texas Panhandle, where long and severe winters are the rule, typically breed only every other year; those living in the warmer southern half of the state produce litters annually.

The female diamond-backed rattlesnake is sexually mature when she is about three years old and approximately 3 feet long (91.4 cm). Although mating normally occurs from March through May, soon after the snakes leave their winter quarters, it is also reported to have taken place as early in the year as January and as late as October 19. The young are usually born sometime in late summer or early fall, though birth dates reported by various herpetologists ranged from June (in the southern part of the snake's range) to October. Nine to 13 inches (22.9–33 cm) long at birth, the newborn serpents number 4 to 25 per litter.

Like the adult males of certain other snakes, those of *C. atrox* often engage in vigorous springtime skirmishes, usually sex-related, by which one of the combatants asserts his dominance over the other without either of them incurring any risk of serious bodily injury. Evidence shows that this generally takes place when a female is nearby. Because of the diamond-backed rattlesnake's large size and the considerable height to which it can raise its forebody during these encounters, male combat in this species is an especially dramatic affair. Such a contest, termed a combat dance, is more akin to a wrestling match than to a bloody brawl, for

throughout the intense struggle no permanent damage is suffered by either contestant (beyond perhaps wounded pride).

During the first few minutes of contact, there is usually a series of sparring maneuvers as each snake tries to gain a height advantage by elevating his head above that of the opponent. Once they have lifted their bodies, the two push firmly against one another and twist their necks together in a kind of abbreviated corkscrew spiral. Such behavior may go on for some time. At the peak of the encounter they elevate their forebodies as high as possible (often equal to a third or more of the snake's total length), arch their raised bodies slightly backward, and push firmly against each other, belly to belly. They now face one another, their heads angled upward at about a 45-degree angle. During the brief time they maintain this posture, the only visible movement is a concordant side-to-side swaying as each snake tries to establish a strategic position. Once a snake succeeds in twisting his head and neck around the nape of his opponent (an advantage giving him the required leverage), he either tries to force the other to the substrate or, with a sudden lateral or downward lashing movement of his forebody too quick and subtle for the human eye to follow, forcefully throws his rival to the ground. The impact of such a fall is sometimes so violent that it results in a loud thud audible several feet away, yet the overpowered snake apparently suffers no injury.

Chances are that before the dance is over, this fantastic scenario will be repeated a number of times, until, finally tiring of the abuse being inflicted on him by his more successful rival, the loser gives up the fight and quickly leaves the arena of contention.

VENOM AND BITE Most of the more than 1,400 estimated (Parrish 1964) venomous snakebites inflicted each year on Texas residents are caused by this species, as are the majority of serious envenomations and most of the fatalities. Several factors, among them a great striking distance, long fangs, and a large venom capacity, account for the negative impact this snake has made on the state's human population. Other elements contributing to the diamondback's ranking as the most dangerous of all Texas serpents

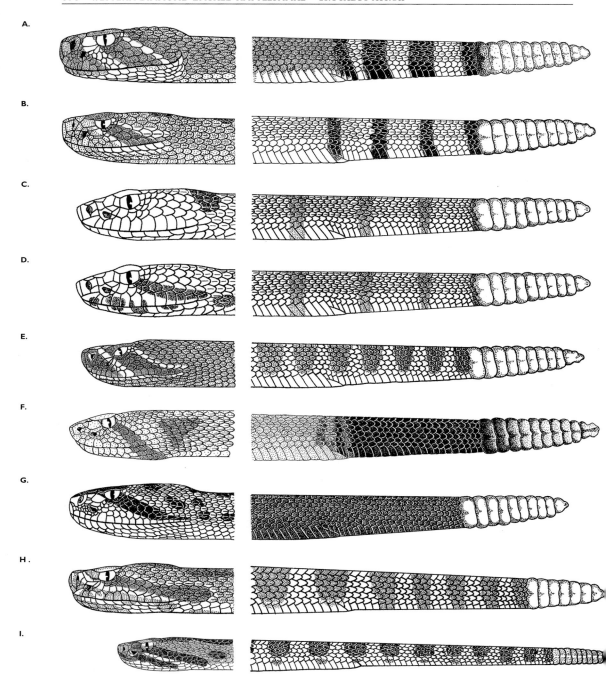

Figure 68. *Lateral head and tail markings of Texas rattlesnakes. (a) Western diamond-backed rattlesnake* (Crotalus atrox). *Pale diagonal stripe behind eye intersects mouthline. Dark tail rings are as wide as the intervening pale spaces. (b) Mojave rattlesnake* (Crotalus scutulatus scutulatus). *Pale diagonal stripe behind eye fails to intersect mouthline. Dark tail rings are narrower than pale interspaces. (c) Banded rock rattlesnake* (Crotalus lepidus klauberi). *Usually no dark diagonal stripe behind eye; normally one or two large, dark spots on back of head. Dark tail rings are much narrower than pale interspaces. (d) Mottled rock rattlesnake* (Crotalus lepidus lepidus). *Dark diagonal stripe behind eye usually present; generally no dark spots on back*

include the snake's continued abundance over much of its present range and its inclination to defend itself vigorously when disturbed. In spite of its ability to injure or kill a human victim, the western diamond-backed rattlesnake, like all other snakes, venomous or not, prefers to avoid confrontation with man.

Its venom is not as lethally toxic as that of the rock rattlers, prairie rattlesnake, Mojave rattlesnake, or coral snake, although it stores a much greater quantity of the toxic substance in its venom glands than do any of the others. Using a variety of extraction methods, from manually squeezing the glands to stimulating them electrically, the maximum yield per adult is reported to range from 600 mg to 1,145 mg of dried weight, the larger amount having been removed from a specimen measuring 5 feet 4 inches (163 cm) long. Klauber (1956) suggests that under ideal conditions as much as 1,500 mg could be extracted from a large western diamond-backed rattlesnake. He also gives 277 mg as an average extraction for this species.

It seems logical to conclude that because of the greater quantity of venom ordinarily delivered by a large rattlesnake, its bite would produce more serious consequences in a human victim than the smaller dose administered by a shorter rattler, all other factors being equal. This, however, is not always the case.

Theakston and Reid (1978), after hearing of a man seriously poisoned by one of three two-year-old western diamond-backed rattlesnakes he kept as pets, were motivated to investigate how so small a snake could produce such dire medical consequences in a grown human. In assaying the qualitative chemical changes in the venom of these specimens

over time, the researchers demonstrated that the lethal toxicity of their venom was actually greatest when the specimens were only 2 months old, declining gradually until it leveled off after the snakes reached 13 months of age. A similar result, incidentally, was noted by Minton (1957), who tested the virulence of a single western diamond-backed rattlesnake's venom over a span of 19 years and concluded that its lethal toxicity decreased by 2.4 times during this period. Theakston and Reid also found that the venom of very young *C. atrox*, because of its defibrinating action, can cause serious internal bleeding in a human victim. As a result, they strongly urge clinicians to monitor carefully the blood-clotting quality of patients bitten by such a snake, since nonclotting blood in this case is a good indication that the offending rattlesnake is less than a year old and, more important, that the victim probably has been injected with a potentially fatal or near-fatal amount of venom. Minton and Weinstein (1986) likewise found a clear disparity between the lethal toxicity of juvenile western diamond-backed rattlesnake venom and that of the adults. Two specimens they examined from North Texas, each less than a year old, had venom 6.6 times as toxic as that of adults from the same area. Variability in venom lethality was also evident among adult snake populations throughout the species' range; the most toxic samples were found in adult diamond-backed rattlesnakes collected in the Big Bend region of Texas, especially those from the base of the Rosillos Mountains.

In a typical case of poisoning by this species, the victim experiences a variety of signs and symptoms, some of which appear immediately, others much later. The first to be

---

of head. Dark tail rings are much narrower than pale interspaces. (e) Prairie rattlesnake (Crotalus viridis viridis). *Pale diagonal stripe behind eye passes above end of mouthline. Dark tail bands are irregular in outline, often narrow. (f) Canebrake rattlesnake* (Crotalus horridus atricaudatus). *Dark diagonal stripe behind eye broadly intersects and sometimes crosses the end of mouthline. Tail and posterior end of body are black. (g) Northern black-tailed rattlesnake* (Crotalus molossus molossus). *Dark diagonal stripe behind eye intersects end of mouthline. Tail is black. (h) Massasauga, western* (Sistrurus catenatus tergeminus) *and desert* (Sistrurus catenatus edwardsi). *Dark diagonal stripe behind eye extends backward onto end of jaw. Dark tail blotches may form rings near rattle. (i) Western pygmy rattlesnake* (Sistrurus miliarius streckeri). *Dark diagonal stripe behind eye extends backward onto end of jaw, and usually a narrower dark stripe, paralleling the first, extends onto the lower jaw; upper half of eye is pale, lower part dark. Tail is relatively slender for a rattlesnake, blotched and ending in a small rattle.*

noted is pain in the bite area, usually intense. Occasionally pain is absent. More often, a serious case of envenomation produces agonizing pain, which begins at the site of the bite and over several hours gradually follows the course of the swelling. Swelling usually appears within 10 or 15 minutes and progresses along the bitten limb, toward the body. The more venom injected, the more severe the swelling. In particularly serious cases, swelling may even reach the body cavity, and the lymph nodes nearest the bite area may become tender and painful to the touch. A bruiselike discoloration also appears at the site of the bite soon after the venom enters the tissues; it ultimately may involve the entire bitten limb. In most instances the pulse rate increases (sometimes doubling), blood pressure drops, and frequently the victim experiences weakness, sweating, faintness, and dizziness. He or she may also suffer nausea and vomiting.

Death, if it occurs, is preceded by the following scenario, as described by Russell (1980): hemoglobin drops during the first 6 to 72 hours after the bite; abdominal bleeding occurs, as well as hemorrhaging in the heart, lungs, kidneys, adrenals, and perhaps also in the brain. Finally, the victim succumbs to acute pulmonary edema. It should be mentioned that unlike the dramatic, sudden-death snakebite episodes usually depicted in motion pictures and on television, human fatalities from pit viper envenomation generally do not occur immediately. They typically take place 6 to 24 hours after the encounter. There are, of course, reports of victims succumbing to western diamond-backed rattlesnake bites in less than an hour, but they are uncommon and often involve small children whose lesser body weight places them at greater risk than adults.

CANEBRAKE RATTLESNAKE
Crotalus horridus atricaudatus
PLATE 186

DESCRIPTION This robust grayish brown, tan, or pinkish gray rattlesnake is marked with jagged-edged, dark brown or black crossbands unevenly margined with lighter pigment. Occasionally some or all of the bands are interrupted on either side of the body, so that each is divided into a large dorsal chevron and two smaller lateral markings. Whatever the pattern, the ground color always darkens toward the rear of the body, becoming uniformly black on the tail (f, p. 376). In addition, a dull, reddish brown stripe extends along the spine, at least on the forward part of the body. On either side of the snake's sharply triangular head, a wide dark brown or brownish yellow band extends obliquely across the cheek from the eye to well behind the end of the mouthline (f, p. 376). The strongly keeled dorsal scales occur in 23 or 25 rows at midbody, and the anal plate is divided. For a description of the rattle, see the western diamond-backed rattlesnake account.

COMPARABLE SNAKES The western diamond-backed rattlesnake, which is unlikely to invade the canebrake's moist woodland habitat, has diamond markings, a light-bordered dark band behind each eye, and a distinctly black-and-white-banded tail. Both the western pygmy rattler and western massasauga can be recognized by the group of large scales and prominent black markings on their crowns, in contrast to the small scales and the absence of markings on top of the canebrake's head. Both possess oval dorsal markings instead of zigzag crossbands, and their tails have dark banding.

SIZE Among Texas rattlesnakes, the canebrake, with a maximum known length of 74½ inches (189.1 cm), ranks second in size only to the western diamond-backed rattler. Adults of this subspecies are generally between 40 and 60 inches (101.6–152.4 cm) long.

HABITAT Primarily a snake of moist lowland forest and hilly woodland near rivers, streams, and lakes, the canebrake ranges across the eastern third of the state from the Red River to the Gulf Coast. Although nowhere abundant, it is evidently as plentiful along the lower reaches of the Trinity,

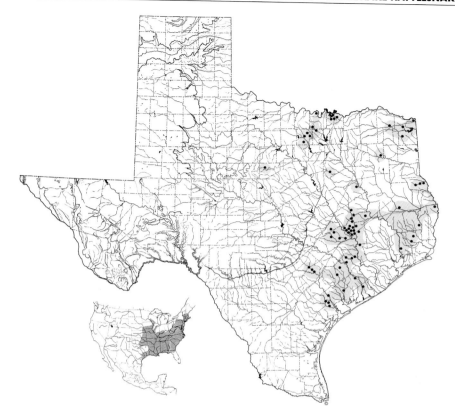

Neches, and Angelina rivers and their numerous tributaries as in any other part of its Texas range. Nearly all of the 35 to 40 canebrake rattlers donated to the Houston Zoo over the last 30 years have come from this region of pine and mixed pine-hardwood forest; most were found less than a mile from some source of permanent water. A number of such specimens came from the river bottoms themselves, others from nearby sandy ridges. According to Gordon Henley (pers. com.), a few were observed in large crevices of sedimentary rock formations that sometimes occur in the otherwise rock-free environment of Angelina County. Canebrake rattlesnakes also inhabit palmetto-covered lowlands and cane thickets, as well as abandoned, brush-covered fields and woodland clearings littered with decaying logs and tree stumps.

According to Cook (1954), Mississippi specimens do not normally occupy dense brush or brier patches, except to escape danger. Instead, they apparently prefer areas in which the undergrowth is thick just above the ground, with relatively open space be-

neath this umbrella of vegetation where they can easily move about. Although seldom encountered in Texas, even by professional herpetologists, the canebrake is sometimes found more frequently in certain other states within the snake's range, such as Louisiana, Mississippi, South Carolina, and the northern part of Florida, especially in ideal coastal habitat. Shevenin (in Klauber 1956), for example, says that in just 15 days, a timber-cutting crew in Louisiana killed 56 canebrakes in a single 40-acre (16.2 ha) stand of forest supporting a heavy undergrowth of palmetto. This may represent the largest number of canebrake rattlesnakes ever found together in so limited an area. During 20 years of fieldwork in extreme southeastern Texas, Ed Guidry (1953), an ardent amateur herpetologist from Port Arthur, observed only two canebrake rattlesnakes.

BEHAVIOR Unlike the excitable diamond-backed rattler, the canebrake is relatively mild-tempered and as a rule not easily aroused. It may simply lie still when approached, hoping to remain undetected, or slowly crawl away in a calculated attempt to avoid a confrontation, its rattle usually silent. A tribute to the snake's unusual tolerance is reported by Dundee and Rossman (1989), who described an encounter with a large specimen that lay coiled among dead leaves near a log and neither rattled nor struck, although two people unwittingly stepped within five inches of the resting serpent. When abruptly alarmed, the snake's tolerance may come to an end, at which time it assumes a defensive stance, its rattle whirring and its head elevated slightly to face the source of its displeasure. If further provoked, it may respond with a swift, sudden strike that is no less effective than the energetic lunge of a western diamond-backed rattler—it just takes the canebrake a little longer to react. Since it is well camouflaged in its woodland environment, generally keeping to the brushy areas of forest usually avoided by man, the canebrake seldom needs to defend itself against a human adversary.

This snake is intimately associated with wet bottomland forests generously littered with hollow logs and decaying tree stumps, both of which it uses as places of shelter. It also hides in the large, ground-level trunk cavities of live and dead standing trees. Near Charleston, South Carolina, Kauffeld (1957) frequently found it snugly coiled in the concave depressions in the tops of large, decaying tree stumps, though the snakes did not occupy just any stump. Those chosen most often had several things in common. First, their decaying, craterlike interiors were deep, held in place by the harder encircling rim of the stump's base, with most of its core previously burned by brush fires. In such bowllike depressions the snakes could easily hide. The preferred stumps were connected to spreading tree roots that decomposed and created a network of tunnels, not only for the snakes but also for some of the small mammals on which they feed. Such tunnel systems were readily accessible through openings inside the hollow stumps.

Spring is the season of greatest activity for the majority of North American serpents, but herpetologists most familiar with the canebrake rattlesnake say it is found abroad chiefly in summer and fall. In neighboring Louisiana, for example, Dundee and Ross-man reported canebrake activity from August to October, with some movement also noted in the spring, as well as in November and December.

Neill (1948) noted that during Georgia's extremely hot and dry late August weather the canebrake rattler meanders toward its winter den, typically moving along well-established routes beside thickly wooded streams. According to Neill, so programmed is this rattlesnake to follow its historical trails that the reptile, often at great risk, frequently crosses roads or cleared land where at one time there was only pristine woodland. Stoically keeping to the same path traveled by its ancestors, it may even cross sizable bodies of water or traverse areas of working farmland and occupied housing developments to reach its ancestral hibernaculum. One such trail wound through pine scrub habitat at the edge of Augusta's city limits, a route probably used by the snakes of the area long before the birth of that now busy metropolis. The place where a migratory trail cuts across a man-made impediment is known to the locals as a rattlesnake crossing. It is here, in early fall, that canebrakes are often discovered and killed by area residents.

Sometimes many trails lead to a single cluster of hibernacula. Neill found such a winter gathering place in southern Richmond County, Georgia. From numerous field observations and local inquiries he determined that dozens of the rattlesnakes converged each fall on a particular cluster of limestone caves in the Savannah River swamps, making their way to the site from many miles around.

Hibernating canebrakes do not always gather in such large groups. Small aggregations of this subspecies sometimes occur, and the more usual winter den contains only a few snakes. Along the coastal lowlands where deep rock formations are absent, the serpents are inclined to hibernate singly or in small groups, often in decaying logs or tree stumps, or in the root systems of large, dead trees whose channels of decomposed wood, made even larger by the activities of small digging mammals, provide adequate spaces in which the snakes can escape the cold. Some canebrakes also find winter refuge in the burrows of small mammals.

FEEDING The snake's diet consists mostly of small mammals such as rabbits, squirrels, chipmunks, gophers, rats, and mice, but occasionally also includes ground-nesting birds. Juvenile canebrakes eat small mammals of appropriate size, including the young of some of the same species taken by the adults, and they are also reported to eat lizards and field sparrows as well as frogs and toads.

In a three-year study of the timber rattler's feeding habits, conducted in Berks County, Pennsylvania, Reinert and his colleagues (1984) discovered several previously unreported details of the species' basic foraging tactics. A central fact to emerge from the study was that the reptile's hunting strategy is intimately associated with fallen logs. Since canebrake and timber rattlesnakes are closely related (some herpetologists consider them taxonomically inseparable), and because both snakes are woodland dwellers occupying areas replete with fallen timber, it seems likely that they use the same feeding strategy when foraging for prey. Beyer (1898), writing about the canebrake rattlesnake in Louisiana, was the first to mention the snake's tendency to coil next to fallen logs, though he apparently did not understand the feeding significance of such behavior.

The snake begins its ambush preparations by searching for a suitable log, one used regularly by small mammals as an elevated pathway. Apparently it finds the right one by flicking its tongue along the top and sides of the

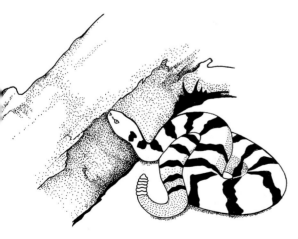

Figure 69. *Timber rattlesnake in typical ambush hunting position along a fallen log.*

log to detect the odor of any prey species that may have recently crossed over it. If for some reason the snake is not satisfied with one particular log, it may continue directly on to another, passing others in between that it decides will not be productive. When the choice is finally made, the snake coils beside the fallen tree trunk with its head held perpendicular to the log's long axis, and sometimes even with the underside of its head, neck, and part of its forebody elevated and resting against the side of the log. Then it settles down to wait for a passing morsel. According to Reinert and his associates, the snake maintains this position at the same spot for an average of 7.3 hours, usually between 9 PM and 8 the next morning. This feeding behavior is in sharp contrast to the foraging pattern of the more active prairie rattlesnake, which is apt to move about between intervals of motionless waiting and seldom remains stationary for such extended periods. The use of fallen logs as a veritable highway by certain small mammals traveling in wooded areas is documented by Douglass and Reinert (1982), who found that approximately 75 percent of 225 logs randomly sampled in the study area were used as a pathway by such animals. Some other prey species such as rabbits, which ordinarily do not use log runways, are probably captured as they move along the forest floor trails that pass close to the logs.

The advantages of log-ambush hunting are several. In the first place, the snake's physical contact with the fallen tree trunk allows the reptile to detect small disturbances made by the approaching animal as it scurries across the top of the log. Even if it fails to pick up such vibrations, the rattlesnake, with its head resting against the side of the log and perpendicular to its long axis, enjoys a clear vista of the raised pathway just above it. From this position it can easily detect the presence of prey, visually and by means of its heat-sensing facial pits.

Reinert and his coworkers suggest that in its persevering ambush behavior, the camouflaged timber rattlesnake, equipped with special senses of prey detection and a remarkably efficient venom-delivery system, is ideally qualified to capture active, wandering prey. For such a sluggish, heavy-bodied snake, this is a significant accomplishment.

REPRODUCTION Gibbons (1972) found that female canebrake rattlers from near Aiken, South Carolina, gave birth to their first litters at three years of age, and males became sexually mature at age four. He also presented evidence pointing to a biennial cycle of reproduction in South Carolina specimens and suggested that some canebrakes may bear young only every third year. The 7 to 17 young per litter, born from late August through September, are 10 to 16 inches (25.4–40.6 cm) long at birth. They are a slightly faded version of the adult.

VENOM AND BITE Because the canebrake rattlesnake generally lives in areas remote from centers of human population, is not abundant in our state, and is often reluctant to strike at sources of passive annoyance, it is seldom the cause of human envenomation in Texas. Nevertheless, its bite can be deadly. Several fatalities caused by this subspecies have been reported for southeastern Texas, including one documented by Guidry that involved a small child bitten near La Belle in Jefferson County. The snake's danger is in its considerable striking range, its relatively long fangs, and its substantial venom output— Glenn and Straight (1982) obtained 244 mg dry weight from one specimen—to say nothing of the unusually toxic venom of certain populations. There is, of course, a certain degree of variation in the venom toxicity within a given snake population, just as there is in venom obtained from the same snake at different times in its life, although the elevated toxicity measured by Glenn and Straight is not the result of such normal variation.

The venom of juvenile canebrakes, like that of some other pit viper young, can actually be more toxic than that of the adults.

This was discovered in a study by Minton (1967), who tested the venom of several canebrakes from the time they were five days old until they reached a year of age. Although the venom of the five-day-old snakes was not even one-third as potent for mice as that of adults, its toxicity gradually increased until at six months of age it had become nearly three times as potent. When the snakes reached one year of age, their venom toxicity had dropped to 1.8 times that of the adults.

Envenomation by this subspecies produces symptoms generally similar to those observed in many other pit viper bites. The canebrake's strongly hemolytic venom, like that of most rattlesnakes, causes pain, hemorrhaging, swelling, ecchymosis, vesiculations, weakness, faintness or dizziness, weak pulse, nausea, and even paralysis. Signs and symptoms manifested in a patient bitten by one of these snakes were reported by Parrish and Thompson (1958). The victim, a 37-year-old male reptile handler working in a large Florida tourist attraction, was struck at the base of the right index finger by only one fang. Even though the offending snake had been milked of its venom only 24 hours earlier, the man experienced a moderately serious level of poisoning. Within just a few minutes there was a burning pain at the site of the bite and the beginning of local swelling. Thirty minutes later the swelling had reached the back of the hand, and in 24 hours it extended almost to the man's shoulder. Other symptoms included cold and clammy skin, facial numbness, and a blood pressure reading of 100 systolic and 76 diastolic; four days after entering the hospital the patient was discharged and suffered no further complications.

MOTTLED ROCK RATTLESNAKE
Crotalus lepidus lepidus
PLATES 187–190

DESCRIPTION This small montane pit viper occurs in a variety of background colors ranging from pale gray to bluish gray, some shade of brown or tan, or even pinkish; the dorsal pattern consists of widely separated narrow, dark, serrated crossbands, which on the fore-

body are often indistinct and blotch-shaped. As the result of small, dark spots and blotches scattered between the crossbands, most specimens have a speckled or dusty appearance, and in some snakes such ancillary markings unite to form smaller, secondary

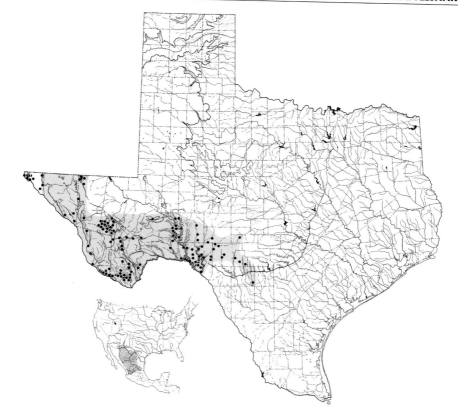

crossbars between the primary series. Widely spaced narrow dark bands cross the tail (d, p. 376). There is usually a dark stripe from each eye to near the end of the mouthline, which is distinct in most snakes, vague or absent in others (d, p. 376). The infants are flecked more heavily with dark spots than the adults, their black crossbands are often indistinct or absent, and their tails are yellowish. The dorsal scales are keeled and in 23 rows at midbody; the anal plate is single. For a description of the rattle, see the western diamond-backed rattlesnake account.

In southwestern Texas, Vincent (1982) identified two distinctly different and geographically separate populations of this subspecies, each displaying its own colors to match the dominant soils and rock formations of its particular habitat. Not only do they occupy different geographic areas, but they are also separated by significant expanses of lowland desert. The easternmost population, occupying the elevated parts of the Edwards and Stockton plateaus where

the limestone rock is predominantly gray and the soils mostly light-colored, consists primarily of matching light gray or bluish gray snakes. In these individuals, the anterior body blotches are mostly faded; some light-toned examples display a nearly chalk-white coloration with scarcely a trace of crossbanding on the forward third of the trunk.

Mottled rock rattlesnakes inhabiting the Davis, Chinati, Sierra Vieja, and Wylie mountains, as well as those living in the upland zones of the Big Bend region, have a strikingly different appearance. Their primary markings are usually more conspicuous and sometimes fairly prominent across the entire length of the snake's body, and in keeping with the dark volcanic soils and rocks that characterize these areas of southwestern Texas, their background colors consist of reddish, pinkish, or buff tones instead of pale gray.

It is not clear what kinds of background colors occur in populations of this subspecies from the Delaware, Guadalupe, Hueco, and

Quitman mountains to the north and west, for adequate specimen samples from these regions are lacking. Consistent with the notion (generally held by zoologists) that narrowly restricted animal populations frequently evolve camouflaging coloration to match the color of their isolated habitats, it is likely that rock rattlesnakes from these mountain ranges, where the substrate is mostly gray, would display a ground color to match. As the result of such natural selection, the serpents' terrain-matching coloration helps to conceal the snakes from detection by predators and also renders them inconspicuous to their color-sensing lizard prey.

COMPARABLE SNAKES No other southwestern Texas rattlesnake species has a dorsal pattern whose primary markings consist of widely spaced, narrow dark crossbands with jagged edges, although the spaces between the bands are often heavily speckled and may even contain smaller secondary bands. This is the only native rattlesnake species in which the preocular scale is vertically divided.

SIZE Although the largest known specimen measured 30½ inches (77.5 cm) long, most adults are less than 2 feet (61 cm) in length.

HABITAT Primarily an inhabitant of craggy ridges, rocky gorges, talus slides, and boulder fields in semiarid to arid environments, this mountain-dwelling rattlesnake usually occurs at elevations ranging from 2,500 feet (762 m) along the eastern portions of its Texas range to 6,800 feet (2,073 m) on Mount Locke in the Davis Mountains and approximately 7,000 feet (2,134 m) in the Chisos Mountains of the Big Bend. Although it normally occupies relatively moist evergreen woodland slopes at higher elevations, it can also be found, often in moderate numbers, along the Pecos and Devil's rivers and their boulder-strewn, tree- and brush-filled tributary canyons, some of the lowest elevations at which it is found. At the eastern end of the snake's geographic range, not far from the small town of Leakey, in Real County, the mottled rock rattler occurs in rugged limestone hills dominated by stands of oak, scrub black walnut, and juniper, along with scattered thickets of mountain laurel and intermittent patches of needle grass. In such habitat, at elevations of 2,500 to 2,750 feet (762–838 m), Theo Tilotte (in Conant 1955) collected as many as 15 specimens in a single summer season. Far-

ther west, in Terrell County, Milstead, Mecham, and McClintock (1950) found mottled rock rattlesnakes in persimmon and shin oak plant associations, mostly along steep rim-rock or at the edges of limestone outcroppings. In the Sierra Vieja mountain range of southwestern Texas, in Presidio County, Jameson and Flury (1949) collected two specimens in the catclaw-grama association and two more in streambeds. Axtell (1959) captured two and saw others in the basalt rubble habitat of the Black Gap area in Brewster County, though none were seen in the nearby limestone formations. According to Michael Forstner (pers. com.), the subspecies prefers habitats in far West Texas that consist of extensive monolithic ledge systems with crevice caves below them, limestone outcroppings containing large fissured areas of rock, and boulder scree slopes.

Beaupre (1995) studied the snake's ecology at two distinctly different sites within Big Bend National Park. The first location, containing a series of limestone gorges emptying into Boquillas Canyon at 1,837 feet (556 m), marked one of the lowest known elevations for this subspecies in Texas. The Grapevine Hills site, at an elevation of 3,398 feet (1,036 m), consisted of an exposed volcanic extrusion associated with several large boulder fields. In spite of similar desert vegetation at both locations (primarily lechuguilla, creosote, and cactus), the Grapevine Hills area contained greater plant cover, experienced more rainfall, and had a lower average monthly air temperature than the Boquillas site. As expected, the background colors of the two snake populations closely matched those of their respective habitats: the Boquillas Canyon serpents possessed an overall gray tone, whereas the Grapevine Hills snakes were rust red.

BEHAVIOR The rock rattlesnake ordinarily is not a pugnacious animal. When first approached, it sometimes remains perfectly still, for it seems to sense that as a result of its camouflaged coloration, it can probably avoid detection by not moving. In Big Bend National Park, Beaupre encountered these cryptic little rattlesnakes most often as they apparently waited in ambush for prey. Such snakes, unless they were touched or prodded, neither rattled nor moved, but some rock rattlers, when threatened by the close approach of man, quickly slipped into the nearest rock shelter.

When midday summer temperatures exceed 85 or 90 degrees F, the rock rattlesnake is seldom encountered in the open. At such times it maintains a comfortable body temperature by crawling beneath rocks and logs, withdrawing into rock crevices, or finding relief in the cool recesses of natural caves. Such resting places are occasionally several feet off the ground: a Real County specimen was discovered as it lay quietly along the 2-foot-high (61.5 cm) lip of a cattle watering trough; another was seen coiled on top of a 4½-foot-high (137 cm) tree stump. Despite the snake's tendency to occupy slightly elevated sites, it apparently seldom climbs into bushes and tree limbs like the larger (sometimes avian-eating) northern black-tailed rattlesnake with which it often shares the same rocky habitat.

Although specimens from the eastern end of the snake's range are generally active in the early morning hours (until 9:30 or 10:00) and again during the hours immediately preceding darkness, populations of this subspecies monitored by Beaupre in Big Bend National Park were encountered during the summer months primarily between 7 AM and 2 PM and again from 6 PM to 11 PM. Of the few rock rattlers he found late at night, most were encountered in August. He also noted an increased capture rate following rains, an extended daily activity period on overcast days, and a decrease in captures during unusually dry years. Several other zoologists have mentioned the snake's predisposition to exit shelters and bask on rocks immediately following summer thunderstorms, even while the rocks are still damp from rains. Often the same rock is used routinely as a basking site, for the reptile's home territory is not extensive compared with that of other larger rattlesnakes, and the probability of finding a suitable perch is perhaps more limited. Beaupre determined that in Big Bend National Park the rock rattler's daily summer movements averaged about 67 feet (20.4 m) a day.

FEEDING Lizards are the snake's chief prey, but small mammals, snakes, and frogs are also eaten by this subspecies. In Terrell County, rock rattlers examined by Milstead and his coworkers contained the following food items: spotted whiptail lizard, eastern tree

lizard, horned lizard, western hook-nosed snake, and cliff frog. In Big Bend National Park, according to Beaupre, the serpent's diet consisted primarily of day-active lizards such as Merriam's canyon lizard, Big Bend tree lizard, southwestern earless lizard, and whiptail lizard, the remains of which were contained in 63.2 percent of the fecal samples he examined. The second most important group of prey species, nocturnal and twilight-active mammals, included kangaroo rats, pocket mice, deer mice, and cotton rats, which were found in 33.3 percent of the sample scats.

Arthropod remains, often contained in the Big Bend fecal samples and once considered secondary prey that were first eaten by lizards, are now known to be normal prey items for this species. That rock rattlers do not regularly include insects in their natural diet is supported by the experience of the late Carl F. Kauffeld (1943). Young rock rattlesnakes he maintained in captivity consistently refused mealworms, small grasshoppers, and earthworms, though they readily consumed juvenile lizards, both alive and dead.

As described by Beaupre, the snake's ambush strategy is to lie motionless on the ground, its body loosely arranged in a widely spaced S coil, with its head angled upward along the side of a rock, across the surface of a boulder, or at a gravel gap in the vegetation. In such surroundings, its color and pattern intimately harmonize with the immediate environment and the rattler is invisible to its potential prey. To render itself even more inconspicuous as it waits for an unsuspecting lizard or mammal to dart within reach of its forward strike or sideways head thrust, the snake often conceals all or part of its body behind a natural corner, in a crevice, or in a fracture of the rocky substrate.

REPRODUCTION Snakes of this subspecies are reported to breed in September or October, followed by the birth of young (2 to 9 per litter) sometime from July through October of the following year. The offspring measure from 6½ to 8½ inches (16.5–21.6 cm) long. In Big Bend National Park, Beaupre found that female rock rattlers inhabiting the Grapevine Hills did not reproduce every year, although one specimen from near Boquillas Canyon gave birth to 3 young in 1991, 3 in 1992, and 4 in 1993. Litter size per female at both places ranged from 2 to 5, averaging 3 or 4.

VENOM AND BITE Although no human death has been attributed to rock rattlesnake venom, several reported bites by this species show that the snake is indeed dangerous to man and probably capable of inflicting a fatal bite. Studies of banded rock rattlesnake venoms from several widely separated points in the snake's range have revealed the presence in some local populations of a dangerous component similar to Mojave toxin (in addition to the hemorrhagic elements found in most rattlesnake venoms) that produces neurological symptoms typically observed in victims of coral snake and some Mojave rattlesnake bites. Although such rock rattlesnakes have a distinct potential to cause a human fa-

tality, the neurotoxic element responsible for their higher lethal toxicity has not yet been found in any Texas populations of *C. lepidus*. Nevertheless, the mottled rock rattlesnake has the capacity to cause serious consequences in man, and a bite from one of these serpents should be treated at a medical facility with the utmost urgency.

In one of the few documented cases of envenomation by this subspecies, A. H. Wright, a renowned herpetologist of his time, reported that after being bitten on the thumb by a specimen he was holding, he experienced considerable swelling of the affected arm, which also affected his lymph glands (Wright and Wright 1957).

BANDED ROCK RATTLESNAKE
Crotalus lepidus klauberi
PLATES 191–193

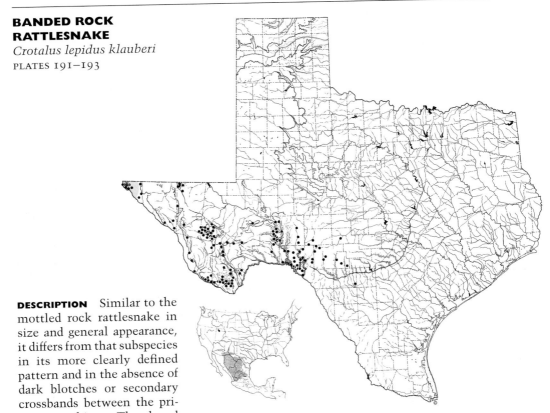

DESCRIPTION Similar to the mottled rock rattlesnake in size and general appearance, it differs from that subspecies in its more clearly defined pattern and in the absence of dark blotches or secondary crossbands between the primary markings. The dorsal crossbands are usually just as distinct on the forebody as they are toward the tail, a large dark nape spot typically marks the back of the crown, and in most specimens there is no dark bar from the eye to the end of the mouthline (c, p. 376). Banded rock rattlesnakes from Arizona generally exhibit a background color

of bluish gray or bluish green, but those from El Paso County, Texas, and adjacent counties of New Mexico represent some of the most stunning examples of this subspecies to be found within the snake's range, their dark dorsal crossbands set boldly against a ground color of tan or light brown. Perhaps even more spectacular are specimens from the Franklin Mountains in Texas, whose jagged, deep black crossbars stand out in vivid contrast to an unblemished dorsal hue of pearl gray. Whatever the background color of such snakes, the dark cheek stripe, usually present in the mottled subspecies, is normally absent or indistinct in the adult banded race; conspicuous only in the infant, it nearly always disappears before the snake reaches maturity. The dorsal scales are keeled and in 23 rows at midbody; the anal plate is single. For a description of the rattle, see the western diamond-backed rattlesnake account.

COMPARABLE SNAKES Among Texas rattlesnakes, only the two subspecies of *C. lepidus* possess widely spaced, narrow dark crossbars along the back and a vertically divided preocular scale on either side of the head.

SIZE Most adults of this moderately small rattlesnake are less than 2 feet (61 cm) long. The largest known specimen measured 32⅝ inches (82.9 cm) in length.

HABITAT This snake ordinarily inhabits fissured rock ledges, rock-strewn canyons, and precipitous talus slides in upland scrub forest or pine-oak woodland at relatively high elevations, preferring open spaces where a gap in the canopy permits sunlight to reach the ground. Elsewhere most banded rock rattlesnake populations inhabit moist forests, but those living in the Franklin Mountains of far West Texas occupy rather sparsely vegetated arid terrain. Although rocks are an essential component of the snake's habitat over most of its range, in Arizona it may be found in grassy meadows some distance from any sizable surface rock formations.

BEHAVIOR Timid and easily alarmed at the approach of man, the banded rock rattler prefers to coil unnoticed in some open, sunlit space until it senses the vibrations of advancing footsteps or detects a threatening movement. At the first sign of danger, it darts for the nearest rock sanctuary, often sounding its rattle along the way. Some observers report that to escape a predator the snake does not always use the nearest refuge but often goes out of its way to reach a familiar sanctuary, one used habitually in time of danger. According to Armstrong and Murphy (1979), several kinds of montane Mexican rattlesnakes they encountered in the field, including examples of this species, often

were so determined to reach their preferred hiding places that they unhesitatingly darted toward the zoologists who stood between them and their familiar shelters.

Another curious aspect of the snake's escape behavior (something observed repeatedly by naturalists) is the reptile's reluctance to crawl any deeper into the rock rubble than the first one or two layers of stone, even though a deeper sanctuary would provide a greater margin of security. Apparently possessed with an innate curiosity, this little rattler nearly always selects the more exposed shelter, frequently the space just under the edge of a solitary large, flat rock or the recess of a horizontal rock crevice from which it can easily observe an approaching intruder. Even when totally concealed beneath such a refuge, the impetuous reptile may betray its presence by rattling whenever the sheltering rock is stepped on or otherwise disturbed. Once silent, only the slightest vibration is necessary to start the snake buzzing again. This was demonstrated in the field by one herpetologist who repeatedly provoked rock rattlesnakes to sound off just by throwing stones at their rocky hiding places.

Depending on elevation, latitude, and the season of the year, rock rattlesnakes are either essentially day-active or nocturnal. Those living in warm desert canyons move about chiefly at night during the summer, whereas rock rattlers occupying the cooler elevations of mountain woodlands probably restrict their midyear activities mostly to the daylight hours. To avoid the oppressively hot midday temperatures of summer, they may come to the surface in mid-morning, retreat into the cool rock rubble during midday, then surface again late in the afternoon. Even during the hottest part of a midsummer day, a light thundershower will usually draw the snakes out of hiding.

FEEDING Lizards, which usually abound in the snake's semiarid habitat, constitute the chief prey of this subspecies; scaly lizards are the most frequently consumed. Small rodents are also considered important items in the serpent's diet, and small snakes and frogs are eaten only occasionally.

The infant snakes are born with the end of the tail a bright yellow; according to Kauffeld (1943), that is probably an adaptation for tail-luring. A captive-born litter of infant banded rock rattlesnakes in his care, although otherwise motionless, slowly waved their elevated yellow-tipped tails in apparent imitation of active insect larvae. From this observation he concluded that the young rattlers manipulate their caudal appendages to lure lizards to within reach of their jaws, as do newborn copperheads and cottonmouths.

REPRODUCTION   In common with many other kinds of snakes, males of this subspecies often engage in ritualized fighting, a behavior performed when two males compete for the attention of a single nearby female. Such an encounter, which never results in serious bodily injury to either contestant, ends when one of the males, usually the smaller of the two, yields to the more forceful actions of the other and promptly slips away. Also see the western diamond-backed rattlesnake account.

Mating in U.S. specimens has been observed in February, June, July, September, and October, with birth of young reported in June, July, and August. Fall matings apparently result in the retention of viable sperm in the female's oviducts until the following spring, at which time ovulation occurs and the eggs are fertilized. The newborn snakes, 2 to 8 per litter, measure 6½ to over 8¾ inches (16.5 – 22.2 cm) long, their sulphur-yellow tail tips becoming progressively darker with each skin shedding, until after about the fourth molt they assume the reddish hue of adult specimens.

VENOM AND BITE   Because this snake occupies rugged and usually inaccessible terrain, visited primarily by naturalists and a few adventurous backpackers, and since it is a timid creature that easily avoids a large intruder such as man, it is infrequently encountered in its mountain habitat and rarely bites humans. Such bites, when they do occur, nearly always happen to amateur or professional herpetologists who are deliberately handling live specimens at the time of the accident. We can find no record of a human fatality resulting from the bite of either this subspecies or the mottled rock rattlesnake, but there is good reason to believe that an accident involving a banded rock rattler could be life-threatening, at least when it involves certain isolated populations within the serpent's geographic range.

Although little is known about the precise biochemical nature of the snake's toxins, studies by Glenn and Straight (1982) reveal that significant variation occurs in the venom's lethal potency among several geographically isolated populations of this wide-ranging species. The biologists discovered, for example, that banded rock rattlesnakes from the Florida Mountains of New Mexico possess venom nearly 9 times more virulent than that of the same subspecies collected in Zacatecas, Mexico. Similar results were obtained by Rael and his coworkers (1992), whose experiments indicated the presence in the more lethal venoms of a neurotoxic component corresponding to the powerful Mojave toxin found in the venoms of some Mojave rattlesnakes. Using mice as laboratory animals, their studies revealed that the venoms of rock rattlesnakes from Chihuahua, Mexico, and some parts of Arizona and New Mexico had 3 to 100 times the lethal toxicity of those from Texas and were on average about 10 times as toxic as that of the western diamond-backed rattler.

Despite the high lethal toxicity of the more virulent venom samples, the individual dry-weight yield extracted mechanically from this species has typically ranged from only 5 to 33 mg. It may be assumed that the relatively small amount of venom ordinarily delivered in a single defensive strike is insufficient to kill a grown human. No doubt the severity of a bite would also be moderated by the smallness of the serpent's fangs, which are too short to penetrate the skin deeply. Scarcely ¼ inch (5 mm) long in the adult, they are clearly better adapted for subduing lizard prey than for inflicting a lethal bite on a large mammal such as man. Among other native pit vipers, only the western pygmy rattlesnake has fangs so small.

Unlike Mojave rattlesnake type A venom, which causes serious neurological consequences in man but creates only minimal hemorrhagic effects, banded rock rattlesnake venom with its Mojave-like component produces both significant neurological symptoms and equally severe hemorrhagic degradation. In at least two well-documented cases of human envenomation by the banded rock rattlesnake, the victims experienced considerable swelling of the bitten extremity and suffered two of the classic neurological symptoms of coral snake poisoning, labored breathing and impaired vision. Bitten on the hand by a banded rock rattler, Robert Hubbard (pers. com.), then a reptile keeper at the Houston Zoological Gardens, was admitted to a local hospital in shock 30 minutes after the bite. His hand and forearm were significantly swollen, and his systolic blood pressure was perilously low (70 mm Hg). He also experienced nausea, chills, vomiting, and severe pain at the bite area, but he eventually recovered. Another case, reported by Klauber (1956), involved an experienced herpetologist

who was struck on the middle finger of his right hand by one fang of a 16-inch-long banded rock rattlesnake. The day after the accident, the swelling extended to the forearm, and the following day it reached the shoulder. A severe and burning pain, which began at the site of the bite on the second day, became nearly unbearable the next day, but then moderated, although five weeks after the accident some swelling persisted, accompanied by numbness and tingling.

NORTHERN BLACK-TAILED RATTLESNAKE
Crotalus molossus molossus
PLATE 194

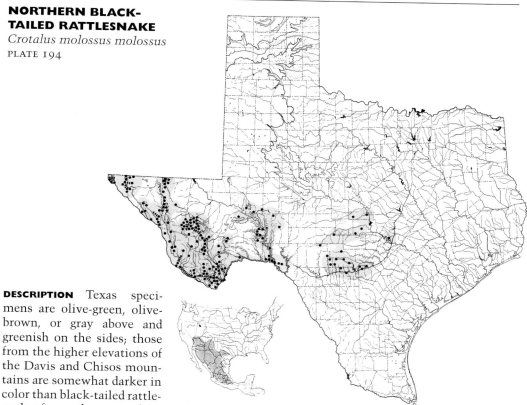

DESCRIPTION Texas specimens are olive-green, olive-brown, or gray above and greenish on the sides; those from the higher elevations of the Davis and Chisos mountains are somewhat darker in color than black-tailed rattlesnakes from other parts of the state. Despite this color variation, the snake can easily be identified by the unique pigmentation of its upper body scales. In the dorsal markings of most other rattlesnakes, two colors often cut randomly across a single scute, producing bicolored scales that are dark on one part and light on the other. In the black-tailed rattlesnake's upper markings, most individual scales are pigmented entirely with a single, solid hue, creating sharply delineated pattern boundaries where rows of

completely pale-colored scales adjoin rows of unicolored dark ones.

Also distinctive is the dark vertebral band on the neck and forebody, which contains numerous prominent, mostly elongate, pale spots of diverse sizes, irregularly spaced down its center. This is followed by a series of jagged, pale-bordered, rhomboid markings, dark brown to nearly black in color, each of which normally contains a small cluster of pale scales on either side of the midline.

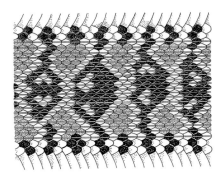

Figure 70. *Body pattern of northern black-tailed rattlesnake, produced by individual unicolored scales.*

Dark vertical bars with uneven edges extend downward from the lateral tips of each blotch nearly to the belly. The blotches, separated dorsally by sizable patches of cream to whitish scales, are most distinct near midbody, becoming narrower posteriorly and gradually more faded. Those close to the tail may be indistinct, resulting in a patternless gray color against which the uniformly black tail stands out in sharp contrast (g, p. 376)—indistinct gray tail bands are visible in juveniles and in some adults.

Also characteristic are the head markings. The dark, reddish brown to blackish coloration on top of the snout and over the forward third of the crown is followed by clusters of dark, generally elongated spots scattered across the light rear part. Conspicuous, too, is a broad, dark brown mask that emanates from the blackish forecrown and runs obliquely downward behind the eye, narrowing gradually to a point near the mouthline (g, p. 376).

Viewed from above, the head is relatively large and rounded at the snout, not sharply arrow-shaped as in the western diamond-backed rattler. The dorsal scales, usually in 27 midbody rows but ranging from 25 to 29, are keeled, and the anal plate is single. For a description of the rattle, see the western diamond-backed rattlesnake account.

COMPARABLE SNAKES Among Texas rattlesnakes, only the black-tailed rattlesnake has the combination of a black forecrown, a dark neck stripe containing patches of pale spots, paired groups of whitish scales in the dark dorsal markings, and a black tail that contrasts sharply against the paler body.

SIZE Although a 52-inch (132.1 cm) black-tailed rattlesnake recently was reported from Kerr County, Texas (Tennant 1984), we believe the most credible record length for Texas is 49½ inches (125.7 cm). A specimen measuring 52²/₅ inches (133.1 cm) in length, collected in Cochise County, Arizona, and reported by Hardy and Greene (1995), represents the longest known specimen for the subspecies. The average adult is between 2½ and 3½ feet (76.2–106.7 cm) long.

HABITAT In Texas the black-tailed rattlesnake inhabits wooded hills and mountains containing myriad rock crevices and stony ridges, although it may sometimes occupy sparsely vegetated low plains and valleys, provided they too possess a rocky substrate. At the eastern end of its range the snake inhabits the rugged central Hill Country, a nearly unbroken continuum of steep-sided sylvan canyons tightly sandwiched between wooded limestone hills and ridges. Here it is moderately abundant, exceeding in numbers its larger cohabiting relative, the formidable western diamond-backed rattlesnake. In such arid habitat, specimens have been taken in Terrell County from thickets of persimmon–shin oak, in stands of cedar-oak, and even in mesquite-creosote flatland; each environment supported sufficient vegetative cover to guarantee the snakes a measure of shade from the hot sun. Not many, however, live in totally open, grassy places. Scattered records show the black-tailed rattlesnake's Texas distribution extending from the Hill Country southwestward to Big Bend National Park, where it is the most common rattlesnake species. In the park itself, it reaches its greatest abundance in the foothills and mountains of the Chisos range at elevations above 4,000 feet (1,219 m), even ascending the slopes of Emory Peak (the area's highest point) to the rock slides at 7,400 feet (2,255 m), barely 145 yards (133 m) from the top. That is not the uppermost limit of its altitudinal distribution in Texas. In the narrow stone canyons and gulches of the Guadalupe Mountains, where it frequents rock slides and dry, rocky streambeds, as well as the leaf-covered floors of pine-oak forest, it makes its way up the mountain slopes to an altitude of at least 8,200 feet (2,499 m).

BEHAVIOR Black-tailed rattlesnakes normally are unaggressive when first confronted by man. There are exceptions, of course, but they are infrequent. The specimen illustrated here seldom ever rattled during handling, nor did it assume a defensive posture even when manipulated with a snake stick to bring it into a natural coiled position to be photographed. Its only assertive response during many hours of being posed was to extend the long, slender tongue downward from the mouth until it was nearly perpendicular to the long axis of the snake's head. In typical black-tailed rattlesnake fashion, the snake then held its tongue motionless for the next 10 to 20 seconds before swinging it slowly up over the snout in a wide, graceful curve until the broadly separated tips barely touched the forecrown. At maximum upward rotation, the tongue ceased nearly all movement, just as it had in the fully extended downward position. After being withdrawn momentarily into the mouth, the tongue abruptly reappeared and the entire cycle was repeated, many times.

Such a display is often continued for as long as the snake feels threatened. At close quarters, this sinister threat-posturing conveys a clear message; it is a tacit warning intended to persuade an enemy to terminate the encounter lest the snake be compelled to strike. Even the boldest adversary senses the menacing implications of the tongue's slow, deliberate movements.

The black-tailed rattlesnake's active season normally extends from early April to at least early November, although during mild winters specimens may be seen occasionally in March and late November as they briefly bask in the warm midday sun. Kauffeld (1943) encountered one out in the open when the ground was still covered with a thin blanket of snow.

Apparently more tolerant of cool temperatures than most other Texas rattlesnakes, this predominantly mountain species seldom moves about during the heat of the day, though it is sometimes active in the early morning and late afternoon, particularly on overcast days. It is also reported to be diurnally active following periods of heavy rainfall. Most of the time, the black-tailed rattlesnake spends its days in a variety of rocky retreats, including the crawl spaces beneath boulders and limestone ledges, or in the endless underground recesses of talus slides and

rock piles, where summertime temperatures are significantly cooler than they are at the surface. In midsummer, such subterranean refuges provide the snakes comfortable sanctuary from the heat of the day, which may also explain why they occasionally inhabit rocky arroyos, particularly after the streambeds have been cooled by runoff from heavy summer showers.

In southeastern Arizona along the foothills of the Tucson Mountains, Beck (1995) tagged three black-tailed rattlesnakes with miniature radio transmitters. His study showed that the serpents occupied an average home range of 8.64 acres (3.5 ha), that they moved approximately 140 feet (43 m) per day during their active season (March 1 to October 15), and that they traveled an average 9.3 miles (15 km) in a single season.

Despite its terrestrial habits, the black-tailed rattlesnake occasionally crawls up into the limbs of bushes and trees, both to bask and to search for nestling birds, an important part of its diet. In Texas, for example, Crimmins (in Klauber 1956) observed a black-tailed rattlesnake perched in a mesquite tree some nine feet (2.7 m) above the ground, and he saw another crawling through the branches of a cedar tree at a similar height.

Near Tucson, Arizona, it seeks winter shelter in the crevices of relatively steep southwest-facing rocky slopes, but elsewhere it also hibernates in caves and mammal burrows.

FEEDING In a field study of the black-tailed rattlesnake's food habits in northeastern Chihuahua, Mexico (a region similar to the snake's southwestern Texas environment), Reynolds and Scott (1982) discovered that fewer kinds of rodents are available to this rattlesnake in its restricted rocky habitat than are ordinarily found in the more diverse environments occupied by the western diamond-backed and Mojave rattlers. They found the black-tailed rattlesnake's most important prey in the study area to be rock pocket mice (25 percent), cactus mice (16.7), and Merriam's kangaroo rats (16.7). Other prey species included wood rats, pocket and deer mice, and a surprisingly large number (16.7 percent) of birds, most of them ground-nesting varieties. The only specific information we can find about this snake's diet in Texas is the report of an Encinal mouse that was taken from the stomach of a Terrell County specimen. Although rodents ordinarily constitute the principal fare of most large rattlesnake species such as this one, juveniles of the same snakes restrict their diets primarily to lizard prey. Lizards are relatively abundant in the arid Southwest, and they are also the right size and shape to be easily swallowed by the young snakes.

REPRODUCTION What little information is recorded about the northern black-tailed rattlesnake's reproductive biology has revealed that this essentially montane species probably mates in the fall, with the sperm maintaining its viability in the female's oviducts until ovulation occurs the following spring, at which time fertilization is achieved. The young snakes, 3 to 16 per litter (average 6 or 7), are born several months later, in July or August. Measuring approximately 9 to 12 inches (22.9–30.5 cm) long at birth, they differ from the adults chiefly in the obscure banding on their black tails.

During the breeding season, the males and females of most snake species remain together only long enough to complete the mating act and then go their separate ways. The following observations, reported by Greene (1990), are therefore somewhat unexpected. After installing miniature radio transmitters in a male and a female black-tailed rattlesnake found together in a wood-rat nest, he monitored the pair. For the next several weeks they were inseparable, basking and traveling together. Only when they entered separate winter dens early in the fall did they part company, leading Greene to suggest that after copulation the male stayed with his mate to prevent her from mating with other males.

VENOM AND BITE Because it is a relatively shy, retiring serpent with a penchant for remote and rugged terrain, the usually mild-mannered black-tailed rattlesnake rarely bites humans. A black-tailed rattlesnake's fangs are proportionately the longest of any native rattlesnake; those of a 4-foot (122 cm) specimen measure more than 1/2 inch (1.3 cm) along the curve, or about the same size as the fangs of a western diamond-backed rattlesnake a foot longer. Add to this the substantial amount of venom that the black-tailed

rattlesnake's sizable venom glands are capable of producing, and it would seem logical to conclude that this is indeed a very dangerous snake. Yet that is not the case. In spite of the high venom yield produced by the adult of this subspecies—calculated by Klauber (1956) to average about 286 mg of dry weight per specimen—the lethal toxicity of the venom when injected into laboratory mice is less than that of most other Texas rattlesnakes, being only 79 percent as potent as the venom of the western diamond-backed rattlesnake. One reason for this is the venom's limited amount of chemical components responsible for severe tissue destruction. Because such components occur in higher percentages in timber, diamond-backed, and prairie rattlesnake venoms, bites from those species ordinarily produce more widespread damage, not only to muscles and subcutaneous tissue but also to various body organs. In recent times, the black-tailed rattlesnake has not caused a single human death, at least in Texas. Not since Amaral (1927) made the first serious effort to study the incidence of venomous snakebite in Texas do we find a documented case of human poisoning caused by this locally abundant pit viper. Russell (1960), on the other hand, reported four cases of black-tailed rattlesnake poisoning that occurred outside Texas, none of which resulted in severe tissue destruction. Hardy et al. (1982) mentioned two instances of envenomation by this snake that did produce intense swelling and ecchymosis of the bitten extremities (perhaps because the rattlesnakes bit with such tenacity that they had to be forcibly removed), but they observed none of the severe tissue necrosis or hemorrhaging into vital organs that would be expected in serious poisoning by certain other Texas pit vipers. In the first case, the victim was bitten at the base of his left index finger by a 21-inch (53.3 cm) specimen, receiving only a single fang puncture; the other patient was bitten on the right wrist by a captive 33-inch (83.8 cm) black-tailed rattlesnake he was holding. Both victims fully recovered, suffering no local tissue destruction, hemorrhaging of blood into vital organs, or loss of limb or digit function.

MOJAVE RATTLESNAKE
*Crotalus scutulatus
scutulatus*
PLATES 195, 196

DESCRIPTION This species shows considerable color variation. Its overall hue may be greenish gray, olive-green, or greenish brown, with diamonds or hexagons down its back, each one circled first with a ring of darker brown scales, then with an outer row of white or cream-colored ones. Every light-colored scale bordering the diamond blotches is garbed in just one color, whereas in most rattlesnakes the same scales often carry two or more colors. Of the two diagonal and parallel white stripes on each side of the snake's head, the rear line begins behind the eye, passing above and beyond the end of the mouthline without intersecting it. The black tail bands are much narrower than the intervening white ones, and except in very young snakes, the bottom half of the base rattle segment is pale yellow and of a lighter hue than the dark brown upper portion (b, p. 376). The presence of only two enlarged scales on top of the head between the large plates over the eyes also characterizes this species. The keeled dorsal scales are in 25 rows at midbody, and the anal plate is single. For a description of the rattle, see the western diamond-backed rattlesnake account.

COMPARABLE SNAKES The western diamond-backed rattlesnake closely resembles the Mojave, but its diamond dorsal markings are not as clearly defined, the black rings on its tail are about the same width as the white ones, the whitish stripe slanting diagonally downward from behind the eye intersects the mouthline, the base rattle segment consists of one color, and on top of the snake's head more than three rows of small scales occupy the space between the enlarged eye plates. In contrast to the angular body blotches of the Mojave, those of both the desert massasauga and prairie rattlesnake are rounded, and each of the white scales bordering them is apt to be intersected by two or more colors (in the Mojave they are nearly always monochromatic). In these snakes the tail lacks the bold black-and-white banding of the Mojave. Although the black-tailed rattlesnake, an inhabitant of rocky woodland, is not likely to be found in the Mojave's open desert habitat, it is easily distinguished from *C. s. scutulatus* by its dark forecrown, a black mask running diagonally backward from its eye, the presence of dark body crossbands with lateral extensions reaching to the snake's belly, and its uniformly black tail.

SIZE A rattlesnake of moderate length and girth, it is generally between 2 and 3 feet (61–91.4 cm) in length. A 51-inch (129.5 cm) specimen represents the most reliable record of maximum size for this species.

HABITAT Although the Mojave rattlesnake occurs in sparsely vegetated arid lowlands, grass-covered flatlands, and less often along the lower mountain slopes below 4,000 feet (1,219 m), it prefers high, barren desertland dotted with creosote bush, mesquite, and cactus. Gehlbach (1981), who has had extensive field experience with our southwestern desert fauna, says it favors both the shortest grass and the fewest shrubs in regions with the lowest elevations. One such place, the area around Big Bend's Terlingua Flats, supports a sizable population of Mojave rattlers. On Mexico's northern plateau it sometimes ranges to unusually high elevations; it was reported by Armstrong and Murphy (1979) from grassland and juniper plains in central Durango at an elevation of approximately 8,000 feet. In California, Bryant and Miller (in Klauber 1956) found it on moderately sloping alluvial fans where soils, intersected by shallow washes, were coarse and rather tightly packed. Whatever the habitat, this rattlesnake tends to avoid severely uneven, rocky terrain and areas of dense vegetation.

BEHAVIOR Not all zoologists familiar with the Mojave rattlesnake characterize its temperament in the same way. Armstrong and Murphy (1979), for example, considered it among the most aggressive rattlesnake species they had encountered, noting that several specimens struck with such force that their entire bodies left the ground. Ernst (1992) likewise described it as very nervous and aggressive, a view shared in part by Lowe, Schwalbe, and Johnson (1986), who called it rather excitable but noted that its defensive stance did not include the same dramatic head-high posture usually performed by the more quick-tempered western diamond-backed rattlesnake. Klauber, on the other hand, considered it less aggressive than the diamondback. Most of the specimens he collected in the desert tried to flee, assuming a defensive posture only when prevented from reaching shelter. Instead of instantly

sounding its rattle at the approach of man, an apprehensive Mojave rattlesnake may occasionally lift its tail and move it slowly and silently from side to side in a ritualistic defensive response. Armstrong and Murphy mentioned another kind of defensive display in which the Mexican subspecies, when provoked, sometimes flattened its neck horizontally in an abbreviated hood.

To protect itself from the serpent-eating desert king snake, the Mojave employs another strategy. When it has identified such a predator, it first tries to flee, but if it cannot escape quickly, the rattler reacts by arching most of its midsection high off the ground, then whacking it down hard against its foe, trying to cut short the predator's attack. For the rattlesnake, this is usually no more than a delaying tactic. In most cases, the king snake relentlessly pursues its victim until the rattler has been seized, constricted in the predator's strong body coils, and devoured.

In its open and mostly shade-free habitat, the Mojave is seldom seen abroad on hot summer days, although on cool, cloudy days it may leave its underground shelter to coil beneath a desert shrub or lie partially concealed along the recesses of a dry mesquite-lined arroyo. During the spring and fall, it usually comes to the surface early in the morning and again late in the afternoon, but on Mexico's northern plateau, particularly at higher elevations, it is often day-active. Writing about the Mojave rattlesnake in the state of Chihuahua, Armstrong and Murphy reported the sighting of one at 11 AM, early in July, on a dirt road near the town of Santa Clara, at an elevation of 6,500 feet (1,988 m). On the windswept tableland of central Durango at an elevation of 8,000 feet (2,446 m), they also encountered this species as it crossed the highway or basked along the edge of the road. Such examples of midday basking are no sign that this species favors higher temperatures; they demonstrate that the snake adjusts its daily activity cycle to fit the local climatic conditions, for at such high elevations the moderate midday temperatures are more comfortable than the chill of night.

The Mojave shows a greater tolerance for cold than other native rattlesnakes, sometimes remaining active when temperatures have dropped as low as 63 F, long after most other species have taken refuge belowground. Klauber, for example, encountered specimens out in the open even when bitterly cold winds were blowing with a force that made walking difficult. During its early evening forays, this species often stops on paved roads to warm itself; the road toppings, especially those of asphalt, retain solar heat for a couple of hours after sundown, even when the air and desert floor have cooled dramatically.

To survive winter's cold, the Mojave crawls into rodent burrows, individually or in pairs, although Lowe and his colleagues stated that in choice locations as many as 11 individuals were found together in a single hibernaculum.

FEEDING The most comprehensive study of this snake's food preferences was made by Reynolds and Scott (1982) in northeastern Chihuahua. It revealed that in this area the Mojave's chief prey consisted of a variety of small mammals. According to these zoologists, the following food animals were taken from 48 Mojave rattlesnakes (frequency as a percentage of the total in parentheses): Merriam's kangaroo rats (27.1), banner-tailed kangaroo rats (12.5), silky pocket mice (12.5), deer mice (10.4), spotted ground squirrels (10.2), insects and millipedes (8.3, taken by young snakes), desert pocket mice (6.2), cactus mice (4.2), nestling black-tailed jackrabbits (4.2), rock pocket mice (2.1), and immature desert cottontails (2.1). The three most frequently consumed prey species (Merriam's and banner-tailed kangaroo rats and the spotted ground squirrel) were also those most abundant in tobosa vegetation, the preferred habitat of the Mojave. Other animals mentioned by Lowe and his coworkers as prey taken by this snake in Arizona include packrats, birds, and an occasional frog or toad. Lizards, they say, are also consumed, but mostly by juvenile Mojaves. Turner confirms (in Tennant 1984) that the snakes also eat road-killed mammals, in a report of a Mojave eating the mutilated remains of a kangaroo rat found lying in the road. In compiling a list of prey animals reported by others, Ernst added leaf-nosed snakes and bird eggs.

REPRODUCTION Little is known about the reproductive biology of this snake. Mating, which has been reported both in the spring and as late in the year as August, results in the birth of 2 to 13 young (average 8 or 9) sometime between mid-July and late September. The infants are 9 to 11 inches (22.9–27.9 cm) long at birth.

VENOM AND BITE The Mojave's most noteworthy attribute is its venom. Studies conducted over the last 25 years, according to Sherman Minton (pers. com.), show that in many individuals of this species the venom is the most toxic of any North American pit viper, even exceeding that of the eastern coral snake. When introduced into mice, and depending on the route of injection, it can be 10 to more than 50 times as lethal as that of the western diamond-backed rattlesnake. Containing a powerful neurotoxic element called Mojave toxin, it targets the victim's myoneural junctions and creates severe neurological degradation that can result in double vision and interfere with the normal functions of speaking and swallowing. It also affects the cardiovascular system, yet it is described as producing only minimal local effects on the tissues. Death, when it does occur, is the result of respiratory failure. Designated as type A venom by Glenn and Straight (1978), the highly dangerous venom containing Mojave toxin is present in *C. s. scutulatus* populations inhabiting southern California, southwestern Utah, southeastern Nevada, parts of western and southern Arizona, and the Big Bend region of Texas. The average venom yield from an adult specimen is reported by Minton and Minton (1969) as between 50 and 90 mg; the same authors estimated that it takes only 10 to 15 mg of the highly toxic substance to kill an adult human.

Not all Mojave rattlesnakes possess such deadly venom. Most of those occupying a wide geographic zone in south-central Arizona between Phoenix and Tucson contain a much less lethal form of venom, known as type B, which lacks the virulent nerve-damaging Mojave toxin. Unlike the A type, it produces dramatic local symptoms typical of pit viper poisoning, including considerable swelling, bleb formation, ecchymosis, and necrosis.

Because the Mojave rattlesnake, one of Texas' most dangerous serpents, is easily confused with the more common western diamond-backed rattlesnake, it is important for persons residing or traveling in the southwestern part of the state to make a careful distinction between the two. If the source of a snakebite is not accurately identified, the relatively mild local effects produced by the more lethal type A Mojave venom may cause an attending physician to underestimate the gravity of a bite. What may at first be diagnosed as a minor case may later prove to be a life-threatening condition, and when critical systemic manifestations finally appear, it

may be too late for the successful administration of antivenin.

Fortunately, this snake is not particularly abundant in Texas, and its distribution is restricted to a relatively small part of the state. If it were even half as common as the western diamond-backed rattler and as widely distributed, the Mojave rattlesnake would represent an extremely serious outdoor hazard for Texans.

PRAIRIE RATTLESNAKE

Crotalus viridis viridis
PLATE 197

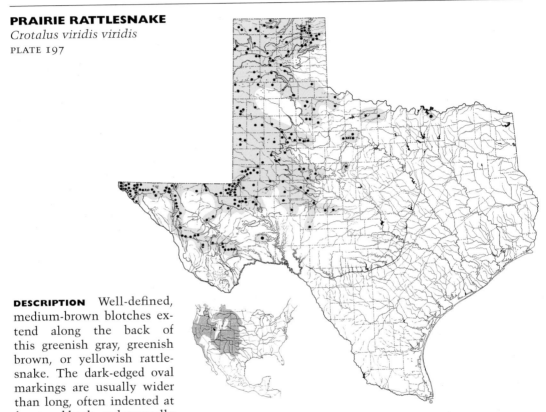

DESCRIPTION Well-defined, medium-brown blotches extend along the back of this greenish gray, greenish brown, or yellowish rattlesnake. The dark-edged oval markings are usually wider than long, often indented at front and back, and generally enclosed by a narrow white border. They become faded, narrow crossbands on the rear of the body, where they merge with the smaller, more discreet lateral blotches. Distinct narrow, dark rings circle the tail; the last one or two rings frequently are black. The lateral head markings provide an additional means of identification. In particular, a narrow white or yellowish stripe on the side of the head runs obliquely downward from in front of the eye to intersect the mouthline; an-

other, nearly parallel to the first, extends from behind the eye to above the end of the mouthline (e, p. 376). In the arrangement of scales on top of the snout, the prairie rattler is unique among Texas rattlesnakes. Only in this species do more than two internasal scales touch the rostral plate. For a description of the rattle, see the western diamond-backed rattlesnake account.

COMPARABLE SNAKES The dark tail rings of both Mojave and western diamond-backed rattlesnakes are black or nearly so, and they contrast strongly with the white spaces that separate them; those of the prairie rattler are mostly faded, like the last few bands on its body. In addition, the oblique, narrow light line behind the diamondback's eye intersects the mouthline, but that of the prairie rattler passes behind it. The body pattern of the rock rattlesnakes, unlike the dorsal ovals of the prairie rattler, consists of widely spaced, narrow, dark crossbands. The caudal append- age of the northern black-tailed rattlesnake is uniformly black (though banded in the very young), and the mask behind its eye is very dark and lacks narrow white margins. Where the prairie rattlesnake's crown is covered by numerous small scales, the massasauga has nine large plates. Among Texas rattlesnakes, only the prairie has more than two internasal scales touching the rostral plate. The plains and dusty hog-nosed snakes, because of their stout bodies and dark dorsal markings, are the nonvenomous snakes most likely to be confused with the prairie rattler, but they are easily identified by their broad necks, sharply upturned snouts, considerable black belly pigment, sharply pointed tails, and ab- sence of rattles.

SIZE A rattlesnake of moderate length, the adult usually ranges between 35 and 45 inches (88.9–114 cm) long. The maximum recorded length is 57 inches (144.8 cm).

HABITAT Although the prairie rattlesnake typically inhabits high grassy plains and as- sociated canyons throughout most of its Texas range, it also occurs sparingly in the more arid southwestern part of the state. It exists, for example, in scattered localities across the sparsely vegetated limestone hills and plateaus marking the southeastern lim- its of its geographic range, and it extends westward from there across the northern edge of the Chihuahuan Desert, where it usu- ally occupies transitional mesquite-grassland habitat and may even be found in dry creo- sote bush scrubland.

Despite its continued survival in such de- pauperate country, it is absent from Big Bend National Park, where it probably lived before man's influence seriously depleted the area's native grasses and with them the prairie rat- tler's prime habitat, for this is essentially a grassland snake. In other parts of southwest-

ern Texas it frequently ascends the rocky hills and bluffs of the lower mountain slopes to elevations above 5,000 feet (1,520 m). Wherever it is found, the prairie rattler in- habits sandy to rocky soils, generally avoid- ing areas of constant wetness such as marshy pond edges, soggy meadows, and damp river valleys.

BEHAVIOR Most herpetologists agree that the prairie rattler is more irritable than most other native rattlesnakes, and when provoked its response will be vigorous, if not vicious.

In their extensive field studies, Duvall and his associates (1985) identified a predictable sequence in the snake's defensive repertoire. They found that when first approached by man, a prairie rattlesnake on the move (par- ticularly if it is away from protective cover) became utterly motionless, its rattle silent, its gaze fixed unerringly on the intruder—all in an obvious attempt to remain inconspicu- ous, yet watchful for any sign of hostility. They also discovered that the same snake encountered near brush or some other form of shelter tended to respond more defiantly than when approached on wide-open prairie, and that rattlesnakes in aggregations, such as those assembled at hibernacula, proved more pugnacious than single animals. When actually threatened, such a snake quickly abandoned its cryptic behavior and rapidly crawled away in a straight-line course from its antagonist, its rattle sounding only briefly, if at all, as it began its withdrawal.

If escape was thwarted, or the threat inten- sified, the rattler escalated its defensive re- sponse in one of two ways. On the one hand, it assumed the classic rattlesnake stand-and- fight posture by planting its body firmly on the ground in a wide, circular loop to support the head and forebody, which could be ele- vated and drawn back into a tight S curve to be unleashed in a sudden forward lunge. At other times it employed a rear-guard action called cocking. In this maneuver, the forward third of the snake's trunk is pulled up into the same sort of S used in the first strike stance. In the cocked position, however, the rear part of the serpent's body is not held sta- tionary as in the more aggressive striking display; instead, by engaging this part of the trunk in a series of constantly shifting coils, the snake backs slowly away from its foe, staring steadfastly at the threat until it is out of danger.

Perhaps the most surprising defensive strategy observed in Duvall's Wyoming study (one totally unexpected by the investigators) was the prairie rattler's unusual head-hiding behavior, used only after the snake's threat posturing failed to turn away a human intruder. Employed in less than 2 percent of the biologists' trial encounters, it was accomplished by simply tucking the head under a midbody coil (generally the widest part of the trunk) in a seemingly submissive action. It was not uncommon for the snake to pop its head back out from under its body coil and, with the mouth wide open and the fangs fully extended, drive home an insidious strike before returning to its head-hiding stance. The in-and-out head-popping often was repeated several times in rapid succession, and a snake frequently executed more than just a single strike from this position.

Another curious head movement, shared by certain other pit vipers, has been observed in this snake. Pit vipers frequently open their mouths widely after feeding, as if yawning, a well-documented behavior long interpreted as a means of stretching and realigning the jaws. More recently, Graves and Duvall (1985) have come to a different conclusion regarding the purpose of this unusual behavior. Noting that mouth gaping was not restricted to feeding events but was employed with even greater frequency when the snakes engaged in social and exploratory activities involving the senses of taste and smell transmitted through the Jacobson's organ in the roof of the snake's mouth, they concluded that mouth gaping must somehow sharpen these senses when they were most needed.

To test this hypothesis, the researchers sealed off the vomeronasal ducts of captive rattlesnakes so that the subjects were unable to detect chemical cues through the Jacobson's organ in the usual way. As expected, the altered snakes, apparently in an effort to clear these passageways, performed a significantly greater number of mouth gapes than specimens not so altered. The investigators concluded that mouth gaping must facilitate the organ's ability to receive odorous molecules from the immediate environment via the searching tongue tips, although just how this is accomplished is not yet clear.

Also believed to aid in the transport of scent particles to the Jacobson's organ is a peculiar head-shaking phenomenon, observed in the prairie rattlesnake by Graves and Duvall and also noted by Tim Jones and Johnny Binder (pers. com.) in the western massasauga. It consists of flicking the head horizontally two or three times in rapid succession, which Graves and Duvall suggest dislodges minute particles from the organ's duct openings or purges fluid from them so that odorous molecules can move unobstructed through the passageway to the inner sensory epithelium.

In its open prairie habitat, this snake shows little inclination to be out in the midday sun when temperatures rise above 90 degrees F, concentrating its foraging efforts instead in the more comfortable late evening and nighttime hours. By day it avoids the fierce solar radiation by coiling in the burrows of prairie dogs, badgers, gophers, kangaroo rats, and other small mammals or by nestling beneath bushy shrubs or prickly pear cactus. For the most part, its daytime wanderings are restricted to the cooler seasons of spring and fall.

Although both latitude and elevation influence to some extent the prairie rattler's active season, across the midlatitudes of its vast geographic range this reptile normally moves about from March to October, spending the rest of the year in winter dormancy. In southern Canada, where winters are severe and protracted, it experiences a reduced period of activity and a correspondingly longer hibernation interlude. Even longer periods of inactivity occur at higher elevations, like those in Colorado's San Luis Valley, where the frigid winters of this 8,000-foot (2,438 m) high region impose on the local rattlesnake populations a remarkable eight-month hibernation cycle. As would be expected, prairie rattlers living in the more moderate climate of the Southwest enjoy a significantly longer active season than those far to the north.

To survive the cold northern winters, this reptile finds refuge in a variety of underground shelters that meet two essential requirements: they must be below the frost line and they must remain free of winter flooding. It is also evident that these snakes show a distinct preference for dens on the south-facing slopes of rocky bluffs, which are well exposed to the sun's warming rays for most of the day. According to Jackley (in Klauber 1956), whose field observations are among the most complete early studies of the prairie rattlesnake's denning behavior, 90 percent of all winter dens used by this snake in South Dakota had such a southern exposure, which is probably true as well of the prairie rattler's rock-crevice Texas dens. He also found that most adults congregated at the same choice dens year after year, hibernating together in groups ranging from 50 to several hundred individuals; the average denning aggregation consisted of approximately 250 snakes.

Other serpents (usually the larger species such as the coachwhip, bull snake, racer, and western diamond-backed rattlesnake) often hibernate in the same dens with the prairie rattlers, particularly in regions where suitable overwintering sites are scarce. Contrary to popular opinion, the rattlers do not magnanimously share their underground retreats with prairie dogs and burrowing owls, either in summer or winter, for these animals constitute the serpents' natural prey species.

Some of the best sites, according to Jackley, were in rock slides on steep bluffs, in fractured banks of deep gullies, in sinkholes that no longer held water, in rock-ledge crevices, and in caves. Because much of the rattler's typical shortgrass prairie habitat in Texas lacks an abundance of deep crevice formations, in this state the reptiles winter primarily in the abandoned mammal burrows that abound on the plains. Most frequently used are the holes excavated by prairie dogs, badgers, and desert tortoises, for they are notably deeper than the tunnels dug by other small prairie animals and thus better protected from subfreezing temperatures. Those of the prairie dog, for example, descend into the ground to a surprising depth of 10 or 12 feet (3.0–32.6 m) and stretch underground horizontally for nearly 50 feet (15 m). Not only must the holes be deep, but also to avoid potential floodwaters most usable burrows are situated on slight elevations. Unlike the permanent rock dens frequently used by

the same snakes year after year, earthen holes unattended and no longer routinely cleared by the original mammalian inhabitants begin to deteriorate in just a few seasons. Consequently, as the tunnels collapse and the blowing sand and dirt drift back into the openings, the rattlers may evict other burrowing mammals from their underground dwellings.

Following the first significant drop in autumnal temperature (usually a light frost in mid-September), adult prairie rattlesnakes at northern latitudes leave their summer habitations and begin the journey to the winter dens. The distance between the two sites is usually no more than 1 or 2 miles (1.6–3.2 km) but in some instances may exceed 5 miles (8 km). Just how a snake locates its remote den is still a matter of conjecture among animal behaviorists. It has been suggested by Landreth (1973) that a rattlesnake uses celestial cues to begin its annual fall migration, after which it follows chemical signals emitted enroute by other rattlesnakes that have reached the hibernaculum before it. Zoologists cannot clearly explain how snakes navigate, but they do agree that the adults are the first to move toward the dens, followed by one- and two-year-olds who find their way by picking up the older snakes' trails. For reasons yet unknown, during the first fall, most young of the year do not travel to the deep communal rock-crevice dens with the older snakes, even though they may have been born only ¼ mile (402 m) away. Instead, the majority survive their initial winter in abandoned mammal burrows. In the snake's Texas plains habitat, where suitable rock formations are generally absent, prairie rattlesnakes of all ages (young of the year included) routinely hibernate in prairie-dog towns.

Whatever the choice of a den, there is always the danger that unforeseen weather conditions will make the snake's journey to its hibernaculum a hazardous one. Klauber (1956), for example, expressed the view that prairie rattlesnakes caught unexpectedly by a sudden freeze on the way to their dens will usually survive the experience, even though partly frozen, if there is a compensatory temperature rise within a few hours, but those trapped above ground during a prolonged freeze are not likely to recover.

Following winter dormancy, prairie rattlers in North Texas usually emerge from their dens sometime in late March or early April to begin a period of laying out, during which numbers of them coil together near the den entrance for several hours each day to bask in the warm spring sun. With the return of cool, late afternoon temperatures, they retreat to the relative warmth of the rock crevices. So long as the daytime temperatures remain agreeable, this daily cycle continues for the next two or three weeks. As the days become warmer and the probability of another freeze diminishes, the serpents leave their den sites to disperse into the surrounding countryside until the next autumn frost brings them back to their dens.

FEEDING Adult prairie rattlesnakes eat a wide variety of mammals, including prairie dogs, ground squirrels, chipmunks, marmots, cottontail rabbits, moles, voles, gophers, wood and kangaroo rats, as well as pocket, white-footed, harvest, and meadow mice. They also consume a relatively large number of ground-dwelling birds, such as doves, mockingbirds, bluebirds, warblers, starlings, juncos, sparrows, meadow and slum larks, lark buntings, lark finches, robins, ravens, grouse, and young pheasants. Where birds are readily available, they may actually represent the most significant part of the prairie rattler's diet. This is borne out by Jackley's discovery of a dozen rattlers near a South Dakota snake den, which apparently had consumed their first meal since leaving hibernation. Only 4 had taken mammals, but 8 had eaten birds, including 4 meadowlarks, 1 towhee, 1 catbird, and 2 horned larks. According to Klauber, even bird eggs are sometimes devoured.

Young snakes, because of their small body girth and mouth-gape limitations, feed almost exclusively on lizards, the remaining prey consisting of frogs and perhaps also some insects. This predilection for lizards was underscored by Perkins (in Klauber 1956), who, while collecting prairie rattlesnakes at their dens near Platteville, Colorado, noted that young of the year regurgitated northern prairie swifts and northern earless lizards when handled. That the adults also occasionally eat lizards was confirmed by Hamilton (1950), who reported the ingestion of eastern short-horned lizards by mature prairie rattlers.

The Wyoming field study by Duvall and his coworkers provides some interesting details about the snake's feeding behavior. In it the investigators revealed how a rattlesnake migrating from its den in the spring traveled along a remarkably straight path, moving fairly continuously each morning and afternoon until it encountered the first active patch of deer mice (the preferred and most common prey species in the study area), which it readily identified by the scent of the rodents' urine or feces. It remained in the vicinity of these mammalian aggregations for the next several weeks, establishing something of a home range in the area while availing itself of the food source. During this time, the snake occupied the rodent burrows almost exclusively. Lying in ambush just inside a tunnel, it faced the opening with its head no more than a foot from the entrance, waiting for an unsuspecting rodent to enter. When it did, there was only a slight chance that it would escape with its life, for the rattler's heat-sensing receptors (the facial pits) quickly detected the mammal's body heat, actuating the reptile's swift strike and leaving little opportunity for the prey to retreat.

REPRODUCTION At more northern latitudes, where the females may breed only every second or third year, mating usually takes place in late summer or fall, with the sperm remaining viable in the female's oviducts until spring ovulation, at which time the eggs are fertilized. Farther south (for example, in Trans-Pecos Texas), where females most likely breed every year, spring copulation probably is the rule, although this has not been documented.

Baxter and Stone (1980) and Jackley found that sometime in August, a month or so before the main body of prairie rattlesnakes arrived at the communal den site, a dozen or more gravid female rattlers came together at a suitable location not far from the den (either a sunny hillside or a place near an appropriate hole or cavity), where they remained until the young were born. Jackley noted that in the absence of rocky terrain, gravid females gave birth to their young in old prairie-dog holes, selecting tunnels at the edge of the dog towns, particularly those kept at least partially open by the diggings of striped gophers or other small rodents. He went on to say that in moderately rolling country the best birthing sites were in old badger and skunk burrows near the ridge tops of prairie-dog towns.

Such aggregations may serve two purposes. First, because the maternal rookeries were usually in open, unshaded locations, the females had ample opportunity to bask directly in the warm sun, thus aiding the development of the unborn young by thermoregulation, an especially important advantage to snakes living at high, cool elevations. For the baby rattlesnakes subsequently born at the rookeries, separation from the main den population benefits them in another way. Detached as they now are from the larger den aggregation, the newborn snakes undoubtedly avoid direct competition with the main body of young adults for the limited food supply. To survive their first winter of life it is important, if not crucial, that the infant snakes secure at least one meal before entering hibernation, for during winter dormancy they may lose as much as 50 percent of their body weight.

Duvall and his group of researchers discovered such a communal birthing rookery of prairie rattlers in the Haystack Mountains of south-central Wyoming, only 300 yards (274.3 m) from the main den. Near the bottom of a river canyon, it occupied 115 square feet (10.6 m²). Its most conspicuous feature was the large, flat rocks honeycombed underneath with abandoned mammal burrows into which the pregnant females could retreat for safety. By August of one year, the herpetologists had counted nine pregnant females at the rookery and two more across a sandy ridge just 59 feet (18 m) away. Most of the snakes gave birth to their young between September 2 and 12. By carefully monitoring the postbirth activities of three female rattlesnakes in the group, the investigators found that although the mother snakes remained close to their respective broods—never moving more than 5½ feet (168 cm) away—they showed no maternal care toward their young. Littermates were even more gregarious than the mothers. Until the young snakes first

shed their skins, some 10 days after birth, they remained huddled together in tight sibling groups near the crack, crevice, or burrow where they had been born.

The survival value of such interlitter aggregations may be explained by the dangers of body-fluid loss. The newborn's skin is considerably more permeable before the first postnatal shedding than after. Staying in close physical contact with one another during this crucial period reduces the individual snake's overall exposure to dry, warm air, making the infants less vulnerable to desiccation than when they coil separately. Once the less permeable new skin is in place, each sibling goes its own way.

Female prairie rattlesnakes bear 4 to 21 young per litter, although the usual brood is estimated by different authors to contain 6 to 12; older snakes generally give birth to larger litters. Of two Randall County, Texas, specimens reported by Werler (1951), one female 32½ inches (83 cm) long contained 12 well-developed embryos; the second, measuring 34 inches (86 cm), held 11. Born sometime during August, September, or early October, the infants are usually between 8½ and 11 inches (21.6–27.9 cm) long.

VENOM AND BITE   Overall, the prairie rattlesnake's venom is estimated to be 2 to 2½ times more toxic than that of the western diamond-backed rattler, although the storage capacity of the snake's venom glands is only about one-ninth that of its larger cousin.

According to Russell et al. (1978), the first and most frequently reported symptoms of *C. viridis* poisoning are pain and swelling at the site of the bite, which typically occur immediately following the accident but may be delayed up to half an hour. An early symptom of most North American rattlesnake bites, such pain ordinarily is less severe in this species than in bites by the diamondback. Russell (1960) treated two exceptional cases of poisoning by the northern Pacific rattler (*C. v. oreganus*), in which the patients described the degree of pain as minor. Envenomation by the prairie rattlesnake and its close allies frequently results in a tingling sensation involving the tongue, mouth, and scalp and occasionally the ends of the fingers and toes as well, symptoms not usually evident following the bites of other Texas pit vipers. Additional signs and symptoms include weakness, giddiness, sweating, faintness, and nausea; in severe cases the victim may experience a weak though rapid pulse, a drop in systemic arterial pressure, respiratory difficulties, and some degree of paralysis. According to Russell, death, when it does occur in humans, results from cardiovascular failure caused by a lethal peptide component in the snake's venom.

DESERT MASSASAUGA

*Sistrurus catenatus
edwardsi*
PLATE 198

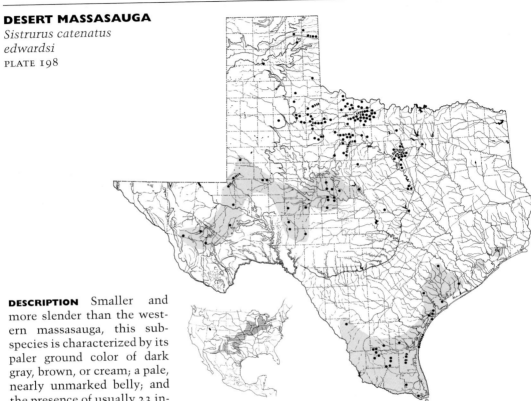

DESCRIPTION Smaller and more slender than the western massasauga, this subspecies is characterized by its paler ground color of dark gray, brown, or cream; a pale, nearly unmarked belly; and the presence of usually 23 instead of 25 dorsal scale rows at midbody. Extending along the length of the snake's back is a row of large, dark brown, oval or circular blotches, each edged in blackish brown. A row of smaller dark spots, usually resembling circular smudges, alternates with the middorsal series, but they are less distinct than the larger ones and they lack the dark borders of the middorsal series. Below them lie two more alternating rows of even smaller dark spots. On top of the head, two somewhat wavy dark brown stripes extend backward from near the eyes to the neck, although in some snakes such markings may be reduced to a pair of large nuchal spots. On either side of the head, a wide, dark brown mask, typically margined above and below by distinct white lines, extends rearward from the eye onto the neck (h, p. 376). The dorsal scales are keeled, and the anal plate is single. For a description of the rattle, see the western diamond-backed rattlesnake account.

COMPARABLE SNAKES In addition to certain features of pattern and coloration, all other Texas rattlesnake species living within the range of the desert massasauga can be distinguished by the mostly small scales covering the top of the head. Mojave and western diamond-backed rattlesnakes also have diamond dorsal markings and distinctly black-and-white-banded tails. The prairie rattler, which lacks a bold, dark mask on either side of the head, has 25 or more midbody dorsal scale rows and more than two internasal scales in contact with the rostral plate. The dark crossbands of the black-tailed rattlesnake continue down the sides of its body to the snake's belly, and its tail is uniformly black. Hog-nosed snakes (particularly the races of the western species) are the nonvenomous serpents most likely to be confused with the desert massasauga. They do not have facial pits, elliptical pupils, or rattles. Moreover, they possess a uniquely flared and upturned snout, a neck fully as large in diameter as the head, and a divided anal plate.

SIZE Among Texas' smallest rattlesnakes, the adults of this subspecies are generally less than 18 inches (45.7 cm) in length. A specimen of record size measured 21⅕ inches (53.8 cm) long.

HABITAT This wide-ranging inhabitant of desert grassland and shortgrass prairie has a curiously discontinuous Texas distribution that includes the west-central part of the state on the one hand and extreme South Texas on the other. In between lie the Stockton and Edwards plateaus and a large stretch of northern Rio Grande Plain thornbrush from which, despite many years of herpetological exploration, no massasaugas have been collected. This region extends from Sutton County in the north to Webb County in the south.

Although in Texas the desert massasauga is primarily a grassland and thornbrush dweller, like the other races of *S. catenatus* it often favors moist areas, such as those near streams, riverbeds, lakes, ponds, and water holes. Along the South Texas coast it can frequently be found in and near grass- and brush-covered sand dunes and grassy meadows.

BEHAVIOR Many field zoologists familiar with this small rattlesnake say it has a relatively even temper, rattling only when necessary to avoid a confrontation. It may, for the same reason, escape into the nearest mammal burrow. When approached too closely or otherwise provoked, it does not hesitate to strike, though not from an elevated S-shaped forebody stance and never with the same frenzy that is the hallmark of many other *Crotalus* species. Instead, it is more likely to deliver a short thrust that extends less than 4 or 5 inches (10–13 cm).

In the upper Panhandle, where long, cold winters are the rule, this species makes its first appearance in April or May. In the rest of the state it may first be encountered on the surface as early in the year as late March. Except in the northwestern Panhandle, where Knopf and Tinkle (1961) found it in greatest abundance during the month of August, in parts of Texas where it has been studied it apparently shows up most often in May and June. According to Lowe, Schwalbe, and Johnson (1986), in Arizona the desert massasauga is active from April into October, the greatest number of specimens being found during the brief summer rainy season.

Throughout the summer months, this primarily nocturnal reptile usually begins its nightly hunting forays at dusk, when it frequently crosses roadways in its search for prey. Since the air and ground temperatures are then turning cooler, the snake often stops to coil on the warm pavement, where heat absorbed earlier in the day normally lasts for a couple of hours after sundown, providing the reptile with a comfortable base on which to rest. As it lies motionless on the warm asphalt, the massasauga is sometimes crushed by passing vehicular traffic. In the spring and fall, when nighttime temperatures are uncomfortably cool, it may prowl on the surface of the ground during the day, hiding in rodent burrows or beneath shrubs, cactus plants, or vegetative debris during periods of inactivity. At times it has been observed to bury itself in loose sand, its body arranged in a tight, circular coil with the head lying near the center. To move more easily over such shifting substrate, it is known to use a sidewinding mode of locomotion. In Arizona, on the other hand, Fowlie (1965) reported seeing specimens in wet environments, sunning on low clumps of grass after recent summer rains.

FEEDING By most accounts, small mammals and lizards constitute the snake's chief prey. In Texas it is said to eat primarily harvest and white-footed mice. Lowe and his colleagues (1986) noted that Arizona specimens consumed chiefly mice and lizards in about equal numbers, with whiptail and earless lizards forming the bulk of its lacertilian prey. Fowlie, who also reported on the food of Arizona massasaugas, mentioned frogs as a primary ingredient in the snake's diet, but he neglected to identify the species involved.

Although none of these reports specifically mentioned toads as prey, it seems likely, based on one of the snake's unusual morphological adaptations, that they constitute an important part of the massasauga's diet when they are available. This modification, consisting of enlarged adrenal glands, permits the snake to consume adult toads without succumbing to their extremely toxic skin-gland secretions, powerful epinephrine and digitaloid compounds to which most snakes are highly sensitive. When ingested or even introduced into a predator's mouth, the toad's toxins are quite capable of killing serpents with adrenal glands of ordinary size. They will easily kill most vertebrate animals up to the size of large dogs, and even bigger animals may be at risk. An incredible fatality from this cause, reported by Smith and White (1955), was that of a man who ate a marine toad in the belief it was some kind of edible frog.

According to the same authors, the skin exudate of adult toads produces two devastating consequences in an affected predator. The first, stimulated by the secretion's epinephrine component, is a dramatically accelerated heartbeat, which alone can prove fatal. Should the victim survive this calamity, the exudate's digitaloid element (the more potent of the two principal toxins) takes over, severely depressing rather than increasing the pulse rate. This is more likely to cause death. It stands to reason that a snake's ability to consume adult toads safely depends on the size of its adrenal glands. Other snakes with oversized adrenal glands include some species of garter and water snakes, and the eastern hog-nosed snake, which has by far the largest such glands of any U.S. serpent, dines almost exclusively on toads. Such snakes are effectively protected from the skin-gland toxins by the ability of their adrenal glands to produce an adequate volume of toxin-neutralizing adrenaline.

REPRODUCTION   Little specific information is available about the reproductive biology of this subspecies. Based on captive specimens, Lowe and his coworkers reported courtship and mating from March into June, noting litter sizes of 5 and 7 young. Born in late August or September, the infant snakes measure about $6^7/_{10}$ inches (17 cm) in length, nearly as long as the smallest newborn young of the largest massasauga subspecies. At birth the young are more boldly patterned than the adults, and the tail tip of the infants is yellowish or pinkish, an apparent adaptation for luring frogs, toads, and lizards to within striking range.

VENOM AND BITE   Since neither the snake's venom yield nor lethal toxicity have been studied, and there are no recorded case histories of bites by this subspecies, we know little about the effects of desert massasauga envenomation in man. Like its close relatives the eastern and western massasaugas, it probably has a highly toxic venom containing a potent neurotoxic component, although this is not certain. If future research reveals that the desert massasauga does indeed possess such a venom, then its bite should be regarded as potentially life-threatening to man. Even then, the snake's relatively short fangs and modest venom supply make death from a bite unlikely, for this is the smallest of the three massasauga subspecies. Besides, it has a spotty distribution, making an encounter with one of these elusive little rattlesnakes highly improbable. See also the western massasauga account.

WESTERN MASSASAUGA
Sistrurus catenatus tergeminus
PLATE 199

DESCRIPTION   A robust snake with a dark tan, pale gray, or brownish gray ground color, the western massasauga displays a longitudinal row of dark gray, dark brown, or nearly blackish ovals down the length of its back, most of them wider than long, some notched in front, but all narrowly margined with gray or white. A row of smaller lateral spots alternates with the primary series, but these markings are less distinct than the larger ones

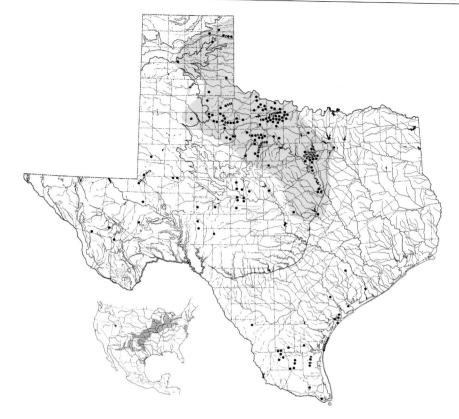

(usually resembling circular black smudges), and they lack the light-colored borders of the middorsal blotches. Below them are two more rows of even smaller spots, each row alternating with its neighbor. A moderate amount of dark pigmentation is distributed along the outer edges of the snake's belly. The darkly pigmented forecrown is followed by a pair of parallel dark stripes that reach backward onto the neck. On each side of the head, a wide, dark mask, bordered above and below by a narrow light line, extends from the eye to the side of the neck (h, p. 376). The keeled dorsal scales are usually arranged in 25 rows at midbody, and the anal plate is single. For a description of the rattle, see the western diamond-backed rattlesnake account.

COMPARABLE SNAKES The western pygmy rattlesnake, whose crown is covered like that of the western massasauga mostly with large plates, is distinguished by its smaller, more widely spaced middorsal blotches, a pale orange stripe down the middle of its back, and an unusually small rattle. All other Texas

rattlesnakes have primarily small scales on top of the head. Within the range of the massasauga, rattlesnake species can be further differentiated: in the canebrake rattler the dorsal markings consist of jagged black crossbands, the tail is solid black or dark brown, and the top of the head bears no distinct dark markings; in the prairie rattlesnake there is no bold, dark mask; and in the western diamond-backed rattler the dorsal markings consist of angular diamonds.

SIZE Averaging only about 18 to 24 inches (46–61 cm) in length, this is one of our smallest native rattlesnakes. The largest known specimen measured 34¾ inches (88.3 cm) long.

HABITAT The snake's Texas distribution includes the gently rolling plains and prairies of the northwestern part of the state from the Caprock Escarpment in the west to the Blackland Prairie in the east, then continues southeastward to Bell and Lampasas counties. Over most of this region it is encountered in both shortgrass and tallgrass prairie, often in association with mesquite, juniper, and overgrazed grassland. All of the 92 specimens collected by Greene and Oliver (1965) in eastern Parker and western Tarrant counties came from rolling tallgrass prairie, although Wright and Wright (1957) described the species' habitat throughout its total range as lowlands, moist areas near rivers and streams, damp sandy places, swampy regions, and meadows. Atkinson and Netting (1927) commented that the Chippewa Indian term "massasauga" (actually two words combined) means great rivermouth, a reference to the eastern subspecies' swampy, estuary environment, yet neither Texas subspecies seems to depend on moisture for its wellbeing. The desert race, however, can be found on some of the state's barrier islands. In the early 1950s, Pug Mullinax (pers. com.), then a state game warden in Rockport, sometimes collected four or five specimens in a single day on San Jose Island, where he found them under clumps of saltgrass and among the island's scattered patches of prickly pear cactus.

Despite the survival of undiminished local populations in areas not severely altered by man, massasauga numbers are decreasing in nearly all parts of the snake's range. There is ample evidence that until recently, it was quite common in some parts of the state. In the early 1900s one Armstrong County farmer killed 50 to 60 of these little rattlers during one wheat-harvesting season alone. Years later, massasaugas were still relatively plentiful in some areas of Texas. On the evening of May 14, 1960, for example, Knopf and Tinkle (1961) collected 15 specimens in Throckmorton County on the road between the towns of Throckmorton and Woodson, a distance of just 16 miles. During nighttime collecting activities, Greene and Oliver found this to be the most abundant serpent on roadways in western Tarrant and eastern Parker counties.

In Texas, as elsewhere within the snake's geographic range, continued alteration of the reptile's open habitat for farmland and suburban housing development has caused a significant decline in the snake's numbers. In Missouri, where the western massasauga's already limited habitat was being further diminished by unsound land-use practices, the

Missouri Department of Conservation declared this serpent an endangered species. Even at Squaw Creek National Wildlife Refuge in northwestern Missouri, an area established specifically to protect native wildlife, the local population of this subspecies, the largest such concentration in the state, was for a time seriously declining as the result of unsound land-management practices that came to light only after they were revealed in a long-term study by Seigel (1986). One such practice involved the release of large, unmanaged herds of cattle onto the prairie, which soon resulted in the loss of natural habitat considered essential to the snake's survival. When the harmful routines were halted in the early 1970s, the area's natural vegetation made a gradual though only partial recovery, as did the local massasauga population. Other contributions to the snake's decline included controlled burning of the cordgrass prairie at times when the rattlesnakes were exposed to the fires, and the mowing of roadside shoulders and dikes when the snakes were likely to be present. The greatest danger to the local reptiles, according to Seigel, was the seasonal influx of tourists who came to observe the multitudes of snow geese and other waterfowl that gather there each fall, resulting in the loss of many specimens to vehicular traffic. It is likely that some of the same factors identified by Seigel in the massasauga's decline at Squaw Creek may also be reducing certain local Texas populations of this native serpent.

BEHAVIOR Described by various collectors as either relatively docile or somewhat irascible, the massasauga shows little tolerance when closely approached, usually coiling when confronted and often rattling in response to any nearby movement. If threatened at close range, it is apt to deliver a short strike (6 or 8 inches in the case of an adult specimen) or attempt to reach its mark by suddenly lashing out sideways. Lacking the elevated forebody stance of a western diamond-backed rattlesnake, its fangs, when extended during a strike, ordinarily reach no higher on a standing human than just above the ankle.

Head-twitching, a peculiar behavior consisting of several quick side-to-side flicks of the head, was first noted in the prairie rattle-snake, but it has been observed as well by Tim Jones and Johnny Binder (pers. com.) in Waco-area massasaugas. Graves and Duvall (1985) believe this cephalic twitching may assist the movement of scent particles from the snake's nostrils to its Jacobson's organ by dislodging the tiny particles from the organ's duct opening or by purging the channel of fluid.

Some of the most detailed information about the snake's natural history has been provided by Richard A. Seigel, whose field studies in northwestern Missouri revealed a number of interesting facts concerning the reptile's seasonal habitat preferences, activity cycles, feeding habits, and reproduction. According to the zoologist, the massasaugas were found abroad from mid-April to late October, chiefly during the daylight hours and for an average 197 days annually during the study period. They were encountered most frequently in April (25.6 percent of captures), May (26.3 percent), and October (18.0 percent), and least often from July to September, although Seigel acknowledged that the samples may have been biased by the maturation of thick plant growth in summer, making the snakes difficult to see during that time of year. During the cooler weather of spring and autumn, the serpents were found on the prowl mainly from noon to 4 PM. In summer, when midday temperatures became too hot for their comfort, 60 percent of the rattlesnakes were encountered between 4 PM and 8 PM. Summer was the only season when the massasaugas frequently became active at night. Unlike the Missouri specimens, those living in north-central Texas and the Texas Panhandle (as well as those studied in south-central Kansas) tended to travel mostly in the early evening and at night.

Besides altering their activity patterns seasonally, the snakes also changed their habitat preferences according to the time of year. Thus, in spring, Seigel discovered them primarily in moist prairies, but as summer approached they moved out of the wet areas and into the drier uplands, where most of them occupied old fields and deciduous woodlands. With the approach of autumn, they returned again to the prairies. Except for massasaugas encountered in Roberts and

Lipscomb counties in the northeastern Texas Panhandle, which were observed to wander in mid-August, most Texas specimens were seen in the open in May and June.

To track their movements in the wild, Reinert and Kodrich (1982) fitted 25 eastern massasaugas with miniature radio transmitters. At the conclusion of their 50-day survey, the zoologists found that the snakes had traveled an average total distance of about 290 feet (88.4 m) and in any single day had moved approximately 30 feet (9.1 m).

The best way to find these rattlesnakes is to drive slowly along seldom-traveled secondary roads between dusk and 10 PM. As long as the air temperature is cooler than the road surface, the snakes are apt to be encountered crawling over the still-warm pavement or resting comfortably on the tepid asphalt with their bodies coiled or loosely extended, as if recently in motion. In a more natural setting, they can be found among rock formations, in stacks of lumber or under individual boards, beneath grass clumps or prickly pear cactus, and under bales of hay. In Illinois, P. W. Smith (1961) sometimes found them under logs and shocks of grain, although most were discovered basking on clumps of grass.

In winter, massasaugas at more northern latitudes find protection from freezing weather by crawling into deep rock crevices, small mammal burrows, crayfish tunnels, and rotting logs. Those of the Texas coastal prairies depend for winter shelter primarily on mammal burrows. In some regions, crayfish burrows apparently constitute the chief refuge for hibernating massasaugas. Vogt (1981) noted that in Wisconsin, specimens of this species typically entered such vertical tunnels to survive the chilly northern winters, coiling snugly (no more than one snake per burrow) just above the water line. In Ohio, a specimen was discovered hibernating with a blue racer under 18 inches of sand and peat.

FEEDING Both vertebrate and invertebrate animals are consumed by the western massasauga, including the following prey species specifically mentioned in the literature: northern short-tailed shrew, silky pocket mouse, hispid pocket mouse, deer mouse, plains harvest mouse, prairie vole, eggs of the lark sparrow, Texas spotted whiptail lizard, ground skink, northern fence lizard, Texas spiny lizard, horned lizard, common garter snake, ground snake, brown snake, lined snake, dusty hog-nosed snake, Rio Grande leopard frog, Cope's gray tree frog, toads, fish, crayfish, centipedes, and insects. That it also eats carrion was documented by Greene and Oliver, who discovered a Texas specimen in the act of trying to swallow a dead hog-nosed snake that was the victim of vehicular traffic.

Although frogs are sometimes mentioned as the snake's chief prey, three of the most detailed studies of this reptile's feeding habits clearly show otherwise. Adult massasaugas eat primarily mammals, and the juveniles consume mostly small snakes and probably also small frogs and lizards. Of particular interest in this regard is the fieldwork of Keenlyne and Beer (1973), whose exhaustive Wisconsin field study disclosed 91 food items from 323 specimens collected along the Chippewa River in Buffalo County. Even in this wet environment, not a single frog was found in the many snakes examined. Nearly 95 percent of the food items consumed by these massasaugas proved to be small rodents, including 78 meadow voles, 4 white-footed mice, 2 meadow jumping mice, and 1 masked shrew. Other prey species consisted of 1 fledgling red-winged blackbird, 4 common garter snakes, and 1 unidentified serpent.

As would be expected, very young rattlesnakes, unable to swallow large mammalian prey, resort to eating the most available quarry of appropriate size, in this case, small garter snakes, which are born at the same time of year as the infant massasaugas and are plentiful then, and are also the right size to be easily swallowed by the juvenile pit vipers.

Judging from evidence presented by Schuett and his colleagues (1984), it can be assumed that small frogs (and perhaps lizards) are also eaten by very young massasaugas when available. The frogs are drawn to the snake by what appears to be an animated larval insect but is instead the snake's wriggling tail tip. To determine if these snakes do indeed use their tails to lure prey, Schuett and his colleagues placed a group of 10-day-old eastern massasaugas in a terrarium with small frogs. Of 15 baby snakes tested, 3 responded. In each case, the infant rattler held its body perfectly still as it undulated and waved its elevated sulphur-yellow tail in an arc of 90 to 180 degrees. Once attracted by the tail movements, the amphibian turned to face the motion, approached it, then either snapped at the snake's tail or seized it in its jaws, sometimes even brazenly trying with its front feet to stuff the caudal member into its mouth. At this point, the snake struck, killed, and ate the frog. Curiously, the prey was never attacked until it had seized the massasauga's tail, even though it was well within the rattler's striking range. Altogether, the snakes successfully lured seven anurans of three species, including green, wood, and northern leopard frogs. Incidentally, tongue-flicking, which ordinarily is used by the snake to identify or track its prey, was not employed during these encounters, presumably to avoid alarming the frog by creating an unnecessary distraction.

REPRODUCTION Western massasaugas, which usually become sexually mature between three and four years of age, mate in the spring or fall, although Howard Reinert (in Ernst 1992) believes that in this species, late summer and fall matings are the rule. In that case the viable sperm is no doubt retained in the female's oviducts until the eggs ovulate the following spring. After a gestation of approximately 110 to 115 days, the 2 to 19 (usually 8 to 10) young per litter are born sometime between mid-July and late September, when they are 7 to 10 inches (17.8–25.4 cm) long. The infants have a lighter ground color than the adults, their dorsal markings are slightly darker, and both their tail tips and base rattle segments are greenish, yellowish, or pale pink.

VENOM AND BITE Endowed with a relatively toxic venom believed to contain some neurotoxic components, the western massasauga can seriously poison a human victim, but its bite rarely causes death in humans. This is partly the result of the snake's relatively short fangs (barely ¼ inch long in the largest specimens) and its conservative venom supply. According to Minton and Minton (1969), the venom averages 25 to 35 mg by dry weight in an adult snake, and they estimate the lethal human dose at 30 to 40 mg. Since rattlesnakes rarely exhaust their venom in one strike, it is unlikely that a massasauga will inject a lethal dose in just a single stab of its fangs.

Symptoms typically associated with massasauga poisoning include immediate, often severe pain at the bite area; some swelling at the site, though usually not extensive; discoloration; a moderate degree of ecchymosis; faintness; and nausea. According to Russell (1980), none of the seven victims of *Sistrurus* poisoning he treated showed any significant changes in their blood picture, and all recov-

ered uneventfully in just a few days. This does not mean that a massasauga bite should be treated as a trivial event. On the contrary, every bite by this species, if it produces signs and symptoms of poisoning, should be seen promptly by a physician experienced in the treatment of such a medical emergency. The lethal toxicity of western massasauga venom has not yet been established, although Glenn and Straight (1982) report that for the closely related eastern race, it is greater than for the majority of other rattlesnakes.

WESTERN PYGMY RATTLESNAKE
Sistrurus miliarius streckeri
PLATE 200

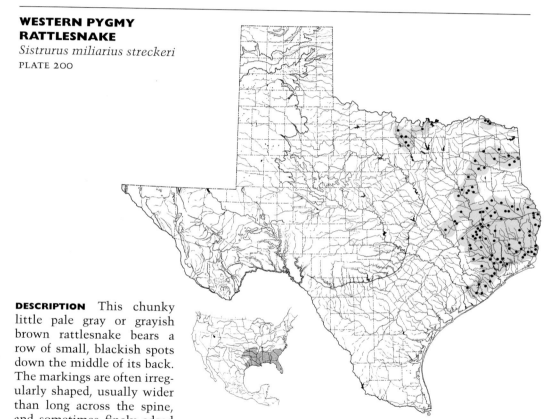

DESCRIPTION This chunky little pale gray or grayish brown rattlesnake bears a row of small, blackish spots down the middle of its back. The markings are often irregularly shaped, usually wider than long across the spine, and sometimes finely edged in white. They are often flanked on either side by a second row of similarly colored spots, more circular than the first, and below them is a third row of alternating dark spots, each of which extends onto the outer edges of the abdomen. In most specimens a pale orange wash occurs between the dorsal blotches without crossing them, giving the impression of an orange stripe running down the center

of the snake's back. The head is conspicuously marked by a pair of slightly wavy, parallel black lines on the crown that extend from between the eyes onto the neck and a black band that runs along each side of the face from the eye to the back of the mouthline (i, p. 376). The tail is indistinctly banded and ends in a tiny rattle. The dorsal scales, usually arranged in 21 (sometimes 23) rows at midbody, are strongly keeled, and the anal plate is single. As in all *Sistrurus*, the top of the head is covered with nine large plates. One of this species' most curious anatomical features is its diminutive rattle; carried at the end of a relatively long, slender tail, it is unique in size among native rattlesnakes. From a distance of only 4 or 5 feet (122–152 cm), the rattle is difficult to hear when in motion, and it is equally hard to see. For a description of rattles, see the western diamond-backed rattlesnake account.

COMPARABLE SNAKES Hog-nosed snakes, which have a distinctly upturned snout, lack both a rattle and the heat-sensing facial cavities of the western pygmy rattler. In addition, they have round instead of elliptical pupils. The much larger dorsal blotches of the western massasauga are closely spaced, and its dorsal scales are arranged in 25 rows at midbody. Both the western diamond-backed and canebrake rattlers can be distinguished by their larger dorsal markings, by the absence of a distinct pattern on their crowns, and by the presence of numerous small scales instead of large plates on top of their heads. The diamondback's tail is boldly banded with black and white; that of the canebrake is all black.

SIZE The adults of this subspecies are usually between 15 and 20 inches (38.1–50.8 cm) long. They have been known to reach a maximum size of 25⅛ inches (63.8 cm).

HABITAT Restricted primarily to the partially wooded or open lowlands of the upper Texas coast and to the hilly second-growth forests of East Texas, this uncommon snake occurs on sandy inland soils and on some of the less permeable coastal substrates, but nearly always close to standing water, which can include river bottoms, lakes, ponds, swamps, marshes, wet pastures, and even rice-field canals and roadside ditches. Of the numerous pygmy rattlesnakes donated to the Houston Zoo over the last 30 years, by far the greatest number have come from near towns and cities scattered throughout the pine-hardwood forest along U.S. Highway 59, from Lake Houston to Nacogdoches. This sporadically distributed serpent is infrequently encountered in Texas, even by professional collectors, and then usually only a specimen at a time. Judging by the observa-

tions of Percy Viosca (in Dundee and Rossman 1989), it may actually be more common than we believe, for in neighboring Louisiana he collected 103 western pygmy rattlesnakes from levees on Delacroix Island, where they had been driven after 12 days of severe flooding.

BEHAVIOR Although this snake demonstrates a fairly wide range of reactions when provoked, with some individuals tolerating a close approach before rattling or striking, we have found that most pygmy rattlers respond to a nearby threat by immediately coiling, if they are not already in such a position, and striking vigorously. The snake's striking distance is limited, for even a determined thrust propels the reptile's head forward only a few inches.

In keeping with its small size, this snake does not normally wander great distances. In Palm Beach County, Florida, for example, where Hudnall (1979) marked and released 50 dusky pygmy rattlesnakes (a subspecies closely related to the western pygmy rattler), he found that some of the serpents had moved only 29½ feet (9 m) from the release site the first time they were recaptured, though others were found as far away as 744 feet (227 m). A male specimen apprehended five times during the 19½ months of the survey traveled an average distance of 589¾ feet (180 m). The average distance covered by two other snakes recaptured three times was 279½ feet (85 m). In another field study, this one involving a gravid female western pygmy rattler in East Texas, Fleet and Kroll (1978) found that after seven recaptures in one month, the snake had wandered little more than 6½ feet (2 m) from its initial collecting site. This figure may not be typical, for female snakes carrying young are often more sedentary than normal.

So long as the air temperature is moderate, in the southern part of its range the pygmy rattlesnake may be found active above ground at almost any time of the year. Johnson (1987) states that in Missouri it is normally active from mid-April to mid-October. Although we have no detailed information about the snake's daily activity pattern, it is believed to be chiefly day-active during the cool days of spring and fall, becoming largely nocturnal during the hot summer months. Hudnall detected a somewhat similar pattern for the closely related dusky pygmy rattler. He found that in southeastern Florida, from March through October, the serpents were active from late afternoon to dusk, but during the cooler months of November and December they moved about mostly in the afternoon. During the first two hours after sunrise, many of them lay coiled in the sun; later in the evening they rested both in the shade on the west side of vegetative cover and in the eroded cuts of a levee.

The natural history of the western pygmy rattlesnake is largely unknown. When late summer or early fall showers periodically drench the pine and pine-hardwood forests of East Texas, the western pygmy rattler may be encountered crawling over the wet pavement of secondary roads. When at rest, it coils in grass clumps, on or under leaf litter, in brush piles, beneath fallen palmetto fronds, and on or under rocks and logs. Some have been found beneath boards, tarpaper, and other kinds of man-made litter or concealed in the burrows of small mammals. Although typically a ground-dwelling snake, a Missouri specimen mentioned by Klauber (1956) was discovered some 26 feet above the ground on the limb of a blackjack oak. This species usually hibernates under logs and in small mammal burrows, although one specimen escaped the cold weather by crawling into a sawdust pile.

FEEDING The snake's varied diet includes both vertebrate and invertebrate prey ranging from insects and spiders to nestling birds and mice. There is some question about the validity of listing invertebrates as normal prey species for this rattler, even when they are found in the snake's digestive tract, for there is always the possibility that such prey (especially hard-shelled beetles) were contained in the stomachs of vertebrate prey before the vertebrates themselves were consumed by the snakes. In such cases it is likely that when the snake is dissected, the frog, lizard, or mouse in its stomach will be in an advanced stage of decomposition and perhaps barely recognizable, whereas the hard-shelled insects are still intact and easily identifiable. On the other hand, soft-bodied insects such as caterpillars and moths are quickly assimilated by the reptile's digestive enzymes. When discovered intact in the reptile's stom-

ach, such creatures almost certainly represent the serpent's primary prey and not a secondary food item contained in the snake's other prey species.

Two field studies in particular provide good clues to the species' natural diet. One, completed in Georgia by Hamilton and Pollack (1955), shows that of 12 Carolina pygmy rattlers with food in their stomachs, 50 percent contained reptiles (5 lizards and 1 snake), 33 percent held centipedes, and 17 percent had mice or voles. The second study, made in Louisiana by R. F. Clark (1949), revealed that instead of consuming primarily reptiles, the local pygmy rattlesnakes ate chiefly amphibians; cricket, bronze, and leopard frogs constituted nearly the entire diet, though one specimen had devoured a small bird. Others report anoles and very small toads as prey. In an unusual departure from the norm, one of Klauber's correspondents claimed to have seen a western pygmy rattler capture small minnows in a shallow slough. If the report is authentic, such prey must be regarded as highly exceptional fare for this species.

Although it has not been verified by an eyewitness account, there is reason to believe that western pygmy rattlesnakes use their pale tail ends as lures, as do juvenile copperheads and cottonmouths. As the tail is held aloft and waved slowly and erratically, it looks to a nearby small frog or lizard like a tasty larval insect waiting to be devoured. When the would-be predator attacks the counterfeit larva, it is quickly seized by the waiting snake and eaten.

REPRODUCTION Because only September matings have been reported for this subspecies of *S. miliarius*, and because the females usually give birth in July and August, it is probable that after copulation the spermatozoa remain viable but inactive in the female's oviducts until the following spring, at which time they fertilize the eggs. The young, in litters of 3 to 32 (usually 4 to 10), normally are 5½ to 7 inches (14–17.8 cm) long at birth.

VENOM AND BITE Over the last 30 years, in the Houston area alone, five persons have been bitten by western pygmy rattlesnakes that each intentionally handled in the belief that it was a harmless juvenile hog-nosed snake.

Even this short-tempered little rattlesnake

usually crawls away from danger if permitted to do so, but if provoked, even slightly, it is apt to launch a strike with the suddenness of a coiled spring. Its striking distance is limited, however, seldom more than 4 or 5 inches (10–13 cm), and its fangs (measuring only $\frac{1}{8}$ to $\frac{3}{16}$ inch long) are not capable of deep penetration. According to Russell (1980), the lethal potency of pygmy rattlesnake venom when administered intravenously in mice is less than that of most other Texas rattlesnake species tested. It is also evident that although the larger eastern races of *S. miliarius* (nearly as big as a full-grown western massasauga) produce venom quantities averaging about 30 mg of dry weight per individual, the glands of the average western pygmy rattler must contain significantly less venom (apparently the amount has not been measured). Snakebite statistics reveal that the western pygmy rattlesnake is responsible for relatively few human snakebites, and a bite from this subspecies, though capable of producing serious medical consequences in man, rarely if ever causes human death. We can find no record of a human fatality from its bite. According to Vick (1971), envenomation usually produces moderate to somewhat severe local symptoms and, in some of the more aggravated cases, may even result in marked systemic consequences such as hemorrhaging, passing of bloody urine, and breathing difficulty. Although most victims suffer pain, swelling (generally not severe), and some nausea, seldom do they experience significant tissue degeneration, nor is there a dramatic change in their blood picture. Unless the patient is a small child or a debilitated older person (which adds to the gravity of any envenomation), most victims recover completely and uneventfully in just a few days.

GLOSSARY

Adrenal gland Either of a pair of small, ductless glands found just above the kidneys of most vertebrate animals, which secretes adrenaline, cortisone, and certain hormones.

Anal plate The rearmost belly scale, usually larger than the preceding abdominal scales, which covers the anal opening and marks the separation of the snake's body from its tail.

Annelid A leech or segmented worm; more specifically in this book, earthworms.

Anterior Pertaining to the forward or head end of an animal.

Antivenin or antivenom A commercially prepared serum that confers a certain degree of immunity against the lethal toxins of specific snake venoms.

Anuran A tailless amphibian; specifically a frog or toad.

Arachnid An arthropod with two body sections and eight legs; namely, scorpions, spiders, mites, and ticks.

Arthropod An invertebrate animal with a segmented body and jointed legs, such as an insect, arachnid, or crustacean.

Biennial Taking place every other year.

Bufonid Referring to the true toads, family Bufonidae.

Carnivorous Feeding only on animal life.

Caudal Pertaining to the tail.

Cloaca In amphibians and reptiles, the common chamber into which the digestive, urinary, and reproductive tracts discharge their contents.

Cold-blooded Refers to an animal without a constant body temperature, one whose body heat is regulated not by its own metabolism but by exposing itself to certain external sources. It may increase its body temperature by basking or lower it by seeking shade. To avoid prolonged subfreezing temperatures in winter, it must hibernate.

Convergent evolution The evolutionary development of distantly related organisms into similar-looking kinds.

Crustacean The class of arthropods that includes shrimp, crayfish, and pill bugs; those with two pairs of antennae and a hard protective outer shell.

Cryptic Difficult to detect in nature by virtue of an animal's concealing color, pattern, or body form.

Defibrination The destruction or removal of fibrin from the blood.

Depauperate Impoverished or destitute.

Desiccate To dry or dehydrate.

Disjunct Discontinuous or separated, as an isolated animal population that formerly was part of a species' continuous geographic range.

Diurnal Active by day.

Dorsal Referring to an organism's back; in the case of a snake, its upper body surface.

Dorsolateral The area between the midback and sides of an animal.

Dorsum The entire upper surface or back of an organism.

Ecchymosis The oozing of blood into the tissues, causing skin discoloration.

Ecosystem In a given environment, a system of interaction among plants and animals with one another and with their surroundings.

Elapid Referring to the family Elapidae, which includes coral snakes, cobras, mambas, and sea snakes, among others.

Endemic Restricted to a limited geographic region.

Envenomation The introduction of venom into an animal, which in snakes is typically accomplished through grooved or hollow fangs.

Epidermis The thin, nonvascular outer layer of skin, which in snakes is periodically shed.

Gastropod Slugs and snails.

Genetics The study of heredity and the transmission of characteristics.

Genus A group of closely related species.

Glutinous Gooey or sticky.

Gravid Pregnant.

Ground color The overall background color of a snake, on which its markings appear to lie.

Gular Pertaining to the throat.

Hemipenis Either of the paired copulatory organs of male snakes and lizards.

Hemotoxic Referring to any venom component that specifically destroys the blood cells and blood vessels.

Herpetoculture Captive maintenance and breeding of reptiles and amphibians.

Herpetofauna Collectively, the species of amphibians and reptiles inhabiting a specific region.

Herpetology The study of amphibians and reptiles.

Hibernaculum An animal's winter quarters.

Home range The area within which an organism usually travels during its normal activities.

Hybrid The offspring of a mating between two different species.

Hylid Referring to the tree frogs, primarily of the genus *Hyla.*

Hypotension Abnormally low blood pressure.

Imago The final, reproductive stage in the physical development of an insect.

Intergrade An intermediate individual that shares the characteristics of two closely related subspecies of the same species.

Interspace The ground color between a snake's primary markings of blotches, bands, or rings.

Invertebrate An animal without a backbone.

Jacobson's organ A sensory organ in reptiles, located in the roof of the mouth, which receives external chemical stimuli transmitted to it by the tongue.

Keel A ridge running lengthwise along the center of a scale.

Keratin A hard, fibrous, nonvascular protein that is the basic material of scales, claws, and a rattlesnake's rattle.

Lacertilian Pertaining to lizards.

Lateral Referring to the side of an organism.

Longitudinal Extending lengthwise.

Median In or of the middle.

Melanistic Having an unusual predominance of black pigmentation.

Microhabitat A small piece of an animal's habitat.

Middorsal The area down the center of the back.

Mimic A species whose form, color, or behavior imitates to its own advantage that of another species; in snakes, a harmless serpent that resembles a venomous species.

Mollusk An invertebrate with a soft, unsegmented body, usually covered with a single or double shell. This phylum includes slugs, snails, clams, oysters, squids, and octopuses.

Morphology The study of the form and structure of plants and animals, especially their outward appearance.

Mortify To decay or become gangrenous.

Mottled Irregularly marked with spots and blotches of various shapes, sizes, or colors.

Mouthline The seam formed by the juncture of a snake's upper and lower lips, which extends from one side of the mouth to the other.

Necrosis The death or decay of tissue.

Neurotoxic Referring to components in snake venom that damage the nervous system, often causing paralysis.

Nominate subspecies An organism whose species and subspecies names are the same.

Nuchal Referring to the back of the neck.

Ophidian Pertaining to snakes.

Ophidiophobia An irrational and excessive fear of snakes.

Ophiophagous Snake-eating.

Orbit The bony cavity within which the eye fits.

Parotoid gland Venom-secreting skin glands, granular and swollen, which lie on either side of a toad's neck above the tympanum.

Permeable Referring to tissues that are easily penetrated by liquids.

Pheromone A chemical released by an animal to provoke a specific behavioral or physiological response from another individual of the same species.

Physiology The study of the functions and activities of cells, tissues, and organs.

Piscine Referring to fish, as in piscine prey.

Population A group of organisms of a single species or subspecies living together in the same geographic area.

Posterior Pertaining to the rear portion of the body.

Postnatal After birth.

Race Subspecies.

Relict population The surviving remnant of a once more widespread population that is now confined to an isolated geographic area.

Rostral Pertaining to the snout or to the scale covering the snout.

Scute A large scale.

Spermatozoa The sperm cells found in semen.

Stereotype A fixed pattern of behavior.

Substrate The surface covering of the ground.

Subterranean Living below the surface of the ground.

Talus A pile of rock fragments at the base of a slope or cliff.

Toxic Poisonous.

Taxonomy The science of identifying and classifying plants and animals.

Translucent Transmitting but diffusing light.

Transverse Extending across the body or limb as opposed to being disposed lengthwise.

Tympanum The external eardrum of certain amphibians and reptiles.

Vent In reptiles and amphibians, the external orifice of the cloaca.

Ventral Pertaining to the underside of an animal.

Vertebral Lying lengthwise along the midline of the back.

Vesiculation The formation of a fluid-filled blister.

Vomeronasal organ Jacobson's organ.

Voucher specimen A specimen of an organism preserved in a permanent scientific collection to verify the species' presence at a particular geographic location.

REFERENCES

Aldridge, R. D. 1979. Seasonal spermatogenesis in sympatric *Crotalus viridis* and *Arizona elegans* in New Mexico. J. Herpetol. 13(2):187–192.

Aleksiuk, M., and K. W. Stewart. 1971. Seasonal changes in the body composition of the garter snake (*Thamnophis sirtalis parietalis*) at northern latitudes. Ecology 52:485–490.

Allen, E. R., and D. Swindell. 1948. Cottonmouth moccasin of Florida. Herpetologica (suppl. 1):1–16.

Alvarez del Toro, M. 1960. Reptiles de Chiapas. Inst. Zool. del Estado. Tuxtla Gutierrez, Chiapas.

Amaral, A. do. 1927. The anti-snake-bite campaign in Texas and in the subtropical United States. Bull. Antivenin Inst. Amer. 1:77–85.

Armstrong, B. L., and J. B. Murphy. 1979. The natural history of Mexican rattlesnakes. Univ. Kansas Mus. Nat. Hist. Spec. Publ. 5:1–88.

Arnold, S. J., and A. F. Bennett. 1984. Behavioral variation in natural populations, 3: Antipredator displays in the garter snake *Thamnophis radix*. Anim. Behav. 32:1108–1118.

Arny, S. A. 1948. A survey of the reptiles and amphibians of the Delta National Wildlife Refuge. Master's thesis, Tulane University, New Orleans, La.

Ashton, R. E., and P. S. Ashton. 1981. Handbook of Reptiles and Amphibians of Florida. Windward Publishing, Miami, Fla.

Atkinson, D. A., and M. G. Netting. 1927. The distribution and habits of the massasauga. Bull. Antivenin Inst. Amer. 1:40–44.

Auffenberg, W. 1948. Airplane introduces *Cemophora coccinea* to Texas. Herpetologica 4(5):212.

———. 1949. The racer *Coluber constrictor stejnegerianus* in Texas. Herpetologica 5(2):53–58.

Axtell, R. W. 1959. Amphibians and reptiles of the Black Gap Wildlife Management Area, Brewster County, Texas. Southwest. Nat. 4(2):88–109.

———. 1969. Another *Ficimia streckeri* from southern Texas. Tex. J. Sci. 20(4):381.

Bailey, V. 1905. Biological survey of Texas. North American Fauna 25.

Ball, R. L. 1990. Captive propagation of the Kansas glossy snake *Arizona e. elegans*. *In* Proceedings of the 14th International Herpetological Symposium, Dallas–Fort Worth, A. W. Zulich, ed.

Banicki, L. H., and R. G. Webb. 1982. Morphological variation of the Texas lyre snake (*Trimorphodon biscutatus vilkinsoni*) from the Franklin Mountains, West Texas. Southwest. Nat. 27(3):321–324.

Barbour, R. W. 1956. A study of the cottonmouth, *Ancistrodon piscivorus leucostoma*, in Kentucky. Trans. Kentucky Acad. Sci. 17:33–41.

Baxter, G. T., and M. D. Stone. 1980. Amphibians and reptiles of Wyoming. Bull. 16, Wyoming Game and Fish Dept., Cheyenne.

Beasom, S. L. 1974. Selectivity of predator control techniques in South Texas. J. Wildl. Mgmt. 38:837–844.

Beaupre, S. J. 1995. Comparative ecology of the mottled rock rattlesnake, *Crotalus lepidus*, in Big Bend National Park. Herpetologica 51(1):45–56.

Beavers, R. A. 1976. Food habits of the western diamondback rattlesnake, *Crotalus atrox*, in Texas. Southwest. Nat. 20:503–515.

Beck, D. D. 1995. Ecology and energetics of three sympatric rattlesnake species in the Sonoran Desert. J. Herpetol. 29(2):211–223.

Bechtel, H. B. 1995. Reptile and Amphibian Variants. Krieger Publishing, Malabar, Fla.

Behler, J., and F. W. King. 1979. The Audubon Society Field Guide to North American Reptiles and Amphibians. Alfred A. Knopf, New York.

Betz, T. 1963. The gross ovarian morphology of the diamond-backed water snake, *Natrix rhombifera*, during the reproductive cycle. Copeia 1963:692–697.

Beyer, G. E. 1898. Observations on the life histories of certain snakes. Amer. Nat. 32:17–24.

Blair, W. F. 1949. The biotic provinces of Texas. Tex. J. Sci. 2(1):93–117.

Blanchard, F. N. 1937. Data on the natural history of the red-bellied snake, *Storeria occipitomaculata* (Storer), in northern Michigan. Copeia 1937:151–162.

Blaney, R. M. 1977. Systematics of the common kingsnake, *Lampropeltis getulus* (Linnaeus). Tulane Studies in Zoology and Botany 19:47–103.

Bogert, C. M., and R. B. Cowles. 1947. Results of the Archbold Expeditions 58: Moisture loss in relation to habitat selection in some Florida reptiles. Amer. Mus. Novitates 1358:1–34.

Bogert, C. M., and V. D. Roth. 1966. Ritualistic combat of male gopher snakes, *Pituophis melanoleucus affinis* (Reptilia, Colubridae). Amer. Mus. Novitates 2245:1–27.

Bolen, E. G., B. McDaniel, and C. Cottom. 1964. Natural history of the black-bellied tree duck (*Dendrocygna autumnalis*) in southern Texas. Southwest. Nat. 9(2):78–88.

Boundy, J. 1995. Maximum lengths of North American snakes. Bull. Chicago Herpetol. Soc. 30:109–122.

Bowers, J. H. 1966. Food habits of the diamondback water snake, *Natrix rhombifera rhombifera*, in Bowie and Red River counties, Texas. Herpetologica 22(3):225–229.

Bragg, A. N. 1960. Is *Heterodon* venomous? Herpetologica 16(2):121–123.

Brauman, R. J., and R. A. Fiorillo. 1995. Natural history notes: *Lampropeltis getula holbrooki* (speckled kingsnake), oophagy. Herpetol. Rev. 26(2):101–102.

Brecke, B. J., J. B. Murphy, and W. Seifert. 1976. An inventory of reproductive and social behavior in captive Baird's rat snakes *Elaphe obsoleta bairdi* (Yarrow). Herpetologica 32(4):389–395.

Breckenridge, W. J. 1944. Reptiles and Amphibians of Minnesota. Univ. Minnesota Press, Minneapolis.

Brisbin, I. L., Jr. 1968. Evidence for the use of postanal musk as an alarm device in the kingsnake, *Lampropeltis getulus*. Herpetologica 24(2):169–170.

Brothers, D. R. 1994. Reproduction: *Elaphe obsoleta* (rat snake). Herpetol. Rev. 25(3):124.

Brown, B. C. 1939. The effect of *Coniophanes* poisoning in man. Copeia 1939(2):109.

———. 1950. An annotated checklist of the reptiles and amphibians of Texas. Baylor University Studies, Waco, Tex.

Brown, E. E. 1979. Stray food records from New York and Michigan snakes. Amer. Midl. Nat. 102:200–203.

Brown, E. V. 1979. Some snake food records from the Carolinas. Brimleyana 1:113–124.

Burger, J., and R. T. Zappalorti. 1986. Nest site selection by pine snakes, *Pituophis melanoleucus*, in the New Jersey pine barrens. Copeia 1986:116–121.

———. 1988. Habitat use in free-ranging pine snakes, *Pituophis melanoleucus*, in the New Jersey Pine Barrens. Herpetologica 44(1):48–55.

———. 1989. Habitat use by pine snakes (*Pituophis melanoleucus*) in the New Jersey Pine Barrens: Individual and sexual variation. J. Herpetol. 23(1):68–73.

———. 1991. Nesting behavior of pine snakes (*Pituophis melanoleucus*) in the New Jersey pine barrens. J. Herpetol. 25(2):152–160.

———. 1992. Philopatry and nesting phenology of pine snakes *Pituophis melanoleucus* in the New Jersey pine barrens. Behav. Ecol. Sociobiology 30:331–336.

Burger, J., et al. 1988. Hibernacula and summer den sites of pine snakes (*Pituophis melanoleucus*) in the New Jersey Pine Barrens. J. Herpetol. 22(4):425–433.

Burger, J., et al., 1992. Subterranean predation on pine snakes (*Pituophis melanoleucus*). J. Herpetol. 26:259–263.

Burghardt, G. M. 1968. Chemical preference studies on newborn snakes of three sympatric species of *Natrix*. Copeia 1968:732–737.

———. 1970. Chemical perception in reptiles. Pp. 241–308 *in* Communication by Chemical Signals, J. W. Johnson, D. G. Moulton, and A. Turk, eds., Appleton-Century-Crofts, New York.

Burghardt, G. M., and H. W. Greene. 1988. Predator stimulation and duration of death feigning in neonate hognose snakes. Animal Behav. 36:1842–1844.

Burkett, R. D. 1966. Natural history of cottonmouth moccasin, *Agkistrodon piscivorus* (Reptilia). Univ. Kansas Publ. Mus. Nat. Hist. 17(9):435–491.

Burt, C. E., and W. L. Hoyle. 1935. Additional records of the reptiles of the central prairie region of the United States. Trans. Kans. Acad. Sci. 37:193–216.

Carl, G. 1981. Reproduction in the captive Brazos water snake, *Nerodia harteri*. Texas J. Sci. 33(1):77–78.

Carpenter, C. C. 1982. The bullsnake as an excavator. J. Herpetol. 16(4):394–401.

———. 1986. An inventory of combat rituals in snakes. Smithsonian Herpetological Information Service 69:1–18.

Carpenter, C. C., and J. C. Gillingham. 1977. A combat ritual between two male speckled kingsnakes (*Lampropeltis getulus holbrooki*: Colubridae, Serpentes) with indications of dominance. Southwest. Nat. 22(4):517–524.

Carr, A. F. 1940. A contribution to the herpetology of Florida. Univ. Florida Publ. Biol. Ser. 3(1):1–118.

Chiszar, D., and H. M. Smith. 1994. Life history notes: *Crotalus viridis viridis*, record rattle-string. Herpetol. Rev. 25(3):123.

Clark, D. R., Jr. 1967. Experiments into selection of soil type, soil moisture level, and temperature by five species of small snakes. Trans. Kansas Acad. Sci. 70(4):490–496.

———. 1970. Age-specific "reproductive efforts" in the worm snake *Carphophis vermis* (Kennicott). Trans. Kansas Acad. Sci. 73:20–24.

———. 1974. The western ribbon snake (*Thamnophis proximus*): Ecology of a Texas population. Herpetologica 30(4):372–379.

Clark, D. R., Jr., and R. R. Fleet. 1976. The rough earth snake (*Virginia striatula*): Ecology of a Texas population. Southwest. Nat. 20(4):467–478.

Clark, D. R., Jr., and G. W. Pendleton. 1995. Texas rat snake (*Elaphe obsoleta lindheimeri*) eggs and hatchlings from a communal nest. Southwest. Nat. 40(2):203–207.

Clark, R. F. 1949. Snakes of the hill parishes of Louisiana. J. Tennessee Acad. Sci. 24:244–261.

Cobb, V. A. 1990. Reproductive notes on the eggs and offspring of *Tantilla gracilis* (Serpentes: Colubridae), with evidence of communal nesting. Southwest. Nat. 35:222–224.

Cochran, P. A. 1987. Life history notes: *Opheodrys aestivus* (smooth green snake). Herpetol. Rev. 18(2):36–37.

Collins, J. T. 1990. Standard Common and Current Scientific Names for North American Amphibians and Reptiles. 3rd ed. Society for the Study of Amphibians and Reptiles, Oxford, Ohio.

———. 1993. Amphibians and Reptiles in Kansas. 3rd ed., rev. University of Kansas Museum of Natural History, Public Education Service, Lawrence.

Collins, J. T., and S. L. Collins. 1991. Reptiles and amphibians of the Cimarron National Grasslands, Morton County, Kansas. U.S. For. Ser., USDA. 60 pp.

Conant, R. 1934. The red-bellied water snake, *Natrix sipedon erythrogaster* (Forster) in Ohio. Ohio J. Sci. 34(1):21–30.

———. 1942. Notes on the young of three recently described snakes, with comments on their relationships. Bull. Chicago Acad. Sci. 6(10):193–200.

———. 1951. The Reptiles of Ohio. 2nd ed. Univ. Notre Dame Press, Notre Dame, Ind.

———. 1955. Notes on three Texas reptiles, including an addition to the fauna of the state. Amer. Mus. Novitates 1726:1–6.

Conant, R., and J. T. Collins. 1991. A Field Guide to the Reptiles and Amphibians of Eastern and Central North America. 3rd ed. Houghton Mifflin, Boston.

Cook, F. A. 1954. Snakes of Mississippi. Mississippi Game and Fish Comm., Jackson. 40 pp.

Cottam, C., W. C. Glazener, and G. G. Raun. 1959. Food of moccasins and rattlesnakes from the Welder Wildlife Refuge, Sinton, Texas. Welder Wildl. Found., Contr. 45. 12 pp.

Cowles, R. R., and C. M. Bogert. 1935. Observations on the California lyre snake, *Trimorphodon vandenburghi* Klauber, with notes on the effectiveness of its venom. Copeia 1935(2):80–85.

———. 1944. A preliminary study of the thermal requirements of desert reptiles. Bull. Amer. Mus. Nat. Hist. 83(5):261–296.

Criddle, S. 1937. Snakes from an ant hill. Copeia 1937:142.

Crimmins, M. L. 1927. Notes on Texas rattlesnakes. Bull. Antivenin Inst. Amer. 1:23–24.

Curran, C. H., and C. F. Kauffeld. 1937. Snakes and Their Ways. Harper and Bros., New York.

Curtis, L. 1949. The snakes of Dallas County, Texas. Field and Lab. 17(1):1–13.

Dalrymple, G. H., and N. G. Reichenbach. 1981. Interactions between the prairie garter snake (*Thamnophis radix*) and the common garter snake (*Thamnophis sirtalis*) in Killdeer Plains, Wyandot County, Ohio. Ohio Biol. Surv., Biol. Notes 15:244–250.

Davenport, J. W. 1943. Fieldbook of the Snakes of Bexar County, Texas, and Vicinity. Witte Memorial Museum, San Antonio, Tex.

Davis, W. B. 1953. Another record of the smooth green snake in Texas. Herpetologica 9(2):165.

Degenhardt, W. G., T. L. Brown, and D. A. Easterla. 1976. The taxonomic status of *Tantilla cucullata* and *Tantilla diabola*. Texas J. Sci. 27(1):226–234.

Degenhardt, W. G., and P. B. Degenhardt. 1965. The host-parasite relationship between *Elaphe subocularis* (Reptilia: Colubridae) and *Aponomma elaphensis* (Acarina: Ixodidae). Southwest. Nat. 10(3):167–178.

Devine, M. C. 1975. Copulatory plugs in snakes: Enforced chastity. Science 187:844–845.

Dice, L. R. 1943. The Biotic Provinces of North America. Univ. Michigan Press, Ann Arbor.

Diener, R. A. 1957. An anatomical study of the plain-bellied water snake. Herpetologica 13:203–211.

Diller, L. V., and R. L. Wallace. 1986. Aspects of the life history and ecology of the desert night snake, *Hypsiglena torquata deserticola*: Colubridae, in southwestern Idaho. Southwest. Nat. 31(1):55–64.

Ditmars, R. L. 1936. The Reptiles of North America. Doubleday, Doran & Co., Garden City, N.Y.

Dixon, J. R. 1987. Amphibians and Reptiles of Texas. Texas A&M Univ. Press. College Station, Tex.

Dixon, J. R., B. D. Greene, and J. M. Mueller. 1988. 1988 Annual Report, Concho Water Snake Natural History Study, for the Colorado River Municipal Water District, Big Springs, Tex. 36 pp.

———. 1989. 1989 Annual Report, Concho Water Snake Natural History Study, for the Colorado River Municipal Water District, Big Springs, Tex. 66 pp.

Dixon, J. R., B. D. Greene, and M. J. Whiting. 1990. 1990 Annual Report, Concho Water Snake Natural History Study, for the Colorado River Municipal Water District, Big Springs, Tex. 69 pp.

Douglass, N. J., and H. K. Reinert. 1982. The utilization of fallen logs as runways by small mammals. Proc. Pennsylvania Acad. Sci. 56:162–164.

Drummond, H. 1983. Aquatic foraging in garter snakes: A comparison of specialists and generalists. Anim. Behav. 86:1–30.

Duellman, W. E. 1958. A monographic study of the colubrid snake genus *Leptodeira*. Bull. Amer. Mus. Nat. Hist. 114(1):1–152.

Dundee, H. A., and W. L. Burger, Jr. 1948. A denning aggregation of the western cottonmouth. Nat. Hist. Misc. (21):1–2.

Dundee, H. A., and M. C. Miller. 1968. Aggregative behavior and habitat conditioning of the prairie ringneck snake, *Diadophis punctatus arnyi*. Tulane Stud. Zool. Bot. 15(2):41–58.

Dundee, H. A., and D. A. Rossman. 1989. The Amphibians and Reptiles of Louisiana. Louisiana State Univ. Press, Baton Rouge.

Dunham, A. E. 1981. Population in a fluctuating environment: The comparative population ecology of the iguanid lizards *Sceloporus merriami* and *Urosaurus ornatus*. Misc. Publ. Mus. Zool. Univ. Michigan 158:1–62.

Duvall, D., M. B. King, and K. J. Gutzwiller. 1985. Behavioral ecology and ethology of the prairie rattlesnake. Natl. Geogr. Res. 1:80–111.

Easterla, D. A. 1975. Reproductive and ecological observations on *Tantilla cucullata* from Big Bend National Park, Texas (Serpentes, Colubridae). Herpetologica 31(2): 234–236.

———. 1989. Amphibians and reptiles checklist, Big Bend National Park, Rio Grande wild and scenic river. Big Bend Nat. Hist. Assoc. leaflet.

Englehardt, G. P. 1932. Notes on poisonous snakes in Texas. Copeia 1932:37–38.

Ernst, C. H. 1992. Venomous Reptiles of North America. Smithsonian Institution Press, Washington, D.C.

Ernst, C. H., and R. W. Barbour. 1989. Snakes of Eastern North America. George Mason Univ. Press, Fairfax, Va.

Ferguson, G. W. 1965. Verification of a population of *Ficimia cana* in north–central Texas. Herpetologica 21(2):156–157.

Ferguson, G. W., and R. M. Thornton. 1984. Oxygen storage capacity and tolerance of submergence of a non-aquatic reptile and an aquatic reptile. Comp. Biochem. Physiol. 774:183–187.

Ficken, R. W., P. E. Matthiae, and R. Horwich. 1971. Eye marks in vertebrates: Aids to vision. Science 173(4000):936–988.

Finneran, L. C. 1948. Reptiles at Branford, Connecticut. Herpetologica 4(4):123–126.

Fitch, H. S. 1956. Temperature responses in free-living amphibians and reptiles in northeastern Kansas. Univ. Kansas Publ. Mus. Nat. Hist. 8:417–476.

———. 1960. Autecology of the copperhead. Univ. Kansas Publ. Mus. Nat. Hist. 13:85–288.

———. 1963a. Natural history of the black rat snake (*Elaphe o. obsoleta*) in Kansas. Copeia 1963:649–658.

———. 1963b. Natural history of the racer *Coluber constrictor.* Univ. Kansas Publ. Mus. Nat. Hist. 15(8):351–468.

———. 1965. An ecological study of the garter snake *Thamnophis sirtalis.* Univ. Kansas Publ. Mus. Nat. Hist. 15:493–564.

———. 1970. Reproductive cycles in lizards and snakes. Univ. Kansas Mus. Nat. Hist. Misc. Publ. (52):1–247.

———. 1975. A demographic study of the ringneck snake (*Diadophis punctatus*) in Kansas. Univ. Kansas Mus. Nat. Hist. Misc. Publ. (62):1–53.

———. 1978. A field study of the prairie kingsnake (*Lampropeltis calligaster*). Trans. Kansas Acad. Sci. 81:354–362.

———. 1985. Variation in clutch size and litter size in New World reptiles. Univ. Kansas Mus. Nat. Hist. Misc. Publ. (76):1–76.

Fitch, H. S., and R. R. Fleet. 1970. Natural history of the milk snake (*Lampropeltis triangulum*) in northeastern Kansas. Herpetologica 26(4):387–396.

Fitch, H. S., and H. W. Shirer. 1971. A radiotelemetric study of spatial relationships in some common snakes. Copeia 1971(1): 118–128.

Fix, J. D., and S. A. Minton, Jr. 1976. Venom extraction and yields from the North American coral snake, *Micrurus fulvius.* Toxicon 14:143–145.

Fleet, R. R., and J. Kroll. 1978. Litter size and parturition behavior in *Sistrurus miliarius streckeri.* Herpetol. Rev. 9(1):11.

Fleharty, E. D. 1967. Comparative ecology of *Thamnophis elegans, T. cyrtopsis,* and *T. rufipunctatus* in New Mexico. Southwest. Nat. 12:207–229.

Force, E. R. 1935. A local study of the opisthoglyph snake *Tantilla gracilis* Baird and Girard. Pap. Michigan Acad. Sci., Arts, Lett. (1934) 20:645–659.

Ford, N. B., V. A. Cobb, and J. Stout. 1991. Species diversity and seasonal abundance of snakes in a mixed pine-hardwood forest of east Texas. Southwest. Nat. 36(2):171–177.

Ford, N. B., and J. P. Karges. 1987. Reproduction in the checkered garter snake, *Thamnophis marcianus,* from southern Texas and northeastern Mexico: Seasonality and evidence for multiple clutches. Southwest. Nat. 32(1):93–101.

Ford, N. B., and J. R. Lowe, Jr. 1984. Sex pheromone source location by garter snakes: A mechanism for detection of direction in non-volatile trails. J. Chem. Ecol. 10:1193–1199.

Fouquette, M. J., Jr. 1954. Food competition among four sympatric species of garter snakes, genus *Thamnophis.* Texas J. Sci. 5(2):172–188.

Fouquette, M. J., Jr., and H. L. Lindsay, Jr.

1955. An ecological survey of reptiles in parts of northwestern Texas. Texas J. Sci. 7(4):402–421.

Fowlie, J. A. 1965. The Snakes of Arizona. Azul Quinta Press, Fallbrook, Calif.

Fox, J. J. 1986. Ecology and management of the bullsnake in the Nebraska Sandhills: Final report. Crescent Lake National Wildlife Refuge. 22 pp.

Freedman, W., and P. M. Catling. 1979. Movements of sympatric species of snakes at Amherstburg, Ontario. Can. Field Nat. 93:399–404.

Froom, B. 1972. The Snakes of Canada. McClelland and Stewart, Ontario.

Gardner, J. B. 1955. A ball of garter snakes. Copeia 1955(4):310.

Garrett, J. M., and D. G. Barker. 1987. A Field Guide to Reptiles and Amphibians of Texas. Texas Monthly Press, Austin.

Garton, J. S., E. W. Harris, and R. A. Brandon. 1970. Descriptive and ecological notes on *Natrix cyclopion* in Illinois. Herpetologica 26:454–461.

Gehlbach, F. R. 1970. Death feigning and erratic behavior in leptotyphlopid, colubrid, and elapid snakes. Herpetologica 26(1):24–34.

———. 1972. Coral snake mimicry reconsidered: The strategy of self-mimicry. Forma et Function 5:311–320.

———. 1974. Evolutionary relationships of southwestern ringneck snakes (*Diadophis punctatus*). Herpetologica 30(2):140–148.

———. 1981. Mountain Islands and Desert Seas: A Natural History of the U.S.-Mexican Borderlands. Texas A&M Univ. Press, College Station, Tex.

Gehlbach, F. R., and R. S. Baldridge. 1987. Live blind snakes (*Leptotyphlops dulcis*) in eastern screech owl (*Otus asio*) nests: A novel commensalism. Oecologia 71:560–563.

Gehlbach, F. R., J. F. Watkins, and J. C. Kroll. 1971. Pheromone trail-following studies of typhlopid, leptotyphlopid, and colubrid snakes. Behavior 90(19):282–294.

Geiser, S. W. 1941. Dr. Benno Mathis: An early Texas herpetologist. Field and Lab. 9(2):37–44.

Gibbons, J. W. 1972. Reproduction, growth, and sexual dimorphism in the canebrake rattlesnake (*Crotalus horridus atricaudatus*). Copeia 1972(2):222–226.

Glenn, J. L., and R. C. Straight. 1978. Mojave rattlesnake, *Crotalus scutulatus*, venom: Variation in toxicity with geographical origin. Toxicon 16(1):81–84.

———. 1982. The rattlesnakes and their venom yield and lethal toxicity. Pp. 3–119 *in* Rattlesnake Venoms: Their Actions and Treatment. A. T. Tu, ed., Marcel Dekker, New York.

Gloyd, H. K. 1938. A case of poisoning from the bite of a black coral snake. Herpetologica 1(5):121–124.

———. 1947. Notes on the courtship and mating behavior of certain snakes. Nat. Hist. Misc. (12):1–4.

Gloyd, H. K., and R. Conant. 1934. The taxonomic status, range, and natural history of Schott's racer. Occ. Papers, Mus. Zool. Univ. Michigan 287:1–17.

———. 1990. Snakes of the *Agkistrodon* complex: A monographic review. Soc. Study Amph. Rept., Contrib. Herpetol. 6.

Glup, S. C., and L. L. McDaniel. 1988. Bullsnake predation on waterfowl nests on Valentine National Wildlife Refuge, Nebraska. USDA Forest Service, Gen. Tech. Rept. RM-154:149–152.

Godley, J. S., R. W. McDiarmid, and N. N. Rojas. 1984. Estimating prey size and number in crayfish-eating snakes, genus *Regina*. Herpetologica 40(1):82–88.

Goldsmith, S. K. 1984. Aspects of the natural history of the rough green snake, *Opheodrys aestivus* (Colubridae). Southwest. Nat. 29(4):445–452.

———. 1986. Feeding behavior of an arboreal insectivorous snake (*Opheodrys aestivus*) (Colubridae). Southwest. Nat. 31(2):246–249.

Goodman, J. D. 1953. Further evidence of the venomous nature of the saliva of *Hypsiglena ochrorhyncha*. Herpetologica 21:283–287.

Graves, B. M., and D. Duvall. 1985. Mouth gaping and head shaking by prairie rattlesnakes are associated with vomeronasal organ olfaction. Copeia 1985(2):496–497.

Green, N. B., and T. K. Pauley. 1987. Amphibians and Reptiles in West Virginia. Univ. Pittsburgh Press.

Greene, B. D. 1993. Life history and ecology of the Concho water snake, *Nerodia har-*

teri paucimaculata. Ph.D. dissertation, Texas A&M Univ., College Station. 134 pp.

Greene, B. D., J. R. Dixon, J. M. Mueller, M. J. Whiting, and O. W. Thornton. 1994. Feeding ecology of the Concho water snake, *Nerodia harteri paucimaculata*. J. Herpetology 28(2):165–172.

Greene, H. W. 1973. Defensive tail display by snakes and amphisbaenians. J. Herpetol. 7(3):143–161.

————. 1984. Feeding behavior and diet of the eastern coral snake, *Micrurus fulvius*. Univ. Kansas Mus. Nat. Hist. Spec. Publ. (10):147–162.

————. 1990. A sound defense of the rattlesnake. Pacific Discovery 43(4):10–19.

Greene, H. W., and R. W. McDiarmid. 1981. Coral snake mimicry: Does it occur? Science 213:1207–1212.

Greene, H. W., and G. V. Oliver, Jr. 1965. Notes on the natural history of the western massasauga. Herpetologica 21(3):225–228.

Guidry, E. V. 1953. Herpetological notes from southeastern Texas. Herpetologica 9(1):49–56.

Haines, T. P. 1940. Delayed fertilization in *Leptodeira annulata polysticta*. Copeia 1940 (2):116–118.

Hall, P. M., and A. J. Meier. 1993. Reproduction and behavior of western mud snakes (*Farancia abacura reinwardtii*) in American alligator nests. Copeia 1993(1):219–222.

Hall, R. J. 1969. Ecological observations on Graham's water snake (*Regina grahami* Baird and Girard). Amer. Midl. Nat. 81:156–163.

Hamilton, W. J., Jr. 1947. Hibernation of the lined snake. Copeia 1947(3):209–210.

————. 1950. Food of the prairie rattlesnake. Herpetologica 6(2):34.

Hamilton, W. J., Jr., and J. A. Pollack. 1955. The food of some crotalid snakes from Fort Benning, Georgia. Nat. Hist. Misc. (140):1–4.

————. 1956. The food of some colubrid snakes from Fort Benning, Georgia. Ecology 37:519–526.

Hammack, S. H. 1991. Life history notes: *Heterodon nasicus kennerlyi* (Mexican hognose snake), oophagy. Herpetol. Rev. 22(4):132.

Hardy, D. L. 1992. A review of first aid measures for pitviper bite in North America with an appraisal of extractor suction and stungun electroshock. Pp. 405–414 *in* Biology of the Pitvipers, Campbell and Brodie III, eds., Selva, Tyler, Tex.

————. 1994. A re-evaluation of suffocation as the cause of death during constriction by snakes. Herpetol. Rev. 25:45–47.

Hardy, D. L., and H. W. Greene. 1995. Natural history notes: *Crotalus molossus molossus* (blacktail rattlesnake), maximum length. Herpetol. Rev. 26(2):101.

Hardy, D. L., M. Jeter, and J. J. Corrigan, Jr. 1982. Envenomation by the northern blacktail rattlesnake (*Crotalus molossus molossus*): Report of two cases and the *in vitro* effects of the venom on fibrinolysis and platelet aggregation. Toxicon 20(2):487–493.

Herreid, C. F. II. 1961. Snakes as predators of bats. Herpetologica 17:271–272.

Hibbard, C. W. 1964. A brooding colony of the blind snake, *Leptotyphlops dulcis dissectus* Cope. Copeia 1964:222.

Hillis, D. M. 1977. An incident of death-feigning in *Sonora semiannulata blanchardi*. Bull. Maryland Herpetol. Soc. 13(2):116–117.

Hobbs, H. H., and M. Whiteman. 1991. Notes on the burrows, behavior, and color of the crayfish *Fallicambarus (F.) devastator* (Decapoda: Cambridae). Southwest. Nat. 36:127–135.

Howell, T. R. 1954. The kingsnake *Lampropeltis getulus holbrooki* preying on the cardinal. Copeia 1954(3):224.

Hudnall, J. A. 1979. Surface activity and horizontal movements in a marked population of *Sistrurus miliarius barbouri*. Bull. Maryland Herpetol. Soc. 15(4):134–138.

Imler, R. H. 1945. Bullsnakes and their control on a Nebraska wildlife refuge. J. Wildl. Mgmt. 9:265–273.

Iverson, J. B. 1990. Nesting and parental care in the mud turtle, *Kinosternon flavescens*. Can J. Zool. 68(2):230–233.

Jacob, J. S., and H. S. McDonald. 1976. Diving bradycardia in four species of North American aquatic snakes. Comp. Biochem. Physiol. 53A:69–72.

Jameson, D. L., and A. G. Flury. 1949. Reptiles and amphibians of the Sierra Vieja. Texas J. Sci. 1(2):54–79.

Johnson, T. R. 1987. The Amphibians and Reptiles of Missouri. Missouri Dept. Conserv., Jefferson City.

Jones, K. B. 1990. Habitat use and predatory behavior of *Thamnophis cyrtopsis* (Serpentes: Colubridae) in a seasonally variable aquatic environment. Southwest. Nat. 35(2): 115–122.

Jones, K. B., and W. G. Whitford. 1989. Feeding behavior of free-roaming *Masticophis flagellum* an efficient ambush predator. Southwest. Nat. 34(4):460–467.

Kassing, E. F. 1961. A life history of the Great Plains ground snake, *Sonora episcopa episcopa* (Kennicott). Texas J. Sci. 13(2):185–203.

Kauffeld, C. F. 1943. Field notes on some Arizona reptiles and amphibians. Amer. Midl. Nat. 29(2):342–359.

———. 1957. Snakes and Snake Hunting. Hanover House, Garden City, N.Y.

Keenlyne, K. D., and J. R. Beer. 1973. Food habits of *Sistrurus catenatus catenatus*. J. Herpetol. 7:382–384.

Kennedy, J. P. 1964. Natural history notes on some snakes of eastern Texas. Texas J. Sci. 16:210–215.

King, K. A. 1975. Unusual food item of the western diamondback rattlesnake (*Crotalus atrox*). Southwest. Nat. 20(3):416–417.

Kirk, V. M. 1969. An observation of a predator–escape technique practiced by a worm snake *Potamophis striatulus* (L.). Turtox News 47:44.

Kitchens, C. S., S. Hunter, and L. H. S. Van Mierop. 1987. Severe myonecrosis in a fatal case of envenomation by the canebrake rattlesnake (*Crotalus horridus atricaudatus*). Toxicon 25:455–458.

Klauber, L. M. 1939. Studies of reptile life in the arid southwest, 1: Night collecting on the desert with ecological statistics. Bull. Zool. Soc. San Diego 14(1):6–64.

———. 1940a. The worm snakes of the genus *Leptotyphlops* in the United States and northern Mexico. Trans. San Diego Soc. Nat. Hist. 9(18):87–162.

———. 1940b. The lyre snakes (genus *Trimorphodon*) of the United States. Trans. San Diego Soc. Nat. Hist. 9:163–194.

———. 1941. The long-nosed snakes of the genus *Rhinocheilus*. Trans. San Diego Soc. Nat. Hist. 9(29):289–332.

———. 1946. The glossy snake, *Arizona*, with descriptions of new subspecies. Trans. San Diego Soc. Nat. Hist. 10:311–398.

———. 1956. Rattlesnakes: Their Habits, Life Histories, and Influence on Mankind. 2 vols. Univ. California Press, Berkeley.

Klemens, M. W. 1993. Amphibians and reptiles of Connecticut and adjacent regions. State Geolog. Nat. Hist. Survey Connecticut, Bull. 112.

Klimstra, W. D. 1959. Food habits of the yellow-bellied king snake in southern Illinois. Herpetologica 15:1–5.

Knight, J. L. 1986. Variation in snout morphology in the North American snake *Pituophis melanoleucus* (Serpentes: Colubridae). J. Herpetol. 20:77–79.

Knight, J. L., and R. K. Loraine. 1986. Notes on turtle egg predation by *Lampropeltis getulus* (Linnaeus) (Reptilia: Colubridae) on the Savannah River Plant, South Carolina. Brimleyana (12):1–4.

Knopf, G. N., and D. W. Tinkle. 1961. The distribution and habits of *Sistrurus catenatus* in northwest Texas. Herpetologica 17(2):126–131.

Kofron, C. P. 1978. Foods and habitats of aquatic snakes (Reptilia, Serpentes) in a Louisiana swamp. J. Herpetol. 12(4):543–554.

Kofron, C. P., and J. R. Dixon. 1980. Observations on aquatic colubrid snake in Texas. Southwest. Nat. 25(1):107–109.

Kroll, J. C. 1971. Combat behavior in male Great Plains ground snakes (*Sonora episcopa episcopa*). Texas J. Sci. 23(2):300.

———. 1973. Comparative physiological ecology of eastern and western hognose snakes, *Heterodon platyrhinos* and *H. nasicus*. Diss. Abst. Int. B34(3):1069.

Lagesse, L. A., and N. B. Ford. 1996. Ontogenetic variation in the diet of the southern copperhead *Agkistrodon contortrix* in northeastern Texas. Texas J. Sci. 48(1):48–54.

Landreth, H. F. 1973. Orientation and behavior of the rattlesnake, *Crotalus atrox*. Copeia 1973(1):26–31.

Laposha, N., and R. Powell. 1982. Life history, *Virginia valeriae*. Herpetol. Rev. 13:97.

Lawson, R., and C. S. Lieb. 1990. Variation and hybridization in *Elaphe bairdi* (Serpentes: Colubridae). J. Herpetol. 24(3):280–292.

Lindner, B. D. 1962. Observations on the natural food preferences of the Mexican black-headed snake, *Tantilla atriceps*. Bull. Phil. Herp. Soc. Oct.-Dec. 1962:32.

Liner, E. A. 1954. The herpetofauna of

Lafayette, Terrebone, and Vermilion parishes, Louisiana. Proc. Louisiana Acad. Sci. 17:65–68.

———. 1977. Letisimulation in *Storeria dekayi limnetes* Anderson. Trans. Kansas Acad. Sci. 80:81–82.

Lowe, C. H., C. R. Schwalbe, and T. B. Johnson. 1986. The venomous reptiles of Arizona. Arizona Game and Fish Dept., Phoenix.

Lynch, W. 1978. Death–feigning in the eastern yellow-bellied racer. Blue Jay 36(2):92–93.

Markel, R. G. 1990. Kingsnakes and Milk Snakes. THF Publ., Neptune City, N.J.

McCallion, J. 1945. Notes on Texas reptiles. Herpetologica 2(7–8):197–198.

McCauley, R. H., Jr. 1945. The Reptiles of Maryland and the District of Columbia. Privately published, Hagerstown, Md.

McComb, W. C., and R. E. Noble. 1981. Herpetofaunal use of natural tree cavities and nest boxes. Wildl. Soc. Bull. 9(4):261–267.

McCoy, C. J., Jr., and F. R. Gehlbach. 1967. Cloacal hemorrhage and the defense display of the colubrid snake *Rhinocheilus lecontei*. Texas J. Sci. 19(4):349–352.

McCrystal, H. K. 1991. The herpetofauna of the Big Bend region. Sonoran Herpetologist 4(4):137–141.

McCrystal, H. K., and J. R. Dixon. 1983. Notes on the eggs and young of Schott's racer, *Masticophis taeniatus schotti* (Serpentes: Colubridae). Texas J. Sci. 35(2):161–163.

McCrystal, H. K., and R. J. Green. 1986. Life history notes: *Agkistrodon contortrix contortrix* (Trans-Pecos copperhead), feeding. Herpetol. Rev. 17:61.

McKinney, C. O., and R. E. Ballinger. 1966. Snake predators of lizards in western Texas. Southwest. Nat. 11(3):410–412.

Meade, G. P. 1934. Feeding *Farancia abacura* in captivity. Copeia 1934(2):91–92.

Mecham, J. S. 1979. The biogeographical relationships of the amphibians and reptiles of the Guadalupe Mountains. Natl. Park Serv. Trans. Proc. Ser. (4):169–179.

Medica, P. A. 1962. The Texas lyre snake, *Trimorphodon vilkinsonii*, in New Mexico. Herpetologica 18(1):65.

Miller, D. 1979. A life history study of the gray-banded kingsnake, *Lampropeltis mexicana alterna*, in Texas. Chihuahuan Desert Res. Inst. Contrib. 87:1–48.

Milstead, W. W., J. S. Mecham, and H. McClintock. 1950. The amphibians and reptiles of the Stockton plateau in northern Terrell County, Texas. Texas J. Sci. 2(4):543–562.

Minton, S. A., Jr. 1956. A new snake of the genus *Tantilla* from west Texas. Fieldiana Zool. 34:449–452.

———. 1957. Variation in yield and toxicity of venom from a rattlesnake (*Crotalus atrox*). Copeia 1957(4):265–268.

———. 1959. Observations on amphibians and reptiles of the Big Bend region of Texas. Southwest. Nat. 3(1–4):28–54.

———. 1967. Observations on toxicity and antigenic makeup of venoms from juvenile snakes. Toxicon 4:294.

———. 1972. Amphibians and reptiles of Indiana. Indiana Acad. Sci. Mongr. 3:1–346.

Minton, S. A., Jr., and M. R. Minton. 1969. Venomous Reptiles. Charles Scribner's Sons, New York.

Minton, S. A., Jr., and S. A. Weinstein. 1986. Geographic and ontogenetic variation in venom of the western diamondback rattlesnake (*Crotalus atrox*). Toxicon 24:71–80.

Moehn, L. D. 1967. A combat dance between two prairie kingsnakes. Copeia 1967(4):480–481.

Morris, M. A. 1982. Activity, reproduction, and growth of *Opheodrys aestivus* in Illinois (Serpentes: Colubridae). Nat. Hist. Misc. (214):1–10.

———. 1985. Envenomation from the bite of *Heterodon nasicus* (Serpentes: Colubridae). Herpetologica 41:361–363.

Mosauer, W. 1932. The amphibians and reptiles of the Guadalupe Mountains of New Mexico and Texas. Occ. Pap. Mus. Zool. Univ. Michigan 246:1–18.

Mount, R. M. 1975. The Reptiles and Amphibians of Alabama. Agr. Exp. Sta., Auburn University, Auburn, Ala.

Mueller, J. M. 1990. Population dynamics of the Concho water snake. Unpub. M.S. thesis, Texas A&M Univ., College Station, 52 pp.

Mulaik, S., and D. Mulaik. 1941. Variation in *Sonora taylori*. Copeia 1941(4):263.

———. 1942. A neglected species of *Coluber*. Copeia 1942(1):13–15.

———. 1943. Observations on *Ficimia streckeri* Taylor. Amer. Midl. Nat. 29(3):796–797.

Murphy, J. B., B. W. Tryon, and B. J. Brecke. 1978. An inventory of reproductive and social behavior in captive gray-banded king-snakes, *Lampropeltis mexicana alterna* (Brown). Herpetologica 34(1):84–93.

Murray, L. T. 1939. Annotated list of amphibians and reptiles from the Chisos Mountains. Contr. Baylor Univ. Mus. 24: 4–16.

Mushinsky, H. R., and J. J. Hebrard. 1977. Food partitioning by five species of water snakes in Louisiana. Herpetologica 33:127–129.

Mushinsky, H. R., J. J. Hebrard, and M. G. Walley. 1980. The role of temperature on the behavioral and ecological associations of sympatric water snakes. Copeia 1980(4): 744–754.

Mushinsky, H. R., and K. H. Lotz. 1980. Chemoreception responses of two sympatric water snakes to extracts of commonly ingested prey species: Ontogenetic and ecological considerations. J. Chem. Ecol. 6:523–535.

Neill, W. T. 1947. Size and habits of the cottonmouth moccasin. Herpetologica 3:203–205.

———. 1948. Hibernation of amphibians and reptiles in Richmond County, Georgia. Herpetologica 4:107–114.

———. 1951. Notes on the natural history of certain North American snakes. Publ. Res. Div. Ross Allen's Rept. Inst. 1:47–60.

———. 1957. Some misconceptions regarding the eastern coral snake, *Micrurus fulvius.* Herpetologica 13:111–118.

Nelson, D. H., and J. W. Gibbons. 1972. Ecology, abundance, and seasonal activity of the scarlet snake, *Cemophora coccinea.* Copeia 1972(3):582–584.

Noble, G. K., and H. J. Clausen. 1936. The aggregation behavior of *Storeria dekayi* and other snakes with especial reference to the sense organs involved. Ecol. Monogr. 6:269–316.

Oldfield, B., and J. J. Moriarty. 1994. Amphibians and Reptiles Native to Minnesota. Univ. Minnesota Press, Minneapolis.

Oliver, J. A. 1955. North American Amphibians and Reptiles. D. Van Nostrand, Princeton, N.J.

———. 1958. Snakes in Fact and Fiction. Macmillan, New York.

Olson, R. E. 1977. Evidence for the species status of Baird's ratsnake. Texas J. Sci. 29(1): 79–84.

Ortenburger, A. I. 1928. The whip snakes and racers: Genera *Masticophis* and *Coluber.* Mem. Univ. Michigan Mus. 1:1–247.

Orth, J. C. 1939. Moth larvae in a copperhead's stomach. Copeia 1939:54–55.

Painter, C. W., P. W. Hyder, and G. Swinford. 1992. Three species new to the herpetofauna of New Mexico. Herp. Rev. 24(4):155–156.

Palmer, W. M., and A. L. Braswell. 1976. Communal egg laying and hatchlings of the rough green snake, *Opheodrys aestivus* (Linnaeus) (Reptilia, Serpentes, Colubridae). J. Herpetol. 10(3):257–259.

———. 1995. Reptiles of North Carolina. Univ. North Carolina Press, Chapel Hill.

Palmer, W. M., and G. Tregembo. 1970. Notes on the natural history of the scarlet snake *Cemophora coccinea copei* Jan in North Carolina. Herpetologica 26:300–302.

Parker, W. S., and W. S. Brown. 1980. Comparative ecology of two colubrid snakes, *Masticophis t. taeniatus* and *Pituophis melanoleucus deserticola* in northern Utah. Milwaukee Pub. Mus. Publ. Biol. Geol. (7):1–104.

Parrish, H. M. 1964. Texas snakebite statistics. Texas State J. Med. 60:592–598.

Parrish, H. M., and R. E. Thompson. 1958. Human envenomation from bites of recently milked rattlesnakes: A report of three cases. Copeia 1958 (2):83–86.

Penn, G. H., Jr. 1943. Herpetological notes from Cameron Parish, Louisiana. Copeia 1943(1):58–59.

Perez, J. C., W. C. Haws, V. E. Garcia, and B. M. Jennings. 1978. Resistance of warm-blooded animals to snake venoms. Toxicon 16:375–384.

Peters, J. A. 1954. The amphibians and reptiles of the coast and coastal sierra of Michoacan, Mexico. Occ. Pap. Mus. Zool. Univ. Michigan 554:1–37.

Pettus, D. 1958. Water relationships in *Natrix sipedon.* Copeia 1958:207–211.

———. 1963. Salinity and subspecies in *Natrix sipedon.* Copeia 1963(3):499–504.

Phelan, Richard. 1976. Texas Wild. Simon and Schuster, New York.

Platt, D. R. 1969. Natural history of the hognose snakes *Heterodon platyrhinos* and *Heterodon nasicus.* Univ. Kansas Publ. Mus. Nat. Hist. 18(4):253–420.

Plummer, M. V. 1976. Communal egg laying and hatchings of the rough green snake, *Opheodrys aestivus* (Linnaeus) (Reptilia, Serpentes, Colubridae). J. Herpetol. 10(3):257–259.

———. 1981. Habitat utilization, diet and movements of a temperate arboreal snake (*Opheodrys aestivus*). J. Herpetol. 15:425–434.

———. 1985. Demography of green snakes (*Opheodrys aestivus*). Herpetologica 41:373–381.

———. 1989. Observations on the nesting ecology of green snakes (*Opheodrys aestivus*). Herpetol. Rev. 20(4):87–89.

———. 1990a. Nesting movements, nesting behavior, and nest sites of green snakes (*Opheodrys aestivus*) revealed by radio telemetry. Herpetologica 46(2):190–195.

———. 1990b. High predation on green snakes, *Opheodrys aestivus*. J. Herpetol. 24(3):327–328.

Plummer, M. V., and N. E. Mills. 1996. Observations on trailing and mating in hognose snakes (*Heterodon platirhinos*) J. Herpetol. 30(1):80–82.

Powell, A. M. 1988. Trees and Shrubs of Trans-Pecos, Texas. Big Bend Nat. Hist. Assoc., Big Bend National Park, Tex.

Price, A. H., and J. L. LaPointe. 1981. Structure–functional aspects of the scent gland in *Lampropeltis getulus splendida*. Copeia 1988(1):138–146.

Punzo, F. 1974. Comparative analysis of the feeding habits of Arizona blind snakes, *Leptotyphlops h. humilis* and *Leptotyphlops d. dulcis*. J. Herpetol. 8(2):153–156.

Rael, E. D., J. D. Johnson, O. Molina, and H. K. McCrystal. 1992. Distribution of a Mojave–like protein in rock rattlesnake (*Crotalus lepidus*) venom. Pp. 163–168 *in* Biology of the Pitvipers, Campbell and Brodie, eds., Selva, Tyler, Tex.

Ramsey, L. W. 1947. Feeding behavior of *Tropidoclonion lineatum*. Herpetologica 4:15–18.

Raun, G. G., and F. R. Gehlbach. 1972. Amphibians and reptiles in Texas. Dallas Mus. Nat. Hist. Bull. 2:1–61.

Reichenbach, N. G., and G. H. Dalrymple. 1986. Energy use, life histories, and the evaluation of potential competition of two species of garter snake. J. Herpetol. 20(2):133–153.

Reichling, S. B. 1988. Herpetological husbandry. Reproduction in captive Louisiana pine snakes, *Pituophis melanoleucus ruthveni*. Herpetol. Rev. 19(4):77–78.

———. 1990. Reproductive traits of the Louisiana pine snake, *Pituophis melanoleucus ruthveni* (Serpentes: Colubridae). Southwest. Nat. 35(2):221–222.

Reid, J. R., and T. E. Lott. 1963. Feeding of a *Leptotyphlops dulcis dulcis* (Baird and Girard). Herpetologica 19:141–142.

Reinert, K., D. Cundall, and L. M. Bushar. 1984. Foraging behavior of the timber rattlesnake, *Crotalus horridus*. Copeia 1984:976–981.

Reinert, H. K., and W. R. Kodrich. 1982. Movements and habitat utilization by the massasauga, *Sistrurus catenatus catenatus*. J. Herpetol. 16:162–171.

Reynolds, R. P., and N. J. Scott, Jr. 1982. Use of a mammalian resource by a Chihuahuan snake community. Pp. 99–118 *in* Herpetological Communities, N. J. Scott, Jr., ed., U.S. Dept. Interior, Fish and Wildl. Ser., Wild. Res. Rep. 13.

Richmond, N. D. 1952. *Opheodrys aestivus* in aquatic habitats in Virginia. Herpetologica 8(1):38.

Ridlehuber, K. T., and N. J. Silvy. 1981. Texas rat snake feeds on Mexican freetail bat and wood duck eggs. Southwest. Nat. 26:70–71.

Rodgers, R. B. 1985. Life history notes: *Heterodon platyrhinos* (eastern hognose snake), behavior. Herpetol. Rev. 16(4):111.

Rojas, N. N., and J. S. Godley. 1979. Tooth morphology in crayfish–eating snakes, genus *Regina*. *In* Abstracts, Joint Annual Meeting, Herpetologists League, Society for the Study of Amphibians and Reptiles, Univ. Tennessee, Knoxville.

Rossi, J. V., and R. Rossi. 1995. Snakes of the United States and Canada: Keeping Them Healthy in Captivity, Vol. 2, Western Area. Krieger Publishing, Malabar, Fla.

Rossman, D. A. 1963. The colubrid snake genus *Thamnophis*: A revision of the *sauritus* group. Bull. Florida St. Mus. Biol. Sci. 7:99–178.

Rossman, D. A., and P. A. Myer. 1990. Behavioral and morphological adaptations for snail extraction in the North American brown snakes (genus *Storeria*). J. Herpetol. 24(4):434–438.

Roze, J. A. 1982. New World coral snakes (*Elapidae*): A taxonomic and biological summary. Mem. Inst. Butantan 46:305–338.

Ruben, J. A. 1977. Some correlates of cranial and cervical morphology with predatory models in snakes. J. Morphol. 152:89–100.

Rudolph, D. C., H. Kyle, and R. N. Conner. 1990. Red-cockaded woodpeckers vs rat snakes: The effectiveness of the resin barrier. Wilson Bull. 102(1):14–22.

Rundquist, E. M., E. Stegall, D. Grow, and P. Gray. 1978. New herpetological records from Kansas. Trans. Kansas Acad. Sci. 81(1): 73–77.

Russell, F. E. 1960. Snake venom poisoning in southern California. California Med. 93:347–350.

———. 1980. Snake Venom Poisoning. Scholium International, Great Neck, New York.

Russell, F. E., C. Gans, and S. A. Minton, Jr. 1978. Poisonous snakes. Clinical Med. 85(2): 13–30.

Russell, F. E., and H. W. Puffer. 1971. Pharmacology of snake venoms. *In* Snake Venoms and Envenomation. Marcel Dekker, New York.

Sabath, M. C., and L. E. Sabath. 1969. Morphological intergradation in Gulf coastal brown snakes, *Storeria dekayi* and *Storeria tropica*. Amer. Midl. Nat. 81(2):148–155.

Sabath, M. C., and R. Worthington. 1959. Eggs and young of certain Texas reptiles. Herpetologica 15(1):31–32.

Savitsky, B. C. 1992. Laboratory studies on piscivory in an opportunistic pitviper, the cottonmouth, *Agkistrodon piscivorus*. Pp. 405–414 *in* Biology of the Pitvipers, Campbell and Brodie, eds., Selva, Tyler, Tex.

Schmidt, K. P. 1929. The Truth about Snake Stories. Field Museum of Natural History, Chicago.

Schmidt, K. P., and D. D. Davis. 1941. Field Book of Snakes of the United States and Canada. Putnam, New York.

Schuett, G. W., D. L. Clark, and F. Kraus. 1984. Feeding mimicry in the rattlesnake *Sistrurus catenatus*, with comments on the evolution of the rattle. Animal Behav. 32:625–626.

Schwartz, J. M., G. F. McCracken, and G. M. Burghardt. 1989. Multiple paternity in wild populations of the garter snake, *Thamnophis sirtalis*. Behav. Ecol. Sociobiol. 25:269–273.

Scott, N. J., T. C. Maxwell, O. K. Thornton, L. A. Fitzgerald, and J. W. Flury. 1989. Distribution, habitat, and future of Harter's water snake, *Nerodia harteri*, in Texas. J. Herpetol. 23(4):373–389.

Secor, S. M. 1995. Ecological aspects of foraging mode for the snakes *Crotalus cerastes* and *Masticophis flagellum*. SSAR Herpetol. Monog. 8:169–186.

Seib, R. L. 1984. Prey use in three syntopic neotropical racers. J. Herpetol. 18(4): 412–420.

Seibert, H. C. 1950. Population density of snakes in an area near Chicago. Copeia 1950: 229–230.

Seibert, H. C., and C. W. Hagen. 1947. Studies on a population of snakes in Illinois. Copeia 1947:6–22.

Seifert, W. 1972. Habitat, variations, and intergradation of the Trans-Pecos copperhead, *Agkistrodon contortrix pictigaster*. Dallas Mus. Nat. Hist. Bull. 2(2):1–10.

Seigel, R. A. 1984. The foraging ecology and resource partitioning of two species of garter snakes. Ph.D. dissertation, Univ. Kansas, Lawrence.

———. 1986. Ecology and conservation of an endangered rattlesnake, *Sistrurus catenatus*, in Missouri, USA. Biol. Conserv. 35:333–346.

Semlitsch, R. D., and G. B. Moran. 1984. Ecology of the redbelly snake (*Storeria occipitomaculata*) using mesic habitats in South Carolina. Amer. Midl. Nat. 111(1):33–40.

Shaw, C. E. 1951. Male combat in American colubrid snakes with remarks on combat in other colubrid and elapid snakes. Herpetologica 7(4):149–168.

Shaw, C. E., and S. Campbell. 1974. Snakes of the American West. Alfred A. Knopf, New York.

Smith, H. M. 1950. Handbook of the amphibians and reptiles of Kansas. Univ. Kansas Mus. Nat. Hist., Misc. Pub. 2:1–336.

———. 1953. Case history of a snake with an irregurgitable artificial egg. Herpetologica 9(2):93–95.

———. 1978. Phenological and other data for the plains red king snake. Colorado Herpetologist 3(1):2–3.

Smith, H. M., J. R. Staley II, and K. Tepedelen. 1994. Populational relationships in the corn snake *Elaphe guttata* (Reptilia: Serpentes). Texas J. Sci. 46(3):259–292.

Smith, H. M., and F. N. White. 1955. Adrenal enlargement and its significance in the hognose snakes (*Heterodon*). Herpetologica 11:137–144.

Smith, P. W. 1961. The amphibians and reptiles of Illinois. Illinois Nat. Hist. Sur. Bull. 28:1–298.

Solorzano, E., and L. Cerdas. 1987. Life history notes: *Drymobius margaritiferus* (speckled racer), reproduction. Herpetol. Rev. 18(4):75–76.

Stebbins, R. C. 1966. A Field Guide to Western Reptiles and Amphibians. Houghton Mifflin, Boston.

Stickel, W. H., and J. B. Cope. 1947. The home ranges and wanderings of snakes. Copeia 1947:127–136.

Strecker, J. K. 1915. Reptiles and amphibians of Texas. Baylor Univ. Bull. 18(4):1–82.

———. 1926a. On the habits of some southern snakes. Contr. Baylor Univ. Mus. 4:3–10.

———. 1926b. Reptiles of the South and Southwest in Folklore. Tex. Folklore Soc., Publ. 5:56–69.

———. 1927. Chapters from the life-histories of Texas reptiles and amphibians, part 2. Contr. Baylor Mus. 10:1–14.

———. 1935. Notes on the pit-vipers in McLennan County, Texas. Baylor Univ. Bull. 38(3):26–28.

Stuart, L. C. 1935. A contribution to a knowledge of the herpetology of a portion of the savanna region of central Peten, Guatemala. Univ. Michigan Mus. Zool. Misc. Publ. 20:1–56.

Surface, H. A. 1906. The serpents of Pennsylvania. Bull. Pennsylvania Dept. Agr., Div. Zool. (4):133–208.

Swain, T. A., and H. M. Smith. 1978. Communal nesting in *Coluber constrictor* in Colorado (Reptilia: Serpentes). Herpetologica 322:175–177.

Taggart, T. W. 1992. Observations on Kansas amphibians and reptiles. Kansas Herpetol. Soc. Nwsl. 88:13–15.

Tanner, W. W. 1985. Snakes of western Chihuahua. Great Basin Nat. 45(4):615–676.

Tanzer, E. C. 1970. Polymorphism in the *mexicana* complex of kingsnakes, with notes on their natural history. Herpetologica 26(4):419–428.

Tennant, A. 1984. The Snakes of Texas. Texas Monthly Press, Austin.

Theakston, R. D. G., and H. A. Reid. 1978.

Changes in the biological properties of venom from *Crotalus atrox* with aging. Period. Biol. 80 (suppl. 1):123–133.

Thomas, R. A., and F. S. Hendricks. 1976. Letisimulation in *Virginia striatula* (Linnaeus). Southwest. Nat. 21(1):123–124.

Tinkle, D. W. 1957. Ecology, maturation, and reproduction of *Thamnophis sauritus proximus*. Ecology 38:69–77.

———. 1959. Observations of reptiles and amphibians in a Louisiana swamp. Amer. Midl. Nat. 62(11):189–205.

True, F. W. 1883. On the bite of the North American coral snakes (genus *Elaps*). Amer. Nat. 17:26–31.

Tryon, B. W., and J. B. Murphy. 1982. Miscellaneous notes on the reproductive biology of reptiles 5: Thirteen varieties of the genus *Lampropeltis*, species *mexicana*, *triangulum*, and *zonata*. Trans. Kansas Acad. Sci. 85(2):96–119.

Turner, E. 1977. Colorful kingsnake of the Trans-Pecos. Texas Parks and Wildlife magazine 45(1):10–11.

Twente, J. W., Jr. 1955. Aspects of a population study of cavern dwelling bats. J. Mammal. 36:379–390.

Uhler, F. M., C. Cottam, and T. E. Clarke. 1939. Food of snakes of the George Washington National Forest, Virginia. Trans. 4th North American Wildl. Conf.: 605–622.

Vaughan, R. K., J. R. Dixon, and R. A. Thomas. 1996. A reevaluation of populations of the corn snake *Elaphe guttata* (Reptilia: Serpentes: Colubridae) in Texas. Texas J. Sci. 48(3):175–190.

Vermersch, T. G., and R. E. Kuntz. 1987. Snakes of South–central Texas. Eakin Press, Austin, Tex.

Vick, V. A. 1971. Symptomology of experimental and clinical envenomation. Pp. 71–86 in Neuropoisons: Their Pathophysiological Actions, Vol. 1, L. L. Simpson, ed., Plenum, New York.

Vincent, J. W. 1982. Color pattern variation in *Crotalus lepidus* (Viperidae) in southwestern Texas. Southwest. Nat. 27(3):263–272.

Vitt, L. J. 1975. Observations on reproduction in five species of Arizona snakes. Herpetologica 31(3):83–84.

Vogt, R. C. 1981. Natural History of Amphibians and Reptiles of Wisconsin. Milwaukee Publ. Mus., Milwaukee, Wisc.

Watkins, J. F. II. 1964. Laboratory experiments on the trail following of army ants of the genus *Neivamyrmex*. J. Kansas Entomol. Soc. 37:22–28.

Watkins, J. F. II, F. R. Gehlbach, and R. S. Baldridge. 1967. Ability of the blind snake, *Leptotyphlops dulcis*, to follow pheromone trails of army ants, *Neivamyrmex nigrescens* and *N. opacithorax*. Southwest. Nat. 12:(4): 455–462.

Webb, R. G. 1970. Reptiles of Oklahoma. Univ. Oklahoma Press, Norman.

Wendelken, P. W. 1978. On prey-specific hunting behavior in the western ribbon snake, *Thamnophis proximus* (Reptilia: Serpentes: Colubridae). J. Herpetol. 12(4):577–578.

Werler, J. E. 1951. Miscellaneous notes on the eggs and young Texas and Mexican reptiles. Zoologica 36:34–48.

———. 1970. Notes on young and eggs of captive reptiles. Inter. Zoo Yearbook 10:105–116.

Wharton, C. H. 1958. The ecology of the cottonmouth *Agkistrodon piscivorus* Lacepede of Sea Horse Key, Florida. Ph.D. dissertation, Univ. Florida.

Whiting, M. J. 1993. Population ecology of the Concho water snake, *Nerodia harteri paucimaculata*, in artificial habitats. M.S. thesis, Texas A&M University, College Station. 137 pp.

Whittier, J. M., and D. Crews. 1986. Ovarian development in red-sided garter snakes, *Thamnophis sirtalis parietalis:* Relationship to mating. Gen. Comp. Physiol. 61:5–12.

Wigginton, E. 1972. The Foxfire Book. Doubleday, New York.

Williams, G. G. 1951. Rat snake overpowers a red-shouldered hawk, *Buteo lineatus*. Auk 68(3):372.

Williams, N. R. 1969. Population ecology of *Natrix harteri*. M.S. thesis, Texas Tech Univ., Lubbock. 51 pp.

Wilson, L. D. 1970. The coachwhip snake, *Masticophis flagellum* (Shaw): Taxonomy and distribution. Tulane Stud. Zool. Bot. 16:31–99.

Wilson, P. 1908. Snake poisoning in the United States: A study based on an analysis of 740 cases. Arch. Int. Med. 1(5):516–570.

Wingert, W. A., T. R. Pattabhiraman, R. Cleland, P. Meyer, R. Pattabhiraman, and F. E. Russell. 1980. Distribution and pathology of copperhead (*Agkistrodon contortrix*) venom. Toxicon 18:591–601.

Wright, A. H., and S. C. Bishop. 1915. A biological reconnaissance of the Okefenokee Swamp in Georgia, 2: Snakes. Proc. Acad. Nat. Sci. Philadelphia 67:139–192.

Wright, A. H., and A. A. Wright. 1957. Handbook of Snakes of the United States and Canada. 2 vols. Comstock Publishing, Ithaca, N.Y.

Yancey, F. D. 1997. Maximum size: *Hypsiglena torquata jani* (Texas night snake). Herpetol. Rev. 28:205.

Yeatman, H. C. 1983. Life history notes: *Virginia valeriae* (eastern smooth snake), defense. Herpetol. Rev. 14(1):22.

Zappalorti, R. T., and J. Burger. 1985. On the importance of disturbed sites to habitat selection by pine snakes in the Pine Barrens of New Jersey. Environ. Conserv. 12(4):358–361.

Zappalorti, R. T., E. W. Johnson, and Z. Lesczynski. 1983. The ecology of the northern pine snake, *Pituophis melanoleucus melanoleucus* (Daudin) (Reptilia, Serpentes, Colubridae), in southern New Jersey, with special notes on habitat and nesting behavior. Chicago Herpetol. Soc. 18(3–4):57–72.

Zappalorti, R. T., and H. K. Reinert. 1994. Artificial refugia as habitat improvement strategy for snake conservation. Pp. 369–375 *in* Captive Management and Conservation of Captive Reptiles, J. P. Murphy, K. Adler, and J. T. Collins, eds., SSAR Publication, Oxford, Ohio.

INDEX OF COMMON NAMES

INDEX OF SCIENTIFIC NAMES

Boldface numbers indicate detailed discussion.